The essays in this volume provide various perspectives on the meanings that different individuals and social groups have attached to their experience of the market. Based on a wide range of literary, artistic, philosophical, and other historical sources, they explore how the norms and practices that market societies foster have been shifting and conflict-ridden. In speaking of the "culture of the market," the authors do not assume that culture is simply a reflection of autonomous economic forces, nor do they suppose that the market is always associated with the same cultural forms, independent of time, place, tradition, and human volition. Yet to speak of the cultural implications of the market is to assume that markets, precisely because they are aspects of culture, have cultural concomitants, and that careful observers are capable of identifying at least some of them. Just what those concomitants are, whether they are best understood as preconditions of market behavior or as results of it, and just how necessary or contingent their connection to market activity may be, are open questions on which the contributors to this volume shed new light.

The culture of the market

Murphy Institute Studies in Political Economy
General Editor: Richard F. Teichgraeber III

The books in this series are occasional volumes sponsored by the Murphy Institute of Political Economy at Tulane University and Cambridge University Press, comprising original essays by leading scholars in the United States and other countries. Each volume considers one of the intellectual preoccupations or analytical procedures currently associated with the term "political economy." The goal of the series is to aid scholars and teachers committed to moving beyond the traditional boundaries of their disciplines in a common search for new insights and new ways of studying the political and economic realities of our time. The series is published with the support of the Tulane–Murphy Foundation.

Other books in the series:

Gordon C. Winston and Richard F. Teichgraeber III, eds., *The boundaries of economics*

John Dunn, ed., *The economic limits to modern politics*

The culture of the market

Historical essays

Edited by

THOMAS L. HASKELL
Rice University

RICHARD F. TEICHGRAEBER III
Tulane University

CAMBRIDGE UNIVERSITY PRESS
Cambridge, New York, Melbourne, Madrid, Cape Town, Singapore,
São Paulo, Delhi, Dubai, Tokyo, Mexico City

Cambridge University Press
The Edinburgh Building, Cambridge CB2 8RU, UK

Published in the United States of America by Cambridge University Press, New York

www.cambridge.org
Information on this title: www.cambridge.org/9780521444682

First published 1993
Reprinted 1995
First paperback edition 1996

A catalogue record for this publication is available from the British Library

ISBN 978-0-521-44468-2 Hardback
ISBN 978-0-521-56478-6 Paperback

Contents

Plates 1–13 follow p. 260. Plate 14 follows p. 396.

Acknowledgments

All but one of the chapters in this volume were presented initially at a conference on The Culture of the Market held at the Murphy Institute of Political Economy, Tulane University, in New Orleans on March 9–11, 1990, on the occasion of a three-month-long visit to the Murphy Institute by Thomas L. Haskell during the winter–spring semester of that year. (Howard Brick's paper on Talcott Parsons was prepared especially for the volume.) Although most of the contributors to this book are historians, the concept of "political economy" that informs both scholarship and teaching sponsored by the Murphy Institute describes a broad field of inquiry in which economists and political scientists, as well as philosophers and historians, are making contributions of shared and equal interest.

The conference was funded by the Tulane–Murphy Foundation and the National Endowment for the Humanities, an independent federal agency. We are particularly grateful to NEH for making possible both the conference and the preparation of this volume. We would like to thank Colin Campbell, Lynn Hunt, Matthew Mancini, Peter Schwartz, R. Jackson Wilson, and many Tulane University scholars, all of whom also participated in the conference. Finally, special thanks should go to Ruth Carter, Program Coordinator at the Murphy Institute, who played a central role at virtually every turn in the editors' production of this volume.

Richard F. Teichgraeber III
Director, Murphy Institute of Political Economy

Contributors

JEAN-CHRISTOPHE AGNEW is Associate Professor of American Studies and History at Yale University. He is the author of *Worlds Apart: The Market and the Theater in Anglo-American Thought, 1550–1750* (1986).

JOYCE APPLEBY is Professor of History at the University of California, Los Angeles. Author of *Economic Thought and Ideology in Seventeenth-Century England* and *Capitalism and a New Social Order,* she has written on liberalism and republicanism in early modern thought. She is a past president of the Organization of American Historians.

HOWARD BRICK, Assistant Professor of History at the University of Oregon, is author of *Daniel Bell and the Decline of Intellectual Radicalism: Social Theory and Political Reconciliation in the 1940s* (1986). He is writing a history of the concept of capitalism in U.S. social theory from 1920 to 1970.

MARILYN R. BROWN is Associate Professor of Art History at Tulane University. She is author of *Gypsies and Other Bohemians: The Myth of the Artist in Nineteenth-Century France* (1985), *An Inventory of the DeGas–Musson Papers at Tulane University* (1991), and a forthcoming book, *Degas and the Business of Art: A Cotton Office in New Orleans.*

JONATHAN DEWALD is Professor of History at the State University of New York at Buffalo. He is the author of *The Formation of a Provincial Nobility: The Magistrates of the Parlement of Rouen, 1499–1610* (1980); *Pont-St.-Pierre, 1398–1789: Lordship, Community, and Capitalism in Early Modern France* (1987); and *Aristocratic Experience and the Origins of Modern Culture: France 1570–1715* (1993).

THOMAS L. HASKELL is McCann Professor of History at Rice University. He is currently at work on a study of agency and responsibility in Anglo-American culture in the eighteenth and nineteenth centuries. He is author of *The Emergence of Professional Social Science: The American Social Science Association and the Nineteenth Century Crisis of Authority* (1977) and of a two-part essay, "Capitalism and the Origins of the Humanitarian Sensibility," which appeared in the *American Historical Review* in 1985. He is editor of *The Authority of Experts: Essays in History and Theory* (1984).

MARGARET C. JACOB is Professor of History in the University at the New School for Social Research, and formerly dean of its college. She is the author of *The Newtonians and the English Revolution* (1976), *The Radical Enlightenment* (1981), *The Cultural Meaning of the Scientific Revolution* (1988), and *Living the Enlightenment* (1991). With J. Appleby and L. Hunt, she is coauthor of *Telling the Truth about History* (1994).

RICHARD B. LATNER is Associate Professor of History at Tulane University and former director of the American Studies Program. He is author of *The Presidency of Andrew Jackson: White House Politics 1829–1837* (1979), and a number of published articles on Jacksonian politics.

WILFRED M. MCCLAY is Associate Professor of History at Tulane University. He is author of *The Masterless: Self and Society in Modern America* (1993). His articles and essays have appeared in the *New England Quarterly, Reviews in American History, American Scholar, Commentary,* and *Virginia Quarterly Review.* He is working on a biography of David Riesman.

CHANDRA MUKERJI is Professor in the Communication Department at the University of California, San Diego, and a member of the Sociology Department and Science Studies Program. She is the author of *From Graven Images: Patterns of Modern Materialism* (1983) and *A Fragile Power: Scientists and the State* (1989); co-editor of *Rethinking Popular Culture* (1991); and author of a number of essays in the sociology of the arts.

WILLIAM M. REDDY is Professor of History and Cultural Anthropology at Duke University. He is author of *The Rise of Market Culture: The Textile Trade and French Society, 1750–1900* (1984) and *Money and Liberty in Modern Europe: A Critique of Historical Understanding* (1987).

RICHARD F. TEICHGRAEBER III is Director of the Murphy Institute of Political Economy and Associate Professor in the Department of History at Tulane University. He is author of *'Free Trade' and Moral Philosophy: Rethinking the Sources of Adam Smith's Wealth of Nations* (1986); his book-length study of the ways in which Emerson and Thoreau understood and experienced the emergence of the market in antebellum America is forthcoming.

MARTIN J. WIENER is Jones Professor of History at Rice University. He is the author of *Between Two Worlds: The Political Thought of Graham Wallas* (1971), *English Culture and the Decline of the Industrial Spirit, 1850–1980* (1981), and *Reconstructing the Criminal: Culture, Law and Policy in England, 1830–1914* (1990).

Introduction: The culture of the market

THOMAS L. HASKELL AND RICHARD F. TEICHGRAEBER III

What should the reader expect to find in a collection of historical essays titled *The Culture of the Market?* Many of the assumptions shaping this volume are evident in the words of the title. Consider, to begin with, the word "culture."

There is one intellectual tradition, unfashionable today among academics but possessed of greater staying power than meets the eye, that understands true culture to embrace only the priceless, only that which is (or ought to be) immune from the tawdry calculations of least cost and maximum utility that notoriously prevail in the marketplace. From that traditional standpoint, often loosely identified with Immanuel Kant or Matthew Arnold, the market is not only a cultural void but an active corrosive agent, obliterating cultivated values wherever it reaches. To anyone firmly wedded to that conception of culture, our title can only be puzzling, for it would seem unnaturally to couple domains of human existence that are mutually exclusive.

Even to speak of "market culture" is tacitly to sever culture's traditional association with transcendent values and define it in a way that is more inclusive and less evaluative – allowing us to speak of the culture of Tanzania as readily as that of France, of low culture as well as high, of the culture of business people and shopkeepers as well as that of aristocrats and priests. This is only to follow common practice, for during the past half century the broad, nonjudgmental conception of culture has become prevalent in most academic circles. "Culture," argued Franz Boas in the characteristically inclusive spirit of twentieth-century anthropology, "may be defined as the totality of the mental and physical reactions and activities that characterize the behavior of the individuals composing a social group collectively and individually in relation to their natural environment, to other groups, to members of the group itself and of each individual to himself."[1] Here culture signifies a whole way of life: institutions, artifacts, rituals, and practices, as well as ideas, images, and texts. Relaxed and tolerant though this standpoint is, even it, as we shall see, is capable of treating the market as an enemy of certain highly valued cultural practices.

The relation between culture and economic activity is, we assume, one not of mutual exclusiveness but, rather, of reciprocal influence and interpenetration, sometimes harmonious, sometimes conflictual. Economic practices are imbedded in culture, aspects of culture. As such, markets can be seen as the effects of certain cultural configurations and the causes of others. In the absence of certain values and practices a market economy cannot come into existence. Once a market economy does exist, its very presence seems to encourage some ways of life and discourage others. There often appears to be a nonvicious circularity between the preconditions for market activity and the consequences of that activity, as if markets, like powerful disturbances in the atmosphere, can in some degree be self-reinforcing, helping to create the very sorts of people and ways of life that they need in order to function effectively. But not every dust devil turns into a cyclone, and not every market grows.[2]

To speak of "the culture of the market," then, is not to assume that culture is merely a reflection of autonomous economic factors, or to suppose that the market is always associated with the same cultural forms, independent of time, place, tradition, or human volition. There is no single "culture of the market." But, on the other hand, not all cultures are equally compatible with the needs of a market economy. To speak of the cultural implications of the market is to assume that markets, precisely because they are aspects of culture, have cultural concomitants, and that we are capable of identifying at least some of them. Just what those concomitants are, whether they are best understood as preconditions of market behavior or as results of it, and just how necessary or contingent their connection to market

[1] Boas, *The Mind of Primitive Man* (New York: Free Press, 1966), 159.

[2] For a strong argument on behalf of the priority of culture over utility – stronger than the one assumed here – see Marshall Sahlins, *Culture and Practical Reason* (Chicago and London: University of Chicago Press, 1976).

activity may be, are open questions, on which the contributors to this volume aspire to shed some light.

Being historians (with the perhaps nominal exception of one historical sociologist), the authors are concerned more with particular times, places, people, and events than with the development of general theoretical perspectives on the relations between markets and culture. Just as we have borrowed the anthropologist's conception of culture without attending to all the technicalities that a specialist might want to explore, so we have borrowed from economics the notion of a market – the second of the two operative words in our title – and used it in decidedly nontechnical ways. Somewhat to the surprise of the organizers of the volume, none of the contributors volunteered a definition of the key term, "market."[3] Perhaps this is just as well. Although the closely affiliated words "market" and "capitalism" are today part of the common parlance of historians, there is no consensus about their meaning. Thus, what the reader needs is not so much a definition as a sense of the range of meanings now current in the field. The next section is intended to meet that need. Having established a range of shared meanings of "market" and related terms, we can then proceed to the essays at hand.

What follows in this introduction is an examination of three conceptions of the market that have been especially influential among histori-

[3] As an alternative to a *definition* of "market," Haskell suggests the following, with tongue not entirely in cheek. Imagine that we knew, for a given society, who was in competition with whom, over what stakes, and with what degree of intensity, in all the multitudinous dimensions of human performance, whether economic or not. We would, in short, know for every conceivable commodity and service who produced it, who consumed it, and how the choices and activities of each producer and consumer influenced prices and thus figured in the lives of all other producers and consumers. Moreover, we would also know for all the dimensions of human performance (whether ordinarily reckoned "economic" or not) which performances were seen (in whose eyes) to be commensurable, and therefore "in competition," such that the performance of one person made a difference, pleasing or displeasing, to "consumers" or to others engaged in the same art, craft, sport, endeavor, form of play, and so on. Such knowledge would enable us to view society as an intricate network of overlapping spheres *within* which human actions appeared commensurable, and therefore competitive, but *between* which no competition could be recognized. Before we could form an image of this complex network and extend it through time, taking account of changes, we would also, of course, have to have at our fingertips a vast amount of knowledge about the changing technology of "action-at-a-distance," all those means by which one person's action can make a difference in the lives of others, whether or not they are physically and temporally proximate. This is not a definition of "the market." But if we possessed such knowledge, we might not need a definition, for the object of our curiosity would already be in view.

ans during the past half century. Our aim has not been to survey the full length and breadth of the emerging field of historical studies devoted to the origin and meaning of market culture. That field, which scarcely existed a decade ago, is thriving; a historical overview of it would undoubtedly serve valuable purposes. But instead of a thin discussion of many works, we have preferred to offer a deeper analysis of the few that aspired to something like theoretical adequacy, and thus set the terms of debate. Our aim has been to triangulate the domain of possible perspectives, as it were. By exploring in some depth the most compelling efforts to conceptualize the market, we hope to convey at once, even to uninitiated readers, the intellectual magnitude of what is at stake in the study of market culture. We live at a time when the long contest between capitalism and socialism seems suddenly to have reached endgame. When the fate of nations hangs in the balance, the cultural implications of the market take on more than scholarly interest.

•

The first of the three conceptions of the market to be examined was articulated by Karl Polanyi in 1944; the second, by C. B. Macpherson in 1962; and the third, by Fernand Braudel in 1979. Polanyi understood the pivotal development of European and world history in the nineteenth century to be the "utopian endeavor of economic liberalism to set up a self-regulating market mechanism."[4] To that effort, profoundly misguided in his view, he attributed not only the breakdown of world economic order after 1900 but two cataclysmic world wars. He conceded, of course, that there was nothing new about markets in the nineteenth century. At least as far back as the later Stone Age, he observed, human beings had gathered to exchange goods through barter, or buying and selling. In a spirit that had Kantian overtones but was also deeply influenced by the anthropological conception of culture, he directed his criticism not against markets as such but against the systematic effort that took place during the nineteenth century, first in England and then on the Continent and in the United States, to reorganize the economy as a self-regulating

[4] Karl Polanyi, *The Great Transformation: The Political and Economic Origins of Our Time* (Boston: Beacon Press, 1957), 21–29.

mechanism, subject to the will of neither the government nor the citizenry.

Throughout most of human history, argued Polanyi, market activity was only an incidental aspect of economic life and the motive of economic self-advancement was firmly subordinated to considerations of social esteem. Rejecting Adam Smith's assumption that all mankind displayed a natural propensity to truck, barter, and exchange, Polanyi, like Max Weber and others before him, insisted that the motive of gain was a European invention of recent origin. Drawing heavily on the anthropology of the 1920s and 1930s, and boldly extrapolating from the current practices of Trobriand islanders to the historical practices of European societies, Polanyi contended that the natural relation of economy to culture was that of part to whole, mere means to surpassingly important ends.

"Man's economy," he wrote, "as a rule, is submerged in his social relationships. He does not act so as to safeguard his individual interest in the possession of material goods; he acts so as to safeguard his social standing, his social claims, his social assets. He values material goods only insofar as they serve this end." When economic considerations are properly imbedded in social relations and shaped by communal ritual, "the premium set on generosity is so great when measured in terms of social prestige as to make any other behavior than utter self-forgetfulness simply not pay."[5] Although the motive of gain seems inescapable, even indispensable, in modern European economies, economic production need not stagnate in its absence, he reported; instead, a sufficiency continues to be produced and distributed according to noneconomic, or only quasi-economic, principles of reciprocity, redistribution, or simply household maintenance. In a strongly prescriptive voice, Polanyi, like Marx before him, hailed Aristotle's "prophetic" distinction between production for use and for gain, and echoed the philosopher's denunciation of the latter as "not natural to man."[6]

Polanyi recognized that European economies by the fifteenth and sixteenth centuries had already moved far beyond simple production for use. But the "great transformation" of which he wrote – the shift from an economy imbedded in social relations to one that cavalierly

[5] Ibid., 46.
[6] Ibid., 53–54.

manipulated social relations as means to its own impersonal ends – did not reach completion even in England, the world's most advanced economy, until 1834. In that year the Poor Law Amendment put an end to the subsidy in aid of wages that the justices of Berkshire, meeting in Speenhamland, had established in 1795, a time of great distress. The repeal of the Speenhamland law did away with "outdoor relief" and what amounted to a paternalistic minimum income, thus for the first time exposing workers to the full fury of a competitive labor market. Polanyi accepted the conclusion of economists that the Speenhamland law – paradoxically and contrary to the intention of its authors – had depressed wages and contributed to the immiseration of the work force. He even conceded that "in the end the free labor market [created by the repeal of Speenhamland], in spite of the inhuman methods employed in creating it, proved financially beneficial to all concerned."[7] Nonetheless, he regarded the repeal of Speenhamland as a "ruthless act of social reform," the effect of which was nothing less than to transform England into the world's first true market economy – and, still more ominously, into the first market society.[8]

> A market economy can exist only in a market society. . . . A market economy must comprise all elements of industry, including land, labor, and money. . . . But labor and land are no other than the human beings themselves of which every society exists and the natural surroundings in which it exists. To include them in the market mechanism means to subordinate the substance of society itself to the market.[9]

Land and money had already become subject to the market before the nineteenth century. The repeal of the Speenhamland law completed the transformation by stripping away the last protective shelter and subjecting man himself to the dictates of the invisible hand. Far from recognizing the peril to which they were exposing their fellow citizens, middle-class reformers, no longer checked by a powerful landed interest, recklessly plunged ahead. Under the banners of "free trade," they tried to perfect the autonomy of the market by bringing about the complete separation of the economic sphere from the politi-

[7] Ibid., 77.

[8] Ibid., 82.

[9] Ibid., 71. For a provocative effort to rethink Polanyi's subject (and a denial that efforts to create a true market in labor ever succeeded), see the work of a contributor to this volume, William M. Reddy, *The Rise of Market Culture: The Textile Trade and French Society, 1750–1900* (Cambridge University Press, 1984).

cal. The birth of modern consciousness, claimed Polanyi, lay in the discovery that fostered the reformer's extravagant hopes: Economic society was subject to laws of neither divine nor human origin. For the sake of comparison with Macpherson and Braudel, Polanyi's extensive definition of a market economy is worth reproducing in full:

> A market economy is an economic system controlled by markets alone; order in the production and distribution of goods is entrusted to this self-regulating mechanism. An economy of this kind derives from the expectation that human beings behave in such a way as to achieve maximum money gains. It assumes markets in which the supply of goods (including services) available at a definite price will equal the demand at that price. It assumes the presence of money, which functions as purchasing power in the hands of its owners. Production will then be controlled by prices, for the profits of those who direct production will depend on them; the distribution of the goods will also depend upon prices, for prices form incomes, and it is with the help of those incomes that the goods produced are distributed amongst the members of society. Under these assumptions order in the production and distribution of goods is ensured by prices alone.
>
> Self-regulation implies that all production is for sale on the market and that all incomes derive from such sales. Accordingly, there are markets for all elements of industry, not only for goods (always including services) but also for labor, land, and money, their prices being called respectively commodity prices, wages, rent, and interest. . . .
>
> A further group of assumptions follows in respect to the state and its policy. Nothing must be allowed to inhibit the formation of markets, nor must incomes be permitted to be formed otherwise than through sales. Neither must there be any interference with the adjustment of prices to changed market conditions – whether the prices are those of goods, labor, land, or money. Hence there must not only be markets for all elements of industry, but no measure or policy must be countenanced that would influence the action of these markets. Neither price, nor supply, nor demand, must be fixed or regulated; only such policies are in order which help to ensure the self-regulation of the market by creating conditions which make the market the only organizing power in the economic sphere.[10]

This definition of a market economy, which closely identifies it with the policy of laissez-faire, was, of course, intended by Polanyi as an ideal type rather than a description of any real society, for he acknowledged – or, rather, insisted – that such an economy was "utopian" and could never be realized. "To allow the market mechanism to be sole director of the fate of human beings and their natural

[10] Polanyi, 68–69.

environment, indeed, even of the amount and use of purchasing power, would result in the demolition of society. . . . Robbed of the protective covering of social institutions, human beings would perish from the effects of social exposure."[11] Driven by an inhuman fantasy that threatened vital interests at every level of society, the admirers of the self-regulating market had only to announce their program to trigger an avalanche of opposition to it.

Thus, for a century following the repeal of Speenhamland, the dynamics of modern society were governed, as Polanyi put it in an often-quoted passage, by a "double movement: the market expanded continuously but this movement was met by a countermovement checking the expansion in definite directions."[12] Socialism, of course, formed part of Polanyi's "countermovement" against the spread of the market, but he used the term broadly, so that it referred not only to the trade union movement and programs aimed at collectivizing the means of production, but also to the entire range of liberal regulatory devices and even to pragmatic measures designed to protect small capitalists from big ones, such as the establishment of central banking systems.[13] At every opportunity Polanyi took pains to reassert what were, perhaps, his most fundamental convictions about the market economy: its "extreme artificiality," in spite of the most seductive appearances to the contrary; and its fundamental incompatibility, not only with humane values but with the most mundane practical arrangements of everyday life.[14]

C. B. Macpherson, the second of the theorists whose influence on historians merits our attention, was no more enamored of the market than Polanyi. The term "market society" is central to the work of both men, and their conceptions of the market are similar at many points, but Macpherson acknowledged no debt to Polanyi and his assumptions about the chronology of development of market society are not easy to reconcile with those of his predecessor.

What Macpherson called "market society" did not come into existence in 1834, the year in which Polanyi claimed that the repeal of Speenhamland created an unsheltered market for labor, but was al-

[11] Ibid., 73.
[12] Ibid., 130.
[13] Ibid., 132.
[14] Ibid., 73.

ready full-blown in England at least as early as 1651, when Thomas Hobbes published *Leviathan.* Indeed, one of the principal argumentative burdens of Macpherson's important and provocative book, *The Political Theory of Possessive Individualism,* was that Hobbes and the Levellers, as well as James Harrington and John Locke – the founding fathers of liberal political theory – all lived in a society thoroughly oriented to the market, and that they had tacitly drawn some of the most important of their theoretical premises from their everyday experience in market transactions. Macpherson displayed far more interest in the empirical details of history and economics than theorists generally do, but in the end he unapologetically subordinated empirical interests to his primary goal: shedding light on the unspoken presuppositions lying deep in the foundations of liberal thought.

That Hobbes's thinking was influenced by the market is impossible to deny, as the following example, quoted by Macpherson, attests:

> The *Value,* or WORTH of a man, is as of all other things, his Price; that is to say, so much as would be given for the use of his Power: and therefore is not absolute; but a thing dependant on the need and judgement of another. . . . And as in other things, so in men, not the seller, but the buyer determines the price. For let a man (as most men do,) rate themselves at the highest Value they can; yet their true Value is no more than it is esteemed by others.[15]

Whether the reliance of Hobbes and other seventeenth-century theorists on market metaphors can carry all the argumentative weight Macpherson heaped upon it is a controverted question.[16] The ultimate success of his argument on this and other points is less important for our purposes than the intriguing and admirably explicit model of market society that he developed in the course of presenting his argument. One suspects that many historians today, if pressed for a definition of the market, would point to Macpherson's threefold distinction between a "Customary, or status society," a "Simple market society," and a "Possessive market society." The reader may wish to

[15] Hobbes, *Leviathan,* quoted in C. B. Macpherson, *The Political Theory of Possessive Individualism: Hobbes to Locke* (London: Oxford University Press, 1962), 37.

[16] For criticisms of Macpherson, see his exchange with Jacob Viner in the *Canadian Journal of Economics and Political Science* 29 (November 1963), 548–66; John Dunn, *The Political Thought of John Locke* (Cambridge: Cambridge University Press, 1969), chs. 16 and 17; and Keith Thomas, "The Social Origins of Hobbes's Political Thought," *Hobbes Studies,* ed. K. C. Brown (Oxford: Oxford University Press, 1965), 186–236.

compare and contrast these three ideal-typical constructions with Polanyi's discussion. "Customary society" appears to correspond to Polanyi's conception of a pre-market society, in which economic affairs are imbedded in and routinely subordinated to social relations. The "Simple market society" corresponds roughly to Polanyi's description of England in the late eighteenth century, or even on the eve of the repeal of Speenhamland, for although the model specifies markets in commodities, money, and land, there is none in human labor. The "Possessive market society" quite closely resembles the final stage depicted by Polanyi, in which the market extends everywhere and no authority is powerful enough to challenge its self-regulating discipline. Following are the essential properties Macpherson (*Possessive Individualism,* 51–54) assigned to each of the three types:

Customary or status society:

a. The productive and regulative work of the society is authoritatively allocated to groups, ranks, classes, or persons. The allocation and performance are enforced by law or custom.
b. Each group, rank, class, or person is confined to a way of working, and is given and permitted only to have a scale of reward appropriate to the performance of his or its function, the appropriateness being determined by the consensus of the community or by the ruling class.
c. There is no unconditional individual property in land. Individual use of land, if any, is conditional on performance of functions allotted by the community or the state, or on the provision of services to a superior. There is hence no market in land.
d. The whole labour force is tied to the land, or to the performance of allotted functions, or (in the case of slaves) to masters. The members of the labour force are thus not free to offer their labour in the market: there is no market in labour.

Simple market society:

a. There is no authoritative allocation of work: individuals are free to expend their energies, skills, and goods as they will.
b. There is no authoritative provision of rewards for work: individuals are not given or guaranteed, by the state or the community, rewards appropriate to their social functions.

c. There is authoritative definition and enforcement of contracts.
d. All individuals seek rationally to maximize their utilities, that is, to get the most satisfaction they can for a given expenditure of energy or goods, or to get a given satisfaction for the least possible expenditure of energy or goods.
e. All individuals have land or other resources on which they may get a living by their labour.

Possessive market society:

[Notice that the simple market society is transformed into the possessive market society by retaining the first four properties; by dropping the fifth, so some individuals do *not* have land or other resources on which they may make a living; and by adding four new properties, which are understood by Macpherson to be the logical prerequisites for the emergence of a fully competitive market in labor. Thus the full list of properties defining the possessive market society is as follows:]

a. There is no authoritative allocation of work.
b. There is no authoritative provision of rewards for work.
c. There is authoritative definition and enforcement of contracts.
d. All individuals seek rationally to maximize their utilities.
e. Each individual's capacity to labour is his own property and is alienable.
f. Land and resources are owned by individuals and are alienable.
g. Some individuals want a higher level of utilities or power than they have.
h. Some individuals have more energy, skill, or possessions, than others.

Unlike Polanyi, Macpherson attached no particular significance to the nineteenth-century policy of laissez-faire, or to that century's fascination with equilibrating mechanisms and homeostatic processes, the quasi-scientific underpinnings that inspired the era's confidence in the capacity of the market to regulate itself. Observing that "one cannot infer from the fact of [government] intervention that the intention is, or that the effect will be, to weaken the system," Macpherson insisted that the possessive market model was perfectly consistent with mercantilist policies such as those that prevailed in Hobbes's lifetime.[17]

[17] Macpherson, *Possessive Individualism,* 58.

Macpherson's aim in laying out the essential properties of the three types of society was, of course, to show that only the third, the possessive market society, corresponded with the presuppositions that Hobbes and the other seventeenth-century liberal thinkers incorporated into their theories. Hobbes and Locke claimed to base their theories of sovereignty and political obligation on man as he was in a pure state of nature, before socialization, but in fact, argued Macpherson, their "natural" man was already steeped in the habits, motives, and perceptions of the marketplace. What Macpherson found most offensive about possessive market society was its tendency to pull even those who were content with their existing level of satisfactions into new rounds of competitive frenzy, if for no other reason than to hold on to the level they had already attained. The limitlessness of competition and the inability of people of moderate disposition to stand apart from it in a world in which everything has its price, damned modern liberal society in Macpherson's eyes.[18]

Under the sway of possessive individualist assumptions, wrote Macpherson, the

> exchange of commodities through the price-making mechanism of the market permeates the relations between individuals, for in this market all possessions, including men's energies, are commodities. In the fundamental matter of getting a living, all individuals are essentially related to each other as possessors of marketable commodities, including their own powers. All must continually offer commodities (in the broadest sense) in the market, in competition with others. . . . It is a society in which those who want more may, and do, continually seek to transfer to themselves some of the power of others, in such a way as to compel everyone to compete for more power, and all this by peaceable and legal methods which do not destroy the society by open force.[19]

The ideological implications of criticizing the market are plain enough. In the writings of both Polanyi and Macpherson, the market stands quite straightforwardly for capitalism. To condemn market society is to condemn capitalism, or at least its excesses, for the market is the most distinctive of all the institutions of a capitalist economy. Polanyi's critical standpoint is the more optimistic of the two, for his target is the reckless ambition to give completely free

[18] Ibid., 53.
[19] Ibid., 55, 59.

sway to the self-regulating capacities of the market, a policy that in spite of its surprising rejuvenation in the past decade has always aroused strong opposition and is unlikely ever to go unchallenged. The evils that he protests do not require the extirpation of markets which, he acknowledges, long antedate the emergence of "market society." Moreover, his criticism is compatible with a wide variety of remedies, ranging from democratic socialism to welfare capitalism. Any intervention by the government in the economy would evidently count as a step in the right direction.

Macpherson's standpoint is more pessimistic, for he traces modern problems into a more distant past and finds the heart of the difficulty in a market-bred conception of freedom and personhood for which there is no obvious or ready-made alternative. The crux of the problem, in his view, is the possessive quality of the assumptions upon which liberal theory was founded.

> Its possessive quality is found in its conception of the individual as essentially the proprietor of his own person or capacities, owing nothing to society for them. The individual was seen neither as a moral whole, nor as part of any larger social whole, but as owner of himself. The relation of ownership, having become for more and more men the critically important relation determining their actual freedom and actual prospect of realizing their full potentialities, was read back into the nature of the individual. The individual, it was thought, is free inasmuch as he is proprietor of his person and capacities.[20]

This is all well and good, but how are we to reconceive freedom and personhood so as to rid them of their possessive, market-infected quality? Can one overcome the taint of possessiveness by merely acknowledging a debt to society for one's capacities, or by stoutly asserting that persons are moral wholes? How are we to avert the danger that if the individual is not proprietor of his own person and capacities, someone else will be?

Macpherson did not pretend it would be easy to safeguard the hard-won liberties of liberal society while ridding it of so subtle and pervasive a malignancy. His central claim was that possessive market society places all individuals in a "continual competitive power relationship" because it construes each person's capacity to labor as his or her own property, which is alienable, and therefore a market com-

[20] Ibid., 3.

modity.[21] But if that is truly the source of our troubles, then certain questions obviously arise, and Macpherson's answers to them were not altogether clear. If a person's capacity to labor were not defined as his or her own property, how would it be defined? How could people's capacity to labor be made inalienable without diminishing their freedom to choose when, where, and under what conditions to work? In order to keep labor from becoming a market commodity, it appears necessary that some other authority, superior to the market, be established to allocate resources and rewards – much as kings and masters did in customary society. Upon whom should we confer such a high trust? If the cultural concomitants of the market are what Macpherson said they are, and if their relation to the market is as much a matter of necessity as he believed them to be, then reform involves very hard choices indeed.

For a much less ominous conception of the market and its cultural consequences, consider the views of Fernand Braudel, the eminent French historian and dean of the "Annales" school. Impatient with theory, as most historians are, Braudel nonetheless embarked upon a major reconceptualization of our problem in his magisterial three-volume work, *Civilization and Capitalism* (1979). The principal novelty of his approach is easily stated and goes straight to the heart of the relations between market and culture that we have been examining. Unlike Polanyi, Macpherson, and many others, Braudel did not regard the market as the distinctive institution of capitalist society. Instead of letting the market stand for capitalism, Braudel deliberately drove a wedge between the two. The "essential message," he said, of his extensive studies, was that capitalism is "distinct from the market economy."[22]

Very much the historian's historian in spite of his frequent gestures of respect for the other human sciences, Braudel eschewed schematization and prided himself on the concrete particularity of his work. His massive study, which encompassed the globe and cited evidence from four centuries of world history, placed such heavy stress on the ubiquity of markets and the virtual universality of exchange activity that it cast doubt on all efforts to chart qualitative

[21] Ibid., 59.

[22] Fernand Braudel, *Civilization and Capitalism: 15th–18th Century,* vol. III, *The Perspective of the World,* trans. Sian Reynolds (New York: Harper & Row, 1984), 620.

change in the history of capitalism, much less to single out decisive moments and critical phases in the Marxian manner. With a characteristic concern for continuity (and more than a trace of ambiguity) he asserted that "exchange is as old as human history" and claimed that "capitalism has been *potentially* visible since the dawn of history."[23] Unpersuaded that the market's relation to other cultural elements was as stable or as necessary as Macpherson assumed, Braudel urged his readers not to be "too quick to assume that capitalism embraces the whole of western society, [or] that it accounts for every stitch of the social fabric."[24] Impressed neither by Weber's thesis crediting Protestant theological innovations with unleashing a flood of acquisitive rationality after the Reformation, nor by Marx's thesis of radical change in the period 1750–1850, Braudel instead depicted capitalism as a slowly changing, "long lived structure," which, he hastened to add, "is not the same thing as an absolutely unchanging reality."[25]

His insistence on the fundamental difference between capitalism and the market economy as such was part and parcel of his stress on continuity:

I found myself constantly faced with a regular contrast between a normal and often routine exchange economy (what the eighteenth century would have called the *natural* economy) and a superior, sophisticated economy (which would have been called *artificial*). I am convinced that this distinction is tangible, that the *agents* and men involved, the actions and the mentalities, are not the same in these different spheres; and that the rules of the market economy regarding, for instance, free competition as described in classical economics, although visible at some levels, operated far less frequently in the upper sphere, which is that of calculations and speculation. At this level, one enters a shadowy zone, a twilight area of activities by the initiated which I believe to lie at the very root of what is encompassed by the word capitalism: the latter being an accumulation of power (one that bases exchange on the balance of strength, as much as, or more than on the reciprocity of needs), a form of social parasitism which, like so many other forms, may or may not be inevitable. In short, there is a hierarchy in the world of trade, even if, as in all

[23] Ibid., II, 225; III, 620 (italics in the original). For an argument that capitalism, or at any rate economic individualism, has a much longer history in England than conventional historiography has recognized, see Alan Macfarlane, *The Origins of English Individualism* (New York: Cambridge University Press, 1978), and *The Culture of Capitalism* (Oxford: Basil Blackwell, 1987). See also the important review essay by K. D. M. Snell, "English Historical Continuity and the Culture of Capitalism: The Work of Alan Macfarlane," *History Workshop*, 27 (Spring, 1989), 154–63.

[24] Braudel, *Civilization and Capitalism,* III, 630.

[25] Ibid., III, 620–21. On Weber, see II, 566–578.

hierarchies, the upper stages could not exist without the lower stages on which they depend.[26]

This nearly timeless, multilevel model of the economy appealed to Braudel precisely because it accommodated random, nondirectional change and the *simultaneous* coexistence of capitalism with traits often described as precapitalist. From this standpoint, a thriving market economy was a necessary, but not a sufficient condition for the emergence of full-blown capitalism. Braudel construed capitalism as a parasitic growth, sinister yet possibly inevitable, which depended on markets but was not constituted by them. He identified it almost entirely with giant corporations, big business, buccaneering raids, boardroom knavery, and other practices and institutions made possible by monopoly power. Monopoly power, in turn, he regarded as alien to the fundamentals of market exchange, though never absent from the marketplace for long. There is considerable irony in this strategy. Instead of identifying capitalism with the spread, intensification, and possibly the ultimate universalization of competition that Macpherson, Polanyi, Max Weber, and so many others have dreaded, Braudel identified it with monopoly – with the subversion of competition, the negation of the free market. On this interpretation, the market itself is held harmless. Instead of being the quintessential institution of a capitalist economy, it becomes a potential cure for at least some of capitalism's excesses. As Braudel put it, a "market economy, the same everywhere, with only minor variations, was the necessary, spontaneously-developing and in fact normal base of any society over a certain size."[27]

Braudel's strategy of separating the market from capitalism, treating the former as a normal feature of large economies, too deeply rooted in authentic human needs to be dispensed with, and the latter as a potentially malignant but controllable parasite, obviously has political implications. He did not hesitate to make them explicit. "If we are prepared to make an unequivocal distinction between the market economy and capitalism," he mused at the end of his final volume, this might "offer us a way of avoiding that 'all or nothing' which politicians are constantly putting to us, as if it were impossible

[26] Ibid., II, 22. Italics in the original.
[27] Ibid., II, 600.

to retain the market economy without giving the monopolies a free hand, or impossible to get rid of monopolies without nationalizing everything in sight."[28]

The three figures we have chosen – Polanyi, Macpherson, and Braudel – more or less box the compass on the relationship between market and culture. The market can be praised or damned; seen as an institution that only recently appeared on the historical scene, or one whose origins are lost in the mists of antiquity; construed as a virtual synonym for capitalism, or something close to its antonym. Some scholars, like Macpherson, see the market necessarily trailing in its wake a large array of cultural consequences, between which we have little freedom to pick and choose; others, like Braudel, stress the fluidity of the connections between culture's various elements and treat the market as a protean, multifaceted phenomenon, more nearly the product of cultural change than its motor. The thirteen authors whose essays are collected in this volume are no more unified in their understandings of key terms such as "market," "capitalism," and "culture," than Polanyi, Macpherson, and Braudel. Whether this wide range of possible meanings is a sign of vitality and free-wheeling intellectual energy, or of simple confusion, remains to be seen. In any case, the reader is forewarned that in the pages that follow one must ask, over and over again, precisely what words mean in the various contexts that each author supplies.

Part I: market regimes old and new

In Jonathan Dewald's "The Ruling Class in the Marketplace: Nobles and Money in Early Modern France" (Chapter 1), the reader will encounter one of this volume's most important recurrent questions, the question of chronology that separated Polanyi, Macpherson, and Braudel. Where should historians draw the line between the norms and practices that define traditional society and the new forms of thought and behavior – especially acquisitiveness and instrumental rationality – we usually associate with the historical movement toward fully developed market economies? In examining how the high French nobility responded to the increasing importance of money in

[28] Ibid., III, 632.

their lives, Dewald argues that instrumental, rational attitudes toward money have had an older and more complex history than we are usually taught to assume. He stresses that it would be a mistake to believe the French nobility were by nature incapable of meeting the challenges that acceptance of the market and monetary exchange involved, and hence docile in the face of the growing success of financiers and other bourgeois. Models of economic rationality and self-control in fact existed among the French nobility as early as the fourteenth century, and Dewald contends that throughout the early modern period the French nobility had little difficulty in recognizing that economic abundance and calculation were necessary to maintain their traditional social status.

Dewald's chief concern here, however, is to describe and account for a partial breakdown of this early regime of aristocratic adaption over the course of the seventeenth century, when the nobles' experience of money became intertwined with their experience of a new form of political power they disliked and sought to escape. By the early seventeenth century, the French monarchy had fully systematized the practice of selling judicial and administrative offices, and venality eventually came to touch military positions, governorships of provinces and small towns, and honorific titles as well. These changes meant that nobles who wished to participate in public life were required to make large financial investments, usually comparable to the cost of a substantial estate or to several years of most nobles' annual revenues. Few noble families, however, could raise the immense sums that a military or court office required. Hence, attaining public office now also entailed heavy borrowing, a practice that placed the nobles within yet another new and complicated set of exchanges with those whose money they used. As a result, Dewald argues, the growing significance of money in court circles came to reinforce rather than undermine the bonds of patronage, since political actors now had greater need of well-placed patrons than ever before. Further complicating matters here was the fact that venality brought the nobility into a new money-based system of public life that as yet had no secure legal protections for private property. In early modern France, landownership too depended heavily on political power and influence, requiring constant defense against litigation and political interference.

Dewald observes that the increasingly effective commercial organization of France, ultimately, did serve to enrich the nobility, even in the face of growing debts and legal burdens, by conferring new exchange value on their vast resources in food and fuel. Yet at the same time he wants to show that the most pressing force for economic change within the lives of the high French nobility – the steadily increasing concentration of political power in the hands of an absolute monarch – had little to do with "the market" as historians usually understand it. Indeed, more immediately important than purely economic calculations, Dewald argues, were new monetary calculations forced upon the nobility by the practice of venality, calculations that led to a sharp decline in the ability of the nobles to control their own finances.

In the end, the French nobility came to despise the credit relations of venality, Dewald concludes, because the system compelled them to depend on wealthier figures for public office. They also disliked the humiliations that landownership entailed, especially the need to "solicit" legal support from social inferiors. In these circumstances, withdrawal or changes of allegiance were very difficult, if not impossible, given often huge commitments of financial resources. But other forms of flight from subordination – especially, opportunities to play with money by gambling – were available. Dewald ends his examination of the French nobles' multidimensional dealings with money by arguing that their increasing readiness to gamble sprang from a new desire to step outside traditional roles that now brought uncertainty and humiliation to most of them.

In "Territorial Gardens: The Convergence of Feudal and Bourgeois Conceptions of Land in Seventeenth-Century French Formal Gardens" (Chapter 2), Chandra Mukerji, like Dewald, finds that the traditional culture of the early modern French nobility was altered to meet both the new ambitions of absolute monarchy and the new opportunities of a developing market economy. Yet where Dewald argues that the mounting costs of adapting left the high nobility deeply uncomfortable in their attitudes toward money, Mukerji contends that they did manage to restructure their economic attitudes and practices in ways that allowed them to retain and enhance their traditional social prestige.

During the seventeenth century, the French nobility designed and built formal gardens that fused their values and interests with those of an emerging French bourgeoisie. While these often stupendous productions became the envy of the Western world, they also served – within France – to advertise and legitimate the authority of a new elite culture in which the different economic attitudes of two social classes converged, yet without jeopardizing the preeminence of the established noble elite. On the one hand, the imposition of order on land made a political statement because gardens were constructed as miniaturized models of the recently centralized French monarchy and its territories. Plotted like territorial maps, they were accessible visual structures for territorial demarcation and display in which a complex, yet also centralized, organization of forests, lawns, canals, and walkways announced a new distribution and use of authority. And yet, while plainly reasserting the preeminent status of noble life, French gardens also put to use techniques of estate development that were contributing in new ways to the power and wealth of France. The extraordinary water system at Versailles, for example, included numerous fountains that spewed jets of water to great heights, thereby highlighting the extraordinary ambitions of the French king. The pumps that actually worked the fountains, however, also displayed the new technological capacities of French mines, where excavation depths had been increased as a result of recent improvements in pumping systems originally designed to dispose of excess water.

In seeking to demonstrate a convergence of feudal and bourgeois conceptions of land in the organization of seventeenth-century French formal gardens, Mukerji clearly does not defend the proposition that the spread of market relations entirely transformed traditional aristocratic practices and self-conceptions. (The importance of commerce was never openly acknowledged in the final designs of formal gardens, and the pervasiveness of military architecture, statuary, and engineering testified to the continuing identification of nobility with military power and prowess.) Yet she also does not suggest that the French king and his court simply overlooked their ties to a society whose well-being was increasingly determined by trade and finance. (Formal gardens were dependent, for example, on France's preeminence in an international horticultural trade, which was both encouraging and profiting from new techniques in locating, shipping, and cultivating tender plants.) What Mukerji, like other contributors to this volume, does show is that the development of market relations has never taken place in a cultural vacuum, but instead has been dependent on a complex cultural mediation. Moreover, although the precise structure of the mediation Mukerji uncovers may have been unique to early modern France, its complexity, as we shall see, was not.

Margaret C. Jacob's essay "Money, Equality, Fraternity: Freemasonry and the Social Order in Eighteenth-century Europe" (Chapter 3) also supports the view that the market initially spread by way of assimilating and transforming traditional institutions, not simply by dismantling them. Like Dewald and Mukerji, she focuses primarily on a reconfiguration of conduct that occurred within elite culture. As Jacob interprets them, Masonic lodges in the eighteenth century were (not unlike French formal gardens in the seventeenth century) points of cultural convergence in which an expanding population of prosperous artisans and wealthy merchants gathered with an older aristocracy of birth. Masonic lodges, however, also sought to redefine the identity of Europe's elite by creating among its members a new form of hierarchy based on elections and rituals that rewarded merit and recognized Masonic brothers as "equals." This new code of sociability within the lodges, Jacob goes on to show, also rested firmly on monetary practices that reflected the growing importance of monetary relations in European society at large, for all members were required to pay substantial fees upon initiation, then again with each honorary "degree" conferred, as well as annual (if not monthly) dues.

Jacob also observes that although many of the practices of Freemasons plainly reflected the growing importance of the market in elite culture, other characteristic aspects of freemasonry had their origins in changes that first unfolded within traditional popular culture, and here she is the first to raise another of this volume's recurrent questions: How did the spread of the market affect the attitudes and institutions of ordinary people? In exploring the surviving manuscript records from one of the first Masonic lodges in Dundee, Scotland, Jacob shows that the roots of freemasonry in fact lay in efforts by ordinary workingmen's craft guilds, in the late seventeenth century, to survive in an economic setting where an expanding market for labor would overwhelm their efforts to regulate wages. The struggles for survival that took place in towns like Dundee ended with the disappearance of guilds as they were gradually transformed into social organizations consisting of and governed by landed gentlemen, wealthy merchants, and nobles. In the process, many of the traditional functions of guilds – which had included policing the economic practices of the particular crafts they represented, as well as protecting their members from powerful lay and ecclesiastical magistrates – were also abandoned. Yet Jacob's paper shows that eighteenth-century Masonic lodges did retain other elements of a once vital guild tradition, including a concern for the moral betterment of its members and old ceremonies of initiation and rituals associated with popular festivals and religious feast days. Masons' dues, for example, were collected not just to cover expenses of running a lodge. They also allowed for the establishment of charitable funds to assist brothers who had fallen on hard times, the provision of loans or outright gifts to brothers or their widows (with Mozart's being perhaps the most famous widow to receive such charity), and wherever possible the distribution of money to the deserving poor.

The complex practices within eighteenth-century Masonic lodges, Jacob concludes, should be understood as activity that opaquely mirrored the new rules and values of the market. For while the lodges certainly did affirm the increasing importance of monetary exchange, they at the same time sought to mitigate some of its negative social effects by providing economic protection for lodge members who happened to fall victim to the vagaries of chance and fortune. Or put another way, the new sociability defined and encouraged by freemasonry flourished in a century when a growing number of Europeans had the money to support it, yet it also sanctioned and provided new remedies for the dire consequences of being moneyless.

Martin J. Wiener's "Market Culture, Reckless Passion, and the Victorian Reconstruction of Punishment" (Chapter 4) also approaches the history of market relations as a development that at first had served to introduce new codes of personal and social conduct into human affairs. Like Jacob, he is interested in understanding how the spread of the market affected popular attitudes and institutions – in this instance, early Victorian views of crime and punishment. For Wiener, however, over the course of the first half of the nineteenth century, the widening and deepening of market relations had become less a matter of new forms of discipline than of new opportunities for compulsive and willful behavior.

The broader question that lies behind Wiener's examination of early Victorian views of criminality, then, is what he calls the "permissive" face of the market. Here he argues that early Victorian feelings about the market were marked by a new and increasingly widespread fear that all traditional checks on individual desires and impulses were now dissolving without effective replacement. Wiener's essay thus complicates a theme shared by the volume's first three chapters – namely, that the initial pattern of change that came with the growth of the market did not represent a break with past values, so much as a process of restructuring those values to serve new ends – by offering a detailed exploration of the ways in which the early Victorians' anxious preoccupation with crime revealed a new fear that Britain's economic progress was no longer being accompanied by moral progress but instead was serving to increase moral disorder.

In early-nineteenth-century Britain, a sharp increase in crime was seen as the most troubling evidence of this disorder. Indeed, Tories, Whigs, and Radicals alike agreed that their age was witnessing an unprecedented wave of crime. Between 1805 (when national criminal statistics were first compiled) and 1842, the number of people brought to trial for indictable offenses rose nearly sevenfold, far exceeding the increase in Britain's population. Wiener goes on to show that, on more careful examination, these new statistics appear to have significantly overstated the situation. Figures on crime against both persons and property were inflated by a combination of improved record keeping, expanded enforcement, and changes in the law that greatly extended criminal liability. (Mere attempts to steal, for example, were thoroughly criminalized and more systematically punished. Similarly, violent behavior was met with diminishing tolerance.) Yet Wiener also emphasizes that it would be a mistake to dismiss early Victorian fears of crime as exaggerated or as simply reflecting a new determination to enforce the rules and values of the marketplace. In fact, the chief concern in early Victorian discussions of all aspects of social policy, he contends, was to contain and master an impulsiveness that the market itself was now assumed to be encouraging and nourishing. As a result, early Victorians also became obsessed with the development of "character," of the individual whose ability to master his or her passions by reflection would provide a remedy for the threat of moral decay posed by the continuing spread of the market.

The reformation of criminal law, Wiener argues, played a central role in building the framework of this new culture dedicated to "character" building. The external controls of imprisonment were now made less brutal and erratic, more uniform and consistent. The convict ship, the gallows, and the pillory were replaced by specified periods of imprisonment; hangings were less frequent and no longer public spectacles. The new modes of punishment in the early Victorian era were, in turn, firmly based on the assumption that if criminals were subject to predictable pains and rewards, and held strictly accountable for their actions, they too could behave like individuals capable of controlling their passions and impulses. In short, Wiener concludes that as people in early Victorian Britain lost faith in the view that moral and economic progress went hand in hand, they looked no longer to the market, but instead to criminal law, to provide aid in the urgent task of developing a new moral regime needed to maintain a respectable, law-abiding society.

Part II: personality and authority in the age of capital

Wiener's examination of the market's "permissive" face and the fears of licentiousness and unconstrained willfulness it aroused leads us into a second group of essays concerned with new forms of personhood and social authority associated with the market. The pre-Victorian image of the criminal as a being of monstrous appetites and unmanageable will differs only in magnitude and lurid details from early images of entrepreneurs, whose sense of power and control over other people's lives carried them far outside established orbits of propriety. Advancing capitalism produced in the early decades of the nineteenth century repeated scenes of "creative destruction," as Joseph Schumpeter called it, in which personal traits of resiliency, adaptiveness, and steely determination took on an importance unknown in traditional society. Communal values of dutifulness and Christian humility could have taken a heavy toll on self-esteem if they had not been counterbalanced by the emergence of new values better suited to change, opportunity, and new departures. How did people raised on one set of values justify lives lived according to another?

The key question, argues Joyce Appleby in "New Cultural Heroes in the Early National Period" (Chapter 5), concerns attitudes toward uncertainty and disruption: "How did those men most directly connected with creating America's commercial society in the early nineteenth century arrive at a constructive appraisal of the constant disruption and uncertainty that attended their lives?" To answer that question she marshals evidence from a group of autobiographies written by men born mainly in the North between 1765 and 1804. No single pattern emerges from such diverse sources, of course, but certain leitmotifs appear again and again, and Appleby offers the following four-part schema as a first approximation to the self-told life story that lay at the heart of an "entrepreneurial culture in the making."

First came an "unforeseen break with childhood expectations," most often a literal passage away from home and journey into unfamiliar lands. Especially striking at this stage is the authors' lack of nostalgia about the lives they left behind, and open anger (or sometimes seething contempt) for the fathers who resisted their departure – and whose own accomplishments fell so far short of their sons'. "What may have begun as a fantasy wish to slay their fathers appears in their life stories as a fait accompli," Appleby writes. Liberated from authority and confining expectations, the authors then often report a second stage marked by "the wonder of a new life prospect," as the world opens before them. Then follows a series of "encounters that teach moral lessons," often with older men whose advice and help substitutes for that of the father. Finally the autobiographies turn to "outcomes and observations," as the authors self-consciously construe their lives as models that their children and others may wish to imitate. At every stage, Appleby stresses the "strong story line" of these tales, and the readiness of the authors to impute to themselves effective power and control over the events of their lives. "Providential thinking," she observes, "figures very weakly in explanations of outcomes."

Appleby also finds in these texts intriguing contrapuntal themes and metaphors that seem designed to cultivate mutuality and ward off envy in the face of rapidly shifting fortunes. Crescendos of self-appreciation are matched by expressions of gratitude toward others; envy is displaced by admiration for what others accomplish. In place of the age-old conception of society as divided between haves and have-nots, a rigid structure of ranks and strata, there emerges a metaphor of society as a smoothly functioning machine with "interacting parts and interchangeable participants," in which there is room for everyone to contribute to the well-being of the whole. Like Max Weber, who sought to show that the desire for endless acquisition was not natural but historical in origin, and Colin Campbell, who has similarly sought to unearth the historical origins of the endless appetite for consumption that fuels capitalist productivity, Appleby traces in these autobiographies a fusion of myth and reality that enabled people to make sense of their lives under dizzying marketplace conditions we call "natural" and take for granted today, but which had little precedent before the nineteenth century.[29]

Richard B. Latner's essay, "Preserving 'The Natural Equality of Rank and Influence' " (Chapter 6), is an exercise in historiographical revision. In retrospect it is clear that Andrew Jackson's America was already embarked on a path toward economic growth, widening disparities between poor and rich, and an urban-industrial future in which the discipline of the market would reach deeply into every life, irrevocably undercutting the yeoman dream of independence and small-scale production. But the Jacksonians (Appleby's autobiographers among them) could not anticipate what lay before them. As so often in history, what they intended and what they wrought were two different things.

Latner suggests that historians in recent years have erred by losing sight of the distinction between intentions and consequences; by assuming that because Jacksonian policies often opened the floodgates of capitalist development, this must also have been the policies' covert intention, no matter how egalitarian and republican their rhetoric. On the contrary, he argues, drawing on an older interpretation by Marvin Meyers, the Jacksonians meant what they said: They admired equality and thought their policies well suited to its achievement.

The crux of the matter is how to interpret their abundant and repetitive praise of what we today would call "equality of opportunity." From our contemporary standpoint the contrast between

[29] Colin Campbell, *The Romantic Ethic and the Spirit of Modern Consumerism* (Oxford: Basil Blackwell, 1987).

"equality of opportunity" and "equality of condition" seems clear and highly charged with political implications. To advocate equality of condition today is to oppose hierarchy; in contrast, the person who advocates equality of opportunity is at least tacitly accepting the ladder of hierarchy, and merely seeking fair access to its higher rungs. Equality of opportunity conforms to the meritocratic principles on which capitalist societies presently operate; equality of condition is potentially subversive of them. But we have no basis, Latner suggests, for supposing that the contrast between these two varieties of equality was clear-cut in the eyes of early-nineteenth-century villagers, who had no inkling of the massive social transformation that the next century and a half would bring.

Being a Jacksonian Democrat and an upstate New York banker, Alexander Bryan Johnson might well have figured among Appleby's entrepreneurs or Latner's egalitarians. But what earns him the close attention of Jean-Christophe Agnew in "Banking on Language: The Currency of Alexander Bryan Johnson" (Chapter 7) is a distinction of a different sort: his authorship of the first American text on the philosophy of language. That a banker should also be a philosopher is intriguing enough. Johnson's special claim on our attention, however, derives from the precise manner in which his everyday life in the marketplace seems to have informed his curiously modern views on language and the highly problematical relationship between words and the world they ostensibly represent.

Agnew is the author of a subtle book on Anglo-American culture 1550–1750, which links the theater – that scene of deliberate and playful misrepresentation – to the growing theatricality of life itself in a culture increasingly oriented to the marketplace, where duplicity is always a danger and all representations are presumed to be in the service of self-interest.[30] Johnson's flashes of skeptical insight, like Herman Melville's strange ruminations in *The Confidence-Man,* supply nineteenth-century evidence for a theme Agnew first observed in the sixteenth: The rise of the market seems to have been closely associated with "crises of representation," in which the real world

[30] *Worlds Apart: The Market and the Theater in Anglo-American Thought, 1550–1750* (Cambridge: Cambridge University Press, 1986).

threatens to dissolve into a sea of appearances, and the self to evaporate, taking on whatever shape shifting occasions may demand.

Johnson's life was strongly marked by false appearances. Once, for example, although the very model of a gentleman, he cunningly concealed authorization for banking operations in a bill that legislators approved, thinking it applied only to the insurance business. He married Abigail Adams, granddaughter of John Adams, and became a member of her church, only to leave it when a church court threatened to chastise him for violating the Sabbath by using the Sunday mail. His son-in-law, whom he entrusted with a responsible position, took advantage of it to embezzle a million dollars. Most striking of all, this English immigrant whose accent helped give him a reputation for gentility, and who led in America an impeccably correct and gentrified life, first as an Episcopalian and then as a Presbyterian, appears in truth to have been a Jew, whose father changed the family name for "purposes of trade."

Johnson's philosophy, reminiscent of Ludwig Wittgenstein's, stressed the artificiality of language and our inability ever to validate the supposed connection between word and thing. It earned him a reputation among those few contemporaries who read his books as an "unflinching nominalist," deeply suspicious of the world of commonsense appearances. Johnson himself explicitly drew connections between the perils of banking and his skeptical views on language: Just as bank notes were the "artificial representatives of specie," he argued, so words were the "artificial representatives of natural phenomena."

Disturbingly esoteric and alien though his philosophical writings seemed in the eyes of his contemporaries, Johnson also wrote essays with titles such as "The Art of Self-Control" and "The Art of Controlling Others" that expounded a kind of sociological instrumentalism, in which language was not only returned to its commonsense status as a tool, but elevated into a tool of remarkable constructive power, becoming constitutive of reality itself. "Mark out for yourself," he once advised his son, "such a character as you desire to possess, and by speaking constantly thereto, you will attain the desired character as certainly as you will a coat, by going to your tailor and ordering it." In this homespun anticipation of postmodern vertigo, wherein it becomes possible to suspect that words constitute the real, rather than imperfectly representing it, we see hints of epistemological instability and an evanescent, protean conception of the self that Agnew suggests may always have lurked beneath the deceptively complacent surface of market culture. That suggestion finds an echo at the end of the volume in Haskell's essay on the relation between capitalism and antiformalism.

Part III: the lens of "high" culture

With Marilyn R. Brown's "An Entrepreneur in Spite of Himself: Edgar Degas and the Market" (Chapter 8), the first of three essays in Part III, we shift our focus to consider relationships between the market and art and literature, forms of imaginative activity typically associated with "culture" in its hierarchical or elitist sense. Like Martin Wiener, Brown is analyzing a response to the market marked by ambivalence and conflict. Her protagonist was often fiercely critical of art's increasingly close ties to the marketplace, yet he was also an artist who became well known within his society, and achieved considerable success in selling paintings that conveyed his critical attitudes. In exploring several of Degas's visual productions – especially *A Cotton Office in New Orleans* (1873) – Brown is careful not to approach his work simply as illustrations of contemporary events and personalities. She does argue, though, that understanding the shifting conditions of patronage and the art market during Degas's lifetime is indispensable to appreciating the complex process by which he came to make his pictures. Moreover, she demonstrates that the disjunctive pictorial focus and unfixed messages about business in his paintings can be interpreted as appealing to, and fulfilling the needs of, an expanding and heterogeneous market for art in nineteenth-century France.

Brown also makes use of Degas's letters and notebooks to explore his attitudes toward his own success and recognition. Degas was profoundly ambivalent about the role of artist-entrepreneur, decrying the fickle nature of success in the artistic market, and railing against new buyers and dealers for creating a culture in which artistic success seemed to take the form of a financial panic. Yet Brown shows too that although Degas's cantankerous attitude toward the new market for art never changed, he did learn how to play the market to his own advantage, thereby becoming "an entrepreneur in spite of himself." Throughout the 1880s, for example, his earnings increased with his growing success in selling through dealers to rich businessmen and industrialists. As his earnings went up, Brown observes, Degas also chose to make fewer paintings, indicating that a now well-established reputation allowed him to benefit from higher prices he commanded for his later works.

Finally, Brown shows that Degas's attitudes toward the market were further complicated by issues of gender. His brothel monotypes, for example, present secretly observed exchanges in pictures that often appear murky and ugly as sex is reduced to commerce and vice versa. The commodity marketed in brothels, of course, was not cotton, but the ambivalence implicit in Degas's earlier paintings of businessmen was also present in his drawings of the "businesswomen" of the French demimonde. His representations of prostitutes oscillate between voyeurism in his choice of subject and point of view and an organization of pictorial space in which the torsos of prostitutes – cropped and stripped of their clothes and individuality – appear as grotesque emblems of the commodity offered for sale. There is a final irony to be found here, Brown notes: Although Degas carefully planned paintings like *A Cotton Office* for sale and exhibition, he kept most of his brothel monotypes for his own private delectation and for the pleasure of select friends.

Richard F. Teichgraeber III in " 'A Yankee Diogenes': Thoreau and the Market" (Chapter 9) is engaged in much the same enterprise as Marilyn Brown. Thoreau once described life in market society as a "life without principle," and yet, like Degas's, his disaffection was by no means consistent or free of paradoxes. While there were radically antimarket implications in his account of his experiment in living at Walden Pond, Thoreau emphasized that the experiment was not to be taken as a guide to social or economic reform. He also recognized the paradox of poverty in the midst of economic progress in antebellum America, yet often said that progress had done more to degrade the affluent than the poor. And finally, to name only one more seeming paradox, Thoreau railed against the commercialization of American life, yet also used the language of business and commerce to convey the joys of an unspoiled natural life.

The many-sidedness of Thoreau's response to the market, his shifting back and forth from criticism to grudging accommodation, Teichgraeber argues, cannot be explained simply by asking whether Thoreau was "for" or "against" the market. Thoreau's attitude, like that of Degas, is better understood as one of ambivalent attachment. Thoreau certainly did not believe the market was the soil in which the greatness of individuals might flourish. Yet he also did not believe, Teichgraeber argues, that life *with* principle dictated unqualified opposition to or complete withdrawal from the market. (Thoreau never advocated voluntary poverty; he suggested it was merely one possibility.) What Thoreau sought in writing *Walden,* Teichgraeber concludes, was to establish an intellectual position that mirrored an actual place he had once made for himself at Walden Pond: a place both outside and inside the market. "Outside" because Thoreau obviously wanted to present himself as an arbiter of its value, but "inside" too because the most he finally expected of his countrymen was acknowledgment of the need for an antipecuniary ethic to restrain their acquisitiveness, and recognition that trade and commerce might become means to higher ends.

William M. Reddy's "Need and Honor in Balzac's *Père Goriot:* Reflections on a Vision of Laissez-Faire Society" (Chapter 10) demonstrates another way in which new approaches to the study of art and literature are enriching our understanding of "high" cultural attitudes and practices within market societies. Like Brown and Teichgraeber, Reddy contends that art and literature are never mimetic in any simple sense; they engage instead in what Stephen Greenblat has called "exchanges" or "negotiations" with the society within which they were born. Such activity, in turn, will yield different messages, depending on the frame of reference we bring to the examination of activities within the realm of "high" culture.

Reddy interprets *Père Goriot* as a novel that illustrates a neglected but long-standing current of thinking about the market in which a focus on the shared hierarchy of "needs" born of our physical nature – that is, we must all breathe, eat, and shelter ourselves from the elements – sets parameters for the functioning and fairness of exchange systems. Balzac did not, Reddy argues, assume that individuals who inhabited nineteenth-century market societies were essentially equal partners, each committed in exactly the same way to increasing his or her advantage or maximizing individual utility. Instead, he differentiated parties to exchange by examining which needs, desires, and preferences they sought to satisfy. *Père Goriot* contains, for example, stories of people who must devote their energy primarily to satisfying their urgent needs, and tells us that in a market society they can do so only by the daily acquiring and spending of money. Balzac's novel also makes it clear, however, that propertyless people face the added burden of finding themselves vulnerable to others whose wealth allows them to come to the market for the purpose of satisfying less pressing goals that, in Reddy's interpretation, cluster around the notion of "honor."

The vision of market society that emerges from *Père Goriot,* Reddy contends, is that of a world in which rich and poor alike are caught up in various sorts of trade-offs between "honor" and need. The majority of Balzac's characters are largely propertyless and choose to escape from want by dishonorable conduct. Some sell their affections, their talents, or their bodies for a square meal or a roof that does not leak. Still others squander meager living allowances to purchase honorable commodities such as opera tickets or stylish clothing. "Honor" is the all-important good in *Père Goriot,* Reddy argues, because it contributes its aura to all commodity forms that signal the availability of economic surpluses. And in market societies political and cultural authority inevitably attach themselves to individuals who have significant surpluses of property.

Yet while honor is all important, Balzac also saw that it remained both remarkably difficult to define and impossible to distinguish from the mere possession of money. Even the already rich and honorable, who decry the fact that money brings honor, cannot themselves escape the fact that their freedom from need in the end only serves to reflect wealth's central role in the logic of honor. Moreover, while Balzac was no feminist, he recognized that the conflict between honor and money was complicated by issues of gender. He consistently presented the women characters in *Père Goriot* as suffering from painful constraints in their behavior that men do not experience. For women in nineteenth-century market societies, "honor" takes on a grim and repressive face, as some suffer near imprisonment at the hands of their husbands, and others embrace exile. The poverty of women, in Balzac's view, remained a subordinate issue, since he believed that they always had at hand dishonorable means to fulfill their needs. Hence, where men in the world of *Père Goriot* at least were still allowed to have ambition, the only course the market left open for women was whether or not they would preserve their sense of honor.

Part IV: agency and structure

Anyone who pursues the issues raised in parts I, II, and III far enough will eventually come up against problems of agency and structure, free will and determinism, freedom and fate. Timeless and universal though these dilemmas may appear to be, there is reason to suspect they are especially salient in societies that rely heavily on the discipline of the marketplace. These are, after all, societies in which people are given unusual latitude to do as they please – but only on the tacit assumption that both internal and external forms of discipline (think of Weber's Protestant ethic and Adam Smith's "invisible hand") are securely in place, ensuring that what people find it pleasing to do will serve the larger interests of allocative efficiency. This is a cultural situation well calculated to breed doubt about the reality of freedom, and to accentuate awareness of structural factors, determinants that subtly shape an actor's sense of what is possible and desirable, without ever thwarting the already formed will. Accordingly, the great debate between capitalism and socialism that has gripped much of the world's population for more than a century has repeatedly come back to certain key questions concerning the status of the self and the authenticity of its experience of autonomy.

The final section of this collection is devoted to three notable intellectuals who grappled with the problem of autonomy in market culture: Talcott Parsons, the leading American sociological theorist of the twentieth century; David Riesman, whose book *The Lonely Crowd* is probably the most widely read sociological text ever published; and John Stuart Mill, the principal nineteenth-century philosopher of liberalism, the political regime most often associated with market culture.

Talcott Parsons's reputation for unreadable prose and an inordinate preoccupation with social order and stability will be hard to shake among those who have never read his important and eminently readable first book, *The Structure of Social Action* (1937), or who know him only through his critics. The latter were legion during the 1960s and 1970s, when Parsons became a kind of whipping boy for a generation of sociologists intent on radicalizing their profession. Thus, Howard Brick's first task in "The Reformist Dimension of Talcott Parsons's Early Social Theory" (Chapter 11) is to correct misapprehension and reestablish the context of Parsons's work before World War II.

The son of a Congregational minister in the social gospel tradition, Talcott Parsons attended Amherst in the heyday of President Alexander Meiklejohn, who made the college a center for progressive politics and institutional economics in the early 1920s. As an undergraduate, Parsons admired the Russian Revolution, identified with the British Labour Party, and was active in left-wing causes, including the defense of President Meiklejohn against trustees who demanded his resignation. As a graduate student in Germany and at the London School of Economics in the mid-1920s, Parsons sought out the company of Harold Laski, R. H. Tawney, Karl Mannheim, Emil Lederer, and other left-of-center scholars and called himself a socialist. His first publication as an instructor in the Harvard Economics Department still displayed the influence of his institutionalist background, although he was by this time convinced, as was Max Weber, of the triumph of marginal utility economists over those of the historical school. Brick calls *The Structure of Social Action,* arguably Parsons's masterpiece, a "late manifestation of the reformist inclinations of the social-scientific intelligentsia in the United States." Although it addressed theoretical questions and was hardly a call to action, it displayed the same "mild left-wing tinge" as Parsons's other youthful work, and took the obsolescence of classical liberalism as one of its founding assumptions.

At the core of the book was Parsons's claim that the thought of Weber, Emile Durkheim, Vilfredo Pareto, and Alfred Marshall all converged on a single, paradigmatic way of understanding human affairs, which Parsons labeled the "voluntaristic theory of action." The chief virtue of the voluntaristic theory, Parsons claimed, was the middle path it traced between the two great theoretical poles of nineteenth-century thought, positivism and idealism. Idealist interpretations had erred by tending to treat human affairs as entirely a matter of ends and norms, thus exaggerating human autonomy and obscuring the force of circumstance. Positivist interpretations had tended to construe conduct exclusively in terms of means and conditions, thus ignoring the subjective experience of choice and reducing persons to mere reflexes of heredity and environment. Parsons's claim, in short, was that the voluntaristic theory of action transcended the terms of the nineteenth-century debate and imputed to human actors just that degree of autonomy they actually enjoyed.

The political standpoint of the book, argues Brick, was not conservative, but meliorist. One of Parsons's most insistent themes, the tendency of utilitarian modes of explanation to decay into deterministic varieties of positivism, thus obscuring the "voluntary" element in human action, echoed left-wing polemics about the crisis of capitalism in the mid-1930s. Given the book's attention to subjective states of mind and the preoccupation with motivation that Parsons displayed both in the book and in articles he wrote during the 1930s, Brick concludes that Parsons's goal at that time was to formulate a "postliberal theory that could explicate the kinds of motivations required to sustain effectively the moral legitimacy of an already emerging collectivized order." What Parsons sought to avoid was the danger of more coercive forms of collectivization, a threat that emanated from both extremes of the political spectrum and seemed all too real during the depression decade, when market discipline promised nothing but despair and misery.

Wilfred M. McClay takes as his subject "The Strange Career of *The Lonely Crowd*" (Chapter 12), the astonishing tour de force by David Riesman, Nathan Glazer, and Reuel Denney that sold more than a million copies and put its principal author on the cover of *Time* magazine in 1954. Trained as a lawyer rather than a sociologist, Riesman was a bright young man of patrician upbringing and boundless energy whose speculative musings on the changing national character somehow struck a powerful chord in the reading public. The two major protagonists in his story were abstract typifications in social psychology, the "inner-directed man" of the nineteenth century and the "other-directed man" of the twentieth. The plot told how the latter displaced the former. Taking Riesman at his word, the *Time* magazine cover artist captured their essential traits by depicting the first as a firm-jawed fellow kept rigidly on course by a gyroscope strapped to his back, and the second as a smiling glad-hander equipped with a radar antenna, the better to adapt himself to the ever-shifting expectations of others.

A third, shadowy figure played a large part in Riesman's argument but eluded iconographic representation. This was the "autonomous" person who, Riesman and his coauthors insisted, was their real ideal. He or she was purposive without being rigid, sensitive to others without being in thrall to them, self-possessed yet keenly aware of the limits of mastery. The cover artist's inability to get a handle on autonomy was shared by other readers and by Riesman himself, who in later years admitted the inadequacy of the book's treatment of autonomy and the ease with which readers conflated it with inner-direction. Lionel Trilling, who gave the book rave reviews, expressed the reaction of many readers when he observed that in comparing inner- with other-direction Riesman had found it impossible not to make inner-direction seem the more attractive, because the more autonomous. "I don't agree with Mr. Riesman that the preference is a mere prejudice which we must guard against. . . . it is still inner-direction that must seem the more fully human, even in its excesses."

The warmth of the public's reaction to *The Lonely Crowd* and the difficulty that authors and readers alike experienced in distinguishing between inner-direction and autonomy suggest to McClay that by the 1950s many people were having second thoughts about the "already emerging collectivized order" that Talcott Parsons and many other intellectuals had hoped to legitimize in the 1930s. From the post–Civil War decades through the New Deal, intellectuals in the United States had striven to set limits to individualism and call attention to the increasingly collectivist realities of urban-industrial life. Although not intended as a repudiation of that project, *The Lonely Crowd* does seem to mark its exhaustion. Inspired more by the antistatist sentiments of refugees from Hitler's Germany than by nostalgia, the book's authors neither anticipated nor desired the surprising revival of classical liberal ideology that culminated in the Republican electoral triumphs of the 1980s. Nonetheless they sounded alarms about conformity, individual initiative, and, of course, autonomy, that have always been the benchmarks of liberalism.

McClay confirms the shallowness of Riesman's conception of autonomy by contrasting it with Kant's more profound treatment a century and a half earlier. But he also gives *The Lonely Crowd* credit for having powers of illumination that reach beyond the limitations of its formal argument. Like surf waters, it moves in different directions at different levels, superficially affirming the new sensitivity to others, even while tacitly celebrating grit and determination; warning of the immense power of social institutions to mold personal character, even while indirectly encouraging confidence in the power of individuals to resist social pressure and become whoever they choose to be. The one great missed opportunity, in McClay's view, is that the authors of *The Lonely Crowd* treated the relation between inner- and other-direction as a succession in time, *from* one *to* the other, when they could have construed it as a matter of contending polarities that wax and wane, but perpetually coexist and may even have a complementary relation to one another. Thus, one might characterize the people of the United States (and other advanced market societies?) not simply as "other-directed" but as perpetually torn between the alternatives of inner- and other-direction, their distinguishing trait being neither the one nor the other, but the sense that life's choices boil down to this great either–or.

The perils of heteronomy figure also in Thomas L. Haskell's essay, "Persons as Uncaused Causes" (Chapter 13). He takes up a theme touched on by many of the volume's authors, that of the insubstantial self, and tries to bring it and its relationship to the market to a focus in the life of one person, John Stuart Mill. A principal architect of liberalism, Mill was a precocious young man who at the age of twenty experienced a "mental crisis" to which he later devoted a surprisingly large part of his *Autobiography.* During his crisis Mill was so deeply impressed with the power of antecedent circumstances to mold human character that he found it impossible to cast himself in a causal role. The philosophical doctrine of necessity, he reported, weighed upon him "like an incubus," temporarily convincing him that he was literally inconsequential, a mere passive object, rather than a free agent.

Observing that all our efforts to praise, blame, or explain depend on perceptions of cause-and-effect relationships, and observing also that those relationships are highly problematical, Haskell proposes to set aside for the moment the ontological concerns that normally propel philosophical inquiry into the question of free will, and construe Mill's crisis in strictly psychological and attributive terms. His aim is to open up for historical examination a deadly serious "game of causal attribution" in which we all participate incessantly, and which has rules that change in time, defining and redefining the form of life of the people who subscribe to them. The rules of this game affect all our thinking and acting, "for they are the rules of change itself; of being and nonbeing; of how things come into, and go out of, existence." Nowhere is causal attribution more vital than in regard to conceptions of the self, for once we know what the self can do or make, and what, in contrast, has made it the particular sort of self it is, we know virtually all there is to know about a self and its relations, free or determined, to the world at large.

Drawing on the explicitly causal language in which Mill discussed his personal crisis, and the equally explicit causal language in which Thomas Carlyle contemporaneously discussed the cultural crisis of an entire world "grown mechanical in head and heart" (an analysis that resonated with personal meaning for Mill), Haskell contends that Mill's crisis was symptomatic of a general upheaval in the rules of the game of causal attribution. That upheaval began in the eighteenth century and was intimately bound up with the rise of a market economy. Unfolding the causal implications both of Max Weber's utilitarian "spirit of capitalism," and of secularization – the death of God, the First Cause and Creator of everything – Haskell suggests that Mill hit upon the right explanation of his crisis when he traced its "origin" to the period of Benthamite enthusiasm just preceding it, when the young man was euphorically confident of his ability to outwit fate and shape the world to his will.

Mill's sudden swing from euphoric voluntarism to fatalistic dejection reproduces in miniature the cultural paradox Haskell's essay is meant to illuminate. The culture of the market simultaneously breeds two contradictory standpoints: the complacency of the "self-made man," who (like Mill on the eve of his crisis) imputes to himself great causal powers that make the world appear to be his oyster; and yet also a potentially bottomless skepticism and fatalism, which arises from the transitivity of causal relations, the liability of anything that can be construed as a *cause* of subsequent events to collapse, perceptually speaking, into an *effect* of antecedent ones (just as Mill's own self did during his crisis). The paradox inheres in the very nature of causal perception, but a market economy makes it common, everyday experience by encouraging a quest for technical mastery and cultivating the habits of remote causal attribution and instrumental rationality necessary to that quest. On this view, the young Mill was an early victim of a malaise that would become culture-wide as the market's new rules of causal attribution displaced older habits of mind. The result today, claims Haskell, is a world of depths and surfaces, beset by repeated controversies between "formalists," who construe causation proximately, and various "antiformalists," who construe it remotely. Discrepant though the interpretations of formalists and antiformalists are, and bitter though the battles between them, the prevailing rules of causal attribution do not decisively privilege either standpoint, leaving us, if anything, even less certain than our ancestors about the location of that elusive boundary that separates free agency from structural determination, autonomy from heteronomy, liberty from necessity.

•

The issues explored in these papers by no means exhaust the range of possibilities, and it should be said again that this volume makes no claims to suggesting the outlines of an overarching theory of market culture. Nor is our purpose to chalk up points for or against the market. Many past historical instances of "the culture of the market" have not survived into our time. Yet it is the changing appearance and complexity of this culture, not its prospects for survival, that interest us most in this volume. Taken together, the essays that follow are best read as a shared effort to demonstrate that the experiences and feelings brought about by the historical development of market societies have been, and still remain, open to a broad range of interpretations. They share, too, what Lynn Hunt has called the two characteristic aspects of a new approach to the challenge of writing cultural history: a close examination of actions, texts, and artifacts, which is accompanied by an open-mindedness to what their examination reveals.[31]

[31] "Introduction: History, Culture, and Text," *The New Cultural History*, ed. Lynn Hunt (Berkeley: University of California Press, 1989), p. 22.

PART I

Market regimes old and new

CHAPTER 1

The ruling class in the marketplace: nobles and money in early modern France

JONATHAN DEWALD

This essay asks how members of the high French nobility responded to the appearance of money in their lives during the seventeenth century. Despite the group's limited social and national dimensions, I believe it can help us to understand a larger problem: How do groups who are in many ways shielded from market forces, and who rely heavily on tradition to understand their lives, enter the capitalist world? What kinds of transformations are needed before tradition ceases to seem an adequate guide, and the rationality of the market comes to replace it? These transformations are difficult because such varied forces bind people to other forms of economic behavior. There are the attachments of habit and fear, which (so social scientists from a variety of disciplines have argued) encourage peasant farmers to retain inefficient economic practices; impoverished groups and societies cannot afford the risks that theoretically more effective techniques may involve.[1] There are also attachments of privilege and greed, which encourage (for instance) aristocracies to use their political power and social status to obtain economic advantages. And there are ethical attachments, which discourage rich and poor alike from the calculating selfishness that market economies may demand. In the case of Europe, these would include the overlapping attachments to

A somewhat different version of this essay appears as part of my book *Aristocratic Experience and the Origins of Modern Culture: France 1570–1715* (Berkeley: University of California Press, 1993). This material is used here with permission of the Press.

[1] A convenient summary of these views is supplied by Eric Wolf, *Peasants* (Englewood Cliffs, 1966); for recent debate about them, Robert P. Weller and Scott E. Guggenheim, *Power and Protest in the Countryside: Rural Unrest in Asia, Europe, and Latin America* (Durham, N.C., 1982), pp. 3–12.

Christian doctrine, to village community, and to the codes of a warrior aristocracy – in their different ways, all inhibited market calculations and individualism.[2]

Indeed, so many forces attach people to premarket economic arrangements that social scientists have seen the advent of monetary exchanges as an especially important, especially disruptive moment in the history of societies. Whatever advantages money and markets may eventually bring, adaptation to them requires that groups give up long-standing advantages, protections, and ethical positions. We may see interpretations of this confrontation as clustering around two interpretive poles, the one represented by Adam Smith and stressing the fundamental likeness of human behavior and inclination, the other represented by Max Weber and stressing fundamental differences among societies. For Smith, the impulse to exchange one's own goods for others' is natural and universal; mankind craves change and advancement, and will respond to whatever opportunities for improvement the outer world accords. Smith believed that the medieval European world offered few such opportunities, less for technological than for political reasons: Violence continually disrupted the exchange process, discouraging economic efforts of all kinds; men could get rich by stealing rather than working. As the progress of civilization brought these impulses under control and as other opportunities widened, though, men and women naturally and quickly responded, exchanging, investing, working, and innovating. For Smith, attachment to the premarket world is essentially a negative phenomenon, resulting from the fear and uncertainty that political oppression brings. Mankind's natural state is one of development.[3]

2 Benjamin Nelson, *The Problem of Usury, from Tribal Brotherhood to Universal Otherhood* (Princeton, 1949). For emphasis on the European nobilities' commitment to such views, see, for instance, George Huppert, *Les Bourgeois Gentilshommes: An Essay on the Definition of Elites in Renaissance France* (Chicago, 1977), and E. P. Thompson, *Whigs and Hunters: The Origins of the Black Act* (New York, 1975). Even Aristotle taught early modern Europeans suspicion of money and exchange, in arguing that money was unnatural and a cause of unnatural behavior. "We seek to define wealth and money-making in different ways . . . ," so taught the *Politics,* "for they *are* different; on the one hand [there is] true wealth, in accordance with nature, belonging to household management, productive; on the other money-making, with no place in nature, belonging to trade and not productive of goods in the full sense."

3 Adam Smith, *Wealth of Nations,* ed. Andrew Skinner (London and Baltimore, 1982). My understanding of these issues is indebted to discussions with Robert Brenner and Thomas Haskell, and to Haskell's chapter in this volume.

For Weber, of course, attachment to economic habits is a much deeper matter, an attachment to ways of life and forms of meaning. In famous formulations, Weber presents stability as people's natural desire; we wish to live as we always have, and we adjust our economic efforts accordingly, earning enough to preserve our traditional ways of life. To do otherwise would require a fundamentally new vision of the world. From this perspective, innovation brings pain to the participants and questions to the social scientist, who must ask how forms of behavior suitable to market exchanges might come into being – and how market participants managed to cope with the experience. Only men and women born into a fully developed capitalist system can find its assumption of relentless economic change in some degree natural – and even about this Weber displays uncertainty.[4]

Smithian and Weberian perspectives thus draw the historian's attention to quite different aspects of the confrontation with the market. Smith leads us to consider political "obstacles" to development and to situate these high in society; in the case of Europe, as Smith presents the story, warlike and larcenous aristocracies had to be controlled before the society's potential energies could be released. Weber situates obstacles to development throughout society, but at several points *The Protestant Ethic* emphasizes those presented by the lower orders, the peasants and others most insulated from cultural innovation.[5] And Weber draws attention to the difficult process of cultural adaptation and displacement that acceptance of the market and of monetary exchanges involved. For Smith, the cultural and psychological costs of market behavior are feeble; experience of the market is mainly liberating, closely associated with release from age-old experiences of violence and inequity. Weber stresses instead the psychological shock of the market's arrival and the range of mental habits that had to be changed to accommodate it.

Few historians today would wholly adopt either Smithian or Weberian perspectives. These are points between which interpretations have clustered, rather than strict alternatives. Yet, at least insofar as

[4] Although Weber presents capitalism as an "immense cosmos," whose rules economic actors have no choice about following, he also stresses the continuing force of religious differences in shaping economic behavior even within his own fully capitalist society: *The Protestant Ethic and the Spirit of Capitalism*, trans. Talcott Parsons (New York, 1958), pp. 54, 35.

[5] E.g. Weber, *The Protestant Ethic*, pp. 56–61.

early modern Europe is concerned, Weberian perspectives have dominated recent interpretive efforts. Scholars such as Jean-Christophe Agnew, Joyce Appleby, and William Reddy in different ways have emphasized the conceptual leap that early modern men and women had to take in order to enter a capitalist world. They needed to set in place a new vision of their world and of proper behavior in it before they could act in new ways. The process was hesitant and in some ways painful. Appleby points to an English retreat from market ideas in the early eighteenth century, and Reddy argues that in France the "rise of market culture" was incomplete well into the nineteenth century.[6] Historians' growing interest in anthropological interpretation has strengthened this Weberian orientation. Thus Jean-Christophe Agnew points to the anxious care with which medieval Europeans walled off their marketplaces – and the dangerous behavior that took place within them – from the ordinary conduct of life, to which the market represented a frightening challenge.[7] Not the Smithian liberation of natural economic impulses, but the destruction and replacement of old relationships and meanings has seemed the most important aspect of early modern confrontations with a money economy.

This essay argues for a different view of early modern Europeans' responses to money, by stressing ways in which nobles' adaptation to a market economy was easier, less troubled, than a Weberian view would suggest. I offer three specific arguments. First, instrumental, rational attitudes toward money had a longer history among the French nobility than many models of economic development suggest. Second, the market and the capitalist economy were only one of the realms in which nobles found themselves forced to adopt monetary calculations. At least as important as purely economic choices were the monetary calculations that the early modern state forced upon French nobles. This was only one of several ways in which the economic sphere of privilege, the world of state service, feudal landownership, and the economic use of political power, was one of discomfort and tension even for those who benefited most from it. As a result, so runs my third argument, French nobles

[6] Joyce Appleby, *Economic Thought and Ideology in Seventeenth-Century England* (Princeton, 1978); William Reddy, *The Rise of Market Culture: The Textile Trade and French Society, 1750–1900* (Cambridge, 1984).

[7] Jean-Christophe Agnew, *Worlds Apart: The Market and the Theater in Anglo-American Thought, 1550–1750* (Cambridge, 1986).

turned readily to forms of behavior that in some ways imitated, in some ways prepared them for, a market economy. In the realm of amusements, they turned to such practices as gambling and masked balls, which offered experiences of anonymity and free exchange; in the realm of property, they retreated from landowning and placed an increasing share of their wealth in government bonds and stocks. In this instance, at least certain aspects of a market economy were indeed felt to be liberating, less because of the energies that it unleashed than because the older economic order was so very oppressive, even to its beneficiaries.

Historians have devoted a good deal of fine research to the quantitative dimensions of nobles' dealings with money, seeking to evaluate successes and failures. They have made it clear that the French nobles cannot be thought of (as literary scholars have tended to do) as representing a precapitalist, decaying economic group, helplessly anxious before the growing success of financiers and other bourgeois and frightened by the properties of money itself.[8]

Such views seem to fit neither recent empirical research nor a theoretical reading of the nobles' economic position. Without seriously arguing the matter, I want here simply to assert that in the long run, nobles could scarcely help being economic winners in the sixteenth and seventeenth centuries. They controlled resources of food and fuel for which the society had an increasingly desperate need, and the increasingly effective commercial organization of their society gave monetary value to properties that previously had been virtually worthless. Forests, for instance, had supplied little revenue in the Middle Ages, but quickly became valuable in the sixteenth century, as a rapidly growing population bought wood for heating and construction. What Adam Smith called "the progress of improvement" conferred a new exchange value on resources that the nobility could previously consume only in "rustic hospitality at home."[9] Most of what we know about their circumstances suggests that in fact the nobles were getting richer, and even the group's complaints suggest

[8] As a recent example, Ralph Albanese, "The Dynamics of Money in Post-Molièresque Comedy," *Stanford French Review*, 7, no. 1 (Spring 1983). See also above, n. 3.

[9] Smith, *Wealth*, pp. 508–12, 335.

rising standards of luxury.[10] A vision of the nobles as wedded to a moral economy, baffled and angry in an increasingly monetized world, seems inappropriate to these circumstances.

Yet a vision of the nobles as increasingly comfortable with economic calculation, as steadily adapting to a monetary economy, seems insufficient as well – partly because certain forms of economic rationality had such long histories by the seventeenth century. In upper Normandy, land was bought and sold about as frequently in the fifteenth century as in the eighteenth, and purchases substantially outnumbered cases of inheritance.[11] Late medieval nobles kept impressive account books, far more orderly than their sixteenth- and seventeenth-century successors.[12] As a more explicit statement of late medieval attitudes to money, we may take Jean Froissart's description of his visit to Gaston de Foix, in southwestern France, at the end of the fourteenth century. Gaston was not a typical nobleman, but Froissart offered him as something better: as a pattern of what a nobleman ought to be. Gaston's economic behavior contributed to this role:

> He always disliked excessive extravagance and required an account of his wealth once every month. He chose twelve prominent men from his country to receive his rents and administer his retainers. For each period of two months, two of them worked in his receiving-office and at the end of that time they were changed and two others took their place. . . . The comptroller brought his accounts to his master on rolls or books, and left them for the Count to look over. He had a number of chests in his private room and from time to time, but not every day, he had money taken from them to give to some lord, knight or squire who had come to visit him, for no man ever left him without receiving a present. He was always increasing his wealth, as a precaution against the hazards of fortune, which he feared. He was approachable and agreeable to everyone, speaking to them kindly and amiably.[13]

[10] I have summarized some of this literature in *Pont-St-Pierre, 1398–1789: Lordship, Community, and Capitalism in Early Modern France* (Berkeley and Los Angeles, 1987); for rising levels of luxury, see, for instance, Gédéon Tallemant des Réaux, *Historiettes,* 2 vols. (Paris, 1960), I, 303.

[11] *Pont-St-Pierre,* pp. 51–52.

[12] A point discussed by Guy Bois, *Crise du féodalisme: économie rurale et démographie en Normandie orientale* (Paris, 1976). For other examples of declining accounting practices in the sixteenth century, André Plaisse, *La baronnie du Neubourg: Essai d'histoire agraire, économique, et sociale* (Paris, 1961); Dewald, *The Formation of a Provincial Nobility: The Magistrates of the Parlement of Rouen, 1499–1610* (Princeton, 1980), pp. 194–95.

[13] Jean Froissart, *Chronicles,* selected, edited and translated by Geoffrey Brereton (London and Baltimore, 1968), pp. 264–65.

Gaston (so Froissart's description suggests) had at his disposal a full range of economic techniques and assumptions. He kept close records, controlled his expenditures, and assumed that his wealth would grow. He and Froissart both believed that wealth was money, rather than lands or retainers, and Gaston at least assumed that only his money would shelter him against unfriendly developments in the future. Neither he nor Froissart perceived contradictions between gentility and hard economic calculation. Record keeping, mistrust of economic agents, and constant accumulation allied easily with hospitality and affability, in fact were their preconditions; abundance and calculation went together. Gaston, to repeat, offers an ideal type rather than a representative case, and perhaps Froissart thought him interesting because unusual. But Gaston's example raises complexities when we seek to define a specifically seventeenth-century stance toward money, for clearly instrumental rationality toward money and calculations of profit had long histories by then. Gaston seems not to fit any of Max Weber's categories of economic action. If he lacked the self-restraining, acquisitive ethic that Weber saw in Benjamin Franklin, he also seems far from "the capitalistic adventurer" whom Weber contrasted with Franklin and whose "activities were predominantly of an irrational and speculative character"; and he seems still farther from Weber's traditional social actor, who wishes "simply to live as he is accustomed to live and to earn as much as is necessary for that purpose."[14] Neither unrestricted greed nor traditional norms governed his monetary dealings. Gaston gave generously to his followers, but his giving reflected hard political calculations; and such generosity made him all the more careful about accumulating and controlling his wealth.

Indeed, it is rather the decline than the advance of control over money that strikes one in following the history of aristocratic economic behavior through the seventeenth century. Aristocratic bookkeeping declined sharply after about 1520, and revived only in the mid-eighteenth century. This decline in nobles' control of their finances had several causes: Fewer nobles managed their estates directly, turning instead to tenant farmers, over whom only loose control was exercised; possibilities for expenditure widened, and keeping track of purchases became more difficult.[15] The sense of control that

[14] Weber, *The Protestant Ethic,* pp. 20, 60.
[15] Above, n. 13.

Gaston displayed survived in some cases, but as an object of surprise rather than admiration. The Grand Condé's father, for instance, "had the soul of a business manager of a great house; no man ever kept his papers in better order." Condé paid his debts on time, followed his lawsuits carefully, and dramatically expanded his family's wealth.[16] I have argued elsewhere that the acquisitiveness and economic successes that Condé embodied were not unusual within the sixteenth- and seventeenth-century aristocracies.[17]

But debts and economic confusion were equally possible, and might arise very quickly. Twenty years after his father's death, the Grand Condé himself had debts of 8 million livres, at a time when leading provincial nobles enjoyed yearly revenues of about 15,000 livres; his servants had received no money for five years, and he himself could barely leave his rooms for the waiting throng of creditors. The financial confusion in which Condé lived did not imply economic decline, at least in the terms that historians have normally used in debating nobles' successes and failures. Despite his unpaid creditors, Condé continued buying land in the 1660s; he and his son the duc d'Enghien were spending about 200,000 livres yearly in beautifying Chantilly; and amidst the wreckage the duc d'Enghien "wished only to reserve for himself 100,000 livres for his clothing and small pleasures" (in the words of a financial advisor).[18] More important, as we shall consider shortly, the Condé in fact managed to extricate themselves from this financial disarray rather easily – and in ways that seem essentially new: through the use of credit markets and the establishment of financial honor as a means of access to those markets. Condé illustrates neither the nobility's economic decline nor a traditionalist's lack of acquisitive impulses. He embodied economic confusion rather than decline; he could not sustain his father's (or Gaston's) overall vision of revenues and expenditures. The difference in some measure reflected their personalities, but it also reflected changing ideals and economic realities. Condé was in many ways the greatest nobleman of his age, an example on whom others modeled their behavior and who appeared, thinly disguised, in contemporary fiction by Mademoiselle de Scudéry and Pierre Corneille. Like Gas-

16 Tallemant des Réaux, *Historiettes,* I, 420.
17 *Pont-St-Pierre,* passim.
18 Léon Lecestre, ed., *Mémoires de Gourville,* 2 vols. (Paris, 1894), II, 34–53.

ton de Foix, then, Condé's example carries more than anecdotal weight, and can suggest ideals prevalent in the world around him. But his example also points to other characteristics of that world. The later seventeenth-century economy was complex, and offered far more temptations for expenditure than even the world of Condé's father, let alone that of Gaston de Foix. It required new kinds of calculation and control, and for these techniques (as we shall see) Condé needed to turn to an outside financial specialist, to whom he eventually handed over his affairs.

Figures like Condé moved in an economic world that was heavily influenced by political power, and we should appreciate these political influences if we are to understand the kinds of economic choices nobles made. Economic and political realms overlapped especially for those nobles who wished to participate in public life. From the early sixteenth century, French kings had sold judicial and administrative offices; by the early seventeenth century, the practice had become fully systematized, with clear rules for inheritance and sale to third parties. By the mid-seventeenth century, venality no longer touched the judicial nobility alone. Military positions, governorships of both whole provinces and small towns, honorific positions at court – all of these required money, more money than even offices in the highest law courts. Aristocratic participation in public life now required a substantial investment, usually comparable to the cost of a substantial estate and to several years of most nobles' annual incomes.[19] Venality thus placed money – but not the market – at the center of public life, and this created significant ethical problems. Intellectuals could justify purchasing offices in terms of Aristotelian ethical tradition, which presented liberal expenditure as a fundamental demand on a public man, and could note the importance of associating power with property; venality ensured that the wealthy would occupy important positions.[20] The practice was so widespread, in any

[19] For examples, Ludovic Lalanne, ed., *Mémoires de Roger de Rabutin comte de Bussy . . .* , 2 vols. (Paris, 1857), I, 207, 312, 313; Tallemant des Réaux, *Historiettes,* II, 193.

[20] *Nicomachean Ethics,* trans. J. A. K. Thompson (London, 1953), pp. 111, 118; Bernard de La Roche Flavin, *Treze livres des Parlemens de France* (Bordeaux, 1617), pp. 349–50; Charles Louis de Secondat de Montesquieu, *The Spirit of the Laws,* ed. David Wallace Carrithers (Berkeley and Los Angeles, 1977), pp. 149–50.

case, that denunciation could only be antisocial, indeed misanthropic. But even defenders, among them Richelieu, agreed that the practice corrupted government functions and ought eventually to be eradicated from a reformed France.[21] Venality demonstrated the fallen nature of political life.

Historians have not given much attention to the venality of military offices, but it seems to have differed from the venality of civil offices chiefly in its looseness of organization. Seventeenth-century civil officials defended their financial interests in office collectively and thus succeeded in institutionalizing the trade in offices. Soldiers and courtiers seem not to have had this kind of protection, and thus their experience of venality was substantially more risk-filled and insecure. There was no Paulette, the system of taxation that regularized inheritance of civil office, and the crown intervened much more frequently in the process of transmission. The crown might prohibit sales for political reasons or merely to assist a favorite; it might forbid individuals to sell offices, or force someone to do so. Richelieu refused Henri de Campion the right to sell his office, on the ground that he was planning to join the comte de Soissons's conspiracy, while the prince de Condé forced Bussy-Rabutin to sell his to one of his favorites.[22]

Clearly nobles who participated in public life needed from the outset to think in the calculating terms of monetary exchange and competition. Aristocratic rhetoric might contrast the world of public life with the world of money, but the contrast was not between monetary and nonmonetary domains; rather, it was between the world of the household – economy in its original sense – and the intensely monetary system of public life. But venality brought nobles into a monetary system of public life without establishing absolute property rights, bringing the need to calculate without clear rules for doing so. In this instance, money entered the nobles' lives independently of the market, indeed in ways that contradicted the assumptions of a market economy.

To attain a public role in the army or at court, further, nearly always required borrowing, for no family could raise the immense

[21] Louis André, ed., *Testament Politique du Cardinal de Richelieu* (Paris, 1947), pp. 230–43; but he too offered conventional defenses of venality as a barrier to intrigue, the excessive patronage of the great, and the presence of the lowborn in high positions.

[22] Marc Fumaroli, ed., *Mémoires de Henri de Campion . . .* (Paris, 1967), p. 135; Lalanne, ed., *Mémoires de Roger de Rabutin,* I, 207; see also I, 159.

sums that military or court office required. This in turn placed nobles within a complicated set of exchanges with those whose cash they used. Before the Fronde, Condé forced Bussy-Rabutin to sell his captaincy, but assured him that "if I wished to buy some property at court or as lieutenant of the king in Burgundy, he offered me his credit and his purse." After the Fronde, still according to Bussy, such credit relations centered on Fouquet. "One was his pensioner, his spy, as soon as one wished, and the shame of this trade did not repell most of the great lords of the court from being on his payroll; those who bought high positions had his purse at their disposal, provided that they bound themselves up with him."[23] The advent of money in public life thus strengthened rather than weakened bonds of patronage, because political actors had greater need of patronage support. In that sense, there was no contradiction between the monetization of public life and traditional forms of dependence. But the dependence that money brought had a highly uncomfortable character, for it so firmly subordinated the client to his financial patron. Withdrawal or change of allegiance was extremely difficult, given such commitments of financial resources.

It is not surprising in these circumstances that "credit" became a central metaphor of seventeenth-century public life. Contemporaries typically described the standing of leading figures in terms of the "credit" they enjoyed. Intendants were asked to describe " 'magistrates of the cities, their reputations, talents, credit, and properties.' "[24] In the mid-1680s Furetière offered three definitions of the term: "Confidence [*croyance*], esteem that one acquires in the public by one's virtue, probity, good faith, and merit; . . . the power, authority, wealth that one acquires by means of that reputation. [For instance] this Minister has acquired a great credit at court over the mind of the Prince; this president has gained credit in his company by his knowledge. ["Credit"] is more ordinarily used in commerce, to describe that mutual lending of money and merchandise, on the reputation of probity and solvency of the businessman."[25] Furetière thus suggested that the term retained its commercial overtones even when used in political contexts; political credit was not yet a dead metaphor.

23 Ibid., I, 207, II, 49.
24 François Bluche, *Louis XIV* (Paris, 1986), pp. 751–52.
25 Antoine Furetière, *Dictionnaire universel* . . . (repr. Geneva, 1970), s.v., "credit."

Money thus permeated seventeenth-century public life as both a practical reality and an organizing metaphor. To avoid the exchange relationship – however uncomfortable – meant to avoid public life altogether. In effect, this was the choice of the miser and the misanthrope, both risible because of their refusal to endure the discomforts of exchange. But at the same time, property itself depended heavily on politics, for property required constant defense against litigation and against direct political interference. Historians have shown how quickly fortunes might collapse in moments of special political strain. Despite the fantastic wealth that Richelieu had accumulated and his eagerness that it pass intact to his heirs, his death brought immediate financial uncertainty: Thirty-five-year-old debts and purchases came under litigious questioning; the crown demanded the restoration of its gifts and refused to honor financial commitments; and family members themselves feuded.[26] The Grands Jours d'Auvergne, when the government sent its commissioners to investigate aristocratic abuses in a backward area, produced comparable effects. Long-standing financial arrangements came under question, and litigation rose dramatically.[27]

But these were only extreme examples of a general situation, for all property was vulnerable to litigious assault. Landowners could expect to be involved in dozens of lawsuits, and their success depended explicitly on political considerations: Litigants were expected to mobilize whatever influence they could to "solicit" their cases. They and their friends were to visit the judges, argue the merits of their cases, perhaps offer bribes, and certainly offer future goodwill and service. Tallemant des Réaux described a widely followed lawsuit at Nantes, in the course of which a group of noble ladies "formed such a cabal with the wives of the councillors and presidents (of the Parlement), for whom they performed every imaginable service, that the girl not only won her case, but afterward was placed on a sort of chariot, crowned with laurel, and paraded thus through the whole city."[28] Bussy-Rabutin wrote to a Parisian judge in 1677 that "my daughter has . . . just learned, monsieur, that you are to be the principal judge

[26] Joseph Bergin, *Cardinal Richelieu: Power and the Pursuit of Wealth* (New Haven, 1985), pp. 264–92.

[27] James Lowth Goldsmith, *Les Salers et les d'Escorailles: Seigneurs de Haute Auvergne, 1500–1789* (Clermont-Ferrand, 1984).

[28] Tallemant des Réaux, *Historiettes,* I, 193.

[*rapporteur*] in a matter that she has before the council; if you knew the joy that she and I have had, you would judge what confidence we have in your ability and your friendship. She has asked that I beg Mme de Sévigné to speak with you on her behalf, but, though I do not dispute her influence with you, I believe that I have enough to act on my own."[29] Even expressions of delicacy in such matters testified to the pervasive role of politics in property matters. In 1607, so his wife reported to her sister, the duc de Bouillon's council in Paris thought one of his lawsuits "of such importance that they have urged him to go do the soliciting himself"; but he "has contented himself with writing to each of the judges and with hoping that his right will protect him."[30] Few displayed such reluctance, though, and for that reason Paris represented – as one of the duchesse de La Trémoille's correspondents put it – "le rendez-vous des playdeuses."[31] Anyone with land had to participate in these efforts, and those with other forms of revenues had still more constant need of them: No one could expect government pensions or salaries to be paid without the constant help of well-placed intermediaries. Again, the interconnectedness of money and public life gave central importance to relations of patronage and friendship.

The presence of such friendships in the workings of property led contemporaries to reflections on the role of chance in human affairs and to social humiliations, for the property owner was invariably a petitioner before those who held even the meanest forms of judicial authority. "What is a gentleman?" asks the rascally petty judge of Racine's *Plaideurs*. "A pillar in the waiting room [*pilier d'antichambre*]. How many of them have you seen – I mean the richest of them – warming their hands in my courtyard."[32] In 1624 the duchesse de La Trémoille found herself indeed forced to wait for hours outside a minister's door, in hopes of securing payment of a pension promised to her son. When finally admitted, she realized that "he was listening to her very casually and that he barely wished to stop [his previous business]; she took him by the arm and said to him, monsieur, one should not treat in this manner persons of my standing." Madame retained a

[29] Quoted in C. Rouben, *Bussy-Rabutin épistolier* (Paris, 1974), p. 43.
[30] A[rchives] N[ationales] 1 AP 333 (La Trémoille papers), 78, July 2, 1607.
[31] AN 1 AP 649, Judith de Chavigny to Madame, n.d., letter no. 4.
[32] Jean Racine, *Oeuvres complètes* (Paris, 1964), 316 (Act 1, Scene 5).

sense of her family's potential power, and told the minister that "someday, you'll have more need of him [her son] than he now has of you," but the interview reduced her to public tears.[33] In view of the political pressures that surrounded litigation, it is not surprising that contemporaries turned to metaphors of chance to describe their experiences. "Whatever hopes the situation and the moment may promise," counseled the La Trémoille's lawyer in 1589, "nonetheless one must always guard oneself against the hazards of fortune, which has great authority over human affairs." In the sixteenth and seventeenth centuries, property ownership itself had elements of a game of chance.[34]

Large property enjoyed no immunity from such risks; in fact its very size and complexity made it especially vulnerable. "If the lawsuits to preserve your rights were decided before a single jurisdiction or province," wrote a lawyer to madame de La Trémoille in 1584, "it would be easier to receive justice; but since that cannot be done, both because of the varied levels of jurisdiction and because of the multitude of properties that you own, no sooner have those in charge of your affairs put them in order in one place, than they are called to another."[35] Constantly distracted from their tasks, the La Trémoille lawyers could not match the effectiveness of the lesser litigants, who could concentrate their energies on the case at hand. Even the most elementary aspects of litigation could pose problems. There was, for instance, the problem of making documents available where they were needed: In 1585 the La Trémoille's lawyer explained that one set had proved too large for the ordinary messenger service between Poitiers and Paris, and thus had to be shipped in barrels, by cart.[36] Large property was vulnerable.

Considerations of this kind help to explain the nervousness that seventeenth-century men and women sometimes expressed about property ownership. In the late seventeenth century, at the end of his adventurous life, Gourville congratulated himself that "my fortunate star has so well led me, that I find myself enjoying abundance without owning either lands or houses that might cause me some small pain in the midst of my pleasure."[37] Already by the mid-seventeenth century,

[33] AN 1 AP 648, Chateauneuf to Monseigneur, February 19, 1624.
[34] AN 1 AP 286, Rouhet to Madame, September 11, 1589.
[35] Ibid., September 9, 1584.
[36] Ibid., Rouhet to Madame, July 30, 1585.
[37] Lecestre, ed., *Mémoires de Gourville,* II, 149.

Gourville's choice had acquired a certain currency. Land retained its powerful attractions, but some important fortunes included little or none of it. Mazarin after the Fronde constituted the Old Regime's largest private fortune, but land amounted to less than 20 percent of his assets; the Fouquet family had virtually none before the 1650s.[38] A century later, these attitudes typified Parisian high society. "I am beginning to think like all the rich people of Paris," wrote one nobleman in 1736. "There is not one of them who wants land. Most of them have only shares or *rentes* on the *Hôtel de Ville*."[39] By the end of the Old Regime, the same outlook could be found in at least some provincial settings as well: In one upper Norman village during the last generation of the Old Regime, nobles sold 227,778 livres of land and bought 26,000 livres.[40] By this point, Paris had a booming stock market as an alternative focus for investment. But already in the later seventeenth century, Daniel Dessert has shown, nobles had begun investing heavily in the French tax farms, using bourgeois financiers as front men.[41] In the early eighteenth century John Law's system seemed to offer still greater opportunities for profiting from the state, and Montesquieu indignantly described the eagerness with which contemporaries sold real property in order to profit from the high returns that the system appeared to offer.[42] Such alternatives seemed especially tempting amidst the declining agricultural prices and rents of the century after 1660.

In France as throughout western Europe, seventeenth- and eighteenth-century landowners thus had a growing array of alternative investments, many of which brought substantially higher returns than land. Yet the retreat from landowning remains an extraordinary fact, for during these same years the French aristocracy became increasingly preoccupied with its feudal origins and with setting itself apart from the bourgeoisie and new nobility.[43] Landowning, as a symbol of

[38] Daniel Dessert, *Fouquet* (Paris, 1987), pp. 206–25, 45–46.
[39] Quoted by Robert Forster, "The Nobility During the French Revolution," *Past and Present*, 37 (July 1967), n. 40.
[40] Dewald, *Pont-St-Pierre*, pp. 68–70.
[41] George Taylor, "The Paris Bourse on the Eve of the Revolution," *American Historical Review*, 67 (July 1962), 951–77; Daniel Dessert, *Argent, pouvoir et société au Grand Siècle* (Paris, 1984).
[42] Charles Louis de Secondat de Montesquieu, *Persian Letters*, trans. J. Robert Loy (Cleveland, 1961), pp. 237–38, 246–48, 282.
[43] For recent discussion of eighteenth-century aristocratic ideologies, Harold A. Ellis, *Boulainvilliers and the French Monarchy: Aristocratic Politics in Early Eighteenth-Century France* (Ithaca, 1988).

familial continuity and distinctively aristocratic modes of life, might be expected to have contributed to these efforts. This in fact happened in England, where the country house became the subject of a celebratory poetic genre and the gentry held so tenaciously to its estates that little appeared on the market.[44] Specific conditions partially explain why this did not happen in France. Above all there were the lures of Paris and the French court, which dimmed the attractiveness of rural life even for those who had no real place with the king. But these years also showed the dangers of turning away from land: The Law System's collapse in 1720 ruined both shareholders in Law's companies and creditors throughout French society, as debtors used worthless bank notes to pay off their loans. Purely practical calculations do not explain nobles' long-term imperviousness to shocks of this kind. Rather, their choice seems to have expressed discomfort at the political uncertainties of landowning and a larger fascination with more fluid exchange relations. In high French society, landed property failed to acquire the symbolic functions it had long played in England because the realm of property could not be seen as beyond the reach of political constraint, as a source of independent identity. Even for its ruling groups, it appears, traditional forms of economic practice posed burdensome anxieties and restraints.

This did not mean that French nobles turned away from land altogether, or that they lost interest in their country houses. The Condé, we have seen, spent a fortune beautifying their palace at Chantilly, and numerous other families behaved in similar ways. As elsewhere in western Europe, the seventeenth century produced a building mania among the French nobles, one that damaged individual fortunes and careers. Louis XIV accused his finance minister Fouquet of spending too much money on his country house, and his foreign minister Arnauld de Pomponne of spending too much time at his, to the neglect of his official duties.[45] The archbishop and moralist Fénelon observed that "one gives oneself to building as to gaming; a house becomes like a mistress."[46] This view of the country house, however,

[44] See, for instance, Don E. Wayne, *Penshurst: The Semiotics of Place and the Poetics of History* (Madison, 1984); Lawrence Stone and Jeanne Fawtier Stone, *An Open Elite?* (New York, 1987).

[45] Dessert, *Fouquet,* pp. 155–57; Bluche, *Louis XIV,* pp. 151–56; Roger-Gailly, ed., *Lettres de Madame de Sévigné,* 3 vols. (Paris, 1955), II, 508.

[46] François de La Mothe-Fénelon, *Oeuvres spirituelles* (Paris, 1954), p. 319.

implied a special view of the countryside: as a focus for consumption, amusement, and expense, a retreat from activity, rather than a center of production and income.

Thus far I have sought to develop two arguments. First, models of economic rationality and self-control already existed among the fourteenth-century nobility, and probably became more difficult to live up to as the early modern period advanced. Second, much of seventeenth-century nobles' experience of money was hopelessly intertwined with their experience of political power. Landowning demanded the constant use of political influence; and public careers of all kinds required nobles to mobilize large sums of money. Such experiences of money in political life doubtless encouraged attitudes of calculation and selfishness that may be thought of as characteristic of market economies. At the same time, these experiences with money came not from outside the traditional social and political order but from within it. Money was a means by which kings and other powerful figures secured obedience and deference, a new mechanism for obtaining the old ends of a feudal society. Far from breaking down, feudal relations (loosely understood) were acquiring a newly burdensome strength in the seventeenth century. It is partly in terms of these burdens that we can understand the nobles' retreat from landownership after about 1650 – though numerous practical calculations contributed as well to the process.

I suggest that we understand a last facet of the nobles' dealings with money in similar terms, as a form of flight from the discomforts of traditional forms of dependency and subordination. This was seventeenth-century nobles' increasing readiness to play with money, to gamble. Contemporaries believed that an unprecedented gambling mania held seventeenth-century courtly society. Although a longstanding pastime, one especially favored among soldiers, it had acquired a new appeal to polite society in the seventeenth century. By the 1690s it had become a stock theme in Parisian comedy and a normal part of aristocratic behavior.[47] Given this rising enthusiasm for gambling, it is striking that none of it seems to have taken place in

[47] See Jean-François Regnard, *Le Joueur,* ed. John Dunkley (Geneva, 1986); Georges Jamati, *La querelle du Joueur: Regnard et Dufresny* (Paris, 1936); Lecestre, ed., *Mémoires de Gourville,* I, 167.

settings that might have emphasized gentry community, social hierarchy, or separation from other social groups. I have encountered no horse racing or other such contests, which became central to nineteenth-century aristocratic life in both England and France. We can easily imagine the appeal of such sports to landed nobilities. They display both property and bloodlines, thus replicating in play deeply held social ideals; they establish as well clear gender boundaries, visible both in the events themselves and in the social forms surrounding them. All of these functions emerged in such events as the nineteenth-century horse race. But seventeenth-century nobles chose instead to gamble in contests and settings that emphasized impersonal social exchange, a relative equality of both class and gender. Both men and women gambled, and they gambled on the numerical abstractions represented by cards and dice. Seventeenth-century gambling was a world of skill and fortune, rather than one of bloodlines, breeding, and property.

This was also a world open to all social classes. Indeed, the combination of social promiscuity with numerical abstraction was one of the principal reasons that gambling disturbed contemporary moralists. Thus La Bruyère: "Everyone says of gambling that it equalizes conditions . . . in a word, it's a reversal of all propriety."[48] "Lansquenet [among the most popular of seventeenth-century games]," offered another late-seventeenth-century writer, "is a sort of badly policed republic, where everyone becomes equal; there is no more subordination; and the last among men, with money in his hands, takes whatever rank his card gives him, and finds himself above a duke and peer."[49] Comedy might present the same view in a more positive light.

> Gaming assembles all: it brings to one place
> The peaceful bourgeois, the marquis turbulent by race.
> The banker's wife . . .
> . . . defeats the . . . duchess
> . . . .
> And though a jealous fate has concealed our worth
> Thus one can avenge the injustices of birth.[50]

[48] La Bruyère, *Oeuvres complètes,* ed. Julien Benda (Paris, 1951), p. 195 (Des biens de la fortune, no. 71).
[49] Quoted Dunkley, ed., *Le Joueur,* 15.
[50] *Le Joueur,* 152.

Conversely, gaming offered separation from social obligations, existence as a free individual, another principal reason that it upset moralists. Georges de La Tour presented the prodigal son as an aristocratic gambler, and in Regnard's *Le Joueur* the gambler has similarly cut himself off from his father and lives in rented rooms; in his excitement at success he forgets as well about his fiancée. Charles Perrault included gaming as one of the forms that a wife's disobedience might take, another disturbing liberation that the gaming table seemed to promise.[51] La Bruyère summarized these images of social atomization in picturing the gamblers associated: "implacable for one another, and irreconcilable enemies while the session lasts, they no longer recognize friendship [*liaisons*], connection [*alliance*], birth or distinctions."[52]

To play cards, so ran the argument, was to experience republican equality, freedom from the constraints of both natural and social position. Gaming encouraged wives and sons to disobey patriarchal authority, and it turned social connectedness into hostile individualism. Obviously the moralists and comedians overstated their case, for much gaming took place within highly restrictive settings, among men and women who knew each other well. Yet the practical workings of cardplaying in fact conformed to the moralists' vision of it, for gambling was widely seen as a way for outsiders to enter society, even the relatively closed society of the royal court. "There is nothing that brings a man more suddenly into fashion, or attracts so much attention to him, as playing for high stakes."[53] La Bruyère meant to be sarcastic, and so did Regnard's play *Le Joueur,* which included a

> marquis *de hazard,* created by lansquenet
> . . .
> Who, it is said, gains much by his play,
> And before a marquis, was once a valet.[54]

But others made the same point in positive terms. "By gambling," Tallemant des Réaux claimed, "young people who have scarcely any property introduce themselves everywhere and find a means of living."[55] Nicolas Faret, whose best-selling *Honnête homme* offered a long series of moralizing clichés for the upwardly mobile, thought

51 Charles Perrault, *Contes,* ed. Jean-Pierre Collinet (Paris, 1981), p. 62.
52 La Bruyère, *Oeuvres,* 196 (Des biens de la fortune, no. 72).
53 Ibid., 393 (De la mode, no. 7).
54 *Le Joueur,* p. 94.
55 *Historiettes,* II, 264.

gaming one of the skills that a young man needed to learn, "because thus he can sometimes mix familiarly" in good company.[56] Excessive gaming might be a dangerous vice, but within limits it represented one of the normal ways by which a young man or woman entered society. Gaming was a means of social mobility, a mechanism by which outsiders broke through social distinctions.

Gaming thus offered experiences of competition, calculation, and freedom from ascribed social roles, experiences in which value rested entirely on the cards that one held and in which activity was directed toward acquisition. Moralists correctly saw these as ways in which gaming undermined the ideals of a society of orders, in which distinctions were clear, permanent, and founded on birth. To be sure, gaming had other dimensions. The gambling table offered chances to display wealth and demonstrate indifference to its loss, indeed to show oneself above mercantile calculations. It allowed for the display of competitive toughness, hence presumably its early appeal to military men; and it was a way of coping with the boredom of both military camp and court. One need not deny the significance of these impulses to emphasize instead the structural patterns of seventeenth-century gambling. As the seventeenth century practiced it, gaming was strikingly detached from the world of landed property, indeed from the countryside altogether; it infringed boundaries of gender and status; and it centered on the pursuit of money. It represented, I suggest, a voluntary withdrawal from the society of orders, a deliberately sought experience of competitive, anonymous social relations.

As such, I think, it should be attached to other forms of seventeenth-century sociability that pointed in the same directions. Masked balls, at which participants interacted anonymously, without knowledge of one another's standing, were one such form, and acquired enormous popularity in the later seventeenth century. "Since masked balls have been invented," reported the duc d'Enghien in 1664, "no one can endure any others; nothing approaches them; there is a liberty without disorder, one places oneself where one wishes, speaks to whom one pleases, and acts as if everyone were equal."[57] Like gambling, the masked ball

[56] Nicolas Faret, *L'Honnête homme, ou l'art de plaire à la cour,* ed. Maurice Magendie (Paris, 1925; repr. Geneva, 1970), p. 17.

[57] Emile Magne, ed., *Le Grand Condé et le duc d'Enghien: Lettres inédites à Marie-Louise de Gonzague, reine de Pologne, sur la cour de Louis XIV (1660–1667)* (Paris, 1920), p. 131.

represented a deliberate experiment in doing without social distinctions. At a greater remove, but with important parallels, there was the growing readiness of noble women and men to write for publication and to encourage others to set their personal lives before the anonymous public that printing implied. Mid-seventeenth-century observers noted the eagerness of high society men and women to appear, thinly disguised, in Mademoiselle de Scudéry's novels.[58] They deplored the fact that "the ease of printing and the passion for writing have infinitely multiplied these [novels]; the least little secretary, working from the memoirs of the loves of his village seigneur, in no time produces a book with whatever disguised names he chooses."[59] Even the king's sister-in-law offered her life story – "all that has happened to me" – to Madame de Lafayette to write out for some form of public consumption.[60] The urge to exchange and the acceptance of anonymous terms of exchange that gaming implied found echoes elsewhere in aristocratic culture.

Molière's misanthrope proposed retreat from the corruptions of city and court to a rural property. The retreat would have been appealing but implausible to contemporaries, for they experienced rural property itself as part of a public world of exchanges and fortune. As a final image of this world, we may return to the prince de Condé and his debts in the later seventeenth century. With their affairs in chaos, the family turned to the financier Gourville for help, and he managed to set things right with surprising speed. Gourville himself was a highly successful gambler, but his reflections on the Condé's finances resemble aspects of the Weberian Benjamin Franklin. The first step in restoring the family's situation involved knowledge and writing. Gourville drew up memoranda of the family's normal expenses and of its income and debts – following his own practice, which was "every morning to examine in detail what I spent the previous day, as I've always done since I've been able." After this acquisition of written knowledge came a second step, a regularization of credit relations. Gourville arranged for regular, biweekly payments of the Condé's

[58] Tallemant des Réaux, *Historiettes,* II, 689.

[59] Henri Coulet, *Le roman jusqu'à la Révolution: anthologie* (Paris, 1968), p. 31.

[60] Madame de Lafayette, *Histoire de Madame Henriette d'Angleterre, la Princess de Montpensier, la Comtesse de Tende,* ed. Claudine Hermann (Paris, 1979), pp. 22–23.

creditors, to replace the earlier clamor in the antechamber; having made his first payment on time, "this gave me a great deal of credit and ease with the others," so that new money could flow in and judicial seizures could be lifted. Gourville described his achievement as a creation of order: as "giving a form to the business affairs of Monsieur le Prince."[61] We may note both the resemblance to and the distance from Gaston de Foix, two and a half centuries earlier. Like Gaston, Gourville proposed an order based on knowledge, counting, and writing, but Gourville's order rested also on credit, and in this it was new. Unlike Gaston, Gourville viewed money as a relationship rather than a thing. Its essence was the confidence of lenders and suppliers, hence the borrower's public image, and with that established, the Condé could resume their amazing train of life. If Gourville was the heir to Gaston's vision of accounting and self-control, the heir to his notion of money's nature was Molière's miser, with his "chère cassette" of coins.

I have argued here that the contrast between Gaston de Foix and Gourville cannot be understood as the rise of self-interest or of economic rationality, or even of a growing comfort with the market economy. What had changed between the fourteenth and the seventeenth centuries was the rise of credit and the need for economic interdependence. The market became more important in the lives of French nobles and less tangible, but (I have argued) nobles encountered money and had monetary calculation thrust upon them because of forces quite removed from the market as historians have usually understood it. Money formed part of the monarchical order's functioning in the mid-seventeenth century. It was a political tool, attaching individuals to the crown and to great men, who could supply the immense sums that entering public life required. As in Gaston's world, money did not necessarily threaten hierarchy. Monetary exchanges, too, need to be seen in their historical specificity, not as an abstract force with an unvarying psychological impact.[62]

In fact, seventeenth-century discomfort with money seems to have resulted as much from the hierarchies and dependencies that attended its use as from the freedoms and individualism that it promoted. No-

[61] Lecestre, ed., *Mémoires de Gourville,* II, 144, 37, 45.

[62] A point suggested in somewhat different terms by Joyce Appleby in her review of Agnew, *Worlds Apart, Albion,* 19, no. 1 (Spring 1987).

bles disliked the credit relations of venality, which forced them to depend on wealthier figures for offices, and they intensely disliked the humiliations that other property ownership entailed, the need to "solicit" legal support from both superiors and inferiors. Such dislikes help us understand nobles' readiness to play with money and with the roles that an unascribed society might offer them, as at the gaming table or the masquerade. "Play" need not suggest only comfort. We can imagine nobles trying out social roles in play situations precisely because they felt uncertain or uncomfortable about them. But they nonetheless sought out these situations as sources of pleasure.

This returns us to the Smithian and Weberian perspectives on economic tradition from which this essay started. I have argued that the traditional economic world, the world of privileges and feudal property, was a surprisingly uncomfortable one for seventeenth-century nobles – precisely those who benefited most from this economic order. It inflicted uncertainties and humiliations on them, and they stepped out of it with corresponding readiness, selling land and playing with an alternative set of roles, those of gambling. I have also argued that some forms of modern economic calculation were already to be found among the fourteenth-century landed aristocracy. With Smith, then, we may stress both the oppressiveness of the old economic regime and the cultural means the nobles had for responding to alternative possibilities. But we have also seen the complicated ways in which these alternatives arrived. For the nobles, there was no mere "penetration" of traditional arrangements by market forces. On the contrary, one of the most important forces working to monetize social relations was the monarchy itself – and it used money to strengthen bonds of dependence. Money had no inherently liberating effects, nor did the nobles' economic calculations necessarily become more effective as the period advanced. Not their advancing economic rationality but their eagerness to escape the old economic order supplies the principal theme in this account. Against the Weberian discomforts of monetary exchange and social fluidity, we need to set the discomforts of power and subordination.

CHAPTER 2

Territorial gardens: the control of land in seventeenth-century French formal gardens

CHANDRA MUKERJI

One of the mysteries of garden history is why gardens in seventeenth-century France grew so dramatically in size and cultural importance. They became highly articulated and deeply structured forms, emerging from châteaux as quasi-architectural features and continuing along pathways and beyond sculpted masses of trees toward the horizon. They delineated living spaces and ceremonial stages beyond the walls of buildings; they constituted a site for an aristocratic way of life that linked social standing to territorial control and the accumulation of property. It seemed that buildings in this historical moment were no longer large enough or complex enough for the new cultural possibilities of the age. Something more was needed to contain the sculpture, fountains, and plants; a bigger stage was required for the elaborate fetes (or even frequent but modest promenades or hunting parties) that were part of court ceremonial life. Land itself needed attention and celebration, requiring ingenious decorative strategies and engineering feats, and embodying new visions of natural order. Enormous energy and passion were harnessed to bring together garden designers, gardeners, trees, shrubs, sculptures, and water systems to facilitate a massive restructuring of hills and valleys. This kind of activity seemed so important that Louis XIV began building the great gardens at Ver-

I would like to thank my research assistant Isabelle Mourré and her colleagues at the Ecole Normale Supérieure de Paysage for early help in conducting this research. I also want to thank Bruno Latour and the CSI at the Ecole Normale Supérieure des Mines for providing an academic home for me while I completed the research. And finally, I would like to thank the Academic Senate Committee on Research from the University of California, San Diego, for the funds that made research in France possible.

sailles before he began expanding the château there.[1] Why was this the case?

To answer the question, we need to step back and examine some of the layers and contradictions building within French culture. A striking amount of social mobility, created by the expansion of trade, was throwing members of the bourgeoisie into the world of the aristocracy.[2] In this socially unstable environment, French formal gardens gained their new scale, shapes, and cultural importance because they could provide a point of convergence (and hence interpenetration) of feudal and bourgeois cultures, both of which placed a high value on landholding. Feudalism, albeit with variations, associated high social standing with political control of domains, and bourgeois culture, to the extent that it existed as more than an ideal type, associated standing with the accumulation of property (private economic control of real property being central to this).[3] Although these cultural constellations were not perfectly associated with specific nobles and bourgeoises, members of both groups shared enough of a cultural obsession with land that they could link ambition to territoriality. In this common culture, members of the two groups could blur the lines between them, while drawing lines on the earth. Land became a site of political alignment where conflicting interests could be displaced into a world of material culture and visually resolved there. The result was the development of a culture of territoriality that gave land new significance and political power.

This obsession with territory, most evident in state land management and measurement, found important political expression on a

[1] The château at Versailles was being only slightly modified when Le Nôtre started important work in the gardens. The famous first fete at Versailles took place before major renovations made the château large enough to function as the center of court life. William Howard Adams, *The French Garden,* New York: George Braziller, 1979, pp. 79–80; H. Franklin Hazlehurst, *Gardens of Illusion,* Nashville: Vanderbilt University Press, 1980, pp. 59–64; Guy Walton, *Louis XIV's Versailles,* Chicago: University of Chicago Press, 1986; Alfred Marie, *Naiscence de Versailles,* Paris: Editions Vincent, Fréal, et Cie., 1968, pp. 26–27.

[2] Orest Ranum, *Paris in the Age of Absolutism,* Bloomington: Indiana University Press, 1979; Perry Anderson, *Lineages of the Absolutist State,* London: Verso, 1974, part I, ch. 4.

[3] For a description of the materialism and private character of French bourgeois culture in the period, see Georges Mangredien, *La Vie quotidienne sous Louis XIV,* Paris: Librairie Hachette, 1948, ch. 3. For a description of aristocratic ceremonial culture and its relationship to gardens in Italy and France in the sixteenth century, see Adams, pp. 63–67.

smaller scale in the organization of the French formal garden, where physical boundaries were clearly delineated (as social ones were being transgressed). In these gardens, disparate plots of land were woven together into a pleasing whole, whose apparent symmetries contained a world of differences. Mixed symbolism was embodied in the statuary and fountains, and walkways in the garden led into and out of parterres (garden beds), and *bosques* (forest "rooms"), presenting the land and its features from different perspectives.[4] These qualities gave the French formal garden a complexity and multivocality that belied its apparent simplicity as an expression of Cartesian rationality or as a marker of French wealth and ambition.[5] They helped present to the world of European politics a physical embodiment of the ability of the French state to manage land and harness its power.

Political culture in early modern France

The political culture of the early modern period clearly needed redefinition with the growth of the modern state. A new culture was needed to make sense of a political world that depended as much on bourgeois wealth as on noble power.[6] A solution to the problem in seventeenth-century France was to extend aristocratic titles to the powerfully wealthy. Early in the century, the state turned to selling estates and titled offices in order to raise money, particularly for war, a practice that provided a means for bourgeois social mobility while serving the military ambitions of the nobility. Such bourgeois mobility into the aristocracy was greater in France than elsewhere in Europe, and as a result the mix of class cultures in the French court was particularly rich and problematic.[7] The practice of selling titles to bourgeois elites became so extensive it called into question traditional

[4] This obscurity was also evident in the painting of the period. See Jennifer Montagu, "The Painted Enigma and French Seventeenth-Century Art," *Journal of the Warburg and Courtauld Institutes,* 1968, 31:307–35.

[5] For a discussion of the mathematization of design in this period and the role of gardens in this movement, see Alberto Pérez-Gómez, *Architecture and the Crisis of Modern Science,* Cambridge, Mass.: MIT Press, 1983.

[6] Ranum, particularly, ch. 12. For the thesis that financiers were recruited into a more feudal culture of statecraft than most histories suggest, see Julian Dent, *Crisis in France: Crown, Financiers, and Society in 17th-Century France,* New York: St. Martin's, 1973, introduction.

[7] Perry Anderson says (p. 94) that in the 1620s, 38 percent of the state's income came from the sale of offices.

ideas of political legitimacy.[8] Buying land to enter the aristocracy, then, undermined feudal bases for aristocratic privilege.

Colbert's solution to the problem (following Mazarin's earlier moves) was to concentrate power and legitimacy within the state: a political institution outside the hands of both the traditional nobles and the new merchant–financier elite.[9] This system of state power is usually considered a form of political culture employed to promote capitalist development while containing the political disruptions resulting from it, solidifying noble legitimacy while simultaneously undermining the definition of aristocracy.[10] But it can also be seen as a system of material manipulation of land that helped erase differences between the two groups that could erode the king's or the state's power. With the development of the absolutist state, France became more a managed territory than a political stage for a small set of noble families. Louis XIV still acted as though his authority were feudal. He saw and projected himself as expressing *personal* will through the state, but both the king and Colbert were extremely wary of other nobles exercising political privilege. They were as concerned about noble autonomy as about the growing power of financiers, and to constrain both groups and channel the king's authority they used material manipulation: canal building, fortress construction, factory

[8] For descriptions of this mobility in France, see Anderson, pp. 94–95; see also John Locke, *Locke's Travels in France,* J. Lough, ed., Cambridge: Cambridge University Press, 1953, pp. 154, 164–67. The problems of legitimacy raised by these practices, albeit in an earlier period, are documented in LeRoy Ladurie, *Carnival in Romans,* New York: George Braziller, 1979.

[9] Anderson, pp. 94–101. For a brief but useful discussion of Colbert's relationship to Mazarin, see Inès Murat, *Colbert,* Cook and Asselt, trans., Charlottesville: University Press of Virginia, 1984, ch. 3. For his role in constructing the French state, see Murat, ch. 6.

[10] This highly centralized and interventionist state took over activities that had been sources of power for the nobility and bourgeoisie. The state no longer derived its military power from the nobility. Instead, it developed a professional army in which members of the aristocracy could serve and maintain their identities as warriors; however, they no longer held the power of the military as they had before, and they shared their world of warriors with nonaristocrats, again blurring the social ranks. At the same time, the world of commerce was linked to the state, reducing the autonomy of merchants and financiers to act in the economic realm. The state took control of many forms of manufacture and most international trade, allowing aristocrats who were prohibited from engaging in trade a way to gain commercial wealth. Both nobles and the bourgeoisie were pressed to seek their power through the state, found places there in which to explore new social possibilities, and gave the state economic and military support. This state became a new kind of vehicle for political action, containing and exploiting bourgeois economic ambition and feudal authority.

sponsorship, warfare, and colonial land management, all of which gave new material form to the state. In this material realm, the state put to work technical fruits of the politicoeconomic changes within French society, which could have strained further the legitimacy of the French elite.[11]

The material culture of state control blurred feudal and commercial cultures effectively; it seemed to celebrate noble power (through the king), while allowing the bourgeoisie more social presence (by increasing the visibility and importance of commercial culture in politics). In this way, material culture entered the politics of the French court, not as a threat to the king or his legitimacy, but as a way to enrich and empower his reign through the state.

Gardens as symbols of state territory

Gardens in seventeenth-century France afford particularly interesting insight into French territoriality because they were developed in large part using techniques from the new French military and the marketplace that were being used elsewhere to define the state's territory and promote its wealth. Worlds of skill – surveying, mining, military engineering, canal building, bridge building, and market gardening – were mobilized for building the gardens outside the royal houses; the resulting gardens demonstrated in a compact form the technical capacities of the French to manage land. When these sites were used in the ceremonial rituals of the period to present France to foreign

[11] Anderson, p. 100; Norbert Elias, *The Court Society,* New York: Pantheon [1969] 1983. The result was a peculiarly French way of integrating the bourgeoisie and the nobility, the market and feudal relations. The two groups did not remain separate as they did in Italy, where different sources of power were cultivated; see Peter Burke, *Venice and Amsterdam,* London: Temple Smith, 1974. Neither did they become merged as a fundamentally bourgeois elite, as in England. (Bourgeois individualism had a long history in England, which understandably led to the success of bourgeois culture in this period. See Alan MacFarlane, *The Origins of English Individualism,* Cambridge: Cambridge University Press, 1978.) Instead, bourgeois culture in France was encapsulated within an aristocratic culture that diverted the bourgeoisie from investing in commerce (getting them to invest in state offices instead) and placed economic development within the hands of a state that gained its legitimacy from the nobility and its Catholicism. The role of Catholicism in this scenario is very interesting. It seems that the acceptance of Protestants coincided with the rise of the bourgeoisie in France, and the revocation of the Edict of Nantes coincided with the successful incorporation of the bourgeoisie into a noble-dominated elite. For a discussion of bourgeois investment in offices over businesses, see Anderson, p. 97.

visitors, they made manifest the capacity of French engineers to place land under technical control and celebrated the beauties of their doing so.

Significantly, the primary techniques available for this purpose came from institutions undergoing the most change in the period: the military and the marketplace, both of which were centrally affected by the growing state. When the military was professionalized and placed under state control, it was dislodged from its position in traditional feudal life as the center of the reciprocal relationship between nobles and the king. The new fighting force was not made up of members of the nobility doing their duty to the crown; rather, it comprised paid fighting men, working for the state. Nobles could and did find roles in the new military, and the culture celebrating military virtues was enhanced rather than undermined by the change. The standing army could, in fact, elaborate military ritual and rationalize strategic planning in ways that had not been possible before. But it was, importantly, a paid army that had no power independent from the king. As such it displaced and replaced feudal forms, and helped produce a vision of French territory as a resource and responsibility of the state – no longer purely the domain of the crown.

The commercial technologies imported into the gardens also marked a world of commerce that, both independently and through the state, was legitimately entering more and more into aristocratic life. The definition of the aristocracy might have excluded trade from the list of legitimate noble employments, but forms of production related to it were not so clearly or consistently banned. Estate management for market purposes, improving the abundance of France, was fully embraced by Henry IV when he encouraged the French to raise silkworms. By the seventeenth century, the plant trade was becoming a commercial enterprise, although it had earlier been almost entirely, and was still in large part, an activity of noble households. Canal and road building were, under Colbert, activities of the state aimed at commercial rationalization, but they were also forms of military engineering with roots in the feudal obligations and abilities of noble families. Pumps for fountains were part of a culture of mines and tunnels that Vauban was incorporating into military strategy, but large water systems, with aqueducts and pipes, were becoming part of urban development necessitated by the growth of larger commercial centers. All these techniques of land management were available to celebrate a common culture of state territoriality only because they were being developed at the cusp between two cultures, both of which took land management as central to their traditional activities.

French royal gardens mobilized these techniques to present a miniaturized model of French state territory, laying out some material dimensions of state power. They contained experimental systems of centralized geographical control over diverse terrains, and they were filled with statues, fountains, grottoes, *bosquets,* and other garden forms that were made distinctively French. In this way, they celebrated French management and use of land.

The territoriality of these gardens is visible enough. Seventeenth-century French formal gardens were made like maps. They expressed human ambitions for managing the land through careful articulation. Like the territorial maps that were becoming common in the period, they were also organized around boundaries, lines marking divisions and defining their relationships at the same time.[12] The rhythms of the gardens were created by low hedges around parterres and stands of trees around *bosquets.* Their geometries were used to integrate diverse elements into a common whole, a corporate or communal space that transcended all the territorial components that went into it.[13] Garden developers only reappropriated land from other and more traditional purposes in order to integrate it into their great formal designs. Fouquet at Vaux-le-Vicomte bought and tore down three villages to make his garden. He also organized eighteen thousand laborers to build that great monument to his territorial ambi-

[12] Thierry Mariage has discovered that the written designs for gardens were often made by surveyors after the practical work of building the gardens was over. This is an interesting way to understand the relationship between material practices and ideals of geometry in the gardens, which were much more inheritors of traditions of technical practice than of ideals of drawing. See "De la validité des documents graphiques pour juger de l'évolution des jardins de Versailles," in Richard Mique, ed., *Les Jardins de Versailles et de Trianon d'André Le Nôtre,* Paris: Réunion des musées nationaux, 1992, pp. 15–18. Mariage demonstrates that practical surveyors were hired for their skills at this kind of drawing, so they could help shape the public image of these gardens as ideal forms. The surveyors presented the practical work of gardeners as continuous with patterns of land management outside the gardens.

[13] For a discussion of geometries and boundaries as territorial markers, see F. Hamilton Hazelhurst, "Le Nostre at Conflans," in Dumbarton Oaks, *The French Formal Garden,* Washington, D.C.: Dumbarton Oaks, 1974.

tions, indicating the quasi-military actions by which the territorial garden was established.[14]

The great garden designer of the period, André Le Nôtre, is frequently described in French histories of the garden as an exponent of a visual form of Cartesian rationality because of the systematic and theoretically inspired vision of control in his overall garden designs. The concepts of design articulated by Jacques Boyceau and used by Le Nôtre and his followers defined ideal gardens as (visually if not always in reality) bilaterally symmetrical, taking complex environments (both natural and architectural) and fitting them within simple geometries of space that contained complex visual elements. They were systems for the rational integration of bounded spaces around centralized vistas.[15]

This system of organizing territories had its counterparts in the French bureaucracy. During the seventeenth century efforts at state formation in France, the different regions were restructured into territories supervised by the *intendants* who tied them to the central state.[16] While in formal gardens old garden plots were superseded by new ones, new political territories were drawn within France to make them fit the new political structure. And while wars were used to expand and rearticulate the boundaries of France, towns and hamlets were being destroyed around châteaux to produce the new great gardens.[17]

Still, contemporary theories of garden design did not connect the organization of parterres and *bosquets* in gardens to the organization of the regions of France. The royal gardener Jacques Boyceau, for example, argued that gardens were meant (in their integration of

[14] See Derek Clifford, *A History of Garden Design,* New York: Praeger, 1963, p. 73.

[15] H. Franklin Hazelhurst, *Jacques Boyceau and the French Formal Garden,* Athens: University of Georgia Press, 1966.

[16] Perry Anderson quotes Kossman, pp. 96–97, on similarities in the Baroque and the French state apparatus. This analysis is extended here to the gardens that developed from Baroque models. See Clifford (p. 71) for the argument that French gardens in the period were not really Baroque. He sees Baroque gardens developing only in Italy, Spain, and central Europe. He sees the use of canals and the flatness of the designs (based on the flat landscape in northern France) as creating a different design tradition in France, one much more closely related to the Netherlands than to Italy (see Clifford, pp. 65, 71). On the idea that French gardens owed much of their style to Dutch models of urban as well as garden design, see Florence Hopper, "The Dutch Classical Garden and André Mollet," *Journal of Garden History,* 2:25–40.

[17] See Clifford, p. 73.

diversity within a strict geometry of space) to realize a vision of the natural: to make apparent the inherent rationality of the natural world and the diversity of its forms.[18] The result was a vision of land that naturalized the imposition of order by projecting a theory of inherent rationality on nature (after it had been controlled through engineering).[19]

This approach to gardens was novel but did not seem jarringly new, since it shared many characteristics with earlier gardens. It was tied in many ways to ideas of the Italian Baroque – a style of art that used symmetries to offset and organize tumultuous lines and problematic forms. French garden designs were originally derived from Italian Baroque models but added to the form a more formal and restrained geometry (I would call it a surveyor's geometry). Such designs reemphasized boundaries around garden beds, which had been denied in earlier gardens as they moved away from the small, square, hedged garden plots of medieval herb gardens. Mannerist, and then Baroque, garden designers wanted something grander and more integrated than small walled gardens would allow, so they built gardens with sweeping vistas and long walkways. French gardens restored the emphasis on boundaries found in late medieval and early Renaissance gardens, but presented them as markers rather than as barriers. They also increased the size of the garden even more, maintaining large central allées but placing around them a complex geometry of bounded garden spaces and intersecting walks.[20]

[18] Hazelhurst, 1966.

[19] This visual structure of centralized, naturalized, and organized complexity may have been tied more by garden writers of the period to science than to politics, but the garden remained a vehicle for political communication. Mariage points out that garden books were post hoc readings of garden projects and hence could be given a veneer of scientism that did not necessarily drive their construction. The exercise of technique (engineering) preceded the activity of showing the orderliness in it (scientific theorizing). See Mariage in Mique, 1992. In the end, the gardens controlled land first and foremost, and spoke to the capacity of the French to control territory. The overt purpose of French royal gardens (the most dramatic of seventeenth-century French formal gardens) was to display the power of the king and of France. The fact that the designs were meant to present natural laws only added to the sense of overwhelming control there. The imposition of order on the land was naturalized, making the order seem all the more irrevocable. The result was a system of territorial demarcation and display in which bits of forest and lawns, canals and walkways, spoke to the distribution and use of power in territorial terms.

[20] For a discussion of Italian Baroque versus French gardens, see Clifford. For a discussion of diversity and centralization in the Baroque, see H. W. Janson, *History of Art,* New York: Abrams, 1962, ch. 6; see also Hauser, *Social History of Art,* New

In another important link to their French antecedents, Italian gardens, like Baroque architectural spaces, were used above all to celebrate power and its centralization. The Mannerist garden in Italy began to break beyond the walls of the Renaissance pleasure garden, making the claims to land in these gardens greater. The house was then resituated within the Baroque garden as the central point for viewing it, and hence was located as a center of power. The resulting garden was clearly part of the culture of absolutism, of centralization and glorification of power through control of complexity, but it was not yet a territorial garden in the sense that the French gardens would become because it had not yet naturalized the expression of power and bureaucratic order through control of land.[21]

The French garden took a new turn as land and its ordering became the central design problem. French garden design was even more elaborately linked to the land-use practices of the period: survey techniques, agricultural systems, and water management techniques. For the most part, seventeenth-century French gardens were in flat, rural areas – not the hillside cities where most Italian gardens were built – and therefore could make better use of the estate development techniques that were improving agricultural output.To alter and lay claim to the landscape, they also took advantage of current forms of military engineering, from surveys to battlement construction.

Techniques that on the large scale were contributing to the political and economic development of France were also used on the small scale in gardens to assert symbolically the glory of French culture and the French court. Just as the French state was building water and road systems to integrate its territory and develop it economically, the royal gardens were given walkways and water systems to unify them

York: Vintage 1951, vol. 2, ch. 8; see also Kossman in Anderson, pp. 96–97. Thierry Mariage also argues that Italian gardens were more affected by French models than earlier scholars have assumed. See Mariage, 1990, ch. 1. The "natural" evolution of garden forms that we see in most art histories may turn out to be more interesting as cultural artifacts than good history.

21 For a discussion of French gardens and the celebration of power in the Baroque, see Clifford, p. 74. There is an interesting link between Clifford's ideas about the French landscape and the gardens, and the argument presented here. Clifford sees French garden designers responding to a physical environment that made land more two- than three-dimensional. That is why it could look more like a map or estate survey without having any cultural reason to do so. But I contend that designers were responding to a social environment with a particular cultural relationship to land, and that the meaning of land was undergoing change.

and make their beauties accessible. And just as the state was trying to acquire new territory (both by expanding its borders and by developing colonies), the gardens at Versailles and elsewhere were enlarged and remodeled on a regular basis to "improve" them.[22]

How could such complex visions of economic and political control of land be integrated in one system of garden design? The historian of French gardens H. Franklin Hazelhurst[23] provides one way to think about this, describing Le Nôtre's works as gardens of "illusion." Although they used simple geometries and were predominantly open, affording apparently clear vistas from which to "read" them, they in fact used complex series of terraces and depressions, trees and allées, that alternately created and hid views, setting multiple visions of the garden for the visitors who walked through them. This allowed different conceptions of the land to be layered upon one another. Surprises were part of the play of the garden, so contradiction was not a problem (unless it undermined the power of the king, and this it did not do). Hence, French gardens put to good political use the passion of illusion that was apparent in the period, and used it in the service of a new political territoriality.[24]

To understand in more concrete terms the territoriality of French

[22] Thierry Mariage discusses the technical bases of garden design in the period in *L'Univers de Le Nostre,* Bruxelles: Pierre Mardaga, 1990. For a description of the great surveys of France that began in the late seventeenth century, see John Wilford, *The Mapmakers,* New York: Vintage, 1981, ch. 8. For the growth of state and estate surveys in the sixteenth and seventeenth centuries, see Mukerji, 1983, pp. 116–28. For a discussion of changing systems for representing land in the period, see Chandra Mukerji, "Visual Language in Science and the Exercise of Power," *Visual Communication,* 1984, 10:30–45. See also Wilford, ch. 8, for a discussion of the French system for representing territory in the National Survey.

[23] Hazelhurst, 1980.

[24] Illusion, too, was part of the cartography of the period. As much as maps were "rational" systems for the representation of space, they were also clearly distorted and ideological devices. Planned water systems for increasing the usable land on an estate could look very good, but not fit the subtleties of the land well enough to work. Nicely rational systems for representing the world on a two-dimensional plane all carried distortions, depending on whether they used projection systems to aid navigation or to create continuities of scale. And maps were not necessarily made to be above politics. They were often designed for making territorial claims more than statements about nature. All one has to do is look at the changing location of the Spice Islands in European maps from the sixteenth and early seventeenth centuries to see how desire and geography were linked. In cartography, illusion was both an unanticipated by-product and a manipulated variable. It should be no surprise that in territorial gardens, the manipulation and revelation of illusion would also be an important part of "rational control" of land. For a discussion of some routine and systematic ideological distortions in maps, see Mukerji, 1984, ch. 3.

gardens, it will be useful to review in detail some ways in which military and market gardening techniques were employed in the gardens at Versailles (and to a minor extent other gardens of the period). The gardens at Versailles were meant to be the central manifestation of seventeenth-century French gardening, and they were the primary royal gardens. Their debts to military and market-gardening techniques clearly demark some ways that noble and commercial values were brought to court, and simultaneously point to means by which the gardens expressed territorial power and control.

Military sources of French garden design

It is easy enough to argue that Louis XIV saw himself in large part as a warrior, as the heir to a noble family whose primary object was to protect and enhance his domain. One only needs to read his memoirs to realize his obsession with geopolitical intrigue and the aggrandizement of French power and territory.[25] He was also the king who founded the first standing army in Europe. Given this as well as his role in the gardens at Versailles, it should be no surprise that gestures toward military prowess played a part in the development of his gardens. The question is how.

One can see symbolic allusions to military images in things as diverse as statuary and garden layout. Adorning the walkways of Versailles, either interspersed with or embodied in statues of classical figures, are equestrian statues and statues of hunters and warriors prepared for battle. They point quite straightforwardly to the military culture of the nobility still in force in the period, and to the king's particular interest in war and hunting; excelling in these was both his great passion and a virtue for men of his social rank. The statuary at court also presented to the world an image of Louis XIV as a great and powerful warrior. The Sun King, Apollo, in the fountain of that name, emerges in his chariot with powerful arms, strong will, and the look of a fine warrior. Such statues both sustained and violated feudal versions of this noble culture. To the extent that they placed warfare and hunting in the hands of classical gods and heroes, they used

[25] Louis XIV, *Mémoires de Louis XIV, écrits par lui-même, composés pour le grand dauphin, son fils, et adressés à ce prince,* J. L. M. de Gain-Montagnac, ed., Paris: Garnery, 1806.

idioms that in feudal times would have been thought barbaric. Putting noble military culture in the language of classicism demonstrated the power of Renaissance categories over a court society that was still glorifying the militarism of earlier feudal culture.

Military imagery pervaded the plantings as well as the statuary of the garden. Old prints show topiary bushes around parterres or fountains cut, not in the familiar cone shape used today, but with three tiers of spheres, the middle sphere having two armlike branches on the side. The resulting bushes look like sentries, standing guard along the edges of garden features. Allées and *bosquets* often had double rows of trees along their boundaries, reproducing the style of planting used on the barricades of French fortified towns. These long lines of trees consituted a kind of symbolic standing army, guarding garden features, just as trees along barricades stood sentry, guarding and standing in for French soldiers, along the walls of Vauban's fortresses.

Suggestively, formal promenades through the gardens sometimes started with a shows of military marching. An itinerary for showing the garden at Versailles to Queen Marie d'Este of England (wife of James II) begins with military drills at the back of the château. Military parading of this sort was an innovation of the professional army that developed at Versailles. Only full-time soldiers could be regularly submitted to such discipline. Given the novelty of these drills, it is no surprise that they would be of interest to visitors. What is provocative is that the marching was, in this case, part of a promenade through the garden, an introduction to the highly disciplined "nature" presented in the garden of Versailles.[26]

These hints of military influence are tantalizing, but a more revealing tie between garden design and military themes lies not in symbols but in uses of military engineering in the formation of the gardens.

[26] For images of the topiary, see the *veues et perspectives* by Pierre Aveline; the clearest views of the topiary are not at Versailles. See the *veue et perspective du château royale de Vincennes* and the one on the *orangerie de Saint-Cloud.* For images of French fortified towns that showed their landscaping, see Nicolas Faucherre, "Outil stratégique ou jouet princier?" in a special section of *Monuments Historiques* dedicated to Les Plans-Relief, 1986 148:38–44. The special section runs pp. 24–48. See also Antoine de Roux, *Perignan à la fin du XVIIe siècle,* Caisse Nationale des Monuments Historiques et des Sites, 1990. For a description of a promenade in which there was military parading, see Christopher Thacker, "La manière de montrer les jardins de Versailles," *Journal of Garden History,* 1972, 1:49–69.

Architectural systems, survey techniques, bridge-building and road-building systems, all were forms of military engineering that had a powerful place in seventeenth-century French garden design.

Military architecture was visible throughout the gardens of Le Nôtre. Although these highly architectural gardens are usually thought to be extensions of châteaux (continuous with civil architecture rather than with systems of fortification), they in fact have many debts to military architecture.

Fortification techniques were used routinely throughout the gardens at Versailles (and other sites where Le Nôtre worked) to hold up terraces and support battlement-like walkways along cascades, over grottoes, and the like. They were formed with grand and sloping walls of stone, exactly the same type used to build the fortified cities around France designed by Vauban and commissioned by the king.[27] The great wall (with double rampways) at the back of Versailles overlooking the fountain of Latona may look simply like a convenient spot for viewing the expanse of the garden below, but it is also like the barricade walls being built for military purposes elsewhere in France. This wall is much more imposing than the gentle terracing at Vaux that preceded it. It is also a more powerful architectural feature than the terraces in such Italian gardens as Tivoli and the Boboli gardens, where taller walls were made more compact and broad terraces were formed with less imposing supports. The wall behind the fountain at Versailles is closer in scale to the walls at Blois and other medieval royal houses in which the separation of military and civil architecture was not yet complete.

This does not mean (I think) that French châteaux and gardens were much more like their medieval predecessors than their Italian counterparts. The beds of Italian gardens still often used the simple geometries of medieval herb gardens, and the garden walls that gave Renaissance Italian gardens their intimacy were relatively thin stone structures, like the walls of medieval cities and castles. In contrast, French garden walls were usually back-filled with earth, like battlement walls (which had to be supported with dirt to withstand the force of cannonballs). Most seventeenth-century garden walls were

[27] See Roux. See also Michel Parent and Jacques Verroust, *Vauban*, Paris: Editions Jacques Fréal, 1971, particularly p. 122 and the appendix, "Notices historiques sur 12 citadelles ou places fortes en bon état de conservation," pp. 288–97.

built along terraces to hold up the earth behind them, or they were built as double walls filled in between with dirt, allowing people to walk along them.

Without intending to, these edifices demonstrated the state of military engineering in France, a France already known for experimenting with military techniques. When soldiers paraded across the terrace above Latona, as they did for Marie d'Este, they could have been marching along the wall of any fortification in France. It was clear enough, of course, that these garden walls had no real defensive purpose; their massively visible rampways made their heights readily accessible. They did not place a barrier between the king and the countryside as castles did, in a way that might suggest the king needed military defenses from the people. The Sun King was supposed to draw people to him, not send them away. Still, the walls expressed the military power of France. Like Vauban's fortified towns, the string of modern fortifications built around French territory under Louis XIV, the gardens at Versailles presented to the world marvels of French engineering that spoke directly to the might of France and its ability to control its territory.[28]

Other aspects of military engineering also showed up in seventeenth-century French gardens. Military skills in building bridges and roads (for moving troops and support materials) were applied to the the design of grottoes, cascades, and walkways. Bridgelike edifices were not wholly products of French culture and engineering (nor were battlement walls, for that matter); they had Italian counterparts. Many innovations in technology for warfare had originated in the warring city-states of Italy or came from classical Roman culture and spread to France from Italy. Hence, much of the military engineering that was furthered in France came from Italian precedents. Still, new military engineering affected less the design of Italian gardens than it did French gardens. Some Italian gardens used arches in

[28] This kind of great wall adds to the sense of power of the garden and château. On the garden side of Versailles, the wall behind Latona is imposing and gives the château a more elevated stance. The same sense of power is associated with the walls in the *avant-cour* at the front of the château. The stones seem to rise up from the streets to raise the château high above street level. At the Trianon side of the canal, a similar effect is produced by the high wall behind the fountain that abuts the end of the canal. A massive face of stone rises up from the water, giving the building above it a remoteness and grandeur. Similarly at Chantilly, a high wall between the courtyard and garden on the grotto side of the garden adds to the military posture of the house.

their walls and grottoes, but, for example, at the grotto in the Boboli gardens, the arches were not of equal heights; a soaring central arch made the grotto look more like a church nave than a bridge or triumphal arch. In contrast, the grotto at Versailles with its three equal and modestly sized arches looked very much like a bridge across the exterior. Even if the triple doors had been single, the grotto would have resembled from the outside a triumphal arch or city door, other forms of military architecture developed by Vauban.

Bridge architecture had a much more practical relation to the gardens at Versailles as well. The gardens were famous for their waterworks (as we shall see), depending for this magnificence on an elaborate series of aqueducts that carried water into Versailles. These structures were bridges of a sort, and show the less visible but equally important role of bridge architecture to the great gardens of the period.[29]

Many cascades and other walled areas overlooking waterworks below were also made much like the battlements of fortresses. (As moats disappeared from the areas directly around houses, bits of this kind of architecture appeared elsewhere in the gardens.) The older noble houses and more recent fortified cities had for protection a combination of battlements, bridges, and water systems that allowed those at the walls clear views of surrounding land along with distance and protection from them.[30] That elevated walkways built from these military features were often set near canals and ponds in seventeenth-century formal gardens suggests again a line of connection between military engineering and the garden. To the extent that these conjunctions of walls and water began to be used to mark important boundaries in the land rather than the setting at the house, they help point out how the new French obsession with land was linked to military techniques for both controlling and overseeing it.

The battlement or parapet form had another and even more unusual site at Versailles: the *jardin potager,* or kitchen garden. This

[29] For a detailed and fascinating description of the activities of a surveyor for an aqueduct project, see M. Picard, *Traite du Nivellement,* Paris: Estienne Michallet, 1684. For a description of the water systems at Versailles, see L. A. Barbet, *Les Grandes Eaux de Versailles,* Paris: H. Dunod et E. Pinat, 1907.

[30] Vauban actually had a complex view of water systems and their value for agriculture and transportation as well as for fortifications. See Parent and Verroust, particularly pp. 179–90.

garden is not usually discussed in art histories of the gardens at Versailles, even though the king was extremely proud of it and took distinguished visitors there. The *jardin potager* was a site in which intensive gardening techniques were furthered, particularly espalier techniques for stretching fruit trees along walls to create earlier and sweeter fruit. Walls were central to the design of this garden. Espalier trees needed them, not just for support but also so they could absorb the reflected and retained heat from the sun on the walls. There was no reason why these walls should be thick enough to walk across, but the king insisted that the garden be built with battlement-type walls all around it and through it, so visitors to the garden could promenade along them and look down at the plants below. The result is that the *jardin potager* resembles a fortification more than any other part of the Versailles gardens. Its walls surrounded and crossed it in a way that clearly resembles the walls at the fortified Château Trompette after it was rebuilt by Louis XIV in 1680. The *plan en relief* of this château produced at Versailles in 1705 shows dramatically the military origins of this sort of design.[31] We shall see later what this architectural structure did to the gardening there. For now, it is enough to think about the symbolic significance of a kitchen garden that was built like a fortress because the king thought it should be surveyed from above.

The usefulness of road- and canal-building techniques first to the state and then to garden design is clear and does not need extended comment. Both road and canal systems were an essential part of creating a unified state, serving economic as well as strategic purposes, so it is not surprising that the military was recruited into engineering and building an expanded transportation system in France. Similarly, the garden was nothing without routes traversing it. The detailed itineraries the king wrote for showing the garden to visitors were like tour books for traveling over the garden's territory, using its elaborate transportation system. Garden paths and canals shared common purpose with the transportation system in France by facilitating movement over a large territory and giving that land a unity.

Surveys were another area of technique central to the state (especially to building a national defense system) and essential to seven-

[31] See the *plan-relief* on display at Les Invalides in Paris.

teenth-century French gardens.[32] Books on surveying techniques from the period make the military value of surveys clear enough by emphasizing their role in strategic military planning and in aiming cannon. The military was the major advocate of national surveys in the period, and also wanted maps of cities and territories in other parts of Europe where France had a strategic interest. This is not to suggest there were no economic needs for surveys. Individual landowners often wanted surveys of their land to plan the development of their estates, but in France (unlike in England) estate surveys were nothing compared to the myriad surveys of principalities and towns in French and foreign territory that the military wanted.[33]

The king at Versailles as well as the Grand Condé and other nobles were fascinated with maps and battle plans. As noblemen, they had been trained as military officers and had saturated themselves with geographical as well as tactical knowledge. One can see evidence of the resulting passion for political geography in the *plans-relief* of cities that were secretly built as military planning devices at Versailles. These great model cities (some of which were probably fifteen feet across) copied in detail the appearance of every house and alleyway, showing topography and plantings, battlements and churches, as well as rivers, roads, and hillsides. They were results of meticulous surveys and drawings of building exteriors.[34]

These *plans-relief* miniatures of the land were employed to contemplate territorial control. Garden designers explicitly created another and surprisingly similar kind of miniature of the land. Formal gardens were massive but nonetheless miniature versions of the natural world that (like the *plans en relief*) combined aesthetic sensitivity with breathtaking scale, and spoke to the French capacity for putting land under control. French formal gardens reappropriated from the world of the military land-use practices designed to control state territory, and used them to control garden spaces. Gardens, the result of care-

[32] As Mariage (1990) points out, these surveys also had commercial uses and hence meaning. But it is important to point out that although in England the survey was used more extensively for estate surveying in this period, in seventeenth-century France surveys had more military uses. See Mukerji, 1983, ch. 3.

[33] Mariage, 1990, pp. 45–59, 68–77; Joseph Konvitz, *Cartography in France, 1660–1848,* Chicago: University of Chicago Press, 1987, ch. 1.

[34] See the *Monuments Historiques* dedicated to Les Plans-Relief, 1986, 148:24–48. See also Antoine de Roux.

ful manipulation of battlements and plantings, had their own canals, walkways, and mounts. All this evidence supports the contention that they provided a model of French territorial control that (as we well know) was presented to visitors to instill in them a new vision of France, its court, and the French state.

French formal gardens may have symbolically presented a model of French territoriality, but they did more than just manipulate symbols of control. They embodied a practical system of territorial control, using a combination of earth-moving and -measuring techniques. The layout of the allées themselves resembled lines in a surveyor's manual. As French gardens moved away from the strict geometries of Italian and early-seventeenth-century French gardens, they abandoned the use of walkways laid out in squares, rectangles, and circles. The new allées were laid out in lines of sight. Diagonal walkways cut across wooded areas and intersected with shorter walks that marked the depths of the forests. The allées were carefully measured and related to others, but they did not form simple geometries. There were economically few walkways to l'Encalade, the Salle du Conseil, the Galerie, and the Colonnade (this in a garden not known for its economy and simplicity). Where the walkways crossed, viewers could quickly gauge the size of the garden simply by looking at the vistas opening and closing around them, and by following the punctuation of sculptures and gates.

Some surveyors were quite clear about the centrality of this view of land to the design of gardens. Sébastian Le Clerc, for example, wrote a book on survey technique for the education of aristocrats.[35] In it, he set up exercises for the students to study. The problems were drawn out in illustrations accompanying the text. Rather than simply drawing the geometrical figures without embellishment, he set them in decorative backgrounds. Sometimes the backgrounds depicted cherubs holding up cloths on which mathematical figures were drawn; more often they presented towns, hills, or gardens with figures drawn in the foreground. The latter were environments where survey techniques could be used. Most of the "naturalistic" backgrounds depicted towns (like the ones displayed in the military

[35] Sébastian Le Clerc, *Pratique de la geometrie sur le papier and sur le terrain,* Paris: chez Thomas Jolly, 1669.

relief plans), but, interestingly, a large portion of them were of formal gardens.[36]

A fascinating thing about these illustrations is what they show about the meanings of the techniques. Many pictures, for example, have aristocratic figures in the background, *all* looking into the scene (away from the viewer) as though trying to survey the land in front of them.[37] Aristocratic readers of the book are invited by these representations to imagine themselves making surveys, and, through the illustrations' backgrounds, they are shown when they might want to do so. The author says explicitly that survey techniques are essential to the military, especially for planning the use of cannons, but his pictures say even more. Some show cities with oriental figures near them. For an aristocracy that still envisioned themselves as noble warriors, with a history of fighting enemies in the Orient where they also faced new trading competition, these pictures of oriental cities ready for survey and control could be a good advertisement for the usefulness of survey techniques. On other pages, illustrations show aristrocrats staring at a fortified town, apparently engaged in some sort of rough survey-by-eye of the town above, perhaps suggesting that mathematical surveys served the common practice of noble fighting men to measure the lay of the land by sight during war. Unusually, one illustration teaches basic geometry against an illustration of merchants standing on a dock, perhaps alluding to their interest in accurate geographical information for long-distance trade. More characteristically, the last section of the book is devoted to military uses of survey, particularly measuring the distance to and the height of structures for aiming cannons at them. Between the pictures of towns for

36 Le Clerc.

37 These figures are not drawn as surveyors measuring the land; they resemble the ladies and gentlemen seen frequently in the "views and perspectives" of châteaux and gardens printed in the period. It is conventional for many "views and perspectives" to have some hunters in the foreground, all looking into the picture toward the château, but they also depict other figures farther in the background facing the foreground. The directionality of the figures in Le Clerc's book stands out in contrast. The Le Clerc figures do not always look in exactly the same direction, but they always have their backs to the viewer. They seem to illustrate both the environments for surveys and the people living in and studying those environments. While "views and perspective" illustrations seem to welcome the viewer into the picture (by setting up eye contact between viewers and figures in the scene), the Le Clerc illustrations set the viewer up as a detached voyeur. The viewer analyzes the scene on paper while those on the paper analyze the space around them, with equal detachment.

surveying and the extended discussions of the military uses of surveys, the book makes clear the primarily military motivation behind developing these techniques.[38]

The inclusion of garden views in these illustrations is extremely provocative. They suggest that surveys of gardens were culturally accepted and expected for garden planning (a point discussed later in this chapter). Here, we should note that gardens were expected by Le Clerc, and presumably by his readers, to be designed with the kinds of techniques familiarly used in the military for detached analysis of land to achieve greater territorial control.

When foreign visitors promenaded in the royal gardens of Versailles, moving from one site to the next, studying views, appreciating statues, and looking at the château from different positions, they were made to survey the gardens, moving and peering through passages in the landscape in precisely the ways that would encourage them to measure the gardens' immensity. As new vistas appeared and disappeared in these "gardens of illusion,"[39] new relationships of space and land were made the focus of their gaze. The gardens' apparent openness made surveying seem simple; their complex control of vision made resurveying necessary at every turn.

Distances were not the only measures to be taken during these walks. As visitors were led from statue to fountain to statue again, admiring the artwork as they went, they were also encouraged to make informal inventories of the wealth on the estate and to measure the taste of the king. The promenade scripts were formally like the medieval pilgrimage maps that defined routes from one landmark to the next, taking the pilgrim from town to town in quest of truth. The difference was that the truth sought in the promenades was achieved through accounting techniques, measures of territory and its riches,

[38] Le Clerc. For a discussion of merchant needs for skills at measuring volume by sight, see Michael Baxandall, *Painting and Experience in Fifteenth-Century Italy,* New York: Oxford University Press, [1972], 1974, pp. 86–94.

Although there was a long-standing tradition in European publishing of decorating books with illustrations that had no strong relation to the text, by the seventeenth century this practice had diminished, and illustrations of the sort in this book, designed specifically to demonstrate exercises from the text, were clearly tailored to the books' content. Hence, their decorative content was intentional and bore some relation to what the author or publisher thought of the intended readership. See Mukerji, 1983, ch. 2.

[39] Hazlehurst, 1980.

rather than through religious narratives. The royal ceremonial walks constrained viewers in a system of *social* control that highlighted the virtuosity of the *technical* control (particularly from military sources) displayed in French seventeenth-century territorial gardens.[40]

Commercial sources of French garden design

At the time when Louis XIV started commissioning the reconstruction of the grounds around Versailles, France had a reputation for wealth and abundance partially embedded in a vibrant gardening tradition. The English pointed equally to the French and the Dutch as exemplary caretakers of tender plants and nurturers of fruits and vegetables. The gardens at Versailles were hardly experiments in market gardening per se, but they did display the commercial skills of French gardeners and were models of superfluidity of every sort. The fountains of the four seasons (central features in the royal promenades) were, on the surface, representations of classical gods, but the deities were placed on beds heaped high with flowers, fruits, grains, and seafood – the harvests of the seasons. The *parterre du Midi* was a collector's paradise of palms and citruses presented in unparalleled variety and beauty. The riches brought to France by the plant trade and market gardening, which helped promote its identity as a wealthy land, were visible both symbolically and actually in the gardens. But interestingly, much of the

[40] The itineraries developed by the king are seen by Thacker (1972) as problematic to use for understanding the gardens because they were developed for *showing* the garden, not explaining it. They told the visitor where to walk in the garden, what objects to look at, and what views to study, yet provided no guide for analyzing the meaning of statues or the significance of the garden's layout.

The itineraries generally had the visitor walk from the back of the château to one of the garden features to the left or right. Following a large semicircular movement, the guide would take visitors to view major fountains or statues. If these were (as they often were) placed at the intersection of walkways, the guide would tell the visitor which way to look in order to appreciate a view or to see the artwork or château from a different angle. This process pointed out to visitors the two major forms: vistas and artworks, as well as spatial designs and the objects punctuating them. Not surprisingly, the vistas encouraged the visitor to look at and think about the garden as a diverse but integrated territory. The artwork drew attention to the new material culture and cultural materialism of the garden. The movement of studying *bosquets*, fountains, or statues, and then once again looking at an important view, encouraged the viewer to consider two elements of control in the garden's design: its spatial and material claims. Although most garden histories do not mention this, these gardens encouraged viewing from multiple perspectives while maintaining a clear system of centralized control.

invisible technique in the garden – the pumps for the fountains, the transportation systems for trees, the aqueducts for the waterworks, and the techniques for preparing the garden areas for planting – was of commercial origin. As a result, much of the effect on French gardens of the world of commerce was masked and lay hidden behind the explicit references to military culture.

The commercial sources of territorial engineering in French formal gardens are brilliantly analyzed in Thierry Mariage's book on Le Nôtre.[41] He argues that Le Nôtre's originality lies less in his individual imagination than in his use of a tradition of French gardening that began with a commercial culture of estate management from more or less the sixteenth century. The nobility became interested in new approaches to their landholdings when low rents were making estates less profitable. Rather than turning to commercial crops like wood to extract new wealth from the land (as the British tended to do in the period),[42] the French (like the Dutch) identified new commercial possibilities in gardening. Many French garden writers reflected upon and helped direct this movement. Olivier de Serres, who wrote a hugely successful book, was the most famous of them. He not only provided helpful advice for growing different types of plants, but established an attitude toward land management that strongly emphasized the details of technique and rational calculation in the use of property.

These ideas of land management were necessarily connected to the international plant trade and the associated repertoire of means for acclimatizing plants. They also presupposed a capitalist trading system within which the products of commercial gardening could be made profitable. Henry IV was sure that if the French aristocracy simply cultivated mulberry trees on their estates and raised silkworms, the wealth of the kingdom would be increased. (Silk was a precious commodity in the textile trade, and textiles were the center of international commerce in the period.) By strict monetarist economic thinking, raising silk was good because it could be exported for gold, bringing bullion into the country, where contemporary economic thinkers felt it belonged.[43]

[41] Mariage 1990; Olivier de Serres, *Le théâtre d'agriculture et mesnages,* Genève: Mat Hiev Berjon, 1611.

[42] Mukerji, 1983, ch. 6.

[43] Mariage, 1990, ch. 1, particularly pp. 7–20.

This view of gardening as economically productive was dropped by the theorists of French formal gardening in the seventeenth century in favor of pleasure gardens that cost money rather than generated wealth; but (according to Mariage) the designs for their gardens were based on some simple tenets that had been established in the commercial estates. The new gardens were enlarged and emerged along a central axis from the center of an open château; they were not inward-looking enclosed Edens or cloister gardens placed outside a fortress. The great vistas and easy access to the gardens, the movement of the garden in an array of measured plots away from the house, and the measured rationality of the overall garden design (not to mention the commercial gardening concept itself) had roots in this commercial moment in estate gardening.

Equally, the physical construction of French formal gardens evolved from a constellation of garden techniques originally developed to help manage the new commercial estates. Urban artisans were brought into the country to build these new houses and gardens. They leveled areas for planting, built retaining walls, drained plots of land, and otherwise engineered an environment on the new estates that would serve gardening. In the process they created aesthetic and technical connections between the countryside and the urban culture of commerce, where the experts on these forms of construction generally lived and worked. The skilled workers who constructed the royal gardens of the late seventeenth century, like their predecessors from a century before, were urban denizens. Many can be found both in the *Livre Commode,* listing artisans available for hire in Paris, and in the *Comptes des Bâtiments,* the account books recording who was paid what for royal building projects, including gardens.[44]

Mariage traces this tradition of gardening in France and calls it a form of uniquely French territorial management. He sees the French garden of the seventeenth century as a place where commercial life and technique entered the aesthetic world and created an image of territory and its rational management in the great French formal gardens. What Mariage does not explore in any depth are the continu-

[44] For a discussion of this connection, see Mariage, 1990, ch. 3, particularly pp. 39–44. Abraham du Pradel, *Le Livre Commode Des Adresses de Paris pour 1692,* Edouard Fournier, ed., Liechtenstein: Kraus Reprint, [Paris 1878] 1979. L. de Laborde, *Comptes des Bâtiments de Roi,* Paris: J. Baur, 1880.

ities between this culture and the military one described earlier in this chapter. He takes them for granted and hence reduces to commercial technique elements of military engineering. Surveys and roads had commercial as well as military significance. In a seamless fashion, building techniques went from the world of fortresses to other kinds of building. But parts of commercial culture did not have strategic elements and did not enter military culture. Significantly, where these techniques entered the gardens, they were much more masked than elements of military engineering.

The reasons for this are simple enough. The commercial vitality of France was of court interest, but the skills of those in the commercial world were not appropriate symbolic markers for the aristocratic culture of the court. Louis XIV wanted the plant trade to fill his gardens with wonders and his table with delicacies, but he did not want the trade itself visible as a marker of the glory of the French state. Getting the plants he wanted for the garden was important, and was a continual problem for Colbert, who was pressed to find novelties for the new seasons. The sensational water system that supplied the elaborate array of fountains was a tribute to commercial engineering traditions, and of undying interest to the king, but the engineering itself had no special interest at court. Military engineering, however, was a visible obsession of noble families and was reproduced both in *plans-reliefs* and in the maps and paintings of battles they commissioned for the walls of their châteaux. The early fruits and vegetables of the *jardin potager* might have delighted the palate and the king's vanity, but they were treated as bounties of nature and expressions of the genius of La Quintinie, not the result of France's strong tradition of market gardening.

The part of commercial culture that was visibly central in the gardens was one not seen as commercial: the statuary. These works were commissioned and paid for, but they were defined and appreciated as part of the Great Tradition, and hence above any commercial meaning. Indeed, they were part of a system of mass production of artworks in the period (that France helped to nurture with the Academy), but in the gardens they marked a continuity between the heights of classical culture and the new levels of culture being nourished in France. The statues were certainly part of a claim about the greatness of France, and its special place as a Catholic kingdom and heir to the traditions of Rome. Commercial culture, devoted to extracting wealth from the land, had no acknowledged place there. Plants and pumps, glass-covered hotbeds and massive orangeries, espalier fruit trees and quiet canals, all were essential parts of French formal gardens in the seventeenth century, but their roots in the commercial culture of France were not highlighted to make territorial claims in the gardens. They embodied techniques of land control without proclaiming political sovereignty over a territory.

The role of the plant trade in the gardens at Versailles helps to underscore not only how the world of commerce made these gardens possible but also how this fact was obscured. Most visibly, the plant trade contributed to the collection of rare trees, particularly palms and citrus trees, that adorned the *parterre du Midi*. These delicate beauties could adorn Versailles only because of advances in the techniques for boxing, shipping, and cultivating tender plants on which the trade depended. These skills emerged from the efforts of amateur botanists, commercial plant merchants, estate gardeners, and scientists who traveled, wrote each other, and often sent each other samples and seeds from plants in different areas of the world. Their activities were supplemented by the work of explorers who collected plant species from continents beyond Europe as they traveled through them. The culture of collection in Europe encouraged this massive transplanting of plant species, and the culture of science provided a strong intellectual rationale for locating varieties from all over the world. The trade itself comprised such a melange of activities, it could hardly be called commerce per se. It was (like the new military) a place where traditional boundaries broke down, and new relations to nature and land management could be explored – through personal exchanges as well as monied ones.

Even the commercial florist Pierre Morin, in his well-known catalog of flowering plants from his garden, was not just writing to prospective buyers. He wrote also as a collector who wanted to advertise the range of his collection of species from all over the world. He was one of many market gardeners located in the faubourgs around Paris (his being the faubourg Saint-Germain) who lived from their gardening skills, commercial abilities, and positions in a network of collectors. Morin's first catalog, published in 1651 during the period of tulip mania in Europe, quite naturally emphasized the flowering bulbs in his collection, particularly tulips, irises, and ranunculas. He cataloged the bulbs by the colors, sizes, and growth patterns of their flowers, the kind of information amateur gardeners would want to know in choosing what to plant. He wrote, then, as a man of commerce of his period who knew where there were expanding markets for his goods.[45] But in 1655, when he put out a revised catalog of flowering plants, he explained that in the intervening years he had received letters from flower collectors from all over the world, asking him about his collection and telling him about theirs. He traded with them for new plants, which he raised in his garden. These flowers, he claimed, had not been seen in France before, and were now on display in his garden for curious Parisians to see (he does not say buy).

Pierre Morin was no botanist, and not a figure at court. He was a businessman who had amassed a huge plant collection. In his books he categorized plants in gardeners' terms (by their culture) rather than botanical terms (by attributes of the plants themselves). He also had nothing to say about garden design. Yet he was part of the plant trade that made French formal gardens so elegant.[46]

The gardens at Versailles depended heavily on the plant trade. The account books show that Colbert authorized huge annual purchases of plants for the garden from the Midi, particularly such sweet-smelling plants as tuberoses and citruses.[47] The collection of orange trees num-

[45] Pierre Morin, *Catalogue de quelques plantes à fleurs qui sont de présent au jardin de Pierre Morin le jeune, dit troisième, fleurist scitué au faubourg Saint Germain proche la Charité,* Paris: François Le Cointe. 1651.

[46] Morin, 1651; Pierre Morin, *Catalogue de quelques plantes à fleurs* (second edition), Paris: François Le Cointe, 1655; Pierre Morin, *Remarques necessaires pour la culture des Fleurs: Diligement observé par P. Morin,* Paris: Charles de Sercy, 1658 (in which he distinguishes between plants for pleasure gardens and those for collectors' gardens); Pierre Morin, *Instruction façile pour connoitre toutes sortes d'orangers et citronniers,* Paris: Charles de Sercy, 1680. In his books on plant culture, Morin distinguished between plants appropriate for pleasure gardens and those for scientific or collectors' gardens. In the 1655 catalog he also made clear that despite his commercial relation to plants and his relatively low social status, he was nevertheless in touch with aristocratic and scientific gardeners through the plant trade, bringing to Paris new species of plant that interested these other gardeners. Although not a court figure, he helped bring to France exactly the kinds of decorative bulbs and scented trees that were popular with Louis XIV and that graced parterres at Versailles close to the château.

[47] Locke (p. 155) describes how orange trees were brought to Paris in the period: "They are all set in square cases and are a great many of them biger then a man's thigh, but most of them with little heads, haveing been lately transported i.e. 2, 3, 4, 5, or 6 years since. They bring them, as he told me, from Italy to Rouen by sea, big as they are, & the better to transport them, cut of the stock where it is entire & not

bered three thousand plants in the Orangerie under Louis XIV. The king loved having flowering citrus in the Hall of Mirrors and his private apartments, so the gardeners at Versailles learned to keep some citrus flowering at all times of the year. To do this, they not only had to learn how to force trees to flower early or late, but they also had to assemble from different parts of the world a large collection of plants that naturally fruited and flowered at different times. The cost of the trees was substantial. The treasury paid the duchesse de la Ferté 2,200 livres for only twenty of them. This was more than the annual pension paid to the head of the *jardin potager,* La Quintinie, who only received 2,000 livres. Many more citruses came from commercial sources in diverse locations, including Flanders and Saint-Denis.[48]

Not all plant transfers brought rare species to Versailles. The soil and drainage at Versailles were so awful that large numbers of trees died each year. The park had relatively few older ones because of the clay soil and lack of good water. Although the gardeners improved both drainage and the soil to some extent, it was still difficult just keeping the trees alive, so replacements were routinely brought in from the mountain forests. In 1688, the royal treasury paid 16,949 livres for 25,000 trees brought to the gardens at Versailles from Compiègne, Flanders, the mountains of Dauphiné, and the forests of Normandy.[49] In 1700, the state paid 1,500 livres for green trees to regenerate the *bosquets* in the gardens. In 1699, the king ordered for the gardens a thousand small trees (four or five feet tall) and two hundred fully grown trees to be taken from the forests at Marly and other locations.[50]

spread into branches, & cut (as the Gardener told me) all the roots. I believe they are most of them cut of, for the boxes seeme not capeable to hold the roots which are necessary for a tree of that bulke as many of them are, & soe, root & branches being cut off, they bring them exposd to the aire like soe many stakes at all times of the yeare without dyeing, but I am afraid in this later part of the story the gardiner made bold with truth." Wed. 7 Jul, 1677. See Jean-Baptiste Colbert, *Lettres, Instructions et Mémoires de Colbert,* Pierre Clément, ed., vol. 5, Paris: Imprimerie Impériale, 1868, pp. 307, 334–35, 353–54, 362.

[48] See James Eugene Farmer, *Versailles and the Court Under Louis XIV,* New York: Century Co., 1905, p. 100.

[49] Farmer, p. 84.

[50] Registre on sont ecrits par dattes les ordres que Le Roy a donez à Monsieur Mansart Surintendant des Bâtiments de sa Majesté par tout ce qui est à faore. à changer, ou à réparer aux chateaux, jardins, petit et grand, Parc de Versailles, Trianon, la mesnagerie et dépendences dudit Versailles. Archives Nationales, Paris, O1# 1809, du 5 Juillet, 1699.

Interestingly, these plant transfers were alternately military and commercial in nature. Sometimes trees were purchased; other times they were moved by soldiers in quasi-military campaigns that tested the military's ability to transport large-sized and large numbers of objects over difficult terrain. Military and commercial worlds converged in this area of the plant trade, but visitors in the garden had no idea that these trees had not grown where they stood. A "natural" world was made by artifice that lay hidden in the secrets of the plant trade.

Major projects for expanding the garden accounted for the most dramatic transfers of trees, but fetes accounted for some notable others. Special garden rooms, or *bosquets,* were constructed specifically for major fetes, and were part of the escalating conspicuous display at court. Le Nôtre, Mansart, and Louis XIV often made dramatic gestures with massive transfers of plants that demonstrated the French ability to make the land realize the king's ambitions and provide abundant wealth and pleasure for the court. Trade might not have been glorified in these plant transfers, but abundance clearly was, and the king's ability to bring precious vegetation from the far corners of his kingdom and beyond made a statement about the quality of his territory that matched claims about his reach.

The water system at Versailles, including the numerous fountains spewing water jets to great heights, was another dramatic aspect of the gardens that highlighted the extraordinary ambition of the king and resulted from the technological capacity of commercial France. When John Locke visited Versailles, he was most impressed by the water system. He found both the number and height of the water jets astounding in part because of the sheer volume of water required to run them. The system of aqueducts, pipes, and pumps was so sophisticated and impressive to his eye that he took careful note of them. Hydraulic engineering was becoming quite sophisticated in seventeenth-century France, so that fountain designers could be quite precise in determining how much water they needed for their fountains and how they had to set water jets to get particular water movements.[51]

[51] Locke. For the hydraulic engineering, see Abbé Pujol, *Traité du mouvement et de la mesure des eaux coulantes and jaillisantes avec un traité preliminaire du mouvement en general* tiré des ouvrages manuscrits du feu M Varignon, Paris 1725; M. Mariotte, *Traité Mouvement des Eaux et des Autres Corps Fluides, Divise en V. parties,* Paris, Chez Jean Jombert, 1708.

The water system at Versailles was even more complex than Locke noticed. There was not only water to feed the fountains, but water that supplied the château, water that fed the canal, water to irrigate the *jardin potager,* and water in lakes and ponds (the menagerie in the early days and the *pièce d'eau des Suisses* later on). This depended on the tradition of highly developed water delivery systems that were developing in commercial centers like Paris. The early plans of the gardens at Versailles are crisscrossed with lines for pipes and drains that testify to the complexity of these systems.[52]

The technologies for these systems did not all come from the same source, but they were drawn primarily from the world of commerce. The pumps that worked the fountains had origins in mines, where excavation depths were limited by water unless pumping systems could dispose of the excess.[53] Pumps were hardly collector's items among the nobility (as military maps were); hence, their employment in the garden was visually hidden and nobles at court could greet the fountains as miraculous delights. At the same time, more bourgeois visitors would applaud the technological skills in their construction as well as the beauty of the result.

Similarly, the waterwheels used to power pumps that lifted water from the rivers to the canals and aqueducts supplying Versailles were also impressive but ignorable ingredients of the garden that came from the world of commerce. Waterwheels had been primary sources of power for mills during the Middle Ages. In the seventeenth century, they were joined with a complex set of pipes and pumps in the machine at Marly, in an attempt to harness the river for the sake of the garden. This machine was a dramatically impressive artifact in itself, but it did not need to be seen in the garden in order for the fountains to be appreciated.[54]

52 See Mariage, 1990, pp. 122–25.

53 Pujol, preface. In joining interest in the practical movement of water to the garden, Pujol says, "Je prends la liberté de vouse presenter ce Traité sure le Mouvement & la Mesure des Eaux. J'ai crû MONSIEUR, qu'une matiere si agréable & si utile ne seroit pas indigne de votre attention. Les differens movemens des Eaux son aujourd'hui le plus bel agrément des principaux Jardins de la France & de l'Italie. La merveilleuse Machine de Marly & les Jets d'eaux sans nombre du magnifique Parc de Versailles, montrent assez que les plus grand Héros & les plus grands Rois en ont fait l'objet de leurs amusemens & de leurs plaisirs. Et pour l'utilité, MONSEIGNEUR, personne n'ignore ce que des Eaux bien conduites & bien ménagées peuvent porter dans un Pays, de richesses & d'abondance . . . ," pp. aij–aiij.

54 A. M. Gondouin, *Sur la Machine de Marly,* Paris: l'Auteur, 1803.

Networks of canals in the garden were another part of the complex water system with commercial roots. Drainage systems using canals were important contemporary measures for increasing the agricultural yield of estates by allowing more land to be brought under cultivation. In the Versailles gardens this kind of land reclamation and development made boggy sections of land productive and dry areas green. Canals were also central means of commercial transportation in the period, and at Versailles canals were used to move visitors to and from the menagerie and Trianon. Even the layout of the garden at Versailles may have had some commercial roots in a form of Dutch garden designs derived from Dutch models of ideal cities, commercially served by canal systems.[55]

Although many techniques with commercial sources were invisible in the garden, canals were dramatically obvious and used ostentatiously during fetes. Why? Perhaps because canals had military as well as commercial significance in the period, acting as one element in the defenses of towns built by Vauban. Canals were thus the perfect markers of the conjunction of commercial and military technologies. The canals in French gardens could be appreciated as a means of transportation by those with interest in market culture, and could be admired as serene but effective barriers by those with more military interests. No wonder the canals were always at the heart of Le Nôtre's gardens, and central to the ceremonial life of the French court.

Canals, pumps, and waterwheels were all systems of technique for improving and developing property that found their way into French formal gardens. They were part of a commercial infrastructure that was transforming life in France and elsewhere. They did not explicitly tout the commercial power of France, but they were admired in the garden in part because they testified to a technological cleverness in France that, in fact, came from the world of commerce. What the king wanted from the water system was not a measure of commercial greatness but breathtaking fountains and immense canals that matched his political ambition. Water was a precious and difficult resource to contain, and the fact that the water system put it in the garden in great abundance was a measure of French power. But what made the water so impressive to some was the technology of its control, and not just the

[55] Hopper.

fact of control, and this technology had commercial roots. Thus the culture of commerce was both apparent in and essential to the value of the garden for impressing some ranks of visitors.

The commercial culture of plants also provided models in garden architecture and plant culture that added to the conspicuous display at Versailles. Structures like the huge Orangerie at Versailles were built to house such tender plants as palms and citruses during the winter; their design was based on ideas about the culture of plants derived in part from the world of science, and in part from market gardening. Europeans had not yet developed glass-roofed greenhouses for tender plants (in the nineteenth-century mold), partially because gardeners had not yet realized that plants needed light as well as warmth in the winter; but they built south-facing windowed structures to capture heat and keep frost off rare trees. The Orangerie at Versailles looks strange to modern eyes because it lies *underneath* a parterre on the side of the château. Its dugout design seems the opposite to what we expect for housing plants, but the large windows and earth insulation provided a kind of solar heating system that could indeed protect the plants during the winter. In its own way, it took advantage of state-of-the-art knowledge about growing tender plants in the cold northern environment, knowledge that was (as we shall see) developing primarily to serve botanical and market gardeners, and that was used to enhance the effectiveness of the plant trade.

The Dutch were the most consistent innovators in building shelters for plants – in part because they were pioneers in both botanical and market gardening. They had developed glass-faced hothouses, called stoves, that had wood-burning furnaces under ledges facing the glass wall. The ledges provided a warm location for potted plants in winter. Stoves were interesting innovations, serving both scientific plant collectors and market gardeners, but they could easily overheat and did not gain popularity in France.[56]

The French used a related technology for plants. Market gardeners had long used hotbeds (made with raw manure placed under the bedding soil) to bring vegetables to table early, and some had experimented with glass covers. Early in the century, Olivier de Serres

[56] The French clearly knew about stoves because at least one book describing them and their uses was available in French. See Van der Groen, *Jardinier hollandais*, Amsterdam: Marc Doornick, 1669.

advocated the use of glass jars, called *cloches,* over hotbeds for growing melons and cucumbers.[57] This French tradition of sheltering and heating tender plants, along with Dutch work with glass, provided the technical basis for the innovations in fruit and vegetable gardening at Versailles that made the *jardin potager* by La Quintinie so famous.[58]

La Quintinie's major contribution to the culture of plants was his development of espalier techniques for spreading fruit trees along walls, so they could take advantage of the sun's warmth reflected off and retained in the walls. To maximize the walls' value, he placed glass fences in front of the espalier trees to contain more of the heat. Over the top and between the glass and the stone walls, he draped thin cloth that allowed air circulation and pest control while also further retaining heat.

The use of glass for raising trees was something already known, seen in *orangeries* and stoves. La Quintinie simply extended the use of glass in the kitchen garden so he could bring fruits and vegetables to table earlier in the season. In this and his other innovations, he not only made use of market gardening techniques, but improved upon them. As the king's *potager,* he had to (and did) bring to the king's table fruits and vegetables *before* they were available commercially, in part because he was given resources that market gardeners could not provide for themselves. While they were strategically using *cloches,* he was given the money to cover *fields* of fruits and vegetables with glass (interestingly, called *serres*). He scaled up systems of market gardening until they were sources for conspicuous display as well as for high-quality fruits and vegetables.[59]

The extent of the conspicuous display in the vegetable garden becomes clearer when we learn that, in the 1690s, the cost of a meter-by-meter-square piece of glass was 2,000 livres. Glass was a rare and difficult commodity, and *serres* commanded vast amounts of it. The conspicuous display in the Hall of Mirrors was continued outside in on the ground of the *jardin potager.* Techniques of market gardening were amplified by the culture of conspicuous consumption at the court.

[57] Serres was one of the earliest proponents of putting plants under glass. He specifically advocated the use of *cloches* or bell jars for melons and cucumbers. He also saw his work as serving the economic development of estates in particular and France in general. See Serres, 1611, section 6, on the *jardin potager.*

[58] Serres; Van der Groen.

[59] Serres.

The debts to commercial culture were so palpable at the *jardin potager* that they were a problem for a court that denied its own debt to the marketplace. La Quintinie helped by going to great pains in his writings to deny any interest in commercial reward from his gardening. He specifically implored other gardeners managing *jardins potagers* to avoid selling excess produce to enrich themselves. That he felt compelled to mention this suggests that many gardeners did the opposite (as they clearly did in England). It also helps explain the king's delight in La Quintinie's character; here was a man who took techniques from the culture of the market while eschewing market values and touting noble ones. At the king's orders, La Quintinie set up a stand to give away excess produce to the poor of Versailles, transforming the potential profit of the gardens into a paternalistic exchange that reproduced some of the feudal relations between a king and his subjects.

However much the king denied the commercial meaning of the *jardin potager* at Versailles, ordinary gardeners saw the value in the innovations there. Jean Laurent, a notary from Laon, used many of the ideas about the culture of fruits espoused by La Quintinie, and dedicated his book on gardening to the head of the *potager.*[60] La Quintinie responded that Laurent could (and probably should) have found a more powerful patron (as another garden writer, Dom Claude Estienne, had done when he dedicated a book on fruit culture to Le Nôtre, who was not in charge of the fruit garden).[61] But Laurent could have seen La Quintinie's value more in commercial than in political terms. Books on raising fruits and vegetables were profitable because they sold to market gardeners and estate gardeners alike.[62] In spite of his claims to the contrary, La Quintinie was acquiring commercially valuable knowledge in managing the *potager:* This is what eventually made his own book on gardening an economic success.

60 Jean Laurent, *Abrégé pour les arbres nain et autres,* Paris: Charles Sercy, 1675.

61 Dom Claude S. Estienne, *Nouvelle instruction pour connoistre les bons fruits selon les mois de l'année,* Paris: Charles Sercy, 1687.

62 The publisher Charles de Sercy specialized in garden books. He advertised a list of ten of them in 1675, including books by Mollet, a royal gardener, and Laurent, the notary and commercial florist. These books clearly had a market and group of authors linking commercial and royal gardeners, and providing publishers with profits. See the advertisement in Laurent's book.

In the *jardin potager* we can see one intersection of feudal and bourgeois conceptions of land. The improvements in gardening techniques owed and contributed much to the market gardening tradition in France, but the king used the garden to increase his patriarchal authority vis-à-vis the poor and made sure the garden had ramparts around it for his promenades. The glass in the garden was used because it was advocated in the world of market gardening for earlier and better produce, yet the extensive use of glass displayed the wealth of the state and its king, not the commercial health of France.

Beyond the *potager,* a similar mix of cultures was unified in the garden. The *bosquets* were decorated by fountains that used hydraulic systems from the commercial world, and the trees there were sometimes brought by commercial means, but they were used for fetes that were drawn from the performance culture of the feudal nobility. In the forests themselves, imported trees sheltered animals to be pursued in hunts.

In formal gardens, as elsewhere, commercial culture in the seventeenth century was providing the French with new means for improvement of land. International trade was bringing new goods to market, including new flowering bulbs and sweet-scented bushes, and in the French formal garden these commercial forces were contained and used to serve in political rituals and models of territorial control.

In the garden, in the military, and in the state, then, the boundaries of feudal and bourgeois culture were blurred to fit the new social complexity of the period. At the material level, traditions of land control were joined to manage the territorial representation of the state. Within this frame there was no sign that the nobility was losing power to the bourgeoisie or that the bourgeoisie might be trading its identity for offices. The object of the order in the gardens was not the social order but natural order, and hence the gardens naturalized orderliness itself, when imposed on the land. This situation contained a moral lesson for those viewing the gardens. In the military, feudal notions of prowess were still admired, but they were there to protect a material manifestation of the state, its territory, and the government that managed it. In the gardens, commercial techniques were brought to improve the land, but their use was symbolically hidden behind military themes and made subservient to the larger goal of territorial control.

The disintegration of the boundary between bourgeois and feudal culture in seventeenth-century French gardens was made apparently unproblematic by the shared obsession with territoriality. Land-use practices from the military and market were fused to present a vision of territorial control that combined careful measurement, fortification, conspicuous decoration, and improvement. The garden became a model of how military and economic intervention in the use of land could yield new kinds of power and cultural beauty. As a metaphor for state intervention and as a model of territorial control under an interventionist state, the garden was a potent piece of political culture that was well used for entertaining state visitors.

The culture presented in these gardens could easily be (and usually has been) identified with Louis XIV and his symbolic representation as the Sun King and Catholic leader of Europe.[63] But this personalized view of the gardens does not take adequate account of the layout of the gardens and the land-use patterns there. Seventeenth-century French gardens developed a maplike quality, an obsession with boundaries and their measured relations, just as the French state was commissioning national surveys to encompass and define itself in mathematical terms. The overall garden, then, was not just a collection of individual fountains or statues that celebrated the king; it presented a new relation to land that was being organized under the state, not the king. The king was presented as the symbol because that was necessary for legitimating the new state, but power was imposed and displayed on the land.

[63] For an elegant and revealing work in this tradition, see J. P. Néraudau, *L'Olympe du roi-soleil,* Paris: Société d'Edition "Les Belles Lettres," 1986, particularly ch. 6.

CHAPTER 3

Money, equality, fraternity: freemasonry and the social order in eighteenth-century Europe

MARGARET C. JACOB

Eighteenth-century philosophical societies invented modern civil society. Historians and philosophers have related the emergence of this "web of autonomous associations, independent of the state" to the spread of a market economy in the West.[1] Without laboring the complex issue of causality between market relations and the emergence of the public and the civil, this essay examines the major secular form of the new sociability, the Masonic lodges of the eighteenth century, in relation to what they tell us about the earliest experience of living as an imagined "equal" in a social context, in this instance voluntarily created, dominated by money and hence the market. In the lodges men and, by midcentury, some women reflected upon the moral and civic order in a forum made possible by dues, negotiated their social relations within the confines of an egalitarian ideology, and, not least, sought through charity and loans to mitigate the vagaries of chance and fortune. At the heart of their ideology lay the belief that status within the realm of the civil should be contingent not upon birth but upon merit.

While reserving membership in this most private of the new public spaces to men and some women both literate and prosperous enough to afford the substantial entry fees and monthly payments, the lodges then sought to redefine the ideological foundations of social identity, to re-create hierarchy through elections and rituals that rewarded merit and rejoiced in the experience of brothers "meeting upon the

[1] The definition is from Charles Taylor, "Modes of Civil Society," *Public Culture*, 3, no. 1, Fall 1990, p. 96. Cf. Jürgen Habermas, "The Public Sphere: An Encyclopedia Article," *New German Critique*, 3, Fall 1974, pp. 45–55.

level."[2] In the European lodges with which I am familiar, from Scotland, the Low Countries, France, Sweden, and Germany, two monetary practices were universally present: Members paid substantial dues, upon initiation, then again with each new "degree" conferred, and, of course, annually, if not monthly. In some lodges these dues were actually described as "taxes." This money in turn was meant to cover the expenses of the lodge. Just as important was the second objective: to establish a charity fund to assist brothers who had fallen on hard times, to make loans or outright gifts to brothers or their widows (Mozart's widow being one of the most famous to receive such charity), and wherever possible to distribute money to the deserving poor, orphans often being high on the list of favored recipients. The Grand Lodge of France in addition gave money to brothers who were ill, or recommended that brothers who were doctors or apothecaries donate free services to other brothers.[3] In one of the earliest continental Masonic documents charity was seen as the inevitable outgrowth of egalitarian sociability: "The spirit of communication, the sweetness of Equality, of support, of mutual aid . . . all these attributes concur to form the Charity found at the essence and foundation of Freemasonry."[4] The lodges were among the very few, perhaps in many places the only, secular and voluntary societies systematically dispensing charity.

Men and women Freemasons, as well as widows of brothers, wrote to the Paris Grand Lodge and appealed for its "generosity" to relieve them in their miserable state.[5] By the 1780s the Grand Lodge had a committee that did nothing else but dispense charity, sometimes on a regular weekly basis.[6] Most needy brothers and sisters received slightly

[2] The complexities of this experience are further explored in my *Living the Enlightenment: Freemasonry and Politics in Eighteenth Century Europe,* New York and Oxford, Oxford University Press, 1991.

[3] *Statuts et réglemens particuliers, de la R.L. des A.R. . . . à l'O[rient] de Paris, 5774* [1774], p. 72: "Outre les secours d'argent la loge aura toujours parmi les membres, un medecin, un chirurgen, un apothicaire. . . ."

[4] Quoted from one of the earliest extant Continental books of constitutions, modeled on the *Constitutions,* London, 1723; Archives du département de la Côte d'Or, Dijon, MS Livre des Constitutions et Reglemens Generaux des Francs et Reçus Maçons en particulier pour La Loge de Lausanne. Aprouvés par tous les Freres le 30me. Decembre MDCCXLI [1741].

[5] Bibliothèque Nationale, Paris, MS FM1. 136, ff. 393–486, for an entire collection of these letters. I quote from them at random.

[6] Bibliothèque National, MS FM1. 136, 1785–1809, demandes de secours.

more than a livre per month "for bread."[7] This was a fairly minimal sum, although sometimes more was awarded. Repeatedly male supplicants refer to the fraternity as a family of which they are legitimate sons. Invariably, they explain, they or their natural families have been stricken with misfortune, disease, accidents at sea, sudden paralysis, limbs lost at war, in short, disasters unforeseen for which they are in no way responsible. "The situation of this brave man is such . . . that he does not merit the bad fortune that he had endured so long in silence."[8] A Parisian, "sister" Dupont, writes that in her extreme need she "dares to flatter herself that her brothers and sisters would bring to her the consolation of humanity."[9] We sense in the letters that the supplicant has literally nowhere else to turn. A widow writes, "I have two small children. We are without bread, without money. . . ." Sometimes the writer is a brother servant who is begging the lodge for work.

Most letters invariably make clear that when good fortune had reigned the writer had been a faithful brother, had risen through many degrees, and always had been a man of merit. Once meritorious and hence, through virtuous conduct, successful, somewhat ironically, only fate and bad luck can be invoked to explain a brother's demise. Many of the correspondents tell that they are far from their place of birth either in France or abroad. These are travelers whose professions, trade or war making, have taken them from their places of birth, from Ireland, Copenhagen, Portugal, and now they are without support. The arguments they give as to why they should be helped vacillate between a plea for generosity, beneficence, in short, voluntary charity, and occasionally the reminder of "the solemn engagement that our contract obliges us to our brothers."[10] After 1789, it should be noted, the tone of the letters changes slightly and we find brothers in need more willing to begin their plea with a reminder of "the indispensable duty" of all brothers to help members in need. Still these more self-assured supplicants note their "chagrin" at being in this situation given "the talents, the work" that had gone into their industry.[11] Another brother noted with self-confidence "my patriotism and my rapport

[7] Bibliothèque Nationale, MS FM1. 136, ff. 393–486; letters asking for charity; and f. 511 et. seq. records of monthly, even weekly, payments.

[8] Ibid., f. 426.

[9] Ibid., f. 431.

[10] Ibid., f. 420, from one Joseph Schwartzmann, originally Danish.

[11] Ibid., f. 486, dated Paris, June 6, 1791.

with General La Fayette [also a member of the society]."[12] Brothers were also quick to point out that they had lived by "a probity and a civil and masonic conduct equally irreproachable." In May 1789 one indigent brother asked the Grand Lodge "to procure for the State a useful citizen" and thus to assist him in publishing "mon histoire philosophique."[13] In whatever year, the supplicants were universally humble and woeful but a few were not shy in reminding their brothers of the contractual obligations that come with virtue and fraternity.

These indigent brothers of the 1780s and early 1790s tell us that they are caught between two worlds: one, essentially paternalistic, where personal loyalty and charity of rich to poor supposedly prevented the unfortunate from starving; the other where men and women of merit, citizens of a commercial and international order, believe they are entitled by their social contract (in this instance within their private enclaves) to a modicum of care when in desperate need. From the letters it would seem that no other agency of church or state was able to provide a sufficient net for men and women who for whatever reason were in danger of falling through, literally, as their letters tell us, of starving to death.

The French lodges were not the only ones to centralize the dispensation of charity. In Belgium the lodges sought in 1779 to establish a general and national treasury for the purpose of dispensing charity.[14] So too did the Dutch lodges in the same period. Before these efforts lodges dispensed charity on a lodge-by-lodge, case-by-case, basis. Thus any lodge's treasury was essential to its functioning and the subject of constant attention. Good manners and timeliness, as well as proper moral conduct, were enforced through a system of fines.[15] In some lodges coins themselves became the actual method of casting votes.[16] In a Dutch lodge of midcentury brothers replaced the older system of black and white "beans" used for voting "by ballot" – one

[12] Ibid., f. 484, 13th day of the 10th month, 5790 [1790], signed Fr. Bernard De Lamarguisie.

[13] Ibid., f. 466, Paris, 15th day of fourth month, 5789 [1789], signed De la Salle.

[14] *Almanach des Francs-Maçons, Pour l'Année commune 1779,* The Hague, van Laak, 1779, p. 25.

[15] B.A. MS 41, Notulen; the records of La Bien Aimée, the main Amsterdam lodge housed at the Library of the Grand Lodge, The Hague.

[16] Ibid., ff. 46–47. On the fees, ff. 62–63. Cf. Brievenarchief, #103, "Project om de harmonie in de . . . verkeezing der Broederen deser Loge vaster te Maken, en meer en meerder aantequeeken."

probably imitative of local guild practices – with a system that used different coins in the negative and affirmative.[17] In one other lodge fines were also imposed for "immoral" behavior, excessive card playing, and sleeping away from home in places of ill repute, as well as for lingering at the lodge after it was formally closed. The beneficiaries of immorality were to be the poor into whose "box" the fines were put.[18] In the Dutch republic brothers asked for charity because of "a series of disasters and fatal incidents."[19] Widows, orphans, and "unlucky sailors who until now, after risking their lives to the benefit and advantage of our city [Amsterdam] have no place to go in their old age," in short, fate's most obvious victims, were the favorite object of Dutch Masonic largesse.[20] In the earliest manifestations of European civil society, both charity and brotherhood had to conform to the ideal of merit; only fate was permitted to intervene, and then only on a case-by-case basis. People might rise through their own merit but they could not fall through their own efforts; if assistance was sought, only chance could be permitted to explain poverty. It was the rare brother – but by the 1780s such did exist – who laid claim to assistance by virtue of the constitution, the contract, that bound him to this society. Even then he sought to make his case compelling.

Of the many voluntary societies that sprang up in the eighteenth century none was more self-reflective, thus ideologically inclined,

[17] Ibid., f. 66, "en goedgevonden ann de Loge te proponeeren, omme het . . . 20th artie: van onse huishoudelyke wett in deser Voege te altereeren, van namentlyk by de Ballotteringe der Vorrgesteede herboven in plaatse van Witte Boonen te gebruyken, koopere penningen, en in plaatse van de swarte Boonen, een stuk geld bedragende de Waarde van dertig stuyvers voor het overige blykt het articel van de wett in zyngeheel dus wel te verstaan . . . 14 Maart 1760."

[18] The Library of the Grand Lodge, The Hague, MS 38.1, "Notulen der Vergaderingen van . . . Concordia Vincit Animos, van den 13 Juli 1755 tot en met 30 Augustus 1761"; written entirely in French although Dutch was also spoken in the lodge. This lodge met in Amsterdam and had in it many men of French origin, among them, and for a time its orator, the abbé Claude Yvon, author of major articles in Diderot's *Encyclopédie* (1751) and one of his confidants. He fled to Amsterdam in 1752.

[19] The Library of the Grand Lodge, The Hague, MS 41:48 (2), December 26, 1767: "zeekere Missive, van den Broaeder Ryk van Vliet, geweezene Meester van de Agtbare Loge De Goede Trouw te Utrecht, ann deeze Nationale Groote Loge geaddrescert, behelzende het verhaal van een meenigte rampspoeden en noodlottige gevallen, denzelve overkomen, waar door tot dat uiterste was gebragt, om onderstand."

[20] The Library of the Grand Lodge, The Hague, minutes of the lodge, *La Bien Aimée,* MS 41:8, f. 86, February 26, 1772; and again, f. 123, "arme, oude of ongelukkige zeelieden."

than the Freemasons. Beginning with the first official publication, *The Constitutions of the Freemasons* (London, 1723), theirs was a blatantly egalitarian rhetoric and a brother's status within the fraternity was claimed to be contingent solely upon merit. The relationship between the new philosophical societies and the material circumstances of their members, an aspect of their material culture, can be pieced together from the financial and literary records of this private fraternal sociability which have been preserved in public and private archives throughout Western Europe. In this essay evidence will come primarily from Scottish, English, and continental lodges in the Netherlands, Belgium, and France.

Within the forum of a selected and closed "temple," Masonic men, among the first Europeans to be deemed equals, self-consciously negotiated their inequality.[21] They came to terms with *anciens régimes,* oligarchic or absolutist, and for the most part sought a compromise that retained and in some cases reinforced social and economic inequalities within an ideological framework that rendered them unstable. At its inception modern civil society embraced an egalitarianism carefully circumscribed by the realities of relative wealth and surplus income. It also sought to mitigate that reality by providing charity, but only to members caught out by fate, never by their own malfaisance or incompetence, and certainly not by their birth.

Money in the form of dues, initiation fees, fines for misconduct, charitable funds and loans, was the instrument by which equality and inequality were negotiated. In every lodge the officer designated as treasurer was a key figure who shared access to the lodge's treasury only with other officers.[22] And these treasuries could sometimes be large. Dues structures varied, obviously, throughout Europe. Yet all the fees share one common characteristic: They were beyond the

[21] [Anon.], *Essai sur les Mysteres et le veritable objet des Franc-Maçons,* second edition, Amsterdam, 1776 (first edition, Paris, 1771), Bibliothèque Nationale, Paris, Res. II 2326 (2, i–v); pp. 18–19: "Les hommes ne sont égaux, ni par la force, ni par les talents, ni par la figure. Chacun a outre cela cette terrible & naturelle inclination de vouloir dominer sur les autres, il seroit impossible de rendre tous les individus parfaitement égaux. L'égalité des franc-maçons consiste à se regarder tous comme frères, & à se rendre réciproquement les devoirs de la bienfaisance & de la charité. La bonne morale est fondée sur cette égalité, et la charité chrétienne a ce même principe pour base. Toute bonne administration politique est un système moral plus fondé sur la subordination qu'on ne le pense."

[22] The Library of the Grand Lodge, The Hague, MS 41:42b, ff. 148a/158a/54, January 11, 1760.

means of the artisan or handworker, all peasants, most servants, and many minor officials.

Some lodges, in Belgium (i.e., the Austrian Netherlands) for instance, comprised only the most elite citizens of their town. In Antwerp two lodges in the 1770s were composed entirely of men classified in the top 8 percent of the city's wealth in one case, or the top 17 percent in the other. Initiation in all three Masonic degrees could cost about 53 florins; at the time an actual mason, for example, a Belgian carpenter or builder, could hope to earn about 110 florins a year.[23] In France lodge dues directly reflected the means of the members, and as a result the French lodges were often deeply segregated by those financial circumstances. The many lodges of Strasbourg have left an excellent set of records, and not least these Alsatian lodges were among the most socially segregated in the country. Most Alsatian noblemen paid an annual poll tax of between 30 and 50 livres; by comparison, Masonic dues were more noticeable and could average 10 livres a month. A domestic servant might hope for an income of about 300 livres per annum. To illustrate the vast distances between the simplicity of the lowly and the grandeur of the great, the lodge La Candeur, which was entirely aristocratic in the 1760s and 1770s, could spend nearly 100 livres on an evening's reception of a new apprentice at which probably no more than thirty men might be present.[24] Of course, many French lodges were composed of middling men and in turn operated on a far humbler scale.

In Britain all lodges required literacy of their members; but, perhaps most important, as early as the 1730s relative affluence was necessary to pay the dues: a few pounds at initiation, and then a few shillings each month.[25] In addition, the membership records from the earliest official London lodges are noticeably high in fellows of the

[23] *Un Siècle de Franc-Maçonnerie dans nos régions 1740–1840,* Galerie CGER, 1983, p. 182; notes by Hugo de Shampheleire.

[24] Bibliothèque Nationale et Universitaire, Strasbourg (cited as B.N.U.), MS 5437, registre des procès-verbaux de la Candeur, 1763–76, f. 25, 1763: "Le Venerable a ensuite proposé d'augmenter le Prix des réceptions d'aprentis et de compagnon qui étoient fixes à quatre louis ou quatre vingt seize livres, et de les porter à cent vingt livres ainsi et six livres pour les Servants."

[25] Bristol Record Office, MS 20535(291), f. 4, five shillings to be paid by each member, each quarter; two guineas plus a sum "for clothing," i.e., gloves and other items of regalia, upon admission.

Royal Society, government ministers, Whig aristocrats, journalists, and not least Huguenot refugees with journalistic or political connections.[26] At a time when the political nation would be defined as the one out of five males who held sufficient property to vote, as well as those literate enough to follow the pamphlet literature that parliamentary politics encouraged, membership in eighteenth-century lodges tended to be confined to such men.

The new private sociability of the eighteenth century rested upon the currency of the market, upon the commercial order. At its British origin and in its many and lavish continental manifestations, Masonic discourse affirmed "the world"; it was almost utopian about its possibilities. Simultaneously, the lodges sought to hold the world at bay, to distance brothers from the "profane," to offer the corrective to vice, self-interest, superstition, pride, and corruption. Every man when he knocked at the door of the temple and sought his initiation was addressed as a "profane." Only after initiation, executed ritually and through a monetary commitment, did a profane become a brother. Once bonded, the private fraternity sought to create a public space. Within a constitutional structure first created by the London lodges and then imitated throughout western Europe, elections were held, the majority was allowed to rule, "taxes" were collected. In the Dutch republic, for example, newly elected masters were presented to their brother-electors after what was described as a "public vote, [and] by being told that they were being presented publicly."[27]

Some years ago the German philosopher Jürgen Habermas articulated the role played by sociability in the creation of the new public sphere. He argued that the public space being delineated in the eigh-

[26] Margaret C. Jacob, *The Radical Enlightenment,* London, Allen & Unwin, 1981, pp. 130–37.

[27] The Library of the Grand Lodge, The Hague, MS 23.1 Kast 158.B, f. 115. The past master of a lodge in Middleburg speaks in French to the new master and his brothers: "Accepter le suffrage publicq que vous avez gagné avec le soin d'un Père tendre, l'application d'un vrai et veritable maçon, un zèlé, capable à donner l'exemple à tous les Frères, et un amour vrai Fraternel pour nôtre auguste Ordre, et sa propagation dans nôtre Province." The orator continues: "Recever le temoignage publicq, que vous avez parfaitement achevé tous les devoirs de cette charge importante: que vous avez sauvé nôtre loge, jusqu'ici dans des situations critiques, où elle s'est trouvée tant par rapport aux circonstances publicques, qu'au peu de zèle, qui nous a animé jusqu'ici."

teenth century was created by and for the European bourgeoisie. The "bourgeois public sphere" was intended to regulate civil society, and it became possible because of "the background experience of a private sphere that had become interiorized human closeness." Out of a more egalitarian intimacy the public sphere arose "as an expansion . . . and . . . completion."[28] Not only the bourgeois family but also, Habermas believes, the habits and practice of commerce created the "public sphere." With extraordinary insight he argues for its appearance first in England in the 1690s, in the aftermath of the political and economic transformations effected by the revolution in England. And he sees the rapid spread of freemasonry, more precisely, as anticipating the adoption throughout Europe of the public sphere as an alternative to absolutism.[29] In his account the lodges were the first places where "the bourgeois met . . . with the socially prestigious but politically uninfluential nobles as 'common' human beings."

Although we do not have to accept Habermas's terminology about the bourgeoisie, especially because it leaves out the many marginal men who were present in the earliest lodges – refugees, actors, in Paris "a Negro who serves as a trumpeter in the King's Guard"[30] – nor endorse his gender blindness, yet we can still acknowledge that his analysis has merit. It does not explain why the values of a more egalitarian intimacy produced a public sphere intended solely for men. Nor does it address the phenomenon of the continental women's lodges. But it does point us to the fact that a politically meaningful public sphere – as well as the first Masonic lodge – did emerge in England during the 1690s, after the establishment of parliamentary government and constitutional monarchy. Habermas offers clues toward finding the relationship between the new sociability and the culture of the market. The bridge between the two, as Habermas intuited, lies through the political and constitutional order that emerged in post-1689 Britain. It remained the dominant model for European reform-

[28] Jürgen Habermas, *The Structural Transformation of the Public Sphere: An Inquiry into a Category of Bourgeois Society,* Cambridge, Mass., MIT Press, 1989, pp. 50–52. German edition first published 1962.

[29] Ibid., p. 35.

[30] Bibliothèque Arsenal, ibid., f. 347, the spy Dadvenel writing on February 5, 1746: "qui c'est Danguy La vielle qui y a presidé comme Le venerable, ou le Maitre de Loge, charpantier, La mussette y etoit il y voit un Negre qui est des menus plaisirs du Roy une trompette des Gardes du Roy[,] un Sergent du Regimen du Roy qui était La supotte de la maitress de la maison." This may have been a different lodge.

ers right up to the autumn of 1789. The structure of the Masonic lodge in Britain and on the Continent was universally constitutional and representative. These political relationships, made possible and reinforced by the perceived role of the lodge as an economic protector in a hostile world, permitted the ideology of equality and fraternity to flourish among men vastly different in status and resources.

Many historians have searched for ways to articulate the relationship between the new philosophical society of the eighteenth century and the origins of modernity. Invariably they have seized upon the political implications of sociability, and either they have been so blinded by their hostility to modernity as to see conspiracy everywhere, or so terrified by the economic implications of egalitarianism as to see communism where, I will argue, liberalism was present. The vast, and largely useless, historiography that treats the Freemasons as the conspirators of the French Revolution began in the 1790s with a revulsion against the democratic implications within the revolution. In his history of Jacobinism (1797) the abbé Barruel seized upon the Freemasons and argued from their writings that the Masonic temple was intended as a public as well as a private space. He believed that as a result, Masonic language about equality, liberty, and fraternity bore relation to the radical and democratic phase of the French Revolution, that is, to Jacobin language. From there, however, he went on to construct an elaborate conspiracy theory that linked Jacobins, philosophes, and Freemasons.[31] Without the paranoia and condemnation, a similar point about the filiation of language was made by the British historian Michael Roberts, writing in the 1970s.[32] In a highly rigorous and scholarly essay, Roberts noted that the slogan "liberty, fraternity and equality" bears closer relation to Masonic sloganizing than it does to any other eighteenth-century antecedent.

But as some modern historians would have it, the similarities between the philosophical society and subversion do not end in words or slogans. In the 1970s, François Furet revived the writings of a Catholic historian and follower of Durkheim, Augustin Cochin (d. 1916),

[31] Abbé Barruel, *Mémoires pour servir à l'Histoire du Jacobinisme,* London, 1797, vol. 2, p. 262. For the influence of the book, see Emily Lorraine de Montluzin, *The Anti-Jacobins, 1798–1800,* New York, St. Martin's Press, 1988.

[32] Michael Roberts, "Liberté, Egalité, Fraternité: Sources and Development of a Slogan," *Tijdschrift voor de Studie van de Verlichting,* vol. 4, no. 3–4, 1976, pp. 329–69.

and drew from them a new, and disturbing, interpretation of the philosophical society and, in particular, of freemasonry. In the hands of Cochin the conspiracy of Barruel became rarefied into the "machine" enforcing ideological purity and harmony. Cochin asserted and Furet elaborated upon the interpretation that in the eighteenth-century lodges, "consensus was produced by a discussion among equals that did not concern real situations but was exclusively devoted to the relationship of individuals with a set of stated goals."[33] Lost, as it were, in the closed universe of its own rhetoric, the lodge became, metaphorically, a "political party that claimed to embody both society and the State, which were now identical." In this analysis the Masonic lodges of the eighteenth century become unwittingly what the police and clergy of France, and elsewhere, had begun, as early as the 1740s, to suspect might happen. In Furet's interpretation the Masonic lodges become the breeding ground for "militant minorities in whom the new legitimacy" might be vested.[34] In Jacobinism, and hence in the philosophical societies that were its imagined antecedent, Furet spied the origins of totalitarian communism.

We can easily concede the point about the filiation of Masonic language, ritual, and symbol, and certain aspects of Jacobin rhetoric. Crane Brinton also made it some years ago.[35] But because European Marxists of the nineteenth century laid claim to the Jacobins, and hence to the radical and democratic impulses within the Enlightenment, does not mean that they, and hence Furet, were right. This essay should demonstrate that the practices of the philosophical society, of which freemasonry was the most important political example, tell us more about the social and economic origins and nature of modern liberal rhetoric and practices, than they do about the communist or the totalitarian. Eighteenth-century private sociability offered

[33] *Interpreting the French Revolution,* trans. Elborg Forster, Cambridge, Cambridge University Press, 1981, p. 179. The translation is based on texts first written in the 1970s.

[34] Ibid., p. 179. Furet refers here to the type of political man who would be needed, and who was found among the Jacobins, to actualize the transition from philosophical power to political power.

[35] Clarence Crane Brinton, *The Jacobins: An Essay in the New History,* New York, Russell & Russell, 1961, p. 14. See also Pierre Lamarque, *Les Francs Maçons aux Etats Généraux de 1789 et à l'Assemblée Nationale,* Paris, EDIMAT, 1981, pp. 6–7. Two hundred of the deputies and 37 of the supplementary deputies (out of a total of 1,165 members and substitute deputies) were Freemasons.

the foil to the market, while at the same time by its ideology and dues structure opaquely mirroring its rules and values.

Masonic rhetoric, principles, and practices, first found in eighteenth-century Britain, were not significantly altered in their basic principles by French, Dutch, and German Masonic commentators with which I am familiar. What holds true for British freemasonry seems to hold true for continental freemasonry, even bearing in mind the wide variety of political postures any lodge could assume well into the 1790s.[36] The transmission of Masonic sociability onto the Continent was the work of various hands: Whig ambassadors like Lord Waldegrave in Paris and Lord Chesterfield in The Hague, scientific experimenters like the Huguenot refugee, Desaguliers, Jacobite exiles like Lord Wharton, the first Paris grand master, as well as "little men" such as were the British merchants in Rotterdam who held the first documented continental lodge in 1721. By the mid-eighteenth century, lodges could be found in all the imperial colonies – Jamaica, Curaçao, and Bengal – for example, as well as in almost every European town and city.[37] In any major city any monthly visitors' book reveals the presence of foreign Masonic visitors: Jean Paul Marat in Amsterdam in 1774,[38] Casanova earlier, as well as travelers on business from Moscow and the slave colony of Surinam. Masonic ideals varied little from country to country, although lodges could have vastly different rituals, social mixes, financial means, and ethos.[39]

[36] For this growing historiography on eighteenth-century freemasonry, see Ran Halévi, *Les Loges maçonniques dans la France d'ancien régime aux origines de la sociabilité démocratique,* Paris, Colin, 1984; Jacques Feneant, *Francs-Maçons et sociétés secrètes en Val de Loire,* Cambray, CLD, 1985; A. Van den Abeele, *In Brugge onder de Acacia: De Vrijmetselaarsloge, "La Parfaite Egalité (1765–1774) en haar leden,* Brugge, 1987; E. Maquestiau, *Histoire de la Libre Pensée au Pays de Liège,* Liège, Association de la Libre Pensée, 1986; W. W. Mijnhardt, "Sociability in Walcheren 1750–1815," *Tijdschrift voor de Studie van de Verlichting en van het Vrije Denken,* vols. 3 and 4, 1984, pp. 289–310 (entire issue devoted to European freemasonry). Hervé Hasquin, ed., *Visages de la Franc-maçonnerie belge du XVIIIe au XXe siècle,* Brussels, Editions de l'Université de Bruxelles, 1985.

[37] On the founding of a lodge in Tardalga, Bengal, see the Library of the Grand Lodge, MS 41:42b, f. 156/149, December 23, 1759.

[38] H. Rodermond, *De Vrijmetselaarsloge La Bien Aimée, Amsterdam, 1745–1985,* The Hague, 1985, p. 38; citing the Visitors' Book (which I have seen) for that year, which does indeed show the signature of Marat.

[39] Sometimes these differences were articulated and the subject of conflict: for example, Bibliothèque Nationale, Paris MS FM2.563, September 27, 1786, letter from the lodge in Maastricht to the provincial Grand Lodge of Liège, f. 4: "les membres de cette loge bourgeoise quoy que tres honnetes citoyens ne sont pas tous de la classe le

They could also reflect class tensions. French aristocratic lodges quarrelled with other lodges, including the Grand Lodge, over the status permitted an actor within that lodge; they wished to negotiate their constitutional standing and legitimacy only with aristocratic members of the "mother lodge."[40] Similarly, the French Grand Lodge required assurance that the large number of merchants in one lodge were of the "best reputation."[41] Ideally lodges were to contain a mixture of social groupings, who paid for their admission and degrees within a scale of donations.[42] These degrees were highly coveted and in the Dutch republic, if not elsewhere, there was a traffic in them by "certain private" persons who made it their profession "to receive somebody for a vile price and clandestinely."[43] Given its international character, however, European freemasonry calls for generalizations that seek not to unravel its tensions and contradictions, either between lodges or between national styles, but, rather, to explain the working of its prevailing and universalist ideology, its egalitarian posture in the world.

Modern Western democratic thought and practice, complete with its contradictions and complexities, was nurtured by the egalitarian rhetoric of eighteenth-century private sociability. And the roots of

plus distinguée n'y la plus opulente . . ." and hence they must husband their finances. They are in serious disagreement with the Liège lodge; f. 31: "mais bientôt le feu de la discorde excité par le pouvoir *souverain* et *despotique* que la Loge de la Constance pretend pouvoir exercer sur nous."

40 Bibliothèque Nationale, Paris, FM 1.111, ff. 401–5, concerning the request for constitutional status from the lodge in Strasbourg, La Candeur, January 10, 1763; f. 405, September 26, 1763: "Nous vous adressons aussi le tableau de notre loge, vous y verrez que la loge de la Candeur ne reçoit que des freres de Nom et d'un Etat honnete, ils ont été etonnés d'apprendre que le frere Litzelmann [the actor] etoit membre de la grande loge." He could come to their lodge as a visitor but never as a member.

41 Bibliothèque Nationale, Paris, MS FM2.426, ff. 28–30; in this instance the Grand Lodge is also questioning the probity of the orator of the lodge, who is an actor; f. 143, letters of 1778.

42 Archives Municipales, Strasbourg, Boite 35/9 Compte Général, 1783–84, for the lodge St. Geneviève [the one being questioned for its high number of merchants]. Prices were as follows: 60 to 72 livres for reception as an apprentice; monthly fees 1.1–10; grade of Elu, 1.36; reception as master, 1.24, etc. In 1784 the lodge received 1,129, paid out 808 livres, and had in reserve 1,339. Cf. Ph. Claus, "Un centre de diffusion des 'Lumières' à Strasbourg: La Librairie Académique (1783–99)," *Revue d'Alsace,* no. 108, 1982, pp. 81–102, and Bertrand Diringer, *Franc-Maçonnerie et Société à Strasbourg au xviiième siècle,* Mémoire de Maîtrise, Université des sciences humaines de Strasbourg, 1980. There were 1,500 masons in the 1780s in this town of 50,000; 10,000 in Paris (population more than 500,000).

43 The Library of the Grand Lodge, MS 41:42b, f. 151e, October 15, 1760.

the Masonic form of sociability lie in the effort by the craft guilds in late seventeenth-century Scotland and England to survive in an economic setting where the market for labor had overwhelmed their efforts to regulate wages. Out of their struggle, as we shall see, emerged a form of genteel sociability that bore little relation to the interests of handworkers or guildsmen. Other interests were to be negotiated in the new lodges, and central to their activities was the effort to mitigate and negotiate the effects of the market, to ameliorate (and obscure) the inherent inequality of monetary transactions, as well as the vast inequalities of birth and rank endemic in every eighteenth-century European society. Birth and money, land and commerce, as well as the professions, met on the Masonic level in almost every cultural enclave, first in Britain and then by the 1730s and 1740s on the Continent, wherever the prosopography of lodges has been determined.[44]

Invariably, but in subtle ways, lodges retained the symbolism of hierarchy but endowed the men who rose in the Masonic "degrees" with deeper levels of virtue and wisdom. In the degree system the lodges reflected the inequities of the old order while laying over them an ultimately incompatible ideology. In 1795 when triumphant French army officers arrived in Amsterdam, their Dutch brothers feted them; they also changed the eighteenth-century ceremonies to reflect the new, French ideal of democracy. The servants in the lodge were now to stand forward as true brothers. Almost invariably place and leadership within the eighteenth-century lodges conformed to rank and place in society, but lodge officers, however aristocratic, were elected and their status defined as contingent upon their merit. Dues for admission could even be different depending on ability to pay, yet, once admitted, men, and even the few women initiated from the 1750s onward, were designated as "equals."[45] Mixed-gender lodges, permitted only on the Continent and then largely within a French-speaking context, could even be led by a "Maître" and "Maî-

[44] For example, see the statistics produced by Maurice Agulhon, *Pénitents et Francs-Maçons de l'ancienne Provence,* Fayard, 1968, pp. 174–75.

[45] See Margaret C. Jacob, "Freemasonry, Women and the Paradox of the Enlightenment," in Institute for Research in History, *Women and the Enlightenment* (Women and History series), Binghamton, N.Y., Haworth Press, 1984, pp. 69–93. Discusses the first known lodge to admit women, largely from among the actresses in the Comédie Française in The Hague.

tresse."[46] The mixed lodges by the 1760s and 1770s were largely aristocratic and their major activity outside the cultivation of virtue within the lodge consisted in the donation of monetary charity to the local poor. Within French freemasonry the Grand Lodge of Paris had an entire administrative structure that did nothing but oversee the awarding of "degrees," a power and source of revenue it jealously guarded.[47] The new sociability flourished where men had the money to support it; at the same time it sought to mitigate the dire consequences of falling into the condition of being moneyless. In the practices of these small civil polities, which is what the lodges sought to be, complete with constitutions, elections, and majority rule, men negotiated the implications of equality. They paid to be equal; they then paid to rise in the wisdom of the philosophical "degrees" of the Masonic order; with money they adjudicated extreme social differences within an ideological framework that recognized only equality and merit.[48] As far from the ideals of nineteenth-century communism as we are, these were liberal communities, if only in the mind.

We want now to observe how one of these first experiments in European liberalism actually worked, to visit a lodge at its Scottish origin, and to relate its evolution and practices to the market circumstances in which it had to operate.[49] To make this visitation I have chosen to tell the story of the lodge in Dundee, Scotland, culled from its largely unexplored eighteenth-century archives. It is logical and

[46] Ibid.; see also Janet M. Burke, "Freemasonry, Friendship and Noblewomen: The Role of the Secret Society in Bringing Enlightenment Thought to Pre-Revolutionary Women Elites," *History of European Ideas,* 10, no. 3, 1989, pp. 283–94.

[47] Bibliothèque Nationale, Paris MS FM1.57, entire box devoted to the records of this unit. See also MS 1.13, f. 308, where the distribution of grades is defined as one of "our principal functions."

[48] [Anon.], *Recueil de discours et poésies maçonniques . . . de la Douce-Union à l'O[rient] de Paris,* 1788, p. 30: "la persuasion intime de nos propres vices n'avoit pas alors fait nâitre en nous le doute des vertus d'autrui; & de là devenoient inutiles & ces bienfeànces hipocrites, qui cachent le mal & ne l'abolissent pas, & ces convenances puériles, qui etouffent la gaieté sous le masque de l'etiquète, & ces distinctions d'une noblesse conventionnelle, imaginaire inventées par l'orgueil, adoptées par la foiblesse & perpetuées par l'habitude ou la sottise. L'égalité des caractères nécessitoit celle des rangs; le desir de vivre dans la concorde, excluoit toute idee de superiorité."

[49] This example is drawn from my *Living the Enlightenment: Freemasonry and Politics in Eighteenth Century Europe,* Chapter 1.

proper to begin in Scotland for there we have the first records that trace the gradual evolution of freemasonry from roughly the 1680s onward, its growth out of the stonemasons' guilds into the gentlemanly lodges of the eighteenth century.

Market forces caused that evolution; in their wake most guilds declined and then disappeared. In Britian only the stonemasons managed to make a transition to an entirely different form of sociability. The reasons for their success are to this day not fully understood, but two elements marked the Masonic guilds off from those of other handworkers: the relative richness of their lore and traditions, and the rather high degree of skill required of master masons. In effect they could and did function as architects. Thus the earliest nonmasons admitted in the 1640s to the guild in England were men of some intellectual and scientific interests, Robert Moray and Elias Ashmole. Later the men admitted were married into families where the father-in-law was a mason, or these nonmasons in some cases had building ventures which they wanted executed or they possessed the means to help masters initiate such ventures.

The Dundee records are rare for their completeness, although other Scottish lodges also left similar archives documenting the transformation from guild to fraternity. The very richness of these records has led the historian who has worked most extensively with the seventeenth-century records, David Stevenson, to argue (too blanketly, I believe) that the freemasonry bequeathed to the eighteenth-century continental Enlightenment was singularly a Scottish invention.[50] By this he means that the transformation from a guild of stonemasons to a society dominated by gentlemen, if not completely devoid of handworkers, occurred first in Scotland and then spread gradually to England. For our purposes here the locus of the evolution hardly matters; rather, it is the process and its outcome that reward scrutiny.

By the 1690s the Dundee lodge had fallen on hard times. Out of economic necessity, it began quite straightforwardly to admit non-

[50] David Stevenson, *The First Freemasons: Scotland's Early Lodges and Their Members,* Aberdeen, Aberdeen University Press, 1988; and by the same author, *The Origins of Freemasonry,* Cambridge, Cambridge University Press, 1988.

craftsmen to membership. That process was undoubtedly related to what happened as the town sank from a once prosperous east coast shipping port to an increasingly impoverished community, threatened with civil disturbance.[51] Its decline began with the sacking of Dundee by a parliamentary army in 1651 and continued throughout the last decades of the seventeenth century as the Atlantic trade and the western ports grew in importance. This pattern was only reversed slowly in the last decades of the eighteenth century with the growth of the linen and clothing industries. Thus, in the period where we can observe at first hand the transformation of a trade guild into a gentlemen's fraternity, all but the richest of Dundee's inhabitants negotiated with poverty and with "ye decaying state of ye Burgh."[52]

A town with a declining population of approximately six thousand, Dundee possessed about a dozen guilds of tradesmen, all strictly arranged by rank and status. The cloth dyers were last in social rank, while the masons, coopers, barbers, wrights, and periwig makers were considered sufficiently skilled to be organized in a cooperative association separate from the other, more menial trades. The merchants were also organized in their own guild, which held considerable political power in the town. By the 1720s the masons contributed to it without being permitted to join.[53] In 1749 a mason applied for admission to the merchants' guild, but "he was objected to because as exercising a handycraft, he cannot be admitted a member of the Guildry, except he give over working as a tradesman, being contrary to several Acts of Parliament."[54] Ironically, that same tradesman would have socialized with merchants in his lodge by this date. In the world of any eighteenth-century town or city rank or status was everywhere palpable. As they evolved, the Masonic lodges of this period reflected those realities, in one sense mitigating them, in another, through conviviality and the rhetoric of harmony and fraternity, obscuring, and hence reinforcing, them.[55]

[51] Alex. J. Warden, ed., *Burgh Laws of Dundee with the History, Statutes and Proceedings of the Guild of Merchants and Fraternities of Craftsmen,* London, 1872, p. 167, for 1697–99.

[52] Ibid., p. 186.

[53] Ibid., p. 177.

[54] Ibid., pp. 193–94.

[55] On the role of the craft guilds, see Anthony Black, *Guilds and Civil Society in European Political Thought from the Twelfth Century to the Present,* Ithaca, N.Y., Cornell University Press, 1984, p. 43. See also the comments of Daniel Mornet on

In the early 1700s the Dundee guild had come to a financial impasse. One solution was to admit nonmasons into the fraternity. Other lodges in Scotland and England had, of course, also admitted nonmasons intermittently throughout the seventeenth century. Indeed, the decision in Dundee was only in keeping with what was by 1700 a fairly commonplace solution to the economic problems then experienced by all craft guilds. In 1713 the Dundee town council, "taking to consideration the great decay of the burgh and houses within the same for want of inhabitants, and for encouraging strangers to come and live among us," decided that anyone marrying into a trade family could enjoy "the privilege of a guild brother."[56] Yet obviously the Dundee masons' guild believed that its "freedoms and privileges" within the town were worth a not insignificant sum, although the ten pounds (Scots) membership fee requested was less than the sixteen pounds paid by a working journeyman to procure his "privileges" and status as a master in the lodge.[57]

The records are clear that preference for admission of noncraftsmen was to be given to relatives of actually "operative" masons. There was a predictably large number of such sons and sons-in-law admitted to the guild during the eighteenth century. They could be of any occupation. By far the largest number of new members who are not practicing masons, but who tell us their occupations, are described as merchants, and also as a clock and watchmaker, a draper, a wright, a maltman, an officer of the excise (1721), a surgeon, and finally, in the 1730s, a supervisor of the excise, a doctor of medicine, a shipmaster, a clerk of the customs, and, most significantly, landed gentlemen of the county who bear the appellation denoting their gentry origin, "honourable." They received the same "freedom" – now uniformly described as "libertys" – and "privileges."

The "liberty" now accorded to gentlemen, merchants, and minor

the way in which freemasonry was imbedded in the French *ancien régime;* Daniel Mornet, *Les Origines intellectuelles de la révolution française (1715–1787),* Paris, Colin, 1933, pp. 375–87.

56 A. J. Warden, ed., *Burgh Laws of Dundee,* pp. 262–63.

57 Archive and Record Centre, Dundee, MS GD/GRW/M 2/1, entry dated May 3, 1711, "from James Cox in part of his freedom, 16:13:4." Total income for that year appears to have been forty-nine pounds. Pounds Scots should be divided by twelve for the equivalent pounds sterling. In the late seventeenth century, skilled masons could be paid three and a half to five pounds Scots per week. For a description of the Dundee lodge, see Stevenson, *The First Freemasons,* pp. 94–97.

officials recalls the distinction, of medieval origin, between the "liberty" of buying and selling in the burgh, once given to burgesses who were also merchants, and the term "freedom," generally accorded to those who were free to work at their hand trade.[58] These distinctions now occurred while a significant number of operative masons continued in the Dundee lodge. It struggled throughout the century, as did the other crafts, to protect and control the labor of its working members, often against the practices employed by local merchants, and to ensure that members would only employ craftsmen duly admitted to the guild. Yet there is also some evidence of tension within the lodge between the working men and their "betters."[59] The Dundee lodge was quite different from one that met in London in the 1730s. It had over one hundred members, of which not one was a working mason and the vast majority were mercantile by trade.[60]

The tensions in the lodge were the perennial effect of Dundee's poverty, which meant the absence of sufficient municipal funds to repair public works, as well as a dearth of capital to repair "ruinous properties . . . owing to the poverty of the owners."[61] There was also the problem of vagrancy and begging, in other words, of social control. Such social and economic problems occurred, however, within a distinct political culture. As the Whig ministry in London led by Sir Robert Walpole in the 1720s came to control Scottish political life, all patronage came under its purview and under the skillful manipulation of its man in Scotland, the earl of Ilay. No office, no agency of revenue collection, from salt to the excise, was small enough to escape Whig domination.[62] Concomitant with, and indeed augmenting, this consolidation of power was a policy of "improvements," which

[58] William Mackay Mackenzie, *The Scottish Burghs,* Edinburgh, Oliver & Boyd, 1949, p. 69, citing a charter of 1364. Occasionally "freedom" and "liberty" were used interchangeably in the sixteenth century, p. 135. Note that women were regularly admitted as burgesses, p. 140.

[59] Stevenson, *The First Freemasons,* p. 97. One version of the *Constitutions,* now extremely rare, *The Old Constitutions Belonging to the Ancient and Honourable Society of Free and Accepted Masons,* London, J. Roberts, 1722, pp. 16–17, encouraged workers to protect their wages and labor and absolutely forbade a mason from taking over the work of another.

[60] Bodleian Library, Oxford, MS Rylands d.9, pp. 119 et. seq., giving names and occupations.

[61] Ibid., pp. 186, 189–90; noted in 1721 and 1735.

[62] See on this process Eric Wehrli, Jr., "Scottish Politics in the Age of Walpole," Ph.D. dissertation, University of Chicago, 1983, pp. 10–11.

established commissions to improve fisheries and manufacturing and to encourage agricultural experimentation and innovation. All these factors favored the gentlemen within the lodge.

By the 1730s the lodge was actively involved in promoting public works projects, contributing generously in 1739 to a fund for building a workhouse for beggars and other poor. In 1730 guildsmen and burgesses had joined in petitioning the magistrates to build a new prison, with a local Mason promptly volunteering to take down the old one for a modest fee.[63] Culture was also imported into the town, and in 1734 Freemasons paraded to the local theater to see a production brought in specially from Edinburgh.[64] Of all the local guilds the Masons were most active in a process of "improvement" that was visible in Dundee by the 1730s, despite its chronic economic problems. Even the appearance of famine in the vicinity in 1741 did not stop the town council two years later from putting up the money to hire a "professor of mathematics and book keeping" for the local public school.[65] The gentlemen Freemasons in Dundee were not necessarily Whigs, but they did promote the political culture of improvement associated with the Whig ascendancy.[66] It is also worth noting, if only in passing, that the habit of clubbing was more pronounced among late-seventeenth-century Whigs in London than it was among their Tory rivals.[67]

More than civic involvement came with the transformation of the lodge from what Masonic histories like to call operative to speculative freemasonry, that is, philosophical as opposed to practiced masonry. What is striking about the process that accompanies the admission of increasingly elite "brothers" is revealed in the new language gradually

[63] Dundee, *Charters, Writs and Public Documents of the Royal Burgh of Dundee . . . 1292–1880,* Dundee, 1880, pp. 147–49. For the workhouse, see Warden, *Burgh Laws,* p. 190, and p. 191 on famine in the vicinity.

[64] James Thomson, *The History of Dundee,* Dundee, Durham & Son, 1874, p. 134.

[65] Warden, *Burgh Laws,* pp. 191–92.

[66] Thomson, *History of Dundee,* p. 119. There is little correlation between the names of known Jacobites in 1745 and the membership lists of the Freemasons, yet note that the name of one Thomas Blair, merchant, can be found in both.

[67] David Allen, "Political Clubs in Restoration London," *Historical Journal,* 19, 1976, pp. 561–80. The association of freemasonry with Whiggery was continued by the Tories; see Simon Robertson Vasey, *The Craftsman, 1726–1752, An Historical and Critical Account,* Ph.D. dissertation, Cambridge University, 1976, pp. 58, 184ff. Cf. Linda J. Colley, "The Loyal Brotherhood and the Cocoa Tree: The London Organization of the Tory Party, 1727–1760," *Historical Journal,* 20, 1977, pp. 77–95.

replacing the traditional guild terminology. In the seventeenth century, guildsmen spoke more often of their statutes and ordinances, not frequently of their laws, and generally the brethren gave "their consent" to the admission of a new member or to the "selection" of their officers.[68] Occasionally, "the mason trade in Dundee being met together have made and constituted" a master to his "privileges."[69] These consisted of the right to regulate wages, settle disputes among members, and be consulted about taxes by the local magistrates.[70] Guilds had the privilege to exercise authority and control in the lodge and in the community, but not to govern. That was the work of local magistrates.

Quite suddenly, and within less than ten years after the admission of merchants and the sellers of commodities, the language of parliamentary procedure, and hence governance, makes its appearance. An officer "was by plurality of votes chosen."[71] By 1718 "the members of the mason craft being convened did unanimously elect and choose" their officers, and in 1734 a quorum was fixed. By the 1730s the "freedom" of the guildsman, traditionally the freedom, upon admission, to practice his craft in the town, has been transformed into the "libertys of the craft." At that same moment (1732) "members [were] unanimously admitted and received into the Society [*sic*] of master masons." This "fraternity" of guildsmen has become a "society" of gentlemen and merchants, now styled as master masons, who vote and elect, who possess their liberty just as craftsmen once possessed their freedom.

In 1734 the transformation was ensured. The power to govern was placed in the hands of the gentlemen Freemasons. The occasion for

[68] Clerk to the Mason Trade, Dundee Mason Trade, Lockit Book, 1659–1960, unfoliated but dated nearly annually from 1659. For similar language, see Harry Carr, *Lodge Mother Kilwinning, No. 0: A Study of the Earliest Minute Books, 1642 to 1842,* London, Quatuor Coronati Lodge, 1961, pp. 27–28; yet see also pp. 34 and 186, where the term "elected" is used in 1645 and henceforth appears intermittently and is synonymous with "chosen." Its usage began to take on the modern meaning in the 1670s as gentry started to take office in the lodge.

[69] Dundee Mason Trade, Register of entries of Masters and Journeymen, 1659–1779, MS GD/GRW/M3/1, December 28, 1667. For the right to confer those privileges, see the records of the Register of Deeds of the Burgh of Dundee, vol. 26, pp. 903–5, dated 1659, printed in *Ars Quatuor Coronatorum,* vol. 99, 1986, pp. 194–95.

[70] Thomson, *History of Dundee,* p. 255. Guildsmen could also refer to their "libertys," a term interchangeable with "freedom"; see Warden, *Burgh Laws,* p. 584 et. seq., on the wrights.

[71] Ibid., entry for December 27, 1708.

this shift of authority over the "government" of the lodge involved both money and labor. Money had been inappropriately lent without proper security. Craftsmen not belonging to the guild had been employed, while the quality of craftsmanship of some operative members was deemed inadequate. At the annual meeting of the year the gentlemen of substance were elected as the officers.[72] The Honorable John, master of Gray, was chosen as master of the lodge, and he was also a local agricultural improver.[73] Suddenly language employed by London Freemasons and first displayed in Anderson's 1723 *Constitutions* is used in full force. Terms appear that are not to be found in the records of the Dundee operative masons: "the Society of Free and Accepted Masons," the "Hon. Society of the Antient Lodge," the "Laws and Regulations for the better and orderly Government of the respective Brethren." Brothers are charged with the task of assembling

> to consider of such Laws and Regulations as shall seem most proper and requisite for the better Government of the Society . . . with full power to them to make and enact in the locked book of the Society such laws as shall seem best for preserving order and unanimity among the Brethren . . . and punishing delinquents of whatever Rank or Degree.

A committee was established to do just that.[74]

For the first time in these seventy and more years of records reference is made to the "secret mysteries of Masonry." It shall no longer be "lawful by any and or number of the brethren of the lodge of this place to initiate or enter any person or persons of what ever degree or quality as they may have access to the knowledge of the antient and secret mysteries of masonry without first apprising the worshipfull, the master of the lodge with whose consent and approbation" a man may be admitted.[75] In this context the secrets refer to the traditional skills of craftsmen as well as to signs and words used by properly initiated guild masons to signal to one another their status, and hence their right to work.

It is significant that only now does emphasis on the "secrets" of freemasonry appear. Secret signs and tokens of membership had been the everyday manner of communicating among craftsmen. The ability

[72] Ibid., December 27, 1734, a doctor, a merchant, and two men of "honourable" rank.
[73] Ibid., p. 125. He introduced potatoes for sale in 1753.
[74] Lockit Book, December 27, 1734.
[75] Ibid., January 3, 1735.

to keep the secrets now became symbolic of devotion to the fraternity, of loyalty and probity. That ability – rather than the practice of those mysteries – became the only means of identifying a true brother. This social cement was mystical only insofar as it was language memorized out of its original context – it now became words and signs used in the bonding of men who were different from one another in nearly every aspect of their lives, save their membership in a constitutionally governed private society. Eventually the "secrets" of freemasonry acquired a metaphoric meaning as brothers rose by degrees toward a veiled, yet constantly unfolding, wisdom and enlightenment. Accompanying this process were ever more elaborate ceremonies conferring status and honor within the lodge.

The process of elaboration that we have witnessed at work in Dundee by the mid-1730s occurred elsewhere in the Scottish, as well as English, lodges. Gentlemen were admitted and elected "masters" of the lodge. Suddenly, whole initiation ceremonies were created to install the master in his "chair," with overtones of ceremonies used to initiate men into the aristocratic and kingly orders, such as the Order of the Garter, or, indeed, with intimations of royal coronations and court ceremonial. In the 1730s, following the practice in England, Scottish lodges instituted "degrees" by which practicing, that is, operative, and nonpracticing members might be distinguished one from another.[76] Not least, in 1736, the thirty-three Scottish lodges, Dundee among them, sent representatives to an assembly that created the Grand Lodge of Scotland, which in turn elected a gentleman grand master, only, incidentally, after he had renounced any hereditary claims on the office.[77] The national government of Scottish freemasonry could now be said to have been put in place. One of its first acts may have been to give constitutional authorization to a foreign lodge that had appealed to it. The lodge was in Amsterdam and its master was the Huguenot refugee and self-described "pantheist" Jean Rousset de Missy.[78]

The records in Dundee also indicate that in the 1730s the lodge

[76] Harry Carr, *Lodge Mother Kilwinning*, pp. 193–95.

[77] Ibid., pp. 228–29.

[78] The Grand Lodge of The Netherlands, archive of La Bien Aimée, B.A. 6, f. 11, dated April 11, 1756, from Rousset de Missy: "La lettre de notre institution etoit du Venerable Linslager, maistre de la loge de Leuwarde, qui en avoit reçu la permission d'Ecosse."

officers further enhanced their authority. In the transformation officers were not only to be nominated and elected, but they were also given the power of oversight in all aspects of craft activity. Nominations were now to be held for "the Election" of officers who shall have the power and authority to appoint a quorum "of the Operative Brethren not exceeding five in number . . . to visit and inspect" the work done by other masons. By 1737 "rolls [were] being called and votes marked" and elections were "carried by a plurality."[79]

In every sense power had decidedly shifted into the hands of the gentlemen Freemasons, who would oversee the work of their operative brethren. Yet in this instance, and in contrast with the hostility shown to the protective practices of the working masons described in the 1723 *Constitutions,* the gentlemen Freemasons of Dundee did continue to protect the "freedom" of their working brethren by permitting only initiated masons to work in the town. Throughout the rest of the century some efforts were made intermittently to restrict the practice of the craft to members of the lodge. The charitable obligations of the lodge also continued to be important,[80] and it proudly maintained its locked pew in the local church. Yet increasingly its records speak of the "liberty" of the Freemason as more and more gentlemen, as well as relatives of practicing masons, are admitted to the society.

From the early eighteenth century the signs of increasing literacy also become more frequent. The marks and rough, uncertain scrawl by which the majority of brethren signed their names in the seventeenth century give way and eventually by the 1750s all but disappear – even among the craftsmen who remain. In the 1650s masons spoke of "the blessings of God" and "the better ordering of our Comonwill," and they made reference to their craft as "the calling."[81] In Dundee these same craftsmen invoked the Trinity, opening their lodge in 1659 with words taken from the so-called Old Charges, rules widely practiced by lodges throughout England: "The might of the father of heaven with the Wisdom of the glorious sone and the grace and goodnes of the holie gost be with us at our beginning. . . ."[82]

[79] Sederunt Book, 1736–1807, December 27, 1737.
[80] Ibid., November 5, 1761.
[81] Register of entries of Masters and Journeymen, 1659–1779, entry for November 27, 1659.
[82] Lockit Book, f. 1; cited by Stevenson, *The First Freemasons*, p. 197, as Inventory 13.1.

Concomitant with evidence of increasing literacy, and fewer operatives, the old religious language all but disappears. In its place stands reference solely to the Newtonian Grand Architect of the Universe. In the 1740s prospective candidates for admission as operatives were tested by "an Essay of an Architecture," now, however, requiring an arithmetic knowledge of Ionic proportions.[83] The imposition of order extended from a simplified conception of the deity to sound fiscal management of the lodge and came to include correct social behavior, and even the professionalism of skills. Fines were occasionally extracted for infringements of the rules concerning employment. By the same token, money was also lent at interest to assist in business ventures with the lodge operating at moments like a bank, an institution that did not come to Dundee until the 1760s.[84]

In this fascinating instance the consolidation of elite culture, a process historians have traced as under way from well back in the seventeenth century,[85] included the assimilation and transformation of one of the most representative institutions of early modern European popular culture. The guild, complete with its myths and rituals, has been embraced only to be transformed. And its most binding, and potentially subversive, practice, secrecy, has been given new meaning. Knowledge of the secrets delineated brothers by their degrees; it also enveloped their private association and made it special. For others, in a different setting, it may also have made it suspect.

A direct evolution out of its seventeenth-century predecessor, the lodge in Dundee might easily be imagined as vastly different from its continental counterparts of the 1730s and beyond. Indeed, in some respects it differed from many London and provincial lodges because of the large number of operative masons remaining in its ranks. Yet after 1734, at their core, the practices and ideals of this private society in Dundee – as revealed in the language it employed – were not fundamentally different from those elaborated upon by the London *Con-*

[83] On the older, less formal procedure of the "essay and sufficient tryall," see Harry Carr, *Lodge Mother Kilwinning,* p. 24.

[84] B. P. Lenman, "The Industrial History of the Dundee Region from the Eighteenth to the Early Twentieth Century," in S. J. Jones, *Dundee and District,* Dundee, British Association for the Advancement of Science, 1968, p. 163.

[85] David Rollinson, "Property, Ideology and Popular Culture in a Gloucestershire Village, 1660–1740," *Past and Present,* no. 93, 1981, pp. 70–79. Cf. Peter Burke, *Popular Culture in Early Modern Europe,* New York, 1978.

stitutions (1723) and in turn imitated with greater and lesser degrees of imagination by countless European lodges.

The importance of the Dundee lodge is that it permits us to watch the unfolding from guild to fraternity. The emergence of a new private society modeled on – indeed, deriving from – the masonic guilds of medieval origin should be understood in relation to an important moment in the history of European political development. For much of European urban history guilds of craftsmen, and even of merchants, provided, as one historian aptly describes it, "the counter-culture to civil society."[86] The guilds were vital participants in town and city life; they functioned to protect their members from the power of the great magistrates, lay and ecclesiastical. Their understanding of freedom and equality was more protectionist and collective than it was individual and purely market. Yet with these qualifications the guilds also played a regulatory role in the commercial life of any city, operating both protectively and coercively in ways that have been described as "ideal . . . to police the workforce."[87] The guilds regulated who might practice "his mystery," that is, the skills of a particular craft at any given moment and place. The relationship between the guild and the free merchant was partly adversarial, partly collaborative. But the guilds' relation to actual governmental authority in urban settings was significantly different. Guilds might administer the policies of local magistrates; but they did not make those policies, although they might indeed be carefully consulted.

In early-eighteenth-century Britain there was, in one sense, nothing "counter-culture" about the new speculative lodges. They embraced the rhetoric of constitutional authority, of the magistrates seated in Parliament. The emergence of these private societies suggests a new political mentality striving for expression within a particular economic, that is, market context. We have arrived at that moment when a political nation exists within one of the European national states. This nation, in possession of voting rights, governed in tandem and in self-confidence with an older aristocracy and a

[86] Anthony Black, *Guilds and Civil Society*, p. 43. See also the comments of Daniel Mornet on the way in which freemasonry was imbedded in the French *ancien régime*, in *Les Origines intellectuelles*, pp. 375–87.

[87] Heather Swanson, "The Illusion of Economic Structure: Craft Guilds in Late Medieval English Towns," *Past and Present*, no. 121, November 1988, p. 39.

constitutionally limited monarchy. In the cities the mercantile elite no longer needed guilds for their protection; in the countryside, the landed gentry expressed their political interests through parliamentary elections. In town and city the power of the old guilds to regulate wages and labor had now been broken. But the collectivist definition of liberty and equality inherent in guild culture – complete with the ambiguities that continental and antirepublican opponents of freemasonry were quick to seize upon – could be given new meaning. It could now pertain to the aspirations of the political nation. Voters and magistrates could meet within the egalitarian shell provided by the guild shorn of its economic authority and in most cases of its workers. In the new Masonic lodges urban gentlemen, as well as small merchants and educated professionals, could practice fraternity, conviviality, and civility while giving expression to a commonly held social vision of their own liberty and equality.

As in all things new, elements from the past, from that once vital guild tradition, were also clearly present. There was the characteristic concern for the moral betterment of all brothers,[88] now largely equated with civility and decorum. The principle of charity was retained, and reinforced. Indeed, it became one of the most attractive reasons for joining a lodge, a hedge against fate for members who might fall on hard times. Or it became an outlet for charitable activities among the most prosperous and economically insulated members of society.

As far as can be determined, the old guild ceremonies of initiation and the ritual associated with festivals and feast days were retained by the British lodges, but vastly elaborated upon. Yet the original purpose of the guild, which was to confer on its members the "freedom and privileges" of practicing their craft, to protect wages, and to confer status and establish place within the larger community, was gradually replaced and a new language was directly substituted for the old. Increasingly the records speak of the "liberty" of the brothers, or lay emphasis on the old term "fraternity," or, in seeking to describe the relationship between all brothers, speak of "equality." Within the confines of this egalitarian vision the working mason was still expected "to hew Stone and Raise Perpendiculars," while the

[88] Ibid., p. 26.

new "Gentleman Mason" must practice "Secrecy, Morality and good Fellowship."[89] In this fascinating instance the medieval guild was reshaped to give expression to the aspirations of the modern, constitutionally governed polity. Gentlemen Freemasons could retain the obligations and privileges granted by their social rank; they could also bond with lesser but literate and reasonably affluent men, and jointly practice secrecy, fellowship, and charity. Within the new British lodges gentlemen, and even aristocrats, expressed their political hegemony while "laboring" to create among themselves an egalitarian culture.

But discrete words are derived from language spoken in a particular context. Early-eighteenth-century Masonic rhetoric was first articulated in the context of postrevolutionary English and Scottish society. This context permitted its ideals to be prescribed for, and identified with, a larger society where, it could be imagined, good order and government prevailed. The "libertys and privileges" bestowed by this fraternal society were no longer considered guarantees against encroachments from the governing civil authorities, nor intended as protection, in normal times, against market forces. Rather, they were seen to be the natural complement of constitutionally governed behavior, the reward for practicing the principles, it was believed, that should govern the civil polity. In this instance, it could be said, the public gave birth to the private, the political and economic permitted the creation of a new social and cultural form.

In eighteenth-century Masonic sociability – more so than in any other versions of the new philosophical sociability – we find a consuming identification with laws and regulations that will ensure order and good government. It is undoubtedly true that the new individualism sanctioned by the seventeenth-century revolution in England "relegated . . . the practical utility and moral legitimacy of corporations, whether towns or guilds, . . . to the shadows."[90] Yet from those shadows emerged a new private society with which mercantile and literate elites could identify. The guild as it evolved into "an honourable fraternity" inspired a new – at moments quasi-religious – form of cor-

[89] D. Knoop, G. P. Jones, and D. Hamer, eds., *The Wilkinson Manuscript*, privately printed, 1946, p. 33, quoting from a Masonic catechism of the 1720s, but possibly from an earlier date.

[90] Black, *Guilds and Civil Society*, p. 153.

poratism, complete with oaths, rituals, regalia, and "secret" truths. As the British *Constitutions* (1723) made clear, the lodges of "free and accepted" Masons specifically renounced any "confederacy of their working brethren" that attempted to fix "work . . . at their own price and wages."[91]

In the creation of this new form of European sociability we have discerned the moment when increasingly large numbers of literate laymen (and eventually some women) could imagine the principles governing the constitutional state as something they could replicate in their own lives, at their leisure. They could re-create its ideal form and live by a constitution, if only playfully. They paid dues for the privilege of doing so, and they were playfully serious about the meaning of this sociability in their own lives. This private polity could reinforce their identity with the "real" state. It could also – and this was the dangerous quality about Masonic sociability in the context of any *ancien régime* – make men restless when their idealism ran counter to the dictum implicit in absolutism or in oligarchy, namely, that identification with the state was reserved only to those chosen by a select few to serve it. In absolutist countries even the phenomenon of voluntary secular fraternizing could be suspect. As the Paris police code put it, clandestine assemblies had been strictly prohibited because in them "enemies of order seek to weaken in people's spirits the principles of religion and of subordination to the Powers, established by God."[92]

Medieval corporatism may in some attenuated sense bear relation to the late-eighteenth-century emergence of trade unionism.[93] By contrast and earlier, elite sociability in the eighteenth-century Masonic form signaled the birth of relative affluence and high literacy as the characteristics of those who made secular civil society their own. We may be startled by the willingness of gentlemen to embrace a craft

[91] *Constitutions*, pp. 35–36.

[92] Thomas Brennan, *Public Drinking and Popular Culture in Eighteenth-Century Paris*, Princeton, Princeton University Press, 1988, pp. 271–72, quoting a police code from midcentury.

[93] [Anon.], *La Muse Maçonne, ou recueil de poésies diverses, odes, cantates et discours . . . par le Fr. D*B****, The Hague, van Laak, 1773, containing *Discours prononcé par le Grand Maitre des Francs-Maçons de France dans la Grand Loge assemblée solennellement à Paris . . . 5740 {1740}*, pp. 113–14. Probably delivered by the Chevalier Ramsay.

guild, but not by the transformations wrought within that institution as a result. The new and nonartisanal brothers of the craft obviously believed that they had the right to alter it, and radically if necessary, should it fail to respond to their identification and their idealism. Eighteenth-century urban gentlemen, so often the buyers and sellers of commodities by virtue of their occupations and leisure, expressed their identification with governance and the civic through the form provided by an originally craft, and urban, institution created by the sellers of labor. Yet this was surely a more fitting form of voluntary association than models that could have been adopted out of mores, fraternal orders, or institutions found among the economically protected estates, the traditional clergy or aristocracy.

The particular experience of the Dundee lodge also teaches us a lesson about eighteenth-century British society and about the new sociability in relation to it. The members of the political nation brought their constitutional and social values to the lodge and then imposed them upon it. They managed also to integrate those values and the authority that went with them in ways that imitated their place in the larger society. Yet in this instance a necessary accommodation was also made to the interests of the wage laborer, albeit within the context of an essentially market relationship. All these relationships of power and authority were negotiated under the mantle of a rhetoric of order, fraternity, and harmony that was deemed to be ancient, yet capable of adaptation. In hindsight we may find little in common between the liberties of a gentleman and the freedom of a stonecutter to sell and also to protect his labor. Yet clearly, in this new formulation, this freedom and that liberty were meant to be equated. We may find this fraternity of medical doctors, gentlemen, excise officers, merchants, master masons, and journeymen stonecutters an improbable locus of "equality" – a term these Dundee records do not use, but do imply. Yet contemporaneous Masonic rhetoric latched on to the term to describe the ideal private society where "all brothers meet upon the level," where each possessed a vote, and where any could be chosen, at least in theory, to be officers.

Originally the guild had been a social setting that controlled economic life. Within that context by 1700 nonmasons in Dundee were admitted by masters and freemen "to all our privileges as free as we are ourselves."[94] In the actual world of local politics that freedom possessed a political meaning to which tradesmen might aspire only if they ceased entirely to be handworkers, no longer to exercise "a handycraft." And in one respect Dundee was no different from any other town or city in western Europe during the eighteenth century. Social place determined access to political influence and power. The rhetoric of liberalism and constitutionalism developed in seventeenth-century England blurred that reality, or offered an ideological challenge to it. How fitting that a guild, as transformed by gentlemen and highly literate professionals, became one of the first institutions wherein that rhetoric was used to bind men of diverse social rank and hence of disparate power. That binding also obscured the social divisions and the inequities of rank and degree endemic to the lives of the men who embraced "equality" and "liberty." In making those divisions less obvious the idealism of freemasonry ironically served to reinforce them. As tradesmen and gentlemen, doctors and merchants, broke bread together and practiced fraternity they obfuscated the real divisions of wealth, education, and social place that existed between them.

The records in Dundee give substance to the rhetorical formulations about fraternity and harmony, the stuff of Masonic idealism, and that rhetoric turns up in countless lodge sermons, speeches, songs, and treatises throughout the eighteenth century. Published orations in Britain also speak a language that was essentially Augustan, that is, court and Whig, and remarkably self-satisfied and complacent about the joys of order and harmony. Yet Masonic rhetoric could also reveal the tensions within that liberal and constitutional order, particularly as these surfaced in the 1760s with the agitation led by John Wilkes against the power and influence of the court oligarchy. His movement appealed particularly to the less affluent among the middling ranks. In Masonic orations of the 1760s we find officers deeply concerned that the lodges not become infected with the social radicalism of the Wilkesite movement. Try as they may to avoid them, the lodges' pursuit of private social harmony possessed public implications.

[94] Warden, *Burgh Laws,* p. 582, citing the manuscript sources of the Dundee masons for 1684 and the admission of one Captain Andrew Smyton, one of the earliest nonmasons to be admitted.

What was true of British rhetoric would remain true for eighteenth-century European freemasonry in general, however vastly different its forms and aspirations. In the pursuit of social harmony the lodge made porous the boundary between the private and the public. Men of a variety of ranks, and eventually some women, could experience a rarefied and idealized version of society within the confines of a private society. Not surprisingly, European Freemasons, speaking a variety of European languages, were remarkably consistent in referring to the public realm when speaking within the confines of their private rhetorical universes.

In Britain the lodges came to be seen as organized around a constitution in the post-1688, or parliamentary, sense of that term. The goal of government by consent within the context of subordination to "legitimate" authority was vigorously pursued by the Grand Lodge of London, and was demanded of all lodges affiliated to it. Records of lodges throughout the first half of the century, from London and the provinces, attest to the seriousness with which they were to

> keep all and every rules, orders and regulations contained in the Book of Constitutions (except such as have been revoked or altered at any quarterly communication or other general meeting). And also all such other orders, regulations and instructions as shall from time to time be transmitted by us . . . our deputy for the time being or by any of our successors, Grand Masters or his deputy.[95]

The day-to-day working of this constitutional order meant elections by ballot; majority rule (except for unanimous vote for admission to a lodge); in all matters, one man one vote; taxes in the form of dues; registration of membership; and, not least, rules of social behavior, of civility and decorum, to prevent anyone bringing "scandal upon the Society." Discipline was enforced through man-made rules and regulations, as well as by social pressure within the lodge, which included fines for drunkenness, swearing, "or giving abusive language." All lodges were expected to give allegiance to the Grand Lodge of London, and hence to its grand master, as well as to the elected officers of each lodge, beginning with the master. Places in a lodge were as-

[95] Bristol Record Office, Bristol, U.K., MS 20535(291). Warrant dated 1738 from the Grand Lodge in London to permit the establishment of a lodge in Tewkesbury; reply from Edward Popham accepting these conditions, same date. For mention of this lodge, see T. O. Haunch, "The Formation, 1717–51," in United Grand Lodge of England, *Grand Lodge, 1717–1967,* Oxford, Oxford University Press, 1967, p. 85.

signed according to seniority of admission ("Masters and Officers excepted"). Brothers asked permission of the master before speaking at formal meetings, and dues had to be paid regularly.

Commonplace rhetoric among British Freemasons always spoke of their being "free and accepted." As one master informed a provincial lodge, "you Voluntary and at your own Request enter into, calling God and the Members then present to witness, that you will never disclose or make known the Secret or Secrets that are then or hereafter shall be discovered to you." Bound together by the secret signs and rituals inherited from guild practice, the brothers, now from a variety of social ranks, in some instances from gentry to tradesmen, were asked to embrace a common moral code. They were admonished always to practice

> good morals. Such as to give to every one his due, to perform to God ourselves and the whole world, whatsoever is owing from the state of our nature and circumstances wherein we are placed. A Freemason should exercise himself in all those humane virtues, which consist in the Dominion of his Reason over his sensative passions and appetites. Such as Patience, Meekness, Temperance, and Chastity; He must be faithful to his promises, sincere in his professions, just and honest in all his dealings.

The obligations of subjects, superiors, fathers, children, husbands, masters, and servants were then simply and straightforwardly asserted. In this rhetoric we find an almost effortless blending of traditional patriarchal values with the new language of constitutionalism and the older traditions of charity and friendship associated with voluntary associations. And should the bylaws of these new lodges "prove insufficient to keep up and support the good government and prosperity of this society then at all times it shall be in the power of the majority of the whole members of this lodge to make and add from time to time all such further and other good and wholesome laws and orders as shall be thought necessary and conducive thereunto."[96] The implication here is that laws and societies – not just the lodge – are human institutions and they can be altered by the will of the majority.

[96] Bristol Record Office, MS 20535(291), unfoliated. The discussion, just quoted, of secrets, virtues, and the duties of subjects and fathers is from a charge given for the year 1739 at the election of officers for 1740. The speaker is the master, one E. Popham, of the lodge in Tewkesbury.

Although entirely private and avoiding any discussion of religion or politics, the typical eighteenth-century British Masonic lodge was in effect a microcosm of the ideal civil polity. With an almost utopian sense of what is possible, the lodges sought to make a better society within the lodge through the virtue of each brother practiced within a constitutional setting. "The natural consequence of such excellent virtues," it was believed, "is promoting the interest of each other."[97] Within this context of order and harmony, self-interest will flourish.

With their interests flourishing such avowedly secular men bonded, feasted, and gave money to a fraternity of equals. They in turn endowed the less-fortunate-through-no-fault-of-their-own with charity. The plight of the less fortunate, however, was distinctive, determined by fate and chance, seen to possess no implications, nor to modify the equality of all men. Presided over by the Grand Architect, the human order contained almost infinite possibilities for improvement and perfectability. Only the preservation of order, harmony, and civility, now internalized through the lessons offered by sociability, was essential. In the 1790s throughout western Europe those mores broke down. Focusing on the Jacobin moment, as have French historians in particular, has led to a misreading of eighteenth-century sociability. Rather than finding in it the impulse to level and hence destroy the modern commercial order, we may now find in the rhetoric and practice of sociability an affirmation of market principles, an almost mindless celebration of the secular, of the prosperous, and of an imagined equality that remains elusive for those without the money needed, then and now, to participate fully in modern civil society.

[97] Bristol Record Office, MS 20535(291), "A Charge by the Master for the Year 1740 at the Election of Officers for the Year 1741," f. 13.

CHAPTER 4

Market culture, reckless passion, and the Victorian reconstruction of punishment

MARTIN J. WIENER

Men ought to command their passions; and if they fail to do so, they ought to suffer for it. The object of the criminal law is to control the passions which prompt men to break it.

– J. F. Stephen, 1864

It has become almost axiomatic to observe that the rapid development of the market in the eighteenth and nineteenth centuries introduced a new discipline into human affairs. Economic historians have highlighted the way the market increasingly subjugated businessmen to its impersonal dictates, rewarding those who best adapted while bankrupting those who failed to adapt. Social historians have focused on the parallel subjugation of workers to a new "wage slavery." Even intellectual and cultural historians have found in the new discipline of the market a key explanatory tool.[1] However, such preoccupation with the "natural" growth of social and personal discipline makes much of past experience a puzzle. If discipline was inexorably advancing, it is hard to understand the intensified fear of "license" and almost obsessive concern for building "character" that pervaded social discourse through most of the nineteenth century.

The mystery can be dispelled if we acknowledge that there was another, "permissive" face of market culture, which has received comparatively little notice from scholars in recent decades. The widening and deepening of market relations meant not only new forms of discipline but also new forms of liberation – of individuals from social constraints, and, within individuals, of impulses and desires from the re-

[1] See, for example, Thomas L. Haskell, "Capitalism and the Origins of the Humanitarian Sensibility," *American Historical Review* 90 (April and June 1985), 339–61, 547–66.

straints of habit, custom and "morality."[2] For one thing, the market stimulated and legitimated acquisitive and consuming impulses.[3] For another, it potentially empowered individuals, for as technological innovations dramatically reduced distances and increased productive power, the effective force of individual actions, which now could be seen to have consequences far beyond one's immediate local and personal world, was multiplied. This multiplied potential power, going along with industrialization, urbanization, the acceleration of migration, and the growing prominence of consumption – all closely tied to market development – nurtured a heady, but anxious, feeling that traditional checks on individual desires and impulses were dissolving.[4]

When they thought directly about it, early Victorians' feelings about the market were often uneasy and conflicted. Although it was sometimes seen as a "civilizing" force, rewarding self-discipline and deferral of gratification, the market was also feared as *encouraging* impulsive, willful behavior.[5] It appeared to do this chiefly in two ways: first, by encouraging the hope of immediate gratification of desires, and stimulating the growth of such desires, thus shifting the psychic balance within individuals in favor of impulse; and second, by similarly shifting social power to the young.[6] As the Liberal barrister

[2] See, for example, Alan Macfarlane, *The Culture of Capitalism* (Cambridge: Cambridge University Press, 1987), p. 119: "It is money, markets and market capitalism that eliminates absolute moralities. Not only is every moral system throughout the world equally valid . . . but, *within* every system, whatever is, is right."

[3] See Joyce Appleby, "New Cultural Heroes in the Early National Period," in this volume.

[4] Of course, the market was only one of the influences operating on early-nineteenth-century Britain, encouraging but by no means the sole cause of the new preoccupation of criminal policy, and of social policy more generally, with character building. For a fuller picture of the shaping and reshaping of modern British criminal policy, see Martin J. Wiener, *Reconstructing the Criminal: Culture, Law and Policy in England 1830–1914* (New York: Cambridge University Press, 1990).

[5] Even the father of market philosophy, Adam Smith, who had in the *Wealth of Nations* dismissed the simpler charge that the market promoted antisocial selfishness, came to worry about its more subtle demoralizing influences. In his 1790 revisions of the *Theory of Moral Sentiments* Smith placed greater stress on the need to reinforce weakening moral influences. Here Lawrence Dickey has seen "the perception that for a commercial society to function properly – in a 'civilized' way – it would have to maintain a high degree of collective vigilance and 'propriety' with regard to its morality" ("Historicizing the 'Adam Smith Problem': Conceptual, Historiographical, and Textual Issues," *Journal of Modern History* 58 [1986], 608). The spread of the market – despite the "hidden hand" – was making moralization more necessary than ever before.

[6] And to women, particularly in creating new alternatives to domestic subordination for young women. See Sally Alexander, "Women's Work in Nineteenth Century

and school inspector Jelinger Symons observed in 1849 after his service on several official inquiries into labor conditions, "the tendency of manufacturing machinery has been to throw the social importance of industry, in great measure, into the hands of children, investing them with consequence and independence before their minds are schooled in self-government. Hence the precocity of the passions and the growth of juvenile vice in manufacturing places."[7] Indeed, much of the support for restricting child labor in these years stemmed from such fears of a market-borne tide of youthful liberation from adult supervision.[8] The popular Bradford Tory factory reformer Parson Bull exhorted the working classes in 1833,

> Parents of Bradford how say you? Do you consent that your little girls and boys when a day older than 13 shall be held in the eyes of the law as independent of you? Is it for your comfort? Is it for their good? Will it mend their morals? Will it strengthen the bonds which hold society together? Oh worse than madness thus to strike at the very root of all social order and to spread the seed of anarchy and confusion all around![9]

London: A Study of the Years 1820–50," in *The Rights and Wrongs of Women,* ed. Juliet Mitchell and Ann Oakley (Harmondsworth: Penguin, 1976); Barbara Taylor, *Eve and the New Jerusalem* (New York: Pantheon, 1983); and John Gillis, *For Better, For Worse: British Marriages, 1600 to the Present* (New York: Oxford University Press, 1985). In the rapidly developing spheres of both production and consumption in New York City in this period, Christine Stansell has seen a weakening of male controls and new "possibilities for a transformed female identity open[ing] up." Christine Stansell, *City of Women: Sex and Class in New York 1789–1860* (New York: Knopf, 1986), p. 128.

7 *Tactics for the Times* (London: J. Ollivier, 1849), p. 49.

8 Such fears were not only bourgeois ones but were also shared by many working-class parents. Stansell has noted that by 1835, twelve years after its establishment, almost half the commitments to the New York House of [Juvenile] Refuge were being initiated by parents. *City of Women,* p. 54.

9 Quoted in Theodore Koditschek, *Class Formation and Urban-Industrial Society* (New York: Cambridge University Press, 1990). Such contemporary perceptions of a shift in the balance of power between generations seem to have had a basis in everyday life. Olive Anderson has noted that "it is now very clear that in [early Victorian] Lancashire textile towns life was exceptionally good for the young, but exceptionally bad for middle-aged and elderly men, although often not for middle-aged and elderly women." The young were better off partly because a wider range of jobs was open to them, but chiefly because the earning power of textile operatives reached its peak in their late teens and twenties. As their dexterity, strength, and endurance declined, middle-aged men had to move into lower-paid jobs, and ended their work careers hawking, street sweeping, and rag gathering. Older women, on the other hand, were often valued as child-minders and housekeepers, since many younger married women worked in the factories. Thus, older men lost relatively in relation to younger men and to women. All this, Anderson observes, was "in considerable contrast to the state of affairs not only in rural areas, but also in non-industrial towns, where widespread parental ownership of the means of production, a restricted labour market,

From a very different political standpoint, the Benthamite public health reformer Edwin Chadwick also feared the growing power of the young and the reckless. Despite the fact that infant mortality in early industrial Britain was far higher than that at later stages of life, what he was most concerned to reduce was *adult* mortality, in the interests of social order. The most dangerous aspect of "noxious physical agencies" for him was that they "acted as obstacles to education and to moral culture":

> In abridging the duration of the adult life of the working classes they check the growth of productive skill, and abridge the amount of social experience and steady moral habits in the community: they substitute for a population that accumulates and preserves instruction and is steadily progressive, a population that is young, inexperienced, ignorant, credulous, irritable, passionate, and dangerous.[10]

Bad sanitary arrangements undermined generational authority : "The disappearance by premature deaths," he noted, "of the heads of families and the older workmen . . . must to some extent involve the necessity of supplying the lapse of staid influence amidst a young population by one description or another of precautionary force." The mobs of Bethnal Green, Bristol, and Manchester, which had recently rampaged, were all youthful: "the great havoc . . . was committed by mere boys."[11]

"License" and "passion" on the one hand, and "character" on the other, became increasingly prominent terms in social discourse. And not only in *social* discourse; in psychological discourse as well a new fear of the passions was making itself felt. Where eighteenth-century physicians had seen sexuality as a powerful but natural part of the human constitution, whose suppression produced many more disorders than its overindulgence, in the early nineteenth century the passions and their proper management became an increasing question of medical concern.[12] With interest focusing on the emotions, the will,

and the predominance in the male labour force of craftsmen, retailers and professional men usually favoured the middle-aged and elderly" ("Suicide and Industrialization," *Past and Present,* no. 86 [February 1980], 165).

10 *Report on the Sanitary Conditions of the Labouring Population* (1842), ed. M. W. Flinn (Edinburgh: Edinburgh University Press, 1965), p. 268.

11 Ibid., pp. 266–67.

12 See Roy Porter, "Love, Sex and Madness in Eighteenth Century England," *Social Research* 53 (Summer 1986), 211–42. John Pickstone has also remarked on the "dualism of early nineteenth-century physiology" and "the presumption that the

rather than the mind, was coming to be seen as the most problematic aspect of human nature. The shift in psychiatric concern from intellectual defect to malfunctions in impulse control was signified by the new concept of "moral insanity."[13] J. C. Prichard, a physician and ethnologist, coined the term in 1833. In this condition, "the passions were under no restraint," and the will was surrendered impetuously to the emotions.[14]

The passions, of course, were natural to all men and women. There seemed to be an instinct-driven "natural man" within even ostensibly civilized persons, lying in wait.[15] The leading midcentury manual of psychiatric medicine observed that "there is a latent devil in the heart of the best of men; and when the restraints of religious feeling, of prudence and self-esteem, are weakened or removed by the operation of mental disease, the fiend breaks loose, and the whole character of the man seems to undergo a sudden and complete transformation."[16]

This dangerous "natural man" had entered secular social discourse with Thomas Malthus, who placed "the passion between the sexes" in a new role of material, as well as moral, nemesis. As is well known, Malthus frontally attacked the general eighteenth-century approval of population growth. But he also challenged the leading strand of Enlightenment thinking that more generally inclined toward a benign view of human instincts. Instead, he argued that the ineradicable instinct of sexuality virtually ensured that population rose to absorb any increase in food supply, preventing any lasting improvement in the condition of society. Malthus's powerful impact on the imagination of his age must be seen as owing to more than his arguments, which were hardly irrefutable and, indeed, were to be disproved by events. Rather, he seems to have touched a raw nerve with his picture

body and its passions are to be kept in check by the rational mind." "Ferrier's Fever to Kay's Cholera: Disease and Social Structure in Cottonopolis," *History of Science* 22 (1984), 413.

13 See Vieda Skultans, *English Madness: Ideas on Insanity 1580–1890* (London, 1979); Andrew Scull, *Museums of Madness: The Social Organization of Insanity in Nineteenth Century England* (New York: St. Martin's Press, 1979).

14 J. C. Prichard, *A Treatise on Insanity* (London, 1835), p. 175.

15 As Vieda Skultans has observed of early Victorian psychiatric thought: "Like the forces of anarchy and disorder, insanity was thought to be a universal presence ready to break loose." "Moral Order and Mental Derangement," in *Symbols and Sentiments*, ed. Ioan Lewis (London: Academic Press, 1977), p. 225.

16 J. C. Bucknill and D. H. Tuke, *A Manual of Psychiatric Medicine* (Philadelphia: Blanchard & Lea, 1858), p. 273.

of human nature commanded by a peremptory instinct that resists accommodation, which can either, in unusual cases, be denied, at the cost of "inextricable unhappiness," or, more commonly, be surrendered to, carrying with it for the mass of the population inevitable immiseration. Indeed, Malthus's implications went even further: Because the sexual drive was strongest in the young, the vitality of youth, not the debility of age, posed the gravest danger to society. As Catherine Gallagher has pointed out, for Malthus "the social body is growing 'old' [and weak] precisely insofar as the actual demographic proportions of the society are increasingly weighted toward youth."[17] "Malthusianism" pointed not only explicitly to the evil consequences of population growth, but also implicitly to the social dangers of youthful energies.

Given these concerns, it is not surprising that a major preoccupation of early Victorian public policy discussion was crime and punishment. Tories, Whigs, and Radicals agreed that the age was witnessing a "constant and uninterrupted increase of crime"[18] against both property and person. While conservatives may have been the most agitated, the liberal *Law Magazine* could refer in passing at midcentury to "the immense increase which has notoriously taken place in the whole catalogue of personal injuries, from common assaults up to attempts to shoot, stab, and poison."[19] Between 1805 (when national criminal statistics began to be compiled) and 1842, the numbers of persons committed to trial for indictable offenses (nontrivial crimes, roughly corresponding to the older category of felonies) rose nearly sevenfold, far outracing the growth of population.[20]

We now understand how these statistics overstated the situation. For crimes against both persons and property, the figures were vastly inflated by a combination of greatly improved record keeping, greatly expanded enforcement, and changes in the law that extended criminal liability. In general, contemporaries' excited accounts of this supposed

[17] "The Body Versus the Social Body in Malthus and Mayhew," *Representations*, no. 14 (Spring 1986), 86.

[18] "The Increase of Crime," *Blackwood's Edinburgh Magazine* LV (January–June 1844), 533.

[19] *Law Magazine* 44 (August–November 1850), 122.

[20] See V. A. C. Gatrell and T. B. Hadden, "Criminal Statistics and Their Interpretation," in *Nineteenth Century Society*, ed. E. A. Wrigley (Cambridge: Cambridge University Press, 1972), pp. 372–74.

"crime wave" are highly misleading. Most offenses during the period of greatest concern, David Philips has concluded, were "prosaic and undramatic, involving small amounts being stolen, squalid robberies, burglaries and assaults, in which roughness was common, but not fatal violence, and in which the items taken were usually small amounts of coal, metal, clothing, food, money or personal possessions."[21]

Yet it would be a mistake to dismiss contemporaneous perceptions as simply exaggerated, for they are deeply revelatory of early Victorian experience and values, and in particular of the centrality of the "license–character" polarity. Liberals as well as conservatives tended to see in their "crime wave" a moral threat more profound even than the insecurity of property and person. Crimes, as Jelinger Symons put it in 1849, were "the offshoots of an extent of moral disease which they by no means accurately measure, but of which they attest the magnitude."[22] Indeed Symons, thoroughly familiar through his service on official investigative commissions with the material deprivation endured by handloom weavers and by miners, and a strong supporter of legislative reform, nonetheless found the central problem of the age to be nonmaterial: what he called "the relaxation of moral restraint."[23] It was significant that the opening remarks to the 1857 founding meeting of the influential Social Science Association dwelled on the threat of "unlicensed appetites, bold, rebellious will, vicious and enthralling habits."[24]

In the same years, the radical social investigator Henry Mayhew noted the paradoxical fact that not only was the material progress of society not being accompanied by a moral progress, but if anything moral disorder was increasing. His social survey, meant to cover all of London society, never got beyond the criminal and quasi criminal. He found habitual criminals, more numerous than ever before, distinguished by an undisciplined and "nomadic" character-structure: "those persons who feel labour to be more irksome than others, owing to their being not only less capable of continued application to

[21] David Philips, *Crime and Authority in Victorian England: The Black Country* (London, 1977), p. 287.

[22] *Tactics for the Times*, p. 15.

[23] Ibid., p. 58.

[24] Sydney Turner, "Responsibility in Aims and Means," *Transactions of the National Association for the Promotion of Social Science 1857*, 5. The Reverend Turner had recently been appointed the first Inspector of Juvenile Reformatories.

one subject or object, but more fond of immediate pleasure, and, consequently, less willing to devote themselves to those pursuits which yield only prospective ones." Left to "natural" forces, he concluded, such indiscipline was more likely to expand than diminish:

> It is a strange ethnological fact that, though many have passed from the steady and regular habits of civilized life, few of those who have once adopted the savage and nomadic form of existence abandon it, notwithstanding its privations, its dangers, and its hardships. This appears to be due mainly to that love of liberty, and that impatience under control, that is more or less common to all minds.[25]

Like the widely read "Newgate novels" of the 1830s and 1840s, the "factual" writings of Mayhew and other early Victorian protosociologists exhibited a melodramatic fascination with unchained impulses and self-will.[26] Indeed, complaints of the immorality of "Newgate" stories focused less on their occasional explaining away of criminality as a product of poverty or social neglect (which has been excessively noted by modern scholars) and more on their intense portrayal of a life of unchecked emotions and immediate gratification. The novelist W. M. Thackeray was characteristic in objecting to this literature not because it justified or excused crime, but because it glamorized it, habituating its predominantly youthful readers to a profitable world of dissoluteness and impulsive violence.

Few social observers felt much confidence in the inevitable retreat of "unlicensed appetites" and "impatience under control" before the disciplines of the market or the factory. It seemed obvious to most contemporaries that moral order required more deliberate social intervention than had yet been applied. Consequently, running throughout early Victorian social policy was the aim of containing and mastering an impulsiveness that the market by itself nourished more than subdued. The social discourse of the state, of voluntary societies and philanthropic individuals, as well as the discourse of personal rela-

[25] Henry Mayhew and John Binny, *The Criminal Prisons of London* (London, 1862), p. 384. Most of this work was written by Mayhew by 1856.

[26] Early Victorian accounts of criminality usually took the form of melodrama. As literary critics have pointed out, melodrama confronts basic anxieties – "the loss of control, the apparent triumph of anarchy" (Winifred Hughes, *The Maniac in the Cellar: Sensation Novels of the 1860s* [Princeton: Princeton University Press, 1980], p. 175). Not surprisingly, therefore, it became a natural stylistic mode for the early Victorian era.

tions, came to center around ways to develop "character" – not so much certain fixed and externally validated standards of behavior, such as aristocratic honor or the plebeian standard of neighborliness, but rather a psychological state, in which the passions were habitually mastered by reflection, the pressures of the present controlled by the perspective of the future. Character would seal the holes in the social and the psychic order daily being eaten through by the acids of the market; its spread would "civilize" market society.

The habitual deferral of imperious present desires for calm future benefit became the most pervasive trope in the dominant modes of moral discourse of the first half of the century, in both their secular and religious manifestations. Evangelicals stressed deferral until the next life, seeking to teach men to ground all action in a profound awareness of eternity. As William Wilberforce declared,

> The great truths revealed in Scripture concerning the unseen world [serve] to rectify the illusions of vision, to bring forward into nearer view those eternal things which from their remoteness are apt to be either wholly overlooked, or to appear but faintly in the utmost bounds of the horizon and to remove backward, and reduce to their true comparative dimensions, the objects of the present life, which are apt to fill the human eye, assuming a false magnitude from their vicinity.[27]

The Utilitarian counterpart of Evangelical "farsightedness" was consequentialism, which was not simply a pragmatic standard (as it later became) but a moral ideal. Despite the thrust inherent in its eighteenth-century origins toward the ratification of existing appetites and desires, nineteenth-century Utilitarians rarely took that path. Instead, they almost always felt a moral imperative to assist (or compel) persons to perceive their long-term interests in the welter of immediate preoccupations. The Benthamite calculator was a man whose attention was habitually focused on distant consequences. Utilitarianism thus sought to habituate men (and women) to consequential thinking, which did not come naturally or easily, which required, and then itself promoted, impulse control. The principle of utility, Bentham's disciple James Mill wrote, "marshalls the duties in their proper order, and will not permit mankind to be deluded, as so long they have been, sottishly to prefer the lower to the higher good, and

[27] *A Practical View of the Prevailing Religious System of Professed Christians* (Boston: Manning & Loring, 1799), pp. 118–19.

to hug the greater evil, from fear of the less." An individual who automatically focused his mind on the long-run consequences of his acts would come to defer gratification. By this means, as Mill argued, he would gain mastery over his "animal nature" that impelled him, to his ultimate harm, toward immediate, usually sensual, gratification.[28] Or, as the economist Nassau Senior (an author of the disciplinarian New Poor Law) put it in 1836, "to abstain from the enjoyment which is in our power, or to seek distant rather than immediate results, are among the most painful [and necessary] exertions of the human will."[29]

As has come out in the debate over the sources of antislavery sentiment, the discourse of character had a complex and ambiguous relation to the discourse of humanity, also waxing in the early nineteenth century. This was true not only cognitively, as has been noticed, but also in affective terms. On the one hand, as in child rearing, the demand for self-discipline could counteract the softer feelings and legitimate the infliction of pain. On the other hand, less obviously but in the long run more decisively, the zeal to rein in the expression of impulses, and in particular those not only of sexuality but also of aggression, nurtured an intolerance of open displays of aggression and open infliction of physical pain. Thus, in seeming contradiction to their dour philosophies, devout Evangelicals and committed Utilitarians took the lead in many humanitarian movements. Macaulay's scornful remark that the Puritans put down bear baiting out of hatred more of the pleasure of the baiters than of the pain of the bear had

[28] *Fragment on Mackintosh,* quoted in William Thomas, *The Philosophic Radicals* (Oxford: Clarendon Press, 1979), pp. 103–4. In his three-volume *History of British India,* Thomas observed, "Mill's method characteristically combines puritanism and utility" (p. 105). But such a method was not as sharp a revision of his master's philosophy as it might seem; James Steintrager has reminded us that Bentham himself juggled description and prescription: "Hedonic calculation, on occasion, might be a description of the way men behave but it ought always to be the norm." *Bentham* (Ithaca, N.Y.: Cornell University Press, 1977), p. 17. That is to say, men *ought* to calculate their long-term advantage (and be aided and pushed into doing so) whether they were presently disposed to or not. Contrary to his twentieth-century interpreters, Bentham had no faith that men would arive at this norm on their own: "I would no more," he cautioned, "use the word liberty in my conversation when I could get another that would answer the purpose, than I would brandy in my diet, if any physician did not order me: both cloud the understanding and inflame the passions." (Quoted in Douglas G. Long, *Bentham on Liberty* [Buffalo: University of Toronto Press, 1977], p. 173.)

[29] *Political Economy* (1836; London, 1872), p. 59.

closer application to his father's, and even his own, generation.[30] A social ideal of character building declared war on the direct indulgence of appetites both sensual and aggressive.

Criminal law was given a key role in this struggle for the psyche. It has often been assumed that the content of the law in the nineteenth century was becoming more morally neutral. In particular, Utilitarianism, with its conception of law as an instrument for satisfying human needs, has been taken to have widened the space between law and morality. As Macaulay observed in drawing up the Indian penal code, the criminal law was not a body of ethics but must content itself with keeping men from doing positive harm, leaving to public opinion and to teachers of morality and religion the office of furnishing men with motives for doing positive good.[31] Such professional modesty, limiting the sphere of law, was often declared by nineteenth-century judges, jurists, and legislators (and accepted by later commentators). Yet, it is misleading to interpret Victorian law thusly. Early Victorian law reform had "evangelical" as well as "utilitarian" dimensions, while Utilitarians themselves usually held an implicit moral agenda rather distinct from the more permissive modern-day utilitarian philosophies. The law was in fact repeatedly used to counteract the "libertine" influences of capitalism. Reformed to provide a clear tariff of penalties that could be calculated on by potential offenders, and efficiently enforced by a new professional police, it was expected to reward the exercise of self-discipline and punish the surrender to impulse.

The principle of individual moral responsibility, which was ever more emphasized, was as much *instrumental* as declarative, as much interventionist as laissez-faire. For people were not necessarily be-

[30] The "character-building" theme was woven through early Victorian humanitarianism. The bishop of St. David's reminded the annual meeting of the Royal Society for the Prevention of Cruelty to Animals in 1846 that their mission was not simply to help animals but, more fundamentally, to improve men (particularly the lower classes): The uneducated man "is after all but a child in the maturity of his physical powers . . . a savage in the midst of all the refinement of our civilization"; the curbing of animal cruelty was an essential step in the moralization of the English populace. Quoted in Brian Harrison, *Peaceable Kingdom* (Oxford: Clarendon Press, 1982), p. 116.

[31] John Clive, *Macaulay: The Shaping of the Historian* (New York: Knopf, 1973), p. 447.

lieved to be responsible in fact; more important, it was accepted that treating men (and even women) thus was the best way of *making* them more so. Reformers were doing more than bringing the law into closer accord with human nature and social realities; they hoped to use the law to *change* that nature and those realities. Law reform would encourage and compel men to focus their minds on the long-run consequences of their acts, and in the process come to defer gratification. Consequentialism would build character. As Patrick Atiyah has noted, the utilitarianism of the founding generations was, in modern philosophic language, "rule" rather than "act" focused, aimed at instilling principled patterns of behavior.[32] Such patterns would produce a more self-restrained character type in the general public, one that deferred immediate gratification and looked toward the distant consequences of actions. This implicit psychological agenda was quite compatible with the growing judicial reluctance to reach decisions solely on the morality of a particular action.

As its foundation in a comparatively stable, localized, and personalized structure of social relationships eroded, the discretionary and particularistic criminal justice of Georgian England was coming to appear both arbitrary and ineffectual.[33] The criminal laws, the reformer Samuel Romilly typically complained, were the "fruits of no regular design but of sudden and angry fits of capricious legislators"[34] – hardly the sort of laws to discourage an apparent epidemic of popular impulsiveness. Reformers consequently trained their guns on this uncertainty and arbitrariness in the law, which

[32] S. Atiyah, *The Rise and Fall of Freedom of Contract* (Oxford: Clarendon Press, 1979), pp. 354–56.

[33] Compared to the system put in place by the Victorians, "Old Regime" criminal justice was highly particularistic, discretionary, and personal. Before the nineteenth century, Thomas Green has concluded, English criminal justice "was not mainly a matter of the application of abstract rules" but was tailored to the particularity of each situation and each offender (*Verdict According to Conscience: Perspectives on the English Criminal Trial Jury 1200–1800* [Chicago: University of Chicago Press, 1985], p. 286). "At every stage in the trial and in the administration of punishment," John Beattie has similarly observed, "the system was shot through with discretionary powers" (*Crime and the Courts in England 1660–1800* [Princeton: Princeton University Press, 1986], p. 406). Yet another scholar has described pre-Victorian justice as "a private and negotiable process involving personal confrontation rather than bureaucratic procedure" (Peter King, "Decision-Making and Decision-Makers in the English Criminal Law 1750–1800," *Historical Journal* 27 [1984], 25).

[34] Quoted in John A. Hostettler, "The Movement for Reform of the Criminal Law in England in the Nineteenth Century," Ph.D. dissertation, University of London, 1983, p. 12.

failed to discourage willfulness in the populace. The vast scope for discretion built into the eighteenth-century system had created, Romilly charged in 1810, a "lottery of justice"; had introduced, Wilberforce put it the following year, "a sort of gambling into vice," teaching men just the wrong lessons – to take a chance, yield to impulse, and think not on consequences.[35]

A fundamental aim of criminal law reform was to teach the right lessons, that is, to think always on consequences. In both civil and criminal law, the principle of fault, and the notion of "intent," was enlarging. One example was the expansion of the definition of unlawful appropriation of property. As A. H. Manchester has noted, judges in the first half of the nineteenth century showed "a readiness to classify as criminal, conduct which formerly they had regarded as no more than sharp practice."[36] By 1860, with minimal parliamentary intervention, the structural principles grounding larceny had been altered, with the effect of greatly enlarging the ordinary individual's potential criminal liability.[37] Mere attempts to steal, and immoral but not manifestly larcenous appropriations, were more thoroughly criminalized.[38] Liability was also beginning earlier: One no longer had to

[35] *1 Parliamentary Debates 19* (Appendix), c. 12 (February 9, 1810); *19*, c. 744 (April 8, 1811). On the reformist assault on discretion, see Randall McGowen, "The Image of Justice and Reform of the Criminal Law in Early 19th Century England," *Buffalo Law Review* 32 (1983), 89–125.

[36] A. H. Manchester, *A Modern Legal History of England and Wales 1750–1950* (London: Butterworth, 1980), p. 204.

[37] This has been most thoroughly examined and forcefully argued by George Fletcher, in "The Metamorphosis of Larceny," *Harvard Law Review* 89, no. 3 (Jan. 1976), 469–530, and *Rethinking Criminal Law* (Boston: Little, Brown, 1978). Although Fletcher gives a class interest explanation for this development – the desire to afford greater protection to property – the shift of attention from harm to intent was one that had many undertones and ramifications, not always supportive of business or capitalist interests (except through rather convoluted reasoning). Judges, magistrates, and others exhibited an attachment to the concept of intent that went beyond its instrumental value for the existing property system.

[38] The shift from harm to intent can be seen in the reinterpretation noted by Fletcher of the rules relating to temporary takings: "The traditional text writers concurred that in the common law, as distinguished from Roman law, a temporary taking was not felonious. As Blackstone put it, 'if a neighbor takes another's plow that is left in the field and uses it upon his own land and then returns it [cases like this] are misdemeanors and trespasses but no felonies.' When Archbold returns to this hypothetical case in 1812, in the first edition of his influential manual on criminal evidence, it is apparent to him that the issue is not whether the goods are in fact returned, but whether at the time of the taking there was an intent to return" ("Metamorphosis," 509).

complete one's plans or efforts to be open to criminal prosecution.[39] Similarly, the nineteenth century spelled out the liability of finders and of receivers by mistake, and relatively invisible acts of misbehavior – such as appropriating lost goods when "reasonably believing" that the owner could be found, or making no effort to return a bank overpayment – became criminal for the first time during the first two-thirds of the century.[40] In other words, outwardly innocent preparations and takings, which the law had previously ignored, could now, if accompanied by a prohibited state of mind, turn out to be criminal. "Crime" began earlier and extended more widely. Such criminalizing of intentions was not only an expression of capitalist interests in more thoroughly protecting property rights, it was also a form of "character building," for it demanded greater "farsightedness," that is, more internalizing of the consequential mentality, throughout the population.

The criminal law increasingly penalized popular recklessness. Even in cases where specific harm had not been intended, heedless, impulsive behavior was being ever more punished; not necessarily by overriding the rule of intent, but by reinterpreting it. The duty of "reasonable care" was being read into a growing number of situations. Already in the second half of the eighteenth century, the proportion of convictions in murder prosecutions was beginning to rise, and even more strikingly, persons charged with manslaughter, who would earlier have been released or been punished very lightly, were becoming more likely to be convicted and imprisoned. John Beattie has perceived "a tougher attitude in the courts toward carelessness that led to death and an anxiety to condemn forms of violence that earlier might have been entirely excused."[41]

Judicial attitudes toward recklessness hardened much further in the nineteenth century. In 1822, the penalties for manslaughter were sub-

[39] Fletcher, "Metamorphosis," 503. This pushing of criminal liability earlier in time, to the stage of conception and preparation of the act, parallels the rise of the executory contract in civil law. As Atiyah has described this latter development, "all contracts came to be seen as consensual . . . binding in their inception. The focal point of contract law shifted from the performance back in time to the 'making' of the contract," in the agreement of the parties, before anything was done about them (*Rise and Fall*, p. 420).

[40] Fletcher, "Metamorphosis," 514–17.

[41] J. M. Beattie, *Crime and the Courts in England 1660–1800*, p. 91.

stantially increased.[42] Moreover, a wider variety of circumstances was being taken to allow an inference of intent to kill – if a deadly weapon were used; if a killing took place in the course of other criminal activity; if a representative of authority (such as a policeman) were attacked; or if death resulted directly from wildly reckless behavior.[43] Legal tolerance for drunkenness was also diminishing. Arrests for public drunkenness rose dramatically through the early and mid-Victorian period. And in cases of homicide, mid-Victorian judges, a recent student of their behavior has noted, "were reluctant to see even chronic alcoholism as precluding malice. . . . Even prisoners with delirium tremens were considered to have retained sufficient reason and self-control to be liable for the consequences of their acts."[44] And even that apostle of noninterference J. S. Mill supported increased criminal sanctions against drunken offenders. Mill urged making drunkenness, in an offender previously convicted of any act of violence under the influence of drink, an aggravating rather than a mitigating factor. "The making himself drunk," Mill pronounced, "in a person whom drunkenness excites to do harm to others, is a crime against others."[45]

[42] James Fitzjames Stephen, *History of the Criminal Law of England* (London, 1883), III, pp. 78–79.

[43] Crime against the person, even without the use of a deadly weapon, could produce the presumption of intent. J. F. Stephen records a typical such case, that of a would-be rapist who stuffed a girl's shawl into her mouth to stifle her cries for help. She suffocated and he was hanged despite his plea that he had not intended to kill her and that, in Stephen's words, "by doing so he frustrated his own object." *History of the Criminal Law, III,* p. 83.

[44] G. R. Chadwick, "Bureaucratic Mercy: The Home Office and the Prerogative of Mercy in Britain, 1860–1910," Ph.D. dissertation, Rice University, 1990, p. 410. Of course, while denied the status of an excuse voiding criminal liability, drunkenness was nonetheless frequently taken (by magistrates more than by judges) to be a mitigating factor in awarding punishment. However, those convicted of murder who claimed drunkenness as an excuse or mitigating factor were very unlikely to be saved from hanging, unless the victim was also drunk. The case of Joseph Bannister is suggestive: In 1877 Bannister killed his wife with a coal ax that he had taken to bed with him, and pleaded insanity. Although the Home Office acknowledged that he had delirium tremens, he was convicted and executed; he presumably demonstrated intent by carrying his ax to bed. By comparison, see this instance reported in the *Gentleman's Magazine* for 1748: "At a Christening at Beddington in Surrey the nurse was so intoxicated that after she had undressed the child, instead of laying it in the cradle, she put it behind a large fire, which burnt it to death in a few minutes. She was examined before a magistrate, and said she was quite stupid and senseless, so that she took the child for a log of wood; on which she was discharged." (Quoted in Roy Porter, "The Drinking Man's Disease: The 'Pre-History' of Alcoholism in Georgian Britain," *British Journal of Addiction 80* [1985], 387.)

[45] *On Liberty* (1859), ed. David Spitz (New York: W. W. Norton, 1975), p. 90. Criminal prosecution of drunkards rose sharply in the decade after Mill wrote.

Impulsive killings – whether while intoxicated or in the heat of passionate reaction to insult – were ever less excused by the bench. Judges were coming to expect a greater degree of self-control, particularly of men. In 1852, Mr. Justice Cresswell, rejecting an accused wife-murderer's plea for reduction of the charge to manslaughter by reason of provocation by taunting language, observed that not only did words form no justification, but death produced by a willful and unprovoked blow was murder, although the blow may have been given in a moment of passion or intoxication.[46] Mr. Justice Keating reiterated the point in an 1869 murder case with a male victim: "Mere [taunting] words, or gestures . . . will not, in point of law, be sufficient to reduce the crime to manslaughter." He rejected the defense that "the prisoner was under the influence of ungovernable passion at the time he struck the blow." Keating observed that

> when the law says that it allows for the infirmity of human nature, it does not say that if a man, without sufficient provocation, gives way to angry passion, and does not use his reason to control it – the law does not say that an act of homicide, intentionally committed under the influence of that passion, is excused or reduced to manslaughter. The law contemplates the case of a reasonable man, and requires that the provocation shall be such as that such a man might naturally be induced, in the anger of the moment, to commit the act. . . . I can discover no proof of such provocation in the evidence.[47]

The "reasonable man" of the Victorian judiciary was more difficult to provoke than had been his Georgian grandfather.

Criminal liability for dangerous behavior grew in negative as well as positive forms. Judges were finding it less acceptable for defendants simply to refrain from the positive doing of harm – more and more, duty was being extended to the taking of precautions and care. Many "strict liability" judgments around midcentury can be understood as not dispensing with the notion of intent, but expanding it to embrace an understood "duty of care." In 1846, a tradesman's lack of knowledge that the tobacco he was selling was adulterated proved

[46] *R. v. Noon* (1852), 6 Cox Crim. Cases 137; the jury, probably focusing on the defendant's apparent drunkenness, found manslaughter. In this area practice was slow to come into line with principle: The taunts of "bad" wives or tavern fellows were frequently allowed as provocation in assault and homicide cases. Nonetheless, the trend through the Victorian era was clearly in the direction of more severe prosecution of such violence.

[47] *R. v. Welsh* (1869) 11 Cox Crim. Cases 336; the prisoner was found guilty and sentenced to death.

insufficient to prevent his conviction. "A prudent man who conducts this business," Chief Baron Pollock observed, "will take care to guard against" such prosecution by examining his goods, or by taking a guaranty from his supplier.[48] Henceforth, tradesmen had greater incentive to become "prudent men." Like "reasonableness," the standard of what constituted "prudence" was rising. Where the criterion of intent was kept, broader standards of behavior were frequently read into it. In an 1848 case, Mr. Justice Coleridge found a neglect of duty by a railway signalman grave enough to constitute a proper charge of manslaughter; the man was convicted.[49] Similarly, two years later, Chief Justice Lord Campbell found that, in a case of a coalpit lift operator, "an act of omission, as well as of commission, may be so criminal as to be the subject of an indictment for manslaughter."[50]

Like the criminal law, punishment was also reconstructed in the war on impulse. Both corporal and capital punishment came under attack. Although the suffering inflicted upon the convicted offender by flogging or hanging was decried, the deepest objection was to the effects upon spectators. Legal violence – like the private violence of the duel – was increasingly felt to be socially dangerous, worsening popular character by legitimating the public expression of violent passions. The whipping post and especially the gallows, by their pornographic spectacle of violence, were seen as stimulating rather than subduing the passions, disordering the minds of spectators and calling forth just such scenes of saturnalia as would confirm the fears of character reformers. Physical punishments, it was argued, spread violence through society: as Dickens remarked, "it is bad for a people to be familiarised with such punishments. . . . The whip is a very contagious kind of thing, and difficult to confine within one set of bounds."[51]

In 1816 the use of the pillory was seriously restricted by statute, and abolished in 1837. In 1820 an act restricted corporal punishment to men. In 1862 public whipping was absolutely prohibited, while

[48] *R. v. Woodrow* (1846), 15 M. & W. 404.

[49] *R. v. Pargeter* (1848), 3 Cox Crim. Cases 191; clearly, however, the defendant was not felt to be as censurable as if he had possessed some more straightforward intent to harm – his sentence was three months' imprisonment.

[50] *R. v. Lowe* (1850), 4 Cox Crim. Cases 449; this man, too, was found guilty.

[51] "Lying Awake," *Household Words,* October 30, 1852, quoted in Philip Collins, *Dickens and Crime* (Bloomington: Indiana University Press, 1962), p. 255.

the remaining corporal punishment was for the first time subjected to specific statutory regulations governing the number of strokes that could be ordered and the manner of their infliction.[52] Even more than public floggings, a public execution was "a disgusting spectacle . . . *shocking* to humanity." "We are," the leading reformer Samuel Romilly declared in 1813, "so constituted by nature, that such spectacles of horror are seldom beheld by any person with impunity." The popular appeal of executions, once an accepted part of their purpose, now frightened many, all the more as economic development was – through the growth of towns and the building of railways – encouraging ever larger execution crowds.[53] Reformers repeatedly denounced "the love of excitement" that nourished the gallows.[54] Even conservatives were becoming uneasy about this; a majority of the more than twelve thousand spectators present in 1845 at the execution of William Howell, the highly respectable *Morning Post* noted unhappily (though while recounting the day's events at considerable length), were "females and boys."[55]

In his 1840 essay "Going to See a Man Hanged" the novelist W. M. Thackeray expressed revulsion not so much at the possible injustice done to the prisoner but at the psychological effect on the spectators. He described the "hideous debauchery" of a public hanging in terms of a pornographic exhibition, a public loss of control over the passions, and an invasion of the integrity of the body, incited by govern-

[52] Leon Radzinowicz and Roger Hood, *A History of English Criminal Law and Its Administration from 1750, Volume 5: The Emergence of Penal Policy* (London: Stevens, 1986), p. 689. Military flogging, traditionally very harsh, began to diminish in the 1820s and fell rapidly in the 1830s (John Dinwiddy, "The Early Nineteenth-Century Campaign Against Flogging in the Army," *English Historical Review 97* [1982], 308–31). In the ancient public schools the frequency and public character of flogging began in the 1830s to abate. At Eton, John Chandos has noted, "gradually flogging ceased to be a literally public entertainment. From crowding into the library to witness the fun, intending spectators had to view or hear the proceedings from outside the door. Then, from about the 1860s, the door was shut and execution became a private event" (*Boys Together: English Public Schools 1800–1864* [London: Hutchinson, 1984], p. 245).

[53] On the enormous – and growing? – popularity of public hangings in the first half of the nineteenth century, see J. M. Golby and A. W. Purdue, *The Civilization of the Crowd: Popular Culture in England 1750–1900* (London: Batsford, 1984), p. 83.

[54] Basil Montagu, *Thoughts upon the Abolition of the Punishment of Death in Cases of Bankruptcy* (1821), quoted in Randall McGowen, "A Powerful Sympathy: Terror, the Prison, and Humanitarian Reform in Early Nineteenth Century Britain," *Journal of British Studies* 25 (1986), 313.

[55] *Morning Post,* January 27, 1845, p. 8.

ment itself.[56] Thackeray's fellow novelist Dickens also "was haunted," Philip Collins has observed, "as much by the bestiality of the crowd as by the obscenity of hanging."[57] In *Barnaby Rudge* (1841), Dickens had shown the extremes meeting, as Dennis, the public hangman, became a leading rioter. The bestial mob of the Gordon Riots was intertwined with and intimately related to the brutal, impulsive Hanoverian state.

Like these traditional punishments, transportation of convicts overseas was coming to appear socially demoralizing. The chairman of the 1838 Select Committee on Transportation, William Molesworth, declared that in Australia

> every kind and gentle feeling of human nature is constantly outraged by the perpetual spectacle of punishment and misery – by the frequent infliction of the lash – by the gangs of slaves in irons – by the horrid details of the penal settlements; till the heart of the [free] immigrant is gradually deadened to the sufferings of others. . . . The whole system of transportation violates the feelings of the adult, barbarizes the habits, and demoralizes the principles of the rising generation; and the result is, to use the expression of a public newspaper, "Sodom and Gomorrah."[58]

Moreover, his committee argued, the convict system's reliance on physical punishments only confirmed the convict's existing enslavement to "animal indulgences." Such reliance "rendered him mentally incapable of looking beyond the present moment, and confined his ideas to the feelings of the next instant." Yet because it was "precisely this habit . . . of disregarding the distant consequences of their actions, which chiefly lead men into the commission of crimes," the existing system was counterproductive.[59]

In 1868, six years after the abolition of public whipping, the spectacle at the apex of traditional punishment, the public hanging, was

[56] "Going to See A Man Hanged," in *Works,* 23 (London: J. M. Dent, n.d.), pp. 106–7.

[57] *Dickens and Crime,* p. 240.

[58] Extract from Molesworth's notes on the Select Committee Report, quoted in Robert Hughes, *The Fatal Shore* (New York: Knopf, 1987), p. 494.

[59] *Report from the Select Committee on Transportation* 1838 [PP 1837–8 XXII], xxii–xxiii. Instead, the government of convicts should aim at "teaching them to look forward to the future and remote effects of their own conduct, and to be guided in their actions by their reasons, instead of merely by their animal instincts and desires" [xliv]. This committee's membership included three Home Secretaries.

ended (although private executions continued undiminished).[60] At the same time, the government step by step backed away from transportation, until, a few months before the last public hanging, the last convict ship departed English shores for Western Australia. By the 1860s, all the penalties that had made up nearly the entire arsenal of Old Regime criminal sentences – the pillory, the whipping post, the gallows and the convict ship – were extinguished. All had come to appear demoralizing in their "arbitrariness" and their tendency to incite dangerous passions. In their place were being put new, more measured forms of secluded punishment that would appeal to the capacity of calculation rather than the passions, to the imagination rather than the senses.

Once the public character of the penalties was done away with, the movements against both corporal and capital punishment rapidly lost strength. Executions were carried out at a remarkably constant rate, of about fifteen per year, from midcentury to World War I.[61] Whipping as a penalty actually revived after its public administration was prohibited in 1862, starting with the Garroters Act of the following year. Similarly, of course, the ending of transportation did not lessen either the severity or the duration of the penal experience. The new sentence of penal servitude replaced periods of bondage in Australia with equivalent or longer periods of incarceration in England. This turn of events powerfully suggests that what had been most widely upsetting about these penalties (beyond the ranks of committed humanitarians) had not been so much the fact of infliction of bodily pain or death upon malefactors but its visibility, and the psychological consequences that were felt to flow from that act of witness. Once out of sight, such penalties fell out of mind.

What replaced the comparatively open and variable Hanoverian mode of penality was the new closed and invariant regime of reformed prisons. Those who were hanged or whipped were now so treated behind prison walls; those who would have been shipped overseas, or publicly punished and then released, were now incarcer-

[60] See Leon Radzinowicz, *History of English Criminal Law and Its Administration, Volume 4* (London: Stevens, 1968), pp. 343–53; David D. Cooper, *The Lesson of the Scaffold: The Public Execution Controversy in Victorian England* (London: Allen Lane, 1974).

[61] Annual criminal statistics.

ated. Existing prisons lost their comparatively "open" character, as the high degree of access of the public to them, and even of their inmates to the outer world, was removed.[62] As the prison would withdraw punishment from public gaze, it would become a "school of moral discipline," that is, a training ground for, and a social representation of, the overcoming of immediate impulses and passions and the reconstruction of character. If consequentialism were to become a psychic reality rather than only a moral philosophy, the future had to be made as foreseeable as possible. There was little point in reducing the uncertainties in apprehension, trial, and sentencing if disposal thereafter were to continue to be random. To produce the effect now sought on criminal and public character, sentences had to be carried out uniformly from jail to jail. Impersonality was a central premise – and promise – of such policies. Uniformity would banish personal vagaries from criminal justice. After 1839, personal relations, whether friendly or hostile, between prisoners and staff were reduced to a minimum: Warders were forbidden to talk to prisoners (other than to give orders), or to get closer than six feet to them. Nor were even warders to talk among themselves.[63] Like prisoners, prison staff were to be constrained by new institutional rules. A new, self-disciplining character ideal was set for them as well: "The humanity of the gaoler should rather be the result of coldness of character than the effect of a quick sensibility. . . . He should be endowed with a patience which obstinacy the most pertinacious could not overcome; a sense of order which is method, rather mechanical than reflective."[64]

[62] See Michael Ignatieff, *A Just Measure of Pain: The Penitentiary in the Industrial Revolution, 1750–1850* (New York: Pantheon Books, 1978); Margaret Delacy, *Prison Reform in Lancashire, 1700–1850: A Study in Local Administration* (Stanford, Calif.: Stanford University Press, 1986); Sean McConville, *A History of English Prison Administration, Volume I: 1750–1877* (Boston: Routledge, 1981); Robin Evans, *The Fabrication of Virtue: English Prison Architecture 1750–1840* (Cambridge: Cambridge University Press, 1982).

[63] See Philip Priestley, *Victorian Prison Lives: English Prison Biography 1830–1914* (London: Methuen, 1985), pp. 255–56, passim.

[64] G. O. Paul, *Considerations on the Defects of Prisons* (1784), p. 54, quoted in Ignatieff, *Just Measure,* p. 104. The Reverend Daniel Nihil praised the separate system that, "by taking away the danger of collision [between warders and prisoners]," reduced the need for fear-inducing warders and was thus "calculated to raise up a new class of prison officers, both men and women, whose chief qualifications will be rather of a moral than of a physical order" (*Prison Discipline in Its Relations to Society and Individuals* [London: Hatchard, 1839], p. 63).

Bentham similarly sought to remove personality from punishment, to the point of envisaging a whipping machine, a rotary flail made of canes and whalebone, which could be made to lash the backs of each offender with the same unvarying force to a preset number of strokes.[65] As Michael Ignatieff observed, "in his conception of pain . . . what was rational was impersonal, and what was impersonal was humane."[66] In general, by the time prison reorganization got under way on a national level, power had come to be seen as most legitimate and most effective when least personal, most "humane" when least "human." As in the courtroom and the police (and, indeed, the "self-acting" New Poor Law), the element of personality was in retreat in the penal world.

The first official prison inspectors, William Crawford and Whitworth Russell, in their influential reports between 1836 and 1846, insisted in a variety of ways that, as Sean McConville has put it, "prison management approached perfection in the same measure as it succeeded in eliminating the human element."[67] These urgings, we can now appreciate, stemmed not from inhumanity but from a deep distrust of human nature: these prison inspectors feared all discretionary power, and sought to circumscribe and delimit it as far as possible. They insisted that discipline must not be influenced, either toward strictness or toward lenity, by the character of the persons by whom it was administered. A good penal system, they argued in 1838, possessed the "capacity of being administered with *exact uniformity* in every prison, unaffected by the diversity of character and disposition which must be expected in the keepers and subordinate officers of the various establishments."[68]

With successive prison acts in 1864, 1865, and 1877, the principles of uniformity and predictability were enshrined in prison administration. A prison became an extremely, almost minutely, regulated environment, in which each inhabitant, prisoner or staff, would know the rules, applicable to all, by which life was governed.[69] By 1885, the

[65] "Principles of Penal Law: Part II: Rationale of Punishment" (1830), *Works of Jeremy Bentham* (Edinburgh: William Tait, 1834), p. 415.

[66] *Just Measure*, p. 76.

[67] McConville, *History*, p. 246.

[68] Quoted in ibid., p. 246, n. 90.

[69] One provision of the 1865 act was for each cell to contain an approved abstract of the many regulations and a copy of the dietary, and a prisoner unable to read was to

head of the now unified prison system could observe that "a sentence of penal servitude is, in its main features, and so far as it concerns the punishment, applied on exactly the same system to every person subjected to it. The previous career and character of the prisoner makes no difference in the punishment to which he is subjected."[70] The Victorian transformation of the prison experience was complete.

Along with becoming predictable, punishment was to be removed from the overly exciting public stage. The prison was well suited for this aim also. The search for means of diminishing the distractions and disruptions of the distrusted personal element in punishment gave a new importance to architecture. Bentham's Panopticon is well known as the archetype of the prison as carefully designed machine. More generally, proponents of separation like the Reverend Daniel Nihil, chaplain and governor of the first national penitentiary, Millbank, turned enthusiastically to physical design, arguing that correct prison design allowed the prison building itself to provide the necessary discipline and take the place of naked force, thus calming rather than inflaming its inmates. Walls would take the place of guards: "Let the hindrances to enjoyment consist of passive and inanimate obstacles, which cannot be made subject to hostility."[71] At the same time, architecture offered aid to solving the new dilemma of how to deter without demoralizing. As Nihil put it, the pains of imprisonment had to be "sufficient to imbue the mind of the community with an abiding consciousness that crime drags punishment after it; and if all the details of suffering be not exposed to public gaze, enough at least should be unveiled to set the imagination at work, and to awaken mysterious and salutory awe."[72] Architecture was especially suited to setting the imagination at work: the necessary pain of punishment, rather than being publicly *displayed* with the ensuing moral dangers, could be *represented* by gloomy, forbidding prison design, especially in exteriors evocative of bastilles. Thus could pun-

have these documents read to him within twenty-four hours of his admission. "There was no excuse," W. L. Burn has observed, "for anyone in any prison not to know his duties, rights and obligations" (*The Age of Equipoise: A Study of the Mid-Victorian Generation* [London: Allen & Unwin, 1964], p. 185).

[70] Edmund Du Cane, *The Punishment and Prevention of Crime* (London: Macmillan, 1885), p. 155.

[71] Nihil, *Prison Discipline,* p. 59. On how architecture was made a significant part of penal policy, see Evans, *The Fabrication of Virtue.*

[72] Nihil, *Prison Discipline,* p. 6.

ishment be internalized and secluded from public passions and still operate on the public imagination.

In the last quarter of the century, the success of the Victorian reconstruction of criminal justice (and of other, related, social policies like the New Poor Law) and, more generally, the spread of an ethos of "respectability" through the populace, diminished fears of reckless passion. In the new, more ordered society, fears of "unlicensed appetites" and "bold, rebellious wills" waned. Such behavior was coming to appear aberrant, rather than expectable in the absence of countering forces. With its root concerns fading, the Victorian discourse of crime and punishment began to lose its "self-evident" quality.

At the same time, continuing economic and technological development was altering capitalism in ways that further reduced the transparency of this discourse. Reorganization came to predominate over disorganization; economic, social, and political life began to be institutionalized and bureaucratized, reducing the scope of individual action and the sense of individual potency. "Managerial" or "collectivist" capitalism began to replace its more individualist early-nineteenth-century forms. The ever-increasing scale and complexity of life left the individual feeling smaller and less effectual, except as part of an institution. As novel technology and the expanding market extended the effective reach of actions, the first psychic effect – a dissolving of old constraints and a sense of expanded powers and potentialities – gradually gave way to growing uncertainty about one's own autonomy. As the effective reach and force of one's own actions grew, so too did the reach and force of others', to impinge upon oneself. The giddy sense of unleashed powers that had excited, and frightened, middle-class early Victorians, was being countered, as the century progressed, by a sense of subjection to the actions of remote others, actions that became increasingly crystallized into impersonal forces. The sharply focused contest between "character" and criminality dissolved.

As pre-Victorian penal discourse, rooted in a comparatively stable, hierarchical, local, and "face-to-face" society, had become unintelligible to early Victorians, so did Victorian penal discourse, with its focus upon rules, discipline, and character building, become to the children of the Victorians. By the 1920s, indeed, the retired reformist head of the Prison Commission could look back on the system he had taken over in 1895 with the same contempt his early Victorian predecessors had bestowed upon the regime they had inherited:

> It seemed to be assumed [Sir Evelyn Ruggles-Brise scornfully observed] that the wit of man could devise no other method of punishment than by deprivation of liberty, by bolts and bars, and darkened cells, and all those devices of regulation and routine on which so much ingenuity was wasted since the day when Howard first called attention to the awful cruelty and barbarism of the prison methods of his day.[73]

Yet perhaps moralist–disciplinarian criminal policy was as understandable a response to the new social forces of the early nineteenth century as the welfarist–collectivist criminal policy of Ruggles-Brise's successors was to the altered social circumstances of the early twentieth century. By now, both have become historical artifacts.

[73] Evelyn Ruggles-Brise, *Prison Reform at Home and Abroad* (London: Macmillan, 1925), p. 10. He continued: "The size and structure of the cell; the form of labour . . . scale of dietary, so nicely adjusted according to the length of sentence, as if the weight of the body were a greater concern and business for the State than the saving of the soul; rules of discipline, by which every movement was regulated according to plan, and woe betide the wretch who deflected by an inch from the prescribed path of conduct. . . . a multitude of details which now seem to us foolish and unnecessary."

PART II

Personality and authority in the age of capital

CHAPTER 5

New cultural heroes in the early national period

JOYCE APPLEBY

This essay poses some questions about a cluster of individuals who grew to manhood during the first three decades of the nineteenth century. Common, but not shared, experiences permit me to speak of them as a group. They responded to opportunities that took them away from home, and through a series of individual choices they made themselves agents of the remarkable changes transforming America. In that first generation after 1789 a society oriented around the free-market economy took shape in America. Because the men in the cluster wrote autobiographies, the personal element in this great enterprise can be explored. To bring the drama of their historical moment into better focus, I want to look briefly at the work of the social theorists Max Weber and Colin Campbell, both of whom have recognized how familiarity with the outcomes of historic change has masked the problematical nature of the origins of our modern, entrepreneurial society.

When Max Weber entitled his classic study *The Protestant Ethic and the Spirit of Capitalism,* he wrenched two terms from their well-understood context and threw them into a frame of reference utterly unexpected and hence provocative. Ethics had theretofore belonged to a secular inquiry about proper behavior, usually associated with a particular profession, whereas spirit evoked religious or poetic connotations..Neither seemed appropriate for discussions of capitalism that referred to a system of practical enactments designed to move labor, land, and their products into optimal channels for profitable distribution. Whether approached as the material manifestation of Western civilization's progress or as evidence of bourgeois dominance in a system of class exploitation, capitalism figured in scholarly debates as part of the accessible world of concrete objects and transparent intentions. The human predispositions that animated economic development were unproblematic in both liberal and socialist interpretations – either a universal drive for self-improvement expressed through the urge to truck and barter, or the will to power of a ruling class taking advantage of new means of production.

Weber redirected attention to the invisible realm of cultural patterns and personal motivations. His genius lay with his insistence that these areas held the key to understanding that most striking of social transformations: the passage of Western nations into modernity. A critical question needed to be framed: How had men (women do not figure in his analysis), reared to respond to a traditional set of social imperatives, been able to incorporate into their lives the exotic values of capitalism? In an effort to defamiliarize the profit motive, Weber had penned his famous line that "man does not by nature wish to earn more and more money but simply to live as he is accustomed and to earn as much as is necessary for that purpose."[1] Rejecting Adam Smith's claim that people carried an inherent impulse toward self-improvement, Weber asserted that human nature does not manifest itself in universal drives, but expresses itself according to the mores of a particular society. One cannot explain capitalism by invoking behavioral patterns that are themselves the consequences of the capitalist era. The historical sequence is out of order. Thus, Weber thrust to the foreground of social inquiry the puzzle of how a traditional society could incubate modern qualities before they were generally admired. But first he had to establish the relevance of socially constructed values in a world not yet attuned to the concepts of culture, ideology, and discourse.

Weber's answer to the question of how traditional society could have promoted alternative ethical perspectives was that it had done so adventitiously and ironically – in the actual case of capitalism, through the unintended consequences of a religious experience powerful enough to break the hold of ingrained customs. It was his Protestants' ardent embrace of a calling, their pleasure-deferring self-discipline, their obsessive rationality, their stern defiance of tradi-

[1] Max Weber, *The Protestant Ethic and the Spirit of Capitalism,* trans. Talcott Parsons, New York, 1958, p. 60.

tional norms, that enabled them to work, save, invest, and produce. Slow to win support, Weber's thesis and its intellectual implications have collected respect as more mechanical explanations for social transformations have lost appeal. Anticipating the late-twentieth-century engagement with cultural mediations, Weber moved questions about external change into the interior realm of human imagination and motivation.

Recently, scholarly attention has passed to the demand side of the economic equation. And again the same epistemological problem must be confronted: how to create curiosity about those social qualities essential to a particular change that are taken for granted after they achieve dominance. Colin Campbell's theoretical exploration of the dynamic behind consumption offers a counterpoise to Weber's classic study. Just as Weber rejected the presumptive logic of the profit motive, so Campbell has scorned the naturalness of people's wanting to consume more and more. As he has stressed, "in non-literate and pre-industrial societies, consumption, like other aspects of life, is largely governed by custom and tradition, and these forces specify a fixed rather than an open-ended notion of wants."[2]

Paying playful tribute to Weber in his title, *The Romantic Ethic and the Spirit of Modern Consumerism,* Campbell has also rejected the conventional scholarly explanations of consumption, that is, that the newly marketed goods offered the means for ordinary people to emulate their social superiors. The insatiable desire for goods, like the wish for more money, represents a profound restructuring of social sensibilities. According to Campbell, consumption as a way of life requires that emotions dominate individual consciousness, attaching themselves to images of pleasure-seeking and self-fashioning through new possessions. Just because the impulse to consume springs from daydreams rather than material wants, it can never be slaked. Modern hedonism, Campbell says, springs from the shift in modern consciousness away from visceral and instant sensations to the more cerebral and imaginative world of the emotions. Like Weber again, he connects this shift to Protestant piety and its peculiar form of sentimentality, individualism, escape, melancholy and fantasy. Displaced onto the plane of the imagined, Campbell explains, consump-

[2] Colin Campbell, *The Romantic Ethic and the Spirit of Modern Consumerism,* Oxford, 1987, pp. 39, 39, 73–74, 88–89.

tion takes on a restless, searching quality that accounts for endlessly repetitive rounds of illusory experience, actual purchases, and inevitable dissatisfaction.

Both Weber and Campbell start with the conundrum that the innovators of capitalism's new productive and consuming activities grew up with values that should have inhibited the elaboration of an expanding commercial system. What is most taken for granted after the new cultural imperatives have been established becomes the phenomenon most in need of explanation for the period before the change. I have introduced Weber and Campbell to orient the reader toward the invisible realm of individual consciousness. My question has focused on the creative destruction – to use Joseph Schumpeter's term – of stable ways of life and their replacement by expectations of sustained innovation and repeated new beginnings: How did those men most directly connected with creating America's commercial society in the early nineteenth century arrive at a constructive appraisal of the constant disruption and uncertainty that attended their lives?

The elaboration of a national market depended on many, many young men leaving the place of their birth and trying their hand at new careers. I am talking now not about the mobilization of labor but of entrepreneurial talents, defined best as the ability to take on novel economic undertakings as personal ventures. The range and sweep of enterprise in this period are awesome, suggesting the widespread willingness to be uprooted, to embark on an uncharted course of action, to take risks with one's resources – above all the resource of one's youth. This receptivity to change cannot be taken for granted, nor does it fit neatly into the analytical categories of production or consumption.

Commercialization and democratization occurred simultaneously in the early decades of the nineteenth century. The establishment of the new government under the Constitution in 1789 coincided with an economic turnaround marking the end of the post–Revolutionary War depression. The funding of the Revolutionary debt executed by Alexander Hamilton created a new pool of capital. The United States also became a safe place for European investors just when the wars of the French Revolution increased demand for American goods and shipping. Had the Federalists passed on their power to like-minded men, the course of economic development would have been guided by government officials attentive to the nation's financial leaders. The intertwined social and economic perceptions of a national elite would have informed policies for the country as a whole. Instead a new political movement explicitly hostile to the exercise of social authority triumphed with the election of Thomas Jefferson in 1800.

As president, Jefferson dismantled the Federalist fiscal program, paying off the debt, reducing taxes, cutting the size of the civil service, and letting the bank charter lapse while popularizing a strict constructionist view of the Constitution. Thus, the fiscal stability achieved in Washington's administrations redounded to the benefit of ordinary men intent on liberating themselves from the restraining control of hierarchical institutions. After Jefferson became president, land sales soared, going from 67,751 acres in 1800 to 497,939 in 1801.[3] Land in the national domain continued to pass into private hands at an annual rate near 500,000 acres. For the next half century the states, shorn by the Constitution of the power to block economic development, took the lead in promoting it, building an infrastructure of banks, roads, and canals while offering bounties, licenses, and charters for promising economic ventures.[4] The genie of popular commercial activity had been let out of the bottle of material limitations and social constraints.

The unity created by the Constitution enabled the new nation to expel the native Americans who lay in the path of territorial expansion. Continued population growth in Europe raised the price of all foodstuffs and created strong incentives for American farmers to plant for the market. More and more of them, even in frontier areas, were drawn into the international trade networks of the Atlantic. Simultaneously, thousands of new manufacturing ventures provided domestic markets for the produce of American farms. The digest of patents put together by the first commissioner of patents reveals just how early American ingenuity began to change the rural landscape with inventions in metallurgy, chemical processes, civil engineering,

[3] Noble E. Cunningham, Jr., *The Process of Government Under Jefferson,* Princeton, 1978, p. 107. See also Arthur H. Cole, "Cyclical and Sectional Variations in the Sale of Public Land," *Review of Economic and Statistics,* 9 (1927), 50.

[4] L. Ray Gunn, *The Decline of Authority: Public Economic Police and Political Development in New York State, 1880–1860,* Ithaca, N.Y., 1988, offers a fascinating account of this process in one state.

grinding mills, hydraulic implements, machine tools, and household conveniences.[5]

Equally impressive was the laying out of new towns and the growth of old cities, especially those of the mid-Atlantic states. We are used to thinking of mushrooming communities on the frontier; what we fail to appreciate is that older towns with growth rates of more than 50 percent per decade were virtually newly fashioned in terms of people, institutions, and the construction of houses, stores, and workplaces. Commerce set the pace for development in the first three decades of the nineteenth century as merchants and shopkeepers scoured the urban hinterlands for the food, fibers, and skins that could be processed into marketable goods for their stores. Although international trade paced American economic growth between 1793 and 1808, domestic consumption led the way in stimulating the American antebellum economy, even taking into account the high level of cotton exports.[6] With commerce came an intensified flow of information as well as goods. The 96 newspapers in 1790 multiplied to 376 twenty years later. In 1810 Americans were buying 22 million newspapers annually, the largest aggregate circulation of any country in the world. Ten years later, the number of newspapers published in America had more than doubled, with literacy expanding apace.[7]

To foreigners, American society offered an ever-changing landscape as people moved, roads were graded, land cleared, and buildings raised in a reconfiguration of the material environment that went on unabated. Two French witnesses have left evocative descriptions of this perpetual-motion society. The Duc de La Rochefoucauld-Liancourt spent thirty-three months in the United States between 1795 and 1797, thirteen of them traveling through the rural areas of New England, Pennsylvania, and New York. What overwhelmed him was the restlessness of Americans. "It is a country in flux; that which is true today as regards its population, its establishments, its prices,

[5] Henry L. Ellsworth, *A Digest of Patents Issued by the United States, from 1790 to January 1, 1839,* Washington, D.C., 1840. See also Kenneth Sokoloff, "Inventive Activity in Early Industrial America: Evidence from Patent Records, 1790–1846," *Journal of Economic History,* 48 (December 1988), 813–50.

[6] Allan R. Pred, *Urban Growth and the Circulation of Information,* Cambridge, Mass., 1973, pp. 107–9.

[7] William Gilmore, "Literacy, The Rise of an Age of Reading, and the Cultural Grammar of Print Communications in America, 1735–1850," *Communication,* 1988 special issue.

its commerce will not be true six months from now." At every tavern La Rochefoucauld encountered farmers on the move to some other place. Mindful of the contrast between their light-footedness and his own countrymen's love of home, he tried to get Americans to comment on this difference by describing the French sense of *propriété,* the word he used to convey their identification with a particular piece of ground. Americans, he reported, could imagine such an attachment, but inevitably they would ask if it did not reveal a lack of enterprise.[8] Thirty years later another perceptive French observer – the young Michel Chevalier – covered much the same territory, geographically and culturally, responding philosophically to the constant churning of Americans:

> If movement and the quick succession of sensations and ideas constitute life, here one lives a hundred fold more than elsewhere; here, all is circulation, motion, and boiling agitation. Experiment follows experiment; enterprise follows enterprise. Riches and poverty follow on each other's traces and each in turn occupies the place of the other.[9]

Better than Americans themselves these foreign observers saw the convergence of novelties in the United States: a new constitutional order accompanied by a reconceptualization of the body politic; the elaboration of national market networks coinciding with technological transformations in manufacturing processes; the creation of a new civil society accelerated and shaped by a revolution in literacy and publishing. The thickening of commercial links and the intensification of manufacturing investment proceeded alongside striking rates of population growth and the dispersal of that population westward. A greater proportion of the American population lived on the frontier in 1810 than at any time before or since.

For Europeans the astounding fact about America was the presence of social order in the absence of social solidarity. Their wonder at this tells us something of the uniqueness of the transformation of a society undertaken by individuals. Like the disposition to earn more money or the propensity to make consumption a major facet of life,

[8] David J. Brandenburg, "A French Aristocrat Looks at American Farming," *Agricultural History,* 32 (1958), 162–63.

[9] Michel Chevalier, *Society, Manners, and Politics in the United States,* John W. Ward, ed., Garden City, N.Y., 1961, p. 299, as cited in L. Ray Gunn, *The Decline of Authority,* Ithaca, N.Y., pp. 10–11.

the functional cohesion of an atomized society cannot be taken for granted, particularly not in a society where everything is in flux and ordinary men and women live "one hundred fold more than elsewhere." The triumphant American ideology itself has obscured the fact that people had to learn to adapt to the ceaseless reallocation of resources and the simultaneous erasure of established ways of living. Indeed, it is another case of explaining a phenomenon by reference to qualities that appeared later. The common interpretation of economic development as progress has predisposed us to anticipate the breakdown of social solidarity and assume the naturalness of people acting as independent agents, moving in and out of voluntary associations while adapting to the impermanence of friends, occupations, and homes. Our histories describe traditional communities only as a prelude to detailing their demise. We are not encouraged to wonder about the personal qualities and practical arrangements that made possible the fashioning of a new social order in the absence of customary ordering mechanisms.

All that was fresh in America existed alongside a rural way of life that embodied centuries-old traditions. To enter the world of novelty was to leave behind a settled order of limited horizons and prescribed rules. I have been posing questions about this movement to a selection of autobiographies written by men who were born between 1765 and 1804. My curiosity has been directed to their personal responses. How, I have asked, did young men, separated from the communities of their youth, acquire the psychological stability and social understanding that permitted them to perform in a society of mobility, novelty, and individualized outcomes?[10] The elaboration and extension of the market in the early decades of the nineteenth century was rapid, unregulated, and marked by sudden reversals of good times and bad. A punishing process of adaptation lay behind the statistics that measure the dynamic economic development of the period. They point to a collective engagement with the speedy exploitation of resources, both human and physical, through private initiatives. Yet the pace of American enterprise was set in large part by the number of men willing to commit

[10] I have integrated these stories with information I have been gathering on voluntary associations formed between 1776 and 1825, the observations from foreign travelers, and the work of other historians of the early republic.

their talents to the effort. How did those men who set out to create a career for themselves deal with the anxiety of risk, and how did they come to terms with success and failure? What roles did other men play in their lives? What affirmations about American society emerge in their reflections about their own histories? Underneath the bustling confusion of a thousand different routes to self-improvement we can see a new set of male ideals emerging. These autobiographies lay bare many of the preconditions for the shifting of loyalties from home and habit to self and progress. They also introduce us to an American entrepreneurial culture in the making.[11]

Too prosaic to be characterized as *Bildungsroman,* these reminiscences nevertheless pivot around the story of a young man making his own way in a society in the process of transformation. The rites of passage to adulthood involve the literal passage away from home. The predominance of this theme suggests that American autobiographies are permanently indebted to the Benjamin Franklin story. Other common features of the autobiographies are worth noting. Their authors were long-lived, more dying in their seventies than any other decadal age. Intuitively this makes sense, for the longer the men lived, the more dramatic the contrast between the world of their youth and that of their old age. The authors also succeeded in establishing families and hence producing the stereotypical prod to memoir writing in the form of an inquisitive child. As prosperous old-timers triumphing over humble beginnings and the biblical dispensation of "three score years and ten," they viewed their lives as successes and took from their success a ratification of the path they followed. Almost all of the autobiographers were northern-born, the preponderance within that group from New England. Because many of them wrote after the Civil War, the absence of an impulse to memorialize a life in the South is not surprising. Although one author coined the neologism "egotistography" for a title, most of them described their

[11] I have relied upon Louis Kaplan, ed., *A Bibliography of American Autobiographies,* Madison, Wis., 1961. My selection of autobiographies is far from a random sampling. Of the 488 written by men and women born between 1765 and 1805, I rejected 300 as irrelevant to my questions. Most of the rejects were written by Protestant clergymen, but there were also in that group the reminiscences of convicted felons and seafaring adventurers. The distribution by denominations indicates that mobility also promoted autobiographical writing among the clergy, for the largest number came from Methodists (42), followed by Baptists (36).

literary effort as something of a task, undertaken with reluctance and dispatched with diffidence. In this connection, it is important to know that these autobiographies were usually published years after their composition, often under the imprimatur of a state historical society.

What can reasonably be extracted from such an untidy body of evidence? There is a great deal of information about how the break with home came about. The creation of a personal identity made during that difficult middle passage from aspiring youth to established adult emerges from these reminiscences as well. Because many of the writers were rural New Englanders, the autobiographies offer clues about the family mores of that much-studied region. Conspicuous too is the autobiographers' conception of character and how it figured in men's lives. Whatever dramatic intensity these narratives possess comes from the readers' awareness that the unformed boy is moving into an equally unformed social environment.

Women's memoirs have been characterized by their depiction of life as a flow of experiences rather than a dramatic account of a life.[12] Their stories often hide the narrator by describing the activities of others. Our sense of gender differences prepares us for this womanly perspective, and the male autobiographies discussed in this essay conform to the distinction. For one thing, they concentrate almost exclusively on a public life. Children figure tangentially in the accounts, which is surprising because the title pages often announce that the memoirs have been prepared for the author's children. The male autobiographies have strong story lines where fresh starts, encounters, and resolutions are most salient. One might schematize them as follows: the unforeseen break with childhood expectations; the wonder of a new life prospect; encounters that teach moral lessons; outcomes and observations. Most of the writers express the belief that their lives have been memorable because of a departure from home that signaled a break with tradition. They perceive their careers to have been fashioned by choice. As they record them, they grope for an understanding of what those choices have revealed about how to conduct one's life.

Let me summarize four such stories. John Ball (1794–1884) grew

[12] Mary Gergen, "Life Stories: Pieces of a Dream," in George Rosenwald and Richard Ochberg, eds., *Storied Lives,* forthcoming, and Domna Stanton, ed., *The Female Autograph,* Chicago, 1984.

up in Hebron, Vermont, an area that had been only recently settled and hence in the remotest part of a remote state. Once a year his father went to Boston to exchange butter and cheese for manufactured items; for all other material needs the family was entirely self-sufficient. Ball formed the intention of leaving home when he was a teenager, accepting without challenge his father's claim to his time until age twenty-one. During his last years at home, he struggled with his father to gain more schooling, and, as he reports, "after much importunity, he consented that I might go into the next town of Groton to a clergyman . . . who kept a kind of private school." Although Hebron was a frontier community, the mold was that of the seventeenth-century settlements with charter families of similar background building farms around a Congregational church. National politics did obtrude with the arrival in 1804 of a Congregational minister inflamed with zeal for the newly elected republicans. This enthusiasm prompted a rebuke from an elder, which Ball carried with him into old age: "Mr. Page, we employ you to preach Jesus Christ and him crucified, but you preach Thomas Jefferson and him justified." Discordant too was the arrival of a "wild religious reformation" brought to town by the Methodists. For Ball the spiritual residue was a skepticism "as to the utility of churches, ministers and all those things."[13]

Crucial to Ball's breakaway from rural New England and its established ways was the decision of his Groton instructor to teach him Latin, an attainment that enabled him to go on to Dartmouth. Perfecting his plans for leaving home, Ball reported the arrangement he made with his older brother whereby "if he would stay and provide well for our parents I would set up no claim from that source," adding that his brother "did stay and worked the old mountain farm while our parents lived." Ball's father lent him a bit of money during his college years, but remained unsympathetic to his desire for an education. Even more remarkable for the era, John's sister, Deborah, also formed a plan for escaping the rural penury of Hebron by learning the tailor's trade, which she plied in nearby Groton.[14] Ball later moved to Troy, New York, where he practiced law for a brief spell before venturing forth as an explorer and land speculator.

[13] John Ball, *Autobiography*, compiled by Kate Ball Powers, Flora Ball Hopkins, and Lucy Ball, Grand Rapids, Mich., 1925, pp. 10–12.
[14] Ball, *Autobiography*, pp. 12–13, 14.

For Samuel Foot (1790–1878) it was soil exhaustion rather than frontier subsistence farming that colored his youth with the dark shades of poverty. Foot's family claimed descent from seventeenth-century founders of Wethersfield, Connecticut. Five generations later his parents eked out a meager existence on a Watertown farm "greatly exhausted by continued cropping." When his father's health gave out, he trained his youngest son, the twelve-year-old Samuel, to take over management of the farm. Seemingly destined for the cycles of plowing, hoeing, cradling, reaping, mowing, and fence mending whose monotonous rounds fashioned his childhood, Foot despaired of his future: "My parents had nothing but the farm, and had been obliged to sell some fifteen acres of that to clear themselves of debt. There seemed to be nothing before me but a life of hard work on the old farm. . . . There appeared to be no hope or prospect of an education for me, nor did I look forward to anything of the kind." Deliverance came with the intervention of his eldest brother, Ebenezer, who arrived back home with a proposal to take fifteen-year-old Samuel on as a law clerk. Like John Ball's father, Foot's parents were unsympathetic to the idea of his leaving home for more schooling. His mother yielded only when her son-in-law agreed to purchase part of the old farm and bring her daughter back to live with them. Ebenezer subsequently arranged for Foot's schooling at Union College, after which – after a long apprenticeship in disciplined and self-denying labors – Foot became a lawyer and then a judge of the New York Court of Appeals.[15]

John Chambers (1780–1852) moved with his family from Pennsylvania to Kentucky after his father had allowed the family farm to fall into ruin. "I was now fourteen years old and my education had been sadly neglected. I could hardly read or write intelligibly, and had passed rapidly and carelessly through the common rules of Arithmetic, and had my language corrupted and mixed up with a sort of 'low' dutch."[16] Chambers's father, characterized as extremely ill-tempered, also took no interest in his son's education. In fact, Chambers remembered deliberately having to ingratiate himself with his father by taking over the care of his cornfield just to secure a roof over his head. When an uncle offered Chambers a legal education in return for

[15] Samuel Foot, *Autobiography,* New York, 1872, p. 11.
[16] John Chambers, *Autobiography,* Iowa City, 1908, pp. 7–8.

clerking in his office, he seized the chance. Swept up in the fervor over the war with Britain in 1812, Chambers became an aide to William Henry Harrison and acquired a patron who eventually appointed him territorial governor of Iowa.

Like Foot, David Dodge (1774–1852) counted Puritan saints among his ancestors. His great-grandfather was a Congregational minister – "a wealthy, learned man" – who settled near Cape Ann. A profligate grandfather dissipated the family fortune, and Dodge's father struggled to find a secure way of life. He undertook to produce "continental wagons" for the revolutionary army and lost his investment in the depreciation of the currency. After the war his parents bought a succession of farms, downgrading in size each time in hopes of escaping the burden of debt that dogged them in their mature years. Dodge recalled how they struggled "with severe labor and rigid economy, to free themselves from debt." In time his father's "spirit of enterprise" seemed to be crushed, by hard service and misfortune. "I, however," he explained to his readers, "being an ambitious lad of about sixteen, was desirous that my parents should sell and move to Western New York, and grow up with some rising village. But they declined, and this led finally to my wandering from home after a season, by their reluctant consent."[17]

Steadily employed as a hired hand, he attended school two months in the winter, but a fortuitous accident left him bedridden, and he decided to study his way out of farming. After the day's work, as he described it, he would "retire to the old kitchen fire-place, put my lamp into the oven, and sitting with my back against it, take my arithmetic, slate and pencil and try to cipher a little." Though still a teenager, Dodge began teaching school and after a year sought a better-paying teaching post in a nearby school district. This provoked his father's opposition and became, as he recalled, "quite a trial as I felt it my duty and desire to comply with his wishes, except in such things as affected my future life." With apparent unawareness of how being a parent had changed his mind, Dodge explained to his own sons that "if I had then possessed my present views of duty to parents, I should have probably learned my father's trade, and lived with him until his descease, being an only son to comfort him."[18] In fact Dodge

[17] David L. Dodge, *Memorial of Mr. David L. Dodge,* Boston, 1854, pp. 19–24.
[18] Dodge, *Memorial,* pp. 34, 45–46.

revealed the characteristic restlessness of the entrepreneur. He turned his self-nurtured love of learning into a career as a teacher from which he was able to launch a successful mercantile enterprise. A pioneer of new retailing techniques, Dodge later tried his hand at manufacturing, pulling back after an initial failure. Having experienced a powerful conversion in one of the revivals sweeping Connecticut in the first decade of the nineteenth century, he became part of the evangelical laity, overseeing the religious life of his clerks and conducting regular prayer meetings for the operatives of his textile factory.[19]

What seems remarkable about these accounts is the display of early independence, with the son's ambition juxtaposed against the father's failure. So dominant a theme suggests a cultural more than a material cause, although the Revolution may have contributed rhetorically and practically to these youthful rebellions. Chambers blamed his father's misfortunes directly on the Revolution: "A man of very remarkable vigor of intellect, prompt and capable," he associated with the officers of the revolutionary army, and "soon fell into intemperate habits (as did a very large proportion of the Officers of the late army). Business was abandoned or so neglected that everything went to ruin."[20]

The Revolution may also have weakened parental authority. Poor parents have never enjoyed the same control over their children as those wealthy enough to exact penalties for insubordination. And the Revolution created more poverty than wealth. Drawing upon family lore, Foot detailed the cost of the Revolution. He reported that his father reponded to every call of the Connecticut militia, and on "two occasions every able-bodied man was taken from Watertown, and my mother was obliged to go into the field and labor to preserve and secure the crops." His parents also suffered from the depreciated currency, a loss Foot captured in his childhood memory of seeing "a large pile of this worthless paper in my father's drawer."[21]

As these autobiographies indicate, the opportunity to quit the family farm is presented as a deliverance. In retrospect, no regret or nostalgia appears. Moving on meant moving out to a larger world.

[19] Ibid., pp. 82–99.
[20] Chambers, *Autobiography,* p. 6.
[21] Foot, *Autobiography,* p. 8.

The remembered hostility of fathers to their sons' ambitions is also arresting. Although Ball depicted his father's resistance to his desire for more schooling with cool detachment, he never reported returning to Hebron to visit his parents. Chambers's dislike of his father retained such a vivacity that the publishers of his autobiography excised passages in which he summed up his father's character. Foot's father disappeared behind his failing health, and it was actually his mother who strove to keep Samuel on the farm, but both parents shared in his remembered resentment.

Fathers were either absent or a disappointing presence. Mothers, on the other hand, figured more positively in these memoirs. Chambers described with great pride his ability at twenty to create a home for his parents. Making his mother comfortable, he reported, was a source of great gratification,

> for I loved & venerated my mother beyond all others of Gods creation, and the arduous & suffering struggle she made to raise her children and keep them together when young, and impress correct principles upon their minds, entitled her to all, and much more than all, I was ever able to do to make her happy.[22]

Ball reflected upon the "the wonderful ability" his mother showed in giving family prayers when his father was absent. "My mother had never been to school at all, but she could read and was very fond of reading, when she could obtain a book and had the time. She had naturally a fine mind, and was ever curious to learn all that could be, within her very limited means. With her aspirations her life was truly hard."[23] Holmes Hinkley, another autobiographer, simply recalled that he never saw much of his father: "I had to rely upon my mother for protection and support, until I was nearly fourteen years old."[24] Foot remembered an interrupted education – "My impression is that I did not go to school in the summer after I was ten years old" – but his mother used "persuasion and reward" to coax him to

[22] Chambers, *Autobiography*, pp. 10–11.

[23] Ball, *Autobiography*, p. 8 See also Walter S. Hinchman, ed., *Holmes Hinkley: An Industrial Pioneer, 1793–1866*, Cambridge, Mass., 1913; Ezra Michener, *Autographical Notes from the Life and Letters of Ezra Michener, M.D.*, Philadelphia, 1893; Thomas Hart Benton, *Thirty Years' View*, New York, 1880, two vols. (originally published 1866); and John W. Bear, *The Life and Travels of John W. Bear*, Baltimore, 1879. An admired father figures in Francis Edwin Corey, *The Autobiography of Francis Edwin Corey*, Chicago, 1892.

[24] *Holmes Hinkley*, pp. 16–17.

read the Bible "through" and learn the Westminster catechism.[25] Thomas Hart Benton described his widowed mother's home as "the abode of temperance, modesty, decorum. A pack of cards was never seen in her house." For this she was rewarded by seeing him taking that place "among the historic men of the country for which she had begun so early to train him," a thought that prompted Benton to suggest that the later life of many men "may depend upon the early cares and guidance of a mother."[26]

More profound than the sentimental admiration for the mother is the denial of the father's contribution to the son's life. What may have begun as a fantasy wish to slay their fathers appears in their life stories as a fait accompli.[27] Thus the autobiographers assumed a command over their narratives that was undoubtedly greater than their command over life. Rendering their fathers as failures was also a way of burning their bridges to a past – a past, moreover, that had prized continuity. Future-oriented even in old age, the autobiographers publicized their shattering of the strongest cultural link binding one generation to another, that of acknowledged respect for a father. If these personal accounts can be construed as the story of America, individualized, then the rejection of the personal authority of the father can be folded into the antiauthoritarian cast of political and religious developments in the new nation.[28] Like the United States, their lives were self-created and self-defined.

Almost without fail in these autobiographical accounts, an older man entered the narrator's life at some critical juncture to suggest schooling, provide credit, or pluck the person from the anonymity of a group of clerks or a cluster of siblings.[29] It is as if the rejected father had to be replaced by another, less entangling male figure, such as a brother, uncle, or family friend. Invariably the rescuer responded to

[25] Foot, *Autobiography,* p. 10.

[26] Benton, *Thirty Years' View,* I:1–iii.

[27] In thinking of the psychoanalytical implications of this conspicuous rejection of fathers, I have been greatly helped by Karl Figlio. A comprehensive exploration of this theme should take into account the birth order of the sons. Dodge and Chambers were only or eldest sons; Foot and Ball were younger ones.

[28] For elaborations of these developments, see Nathan Hatch, *The Americanization of Christianity,* New York, 1989; Richard Brown, *Knowledge Is Power,* New York, 1989; and Joyce Appleby, *Capitalism and a New Social Order: The Republican Vision of the Jeffersonians,* New York, 1984.

[29] George Wallace Jones, "Autobiography," in John Carl Parish, *George Wallace Jones,* Iowa City, 1912; Burton, *Reminiscences;* Chambers, *Autobiography.*

evidence of intelligence. Education was always the passkey to a larger world. Schooling beyond the elemental level of rural competence enabled Ball, Chambers, and Foot to become lawyers. Schooling also offered jobs. Ball worked his way through Dartmouth teaching school, while Dodge earned enough in teaching to launch himself as an auctioneer and retailer. Antoher autobiographer, Anson Jones, left the poor Berkshire farm of his father because he could support himself teaching in country schools while he studied medicine.[30]

The autobiographers emphasized their youthful appreciation of learning, underscoring the role that both intelligence and knowledge had come to play in the social construction of opportunity. Tench Coxe conveyed this well in a political reflection he shared with a correspondent: "Montesquieu spoke not more than half the truth when he affirmed virtue to be the *cardinal principle* of Republics. *Intelligence* in the Body of the people is quite as important."[31] In a more personal vein, the western Pennsylvania political leader William Findley, reminiscing about his life, noted that he had had "one set of acquaintances and they were generally the most intelligent and respectable in the place."[32] More poignantly, Henry Marie Brackenridge recalled that his father, the eccentric Hugh Henry Brackenridge, devoted to his books and business, had taken little notice of young Henry "until he heard very favorable accounts of my capacity."[33]

While the autobiographers acknowledge that it took someone to recognize their native ability, they also point up their own responsiveness to opportunity. "By attention and close application I got to be head man of the place," the inventor Holmes Hinkley reported of his first job in a machine shop.[34] Chambers when he was delivered from an unpromising family situation affirmed his own youthful sense of responsibility: "I applied myself with unremitting attention to the business of the office, and at the end of six months . . . was able to do

[30] Anson Jones, *Memoranda and Official Correspondence Relating to the Republic of Texas,* New York, 1859, pp. 3–5.

[31] Coxe to Nathaniel Gilman, July 23, 1796, as quoted in Jacob E. Cooke, *Tench Coxe and the Early Republic,* Chapel Hill, N.C., 1978.

[32] "William Findley of Westmoreland, Pa.," *Pennsylvania Magazine of History and Biography,* 5 (1881), 440. The memoir appears in a letter to Governor William Plumer of New Hampshire, February 27, 1812.

[33] H. M. Brackenridge, *Recollections of Persons and Places in the West,* Philadelphia, 1868, p. 11.

[34] *Holmes Hinkley,* p. 21.

all the duties of the office with very little instruction from anybody."[35] William Seward recalled unashamedly how nothing could "subdue by aspirations," not even his father's rebuke when he boasted that he wished to match his achievements.[36] After detailing how he wrested a higher salary from a rural teaching district, Dodge rather patronizingly addressed his family readers with a little peroration about his pluck: "Now, dear children, I would not recommend to you for imitation my self-confidence, without important qualifications, for I had been obliged to rely almost wholly upon my own resources, and when I had an object in view I had devoted so much consideration to it that I generally obtained it, and in consequence, I had become too self-sufficient."[37] Such affirmations stand out against the more conventional self-flagellation one finds in diaries. Indeed, Foot did lament his failing to order his wandering thoughts around the attainment of "practical objects," but he did so significantly in diary passages that he incorporated into his autobiography.[38]

This countrapuntal theme of gratitude and self-appreciation conveys an important clue about these men's acceptance of America's emerging capitalist culture. Rivalries, at least in retrospect, are muted by a sense of mutuality; envy is displaced by admiration. Old competitors at the bar or in commerce are safely folded back into friendship at the career's end. The exertions necessary to make one's way figure as profitable investments of time and hope in a basically worthwhile enterprise. Implicit in the authors' acceptance of the hardship of charting a life course without models is the reasonableness of the exchange.

Two powerful psychological forces seemed to be at work to neutralize the effects of changing fortunes: The first was the capacity to admire those who succeeded; the second, the tendency to claim oneself as the producer of any success that came one's way. Providential thinking figures very weakly in explanations of outcomes; the triumphs are man-made. Heroes large and small are lauded, especially for the economic character of their achievements. Typical is Gideon Burton's praise of public men for their facilitation of private endeav-

[35] Chambers, *Autobiography,* p. 10.

[36] William Seward, *Autobiography of William H. Seward, from 1801 to 1834,* New York, 1891, p. 21.

[37] Dodge, *Memorial,* pp. 47–48.

[38] Foot, *Autobiography,* pp. 54–55.

ors: DeWitt Clinton rose to fame as the great patron of the Erie Canal. Cincinnati acquired the beauty of Philadelphia because of David Griffin, "a man of great enterprise." A statue to Henry Clay is raised along the National Road because it was he who secured the charter. Taking his sons to catch a glimpse of Clay as his boat pulled away from the Philadelphia wharf, Gideon Burton told them that Clay was the greatest man living because he was "the father of the American system, that made our country free from England and other manufacturing nations . . . to this day the mention of his name kindles a glow in my heart."[39]

The autobiographers and their heroes shared a common drama in overcoming the temptations of dissipation. The liminal trial reported by most of these memoir writers was learning to avoid self-indulgence. Dissolute relatives and companions provide monitory foils, often in connection with the author's own struggle to shed bad habits. Drunkenness and gambling figure as the sinister lures to a degraded life. Chambers ascribed his father's ruin to the intemperate habits he picked up from the officers of the Continental Army. Later on, when he undertook the ordering of Harrison's military papers, he scornfully described the men assigned him as "drunken lawyers who having ruined themselves by their intemperance took shelter from starvation by enlisting." His wife's suitors ended up "before middle age in great poverty and perfectly besotted."[40] Thus did he stud his autobiography with the object lessons of his life. Anson Jones detailed how failure dogged him as he went from Massachusetts to New York and then to Louisiana trying to establish a medical practice. Perhaps no truer mark of desperation could be noted than his report that he moved to Texas to escape the gambling and drinking fashionable in New Orleans.[41]

Foot had the most dramatic encounter with vice when he discovered that his benefactor, his "kind, warm-hearted, generous and talented brother," was addicted to gambling.[42] Cosigning his brother's notes, Foot went to jail when his brother's early death left him saddled with debts. Foot and Dodge interpreted their struggle with temp-

39 Gideon Burton, *Reminiscences,* Cincinnati, 1895, pp. 23, 16, 24.
40 Chambers, *Autobiography,* p. 20.
41 Jones, *Memoranda,* p. 10. Since Jones became governor of Texas the move can be presumed to have been therapeutic.
42 Ibid., pp. 21, 27, 31.

tation in the language of their evangelical religious commitments, while others found in a mother or a friend the model for self-discipline. For all, the fight against intemperance and indolence formed a major life theme in which personal rectitude and economic well-being were closely tied. As if to highlight its centrality, Chambers ended his memoirs with a sober assessment of the prevalence of dissipation:

> I have yet to see wealth pass by descent beyond the third generation, but I have seen & see every day the second generation who has squandered the labours of their predecessors . . . in miserable low degrading dissapation. . . . I pray to God to guard my descendents against evil habits, but especially against drunkenness & gambling.[43]

My initial question dealt with the psychological resiliency that enabled young men to enter the entrepreneurial vanguard of America's developing economy. Whether it was a loose attachment to home, or a positive impulse to deny paternal authority, the capacity to sever the actual emotional links to the family seems an important factor. Perhaps, as suggested earlier, poverty eroded parental pride and filial attachment in addition to offering a repellent contrast to the fortunes that might be garnered elsewhere. The early signs of intelligence that aroused the attention of outsiders formed an important element in the social transaction that effected the break with home. Intelligence, an aptitude for learning, an early gift for reading, a yearning for more schooling – these were the notes that, in retrospect, orchestrated the movement from home and justified the rupture, if not in the eyes of parents, clearly for the departing sons.[44]

There is considerable evidence that Americans enjoyed moving from place to place, as though that dynamic of emotionally charged daydreaming that Colin Campbell named the root cause of modern consumerism influenced as well the career decisions of these young men. They appeared to find little satisfaction in settling down, preferring instead to imagine yet another locus of opportunity. Dodge's early career as an auctioneer and operator of "cheap stores" found him resettling every two or three years in what were judged promising commercial centers in New York and Connecticut. Large num-

[43] Chambers, *Autobiography*, p. 31.

[44] Curiously, several of the autobiographers spoke of their small size, their frailty, and their poor health as goads to their efforts to escape the arduous labor of farming.

bers of New Englanders migrated to the Deep South; enough went to South Carolina to form the first of many New England merchant societies. Both Hinkley and Ball worked for stints in the Deep South, Hinkley leading slaves and horses to a Natchez plantation and Ball teaching school in Darien, Georgia.[45] The wanderlust of Ball deserves recounting.

It was Ball who grew up in Hebron, Vermont, and worked his way through Dartmouth as a summertime schoolteacher. What makes his memoirs particularly fascinating are the adventitious adventures this otherwise modest man enjoyed. After graduation from Dartmouth – his years paralleled the political controversy between the State of New Hampshire and the Dartmouth trustees – he studied law in Troy, New York. He attended the New York Supreme Court in Utica to get his certificate, arriving the day that an elderly Aaron Burr was trying a case. Bored by the study of law after a few years, he decided to follow the Oregon Trail to the Pacific. Frequently ruminating about his own diffidence, Ball made up for his lack of assertiveness by his luck in falling in with famous people. When he visited Washington on his way to join up with a contingent of John Jacob Astor's Oregon men, he dropped around the Supreme Court on the day John Marshall delivered his celebrated decision in the Cherokee case. Ball berated himself for not calling on his former classmate Rufus Choate. "I could have renewed by acquaintance," he mused, "but no, I poked about as a stranger. And as such presumed to call on General Jackson at the White House without any introduction. He however received me kindly." Taking a boat from Pittsburgh to Cincinnati, he discovered Lyman Beecher among the passengers, a fortuitous encounter that was only trumped by his return passage around Cape Horn, when he signed on as a clerk for an American man-of-war commanded by Lieutenant David Farragut.[46]

Ball's career took its most interesting turn when he returned to Troy in 1836, well traveled but still unsettled at forty-one. At that juncture in his life, four local men proposed that he use his woodsman's skills to ferret out good land investments in the new territory of Michigan. Ball thought it strange "that so sober men as those should have yielded to the mania that so pervaded the country," but he fell in

[45] *Holmes Hinkley*, pp. 18–19; Ball, *Autobiography*, p. 42.
[46] Ibid., pp. 61–62, 123.

with their plans and went to Michigan, where he became a land developer, state legislator, and community builder. Settling in Grand Rapids, he met a schoolteacher drawn to Michigan from New York who "exchanged her tutorship of a full room of young girls and boys for one old boy, myself." And so, at fifty-six, Ball began a family that numbered five by the time he was seventy-seven.[47]

There were some mighty levelers in this ebullient society driven by ingenuity, effort, and risk taking. Debt was one of them, and it figured in almost every autobiography. Foot went to prison for his brother's gambling debts. Jones had to declare bankruptcy when he was sued for his board as a medical student.[48] Chambers lost $20,000 in a rope-walk venture. His account of this conveys well the stoicism about indebtedness: "I kept my business to myself and maintained my credit until I struggled pretty well through my indebtedness, living economically and wasting nothing."[49] Getting established often meant losing wages when employers went broke or partners abandoned the common enterprise. Hinkley reported such a loss laconically when he described how his partner in a machinist shop deserted him when he "got sick of life, and hanged himself."[50] Success was the great discriminator among the many ventures that transformed American society, but its permanence was never assumed. Failure – or at least temporary failures – dogged men's lives. In these routine defeats a kind of freemasonry of aspiring entrepreneurs took shape, nurtured by the awareness that financial reverses were the inescapable companion of success. Thus, both success and failure cemented the emotional attachment to American opportunity.

What needs to be considered is how potentially disruptive this general, pell-mell pursuit of riches might have been had those who lost in the scramble for resources organized against the system that failed them. That such patterned hostility did not develop suggests that Americans imagined the individual's engagement with chance and choice in a particularly benign way. Important here were the ideal of productivity and the recognition of the interdependence of productive sectors of the economy. To elaborate these truths the traditional image

[47] Ibid., pp. 133–231.
[48] Jones, *Memoranda,* pp. 5–6.
[49] Chambers, *Autobiography,* p. 16.
[50] *Holmes Hinkley,* p. 22.

of society as divided among rich, poor, and middling had to give way to one in which representatives of occupations – farmers, lawyers, schoolteachers, manufacturers, and merchants – interacted to create general prosperity. The age-old concept of a structure with divisions of ranks and strata was supplanted by that of a machine with interacting parts and interchangeable participants. Repeated in orations and pamphlets, by mechanics in their association meetings and merchants in their economic tracts, the truths about a perpetually improving social engine were hammered home: Farmers who produced agricultural surpluses could buy better tools; manufacturers who reinvested the profits from selling those goods expanded output; merchants who sold the farmers' crops and manufactured goods enhanced the size and efficiency of the market.[51] Just how thoroughly personalized America's economic well-being could be made is exemplified by Francis Corey, who entertained the idea that his father in having him, a tenth child, might have acted upon "a patriotic impulse" to add another workman to the underpopulated United States![52]

Articulated in didactic literature, this vision of a society of mutually accommodating workers no doubt appealed to a vast number of ordinary men and women because it leveled their social superiors. As Samuel Latham Mitchill explained in a 1793 oration, since all citizens are equal the only inequality that exists arises necessarily from office, talents, or wealth. As the road "is open for every one to aspire to these, it is by the exercise of one or more of his rights that a man acquires these means of influence."[53] Forty years later Frederic W. Lincoln, Jr., a self-made instrument maker in Boston, echoed Mitchill's view that the road was open to all. Defining a capitalist as any man whose income is more than his expenses, Lincoln described the creation of capitalists as a continuous process.

> The laborer of to-day is the capitalist of tomorrow, and the son of the man who yesterday rolled in affluence, is today working for his daily bread. Every

[51] I am indebted to Gary J. Kornblith, "Self-Made Men: The Development of Middling-Class Consciousness in New England," *Massachusetts Review*, 26 (1985), 461–74, for the development of this idea.

[52] Corey, *Autobiography*.

[53] Samuel Latham Mitchill, *An Oration Before the Society of Black Friars*, New York, 1793, pp. 19–20. It is perhaps fitting for a man like Mitchill of reputed encyclopedic knowledge, living in such a turbulent time, that he should be called "a chaos of knowledge."

man stands upon his own merits, – upon his own habits of industry and frugality; – industry in acquiring, frugality in expanding the fruits of his labors. The fact that he may become a capitalist, is a spur to exertion to the very newsboy in our streets.[54]

One more quality about the autobiographers' lives deserves attention: the way in which they reconfigured public and private space. Only in the United States did the creation of a new civil society accompany the economic changes of the early industrial period. Only here did the decisions that individuals made about their personal lives play so large a part in shaping the character of public institutions. In the absence of a presiding upper class, an established church, and a fully articulated government, personal undertakings did the work of authority. And if these autobiographers are typical, people quite unselfconsciously mingled their private ambitions with public engagements. They practiced law, sought out land investments, and developed mercantile opertions while simultaneously serving in their legislatures, participating in revivals, and organizing reform movements.[55] Even their exaltation of heroes merged the public with the private – the statesman who championed internal improvements, the local merchant who beautified the city.

I have noted several times that the autobiographies described young adolescents moving into an unknown future without a model. However, they did evince a priori notions about the need for direction. Here Weber's Protestant ethic is in evidence, for in retrospect the authors discerned rational plans as moving forces. Confronted with the need to organize a narrative from the flow of remembered experience, the narrators located patterns of meaning in the sequence of events they recorded. Typical of this artistic invention is the linking of a childhood experience with a commitment that resonated throughout the adult life. For Ball, religious doubts that he traced to a childhood experience with a Vermont revival won him to the cause of toleration, which he acted upon years later as a Michigan schoolboard member.[56]

[54] Frederic W. Lincoln, Jr., *An Address Delivered Before the Massachusetts Charitable Mechanic Association,* Boston, 1845, p. 20, as cited in Kornblith, "Self-Made Men," p. 469.

[55] Pertinent here is the constant churning through the New York State Legislature of new officeholders described in Gunn, *Decline of Authority,* pp. 73–74. First-term legislators went from 32 percent in the 1780s to 83 percent in the 1840s.

[56] Ball, *Autobiography,* pp. 10, 154–55.

Ezra Michener, a Quaker doctor, became an ardent member of the early temperance movement because, as he explained it, he had had to struggle to overcome a passion for liquor induced by the alcohol-laced medicine he was given as a child.[57]

In the autobiography of David Dodge, his career as a successful Connecticut dry goods merchant is presented in tandem with his spiritual groping toward a renunciation of war. A Presbyterian, Dodge organized the New York Peace Society in 1815. Mingling advice to his merchant sons with reflections on his path to pacifist convictions, Dodge recalled the ambivalent response he felt as a boy when a neighbor called out the veterans of his Continental Army regiment to parade for the village. The "evil" of listening to martial music and responding to the gaudy trappings of military reviews pricked Dodge's conscience until finally he turned his private doubts about arming himself against bandits into a public testament against war. Running through this story about a pioneering pacifist are Dodge's recollections of the waning and waxing of his religious fervor, the organizational techniques of the peace society, the opening of new "cash" stores, the starting up of a cotton factory, and the spiritual state of the clerks and "laboring men" in his employ.[58] These lives reflect the emerging civil society in which business enterprises, voluntary societies, religious observances and political involvement are welded together because the men behind them do not recognize any boundaries walling off one activity from the other.

The autobiography is clearly a genre well suited to the reflections of the successful. The backward glance of the aged inventor, town settler, factory founder, irradiates the wider plane of opportunity. These Americans wrote about their country as the locus for beneficial exchanges of talents and riches. Within this image of an improving America, the personal qualities of intelligence, honesty, and enterprise appear to be animating the social whole. Accordingly, successful, productive, inventive individuals became powerful nodes of attention and admiration. Their lives served as models of innovation in a society losing all desire to replicate past ways of doing things. We could call these autobiographies a kind of cultural capital, which was accumulating in America alongside the investment funds for industry.

[57] Michener, *Autobiographical Notes,* pp. 3, 11, 35–36.
[58] Dodge, *Memorial,* passim.

Missing from this autobiographical chorus are the voices of artisans whose way of life was being undermined by industrial change. Nor are there memoirs from the vast numbers of young farm workers who moved from the countryside into factory employment. Their disinvestment of hope failed to produce its own autobiographical literature. Laments about the diminishing chances of success and the personal disappointments that entailed were more likely to find expression in ballads. The autobiographies offered a template instead for the fiction of success with its new cultural hero, the self-made man. The invitation to be nostalgic about a bygone era was declined in favor of projecting the autobiographers' story line upon the future. Myth and reality fused as the easy access to opportunity, the just reward of virtue, the irrepressible pluck in the face of adversity – so forcefully depicted in these first-person accounts from the nation's charter entrepreneurs – sank deep into public consciousness as the characteristics that defined America.

CHAPTER 6

Preserving "the natural equality of rank and influence": liberalism, republicanism, and equality of condition in Jacksonian politics

RICHARD B. LATNER

The Jacksonian period occupies a central place in the emergence of market capitalism in the United States. The opening of the Cotton Kingdom, the expansion of the frontier, the rise of the factory system, and the canal and railroad boom were among the developments that revolutionized economic life after the War of 1812. The quickening pace of enterprise was matched by the release of individualistic and acquisitive energies, enduringly depicted by Alexis de Tocqueville in his portrait of Jacksonian Americans. At the same time, politics became more democratic with the expansion of suffrage, the appearance of mass political parties, and a new popular style of campaigning.[1]

The author would like to acknowledge the assistance of research grants from the American Philosophical Society and The Murphy Institute of Political Economy at Tulane University in facilitating this study.

[1] The literature on economic, social, and political changes in the Jacksonian period is vast, but especially helpful are: George Rogers Taylor, *The Transportation Revolution,* 1815–1860 (New York, 1951); Sean Wilentz, *Chants Democratic: New York City and the Rise of the American Working Class, 1788–1850* (New York, 1984); Robert V. Remini, *The Election of Andrew Jackson* (Philadelphia, 1963); Ronald P. Formisano, "Deferential-Participant Politics: The Early Republic's Political Culture, 1789–1840," *American Political Science Review,* 68 (June 1974), 473–87. Edward Pessen, *Jacksonian America: Society, Personality, and Politics,* rev. ed. (Urbana, Ill., 1985), though opinionated, is still a useful guide. Harry Watson perceptively develops the idea of a "Market Revolution" to signify the broad changes in economic and social relationships that occurred in the antebellum period. See Harry L. Watson, *Liberty and Power: The Politics of Jacksonian America* (New York, 1990). For Tocqueville, a recent translation is Alexis de Tocqueville, *Democracy in America,* trans. George Lawrence and ed. J. P. Mayer (New York, 1966). It should be read in conjunction with Sean Wilentz, "Many Democracies: On Tocqueville and Jacksonian America," in Abraham S. Eisenstadt, ed., *Reconsidering Tocqueville's Democracy in America* (New Brunswick, N.J., 1988), 207–28.

This new economic order was a source of pride and nationalistic boasting, as nineteenth-century Americans considered themselves the special beneficiaries of an age of progress. At the same time, however, these changes inspired fear and anxiety. "A cloud habitually hung on their brow, and they seemed serious and almost sad even in their pleasures," Tocqueville observed of a people who should have been "the happiest to be found in the world."[2] There were many concerns: fear of losing wealth and social standing in a more fluid social order, fear of losing power and personal independence to those made powerful by the workings of the market; fear of the unpredictable gyrations of an economy sensitive to forces ever more remote and impersonal; and fear that rewards and rank would increasingly be determined by artificial means rather than natural talent.

Issues relating to the market revolution inevitably intruded into politics. Indeed, for the next hundred years, American politics would, to a great extent, revolve around questions of tariffs, internal improvements, land distribution, corporate charter laws, and especially money and banking. It was in this context that the subject of equality rose to the forefront of Jacksonian political debate. Egalitarianism, a theme that had occupied a peripheral place in the Revolutionary age of the 1770s and 1780s, became a central feature of political ideology during the 1830s, rhetorically binding on Whig and Democrat alike. Candidates of varying political hues, from patrician to populist, paid homage to egalitarian ideals or suffered rebuke from an aroused electorate.

Despite the pivotal position of egalitarian themes in Jacksonian politics, historians have devoted surprisingly little attention to exploring their economic and social dimensions. Much is known about the political changes that nourished egalitarianism, such as the gradual emergence of universal adult white male suffrage.[3] But less consideration has been given to understanding what Jacksonian Americans meant when they spoke about economic and social equality. In particular, historians have ignored or discounted the ideal of equality of condition as germane to Jacksonian politics.

Indeed, scholarly inattention to issues of distributional equality

[2] Tocqueville, *Democracy in America,* 536.

[3] Chilton Williamson, *American Suffrage from Property to Democracy, 1760–1860* (Princeton, 1960).

seems more generally to characterize the field of political economy. In one of the few full-scale explorations of the sources and meanings of equality in American history, J. R. Pole notes that while some of the most glaring inequalities in American life have always been economic, a "remarkably small proportion" of the public debate relating to equality has focused on the maldistribution of wealth. In Jackson's own day, John C. Calhoun, a serious if selective student of politics, called "the great question of the distribution of wealth [the] least explored, and the most important of any in the whole range of political economy."[4]

Scholarly and public neglect of distributional issues can be attributed in good part to the pervasiveness of liberalism and its associated themes of equal opportunity and competition as an explanatory framework for American history. The conviction that equality of opportunity lies at the core of the American belief in equality is so widespread among investigators of nineteenth- and twentieth-century political culture that there has been little incentive for close examination of Jacksonian thinking.[5] There is, undoubtedly, some degree of ambiguity and tension within the general American celebration of equal opportunity. Irving Kristol notes that the Americans only reluctantly sanction the inequality of condition that inevitably results from equality of opportunity.[6] But equality of opportunity remains central to the American Creed. Many an American reformer has called attention to

[4] J. R. Pole, *The Pursuit of Equality in American History* (Berkeley, 1978), xi. *Register of Debates,* 23rd Cong., 1st sess., January 13, 1833, 218. For a recent discussion of income inequality in the United States, see Colin D. Campbell, *Income Redistribution* (Washington, D.C., 1977), especially the exchange between Robert Nisbet and Henry J. Aaron, 179–96, 210–13.

[5] Seymour Martin Lipset argues that achievement, competition, and equality of opportunity "remain at the core of American values." See Lipset, *The First New Nation: The United States in Historical and Comparative Perspective,* rev. ed. (New York, 1979), 115. Especially pertinent on the influence of liberalism in American history is Louis Hartz, *The Liberal Tradition in America* (New York, 1955); Garry Wills, *Nixon Agonistes, The Crisis of the Self-Made Man* (Boston, 1969); and most recently John P. Diggins, *The Lost Soul of American Politics: Virtue, Self-Interest, and the Foundations of Liberalism* (New York, 1984).

[6] Irving Kristol, "Equality as an Ideal," in *The International Encyclopedia of the Social Sciences,* 18 vols. (New York, 1968–79), 5:110. Seymour Martin Lipset similarly discerns that equality of opportunity can at times conflict with liberal values of individualism and autonomy. Opportunity can yield inequalities of wealth and power that, in turn, may undermine egalitarianism. These class distinctions and inequities often lead to efforts to check injustices that arise from unfettered activity. See Lipset, *First New Nation,* xxxiii, 102–3.

the maldistribution of wealth or privilege, not in order to do away with the ladder of hierarchy, but in hopes of equalizing access to its higher rungs. Thus, even those who decry social and economic disparities sustain the competitive framework that generated class and other distinctions in the first place. As one recent European observer aptly remarks, "The United States was dedicated to the proposition that all men are born free, but equality is something else."[7]

With few exceptions, historians have taken it for granted that when Jacksonians talked about equality, they exclusively meant equality of opportunity. The so-called Columbia, or entrepreneurial, school, identified Jacksonian ideology closely with the release of individualistic and acquisitive energies attending the emergence of the liberal market economy. Richard Hofstadter typifies this position in arguing that the environment from which Jackson emerged, the frontier, was "not given to leveling equalitarianism" but, rather, to the ideal of the self-made man. The Jacksonian movement, in this view, was the product of expanding opportunities and the desire to enlarge them still farther by removing residual restrictions and privileges. Jacksonian Democracy, Hofstadter asserts, was "essentially a movement of laissez-faire" and of "liberated capitalism." Hofstadter's ideas echo in recent scholarship. John Patrick Diggins has similarly affirmed that America has always been a "liberal society," and that Whig–Democratic battles took place within the context of "ascendant capitalism."[8]

[7] The Edinburgh *Scotsman* quoted in Roland Berthoff, "Peasants and Artisans, Puritans and Republicans: Personal Liberty and Communal Equality in American History," *Journal of American History,* 69 (Dec. 1982), 484. Commentators often apply the metaphor of a race to describe the American commitment to equality of opportunity. At various times, particularly conservative eras, Americans emphasize the free movement around a track, whereby everyone runs under the same rules. In times of protest or reform, however, Americans acknowledge the inequalities that emerge from the race, and argue the need for a fairer race by having everyone line up more equally at the start of the contest. However, *both* views share a commitment to competition and equal opportunity, what Garry Wills calls the "emulative ethic" of a market system. As the economist Arthur M. Okun observes, efforts to promote equality of opportunity "accept an individualistic, achievement-oriented, and essentially competitive economy in which prizes will be given and a variety of hierarchies will continue to exist." See Wills, *Nixon Agonistes,* 221–26; Arthur M. Okun, *Equality and Efficiency: The Big Tradeoff* (Washington, D.C., 1975), 85–86.

[8] Richard Hofstadter, *The American Political Tradition and the Men Who Made It* (New York, 1948), 47, 55; Diggins, *Lost Soul,* 4, 108. Other studies that emphasize, although with different nuances, the relationship among Jackson, the emergence of capitalism, and equality of opportunity are Pole, *Pursuit of Equality,* 2, 143–47; Bray Hammond, *Banks and Politics in America from the Revolution to the Civil War*

Marvin Meyers's *The Jacksonian Persuasion,* arguably still the most perceptive and persuasive study of Jacksonian political thinking, follows the Columbia school insofar as it grounds the Jackson party in the movement to extend the realm of "laissez-faire capitalism and its culture in America." Yet Meyers recognizes that Jacksonian spokesmen did not employ the language of energetic and aggressive men-on-the-make but, rather, harked back nostalgically to the ideals of a chaste agrarian republic. In capturing the Democratic "fears and resentments" about the market, as compared to the more optimistic Whig "hopes," Meyers offers a view of party conflict that persuasively undercuts the idea that Democrats were unadulterated market enthusiasts. Ambivalent though Meyers's Jacksonians are, it is important to note that they remain fully immersed in a market society. Eager to scourge sources of corruption, such as the Monster Bank, they also yearn for the "goods" provided by the market. The Jacksonians were, in effect, "censuring their own economic attitudes and actions," and their complaints about banks and monopolies were too abstract and diffuse to pose any serious threat to the advance of capitalism. Jacksonian political rhetoric was, according to Meyers, excessive and "out of all proportion" to their interests.[9]

Much has been gained by recognizing that Jacksonian rhetoric about equality and democracy sometimes meant the equalization of economic opportunity and the "democratizations of business." Nor can it be doubted that, despite its egalitarian rhetoric, the Jacksonian era was marked by great and growing disparities of wealth rather than equality of condition. Third parties often charged the major parties with responsibility for this situation, and advanced radically egalitarian doctrines, including arguments for equality of condition. Yet to conclude that the Jacksonians were nothing more than capitalists and political opportunists is to make the thoughts and actions of the Jacksonians unintelligible. Edward Pessen, for example, argues that the Jackson Democratic

(Princeton, 1957); John William Ward, *Andrew Jackson: Symbol for an Age* (New York, 1955); Pessen, *Jacksonian America,* and Edward Pessen, "Society and Politics in the Jacksonian Era," *Register of the Kentucky Historical Society,* 82 (Winter 1984), 1–27; Rush Welter, *The Mind of America: 1820–1860* (New York, 1975); and Charles Redenius, *The American Ideal of Equality: From Jefferson's Declaration to the Burger Court* (Port Washington, N.Y., 1981), ch. 3.

[9] Marvin Meyers, *The Jacksonian Persuasion: Politics and Belief.* 2d ed. rev. (Stanford, 1960), 9–13, 32, 121–27, 141.

Party was hypocritical in its egalitarian professions. Its leaders were "ideological conservatives" who demonstrated "sympathy toward the prevailing arrangements, institutions, and inequities that characterized liberal capitalism in Jacksonian America." Party leadership came from the upper classes, and the party's philosophy "spoke to the interests of the social, economic, and occupational groups represented by their leaders." As for Jackson himself, he was "in large part humbug," Pessen concludes. Such a view ignores the authentic egalitarianism inspired by liberal and republican sentiments and renders the party's self-image nothing more than a massive self-deception.[10]

To be sure, a number of historians have claimed that the Jacksonians were sincerely concerned with the distributional problems brought about by economic growth. Arthur Schlesinger, Jr.'s classic *The Age of Jackson* develops the theme of the Jackson movement as an egalitarian challenge to the power of the business community by other groups, particularly intellectuals and workingmen.[11] But Schlesinger is too quick to associate Jacksonianism with New Deal liberalism and to accept equality of opportunity as its fundamental value. Schlesinger's Jacksonians operate in the context of a liberal marketplace society, "advocating government intervention in order to restore competition" rather than consciously promoting equality of condition.[12] More recently, Robert Remini, revitalizing this Progressive tradition, better captures the Jacksonian debt to republican and agrarian principles. But he, too, argues their exclusive devotion to equal rights and opportunity as distinct from "absolute equality."[13]

To date, only John Ashworth has suggested that the followers of Jackson were interested in something more than equality of opportu-

[10] Hammond, *Banks and Politics,* 327–29, 408–10, 442–43; Lee Benson, *The Concept of Jacksonian Democracy: New York as a Test Case* (Princeton, 1961), 18–20, 329–38; Wilentz, *Chants Democratic,* 102–3, 172–75, 188–90; Edward Pessen, *Most Uncommon Jacksonians: The Radical Leaders of the Early Labor Movement* (Albany, N.Y., 1967), 202–3; Pessen, "Society and Politics," 17, 21, 26; Pessen, *Jacksonian America,* 222–32, 240. Pessen portrays the Whig Party in similar terms but considers the Jacksonians especially hypocritical in light of their professed love of the common man.

[11] Arthur Schlesinger, Jr., *The Age of Jackson* (Boston, 1945), 263, 306–8.

[12] Ibid., 314–16, quote on p. 316.

[13] Robert V. Remini, *Andrew Jackson and the Course of American Democracy, 1833–1845,* vol. 3 (New York, 1984), 6, 92–93. For Remini's defense of the Progressive and New Deal interpretation of Jackson, see ibid., xv.

nity. Like such neo-Progressives as Remini, Ashworth argues that Jacksonian Democrats were clearly reformers who promoted democracy and equality. But Ashworth also contends that there was a genuine "leveling thrust" in Jacksonian Democracy, which implied a society of "substantial equality of wealth." Ashworth acknowledges that equality of opportunity operated in Jacksonian ideology, but so, too, did the idea of equality of condition.[14]

Ashworth's claim for the Democratic party's dedication to a leveling equality is based largely on evidence from the period after 1837, when hard times may have evoked the Jacksonians' concern for equality of condition. Was equality of condition also a central concern of party politics before the Panic of 1837? An examination of the years surrounding Jackson's presidency will establish that historians have likewise exaggerated the theme of equality of opportunity and neglected the theme of equality of condition for this earlier period as well. Uncovering the theme of equality of condition is especially significant because this was the formative period of party development when the Democratic and Whig organizations initially established their platforms and ideologies.

Moreover, the sources of the Democratic Party's egalitarianism need further clarification. Ashworth locates Jacksonian leveling in the liberal ideology of self-interest and an "undifferentiated atomized society." But recent studies of the persistence of republican and agrarian thinking in the nineteenth century suggest that these ideological influences also contributed to the party's egalitarian posture.[15] Selectively drawing upon the liberal, republican, and agrarian traditions, the Jacksonians formulated an egalitarian appeal that found a responsive audience among Americans anxiously contending with the market revolution.

[14] John Ashworth, "The Jacksonian as Leveller," *Journal of American Studies,* 14 (Dec. 1980), 409, 412. Ashworth presents a fuller version of his perceptive analysis of party ideology in John Ashworth, *"Agrarians" and "Aristocrats": Party Political Ideology in the United States, 1837–1846* (London, 1983), esp. 24–29, 50–51, 269–71. The recently published study by Lawrence Frederick Kohl, *The Politics of Individualism: Parties and the American Character in the Jacksonian Era* (New York, 1989), provides a valuable exploration of the issue of economic equality in Jacksonian politics, and lends persuasive support to Ashworth's contention that the Jacksonians were sincerely concerned about inequality of condition. It is less helpful on the intellectual sources of the Whig and Democratic positions.

[15] Ashworth, *"Agrarians" and "Aristocrats,"* 20–21, 30, 203–4.

For Jacksonian Democrats, the definition of a republic began with the idea of majority rule and equal political rights. The "first principle of our system," Jackson announced in his first annual message, is "*that the majority is to govern.*" Given exalted status by Jackson's followers after John Quincy Adams's "corrupt bargain" election to the presidency, the principle of majority rule was considered indistinguishable from equality of rights; its antagonistic counterparts were aristocracy and monarchy, which represented the rule of the few. Republicanism, according to the official Jackson newspaper, the Washington *Globe,* was government "of a majority," and the "free exercise of their reason and will."[16]

There is considerable truth to the standard historical account that along with equal political rights, the Jacksonians also prized equality of opportunity. Andrew Jackson's frequently cited conclusion to his Bank Veto message best exemplifies this basic Democratic tenet. Rooted in the Lockean liberal notion of "competitive equality," which recognized that differences in virtue, industry, and rational capacity generated inequality of property and wealth, the document scored the Bank of the United States (BUS) for violating the principle of equal opportunity. "It is to be regretted that the rich and powerful too often bend the acts of government to their selfish purposes," Jackson argued.

> Distinctions in society will always exist under every just government. Equality of talents, of education, or of wealth can not be produced by human institutions. In the full enjoyment of the gifts of Heaven and the fruits of superior industry, economy, and virtue, every man is equally entitled to protection by law; but when the laws undertake to add to these natural and just advantages artificial distinctions, to grant titles, gratuities, and exclusive privi-

[16] Robert V. Remini, *The Legacy of Andrew Jackson: Essays on Democracy, Indian Removal, and Slavery* (Baton Rouge, 1988), 13–23; James D. Richardson, ed., *A Compilation of Messages and Papers of the Presidents,* 20 vols. (New York, 1897), 3:1011; Washington *Globe,* April 6, 1833. See also William Leggett, *A Collection of the Political Writings of William Leggett,* ed. Theodore Sedgwick, Jr., 2 vols. (New York, 1840), 2:72; and Amos Kendall, *Autobiography of Amos Kendall,* ed. William Stickney (Boston, 1872), 431. As is often noted, the Jacksonian evocation of equal political rights did not apply to blacks, women, or native Americans. "It never entered Jackson's thinking that the suffrage might be extended to other races and the other sex." Remini, *Legacy of Andrew Jackson,* 41. See also George M. Fredrickson, *The Black Image in the White Mind: The Debate on Afro-American Character and Destiny, 1817–1914* (New York, 1971), 90–92.

leges, to make the rich richer and the potent more powerful, the humble members of society – the farmers, mechanics, and laborers – who have neither the time nor the means of securing like favors to themselves, have a right to complain of the injustice of their Government.[17]

Democrats were also quick to deny any radical objectives to redistribute property when, as was often the case, they were charged with leveling or "agrarianism" because of their attacks against monopoly and special privilege. Jackson called the idea of leveling "odious," and criticized the provisions of one Whig legislative proposal as "liable to all the objections which apply to the principle of an equal division of property."[18] Denials of "agrarian" or leveling doctrines became a stock item in the Democratic Party's creed during Jackson's presidency, and shortly after he left office, the new and influential *United States Magazine and Democratic Review* reiterated the party's liberal ideals in announcing that "We are no agrarians – no levellers. It would be as impracticable to produce an absolute equality of condition among men as it would be to produce an absolute equality of stature; and if it were practicable, it would not be desirable." The Democrats, therefore, loudly proclaimed their innocence of being "levelers," just as the Whigs denied being "aristocrats."[19]

However, Democratic disclaimers of leveling do not tell the whole story. Along with avowing principles of competitive equality and economic distinction, they affirmed a commitment to relative equality of

[17] Richardson, ed., *Messages and Papers,* 3:1153. Diggins, *Lost Soul,* 117–18. On John Locke and the theory of liberalism, see C. B. Macpherson, *The Political Theory of Possessive Individualism* (Oxford, 1962), 1–3. Macpherson uses the phrase "possessive individualism" to characterize the essential element of liberalism. See also Sanford A. Lakoff, *Equality in Political Philosophy* (Cambridge, Mass., 1964), 92, 100–101, 211.

[18] Richardson, ed., *Messages and Papers,* 3:1460. "Agrarian" in this negative sense was synonymous with leveling. "Agrarian" was also a positive concept, often associated with Thomas Jefferson, that celebrated the virtues of agriculture. I have sometimes used the phrase "Jeffersonian agrarianism" to distinguish the two ideas, but the context should make clear which "agrarianism" is under discussion.

[19] *The United States Magazine and Democratic Review,* 6 (Dec. 1939), 461. In 1841, when Harper and Brothers published George Sidney Camp's *Democracy,* a book intended as the first popular elucidation of "the democratic *theory,*" Camp distinguished "republicanism," a word he used interchangeably with "democracy," from "a levelling spirit" or "agrarian measures." Democracy demanded "not an equality in the circumstances, but an equality in the rights of mankind." George S. Camp, *Democracy* (New York, 1841), iii, 155, 221. See also, Leggett, *Political Writings,* 2:176, 199; Theodore Sedgwick, *Public and Private Economy,* 3 vols. (1836–39), rept. with introduction by Joseph Dorfman (Clifton, N.J., 1974), 2:88.

wealth as a necessary, instrumental condition for maintaining political liberty. Sometimes explicit, often implicit in their expectations of policy outcomes, equality meant for Jacksonians something more than providing each person with an equal chance to compete in the marketplace, to line up more or less equally at the start of a race for material possessions. It also meant that excessive inequality was *inherently* dangerous to republican liberty. Indeed, the very fact that Democrats had to deny the label of "leveler" testifies to the strength of the popular impression that they were, in fact, advocates of leveling.

There is no necessary inconsistency between Democratic disclaimers of economic leveling and a commitment to equality of condition. When Jackson Democrats condemned leveling or agrarianism, they invariably meant an absolute equality of condition. Such an unequivocal definition of equality, however, is a caricature. "To make equality a synonym for the absence of all distinctions is not to define any of the real proposals of equality," Sanford A. Lakoff explains.[20] Moreover, it is not necessary to argue that all Democrats subscribed to the virtues of relative equality of condition in order for the principle to have had a bearing on policy. Both parties were composed of factions and interests, some of which were undeniably acquisitive in spirit.[21] Nevertheless, for the key group of Democrats surrounding Jackson who ran the party, equality of outcomes, as well as equality of rights and opportunity, was a necessary condition for sustaining republican liberty.

The existence of multiple kinds and degrees of egalitarianism testifies to the complexity of political discourse in nineteenth-century America. Historians have generally been too accepting of Tocqueville's depiction of Jacksonian Americans as uniformly liberal and market-oriented.[22] Other political traditions remained viable in post-Revolutionary America. In particular, by selectively drawing upon and adapting both classical republican and Jeffersonian agrarian tradi-

[20] Lakoff, *Equality,* 6, 62–66.

[21] For an excellent description of Democratic Party factions in the states following the Panic of 1837, see James Roger Sharp, *The Jacksonians Versus the Banks: Politics in the States after the Panic of 1837* (New York, 1970).

[22] For a recent appraisal of Tocqueville's portrait of Jacksonian America, see Wilentz, "Many Democracies," 220–25. Edward Pessen challenges Tocqueville's egalitarian thesis, noting that the antebellum period was characterized by growing inequality of wealth. See Edward Pessen, *Riches, Class, and Power Before the Civil War* (Lexington, Mass., 1973), 302–6.

tions, the Jacksonains found means to identify and resist aspects of their changing society that posed real and substantial dangers to freedom.

Liberalism, republicanism, and Jeffersonian agrarian ideals were at once distinct, conflicting, and mutually reinforcing ideological influences. As James T. Kloppenberg cogently argues, the advance of liberal ideas associated with Locke and Adam Smith carried pronounced idealistic and egalitarian implications, upon which Americans often seized. In the name of expanded individual economic and political rights, liberalism attacked hierarchy and privilege. In association with Scottish common sense philosophy, it contained moral strictures that checked self-interest and sanctioned a middling comfort. To be sure, liberalism promoted the ideal of equality of opportunity and justified disparities of wealth resulting from differing talents and industry, but it also harmonized with agrarian and republican notions that liberty depended on the widespread dispersal and relative equality of property. Early-nineteenth-century liberalism narrowly circumscribed admissible economic inequality, and its political and economic egalitarianism need not be discounted in order to establish the relevance of other vocabularies.[23]

Nevertheless, much of the Jacksonian concern for equality of condition was based on an egalitarian reading of republican and agrarian ideas. Like their Revolutionary mentors, Jacksonian Americans probed the economic and moral bases of a republican polity.[24] As Marvin Meyers sensitively discerned years ago, Jacksonian political

[23] James T. Kloppenberg. "The Virtues of Liberalism: Christianity, Republicanism, and Ethics in Early American Political Discourse," *Journal of American History,* 74 (June 1987), 15–19, 27–28; Lakoff, *Equality,* 100–101; Joyce Appleby, "The Social Origins of American Revolutionary Ideology," *Journal of American History,* 64 (Mar. 1978), 945, 951–58; Lance Banning, "Jeffersonian Ideology Revisited: Liberal and Classical Ideas in the New American Republic," *William and Mary Quarterly,* 43 (Jan. 1986), 12–19. For a provocative argument that capitalism and a market economy are not incompatible with distributive justice, see Jonathan Riley, "Justice Under Capitalism," in *Markets and Justice: NOMOS XXXI,* ed. J. Chapman and J. R. Pennock (New York, 1989), 147. Although liberalism and the market carried leveling tendencies that helped undermine the traditional colonial social order, there were distinct limits to this egalitarianism. For Adam Smith's candid recognition of inequality and the need for government to protect property from "the indignation of the poor," see *An Inquiry into the Nature and Causes of the Wealth of Nations,* ed. Richard F. Teichgraeber III (New York: Modern Library, 1985), 375–76.

[24] Drew R. McCoy, *The Elusive Republic: Political Economy in Jeffersonian America* (Chapel Hill, N.C., 1980), 7.

discourse was replete with references to republican anxieties about virtue, corruption, and liberty.

Republicanism was a supple intellectual formulation, but it generally signified a set of ideas centered on both the proper arrangement of political institutions and the cultivation of a virtuous citizenry, so as best to assure liberty. Republican doctrine celebrated the autonomous citizen whose property holdings were sufficient to avoid dependency on others. It required the maintenance of public and private virtue, a concept that involved among other things the sacrifice of individual self-interest on behalf of the community's common good. Republicanism's posture toward the market and capitalism was ambivalent. By the late eighteenth century, American republicans accepted elements of commerce, manufacturing, and business, but were highly suspicious of those features, such as public debt, speculation, and financial manipulation, that entailed corruption and dependency, vice, and luxury. Republican doctrine additionally condemned standing armies and excessive governmental power.[25]

Although much of its vocabulary and concerns remained constant, republicanism necessarily adjusted to changing times and circumstances. In America, republicanism acquired an egalitarian gloss. Hierarchical and elitist aspects of classical republicanism, which, for

[25] The literature on republicanism in early American history is vast. I have especially relied on three recent essays that, while sympathetic to the republican thesis, also afford a useful overview of the many points of historiographic contention. These are: John Ashworth, "The Jeffersonians: Classical Republicans or Liberal Capitalists?" *Journal of American Studies,* 18 (Dec. 1984), 425–35; Robert E. Shalhope, "Republicanism and Early American Historiography," *William and Mary Quarterly,* 39 (Apr. 1982), 334–56; and Banning, "Jeffersonian Ideology Revisited," 3–19. Particularly helpful in understanding the applicability of republican concepts to early American politics is Gordon Wood, *The Creation of the American Republic: 1776–1787* (Chapel Hill, N. C., 1969); Lance Banning, *The Jeffersonian Persuasion: Evolution of a Party Ideology* (Ithaca, N. Y., 1978); and McCoy, *Elusive Republic.* The leading dissenter from the republican interpretation is Joyce Appleby. See especially Joyce Appleby, *Capitalism and a New Social Order: The Republican Vision of the 1790s* (New York, 1984); Appleby, "What Is Still American in the Political Philosophy of Thomas Jefferson," *William and Mary Quarterly,* 39 (Apr. 1982), 287–309; Appleby, "Commercial Farming and the 'Agrarian Myth' in the Early Republic," *Journal of American History,* 68 (Mar. 1982), 833–49; and Appleby, "Social Origins," 935–58. For other dissenters, see Diggins, *Lost Soul;* and Isaac Kramnick, "Republican Revisionism Revisited," *American Historical Review,* 87 (June 1982), 629–64. Still indispensable for understanding the debate over republicanism is J. G. A. Pocock, *The Machiavellian Moment: Florentine Political Thought and the Atlantic Republican Tradition* (Princeton, 1975) and Pocock, *Politics, Language and Time: Essays on Political Thought and History* (New York, 1971).

example, limited citizenship to a select world of property holders, were modified and adjusted to suit a society of more extensive landholding and political participation. Thus, in the Revolutionary period, republicanism often carried the egalitarian assumption that widespread disparities of wealth undermined political equality and republican virtue, and liberty could not long remain operative in an environment in which excessive inequality of fortunes existed. Equality, in David Ramsay's words, was the "life and soul" of republicanism. In this sense, equality was part of a system of thought about politics and social conditions that best guaranteed liberty, rather than a theory of individual justice.[26]

Republican ideology recognized that some degree of social and economic inequality was inevitable in a republic, since wisdom, virtue, and industriousness were not equally distributed among the people. But where avenues of social ascent remained open, and merit, rather than birth, dictated mobility, distinctions were not expected to be great. A society in which there would be none too rich and none too poor assured social harmony and public virtue. Republican ideals contrasted the relative equality of wealth and power that accompanied a society of autonomous and economically competent citizens of the New World with the social decay and political corruption of Europe.[27]

Americans of the Revolutionary generation derived their egalitarian reading of republicanism from various sources, often interpreting them in a highly selective and distorted way. A significant influence was James Harrington and his successors, who conveyed the idea that property was essentially landed, and its purpose was to make men independent in arms and citizenship. Autonomy and virtue depended

[26] McCoy, *Elusive Republic,* 6–7; Wood, *Creation of the American Republic,* 70 (Ramsey quote); Cathy Matson and Peter Onuf, "Toward a Republican Empire: Interest and Ideology in Revolutionary America," *American Quarterly,* 37 (Fall 1987), 519. As John Ashworth observes, classical republicanism was not monolithic in its structure of beliefs. It provided different lessons as to the inevitability of political degeneration, or the degree of inequality and deference appropriate to a community. My argument is that an egalitarian reading of republicanism was both available and influential in American political thought in Jacksonian politics. Whether such a reading of the classical republican tradition was "correct" is, however significant, a separate matter. Different groups of Americans selectively adopted and adjusted republican concerns and ideas for their use. See Ashworth, "The Jeffersonians," 427–31; also Banning, "Jeffersonian Ideology Revisited," 9–11.

[27] McCoy, *Elusive Republic,* 61–62; 236–38; Banning, "Jeffersonian Ideology Revisited," 16; Wood, *Creation of the American Republic,* 72–74.

on property, and the aim of the legislator was to ensure a distribution of property in which as many people as possible shared authority and avoided dependence on another's power. In *The Commonwealth of Oceana* (1656), Harrington proposed an agrarian law to limit acquisitiveness, ensure divisibility of inheritance, and remedy the maldistribution of land.[28]

By no means did Harrington advocate extreme equality in property or social relations. He argued that political equality did not entail an absolute equality of estates, and he favored a deferential recognition of superior talent and virtue. Nevertheless, his association of property with independence and virtue, and his provision for widespread landholding, clearly rested personal autonomy on a material foundation. In America, where landholding was more extensive than in England, such ideas carried egalitarian implications. Thus, Noah Webster echoed Harrington when he announced that "an equality of property, with a necessity of alienation, constantly operating to destroy combinations of powerful families, is the very *soul of a republic.*"[29]

There was also a distinct outcropping of economic egalitarianism among ordinary American republican citizens in the last third of the eighteenth century. Small farmers and artisans believed that economic exchange had moral and ethical dimensions, which should operate in the direction of equality. This "new moral economy" of the revolutionary and immediate post-Revolutionary eras reinforced republican concerns about disparities of wealth. While conservatives like John Adams relied on equality of opportunity to minimize class disparities, more radical republicans insisted that government actively protect the poor in order to assure opportunity as well as personal independence.[30]

[28] J. G. A. Pocock, ed., *The Political Works of James Harrington* (Cambridge, 1977), 61–62, 122, 145–46. Pocock identifies Harrington as the "central figure" among the English " 'classical republicans.' " See J. G. A. Pocock, *Politics, Language and Time,* 108. Harrington's association of the form of government with the distribution of property is also discussed by C. B. Macpherson. Unlike Pocock, Macpherson argues that Harrington's agrarian law indicates an acceptance of a bourgeois notion of equality of opportunity. See Macpherson, *Possessive Individualism,* ch. 4, esp. 186–88.

[29] Macpherson, *Possessive Individualism,* 167–69, 176. Webster is quoted by J. G. A. Pocock, in Pocock, ed., *Political Works,* 150.

[30] Ruth Bogin, "Petitioning and the New Moral Economy of Post-Revolutionary America," *William and Mary Quarterly,* 45 (July 1988), 392–403, 422–23; Dorothy Ross, "The Liberal Tradition Revisited and the Republican Tradition Addressed," in *New Directions in American Intellectual History,* ed. John Higham and Paul K. Conkin

Republicanism's emphasis on the independent freeholder as the basis of citizenship, autonomy, and virtue neatly blended into American agrarian ideals. Indeed, it was during the Revolutionary period, according to Leo Marx, that the pastoral tradition took firm hold on the popular imagination, and became part of the political and social ideology associated with Thomas Jefferson.[31] Jeffersonianism celebrated a society of extensive, as well as relatively equal, landholding. "It is not too soon to provide by every possible means that as few as possible shall be without a little portion of land," Jefferson once advised James Madison, because the "small landholders are the most precious part of the state." For Americans, agriculture's ability to produce a society of middling comfort and virtue among property holders was the surest means to promote republican institutions. "The wealth acquired by speculation and plunder is fugacious in its nature and fills society with the spirit of gambling," Jefferson observed, but "the moderate and sure income of husbandry begets permanent improvement, quiet life, and orderly conduct both public and private."[32]

The Jeffersonian agrarian ideal, like republicanism, was not necessarily economically stagnant or anticapitalistic. It accommodated itself to a degree of commerce and manufacturing, and sometimes encouraged expansionist efforts to incorporate more land into the American empire of liberty. Such concessions to capitalism, however, did not banish suspicions of the individualistic ethic associated with

(Baltimore, 1979), 120. See also Eric Foner's discussion of "a respectable tradition" of egalitarianism that emerged during the American Revolution, in Foner, *Tom Paine and Revolutionary America* (New York, 1976), 123–26. For an analysis of the importance of one group of British and Irish political émigrés in the 1790s in modifying classical republican notions among Jeffersonian Republicans, see Michael Curey, "Thomas Paine's Apostles: Radical Emigrés and the Triumph of Jeffersonian Republicanism," *William and Mary Quarterly,* 44 (Oct. 1987), 661–88.

31 Leo Marx, *The Machine in the Garden: Technology and the Pastoral Ideal in America* (New York, 1964), ch. 3; McCoy, *Elusive Republic,* 68–69; Pocock, ed., *Political Works,* 151–52; Pocock, *Machiavellian Moment,* 534. J. G. A. Pocock views the myth of the garden as a part of the history of civic humanism. See Pocock, *Politics, Language and Time,* 97–99.

32 Thomas Jefferson to James Madison, October 28, 1785, in Thomas Jefferson, *The Papers of Thomas Jefferson,* ed. Julian P. Boyd and Charles T. Cullen, 22 vols. (Princeton, 1950–86), 8:681–82; Jefferson to George Washington, August 14, 1787, Jefferson, *Papers,* 10:38. See Richard K. Matthews, *The Radical Politics of Thomas Jefferson: A Revisionist View* (Lawrence, Kans., 1984), 27–29, 33; McCoy, *Elusive Republic,* 66, 237; Shalhope, "Republicanism and Early American Historiography," 348.

market exchange. Market transactions too readily encouraged self-interest rather than virtue, dissociating private means from public ends. Agrarian sentiments, therefore, aroused distrust and fear of the corruption, decay, and loss of personal autonomy that seemed to trail in the wake of commerce and manufacturing. As a result, Jeffersonian adjustments to evolving and expanding commercial networks always remained circumscribed within agrarianism's broader moral and ethical ideals, such as moderate wealth, public virtue, morality, and personal autonomy.[33]

The association of republicanism and agrarianism, and their connection with the Jacksonian movement, is evident in the teachings of the Virginia planter, agricultural reformer, political theorist, and occasional officeholder John Taylor. Taylor, who died in 1824, has been dismissed as a reactionary at odds with nineteenth-century progress, and Arthur Schlesinger, Jr., has cautioned against exaggerating his contribution to the Jacksonians. But Taylor's "pastoral republicanism" helped establish a conceptual framework and vocabulary for Jacksonian politics. Thomas Hart Benton, a central figure in Jackson's banking and currency policies, recalled Taylor's high intellectual and personal reputation, and described the Virginian as "the ideal of a republican statesman." As C. William Hill, Jr., has concluded, the similarity of tone and language, and the wide area of policy agreement, between Taylor and the Jacksonians suggests a direct line of influence.[34]

[33] McCoy, *Elusive Republic,* 75; Banning, "Jeffersonian Ideology Revisited," 6; Andrew W. Foshee, "Jeffersonian Political Economy and the Classical Republican Tradition: Jefferson, Taylor, and the Agrarian Republic," *History of Political Economy,* 17 (Winter 1985), 526. The degree to which Jefferson and his followers were capitalistic, anticapitalistic, or precapitalistic is a significant area of disagreement among historians. For a discussion of the problems of definition and evidence involved in the debate, see the exchange between Lance Banning and Joyce Appleby. Banning, "Jeffersonian Ideology Revisited," esp. 4–10; and Joyce Appleby, "Republicanism in Old and New Contexts," *William and Mary Quarterly,* 43 (Jan. 1986), esp. 31–34. Also pertinent is Ashworth, "The Jeffersonians," 430–32.

[34] Paul Conkin claims that Taylor "cast his imprecations against practically every innovation in American life from 1787 until his death in 1824." Paul K. Conkin, *Prophets of Prosperity: America's First Political Economists* (Bloomington, Ind., 1980), 43. Schlesinger, *Age of Jackson,* 308–9; Thomas Hart Benton, *Thirty Years' View,* 2 vols. (New York, 1854) 1:45; C. William Hill, Jr., *The Political Theory of John Taylor of Caroline* (Rutherford, N.J., 1977), 304–8; Robert E. Shalhope, *John Taylor of Caroline: Pastoral Republican* (Columbia, S.C., 1980), 3–4, 9, 216, 405. Taylor was a member of the Old Republican wing of the Jeffersonian Republican Party, a group with which Jackson identified himself early in his political career. See Richard B. Latner, *The Presidency of Andrew Jackson: White House Politics, 1829–1837* (Ath-

Taylor was an agrarian republican who sought to accommodate commerce and manufacturing within a predominantly agricultural society. Agriculture was primary, for it was in the cultivation of the soil that Taylor found the values of social cohesion and virtue that best sustained republican institutions. Taylor's brand of republicanism owed little to the classical form that emphasized the proper balancing of social orders or institutions. For Taylor, as for Jefferson, republican government primarily signified moral character and a commitment to advance the public good. He defined a republic as a "government, which, being founded in good moral principles . . . will produce publick, common, or national benefit."[35]

An essential element of republics was a proper distribution of property. In relating property to republicanism, Taylor made clear his detestation of any "system of levelling property among orders or among individuals." The distribution of property should, instead, be left "to industry and talents," and, since people had "unequal moral and physical powers and wants," nature did not provide for absolute equality of condition. Yet Taylor was not advocating the unrestricted, self-interested pursuit of opportunity, which could generate large-scale inequalities. He denounced "avarice" as an "evil," and, unlike Madison, who would stimulate vices in order to check them, Taylor sought to "suppress" vices such as avarice by basing government on "good" moral principles. Further, Taylor assumed that without artificial or legal stimulation, differences in human qualities would not generate significant inequalities. When allocated according to the differing physical and moral qualities of people, property would be distributed neither "too unequal[ly]" nor "too equally."[36]

ens, Ga., 1979), 25; and Norman K. Risjord, *The Old Republicans: Southern Conservatism in the Age of Jefferson* (New York, 1965), 262.

35 Foshee, "Jeffersonian Political Economy," 526; John Taylor, *An Inquiry into the Principles and Policy of the Government of the United States,* ed. Lorin Baritz (Indianapolis, 1969), 98, 66, 493. Also useful in understanding Taylor is Duncan MacLeod, "The Political Economy of John Taylor of Caroline," *Journal of American Studies,* 14 (Dec. 1980), 387–405. Taylor explicitly denied he was an enemy to manufactures. See John Taylor, *Arator,* ed. M. E. Bradford (Indianapolis, 1977), 86–87.

36 Taylor, *An Inquiry,* 122, 559, 106, 246, 482, 531, 244, 544. MacLeod, "The Political Economy of John Taylor," 404. Richard L. Bushman explains that the prevalence of independent freeholding made Americans more concerned about dependence than inequality. Owing to the extensiveness of freeholding, Americans considered inequalities to be "harmless." See Richard L. Bushman, " 'This New Man': Dependence and Independence, 1776," in Richard L. Bushman et al., eds., *Uprooted Americans: Essays to Honor Oscar Handlin* (Boston, 1979), 91–93.

Such a natural division of property and knowledge was essential to preserve liberty. "Is an accumulation of wealth and knowledge by law in a few hands, to be found in any recipe for making a free republick?" he asked.[37] Quoting John Adams, Taylor considered wealth the "great machine for governing the world" and a major cause of national discontent. The accumulation of a disproportionate share of wealth into a few hands was as dangerous to republicanism as an imbalance of political rights. "As power follows wealth, the majority must have wealth or lose power," Taylor continued. "If wealth is accumulated in the hands of a few . . . it carries the power also; and a government becomes as certainly aristocratical, by a monopoly of wealth, as by a monopoly of arms. A minority, obtaining a majority of wealth or arms in any mode, becomes the government." In order to sustain "a democratick republick," it was therefore essential that "wealth, like suffrage . . . be considerably distributed."[38]

Taylor directed much of his attention to the "evil moral principles" that endangered government. His special enmity was reserved for the transfer of property by law, which he defined as "aristocracy." There were different kinds of aristocracies, such as earlier ones based on religion and title. But the present-day and most dangerous form, the so-called aristocracy of the third age, was that of "paper and patronage." This aristocracy favored "artificial property," such as "paper stock, office, and corporate privileges," legal entities capable of manipulation by government action. Whereas an agrarian society helped sustain a proper division of property and power, the paper and patronage system produced dangerous concentrations of both. Given the dangers posed by the new aristocracy, Taylor considered the use of the law to amass property more pernicious than proposals to equalize property.[39]

While Taylor was highly critical of energetic and powerful government, the very existence of an aristocracy of paper and patronage using law to transfer wealth made it imperative that government be active as a counterweight. The purpose of government was to "protect individuals against these very associations" of paper capitalists, and Taylor ridiculed the laissez-faire pretenses of corporations that,

[37] Taylor, *An Inquiry,* 530–31, 230–31.
[38] Ibid., 149–50, 241.
[39] Ibid., 342, 33–34; 46–47, 480, 245, 483; Conkin, *Prophets of Prosperity,* 55.

protected by law, advised that individuals be left alone by government. Somewhat paradoxically, therefore, society preserved republican liberty by using government to eliminate, or at least limit, the law as an instrument to transfer property and wealth.[40]

Taylor's writings and influence suggest that republican and agrarian currents of thought extended beyond the immediate post-Revolutionary period. Most historians conclude that the evident triumph of market values in the period after the War of 1812 signaled the virtual demise of republican and agrarian traditions. The new political system, according to Edward Pessen, was based on expediency not principle, and the "rampant opportunism" of its leaders was "in accord with the spirit of the times." What remained of republicanism was, at best, merely a "bastard" variety, which retained some of the vocabulary of classical republicanism but stretched and distorted its terms to fit the new market economy.[41]

Yet the persistence of Taylor's concerns and vocabulary into the 1830s argues otherwise. Drawing upon the legacy of republicanism, Jacksonian Democrats celebrated virtue (public and private) and honored the common good; they decried excessive government and corrupt links with private interests, especially financial and monetary; and they upheld a relative equality of condition as a prerequisite to republican society. "No free government can stand without virtue in the people and a lofty spirit of patriotism, and if the sordid feelings of mere selfishness shall usurp the place which ought to be filled by public spirit, the legislation of Congress will soon be converted into a scramble for personal and sectional advantages," Jackson explained in his final address to the American people. He warned that endangerment to liberty was most likely to come from internal decay, "from cupidity, from corruption, from disappointed ambition and inordinate thirst for power." Among the great sources of power and corruption, but by no means the only one, was the "moneyed interest." The

[40] Taylor, *An Inquiry,* 335–56, 559.

[41] Steven Watts, *The Republic Reborn: War and the Making of Liberal America, 1790–1820* (Baltimore, 1987), xvii–xviii, 2–16, 298–321; Banning, *Jeffersonian Persuasion,* 299–302; Wood, *Creation of the American Republic,* 606–15; Pessen, *Jacksonian America,* 170, 196. For the expression "bastard republicanism," see the stimulating essay by Roland Berthoff, "Peasants and Artisans," 585. See also Berthoff's essay "Independence and Attachment, Virtue and Interest: From Republican Citizen to Free Enterpriser, 1787–1837," in Bushman et al., eds., *Uprooted Americans,* 97–124.

paper money system was "an engine to undermine . . . free institutions," and Jackson cautioned against those who were prepared to use it to "engross all power in the hands of the few and to govern by corruption or force." To be sure, by the 1830s, republicanism had evolved even farther from its classical aristocratic and elitist roots. It was increasingly synonymous with democracy and majority rule.[42] Nevertheless, republican and agrarian traditions continued to operate in a coherent fashion, alerting Americans to genuine social problems that were emerging in their midst.

For the most part, republican and agrarian ideals of equality remained in precarious balance with liberalism's emphasis on self-interest and the legitimacy of distinctions consequent to equal opportunity. What especially maintained this equipoise was the comforting notion that there existed natural and inherent limits to whatever inequality resulted from legitimate competition. Adherents of what the sociologist Pierre L. van den Berghe has called "Herrenvolk democracy," the Jacksonians minimized innate differences between whites while drawing a sharp line between white people and other races. Since whites were relatively equal in natural attributes, gross distinctions were largely the product of artificial circumstances, such as unjust laws and corruption. Jacksonians therefore assumed that relative equality was the natural condition of society, and that it complemented, rather than conflicted with, equal rights. Violations of equal rights and opportunity, however, distorted and eroded this essential foundation of republican liberty.[43]

[42] It is evident that Jackson was using the words "corruption" and "virtue" in a republican context to note the kind of social and political decay in a republic that accompanied a decline of public spirit. He was not referring simply to codes of personal moral behavior. See Richardson, ed., *Messages and Papers,* 4: 1520–26; and Watson, *Liberty and Power,* 43–51. The transformation of republicanism into democratic majoritarianism is discussed in Remini, *Andrew Jackson and American Democracy,* esp. xiv, 337–46; and Remini, *Legacy of Andrew Jackson,* esp. 7–9, 22–27. The persistent but changing nature of republicanism after 1815 is argued by William E. Gienapp, who explores the significance of the concept of a Slave Power conspiracy in the 1850s as an expression of republicanism's hostility to aristocracy. See William E. Gienapp, "The Republican Party and the Slave Power," in *Race and Slavery in America: Essays in Honor of Kenneth M. Stampp,* ed. Robert H. Abzug and Stephen E. Maizlish (Lexington, Ky., 1986), 59–64.

[43] For "Herrenvolk democracy," see Pierre L. van den Berghe, *Race and Racism: A Comparative Perspective* (New York, 1967), 17–18, 77–80; and Fredrickson, *Black Image in the White Mind,* 43–70. To the degree that liberalism's commitment to self-interest and opportunity assumes that inequality in society is natural, it offered a

Evidence of Jacksonian egalitarian sentiments comes in part from leading Democratic political economists and publicists, who artfully blended agrarian and republican devotion to a relatively equal community of citizens, alongside liberal endorsements of the pursuit of opportunity. Although not political decision makers themselves, their ideas were widely circulated in newspapers and books, and can be taken to reflect the party's political culture. In some cases, they directly influenced the thinking of politicians.[44]

William M. Gouge was probably the ablest and most prominent theorist of the Jacksonian hard-money point of view. A Philadelphia journalist, publisher, and Treasury Department employee, Gouge specialized in money and banking, the central policy issues around which the debate on equality revolved. His attacks on paper money banking directly contributed to Jackson's assault against the BUS and excessive paper issues.[45]

Gouge's classic *A Short History of Paper Money Banking in the United States* (1833) was a strident condemnation of corporate privilege, especially in paper money banking. It was a best seller of its day, and Paul Conkin claims that *A Short History* was the most widely read American book on serious economic issues prior to Henry George's *Progress and Poverty.* In it, Gouge charged that the paper system violated equal rights, contributed to moral corruption, and interfered with healthy economic growth. Banks owed their influence to special acts of legislation and the government's reception of their notes. The granting of such "exclusive privileges," he alleged, was "repugnant to the fundamental principles of American Government." Furthermore, banking practices debased the moral standards of the country by encouraging excessive desire for luxury

different starting point of social analysis from that adopted by leading Jacksonians. They tended to begin with the principle of relative equality. However, both approaches shared the view that a limited degree of inequality was inevitable.

44 Jacksonian-era political economists are treated in Joseph Dorfman, *The Economic Mind in American Civilization,* 5 vols. (New York, 1946–59), vol. 2; and more recently in Conkin, *Prophets of Prosperity.* My treatment owes a great deal to the discussion of political economists found in Marvin Meyers. See Meyers *Jacksonian Persuasion,* chs. 8–10.

45 On Gouge, see Joseph Dorfman's introductory essay in William M. Gouge, *A Short History of Paper Money and Banking in the United States* (1833; reprint ed., New York, 1968), 5–26; Benjamin G. Rader, "William M. Gouge: Jacksonian Theorist," *Pennsylvania History,* 30 (Oct. 1963), 443–53; and Conkin, *Prophets of Prosperity,* 207–15.

and wealth, and impeded economic progress by promoting "successive 'expansions' and 'contractions.' "[46]

Gouge also drew attention to the banking system's adverse effect on the nation's distribution of wealth. "We have heretofore been too disregardful of the fact, that social order is quite as dependent on the laws which regulate the distribution of wealth, as on political organization," he argued. Banks were the "chief regulating cause" of the country's distribution of wealth and, consequently, merited "particular attention."[47] According to Gouge, the paper money system distorted the allocation of wealth by creating an artificial arrangement of rewards and punishments. In effect, corporate banking privileges, based on political favor, inverted the operation of the "natural and just" causes of wealth and poverty. Banking institutions, Gouge claimed, laid the foundation of "an *artificial* inequality of wealth" whereby the wealth of a few increased "in the ratio of compound interest," while the rest of the community found its wealth reduced and impoverished. Like Taylor, Gouge argued that the paper system was the modern equivalent of the feudal system, dividing the community "into distinct classes" and corrupting its "morals and manners."[48]

Eliminating the paper system would not produce a society of uniform and absolute equality. In the best or ideal society, where laws and institutions were few, unobtrusive, and impartial, inequality of condition would remain. Proceeding from mental, physical, and personality differences, this "natural inequality" was neither evil nor unjust. The "honest capitalist" and the "honest laborer" had the natural right to profit from the immediate product of their labor. Their claims were "equally sacred," and constituted no injustice to the "idle and improvident." Indeed, Gouge argued, the sight of one man enjoying the reward of his good conduct "would induce others to imitate his example."[49]

Yet Gouge's defense of free competition and inequality operated within the broader context of a basic moral commitment to an egalitarian society. Indeed, it was because Gouge sought an egalitarian social order that he advocated equal rights and laws; laissez-faire principles

[46] Conkin, *Prophets of Prosperity,* 208. Gouge, *Short History of Paper Money,* 41, 85, 136.

[47] Gouge, *Short History of Paper Money,* 2, 235; Rader, "William M. Gouge," 451–53.

[48] Gouge, *Short History of Paper Money,* 89–90, 29–32, 91, 228.

[49] Ibid., 91, 133.

prevented the use of law for personal enrichment at the expense of others. Gouge preferred that personal wealth be accumulated slowly and be based on work, and that differences in wealth should be "natural" and, therefore, relatively minor. In short, he valued a middle-ground society that, like its individual members, was characterized by moderate prosperity honestly gained. It is a general maxim, he announced, that "too much or too little wealth, is injurious to the character of the individual, and, when it extends through a community, it is injurious to the character of that community."[50]

In order to reform abuses, some government activity was essential. Government had the "duty" to preserve the "natural equality of men," so far as "equal laws and equal rights and privileges" permitted. Government, therefore, had to "get rid" of the "*instruments* of evil," paper money and money corporations. Only when the "excrescences" that generated artificial inequality were removed would the American republican form of government become "THE PRAISE OF ALL THE EARTH." The leadership of this movement would come from the "farmers and mechanics," those who were least entangled in the meshes of the paper system. Like Taylor, Gouge looked for republican virtue primarily "in the country," where corruption had not yet spread.[51]

A similar mixture of liberal economics and classical republican influences is found in the writings and speeches of Theodore Sedgwick. Sedgwick, scion of an illustrious Revolutionary patriot and leader of the Massachusetts Federalist Party and bar, was himself a former Federalist who eventually settled in the Jacksonian party. His popular reputation was based not on his political deeds (he never held a prominent national office), but on his reputation as a writer on economic matters. His most famous publication, *Public and Private Economy,* was intended as "a popular work" on political economy, written expressly "for the people." It was issued in three volumes between 1836 and 1839.[52]

Sedgwick's stated objective of showing "the value of property, or

[50] Ibid., 96–97.
[51] Ibid., 229–35.
[52] For assessments of Sedgwick's life and views, see the introductory essay by Joseph Dorfman to Sedgwick, *Public and Private Economy.* Sedgwick's statement of purpose is quoted by Dorfman, ibid., 18. See also Meyers, *Jacksonian Persuasion,* ch. 8, esp. 125–26; Conkin, *Prophets of Prosperity,* 203.

wealth, and how it may be acquired," points toward an acceptance of the market, self-interest, and equal opportunity. Property represented progress and civilization. It was the essential condition for prosperity and happiness, and the means by which mankind developed out of the condition of savage to that of citizen. Sedgwick favored any productive activity by which wealth was increased, whether manufacturing, commerce, or transportation improvements. Consequently, he opposed artificial barriers that impeded its pursuit. Like Taylor and Gouge, he decried "monopolies, abuses, [and] privileges" in the public and private sectors as inimical to "*an immense increase of wealth.*"[53]

Sedgwick, however, devoted relatively little attention to the institutional and legal problems that haunted Gouge. Instead, he focused on individual improvement and character, the need for virtue in the people. He advanced the doctrine of "*self-elevation,*" calling it one of the "grand distinctions" of Americans as compared to other people. Self-elevation depended on the acquisition of property, virtue, and education, with property being the most important of the three elements.[54]

Perhaps reflecting the conservative, hierarchical bias of his Federalist background, Sedgwick held that there always were, and should be, class distinctions. "As there must be higher and lower classes," he wrote, "it is Providence that assigns us our places in the one or the other." This inequality, however, was justified only as a consequence of natural or providential distinctions, not when produced by institutions and laws. "Nature's equality" existed when men obtained property according to "their talents, and industry, and economy," he argued. It resulted from an environment of "free competition to all," in which workers secured the rewards of their labor.[55]

This language of self-elevation and inevitable class distinctions seems in retrospect to have paved the way toward a competitive, highly individualistic liberal order. But Sedgwick's own expectation was different. He looked, instead, toward the revitalization of a republican community based on relative equality and Christian virtues. Citizens were not atoms of self-interest, but self-restraining moral

[53] Sedgwick, *Public and Private Economy,* 1:13, 19; 2:86–87; 3:198; Meyers, *Jacksonian Persuasion,* 136.

[54] Sedgwick, *Public and Private Economy,* 1:225.

[55] Ibid., 1:23, 234, 83–84.

beings, autonomous and happy. Wealth per se was not desirable, especially when corruptly gained and associated with sensuality, luxury, and vice.[56]

Indeed, vice was the basis of despotic governments, whereas virtue and republicanism were "synonymous." To Sedgwick, there was "no hope" of preserving liberty without virtue. And to secure virtue and republican government, it was essential to have personal autonomy and independence. These qualities, in turn, were founded on property. The structure was interconnected and mutually reinforcing: from property to autonomy to virtue to liberty. "Independence is secured by our property," Sedgwick explained. "We have gained our *political* independence," he continued, "but there is another, and that is independence of mind." Property brought independence and "dignity" as well as affluence, making workers "the arbiters of their own destiny." A free people could only hope to support their institutions by their virtues, and "a reasonable independence" was the "greatest security to these virtues that can be thought of." The aim of property, therefore, was not to enrich a person but to "contribute to the public good in some way or other."[57]

Despite his acceptance of all useful production, even commerce and manufacturing, Sedgwick, like Taylor, identified agriculture as most congruent with a virtuous citizenry. Both philosophy and common sense, he claimed, agreed on "the superior virtue of the independent cultivator of the earth." Other classes, such as merchants, physicians, and manufacturers, were richer, but the "benign power" that sprang from the regular tilling of the earth by the owners of it made farmers superior in "morals and intelligence."[58]

Sedgwick directly linked this agrarian ideal with republicanism, contending that the countryside was the continuing source of America's ability to ward off European decadence. "We came to these desolate shores as lovers of republicanism," he explained, and have continually advanced into the country, "always carrying our republicanism with us." He predicted that city and countryside would meld as cities profited by the countryside's "more virtuous simplicity" and the country learned from the city's "superior refinements." "Let the

[56] Ibid., 2:115–16; 1:114.
[57] Ibid., 2:168; 1:21–22; 2:86; 1:184; 2:114, 49–50; 1:124.
[58] Ibid., 1:222, 223.

country exert that moral superiority over the great cities which is a new power here," he urged.[59]

If property, particularly in its landed form, was the foundation of republican government, what distribution of it best maintained liberty? Sedgwick ridiculed agrarian leveling. "People ought to be ashamed to be frightened at it, or even to talk of it," he asserted. Yet his own intellectual edifice was built upon the assumption of a wide and relatively equal distribution of property. It was "moderate property," or "comfortable property," that best secured virtue and provided a bulwark against temptation. Those of "middling property," who constituted "nine-tenths of the population," were the real people and held the fate of the nation in their hands. The cardinal point of studying political economy, he declared, was to teach "how property may be more equally destributed [*sic*]" so that a more just distribution of property among the population of farmers, mechanics, and laborers would release their productive energies and increase the nation's wealth.[60]

To establish greater equality, it was necessary to strengthen Christian morality and virtue, as well as to eliminate privilege and monopoly. Proper principles would yield a greater equality of condition than presently existed, based on a "natural" and "just" division, rather than the "ill-gotten, *disproportioned* wealth" that resulted from "unfair dealings . . . fraud . . . oppression . . . monopoly" and other evils. "Equality of condition, or as much of that as is attainable, with freedom to all to exercise their genius and industry for their own advantage, must be the law," he explained. "By equalizing property as far as it can be equalized in a state of freedom," productive labor and equitable laws would produce the greatest happiness for the greatest number.[61]

Sedgwick simply assumed that increasing property by productive labor helped equalize it. "Virtuous, profitable labour," he claimed, increased property, and "by increasing property" did all it could "to equalize it." On the other hand, the disparity of wealth found in an aristocratic system like England's was so great and so extensive that it "never could exist in a state of freedom." Virtue and equal rights,

[59] Ibid., 1:223, 3:156.
[60] Ibid., 2:88; 1:21, 243, 41.
[61] Ibid., 3:143, 2:86; 1:15; 2:122.

then, were inextricably linked to the increase and general diffusion of property, and to a relative equality of condition. "Let the people, then, Heaven directed, work out their own salvation!" he urged. "Let them keep their minds constantly turned to their pole star, the great principle of a more equal division of property, to be brought about by their own improvement in virtue."[62]

Sedgwick, in effect, sketched an unbroken circle of improvement that guaranteed liberty. Virtue increased the amount of property, which brought about its more equal division, while a more equal division of property brought forth increased virtue. Breaking the bonds of privilege and encouraging "self-elevation," did not, in the end, yield a libertarian rush for self-interested riches or inequality. Instead, virtue, personal autonomy, and equal laws produced a relatively equal society composed of productive, free, and happy citizens. In a "natural" social order, there would be some, moderate inequality based on personal distinction. But immoderate inequality could only be artificial, the result of privilege or vice. By different routes, Sedgwick and Gouge both arrived at similar conclusions regarding the relationship between republicanism and equality of conditions.[63]

From the editorial chair of the New York *Evening Post* and the *Plaindealer,* the Democratic journalist William Leggett lent additional testimony to the concern about equality of condition in Jacksonian America. During his brief career (he died in 1839 at the age of thirty-seven), Leggett was both heralded and condemned as a leading publicist of laissez-faire, antimonopoly, and antiprivilege tenets. No one was a more determined advocate of private rights and property.[64] Like other Jacksonians, he categorically denied the charge of "agrarianism" and accepted inequality when it resulted from "natural causes." But like Gouge, Leggett's attack on corporations, monopolies, and other government restraints on liberty reflected a conviction that legal privilege in any form upset the natural and roughly egalitarian order of society. By distorting economic relationships, these ac-

[62] Ibid., 2:138, 123, 178.

[63] Ibid., 3:142–43.

[64] For differing assessments of Leggett's career and significance, see Richard Hofstadter, "William Leggett, Spokesman of Jacksonian Democracy," *Political Science Quarterly,* 58 (Dec. 1943), 581–94; and Carl Degler, "The Locofocos: Urban 'Agrarians,' " *Journal of Economic History,* 16 (Sept. 1956), 322–33. Especially helpful is Marvin Meyers's discussion, in *Jacksonian Persuasion,* ch. 9.

tions generated inequality of condition and class conflict. Inequality, in turn, undermined republicanism and liberty.[65]

American democracy, to Leggett, was more than the idea of government by the majority. Liberty was inseparable from proper economic and social principles, and the special economic correlative of political democracy was equal protection. Equal protection, or equal rights, was the only legitimate end of government. When erroneous principles prevailed, when violations of equal rights occurred, whether in banking or other areas, an inequality of condition arose that was incompatible with liberty. The practice of granting privileges was "the fruitful source of those inequalities of human condition – those extremes of wealth and poverty, so uniformly fatal to the liberties of mankind," he maintained. Acts of "partial legislation" were "undemocratic" and subversive of equal rights. They were "calculated to create artificial inequality in human condition; to elevate the few and depress the many; and, in their final operation, to build up a powerful aristocracy, and overthrow the whole frame of democratic government."[66]

Like other Jacksonians, Leggett distinguished between natural and artificial social arrangements. The "natural system" was based upon equal rights, while governments which denied equal rights substituted "an artificial system for that of nature." In the natural order of things, wealth would be accumulated gradually from a "regular vocation." There would be inequality, but Leggett assumed it would be moderate. Large-scale inequality was due to legal privilege, to monopolies and special charters such as existed in the banking system. Privilege increased the wealth of the rich and rendered "more abject and oppressive" the poverty of the poor. Such "intermeddling" was "artificial," and merited condemnation. Thus, Leggett attributed the "vast disparity of condition" in America to a "great and pervading error in our system," the bestowing of privileges on some, while denying them to others.[67]

[65] Leggett, *Political Writings,* 2:80, 164.

[66] Ibid., 2:109; 1:78, 85.

[67] William Leggett, *Democratick Editorials: Essays in Jacksonian Political Economy by William Leggett,* ed. Lawrence H. White (Indianapolis, 1984), 178; Leggett, *Political Writings,* 2:87; 1:41; 2:164. Rush Welter notes the egalitarianism embodied in the Jacksonian concept of the self-made man, who "inhabited a society of substantial equals in which it could be taken for granted that honest labor would bring only relatively limited rewards." A "natural economy" would not result in grave social distinctions. See Welter, *Mind of America,* 86.

Doubtless influenced by John Taylor's rhetorical flourishes, Leggett identified the country's "privileged orders" as the "scrip nobility . . . aristocrats, clothed with special immunities." They controlled, indirectly but surely, the political power of the state, monopolized the most copious sources of profit, and exploited labor. This most affluent class did not receive its wealth by "patient industry" or "superior wisdom," or even by inheritance. Most derived their "princely fortunes" from "special privileges." As Marvin Meyers observes, Leggett effectively molded the vocabulary of laissez-faire economics and Jeffersonian liberalism into a class appeal. He pointed to the corruption of the legislative process as the means by which certain groups transformed equality of rights and condition into a system of speculation, privilege, class exploitation, and excessive inequality. Little wonder that he was charged with radicalism.[68]

The writings of Taylor, Sedgwick, Gouge, and Leggett were virtually all produced before the onset of the Panic of 1837. They demonstrate the egalitarian assumptions of the Jacksonians when party ideology was first formulated.[69] Significantly, these ideas show a remarkable agreement with those of John L. O'Sullivan, the influential editor of *The United States Magazine and Democratic Review.* O'Sullivan's journal, which first appeared in 1837, aspired to be a respectable intellectual publication with Democratic sympathies (some thought the concept self-contradictory). It coincided with Martin Van Buren's presidency and the more militant antibanking campaign that flared during economic hard times. A brief look at O'Sullivan's views about equality shows that the Democratic Party's concern for distributive justice was not just a response to the economy's downturn; it also reflected assumptions about equality and republicanism imbedded in the party's makeup from the outset.[70]

O'Sullivan struck a by now familiar note in basing republican self-government on extensive property holding, equal rights, a virtuous citizenry, and relative equality of condition. "A democratic government, the leading principle of which is political equality," he con-

68 Leggett, *Political Writings,* 2:123; Meyers, *Jacksonian Persuasion,* 141; Hill, *Political Theory of John Taylor,* 304–8.

69 The last two volumes of Sedgwick's work were actually published in 1838 and 1839, but they largely elaborated ideas found in the first volume, published in 1836.

70 For O'Sullivan, see Schlesinger, Jr., *Age of Jackson,* 371–73; Welter, *Mind of America,* 177–78.

tended, "is the natural expression of a general equality of condition and especially of property among the people." Where equality of condition and property existed, democratic government was "real, substantial, and . . . permanent." O'Sullivan warned that legislation favoring the accumulation or concentration of property, such as monopolistic banking charters, was "anti-democratic" and tended to "the subversion of the present form of government."[71] Widespread property holding, "the general prevalence of the means of comfortable living," was "essential" to the preservation of self-government in America. "If an essential inequality of condition should ever take place among the people of the United States," he cautioned, "the principle of *aristocracy* would immediately prevail in the government." O'Sullivan referred to a "happy mediocrity of fortune which is so favorable to the practice of Christian and republican virtues."[72]

Like the others, O'Sullivan categorically denied that equality would be gained at the expense of property rights. "We are no agrarians – no levellers," he announced. An "absolute equality of condition" was neither practical nor desirable, given differences in ability, industry, economy, enterprise, and other circumstances "which human legislation cannot control, and ought not to attempt to control." Yet it is evident that O'Sullivan assumed that "free competition" and equal rights would in fact produce both orderly progress and relative equality. Equal rights and personal autonomy, he argued, "tend to equalize the distribution of wealth." They "lessen dependence" and "more equitably" apportion property to eliminate the present contrasts created by "overgrown affluence and wretched poverty."[73]

O'Sullivan, who was familiar with the writings of Gouge and Taylor, also attributed excessive, or "artificial," inequality to improper laws and principles. These produced "artificial distinctions" in society, enriching a few and impoverishing the rest of the community. Monopolies, paper money banking, and the credit system skewed the distribution of property and produced fluctuations of fortune. Moreover, they also generated such evils as intemperance, poverty, and the "love of finery" that eroded the moral fabric of the republic. "Virtue

[71] *The United States Magazine and Democratic Review,* 2 (July 1838), 349–50.
[72] Ibid., 6 (Aug. 1839), 114; 2 (July 1838), 351; 6 (Dec. 1839), 457.
[73] Ibid., 2 (July 1838), 345; 6 (Dec. 1839), 461–62; 1 (Oct. 1837), 6–7; 6 (Sept. 1839), 215.

is the soul of a republic," he announced, but the "artificial inequality of wealth" and the fluctuations of fortune produced by false principles yielded instead a "moral canker." When government, therefore, adopted partial laws, it began a course of "injustice and fraud" that opened the way for corruption and oppression.[74]

Concern about distributional equality was not limited to Jacksonian journalists and political economists. It also influenced politicians and public policy during Jackson's presidency. Although sometimes portrayed as opportunists solely motivated by power and patronage, leading Jacksonian politicians considered equality of condition instrumental to the continued success of republicanism. Convinced that government action could and should be employed to maintain ostensibly "natural" conditions, Democratic politicos often portrayed themselves as warring against vested interests that, by "artificial" means, accumulated wealth incompatible with republican virtue and free institutions. By drawing upon long-standing, deeply cherished political values, such egalitarian appeals were doubtless good politics. But their rhetoric also recognized that America was, in fact, showing worrisome signs of social and economic stratification. A Democratic essayist called attention to "the growing progress of inequality" in the country, and Mississippi's Jacksonian leader, John F. Claiborne, observed that "the inequality of wealth, the artificial distinctions of society, and the contrasts of plenty and privation, were painfully visible" in "large cities and manufacturing towns."[75]

The relationship between public policy and equality of condition was the central focus of a remarkable speech delivered by Representative John Bell of Tennessee during the 1832 tariff debates. Bell, at that time a staunch Democrat, attacked protective tariffs and the entire American System. That system, he charged, was actually a misnomer. It was not American but, rather, a "European system transferred to America" that would replicate a political and social

[74] Ibid., 6 (Dec. 1839), 452; 6 (July 1839), 12; 6 (Dec. 1839), 457–59; 7 (Mar. 1840), 227; 6 (Sept. 1839), 214.

[75] "Franklin," in Washington *Globe*, April 23, 1835; *Register of Debates*, 24th Cong., 2nd sess., January 4, 1837, 1249. For the trend toward increased inequality of wealth in antebellum America, see Pessen, *Riches, Class, and Power*, 41–43, 304; Jeffrey G. Williamson and Peter H. Lindert, *American Inequality: A Macroeconomic History* (New York, 1980), 46, 62; Gavin Wright, *The Political Economy of the Cotton South: Households, Markets, and Wealth in the Nineteenth Century* (New York, 1978), 24–42.

order based on inequality of condition. A "true" American system, Bell argued, would be based, instead, on the principle of a "perfect equality of rank, rights, and privileges." Government would achieve this "by discouraging the accumulation of great wealth in the hands of individual citizens."[76]

Bell rejected the notion that government should be primarily concerned with the increase of national wealth; it must also consider the matter of the distribution of wealth. Better, he declared, to add less to the stock of national wealth rather than have it distributed, as in Europe, into the hands of a few. "I affirm," he announced, "that every addition made to the stock of national wealth by the accumulation of overgrown individual fortunes, is a positive national evil. All such unequal and disproportioned fortunes are, in general, so much added to the resources of the enemies of free and just Governments." The principles of political economy must be compatible with America's political institutions, which meant that the production of wealth must also "secure the equal distribution of wealth."[77]

Bell conceded that absolute equality of condition was impracticable and unattainable in any society based on private property. Yet the principle of public responsibility for greater equality remained operative. "To counteract the tendency to inequality in all societies, and as far as practicable to prevent the mischievous effect of this necessary constitution of society, by a wise policy adapted to this end, is, or should be, the care of every man employed in the direction of public affairs," he declared.[78]

Directing this argument to the tariff issue, Bell claimed that it was imperative to resist the protecting system that distributed wealth disproportionately "in the hands of the few." The protective system, Bell concluded, hurt the South, and produced inequality in the North. "The poor are made poorer, and the rich richer."[79] Bell succinctly captured the broad egalitarian assumptions that underlay Jacksonian ideology, and the party's mouthpiece, the Washington *Globe,* ap-

[76] *Register of Debates,* 22nd Cong., 1st sess., June 8, 1832, 3357. During Jackson's second term Bell moved into the Whig Party, largely over the president's continued assaults against the BUS and his hard-money preferences. See Joseph Howard Parks, *John Bell of Tennessee* (Baton Rouge, 1950), 80–82.

[77] Ibid., 3359.

[78] Ibid., 3359–60.

[79] Ibid., 3361, 3384.

plauded his effort as "admirable" and "statesman-like" in its view of the "general and permanent good."[80]

Bell's argument was echoed by other southern Democrats. Although some of them would soon join the Whigs in the aftermath of nullification, they, too, linked protection to distributional inequality. Felix Grundy of Tennessee, who would remain a loyal Jacksonian, charged that protective tariffs acted inequitably by taxing the poor while rewarding the "privileged order." Willie P. Mangum of North Carolina likewise explained that the tariff system promoted "inequality . . . upon the different avocations" as well as between sections. And Jackson himself, in urging lower rates, remarked that many Americans criticized protection as "tending to concentrate wealth into a few hands" and as creating "those germs of dependence and vice which in other countries have characterized the existence of monopolies and proved so destructive of liberty and the general good." As the *Globe* summarized the Democratic viewpoint, the tariff system sustained "monopolies in the hands of a few, by levying . . . a tax on the many."[81]

Similarly, in their war against the BUS, and their more generalized antibanking and hard-money campaign, Democrats claimed they had uncovered a veritable fount of artifice and privileged aggrandizement. During Jackson's first term this egalitarian theme was relatively mute, but it nevertheless sounded on a number of occasions. In his famous Bank Veto message, for example, when Jackson eloquently defended natural distinctions in society, he also denounced "artificial distinctions" and "exclusive privileges," which made the "rich richer and the potent more powerful."[82]

It was during Jackson's second administration, as the national bank debate spilled over into topics of paper money, state banking,

[80] Washington *Globe,* June 11, 1832. See also Richardson, ed., *Messages and Papers,* 4:1523, 1525.

[81] *Register of Debates,* 22nd Cong., 1st sess., February 15, 1832, 406; ibid., 22nd Cong., 1st sess., February 7, 1832, 311–14, 326; ibid., 22nd Cong., 1st sess., February 21, 1832, 440; Washington *Globe,* July 27, 1832. See also Washington *Globe,* April 25, 1832. John Ashworth suggests a special relationship between the South and republicanism during the Jeffersonian era. Ashworth, "The Jeffersonians," 433–35.

[82] Richardson, ed., *Messages and Papers,* 3:1153. For other examples of the Jacksonians' association of the BUS with inequality, see *Register of Debates,* 21st Cong., 2nd sess., February 2, 1831, 53–54, 74; *Register of Debates,* 22nd Cong., 1st sess., March 13, 1832, 2135–36; *Register of Debates,* 22nd Cong., 1st sess., July 11, 1832, 1240.

and the nature of the credit system, that Democratic assaults against legislative-induced inequality blossomed. After Jackson's removal of the deposits from the BUS, Pennsylvania Democrat John Galbraith denounced the excessive issues of paper money by state banks as "rapidly building up a mushroom aristocracy in the country, of a most dangerous and destructive character, and bearing down the most dear and sacred principles of our republican fabric." In an ideal community, Galbraith explained, circulating capital was consistent with production, and everyone acquired property "just in proportion to his industry and economy." But when a bank was introduced into this setting, it brought speculation, boom, contraction, and unsettled economic conditions, so that the community was "kept in a constant fever." As a result, "the few" who managed its concerns grew daily richer, becoming "the lords and disposers of the property of others," while their more industrious neighbors became "slaves."[83]

The "Address of the Republican Members of Congress from the State of New York" in 1834 made a similar point. The congressmen charged the BUS with "multiplying the instances of poverty and want on the one hand, and of bloated wealth on the other," thereby aggravating "the disparities of condition" which already existed.[84] The Massachusetts intellectual and politician George Bancroft cited as "the great objection" to the BUS, "its tendency to promote extreme inequalities in point of fortune." The association of the BUS with concentrated wealth and political power represented the "most baleful" of all heresies, according to Bancroft. History demonstrated that the joining of political power and privileged wealth introduced corruption in government and "extremes of inequality" in the distribution of

[83] *Register of Debates,* 24th Cong., 2nd sess., Appendix, March 3, 1837, 149–50. See also James Buchanan's speech on the credit system, ibid., 24th Cong., 1st sess., March 28, 1836, 1004. A Boston newspaper condemned the existence of "a most powerful and concentrated monied aristocracy," dangerous to the stability of government and the liberties of the people. It warned that as the economy developed, and particularly as manufacturing grew, the country's increased wealth would "become more and more unequally divided, and more and more concentrated among a certain class." The editor ominously forecast that the independence of the common people would diminish until they became " 'white slaves', as our manufacturers now style the British operatives, the mere creatures of their wealthy masters." Somewhat fatalistically conceding that a trend in this direction was "natural and unavoidable," the paper charged that the American System, including banks and high tariffs "rapidly" hastened the crisis. *Boston Commercial Gazette,* quoted in Washington *Globe,* November 12, 1833.

[84] Quoted in Washington *Globe,* July 19, 1834.

property.[85] The Washington *Globe* "cheerfully" approved every word of Bancroft's analysis and published a series of essays by "SPECTATOR," which affirmed that "partial legislation" led to "systems of extreme inequality," whereas the peace and good order of the American republic depended on "our greater equality of condition" than in Europe.[86]

Although this political analysis is intended to be suggestive rather than conclusive, it is evident that Jacksonian politicians and policy makers considered equality of condition instrumental to the continued success of republicanism. Further evidence could readily be obtained to demonstrate a consistent connection between ideology and policy.[87] Of course, there will always be a gap in politics between rhetoric and action. But to conclude, as do some historians, that "Democratic policies which contradicted Democratic pronouncements do not inspire respect for the latter as serious statements of intentions" ignores the frequent occasions when principles and program coincided.[88]

Indeed, the idea that a proper distribution of wealth was the foundation of a free society also influenced the opposition Whig Party. For the most part, historians have characterized Whigs as the party of economic development, enterprise, and equal opportunity. Conservative and paternalistic, they celebrated the benefits of economic growth, worried little about its distributional consequences, and chastised Jackson and the Democratic Party for appealing to class prejudice and threatening the security of property. The Whigs envisioned a morally and economically progressive America, united by the harmo-

[85] Washington *Globe,* November 13, 1834.

[86] Washington *Globe,* November 13, 1834; February 12, 1834; April 3, 1835; March 27, 1835. See also Washington *Globe,* April 23, 1835; October 26, 1835.

[87] For the egalitarian influences in the Democracy's land policy, for example, see Richardson, ed., *Messages and Papers,* 3:1108, 1163, 1287; Washington *Globe,* July 3, July 8, and July 12, 1833, "One of the People," November 7, 1835. *Register of Debates,* 21st Cong., 1st sess., May 5, 1830, 415; ibid., 24th Cong., 1st sess., April 29, 1836, 1355; ibid., 24th Cong., 1st sess., April 25, 1836, 3362–63; ibid., 24th Cong., 2nd sess., January 14, 1837, 420–23. For a recent analysis of sectional and political considerations in Jacksonian land policy, see Daniel Feller, *The Public Lands in Jacksonian Politics* (Madison, Wis., 1984), esp. 189–94.

[88] Pessen, *Jacksonian America,* 213. Pessen concedes a limited range of ideological sincerity among party leaders, noting that "it is rare that the career even of a political chameleon is marked by total unscrupulousness or by actions, no matter how self-interested, bearing no relation whatever to the sympathies of the actor." See ibid., 192.

nious interdependency of classes and sections, and guided by wise and high-minded leaders. Credit, banks, transportation improvements, and tariffs were the engines of the economic prosperity that Whigs considered the foundation of a free society.[89]

To be sure, Whigs often sounded these very themes.[90] Yet Whig leaders also explicitly endorsed the concept of relative equality of outcomes and often turned the Jacksonian argument on its head, asserting that Jackson's policies gave rise to inequality and threatened republican institutions. During the Panic Session of 1833–34, Chilton Allan of Kentucky denounced the administration for instituting a revolution in government policy. "It has heretofore been the object of our statesmen to cause, as far as practicable, a general and equal diffusion of money and property among the people," he explained. "The extremes of wealth and poverty have ever been unfriendly and adverse to the spirit of our free republican institutions." However, he predicted, removing the government's deposits from the BUS, by concentrating the nation's wealth in a few cities, would have the opposite effect. It would "cause an unequal distribution of property; and would throw wealth in the hands of the few, at the expense of the many." Removal, in short, was a plan "to make the rich richer, and the poor poorer."[91] This ironic reversal of the Jacksonians' egalitarian defense of removal was echoed by other Whigs.[92]

[89] No attempt is made here to treat the Whig view of equality thoroughly. That subject merits more extensive investigation than it has yet received. A good start can be made by consulting Ashworth, *"Agrarians" and "Aristocrats,"* 82–84; Kohl, *Politics of Individualism.* 186–227; Glyndon G. Van Deusen, "Some Aspects of Whig Thought and Theory in the Jacksonian Period," *American Historical Review,* 63 (Jan. 1958), 310–14, 319; Daniel Walker Howe, *The Political Culture of the American Whigs* (Chicago, 1979), 9, 101–2, 138–39, Welter, *Mind of America,* 113–17; Conkin, *Prophets of Prosperity,* 202; Meyers, *Jacksonian Persuasion,* 9–10.

[90] See, for example, *National Intelligencer,* August 25, 1832; *Portland Daily Advertiser,* quoted in *National Intelligencer,* August 8, 1832; Nicholas Biddle to Henry Clay, August 1, 1832, Henry Clay, *The Papers of Henry Clay,* ed. Robert Seager II and Melba Porter Hay, 9 vols. to date (Lexington, Ky., 1959–), 8:556; Philip Hone, *The Diary of Philip Hone: 1828–1851,* ed. Allan Nevins, 2 vols. (New York, 1927), 1:119 (entry for November 6, 1834); Harriet Martineau, *Society in America,* ed. Seymour Martin Lipset (1962; rept., New Brunswick, N.J., 1981), 61.

[91] *Register of Debates,* 23rd Cong., 1st sess., April 3, 1834, 349–50. A few Whigs ventured this theme earlier, in the aftermath of the Bank Veto, claiming that Jackson's decision would "make the rich richer and the poor poorer," and destroy the incentive to labor. See *National Intelligencer,* October 20, 1832.

[92] *Register of Debates,* 23rd Cong., 1st sess., May 19, 1834, 4173 (speech of Highland Hall); ibid., February 3, 1834, 2587 (speech of Dudley Selden). Whigs directly connected the credit system to liberty. Credit, announced Senator Nathaniel Tallmadge of

Whigs, too, assumed that good laws and policies ensured relative equality, rather than inequality. They clashed with the Democrats as to what constituted good policy, but they agreed with their opponents that its goal should be a rough equality of condition. As Daniel Webster put it, laws "should favor the distribution of property to the end that the number of the very rich, and the number of the poor, may both be diminished, as far as practicable, consistently with the rights of industry and property." Edward Everett of Massachusetts made the same point. "I regard equality of condition and fortune as the happiest state of society, and those political institutions as immeasurably the wisest and best which tend to produce it," he proclaimed. Economic development and the creation of wealth would assure a broad distribution of property and lift the poor out of poverty. For Whigs, greater equality naturally resulted from the creation of new wealth rather than from attacks on the well-to-do or limitations on government policies to promote economic progress.[93]

Even if this were merely cynical pandering to gain votes, it would still demonstrate the egalitarian assumptions of the electorate to which politicians catered. But it appears likely that Whigs, too, shared the vision of a society of widespread and relatively equal property holding. There never could be an intelligent and virtuous people who were also "a poor and idle people, badly employed, and badly paid," Webster asserted. "Who would be safe, in any community, where political power is in the hands of the many, and property in the hands of the few?"[94]

The idea that excessive inequality of condition endangered republican institutions was, then, a salient element in Jacksonian America's

New York, was found to exist and exert an influence in society " 'in proportion to the freedom enjoyed by any People.' " Quoted in *National Intelligencer,* July 13, 1836.

93 Webster to James Brooks, August 5, 1834, Daniel Webster, *The Papers of Daniel Webster: Correspondence,* ed. Charles M. Wiltse and Harold D. Moser, 7 vols. (Hanover, N.H., 1974–86), 3:359; Edward Everett, "Accumulation, Property, Capital, Credit," an address delivered before the Mercantile Library Association, September 13, 1838, in Edward Everett, *Orations and Speeches,* 2 vols. (Boston, 1850), 2:302–3; Kohl, *Politics of Individualism,* 208–14. See also *National Intelligencer,* December 2, 1836, April 6, 1837.

94 "Address of the Friends of Domestic Industry," in *National Intelligencer,* November 14, 1831; *Register of Debates,* 22nd Cong., 1st sess., June 16, 1832, 3617–18; ibid., 22nd Cong., 1st sess., June 6, 1832, 3310; Webster quoted in *National Intelligencer,* September 24, 1833.

political culture. Contrary to most historical accounts, distributional equality was not the exclusive concern of workingmen and their intellectual spokesmen, although these groups were generally more insistent and articulate in addressing this issue. Spokesmen of both major parties also avowed the principle that a widespread and relatively equal diffusion of property was a necessary condition to the establishment and maintenance of a free society.

It is also evident that the Jacksonians found it more congenial to point the finger at conditions that promoted excessive inequality than to explain how their principles of equal rights, limited government, and free competition would bring about greater equality. Perhaps this is just one more Jacksonian paradox: A party devoted to the ideal of relative equality of condition rested much of its hopes on principles that not only generated more inequality, but helped "clear the path for laissez-faire capitalism," which eventually destroyed their cherished agrarian order. Less sympathetic historians simply reproach the Jacksonians for their alleged "indifference to the pervasive inequities that disfigured the era."[95]

These views do not really explain why the Jacksonians assumed that their ideals would yield more, rather than less, equality. A better approach would be to appreciate more fully the complexity and contingency of the market revolution then under way. In retrospect, the inexorable trend toward factory production, commercial agriculture, and a cash economy validated Thoreau's image of technology and commerce as an "Atropos" that never turns aside. But in the 1830s the outlines of the new economy were relatively recent and unevenly distributed; many of its outcomes, such as increased class stratification and inequality, were not yet fully realized and fixed. In the 1820s and beyond, a considerable degree of economic activity remained within the confines of a local, household economy. Production remained geared to family consumption, and exchange relationships involved complex networks of neighbors and kin, as well as market trading. Barter and noncash payments coexisted in varying ratios with monetary transactions. This world, a jumble of elements both modern and traditional, was familiar and proximate to political leaders of the Jacksonian era.

[95] Lawrence F. Kohl has aptly styled Jacksonian rhetoric as "accusatory." See Kohl, *Politics of Individualism,* 21–28. Meyers, *Jacksonian Persuasion,* viii, 12, 102, skillfully employs the concept of paradox to explain the Jacksonians. Pessen, "Society and Politics," 26, is more critical.

They were mature men by the time they had gained power, and their values and thinking were considerably shaped by assumptions best suited to the less complex and dynamic economy of earlier times.[96]

In this context, the Jacksonians worried little about controlling inequality that resulted from competition between persons of dissimilar talents, strength, and education. They assumed that under "natural" conditions, where innate differences among whites were few, property holding would be extensive and disparities of wealth few. What the Jacksonians did not worry about were the "artificial" conditions that generated excess inequality. Since, in their view, a social order composed of moral, self-restrained citizens would naturally display only a "happy mediocrity" of fortunes, extremes of wealth and poverty could only be evidence of bad laws and improper principles. Legislation, O'Sullivan asserted, was "the fruitful parent of nine-tenths of all the evil, moral and physical, by which mankind has been afflicted since the creation of the world, and by which human nature has been self-degraded, fettered, and oppressed." The *Globe* fully agreed. Poverty, it announced, was "nine cases out of ten," the result of personal considerations, such as misfortune, or of "bad government, sacrificing the many to the few."[97]

Such criticism of legislation presented contradictory lessons for government. On the one hand, active government tended to exacerbate inequality by working in favor of the rich. When government veered from its proper role of equal protection and equal rights, Leggett warned, its power would always be exercised for the "exclusive benefit of wealth." Thus the Jacksonians reaffirmed traditional republican and Jeffersonian hostility to power.[98]

[96] Clarence H. Danhof, *Change in Agriculture: The Northern United States, 1820–1870* (Cambridge, Mass., 1969), 21. On the continuing significance of the household economy in antebellum America, see Christopher Clark, "Household Economy, Market Exchange, and the Rise of Capitalism in the Connecticut Valley, 1800–1860," *Journal of Social History,* 13 (Winter 1979), 169–89; Harry L. Watson, "Conflict and Collaboration: Yeomen, Slaveholders, and Politics in the Antebellum South," *Social History,* 10 (Oct. 1985), 285–89; J. Mills Thornton III, "The Ethic of Subsistence and the Origins of Southern Secession," *Tennessee Historical Quarterly,* 48 (Summer 1989), 74–79; Robert A. Gross, "Culture and Cultivation: Agriculture and Society in Thoreau's Concord," *Journal of American History,* 69 (June 1982), 42–43, 53–55; and Wilentz, "Many Democracies," 225.

[97] *The United States Magazine and Democratic Review,* 1 (Oct. 1837), 6; Washington *Globe,* November 24, 1835. See also "Franklin," quoted in Washington *Globe,* April 23, 1835.

[98] Leggett, *Political Writings,* 1:165.

On the other hand, if government were limited, it need not, indeed must not, be weak. Government should intervene and remove conditions, especially those founded on special privilege, that operated to promote excessive inequality. Democrats justified these periodic assertions of power by the right of the majority to defend liberty against those who would bend government to their special interests. Recalling the republican maxim that "eternal vigilance by the people is the price of liberty," Jackson advised that it would require "steady and persevering exertions" on their part to be rid of the "iniquities and mischiefs" of the paper system, the spirit of monopoly, and other abuses.[99] Government could not create a society of absolute equality, but by destroying privileged institutions and monopolies, it could provide for that *greater* degree of equality of condition essential to upholding republican virtue and institutions.[100]

It is becoming increasingly apparent that the Democratic Party's popular appeal in the 1830s was due largely to its ability to express, through republican and agrarian, as well as liberal, themes, the concerns of numerous Americans about the dangers posed by the market revolution. Recent studies, by Christopher Clark, Lacy K. Ford, Jr., Steven Hahn, J. Mills Thornton, Harry L. Watson, and Gavin Wright, among others, establish that rapid advances in trade, manufacturing, and commercial agriculture did not immediately transform America into a uniform, homogeneous market economy. In many regions, as far apart as the upcountry South and the Connecticut Valley in Massachusetts, where the local economy mixed commercial and monetary exchange along with household production, subsistence practices, and nonmonetary transactions, yeoman farmers engaged in what Gavin Wright calls "safety-first behavior." Their basic goal of preserving the family's landed independence dictated an aversion to the risks of commercial crop agriculture. A considerable number of rural and small-town Americans were thus in, but not entirely of, expanding exchange networks.[101]

[99] *Register of Debates,* 24th Cong., 1st sess., April 28, 1836, 3430–33, 3436; Richardson, ed., *Messages and Papers,* 4:1523, 1525.

[100] Ibid., 1:85; 2:164; Gouge, *Short History of Paper Money,* 235.

[101] In addition to the material cited in note 79, see Steven Hahn, *The Roots of Southern Populism: Yeoman Farmers and the Transformation of the Georgia Upcountry, 1850–1890* (New York, 1983); Gregory H. Nobles, "Commerce and Community: A

The actual social and economic structure of these communities strongly resembled the ideals portrayed in republican thinking, particularly in its agrarian formulation. Personal independence and autonomy rested upon a system of widespread ownership of land and productive property. A keen sense of interdependence and community standards coexisted with an ethic of personal autonomy and antiauthoritarianism. The value system of these "small communities of producers" resembled the "small producer" republicanism of urban artisans and mechanics who resisted market innovations that transformed autonomous craftsmen into dependent wage laborers, commodities themselves.[102]

There is no need to romanticize this culture, which could be virulently racist, hostile to humanitarian reform, contentious, and narrowly tradition-bound. It had its opportunistic, self-interested, and profit-minded side as well. But it was also a society that worried that credit, banking, protective tariffs, and other institutional signs of economic "progress" endangered local autonomy and personal liberty. Jacksonian politics was, in part, a "safety-first" politics, which suspected market advances because the web of credit and cash could easily subvert that political economy of widespread and relatively equal property holding necessary to maintain liberty.[103]

In the end, Democrats failed to slow the pace of economic change or to halt the growing inequality of wealth. Indeed, by the mid-1840s, with the return of prosperity following the Panic of 1837, Democrats in increasing numbers accommodated themselves to an economy of enterprise, often collaborating with the more entrepreneurially oriented Whig Party to work out a rough consensus on issues of credit

Case Study of the Rural Broommaking Business in Antebellum Massachusetts," *Journal of the Early Republic*, 4 (Fall 1984), 287–308; Lacy K. Ford, Jr., *Origins of Southern Radicalism: The South Carolina Upcountry, 1800–1860* (New York, 1988); Wright, *Political Economy of the Cotton South*, 62–74; J. Mills Thornton III, *Politics and Power in a Slave Society: Alabama, 1800–1860* (Baton Rouge, 1978); and Harry L. Watson, *Jacksonian Politics and Community Conflict: The Emergence of the Second American Party System in Cumberland County, North Carolina* (Baton Rouge, 1981).

102 The following discussion draws heavily upon Ford, *Southern Radicalism*, 50–52; Hahn, *Roots of Southern Populism*, 2–11, 50–53, 85; Thornton, "Ethic of Subsistence," 74–79; Watson, "Conflict and Collaboration," 277–85; and Wilentz, *Chants Democratic*, 3–5, 95–103.

103 For a balanced view of this small-producer society, see Hahn, *Roots of Populism*, 52–58.

and banking.[104] The unfolding of these events indicates the limits of the party's egalitarian claims. Their vision was not only defective in its racial exclusiveness, but when events belied expectations, and inequality grew regardless of party or policy, there was no soul-searching reexamination of their assumptions about distributional equality. Democrats failed to appreciate the tenacity with which capitalism and rapid economic growth generated inequality. Assuming that equality of opportunity perfectly harmonized with equality of condition, they overlooked how asymmetries of wealth and power produced by capitalism necessitated interventionist governmental policies specifically designed to redistribute power and wealth.[105]

This disparity between aims and consequences undeniably exposes the Jacksonians to the charge of naiveté, but it does not gainsay the sincerity of their intentions or the plausibility of their case. To scold the Jacksonians for failing to comprehend the full implications of an economic revolution that was just under way would be to miss the degree to which they made equality a consideration in their political calculations and a component of their political ideology. Although success eluded them, Jacksonian Democrats articulated a vision of an egalitarian society characterized by extensive and relatively equal property holding.

104 Sharp, *Jacksonians Versus the Banks,* 327–29.
105 Welter, *Mind of America,* 99–100. For a discussion of asymmetrical relationships in a money economy, see William M. Reddy, *Money and Liberty in Modern Europe: A Critique of Historical Understanding* (New York, 1987).

CHAPTER 7

Banking on language: the currency of Alexander Bryan Johnson

JEAN-CHRISTOPHE AGNEW

"A penny for your thoughts, my fine fellow." The phrase is an innocent enough gambit in ordinary discourse, but when Herman Melville puts those familiar words in the mouth of the infamous trickster figure who dominates his last novel, *The Confidence-Man* (1857), he manages to convert the small change of American conversation into surprisingly dubious coin.[1] And even though the minor panic the offered penny arouses in the "fine fellow" is, like so much else in the novel, momentary, Melville's larger and typically paradoxical point lingers – that while thoughts may appear as catchpenny commodities in the marketplace of American culture, their exchange can turn out to be quite dear. To put Melville's point another way, commerce cheapens *and* deepens meaning at the same time, multiplying and complicating cultural exchange in such a way as to render its currency – language – at once reassuringly standardized and disturbingly defamiliarized.

If this paradox is indeed what Melville intended in *The Confidence-Man,* and the text is guileful enough to allow such a reading, then it is a point that might also be brought to bear upon the history and historiography of market culture in the United States. American intellectual and cultural historians have long toiled in the shadow cast by the nation's commercial reputation, and few of them have not at one time or another had to defend the value of American thought against the pennies offered up by amused Eurocentric colleagues. Even when that condescension has shifted from a dismissive comment on, say,

This essay is dedicated to Christopher Lasch.

[1] Herman Melville, *The Confidence-Man: His Masquerade,* ed. H. Bruce Franklin (Indianapolis: Bobbs-Merrill, 1967), 183.

William James's "cash value" of ideas to the more recent enthusiasm for the pragmatic tradition, the assumption remains unshaken that American thought is so steeped in American soil as to require a special effort at extraction, cracking, and refining (usually with imported equipment) before it can become, if you will, "theory." The assumption grows even stronger in the case of Anglo-American social and political thought, for whether the theory in question is republican or Lockean, we have been encouraged – by Bernard Bailyn as much as by Louis Hartz – to think of its domestic variations as fragmentary, if not irrational. To explore one American philosopher's reflections in and about the market, then, as I do in this essay, is to plunge directly into the environmentalist or contextualist difficulties that have vexed American intellectual historians for so long.[2] Whether I recover a pearl or just another oyster remains to be seen.

Of course, one might simply finesse the intellectual embarrassments of the American context by treating them as assets rather than liabilities. So Daniel Boorstin did in *The Genius of American Politics* (1953), where he argued that "our theory is always implicit in our institutions." Ideology was a peculiarly European product; the widely accepted "givenness" of American conditions, he insisted, had so shaped American experience as to remove the need to theorize those conditions in any systematic manner. At best, the American sense of givenness had "nourished in a very special way and to an extraordinary degree our feeling for the principle of social science which I . . . call the 'seamlessness' of culture."[3] In effect Boorstin proposed the culture concept (and with it, cultural history) as a typically antitheoretical reflection of and on American life, a kind of discount Hegelianism in which the American Genius discovered that, like Molière's Monsieur Jourdain, it had been speaking anthropology all its life without knowing it. To clinch

[2] For a recent discussion of intellectual provincialism, see the preface to David A. Hollinger, *In the American Province: Studies in the History and Historiography of Ideas* (Baltimore: Johns Hopkins University Press, 1985), vii–viii; on the question of contextualism, see, for example, John Higham and Paul K. Conkin, eds., *New Directions in American Intellectual History* (Baltimore: Johns Hopkins University Press, 1979); Robert Darnton, "Intellectual and Cultural History," in *The Kiss of Lamourette: Reflections in Cultural History* (New York: Norton, 1990), 191–218; John Patrick Diggins, "The Oyster and the Pearl: The Problem of Contextualism in Intellectual History," *History and Theory,* 23 (May 1984), 151–69.

[3] Daniel J. Boorstin, *The Genius of American Politics* (Chicago: University of Chicago Press, 1953), 9, 6.

this hostility toward the idolatry of systematic or rationalist thought, Boorstin opened and closed his book with the story of the invasion of the Temple of Solomon in 63 B.C. and of Pompey's subsequent discovery that the temple was empty. "This was," Boorstin concluded, "a symbol of the absence of idolatry, which was the essential truth of Judaism." "Perhaps," he added, "the same surprise awaits the student of American culture, if he finally manages to penetrate the arcanum of our belief."[4]

A somewhat less Ozlike but still strongly contextual approach to the theoretical arcanum of American culture – particularly its market culture – appeared two years later in Louis Hartz's *Liberal Tradition in America.* There he explained the hegemony of liberalism – a "nightmare dream" in which "meaningful thought was practically impossible" – as the product of "a remarkable collusion between Locke and the New World."

> Had it been merely the liberal spirit alone which inspired the American farmer to become capitalistically oriented, to repudiate save for a few early remnants the village organization of Europe, to produce for a market and even to enter capitalist occupations on the side. . . , then the difficulties he had encountered would have been greater than they were. But where land was abundant and the voyage to the New World itself a claim to independence, the spirit which repudiated peasantry and tenantry flourished with remarkable ease.[5]

Lockeanism defined the outer limits of the American political imagination, in other words, because its precepts were "too real, too empirical, too historical in America to attack."[6] Given the close fit between liberal concept and market context – between word and thing – antebellum Americans, Hartz argued, were unable to fathom any social or political possibilities beyond "the idea of democratic capitalism." Theirs was a society "where virtually everyone, including the nascent industrial worker, ha[d] the mentality of an independent entrepreneur."[7] American culture was, in short, a mo-

[4] Ibid., ii, 170; for a cultural context to Boorstin's parallelism between Judaism and the American genius, see John Murray Cuddihy, *No Offense: Civil Religion and Protestant Taste* (New York: Seabury Press, 1978).

[5] Louis Hartz, *The Liberal Tradition in America* (New York: Harcourt Brace Jovanovich, 1955), 153, 17–18.

[6] Ibid., 153.

[7] Ibid., 110–13, 89.

noculture because American soil lacked the sediment of earlier (i.e., "feudal") modes of production and exchange.

Today, Boorstin's and Hartz's portraits of he peculiarities of the Americans have been significantly retouched. Social and intellectual historians have not only consigned the liberal tradition to the margins of the picture, but they have also transformed its so-called agrarian myth from the self-flattering mask of entrepreneurial capitalists to the self-critical ideal of village republicans.[8] Furthermore, as Robert Shalhope and Joyce Appleby have observed, "myth" and "ideology" themselves have gradually lost their conventional meaning as representations of historical reality and, in their new guise as autonomous cultural systems, have become the most decisive constituents of that reality for historians.[9] Where Boorstin and Hartz saw the liberal tradition merging into the modern and individuated social environment of the New World it had philosophically prefigured, later historians have preferred to see that same environment itself dissolving, if only temporarily, into the classical and communal categories of an even more ancient republican tradition. After thirty-five years of more or less continuous use, Boorstin's notion of a seamless culture has quietly appropriated for itself and into itself the same practical, enterprising, and "constructive" powers he once believed had called the concept into being.

Not everyone has fallen in with this view, however. Skeptical of the claims made on behalf of a hegemonic American republican tradition and skeptical as well of the hermetic culturalist assumptions used to make them, Joyce Appleby has recently argued for the vitality of the Lockean spirit in the early national period and has traced that vitality, once again, to what Boorstin called "the peculiar and unrepeatable

[8] I will not rehearse the relevant bibliography, which is vast, but an interesting recent effort to trump the Lockean–Republican debate by means of social psychology is Steven Watts, *The Republic Reborn: War and the Making of Liberal America, 1790–1820* (Baltimore: Johns Hopkins University Press, 1987); Watts traces the origins of a "culture of capitalism" through the workings of "half-conscious motives, unintended consequences, frequent self-deceptions, and new meanings for old words" (xviii, xxii).

[9] See Robert E. Shalhope, "Republicanism and Early American Historiography," *William and Mary Quarterly,* 3rd Ser., 39 (April 1982), 354–56; Joyce Appleby, "Value and Society," in *Colonial British America: Essays in the New History of the Early Modern Era,* ed. Jack P. Greene and J.R. Pole (Baltimore: Johns Hopkins University Press, 1984), 290–316; "Republicanism and Ideology," *American Quarterly,* 37 (Fall 1985), 461–73.

combination of historical circumstances" in which Americans found themselves.[10] "The wealth and fluidity of early American society," Appleby points out, "made it possible to think of the economists' description of the market as a template for society." Actual commercial opportunities in the New World vindicated the Smithian model in American eyes, and once vindicated, the model in turn sanctioned the further exploitation of those opportunities. "Capitalism," Appleby concludes, "thus disclosed itself in a benign and visionary way to Republicans, who drew from its dynamic operation the promise of a new age for ordinary men."[11] When juxtaposed to the realities of, say, an expanding American grain trade, post-Revolutionary republicanism looks less like an instance of cultural lag or cultural resistance than an exercise in cultural collaboration or, as Hartz might have put it, collusion.[12] In the early republic, Appleby reminds us, commerce and culture did not undermine one another; they underwrote one another. Americans opened their purses and their minds – their pennies and their thoughts – at the same time.

Whatever its affinities with Boorstin's and Hartz's work, Appleby's is not an effort to restore the consensus paradigm to contemporary historiography. To the contrary, she sees the ideological contest of the early republic as one between competing visions, visions that were neither imprisoned by the constraints of language nor bound by the imperatives of class interest but that were instead variously responsive to (and responsible for) the volatile facts of American social and material life. She draws an analytic distinction between republicanism and capitalism – between words and things – while refusing to see the former as the successful or shattered container of the latter.[13] In

[10] Boorstin, *Genius,* 1.

[11] Joyce Appleby, *Capitalism and a New Social Order: The Republican Vision of the 1790s* (New York: New York University Press, 1984), 50.

[12] See Joyce Appleby, "Commercial Farming and the 'Agrarian Myth' in the Early Republic," *Journal of American History,* 68 (March 1982), 833–49. "It was exactly the promise of progressive agricultural development that fueled his [Jefferson's] hopes that ordinary men might escape the tyranny of their social superiors both as employers and magistrates" (844–45).

[13] "Words and things" oversimplifies Appleby's distinction – "accounts and experiences" might serve better – but I keep to the phrase in order to come back to it in another context. One difficulty with the word "capitalist" is that it can refer simultaneously to certain economic relations and to the attitudes and perspectives bred by and brought to those relationships. As Appleby puts the question in relation to historical consciousness: "Men and women cannot be separated from their experience, but they can be detached from interpretations of that experience" (*Capitalism,* 79).

place of the closed models of symbolic life favored by interpretive anthropologists and ordinary language philosophers, she proposes an open, improvisational model of a burgeoning market culture created and sustained by what she calls a new "kind of man."[14] Needless to say, the identity of this new American remains almost as elusive as the republic he supported, and some historians have challenged Appleby's choice of examples.[15] But if one is interested in reconstructing a social and cultural history of the market, then biography, as David Davis remarked some time ago, can be a rewarding place to begin.[16] And if one is especially curious, as I am, to sort out the various ways in which Americans translated their experience of market culture into a more systematically articulated "vision" – into, say, philosophy, literature, or politics – then biography offers an especially privileged vantage point from which to watch such processes at work.[17]

Alexander Bryan Johnson, who spent the greater part of his life (1786–1867) as a modest local banker in upstate New York, could well have sat for Hartz's and Appleby's portrait of the democratic capitalist, the new "kind of man" for whom the marketplace offered a means of shedding the past and, as it were, growing with the country. As an English immigrant, though, it would be more accurate to say that he grew *into* the country, and for that same reason Johnson's prolonged acculturation throws a special light on the larger process by which unfamiliar commercial practices, relations, and values were "naturalized" in early-nineteenth-century America. Retrospect reveals Johnson to have been an extraordinary figure, but that, after all, is what retrospect most often does. In Johnson's case, however, hindsight came rather late. During his lifetime he never saw himself as anything other than a man condemned to unearned and unwanted intellectual obscurity. In this, one supposes, he was quite ordinary. What makes him interesting to us, if not to his contemporaries, then, are the life worlds that may be said to have met in him, the social,

[14] Ibid., 4.

[15] See, for example, John Ashworth, "The Jeffersonians: Classical Republicans or Liberal Capitalists?" *Journal of American Studies*, 18 (December 1984), 425–35.

[16] David Brion Davis, "Some Recent Directions in American Cultural History," *American Historical Review*, 73 (February 1968), 704–5.

[17] A fine recent example of this kind of inquiry is R. Jackson Wilson's *Figures of Speech: American Writers and the Literary Marketplace, from Benjamin Franklin to Emily Dickinson* (New York: Knopf, 1989).

economic, and cultural conjunctures that structured his autobiography. For A. B. Johnson was not just a simple country banker; he was also the country's first philosopher of language, and, as we shall see, the connections between his thinking on markets and his thinking on meaning were more than proximate: They were intimate.

I

Alexander Bryan Johnson was born the son of Bryan and Leah Johnson in Gosport, England, in 1786. A channel port situated opposite the Isle of Wight, Gosport housed a mobile population of British sailors and officers, many of whom knew Bryan Johnson as a broker who handled their wages and prize money while they were away at sea. When Alexander was eleven years old, his father emigrated to the United States to begin a new career. He landed in New York City, which was then in the grip of a yellow fever epidemic, and quickly made his way upstate to Old Fort Schuyler, later to be called Utica. There Bryan Johnson established a store that soon made him one of the town's most prosperous men. Four years later, in 1801, his wife and son, having waited patiently for Bryan's instructions, decided to leave London for America. Alexander was about two months shy of fifteen when he arrived in New York, with little schooling and no particular sense of vocation. Conscious that his English background had won for him a reputation for greater learning than he actually possessed, the young boy grappled with dictionaries, grammars, and other works in order to measure up to this unearned esteem and, no less importantly, to rise above the position of storekeeper. Still, his father's affluence and amiability enabled Alexander to defer decisions about calling and marriage until his late twenties, leaving him to drift, almost insensibly, from bookkeeping to the law and ultimately to banking.[18]

Because of his wealth and status in the community, the young man soon found himself invited to comment on the major political and religious debates of his time and place. Angered by Whig condescen-

[18] The details of A. B. Johnson's life are available in his own 1,200-page autobiography, a fair copy of which is on permanent loan to the library of Hamilton College, Clinton, New York, and in Charles L. Todd and Robert Sonkin, *Alexander Bryan Johnson, Philosophical Banker* (Syracuse, N.Y.: Syracuse University Press, 1977).

sion toward the political ambitions of recent immigrants like himself, Johnson would later become a fervent Jacksonian Democrat and Texas annexationist. But he was already sufficiently emboldened during the 1820s to join the Lyceum movement, where he held forth on such subjects as language, banking, and the American Colonization Society. He also stepped forward as an active promoter of the Erie Canal and of the cause of Polish revolutionaries, the last at the request of Lafayette, whom Johnson entertained during the general's triumphal visit to the canal in 1825. Perhaps his greatest social triumph, though, had come more than a decade earlier, with his marriage in 1814 to John Adams's granddaughter Abigail; Johnson was then twenty-eight and Abigail barely sixteen. The match began as a marriage of convenience entered into dispassionately on both sides, but it eventually grew into a devoted union that was ended only by Abigail's death in 1835. It was she who brought Johnson into a long-term correspondence with both John and John Quincy Adams, and it was she as well who led him to leave his father's Episcopal church for the Presbyterian church. There, during the revivals that swept through the Burned-Over District of upstate New York in the mid-1820s, Johnson first heard Charles Finney preach. Soon thereafter he was elected president of both the Union Tract Society and the Oneida Evangelical Society. Johnson may have come to Utica at the beginning of the century, but he had not really "arrived" until 1825.

After Abigail's death, Johnson was married again, to Eliza Masters. When she died in a fire seventeen years later, he resigned his thirty-six-year presidency of the Utica branch of the Ontario Bank of Canandaigua, abandoned his short-story writing for the *Knickerbocker Magazine,* and journeyed to Europe. Though a new banking venture failed within a year and a half, Johnson was nonetheless able at his death to leave his third wife (Mary Livingston) and many children a large fortune and an obituary that praised his "vigilant care" of bank funds and that described the manner of his life as "correct and pure."[19]

Uticans remembered Johnson as a shy and reclusive figure, austere, formal, always punctual, and scrupulously honest in every aspect of

[19] Quoted in David Rynin, introduction to Alexander Bryan Johnson, *A Treatise on Language* (1836; rpt. New York: Dover, 1968), 113; see also Moses Mears Bagg, *Memorial History of Utica* (Syracuse, N.Y.: D. Mason, 1892), 113.

his public life. Indeed, the image sketched of him in his memorials is of a stereotypical provincial banker, with the exception (and perhaps that not even an exception) of his unflagging interest in philosophy. "He was aware that he had the reputation of being mainly devoted to making money," one obituary recalled. But that bothered him little. "He wanted money for independence, – to obtain time to write and for the comfort of his family."[20] If anything, this genteel separation between public and private life, or between commercial and literary ambition, strengthened the impression of his fundamental soundness as a man of business and a man of letters. If a man "wants to be more than a banker," Johnson once warned his colleagues in the profession, "he should cease from being a banker."[21]

But Johnson was a man who always longed to be more than a banker, and notwithstanding his neighbors' willingness to see in him the same sharp division he saw in himself, Johnson's thoughts on philosophy were never far removed from his thoughts on banking. As Johnson himself phrased it, "The labors of the counting room and the study were constantly intermingled and often the sheet of a treatise in hand and a current balance sheet might be seen on the table together."[22] Even the manuscript autobiography that he left behind at his death mixed personal reminiscences with various receipts, expense accounts, and private correspondence. Whatever the subject and whatever the genre, A. B. Johnson's writings were nothing if not intertextual. And that intertextuality, I would submit, registered the presence and in a certain respect the future of an American market culture. In his writing as in his life, Alexander Bryan Johnson's commercial bent was one with his linguistic turn.

It was for the Utica Lyceum in 1825 that Johnson first prepared his thoughts on the place and limits of language. The course of lectures, published three years later as *The Philosophy of Human Knowledge,*

[20] Quoted in Rynin, introduction to Johnson, *Treatise,* 113.

[21] A. B. Johnson, *A Treatise on Banking, the Duties of a Banker, and His Personal Requisites Therefor, in The Banker's Common-Place Book,* ed. J. Smith Homans (Boston: Phillips, Sampson, 1851), 48. "These and other speculations," Johnson wrote, "interfered less with my law studies and with my banking than most persons would imagine, for I carried them on at intervals of business; and the moment any call of business interrupted my study, I intermitted the study and attended to the business – so that business and study became a relaxation of each other" (quoted in Todd and Sonkin, *Johnson,* 106).

[22] Bagg, *Memorial History,* 576.

or A Treatise on Language, situated itself squarely within the then dominant traditions of British empiricism and Common-Sense philosophy.[23] For instance, Johnson shared Francis Bacon's view that words were the "idols of the marketplace," which was to say "the tokens current and accepted for conceits, as moneys are for values."[24] In place of conceits, however, Johnson probably would have substituted a phrase like "the sensible experience of the natural world." As bank notes were the "artificial representatives of specie," he argued, so words were the "artificial representatives of natural phenomena." He wrote:

> We employ words as though they possess, like specie an intrinsick and natural value; rather than as though they possess like bank notes, a merely conventional, artificial, and representative value. We must convert our words into the natural realities which the words represent, if we would understand accurately their value. Some banks, when you present their notes for redemption, will pay you in other bank notes; but we must not confound such a payment with an actual liquidation in specie. We shall possess, in the new notes, nothing but the representatives of specie. In like manner, when you seek the meaning of a word, you may obtain its conversion into other words, or into some verbal thoughts; but you must not confound such a meaning with the phenomena of nature. You will still possess in the new words, nothing but the representatives of natural existence.[25]

This was a hard-money approach to language, if ever there was one. The direct and unmediated experience of the world was for Johnson the only true metal of life. At best words were a more or less inaccurate likeness or counterfeit of the sensible world, so that their value depended on the readiness of individuals to square, redeem, or, in a sense, liquidate them into the particular sensible phenomena they

[23] A. B. Johnson, *The Philosophy of Human Knowledge, or A Treatise on Language* (New York: G. & C. Carvill, 1828); a revised and expanded edition appeared as *A Treatise on Language: or the Relation Which Words Bear to Things* (New York: Harper & Bros., 1836) and is reprinted in a conflated edition (1947, 1950; rpt. New York: Dover, 1968), to which I refer in the remainder of this essay. For the influence of British thinkers on contemporary American thought, see D. H. Meyer, *The Instructed Conscience: The Shaping of the American National Ethic* (Philadelphia: University of Pennsylvania Press, 1972); Henry F. May, *The Enlightenment in America* (New York: Oxford University Press, 1976), Part IV.

[24] Francis Bacon, "The Advancement of Learning," *Works,* ed. James Spedding, Robert L. Ellis, and Douglas D. Heath, 14 vols. (London: Longman's, 1857–74), III:400.

[25] Johnson, *Treatise,* 174; see also *The Meaning of Words: Analyzed into Words and Unverbal Things Classified into Intellections, Sensations and Emotions* (New York: D. Appleton, 1854), 215.

designated. Words referred not to ideas, as in Locke, or to classes of appearances, as in Hume, but to the concrete objects of experience. Words were like mirrors: social conventions that were empty in themselves but that possessed as many potential meanings as the objects placed before them.[26] Anticipating Franz Boas's own examples of cultural discriminations, Johnson noted that the word "white" was often used to describe quite different instantiations of the color. "A perfect language should have a separate word for each of these appearances, and a separate word for every other phenomenon," but such a language, he conceded, would be "too copious for our memory."[27] Proper words were for Johnson proper names, but he also understood that the more proper and differentiated language grew, the more unwieldy it became.[28] For all his confident allusions to the touchstone of sensible reality, his exposition of the limits of language threatened to push that reality even farther out of reach – at least outside the grasp of common discourse.

A revised and expanded version of *The Philosophy of Human Knowledge* appeared in 1836 as *A Treatise on Language,* and then again in 1854 as *The Meaning of Words.* Together, the three volumes proposed what has been called a referential, designative, or verificationist theory of language: a theory holding that the meaning of words lies outside language, that knowledge is of direct acquaintance (and thus verifiable only in that way), and that in view of the failings of language, one can therefore have no theory of this acquaintance. Johnson's impatience with the insubordinacies of language – its tendency to abstract and arbitrate what it can only imperfectly represent – resembled Kant's well-known misgivings over the pretensions of the understanding. But, to tease out Johnson's own monetary metaphor, his impatience likewise mimicked his characteristically Jacksonian indignation at the pretensions of a National Bank to control grass-roots transactions in local banknotes. "Language," he declared, "has usurped over nature a superiority which is so inveterate and unsuspected, that we constantly appeal to words for the interpretation of natural existences, instead of appealing to natural

[26] Johnson, *Treatise,* 113–14.

[27] Ibid., 113.

[28] David Rynin discusses Johnson's indifference to the fact that most names are common, not proper, names, in the critical essay that accompanies Johnson's *Treatise,* 371.

existences for the interpretation of words."[29] Overall, Johnson's work projected a sense of growing impoverishment as one moved away from the infinite multiplicity and particularity of nature, through the basic duality of the senses (seeing and feeling), to the fallacious unity of the intellect as envehicled in language. John Quincy Adams was very much on the mark, then, when he wrote to his relative by marriage to say: "Your subject, if I understand you, is the inherent imperfection of language by its undertaking to generalize that which nature produces individually."[30]

A. B. Johnson's philosophy thus struck his contemporaries, as it does us, as the work of an unflinching nominalist, a thinker hostile to the reifying powers of language and, correspondingly, to the kind of free-lance theorizing such powers authorized. "I desire particularly to remark in relation to theories," he wrote in 1854, "and I solicit for the remark much attention – that every theory is a fiction to the extent that we employ it to materialize a modus operandi that is only intellectually conceived, and such a materialization is the object of every theory." Beyond the sensible world to which they referred, theories were but words, and beyond words, they were nothing.[31] As for fictions, taken in the literal sense, Johnson could not have been more contemptuous. "When I accidently cast my eyes on these modern fictions," he wrote, "and see, as in one of Scott's novels, snares preparing, trapdoors constructing to immure to destruction some beautiful and faultless woman, I as uniformly and indignantly cast from me the book, as I should an invitation from some South Sea cannibal to make a dinner with him on a human victim."[32] Of course, Johnson had in mind the peculiarly exotic contrivances of the contemporary romance, but his analogy nonetheless betrayed a deeper anxiety regarding the power of imaginative language both to cannibalize the real world and to command the reader's complicity in the act.

Taking these thoughts, opinions, and prejudices together, one might suppose Johnson a representative man: a hard-headed, Yankee businessman and philosophizer – a man determined to count the crackers in the barrel before generalizing about them. Yet despite his

[29] Johnson, *Treatise,* 56.
[30] Quoted in Todd and Sonkin, *Johnson,* 115.
[31] Johnson, *Meaning of Words,* 215.
[32] Quoted in Todd and Sonkin, *Johnson,* 194.

commonsense embrace of the external world and his commonsense suspicion of the wiles of words, the *Treatise* went largely unread. In the literary marketplace of antebellum America, few pennies were ever offered for Johnson's thoughts, with the result that the disgruntled banker was repeatedly obliged to shoulder the full cost of publication. "American books do not sell in America," a sympathetic John Quincy Adams explained to him.[33] "Your books seem too *deep* for the common reader," his publisher added.[34] But Johnson was not mollified. Had John Milton "written his books at Utica," he grumbled, "he would have been unknown still, even here, and not great anywhere. With us the love of glory no sooner kindles itself into a little blaze than the damp around us extinguishes it forever."[35] A plausible rationale for Johnson, perhaps, but not as persuasive for anyone looking back upon his work from the twentieth century.

From that standpoint – or blindspot – Johnson's *Treatise* seems very much an artifact of its time and place. Throughout the patient and deliberate exposition of his argument, Johnson projected the image of a sensible but ever vigilant, Locofoco Democrat; a figure alert to the diverse "currencies" in which his society trafficked and their tendency to arrogate to themselves the reality of the world they represented and the powers of the agents who had fabricated them. Indeed, when placed before the mirror of contemporary politics, Johnson's work most closely resembles Andrew Jackson's infamously deflationary Specie Circular (1836), which had prohibited the sale of public lands for anything other than gold or silver. One suspects that had more of Johnson's contemporaries taken the time to read his *Treatise,* they too might have found it similarly deflating. Perhaps that is why Timothy Flint, one of Johnson's more enthusiastic reviewers, wondered out loud about the local response to the banker's lectures. "What an audience must that of the Utica Lyceum have been," he wrote, "to have patiently followed this gentleman through his acute and fine spun, and sometimes darkly woven disquisitions."[36]

[33] Quoted in ibid., 115.

[34] Letter from Derby & Jackson to A. B. Johnson, January 7, 1857; Alexander Bryan Johnson Papers, Manuscripts and Archives, Sterling Memorial Library, Yale University, Box 4, Folder 21.

[35] Quoted in Todd and Sonkin, *Johnson,* 189.

[36] Timothy Flint, "The Philosophy of Human Knowledge," *Western Monthly Review,* 2 (March 1829), 577.

As it happened, though, the audience did not follow Johnson's disquisitions very far; he was in fact never invited back after his first lecture. Moreover, of the very, very few who, like Flint, actually read and reviewed Johnson's philosophical work, most balked at the implications of his nominalist posture for natural theology. Even the Connecticut theologian Horace Bushnell remarked on the banker's indifference to language as a "vehicle of spirit, thought, and sentiment."[37] What "dampness" there was in Utica, then, was most likely found in the spiritual wilderness of Johnson's own nominalism, which, taken to heart, might well have extinguished the evangelical fires of his local audience.

Twentieth-century commentators have echoed these earlier critics, though without the corresponding note of moral judgment. Johnson's theory of language, they complain, was too much of its time and place and therefore disappointingly incomplete. His interest in language was primarily lexical and extremely limited at that. He consistently ignored the functions of nondesignative words, for instance, and of nondeclarative sentences as well. And because he looked upon language as a collection of symbols rather than as a system of rules, he therefore subscribed (as Bushnell noted) to a severely limited definition of knowledge.[38] To put the brief against him in modern shorthand, Johnson's *Treatise on Language* represents a minor example of prestructuralist (or pre-Saussurean) linguistic theory founded on an outmoded metaphysics of presence. Case dismissed.

But the case for Johnson's obscurity may not be so easily disposed of by treating him as no more than a backwater disciple of the didactic enlightenment. True, his turn toward language in the *Treatise* may have fallen short of late-twentieth-century expectations, but the move was nonetheless more radical than his contemporaries could have appreciated. For all its shortcomings, Johnson's work may be said to "anticipate" many of the philosophical positions later taken by Mach, Vaihinger, Bridgman, Dewey, and the logical positivists. Johnson's *Treatise* even foreshadowed Wittgenstein's *Tractatus* when it warned

[37] Horace Bushnell, *God in Christ* (1849; New York: Charles Scribner's Sons, 1907), 43–44.

[38] See Max Black, "Johnson's Language Theories in Modern Perspective," in *Language and Value,* ed. Charles L. Todd and Russell T. Blackwood (New York: Greenwood, 1969), 49–66; Lars Gustafasson, "Note," in ibid., 67–69; Rynin, "Introduction" and "Critical Essay," in Johnson, *Treatise.*

that language could not express its own limits.[39] And, like the British critics C. K. Ogden and I. A. Richards, Johnson was quite prepared to treat language as an emotive, moral, or poetic vehicle when the stakes were other than epistemological. All this while he patiently pored over the books of the Oneida Evangelical Society and the Ontario Bank.

Utica's bemusement with A. B. Johnson's philosophy, however, did not grow out of the skeptical implications of his arguments, for only his closest readers – Flint and Bushnell – chose to draw them out. Whatever Johnson may have thought about the fictions of religion, he never rejected natural theology, and whatever he may have thought about the fictions of commerce, he never opposed soft money. To the contrary, one could more plausibly argue that Johnson owed both his notoriety as a banker and his obscurity as a philosopher to the fictions he deliberately embraced in his life and in his work. And not least of these fictions was the "fine spun" and "darkly woven" style in which life and work alike were presented – a style that makes it difficult to distinguish his treatises on language from those on banking.

By exploring Johnson's fictions further, then, one may begin to sort out some of the ways in which biography and history intersect in a burgeoning market society. In other words, by examining the genius of an upstate banker as he made himself in antebellum New York, one may in turn throw some light on the genius of market culture as it made itself in antebellum America. In this mutual fashioning between self and society, the supreme fiction may very well have been that of the marketplace as commonplace, for by means of this assumption the new poetry of capitalism could remain folded within the more familiar envelope of its ledgerbook prose. A. B. Johnson's commercial career camouflaged – perhaps even from himself – the same skeptical philosophical possibilities it had opened up to him; and those possibilities, in turn, went largely unremarked, not so much because they seemed so unthinkable (Hartz) or so unnecessary (Boorstin) but because, expressed as they were in the labored expository style of the economic treatise, they seemed so unremarkable. In short, A. B. Johnson's writings eluded notice because, like Poe's purloined letter,

[39] Rynin, "Introduction," 19–23.

they lay for so long in plain view on the writing table of American market society.

II

Despite Johnson's inherited wealth and his family background in English commerce, there was nothing simple or easy about his acculturation to the world of the Burned-Over District. Utica, as an irate Universalist clergyman once described it, was "one of the most perfect hot-beds of Calvinist superstition and Orthodox dogmatism that could be found on the continent of America."[40] The personal and social dilemmas associated with commercialization and the formation of an urban, immigrant working class had left a substantial portion of the native population open to a revival movement that promised self-purification, communal reaffirmation, and social control. Thus, spurred by the influx of Irish Catholic workers on the Erie Canal, a sabbatarian movement sprang up in Utica and Rochester in the late 1820s to organize Sunday boycotts of local boats and stages. As Paul Johnson and Mary Ryan have shown, revivalism sought to cauterize the social wounds opened up by class differentiation, household transformation, and the threat of unrestrained ambition.[41] Whiggery, revivalism's complementary political expression, strove to bring such conflict within the compass of a purified public authority, whose range of concern extended from money to language, from Nicholas Biddle's bank to Noah Webster's dictionary.[42]

Set within this context of provincial revivalism, commercial expansion, and political Whiggery, the young Johnson's nagging sense of

[40] George Rogers quoted in Whitney R. Cross, *The Burned-Over District: The Social and Intellectual History of Enthusiastic Religion in Western New York, 1800–1850* (Ithaca, N.Y.: Cornell University Press, 1950), 44.

[41] Paul Johnson, *A Shopkeeper's Millennium: Society and Revivals in Rochester, New York, 1815–1837* (New York: Hill & Wang, 1978); Mary P. Ryan, *Cradle of the Middle Class: The Family in Oneida County, New York, 1790–1865* (Cambridge: Cambridge University Press, 1981), esp. ch. 2.

[42] On Webster's Whig approach to language, see Richard M. Rollins, "Words as Social Control: Noah Webster and the Creation of the American Dictionary," *American Quarterly*, 28 (Fall 1976), 415–30; *The Long Journey of Noah Webster* (Philadelphia: University of Pennsylvania Press, 1980), esp. ch. 8; on sabbatarianism and upstate New York politics, see Bertram Wyatt-Brown, "Prelude to Abolition: Sabbatarian Politics and the Rise of the Second Party System," *Journal of American History*, 58 (September 1971), 328–35.

unease and ambivalence toward Utica becomes comprehensible. By his own account he had been exceptionally slow to arrive at his calling as a banker, "being the only idler in the village."[43] Moreover, he was, like the Irish whom he patronized, only an immigrant, an embarrassment that was brought home sharply to him when he watched helplessly as Rufus King and other local Whigs quashed his effort to get a bill passed allowing naturalized citizens to run for governor. So Johnson became a Democratic businessman in a region where, for example, certain banks were known to refuse service to party members. As Dixon Ryan Fox put it, "It was not considered 'elegant" to be a Democrat in Utica."[44] Yet when Johnson sought a legislative charter for his own bank – something nearly impossible to achieve in the teens – he looked to the Democrat Aaron Burr for his model. Fifteen years earlier Burr had secured a charter for his Bank of Manhattan by concealing its authorization within the wording of a bill permitting the construction of a New York City reservoir. In like manner, the young Johnson wrote up a charter for the Utica Insurance Company, which, in the words of a local historian, "was so cunningly worded that, while it seemed to convey only permission to insure property, it in reality granted the privilege of banking also."[45] Johnson later reported his linguistic triumph in his autobiography, recalling somewhat shamefacedly that "while the bill was being read by sections in Committee of the Whole its meaning seemed so glaring to me that I wondered anybody could avoid seeing it." But, he added, "the meaning of words is in the intellect of the hearer, and they, suspecting nothing but an Insurance Company, saw nothing more."[46] Soon thereafter a bank war ensued, with rival institutions collecting and speedily returning each other's notes. As a result, the Whigs revised the law, eliminating Johnson's loophole and forcing him to close his doors in 1818. His brilliant fiction had collapsed.

Yet another fiction collapsed for Johnson when, in 1834, he inadvertently revealed to his neighbors that he had been instrumental in

[43] Quoted in Todd and Sonkin, *Johnson,* 45.

[44] Alexander Bryan Johnson, *A Guide to the Right Understanding of Our American Union, or Political, Economic and Literary Miscellanies* (1857: rpt. New York: Greenwood Press, 1968), 29; Dixon Ryan Fox, *The Decline of Aristocracy in the Politics of New York, 1801–1840* (1919; rev. ed. New York: Harper & Row, 1965), 56, 78–79.

[45] Bagg, *Memorial History,* 573.

[46] Quoted in Todd and Sonkin, *Johnson,* 95–96.

initiating Sunday mail service for his banking business. A few chilly confrontations with the Presbyterian elders led to the threat of a church trial. Johnson declined to submit to the proceeding, refusing to defend himself before a jury he regarded as little more than a Whig cabal out to police his political beliefs. Instead, he left the Presbyterians as an excommunicant in order to rejoin his father's elite Episcopalian church. According to Mary Ryan, Johnson's break with his wife's church "dealt a major blow to the system of church hegemony over individual opinions and private morals."[47] With his departure, church courts fell into disuse as instruments of social control in the district, and liberalism chalked up another victory against the claims of communal and traditional authority.

That the otherwise reclusive Johnson chose to brave the censure of his community on the sabbatarian issue is not entirely surprising in the light of his commitments to his bank and his party, neither of which wished to see the movements of commerce interrupted. But his firmness on this question, indeed his readiness to risk the very notoriety from which his fictions had thus far protected him, bespoke an estrangement that ran deeper than his immediate political and commercial interests – an estrangement that ran beneath the fiction to which he cleaved all his life, namely, the fiction of his ancestry. For A. B. Johnson was neither Presbyterian nor Episcopalian; he was Jewish. Years before in England his father had changed the family name, we are told, "for purposes of trade."[48] In fact, we do not know the original family name for Johnson took pains to ink it out in every piece of correspondence he preserved from the cousin he had left behind in England. She addressed him affectionately as Cousin Zalick or Zalig, but beyond this faint clue, the genealogical and etymological trail vanishes.[49] Thus, the most proper of names turns out to be the most detached of signifiers. "Alexander Bryan Johnson" was a linguistic fiction whose meaning lay beyond verification in the sensible world of upstate New York; absent that proof, the meaning

[47] Ryan, *Cradle of Middle Class,* 115–116.
[48] Charles Lockwood, "Introduction" to *Language and Value,* ed. Todd and Blackwood, xxi.
[49] See, for example, letters from Rachel Robinson to A. B. Johnson, March 12, 1856, and December 17, 1857, in Alexander Bryan Johnson Papers, Box 3, Folder y; Box 4, Folder 33.

of Johnson's name, like that of his Utica Insurance Company, lay entirely in the "intellect of the hearer."

There was, of course, nothing particularly new or extraordinary about Johnson's fiction. As Werner Sollors has pointed out, most ethnic narratives in America have oscillated between the poles of descent and consent, between the claims of lineage and the freedom of marriage, or between the entailments of heredity and the promise of contract.[50] And if these have been the compass points of Americanization over time, then Johnson's loyalties never wavered from the true North of consent. He was – in Appleby's and Hartz's terms – a liberal through and through: confident in the rational, self-regulative capacity of individuals to escape the past and to promote the general welfare through their private activity. "Every man is constituted by Providence an independent sovereignty," he once wrote. "He is termed a little world."[51] From his marriage to his business to his politics to his philosophy, he invariably affirmed the self-fulfilling powers of individual choice over the self-constraining claims of community or tradition. Drawn up in the marketplace of ordinary discourse, linguistic fictions amounted to convenient commercial instruments by means of which a man might bargain with an intractable past and an uncertain future. In the worlds of science and philosophy, words were not to be confused with things. Society, politics, and commerce, however, did not operate upon such distinctions. There, words might become things in their own right; indeed, they might become the condition of all other rights: a property qualification, so to speak, for the franchise granted by a liberal American culture. This Johnson seemed to suggest when, at the time of his excommunication, he wrote to an Albany newspaper in defense of universal white male suffrage. "A stammerer may by effort become eloquent," he reminded his readers; "but when we are required to overcome the defects of ancestry, we are without hope, and hence without motive and improvement."[52]

Hope, ambition, and confidence thus loosened, not to say liberal-

[50] Werner Sollors, *Beyond Ethnicity: Consent and Descent in American Culture* (New York: Oxford University Press, 1986).

[51] Alexander Bryan Johnson, *Religion in its Relation to the Present Life* (1840; rpt. New York: Greenwood, 1968), 91.

[52] "Letter of A. B. Johnson, Esqu.," *Albany Argus Extra*, October 17, 1834, 4.

ized, Johnson's harsh philosophical strictures on language, for just as his economic nominalism never went so far as to celebrate a hard-money position (he has been described as a Keynesian *avant la lettre*), so his epistemological nominalism never went so far as to alter his belief in the judicious use of fictions in a pecuniary society. This conviction was never more visible than in Johnson's *Encyclopedia of Instruction,* published in the same year as Melville's *The Confidence-Man.* The coincidence of the two works is striking not only for the unities of time and place they shared (the Confidence-Man was probably based on a real figure operating in the Albany area), but also for the themes and possibilities they entertained.[53] So closely do the two authors resemble one another when discoursing on the theatricality of contemporary life and literature that Johnson's ponderous pronouncements meld almost imperceptibly into Melville's deadpan ironies: As Johnson wrote:

> We commend the conjuror who admits that his tricks are sleight of hand, while we imprison the fortune-teller who performs kindred tricks as veritable necromancy. Still a man who employs a fiction as a sort of intellectual condiment is not compelled to announce its imaginative origin, any more than "Snug the Joiner" was bound to assure his audience that he was not a real lion. But the partition is not always obvious between the tweedle-dum that is allowable and the tweedle-dee that is disreputable.[54]

Johnson's obscure partition between the allowable and the disreputable fiction again suggests the limits of his nominalism, not least of which was his readiness to suspend disbelief in the hope of intellectual (and other) "condiments." In fact, when Johnson turned his thoughts from physical to "moral" science, his thoughts themselves seemed to turn as if on a slightly altered axis. That shift first appeared in a series of five lectures published in 1840 under the title *Religion in its Relation to the Present Life.* There he argued that while man remained under the care of Providence, he could still benefit from what he

[53] Johannes Dietrich Bergmann, "The Original Confidence Man," *American Quarterly,* 21 (Fall 1969), 871–73; Paul Smith, "The Confidence-Man and the Literary World of New York," *Nineteenth-Century Fiction,* 16 (March 1962), 329–37.

[54] Alexander Bryan Johnson, *An Encyclopedia of Instruction: or Apologues and Breviats on Men and Manners* (New York: Derby & Jackson, 1857), 208. Compare Melville: "Strange, that in a work of amusement, this severe fidelity to real life should be exacted by any one, who, by taking up such a work, sufficiently shows that he is not unwilling to drop real life, and turn, for a time, to something different" (*Confidence-Man,* 259).

called "moral science." That science consisted in "nothing but a knowledge of the natural consequences which certain actions produce just as the science of medicine is a knowledge of the natural effects which certain things produce."[55] Just because of these effects, morality forbade even the "semblance of evil actions," a point Johnson illustrated with a thinly veiled autobiographical memory. "A young man who saunters through our streets because he possesses at the moment no occupation, is gaining the character which is to prevent his ever obtaining any occupation."[56] Social meaning, like reputation, lay in the intellect of the hearer, and viewer.

For these reasons, Johnson's instructional writings insisted that his readers attempt to anticipate the social responses to the conduct they contemplated. His lecture on "The Art of Controlling Others" took care to say that "no station is so exalted as to disregard the sentiments and feelings of mankind, and that to obtain in our favor the sentiments and feelings that we desire, we must rely on other means than power, station, physical force, or wealth." As a first step "to a control of the feelings of the world," he added, "a man must know what conduct will excite in other men the feelings that he desires."[57] The passage reflects his reading of Adam Smith's *Theory of Moral Sentiments,* but it also betrays the extraordinary strain Johnson himself must have felt in building his bank and his character – to borrow Stanislavski's phrase – upon the open-air stage of the Burned-Over District. A hint of the cost exacted by Johnson's effort to conform to the "sentiments and feelings of mankind" emerges almost subliminally in a letter Johnson addressed to John Adams almost a decade after Adams's granddaughter had brought her husband into the Presbyterian fold:

> [T]o become a Presbyterian in this region is like a formal notice to the world, that your conduct and conversation are to be more rigidly correct than that of the ordinary man; that slander, irascibility, misanthropy, uncharitableness, revenge, dissipation, covetousness, etc. are not to be indulged in or secretly practiced in any instance. I admit there is something pharisaical in all this, but it has, with me at least, much practical effect; and I frequently restrain some

[55] Johnson, *Religion in its Relation to the Present Life,* 45.
[56] Ibid., 54–55; "character" is here understood as "credit" or "reputation"; Franklin, of course, makes a very similar observation in his autobiography.
[57] Ibid., 103.

ill-natured speech or feeling by a reflection that it will disgrace me as being out of character.[58]

With his father's name and his father's help, he had built that character; the problem, as Emerson once pointed out, was to live in it. Here Johnson's model of society reproduced his model of language. "Society is like a spacious hall hung with mirrors around and above," he argued. "You may address yourself to any one mirror; but, if you contemptuously yawn before it, all the others will return the yawn." We may recognize in this analogy the familiar picture of a fun house, but Johnson probably imagined something closer to the biblical House of Mirth. Miscues, stammers, stage fright – any sign of insincerity represented a capital risk for him in the intense moral and pecuniary economy of upstate New York. "You are masquerading before others who have masqueraded themselves," he warned. "They know every turn of the game as skilfully as you."[59] Neither Smith nor Melville could have put his predicament better; nor would they have arrived at his solution.

III

How was this elaborate language-game of society and commerce to be won, then, if sincerity itself was not something one could directly will? For an answer, Johnson turned, ironically, to the same romances whose morbid and cruel "fictions" had presumably led him to cast them aside. In particular he seized upon Walter Scott's *Kenilworth* (1821), a rather long-winded tale of conspiracy, poison, duels, and trapdoors. "The words of the narrative will, as an essential part of their meaning, excite the feelings," he wrote. "Like the sounds of an organ, our feelings must burst forth if you press the proper key; and among the objects which can thus press us, none is so effective over a man's feelings as his own words, thoughts, and actions."[60] Hidden behind the exotic props of the romance, Johnson had discovered an

[58] Letter of 1823 quoted by David Ellis, "Alexander Bryan Johnson: Reform and Religion," in *Language and Value,* ed. Todd and Blackwood, 169.

[59] Johnson, *Religion,* 127, 109; on the problem of theatricality in antebellum middle-class life, see Karen Halttunen, *Confidence-Men and Painted Women: A Study of Middle-Class Culture in America, 1830–1870* (New Haven: Yale University Press, 1982).

[60] Johnson, *Religion,* 131.

even more intriguing linguistic device: poetic effect. Properly understood, the bane of physical science could become the blessing of moral science. The dubious means by which an author invited the moral complicity of his readers in his fictions could be turned by those same readers into an excercise in their own virtuous self-fashioning. By treating feeling itself as a language skill, one could effectively sidestep the awkward gap between word and thought or between word and deed. It was a step Johnson must have made many times for he did not blink in his description of it:

> Every feeling gives to our appearance a peculiar look, to our voice a peculiar tone, to our language a peculiar phraseology, to our limbs a peculiar action, to our thoughts a peculiar tendency. These natural associates of every feeling are so familiar to our experience, that we tell by a glance the feeling which is present with any person, be it love or anger, pride or humility, hope or despair. . . . A theatrical performer can imitate them with corresponding intonations of voice and motions of limbs. . . . we are so constituted that the feeling of sympathy will arise in us when we assume the look, tone, and actions that belong to sympathy. I can assert the like to be a general rule, and that a man can excite in himself any feeling if he will speak, look, and act as if he already possessed the feeling.[61]

"You may ask," Johnson added proleptically, "whether I intend to recommend hypocrisy, since I require a man to act and speak differently from what his feelings may dictate. I answer no. I wish him to profess all that is virtuous, and to act conformably to the profession." But this was scarcely an answer, since the word "act" contained just those troubling hints of impersonation that Johnson's behavioral formula supposedly resolved. Moreover, the formula itself worked only when "profession" and "act" – saying and doing – amounted to the same thing in practice, which is to say, a self-fulfilling speech act. In effect, Johnson proposed to treat discourse itself as if it were a promissory note drawn on the sentiments within and issued to the society without in the confidence that the circle of credit would remain forever unbroken. And it would remain unbroken, he believed, precisely because humans were so constituted that the language of feeling performed what it promised, as it were, in the same breath. By

[61] Ibid., 131–33, 141–42. "So intimate is the connection between our feelings and our language, that men are to a great extent estimated by their professions. Actions are a more equivocal exponent of character than professions." *Encyclopedia of Instruction,* 381.

founding a bank, by marrying an Adams, by joining a church, one was doing something more than serving "a formal notice to the world"; one was also drafting a chain letter to oneself, or rather to the selves one would become over time. Without the slightest touch of irony, *Religion in its Relation to the Present Life* pictured American society as a place where confidence fed upon the assurance of a redemption forever deferred.

Nowhere was Johnson's enthrallment with the powers of language more striking than in his conclusion to *Religion.* "We can accomplish what is the equivalent to controlling the events of life," he crowed; "we can control the effect which the events of life shall produce on us."[62] And by so doing, individuals could move beyond the control of emotions to the manipulation of conviction itself.

> Even belief, which the Bible implicitly exacts and which we often deem the most unreasonable of its exactions, being, we affirm, entirely beyond our control, is as tractable as any other of our feelings. We may believe in opposition to the clearest revelations of our intellect, and nothing is more common. . . . If you would not feel unbelief, avoid the words, thoughts, and actions which unbelief would dictate.[63]

This passage would seem to place us much closer to William James, not to mention Dale Carnegie and Norman Vincent Peale, than to Johnson's own *Treatise on Language.*[64] Nothing in the *Treatise,* for example, could have been construed as endorsing the power of language to block thought, yet this was exactly what Johnson's "Art of Self-Control" commended. He called that art "moral alchemy," and he was right, for by means of it, language – the fool's gold of the *Treatise* – was converted into the most valuable currency of all. No longer did Johnson invoke the reality of things as proof against the pretensions of words. Nor did he instruct his readers to adjust their language to the diverse sensible data of their feelings. Instead, he urged them to adapt their sentiments, or, more accurately, to let their sentiments adapt themselves to their language. Johnson's "Art" had turned language from a "defective medium" into a happy medium.

Is it possible, then, to reconcile Johnson's philosophical nomi-

[62] Ibid., 164.

[63] Ibid., 139, 145.

[64] See David Rynin, "Alexander Bryan Johnson's Treatise on Morality," in *Language and Value,* ed. Todd and Blackwood, 46; and David Ellis, "Reform and Religion," in ibid., 176–77.

nalism with his sociological instrumentalism? Or is the incongruity but one more instance of the antirationalist or irrational genius of American culture? Without begging the question, one might begin by considering Johnson, as others have, as a prototypical logical positivist, and thereby treat his seemingly contradictory views of language as anticipating the twentieth-century, analytic distinction between scientific and emotive discourse: what the critic I. A. Richards termed the "two uses of language."[65] "Anticipation" is, of course, a connection imposed by hindsight; "affinity" might be more appropriate. But even if we regard Johnson's contribution to modern philosophy's linguistic turn as largely honorific, owing more to the belated generosity of posterity than to his precocious influence upon it, this does not dispose of the possibility that the turn he did take in the 1820s responded to some of the same perceived problems as the turn European philosophers made a century later.

It is a long journey, to be sure, from Johnson's Utica to Wittgenstein's Vienna and from the *Treatise* to the *Tractatus*. Still, the affinities the two works do exhibit suggest how plausible it may have seemed to magnify the role of linguistic fictions at the moment of an empire's rise as at the moment of its collapse. Further, when one contemplates Wittgenstein's subsequent movement away from the sharp cognitive–emotive dichotomies of his *Tractatus* toward his pragmatic, behavioral, if not anthropological notion of language games, then his resemblance to Johnson seems even more striking. "Man exists in a world of his own creation," Johnson once wrote. "He cannot step, but on ground transformed by culture. . . . His language, actions, sentiments, and desires, are nearly all factitious."[66] Johnson, the *bourgeois gentilhomme,* had discovered Boorstin's seamless culture concept, only he had done so as an observation on the constructed quality of American experience, not on its "givenness."

But what is perhaps most intriguing about Johnson's remarks on

[65] I. A. Richards, *Principles of Literary Criticism* (New York: Harcourt, Brace & World, 1925), ch. xxxiv; interestingly, Richards's colleague Charles Ogden reconstructed a parallel "tradition" on the other side of the Atlantic when he discovered Jeremy Bentham's "Theory of Fictions"; although Johnson's ideas bear a striking resemblance to some of Bentham's, there is no evidence that he read (or could have read) anything other than Bentham's defense of usury, which he opposed; cf. C. K. Ogden, *Bentham's Theory of Fictions* (London: Kegan Paul, Trench, Trubner, 1932).

[66] Johnson, *Treatise on Language,* 29.

the factitiousness of ordinary life is that he chose to make them not where one might expect – in his instrumentalist essay on "The Art of Self Control" – but, rather, on the opening page of his nominalist *Treatise on Language.* So while one must concede the tension that existed between a philosophy that warned against the misdirections of language and one that, in effect, embraced them, there may be other grounds for treating his sociological instrumentalism as a logical corollary to his epistemological nominalism. For, whatever else may be said of these two positions, both of them recognized discourse – that is, language in its broadest, most active sense – as an autonomous power: a socially constructed power, like bank notes, and consequently (on that analogy) a power that could also stand over and against its creators as an external, even alien, force.

It is that embryonic sense of the performative (or promissory) force of language that places Johnson squarely in the ranks of the new "kind of men" of his age – Appleby's liberal capitalists.[67] Johnson was, after all, an entrepreneur of the urban frontier, and as such he realized that promotion and development were to be, in Suzan Kuhlmann's words, "an effort of language, even at times an enterprise in which language took the place of a salable commodity."[68] "Mark out for yourself," he once advised his son, "such a character as you desire to possess, and by speaking consonantly thereto, you will attain the desired character as certainly as you will a coat, after going to your tailor and ordering it."[69] Such instruction was, in Mary Ryan's words, the "moral capital" parents bequeathed to their children in upstate New York: a new kind of "family collateral . . . honored not just in heaven but in the commercial marketplace of Utica as well."[70] If some clergyman were put off by the double service Johnson's metaphorical coat performed, perhaps that was because the fit felt too close for comfort.[71]

[67] For an illuminating discussion of the "promising self" in Melville's *Confidence-Man,* see Wai-chee Dimock, *Empire for Liberty: Melville and the Poetics of Individualism* (Princeton: Princeton University Press, 1989), 195–99.

[68] Suzan Kuhlmann, *Knave, Fool, and Genius: The Confidence Man as He Appears in Nineteenth-Century American Fiction* (Chapel Hill: University of North Carolina Press, 1973), 50.

[69] Johnson, *Encyclopedia of Instruction,* 318; the advice or "breviat" portions of the book originally had been composed as letters to his children; see Todd and Sonkin, *Johnson,* 327–28.

[70] Ryan, *Cradle of the Middle Class,* 141.

[71] *Religion in its Relation to the Present Life* was briefly considered by Harpers for inclusion in its popular "Family Library," but the idea was laid aside after a minister

Close as it might have seemed, though, Johnson's conception of language was not the only model available to antebellum Americans, and it drew scarcely a fraction of the attention given to Noah Webster's work. Yet the difference between the two figures only confirms the cultural dead end toward which Webster's famous dictionary led and the open road toward which Johnson's otherwise forgotten treatise looked. For Webster (as for Johnson's local nemesis, Rufus King) the truth of a word was a matter of its God-given etymology, not of its social consequences, which explains why he looked to his dictionary to restore the meaning of such lost republican virtues as deference, discipline, quiescence, and piety.[72] For Johnson, on the other hand, words were tokens of exchange, to be judged by their consequences rather than their "defects of ancestry." Where Webster's approach looked backward, Johnson's looked forward; where Webster was diagnostic, Johnson was prognostic. Where Webster wanted life "as it was," Johnson wanted it simply "as it were."

It is this unwavering commitment – in his life as in his work – to the subjunctive mood, to the self-fulfilling power of an ineradicably hypothetical or fictional language that marks Alexander Bryan Johnson as a man both in and out of his time. Had he not been *where* he was and thus exposed, as he was, to the peculiar commercial fictions of a developing market society, he might never have arrived at a view of discourse so complacently modeled in its image. And had he not been *who* he was, he might never have pushed the implications of that model in the direction and to the limits that he did. In the measure that Adam Smith's "reasoning about human nature was itself a product of commercial society," so A. B. Johnson's was as well.[73] Context and concept were intimately linked in his career, they formed and informed one another; yet the ideas generated from this mutual exchange remained sufficiently autonomous, sufficiently original, to speak beyond their time and place, to add their degree or two to the

enlisted to appraise the work objected to it on the grounds that it taught hypocrisy; Todd and Sonkin, *Johnson*, 274.

72 Rollins, "Words as Social Control," 421–30; David Hackett Fischer, *The Revolution of American Conservatism* (New York: Harper & Row, 1965), Appendix II, 303–4; Webster adamantly opposed universal white male suffrage; King, as I noted earlier, had reportedly quashed Johnson's effort to have the New York Legislature pass an amendment allowing naturalized citizens to run for governor.

73 Appleby, *Capitalism*, 26–27.

linguistic turn. If this does not demonstrate Johnson's genius, it does suggest the genius of market culture.

That genius, it need only be added, cannot be reduced to the inspiration of the provincial booster. Diffident, formal, at times even testy, Alexander Bryan Johnson would have made an awkward companion for a Barnum or a Babbitt, and the unrelievedly skeptical nominalism lying at the heart of his *Treatise* cannot be wished away. That was the dark underside of his otherwise sanguine view of fictions, the call for collateral that balanced his faith in credit. Historians like Joyce Appleby and sociologists like Colin Campbell are thus right to point to the hopeful, speculative, subjunctive mood of liberalism and romanticism as a cultural characteristic of early Anglo-American capitalism.[74] But they need not look outside that culture – to republicanism or to aristocracy, for example – to find suspicion and hostility toward that same mood. Confidence and mistrust, speculation and panic, have long operated as the dialectical poles of market culture, and it is doubtless the fundamental instability or risk embodied in these paired terms that has endowed that culture's forms with the autonomous, vital force they seem at times to possess. When Pompey entered the Temple of Solomon, as Daniel Boorstin tells us, he found nothing within. We do not know if Johnson ever pried open the arcanum of his belief, but if he did, he probably found only words, the idols of his marketplace.

In 1857, the year of Melville's *Confidence-Man,* Alexander Bryan Johnson discovered that his son-in-law, James Lynch, had used his position as cashier in Johnson's bank to embezzle close to a million dollars under his very nose. Considering Johnson's scrupulous honesty, this was scarcely justice, but considering his doctrines, it was certainly poetic. Having banked on language all his life, Johnson at last found to his chagrin that someone else had cooked the books. Once the theft was disclosed, of course, the bank was ruined, and Johnson's financial career, like his philosophical career, went into eclipse. He spent his remaining years striving to pay off his debts, striving, that is, to keep good his word and with it, his name.

[74] See Colin Campbell, *The Romantic Ethic and the Spirit of Modern Consumerism* (Oxford: Basil Blackwell, 1987), especially his discussion of the importance of the "as if" response to what he calls "modern, autonomous, imaginative hedonism," and his treatment of the conventionalization of feeling and belief, pp. 82–83, 131–37.

PART III

The lens of "high" culture

Plate 1. Edgar Degas, *A Cotton Office in New Orleans*. 1873, oil on canvas, 73 × 92 cm. Pau, Musée des Beaux-Arts. Giraudon/Art Resource, N.Y. Used by permission.

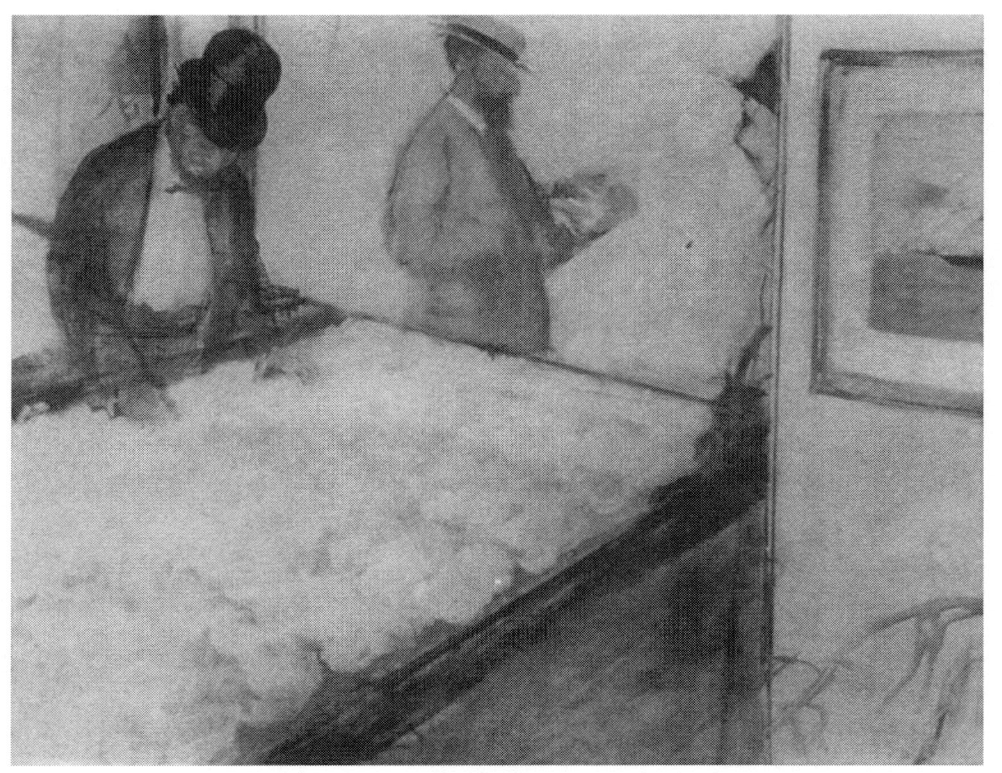

Plate 2. Edgar Degas, *Cotton Merchants*. 1873, oil on canvas, 58.4 × 71.1 cm. Cambridge, Mass., courtesy of The Fogg Art Museum, Harvard University. Gift of Herbert N. Straus. Used by permission.

Plate 3. Edgar Degas, *A Woman Ironing* (*Silhouette*). Ca. 1874, oil on canvas, 54 × 39.4 cm. New York, The Metropolitan Museum of Art. Bequest of Mrs. H. O. Havemeyer, 1929, The H. O. Havemeyer Collection (29.100.46).

Plate 4. Louise Abbéma, *The Luncheon in the Conservatory.* 1877, oil on canvas, 194 × 308 cm. Pau, Musée des Beaux-Arts. Used by permission.

Plate 5. Edgar Degas, *Sulking* (*The Banker*). Ca. 1873–74, oil on canvas, 32.4 × 46.4 cm. New York, The Metropolitan Museum of Art. Bequest of Mrs. H. O. Havemeyer, 1929, The H. O. Havemeyer Collection (29.100.43). All rights reserved, The Metropolitan Museum of Art. Used by permission.

Plate 6. Edgar Degas, *Portrait of Henri Rouart in Front of His Factory.* Ca. 1875, oil on canvas, 65.6 × 50.5 cm. Pittsburgh, The Carnegie Museum of Art. Acquired through the generosity of the Sarah Mellon Scaife family (69.44). Used by permission.

Plate 7. Edgar Degas, *Portrait of Hermann de Clermont.* Ca. 1876–79, black chalk with white highlights on blue paper, 48 × 31.5 cm. Copenhagen, Statens Museum for Kunst. Used by permission.

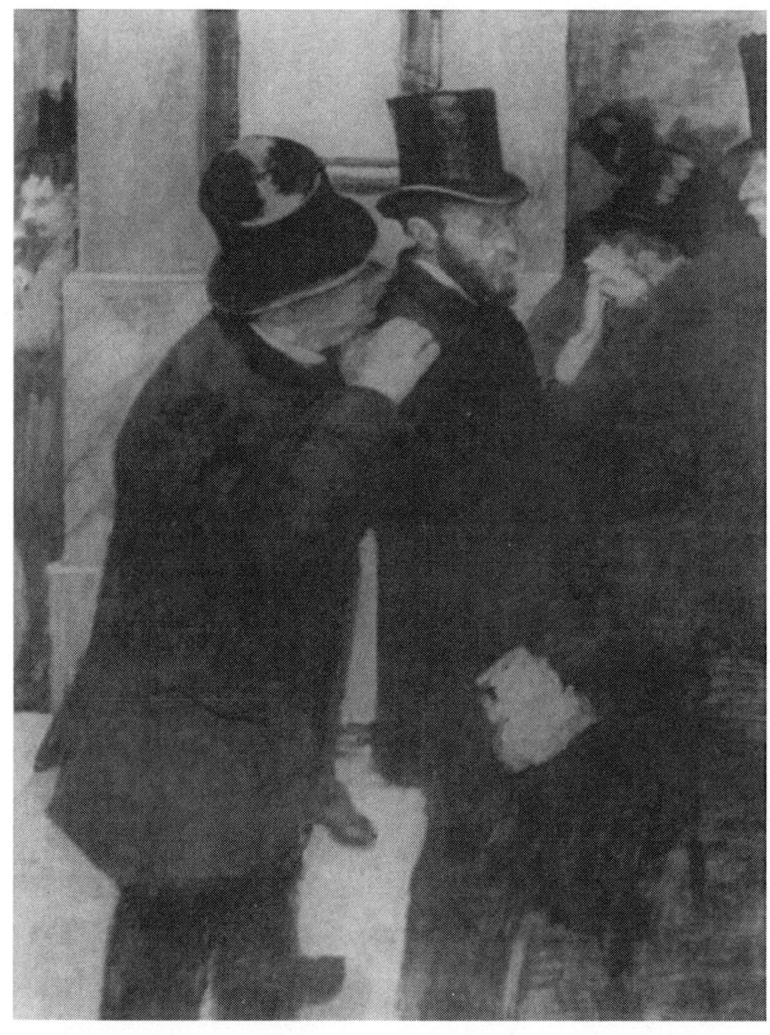

Plate 8. Edgar Degas, *Portraits, At the Stock Exchange.* 1879, oil on canvas, 100 × 82 cm. Paris Musée d'Orsay. Giraudon/Art Resource, N.Y. Used by permission.

Plate 9. Honoré Daumier, *Robert Macaire Boursier.* 1837, lithograph, 22.8 × 21 cm. Paris, Bibliothèque Nationale. Phot. Bibl. Nat. Paris. Used by permission.

Plate 10. Edgar Degas, *Pauline and Virginie Conversing with Admirers* (for *La Famille Cardinal* by Ludovic Halévy). Ca. 1880–83, monotype, 21.5 × 16 cm. Cambridge, Mass., courtesy of The Fogg Art Museum, Harvard University. Bequest of Meta and Paul J. Sachs. Used by permission.

Plate 11. Edgar Degas, *In the Salon*. Ca. 1879–80, monotype, 15.9 × 21.6 cm. Paris, Musée Picasso. Used by permission.

Plate 12. Edgar Degas, *The Madam's Birthday.* Ca. 1879–80, monotype, 11.5 × 15.9 cm. Location unknown [Janis no. 88].

Plate 13. Edgar Degas, *The Millinery Shop*. Ca. 1882–86, oil on canvas, 100 × 110.7 cm. Chicago, The Art Institute of Chicago, Mr. and Mrs. Lewis Larned Coburn Memorial Collection. Scala/Art Resource, N.Y. Used by permission.

CHAPTER 8

An entrepreneur in spite of himself: Edgar Degas and the market

MARILYN R. BROWN

Art historians who engage in interdisciplinary dialogue with colleagues from other fields can on occasion be accused of treating works of art as having an autonomous teleology remote from the cultures that produced them. "In revenge," as the French say, art historians can accuse historians and social scientists of utilizing art merely to illustrate events from social or political history. Such use, the argument goes, is confined to the subject matter of art rather than to the inner workings of its form. An interdisciplinary truce of sorts can be struck by agreeing that the interdependence of content and formal structure be taken into consideration in attempting to understand works of art in relation to history.[1]

Many art historians work in an interdisciplinary manner, taking cultural, social, and economic history into consideration as much as pictorial structure in the interpretation of works of art. For well over a decade, there has been a felt need within the practice of art history in general, and within the field of nineteenth-century French art history in particular, to reevaluate historical interrelationships between, on the one hand, subject, form, and meaning, and, on the other hand, shifting conditions of politics, patronage, and the art market.

[1] See the introductory comments by Robert L. Herbert, "Industry in the Changing Landscape from Daubigny to Monet," in John M. Merriman, ed., *French Cities in the Nineteenth Century* (London, 1982), pp. 139–40. For a comparable discussion of interdisciplinary dialogue between history and literary criticism, see Joan Wallach Scott, *Gender and the Politics of History* (New York, 1988), pp. 8–9. For a more theoretical plea for a resolution between literary (artistic) "form" and "field," see Pierre Bourdieu, "Flaubert's Point of View," in Phillipe Desan, Priscilla Parkhurst Ferguson, and Wendy Griswold, eds., *Literature and Social Practice* (Chicago, 1989), pp. 211–34, especially p. 216.

As attempts are made to integrate art and history more fully, however, it should be borne in mind that the making of a picture is a complex process: not simply a direct reflection or illustration of historical contexts, it is, rather, a social construction in which elements derived from historical circumstances are manipulated into meanings. (Inevitably, as art historians have learned from their colleagues in literary theory, historical meanings encoded in works of art are ambiguous and may shift, in discontinuous fashion, depending on audiences.) From the point of view of art history, then, culture can be seen not only as a given body of beliefs and practices sustained by a particular social organization, but also as an ongoing process of representation, a self-conscious invention of the world.[2]

In recent years art historians in the modern field have been reassessing the presumed "oppositional" stance of the French Impressionist avant-garde, which was traditionally seen as having rebelled against the *retardataire* subjects and styles promoted and sanctioned by the state-supported Academy. Although this view has its truth, especially as regards Academic style and subjects, the Impressionists are now also interpreted as appealing to, and fulfilling the needs of, an expanding and increasingly heterogeneous, middle-class, capitalist audience. With their chosen economic association as a cooperative enterprise, their independent exhibits in the heart of commercial Paris (in the area of the grand boulevards: the vicinity of luxury commodity trades, department stores, and the stock exchange), and their marketing strategies based on the emergence of the commercial art dealer, the Impressionists are seen to have forged a new free-market system that was independent of the centralized state art bureaucracy. In so doing, the artists speculatively engaged in artistic innovations that were likely to appeal directly to the entrepreneurial clients who, they hoped, would purchase their works as investments. According to this interpretation, the Impressionists' individuality, originality, and progressive aesthetics became their market value. Yet their economic uncertainty attested to the as yet incomplete development of the new laissez-faire marketing system in the arts, in which the artist was to be

[2] Such issues were addressed in an art history session chaired by Ann Bermingham entitled "The Invention of Culture, 1760–1900," held at the national College Art Association conference in New York, February 15, 1990.

seen as a middle-class professional rather than as either a protégé of the state or a rebellious bohemian.[3]

In the meantime, there was considerable overlap between market institutions and artists' own self-organized formations. (Durand-Ruel, for example, acted as dealer for many of the Impressionists and also allowed their independent exhibition to be held on the premises of his financially troubled gallery in 1876.) The general transition from what Raymond Williams calls the artisanal (direct sale) to the postartisanal (intermediary-dependent) phases of the commercialization of art was not a clear, linear progression. The artists engaged in several modes of market production simultaneously, including the artisanal and postartisanal as well as older forms of patronal relations, involving commissions.[4] The uncertainty of exchange was compounded by a factor that set the avant-garde art market apart from other markets: namely, an extreme ambiguity concerning the value of the objects sold. Value was not attributed on the basis of production costs, as in other markets, and was only partly based on merchandis-

[3] For a historiographic overview, see John House, "Impressionism and History: The Rewald Legacy," *Art History,* 9, no. 3 (September 1986), 369–76. For an overview of patronage during the period in question, see Albert Boime, "Entrepreneurial Patronage in Nineteenth-Century France," in Edward C. Carter II, Robert Forster, and Joseph N. Moody, *Enterprise and Entrepreneurs in Nineteenth- and Twentieth-Century France* (Baltimore and London, 1976), pp. 137–207. Research on the "new dealer–critic system" and the patronage of Impressionism was pioneered by Harrison C. White and Cynthia A. White, *Canvases and Careers: Institutional Change in the French Painting World* (New York, 1965), especially chs. 3 and 4. See also Merete Bodelsen, "Early Impressionist Sales 1874–94 in the Light of Some Unpublished 'Procès-verbaux,' " *Burlington Magazine,* 110 (June 1968), 331–48. Douglas Cooper, "Early Collectors of Impressionist Painting," in Michel Strauss, ed., *Impressionism and Modern Art: The Season at Sotheby Parke Bernet* (London and New York, 1974), pp. vii–xv, reiterates the importance of examining the role of patronage in the emergence of Impressionism, but upholds modernist myths by stressing the supposedly heroic risks taken by early amateurs of Impressionism "in the face of great hostility" (p. viii), excluding consideration of their entrepreneurial acumen and financial profit. For recent critical analyses of speculative strategies in the marketing of individualism and originality in the art world of this period, see Nicholas Green, "Dealing in Temperaments: Economic Transformation of the Artistic Field in France During the Second Half of the Nineteenth Century," *Art History,* 10, no. 1 (March 1987), 59–78; idem, "Circuits of Production, Circuits of Consumption: The Case of Mid-Nineteenth-Century French Art Dealing," *Art Journal,* 48, no. 1 (Spring 1989), 29–34; Robert L. Herbert, "Impressionism, Originality and Laissez-Faire," *Radical History Review,* 38 (1987), 7–15; see also idem, *Impressionism: Art, Leisure, and Parisian Society* (New Haven and London, 1988), pp. 14–16, on the grand boulevards as the location of the Impressionist exhibits.

[4] Raymond Williams, *The Sociology of Culture* (New York, 1982), pp. 35–46.

ing costs.[5] Instead, value was attributed on the basis of evaluations of quality by experts and by journalistic critical opinion – equally mutable arbiters of taste – and by provenance: the accretion of records of exhibitions in galleries, previous ownership, and museum acceptance.

This chapter looks at one specific artist, Edgar Degas, his financial insecurity, and his ambivalent attitudes toward the market as expressed in his representations of it. The essay has grown out of articles and a book on Degas's painting *A Cotton Office in New Orleans* (1873), one of the most significant visual representations of nineteenth-century capitalism and, in 1878, the first painting by an Impressionist to be purchased by a museum.[6] I begin by summarizing salient points of my interpretation of *A Cotton Office* and proceed to examine Degas's other visual representations of businesspeople in a sequence of pictures initiated by, and thematically related to, the New Orleans picture. My assessment traces the evolution of a critique of the market and of art's relationship to it, even as the artist achieved a relative success in selling his work. The trajectory of these visual images of business is evaluated in light of the artist's conflicted and increasingly rebarbative attitudes toward the market (art and otherwise) as expressed in his letters and notebooks.

Although by the end of the 1870s Degas referred rather bitterly to selling what he called *mes articles,*[7] it is apparent that between 1873 and 1878 he consciously planned and eventually succeeded in satisfy-

[5] For more recent developments of this phenomenon, see, for example, Diana Crane, *The Transformation of the Avant-Garde: The New York Art World. 1940–1985* (Chicago and London, 1987), pp. 110–36; Robert Jensen, "The Avant-Garde and the Trade in Art," *Art Journal,* 47, no. 4 (Winter 1988), 360–67.

[6] "Degas and *A Cotton Office in New Orleans,*" *Burlington Magazine,* 130 (March 1988), 216–21; "The DeGas–Musson Papers at Tulane University," *Art Bulletin,* 72, no. 1 (March 1990), 118–30; *The DeGas–Musson Family Papers: An Annotated Inventory* (New Orleans, 1991); *Degas and the Business of Art: 'A Cotton Office in New Orleans,'* forthcoming as a College Art Association Monograph on the Fine Arts, Pennsylvania State University Press. I would like to express my thanks to the American Council of Learned Societies and the Tulane University Committee on Research for supporting this work, and to Thomas Haskell and Richard Teichgraeber for making helpful comments on the current essay.

[7] The earliest use of the term seems to have been in April–May, 1879, in a letter to artist Félix Bracquemond: Marcel Guérin, ed., *Lettres de Degas* (Paris, 1945), p. 43; see also pp. 59, 61; in the English translation, *Degas Letters,* trans. Marguerite Kay (Oxford, 1947), see p. 190. See also Ambroise Vollard, *Degas (1834–1917)* (Paris, 1924), pp. 66–67. On the common use of the terms *articles de Paris* and *articles de nouveauté* to refer to commodities sold in the arcades and shops of Paris during the July Monarchy, see Rémy G. Saisselin, *The Bourgeois and the Bibelot* (New Brunswick, N.J., 1984), p. 25.

ing a projected future market with *A Cotton Office in New Orleans* (Plate 1). In so doing, the artist seemingly took the marketing of cotton in New Orleans as both subject and commercial paradigm, occasionally and sarcastically referring to the picture itself (in letters to the dealer Deschamps) as *mon coton,*[8] that is, as the cotton commodity it represented. He encountered unforeseen complications in the venture; and during the course of the five years between production and sale, his market, audience, and, apparently, the accumulated social meanings of his picture shifted. Yet the artist's disjunctive pictorial form and unfixed messages about business were sufficiently ambiguous to appeal to different audiences for different reasons. Degas's official success in selling *A Cotton Office* in 1878 marked an important juncture in the trajectory of his career as it progressed from the economically troubled initial years of his participation in the Impressionist movement (beginning in 1874), toward his increasing recognition and improving financial stability during the 1880s.

The very subject matter of the New Orleans picture, represented "objectively" as an exclusively masculine preserve of leisurely capitalist enterprise, was carefully chosen to appeal to a particular market with a given set of social and economic assumptions. The letters Degas wrote from New Orleans at the time he was executing the work in February 1873 establish that he intended to sell the picture to a specific textile manufacturer, one William Cottrill, of Manchester, England – a city known at the time as "cottonopolis." The letters make it clear that Degas was willing to paint a subject he hoped (or speculated) would appeal to this client and that he was willing to negotiate with two dealers – Agnew and Durand-Ruel – behind each other's backs to accomplish his goal. He was even willing to alter his style to suit his market by painting the final version of *A Cotton Office* with a more finished *facture* than that of the sketch version (Plate 2), which he described as "more spontaneous, better art." He implied that the more detailed, tighter version, albeit less innovative, would have a better chance on the British market.[9]

[8] Degas's letters to Charles W. Deschamps, June 1 and 16, 1876, Archives Durand-Ruel, Paris; partially translated in Denys Sutton, *Edgar Degas: Life and Work* (New York, 1986), p. 115; transcribed in Musée d'Orsay, *Degas inédit: Actes du colloque Degas* (Paris, 1989), pp. 436–37. See also below, note 20.

[9] Kay, trans., *Letters,* no. 6, pp. 29–30. See also no. 3, pp. 18–19; no. 7, p. 33; no. 8, pp. 34–5.

An examination of the immediate historical context of Degas's entrepreneurial efforts – that is, the world markets for cotton and art, both of which were shaken by an international stock market crash during the very year the artist was painting his picture – suggests why his venture failed, for reasons both aesthetic and economic. For one thing, William Cottrill, like other new industrialist collectors in Britain, had a decidedly nostalgic preference for preindustrial landscapes and moralizing rural genre scenes. (He owned no representations of the cotton industry that funded his art investments.) Although there was a commercial and industrial logic in Degas's plan to sell a painting representing the marketing of raw cotton to a cotton manufacturer, the artist seemed to be basing his venture less on what Manchester industrialists actually collected than on what they professed economically – that is, the laissez-faire ideals of the Manchester "school." In any case, he incorrectly assumed that a Manchester collector would automatically be drawn to a representation of his own form of life. Meanwhile, for reasons of apparent financial instability (some of them probably stemming from the aftereffects of the cotton famine produced by the American Civil War), Cottrill sold his mansion and his entire picture collection in April 1873, and Degas's envisioned deal was off.[10]

[10] See Brown, *A Cotton Office,* ch. 1. For information on Cottrill, see *Manchester and Salford Census* (1871), Broughton, sec. 16, p. 34; *Manchester of Today: Business Men and Commercial Interests, Wealth and Growth, Historical, Statistical, Biographical* (London, 1888), p. 100; J. Worrall, *The Cotton Spinner's and Manufacturer's Directory for Lancashire* (Manchester, 1884), p. 47; W. B. Tracy and W. T. Pike, *Manchester and Salford at the Close of the Nineteenth Century: Contemporary Biographies* (Brighton, 1899), p. 107; "Visits to Private Galleries. The Collection of W. Cottrill, Esq., Singleton House, Higher Broughton, Manchester," *Art Journal,* new series, 9 (1870), 68–70; 10 (1871), 36, 72, 80; 11 (1872), 68, 92; Christie's, *Catalogue of the Highly Important Collection of Modern Pictures and Water-Colour Drawings of William Cottrill, Esq., Who Has Disposed of His Residence, Singleton House, Higher Broughton, Manchester* (London, 1873). On the collecting habits of Manchester cotton manufacturers, see G. Agnew, *Agnew's 1817–1867* (London, 1967), p. 10; C. P. Darcy, *The Encouragement of the Fine Arts in Lancashire 1760–1860* (Manchester, 1976), pp. 154–55; A. Howe, *The Cotton Masters 1830–1860* (Oxford, 1984), pp. 296–301; E. Conran, "Art Collections," in J. H. G. Archer, ed., *Art and Architecture in Victorian Manchester* (Manchester, 1985), pp. 65–80. On the Manchester "school" of economics, see William D. Grampp, *The Manchester School of Economics* (Stanford and London, 1960). On its influence in France, see Arthur Louis Dunham, *The Anglo-French Treaty of Commerce of 1860 and the Progress of the Industrial Revolution in France* (Ann Arbor, 1930); Adeline Daumard, "L'Etat libéral et le libéralisme économique," in Pierre Léon et al., *Histoire économique et sociale de la France, III; L'avènement de l'ère industrielle 1789–années 1880* (Paris,

What Degas's letters from New Orleans failed to state, as they projected the (eventually unsuccessful) marketing venture, was that the very firm depicted in *A Cotton Office* – a cotton factoring company that belonged to the artist's American uncle, Michel Musson – actually dissolved business at exactly the time he was painting his picture and writing his apparently optimistic, entrepreneurial letters. This was not an unusual occurrence during the period of Reconstruction, when small, antebellum-style cotton factors were being made obsolete by the more impersonal and speculative system of modern cotton exchanges. The situation was exacerbated by the fact that Degas's family, on both sides of the Atlantic, had earlier lost money in ill-advised investments in Confederate bonds. It seems likely that under the circumstances of business instability – something of which is conveyed by the asymmetrical composition of the painting, in the palpable tension between casual order and scattered dislocation – the artist could find more than a passing analogy between the cotton commodity he depicted and the painted *article* he hoped to sell.[11]

Chronically troubled family finances during the period following the dissolution of his uncle's cotton firm in 1873 made the need to sell this and other pictures more pressing for the artist. The fortunes of dealer Paul Durand-Ruel (on whose gallery Degas and the Impressionists depended most heavily), meanwhile plunged in the wake of the stock market crash of 1873. The dealer was forced to suspend most of his purchases in 1874, something that no doubt helped catalyze the formation of the first Impressionist group exhibition that year. Degas continued to try to sell *A Cotton Office* in Britain during 1874–75. During the same time, 1874–76, Degas's father's bank (in Paris and Naples) failed and was liquidated. In addition to problematic economic circumstances following the crash, his father's bank,

1876), pp. 137–60, especially pp. 157–58. On the stock market crash of 1873, see E. J. Hobsbawm, *The Age of Capital 1848–1875* (London, 1977), p. 17; see also S. B. Saul, *The Myth of the Great Depression 1873–1896* (London, 1969).

11 See Brown, *A Cotton Office,* ch. 1. The dissolution of Musson's firm was formally announced in *The Daily Picayune,* February 1, 1873, p. 5, and is confirmed in the DeGas–Musson Papers in the Tulane University Library, New Orleans, ms. 226, box IV, folder 21. For the earlier investments in Confederate bonds, see box I, folders 46, 61, 63, 68, 69, 71, 72, box II, folders 1, 3, 8, 13, 15. On cotton factors and cotton exchanges, see, among others, Harold D. Woodman, *King Cotton and His Retainers: Financing and Marketing the Cotton Crop of the South, 1800–1925* (Lexington, 1968); James E. Boyle, *Cotton and the New Orleans Cotton Exchange: A Century of Commercial Evolution* (New York, 1934).

like other family banks at the time in France, suffered from, and was outmoded by, the emergence of larger and more anonymous credit banks like Crédit Mobilier and Crédit Lyonnais. Degas's brothers meanwhile accrued various debts, including one very large claim resulting from René Degas's ventures in cotton futures. In 1875, Achille DeGas was involved in a shooting incident on the steps of the Paris stock exchange, an event that, along with the ensuing court case, encumbered the family, and specifically the artist, with even more financial woes and wounded pride. By 1876 the artist and several members of his immediate family were reportedly barely subsisting as they sought to settle debts, stave off suits, and save the family honor.[12]

It was under these circumstances that *A Cotton Office in New Orleans* was exhibited in the second Impressionist show in Paris in 1876. Analysis of critical reviews at that time indicates that it received, for the most part, a more positive response than other less finished pictures. But its relative success was a conservative one. In the picture's slick *facture,* in which the avant-garde apologist Emile Zola saw a compromise of progressive painterly style, conservative Parisian critics saw a draftsmanlike confirmation of accurate bourgeois realism. They preferred this painting's "clean," "masculine" representation of individualistic American entrepreneurs to the more sketchy form and

[12] See Brown, *A Cotton Office,* chs. 2, 3. On the financial difficulties of dealer Durand-Ruel during the 1870s, see White and White, *Canvases and Careers,* pp. 135–41. Evidence of the money troubles of Degas's family is found in the DeGas–Musson Papers (see note 11), box II, folders 23, 63, 65; box III, folders 1, 7, 13. On Achille Degas's shooting incident at the Bourse, see "Le Drame de la Bourse," *Paris-Journal,* August 21, 1875, pp. 1–2; "Gazette judiciaire: Tribunal correctionnel de la Seine: L'Affaire Legrand-Degas," ibid., September 26, 1875, p. 3; "Informations," *Le Figaro,* August 20, 1875, p. 3; ibid., August 21, 1875, p. 3; Fernand de Rodays, "Gazette des tribunaux: Police correctionnelle: Affaire Legrand et Degas. – Les Coups de revolver de la place de la Bourse," ibid., September 26, 1875, p. 3. The most detailed recent account is in Roy McMullen, *Degas: His Life, Times, and Work* (Boston, 1984), pp. 250–51; see also Grand Palais, *Degas* (Paris, 1988), p. 214. On the shift from small to large banks and on the fortunes of family businesses in France in the late nineteenth century, see David S. Landes, "French Entrepreneurship and Industrial Growth in the Nineteenth Century," *Journal of Economic History,* 9 (1949), 45–61; idem, "Vieille banque et banque nouvelle: la révolution financière du dix-neuvième siècle," *Revue d'Histoire moderne et contemporaine* (1956), 204–22. Michael Miller argues that the French family firm could be more flexible in the face of dynamic business change than Landes would have it. He cites the example of the Boucicaut family (whose fortunes were, however, considerably different from those of the Degas family). See his *The Bon Marché: Bourgeois Culture and the Department Store 1869–1920* (Princeton, 1981), pp. 11–14, 127–29.

working-class, feminine subject matter of Degas's laundresses (including Plate 3), which they described as coarse and "dirty."[13] The stylistic strategy the artist adopted without success for his elusive Manchester client thus seemed to gain him a qualified acceptance among conservative critics in Paris, but lost him the support of a key defender of the avant-garde. And Degas remained unable to sell the picture, either at the exhibition or immediately afterward, when he renewed efforts to market it in London through the dealer Deschamps, a former associate of Durand-Ruel.[14]

Through the influence of two well-connected friends, Paul Lafond and Alphonse Cherfils, Degas finally succeeded in selling the picture in 1878 to the newly founded museum in the city of Pau, a winter resort in the Pyrenees. Lafond and Cherfils were the secretary and vice-president, respectively, of the Société des Amis des Arts in Pau. The annual exhibits they helped organize in Pau served in some respects as a marketing outlet for Impressionist pictures that failed to sell in Paris, either in the Impressionist exhibitions or in Durand-Ruel's gallery.[15] Lafond and Cherfils seemed to have functioned as provincial impresarios of the avant-garde. When Degas's *A Cotton Office* was exhibited in Pau in 1878, there was a critical campaign in the Palois press, some of the positive remarks coming, evidently, from the hand of Lafond. Funding for its subsequent purchase was provided by the will of one Emile Noulibos, a philanthropic lawyer and scion of an old linen and cotton-textile manufacturing family in Pau, to whom the painting was probably deemed an appropriate homage. But Noulibos's family's had reinvested its money in real estate once its relatively small textile busi-

[13] See Brown, *A Cotton Office,* ch. 2, for analysis of some thirty-nine critical reviews in 1876, including Emile Zola, "Deux Expositions d'art au mois de mai: Salon de 1876 et deuxième exposition impressionniste," in Russian in *Viestnik Evropy (Le Message de l'Europe)* [Saint Petersburg], in French in Emile Zola, *Le Bon combat de Courbet aux impressionnistes; Anthologie d'écrits sur l'art,* ed. Jean-Paul Bouillon (Paris, 1974), pp. 172–76. The more conservative reviews include Marius Chaumelin, "Actualités: L'Exposition des intransigeants," *La Gazette des étrangers,* April 8, 1876, pp. 1–2; Louis Enault, "Mouvement artistique: L'Exposition des intransigeants dans la galerie Durand-Ruelle [*sic*]," *Le Constitutionnel,* April 10, 1876, p. 2.

[14] See Brown, *A Cotton Office,* ch. 3. For the relevant letters to Deschamps, see above, note 8; also Theodore Reff, "Some Unpublished Letters of Degas," *Art Bulletin,* 50 (March 1968), p. 90.

[15] One suspects (although this cannot be documented by materials in the Archives Durand-Ruel in Paris) a connection or arrangement with Durand-Ruel, who was financially troubled throughout the 1870s.

ness, dating from artisanal beginnings in the late eighteenth century, had been supplanted by a bigger industry, Palois tourism. And Degas's painting was likewise compatible with the needs of the new industry. In this venue, the painting's leisurely (and American) aspects appealed to wealthy audiences of foreign visitors (including many touring Americans) who came to Pau to seek recreation and cultural distraction – art included. In this respect, Degas's picture worked in tandem with the other major painting purchased the same year by the museum in Pau with Noulibos's funding: *Le Déjeuner dans la serre* by the Salon Impressionist Louise Abbéma (Plate 4). Painted with a similarly tidy *facture,* Degas's canvas depicted the leisurely making of money by men in public and Abbéma's, the leisurely enjoyment of it by men and women in private.[16]

In Pau, the curious tensions built into the formal structure of *A Cotton Office* could be either overlooked or positively embraced as "innovative," even in the face of occasionally recalcitrant criticism. The combination of physiognomic individualism and perspectival disjunction in which Parisian critic Edmond Duranty, for one, read progressive and innovative evidence of modernism was precisely what proved disconcerting to an anonymous journalist in Pau, who seemed to see in the New Orleans picture an uneasy image of his own prosaic world thrown out of joint.[17] Such discontinuous readings by Degas's contemporaries surely attest to the formal ambiguities and open-ended meanings the artist incorporated into the painting. The same peculiarities of its scattered form and atomized figures, in which some interpreters today read traces of a shift from human to financial relations and evidence of the artist's own ambivalence about capital-

[16] See Brown, *A Cotton Office,* ch. 3. Relevant materials in the Archives municipales de Pau include Sér. 2L 1/2 (Noulibos's will); mayoral correspondence, February 26, and March 22–23, 27, 1878 (letters concerning the committee that chose Degas's painting); R278/3, nos. 127–28 (letters concerning the purchase of Degas's painting); related documents are in the collection of the Musée des Beaux-Arts, Pau. See also Charles Le Coeur, *Les Institutions artistiques de la ville de Pau (1863–1880)* (Pau, 1880). Lafond's defense of Degas and the Impressionists was published as "Exposition des Amis des Arts," *Journal des étrangers* [Pau], February 9, 1878, p. 2. On the commercial and cultural changes in Pau, see, among others, Pierre Tucoo-Chala, et al., *Pau, ville anglaise: du Romantisme à la belle époque* (Pau, 1978).

[17] See Brown, *A Cotton Office,* chs. 2, 3; Edmond Duranty, *La Nouvelle peinture à propos du groupe d'artistes qui expose dans les galeries Durand-Ruel* (Paris, 1876), translated in Charles S. Moffett et al., *The New Painting: Impressionism (1874–1886)* (San Francisco, 1986), pp. 43–45; cf. anonymous, "Exposition des Amis des Arts," *Journal des étrangers* [Pau], February 23, 1878, p. 2.

ism,[18] seemingly contributed, in 1878, to its "innovative" cachet in Pau. Indeed, progressive notions of creative freedom, individualism, originality, and restrained formal novelty, reinforced by entrepreneurial content, seem to have been precisely what appealed to Degas's buyers.

The "right" market was eventually found. Since the 2,000 francs the artist received for the New Orleans picture (an amount equivalent to one-fourth the Noulibos museum revenues for that year) was considerably below the 5,000 francs Degas had estimated as the value of the painting when it was exhibited, the museum perhaps felt it had made a good bargain. The 2,000 francs was not the largest sum Degas had yet received for a single work: in 1874 the opera singer Jean-Baptiste Faure had paid twice as much for a version of *The Dance Class* (Metropolitan Museum of Art, New York). But sales of such magnitude were infrequent during the 1870s, and, given the Degas family's finances, the money from Pau was undoubtedly welcome, as was the recognition.[19] It is evident, though, that in the midst of shifting economic conditions, Degas's search for an appropriate market for *A Cotton Office* was, like his family's business, characterized by halting and occasionally miscalculated strategies. The private and public meanings of the painting likewise shifted, in discontinuous fashion, between the point of initial production and that of eventual consumption. Under the circumstances, Degas's unfixed and even mixed messages about business apparently became, among other things, his most successful (if unwitting) marketing strategy.

Despite the successful outcome of Degas's venture, questions remain about the nature of his attitudes toward his capitalist clients and toward his own commercial transactions as an artist-entrepreneur. The fact that exact answers cannot be empirically documented does not subtract from the importance of asking the questions and looking at circumstantial evidence for clues. In Degas's case, individual behavior, vocation, and creation were connected, in a complicated social dialogue, with family, commerce, publicity, and economics. When translated from the realm of business, through the filter of family, into an apparently detached aesthetic realm, the operative notions of

[18] Herbert, *Impressionism*, pp. 52–55; Carol Armstrong, *Odd Man Out: Readings in the Work and Reputation of Edgar Degas* (Chicago, 1991), pp. 32–34.

[19] On March 31, 1878, Degas wrote the curator of the museum in Pau (document cited in note 16): "Il faut aussi vous avouer que c'est la première fois que cela m'arrive qu'un musée me distingue et que cet *officiel* me surprend et me flatte assez fort."

entrepreneurial progress and individual freedom became all the more powerfully, if problematically, expressed. Far from a passive illustration or recording, his paintings were an active reconstitution of observed social "facts," offering the critical insights of someone assessing the market from the inside.

The official recognition Degas received in Pau in 1878 heralded the gradual (if uneven) upswing of his own financial status during the 1880s. But his attitudes toward official success and recognition remained mixed. The biggest fly in the ointment continued to be the necessary business of marketing his art. Letters ranging throughout the decade of the 1870s convey how he cast himself, if occasionally self-mockingly, in a successful entrepreneurial role.[20] The veneer of success is undercut, however, by letters from the same period to dealers and collectors (most notably the dealer Deschamps and the collector Faure), in which he complained, often bitterly, about dire financial straits.[21] It is further undercut by an earlier statement in his *Notebooks* from the spring of 1856, which revealed deep-seated misgivings about perceived relationships between art and commerce:

It seems to me that today if you want to produce art seriously and make for yourself a little corner of originality, or at least keep for yourself a thoroughly

[20] In about 1869, for example, in a letter to the model Emma Dobigny, he concocted an elaborate metaphor of the artist as shopkeeper. See Reff, "Letters," p. 91. Later, on May 13, 1879, he wrote in a more serious vein to Félix Bracquemond, discussing how plans for the projected journal *Le Jour et la Nuit* should be arranged "so that we can show our capitalists some definite programme." See *Letters* (as cited in note 7), no. 27, p. 51. The "capitalists" he referred to included the banker and collector Ernest May, discussed below. A letter written by Achille DeGas to Michel Musson on February 16, 1869 (DeGas–Musson Papers, box II, folder 29), recounted how Edgar, accompanying Achille on a business trip to Brussels, sold some of his pictures and was offered a contract by the picture dealer [Arthur] Stevens of 12,000 francs a year: "Décidément le voilà lancé . . . il l'a bien mérité depuis le temps qu'il travaille comme un nègre et avec si peu de profit jusqu'alors. Mais cette carrière de peintre est bien la plus difficile que existe, et que de temps il faut pour établir la réputation; une fois là, par exemple, cela va tout seul." Achille hoped that Edgar's deal would signal an upswing in the family's luck in business. But according to P. A. Lemoisne, *Degas et son oeuvre* (Paris, 1946–49), 1, p. 233, note 71, the artist evidently did not accept the contract.

[21] For example, on June 16, 1874, he wrote to Deschamps (see note 8): "Et puis mon coton? Faites donc tout votre possible pour m'en *fixer un prix,* même au-dessous de ce que je vous avais dit. J'ai besoin d'argent, je ne [façonne?] plus là-dessus. *Et le temps presse plus que jamais.*" In March 1877 he wrote to Faure (*Letters,* as cited in note 7, no. 20, pp. 45–46): "Your pictures would have been finished a long time ago if I were not forced every day to do something to earn money. You cannot imagine the burdens of all kinds that overwhelm me. Tomorrow is the 15th. I am going to make a small payment and shall have a short respite until the end of the month."

guiltless personality, you must immerse yourself in solitude. There is too much tittle-tattle. It's as if pictures were being painted by stock exchange players, by friction from people avid for profits. Apparently you are supposed to rely on the mind and the ideas of your neighbor in order to do anything at all, much as a businessman requires the capital of other people in order to earn a sou. All these transactions put your mind on edge and falsify your judgment.[22]

This early acknowledgement of a desire for artistic isolation, which probably drew as much on Romantic myths of the solitary genius-hero as on the artist's own socially formulated personality and first-hand observation of business, was necessarily set aside when in 1874 Degas enthusiastically joined the Impressionists. The group's original title was *Société anonyme coopérative à capital variable,* and its members joined forces for the specific purpose of selling their works through collective exhibitions. By 1876, when Edmond Duranty implied in his review of the second Impressionist show that Degas lacked interest in being a businessman like everybody else, including other Impressionists,[23] either the critic was protesting too much or the artist had indeed become something of an entrepreneur *malgré lui.* That the uncomfortable nature of this role was seriously exacerbated by family financial reverses is attested to by a comment about Degas in a letter of January 24, 1881, from the artist Gustave Caillebotte to his fellow Impressionist Camille Pissarro:

Before his financial losses was he really different from what he is today? Ask all who knew him, beginning with yourself. No, this man has gone sour. He doesn't hold the big place that he ought to according to his talent and, although he will never admit it, he bears the whole world a grudge.[24]

Degas himself admitted in a letter of December 19, 1884, to his friend the sculptor Paul-Albert Bartholomé: "It's that deep down I don't have much heart. And what I had hasn't been increased by family afflictions."[25]

[22] Theodore Reff, *The Notebooks of Edgar Degas* (Oxford, 1976), I, pp. 50–51 (notebook 6, p. 83): "Il me semble qu'aujourd'hui si on veut faire sérieusement de l'art et se faire un petit coin à soi, original, ou du moins se garder la plus innocente personnalité, il faut se retremper dans la solitude. Il y a trop de cancans. On dirait que les tableaux se font comme les jeux de bourse par le frottement des gens avides de gagner. On a autant besoin pour ainsi dire de l'esprit et des idées de son voisin pour faire quoi que ce soit que les gens d'affaires ont besoin des capitaux des autres pour gagner un sou. Tout ce commerce vous aiguise l'esprit et vous fausse le jugement."

[23] Duranty, *La Nouvelle peinture,* p. 44.

[24] Letter quoted by John Rewald, *History of Impressionism* (New York, 1973), p. 448.

[25] *Lettres* (see note 7), no. 68, p. 99.

During the years following the official acceptance of *A Cotton Office in New Orleans,* the artist, his admirers, and biographers increasingly promoted a mythical, antiheroic Degas persona – an ironic, difficult, and self-negating reputation constructed from fragmentary and aphoristic *bons mots.*[26] The recurring themes of the myth inevitably included the painter's blistering diatribes against the art market and commerce in general and his reputed dislike of money transactions for profit – to the degree that, as he eventually became an avid collector of art, he reportedly preferred to exchange his own work with picture dealers for that of his favorite old and modern masters. In 1890, George Moore, for example, paraphrased Degas's analysis of speculation in the market for modern art: "A man buys a picture not because he read an article in a newspaper, but because a friend, who he thinks knows something about pictures, told him it would be worth twice as much ten years hence as it is worth today."[27] Recognizing the increasingly speculative and fickle nature of artistic fame, Degas made his often quoted quip to the artist Jean-Louis Forain: "There are successes that take the form of a panic."[28] Yet he somehow felt left out of the limelight and, according to Moore, confided to a younger acquaintance, "De mon temps on n'arrivait pas."[29]

As such secondhand accounts would have it, Degas seemed to visit the ire stemming from his mixed emotions about *arrivisme* (and the lack thereof) on dealers, amateurs, and buyers. According to Oscar Wilde, Degas claimed that when British painter Walter Sickert surprised him at his studio in 1883, Degas's first thought had been, "Here at last is the Englishman who is going to buy all my pictures." Yet, according to Sickert, Degas refused to admit him, claiming bronchitis as an excuse.[30] Paul Lafond recounted in his biography of Degas

26 See Armstrong, *Odd Man Out,* ch. 5, "The Myth of Degas." Compilations of the bons mots (with varying degrees of documentation) include: Charles Etienne, "Les Mots de Degas," *La Renaissance de l'art français et des industries de luxe* (April 1918), pp. 3–7; Jeanne Raunay, "Degas, Souvenirs anecdotiques," *La Revue de France,* March 15, 1931, pp. 263–82; April 1, 1931, pp. 469–83; April 15, 1931, pp. 619–32; Jean-Marie Lhote, *Les Mots de Degas* (Paris, 1967), n. p.; and Françoise Sevin, "Degas à travers ses mots," *Gazette des Beaux-Arts,* 86 (July–August 1975), 18–46.

27 George Moore, "Degas: The Painter of Modern Life," *Magazine of Art* (1890), 419.

28 Quoted by Daniel Halévy, *Degas parle* (Paris and Geneva, 1960), p. 159.

29 Moore, "Degas," p. 420: "In my day one did not succeed."

30 Walter Sickert, "Degas," *Burlington Magazine,* 31 (1917), 184. Degas later did receive Sickert after the British artist showed him a catalogue conveyed from Whistler.

how the artist stubbornly refused to admit buyers to his studio or to discuss or debate prices. (To get rid of one particularly insistent rich American collector, he supposedly reiterated quite adamantly that he charged a fixed price for each of his works, whatever the size or medium: 100,000 francs.)[31] According to his niece, Degas barked at one would-be buyer at his door: "Here we don't sell; we work."[32] The dealer Vollard (who sold works by, among others, Cézanne and Picasso) recalled Degas's royal riposte to a painter who asked him whether or not a painting is a luxury item (*objet de luxe*): "Yours perhaps. Ours is an object of first necessity."[33] And so on. But at one point in the continuing tirade against the market-minded bourgeoisie, Degas reportedly paused, in February 1889, to admit to his friends the Halévys, "Au fond, je suis très bourgeois!"[34]

That Degas's gradually achieved, if uneven, financial success and public recognition were not welcomed by him (or so he claimed) is further attested to by two accounts from the 1890s. On February 14, 1892, after having been asked by Roujon, the new director of the ministry of fine arts, to permit one of his pictures to be placed in the Luxembourg Museum, Degas held forth to Halévy on the topic of official recognition. He employed the trusty bon mot as a form of refusal – to deliver himself from what he evidently saw as a form of economic determinism:

> I told him [Roujon] no, of course. These people would like to make me believe I have arrived. Arrived, what does that mean? . . . To arrive is to be on a wall next to a portrait of a woman by Bouguereau. . . . They have the chessboard of the fine arts on their table, and we artists are the pieces. They push this pawn and then that pawn. I am not a pawn. I do not want to be pushed.[35]

31 Paul Lafond, *Degas* (Paris, 1918–19), I, p. 153.

32 Jeanne Fevre, *Mon oncle Degas* (Geneva, 1949), p. 68: "Ici on ne vend pas; on travaille." According to Etienne, "Les Mot de Degas," p. 4, Degas told another visiting collector "Je sens déjà vos mains dans mes poches."

33 Ambroise Vollard, *Degas (1834–1917)* (Paris, 1924), p. 29.

34 Halévy, *Degas parle,* p. 29: "Fundamentally, I am very bourgeois." Later, in early January 1896, Degas reportedly said (p. 94): "Ce qui m'intéresse, moi, c'est le travail, c'est le commerce, c'est l'armée!" See also Raunay, "Degas," p. 482, and Georges Rivière, *M. Degas, bourgeois de Paris* (Paris, 1935).

35 *Letters* (see note 7), appendix, pp. 273–74: "Je lui ai dit non, bien sûr. Ces gens voudraient me faire croire que je suis arrivé. Arrivé, qu'est-ce que cela veut dire? . . . C'est être sur un mur à côté d'une dame de Bouguereau. . . . Ils ont l'échiquier des beaux-arts sur leur table et nous, les artistes, nous sommes les pièces . . . ils poussent ce pion-là, puis ci pion-là . . . Je ne suis pas un pion, je ne veux pas qu'on me pousse!"

Some years later, after the Caillebotte bequest had been accepted and exhibited at the Luxembourg Museum beginning in 1897, the sculptor Bartholomé wrote to Paul Lafond on March 15, 1899, of their mutual friend's continuing harangues on the same topic:

> Degas is fine, fumes to see himself in the Luxembourg, and the fact is, in my opinion, that he does not appear there under the kind of circumstances he should. . . . *Never exhibiting* by choice, his works nonetheless figure in all the exhibitions, without his having selected what appears in them and he [remarks] how the museums (except Pau) do not contain what he would have wanted to see in them. Our disputes on this subject are constant.[36]

In addition to tasting some sour grapes, it seems that Degas felt the exhibition of his work was moving out of his personal control.

The adroit irony and human poignance that emerge from such pieced-together anecdotes and aphorisms make their litany delightfully repeatable. But they should also be tested critically against other available documentation of Degas's relationship to the art market and against the artist's own visual construction of business. The witty parries and self-mocking repartee of the bons mots were often noticeably absent from Degas's many letters to dealer Durand-Ruel, whom he essentially used as a banker during the 1880s and subsequent years. Instead, the recurring theme was – as in letters to the dealer Deschamps during the 1870s – Degas's continuing distaste for the necessity of money grubbing. A letter of 1884–85 is exemplary of many others ranging well into the early twentieth century: "For want of big money send me small, by Prosper, tomorrow Thursday. Damnable life. I am finishing your devilish pictures."[37] Yet his ranting letters

[36] Letter possibly dated 1897 rather than 1899. Denys Sutton and Jean Adhémar, "Lettres inédites de Degas à Paul Lafond et autres documents," *Gazette des Beaux-Arts,* sixth period, 109 (April 1987), 174: "Degas va bien, rage de se voir au Luxembourg, et le fait est selon moi qu'il n'y est pas dans les conditions où il devrait y figurer. . . . *N'exposant jamais* il figure dans toutes les expositions, sans choisir ce qui y paraît, et que les musées (sauf Pau) n'auront pas ce qu'il aurait pu désirer y voir. Nos disputes à ce sujet sont constantes."

[37] *Letters* (see note 7), no. 64, p. 82. Cf. no. 71, p. 89, to Henri Rouart from about the same time (ca. 1884): "I have made a few sales which will secure me until the end of this year. So all is not disheartening." But the complaints to Durand-Ruel continued. During the summer of 1884 (no. 76, p. 94), he asked Durand-Ruel for money supposedly to save him from tax seizure and sighed: "Ah well! I shall stuff you with my products this winter and you for your part will stuff me with money. It is much too irritating and humiliating to run after every five franc piece as I do." An irony is that Degas was doing comfortably enough financially to send his maid to pick up the money. Again sending her to the dealer on October 10, 1890 (no. 155, pp. 161–62),

to the dealer eventually assumed, as Degas made more money, the rather predictable and artificial acerbity of harangues between aging married couples who argue out of cumulative habit.

That he continued to be troubled by an increasingly diverse and complicated set of mediations between his individual work and his public is indicated by a subsequent letter to Lafond (now curator of the museum in Pau) in which he railed about the unauthorized exhibition of *A Cotton Office* in Paris at the *Centennale d'art français* in 1900:

> It is a matter, Lafond, of knowing whether the Musée de Pau was solicited to lend its painting of the *Cotonniers* to that exhibit. It is a matter of stopping that shipment, about which I was not consulted. Will you please be so kind as to take care of it, and to respect my independence over and above your professional connections?[38]

When Lafond proceeded to send the painting to Paris over Degas's opposition, the artist was reportedly furious and evidently even considered, but did not pursue, bringing suit. Bartholomé, who described his friend's agitated state to Lafond, said he offered Degas the following advice: "Since he [Degas] is not the master of the dealer who sells his pictures why should he be the master of the amateurs

he said, not without sarcasm: "I should like you to give her 200 for which I shall bring you repayment in objects done by my hand." Commodification was again on his mind in about 1894–95 (no. 197, p. 190) when he wrote the dealer asking for 300 francs ("Always money") and adding haughtily: "I am not leaving your articles." By August 10, 1904 (no. 258, p. 222), he was asking for a much larger sum (3,500 francs to pay a creditor), but was still nattering: "I am working like a galley slave, so as to be able to give you something soon. I am reflecting bitterly on the art, with which I managed to grow old without ever having found out how to earn money." In an undated letter of about 1908–9 (no. 271, p. 228), he had, in his mid-seventies, achieved a certain ironic acceptance: "Take care, I am going to raise my prices. Life is getting very short, and it takes too long to earn money. . . . Perhaps we shall both achieve wealth, at the moment when we no longer need it! – So let it be."

38 Sutton and Adhémar, "Lettres inédites," p. 175: "Il s'agit, Lafond, de savoir si le Musée de Pau a été sollicité de prêter son tableau des *Cotonniers* à cette concentration. Il s'agit d'empêcher ce voyage, pour lequel je n'ai pas été consulté. Aurez-vous la bonté de vous en occuper, et de préférer le soin de mon indépendance à toute relation utile ou agréable?" In my forthcoming book, I suggest biographical reasons Degas would not have wanted the New Orleans picture to be shown in Paris – reasons having to do with family ruptures across the Atlantic caused by, among other things, René Degas's desertion of his wife and children in New Orleans, and by Edgar Degas's refusal to help his New Orleanian uncle, Michel Musson, oversee the care of Musson's brother Eugène (likewise the artist's maternal uncle), who, since 1876, had been committed to the insane asylum at Charenton in France.

who buy them."[39] But Degas was evidently so disturbed by the principle involved that he refused to attend the opening of the Centennial exhibit or have anything to do with it. Although the contretemps between Degas and Lafond blew over without ending their friendship, it illustrates the artist's complicated attitudes toward success and recognition. Even as he succeeded commercially, Degas was apparently finding his stated ideal of independence translated into, and in some ways compromised by, the laissez-faire competition and unrestricted speculation of the open market. As Raymond Williams has suggested, such artistic claims to "freedom" were much more commonly made after, and in response to, the institution of dominant market relations.[40]

Earlier, during the 1870s, within a sequence of pictures initiated by, and thematically related to, *A Cotton Office in New Orleans,* Degas had constructed a visual assessment of the business world. The evolution of these ostensibly detached representations cumulatively constitutes an emerging, albeit discontinuous and nonsystematic, critique of commerce and of art's relationship to it. The arbitrarily posed yet enigmatic painting *Sulking* (occasionally called *The Banker*) (Plate 5) is recognized as an expression of modern psychological tensions owing something to the experiences of the Degas family business.[41] Probably painted in about 1873–74, this picture utilizes acutely observed physiognomy, as well as the wittily interposed British racing print (of the type that was inspiring the racetrack paintings Degas was producing and beginning to sell at the time), to suggest both an ambiguous rift and a tense relationship between physically adjacent but emotionally disjunctive protagonists located in a commercial of-

[39] Ibid., "Puisqu'il n'est pas le maître du marchand qui vend ses tableaux pourquoi serait-il le maître des amateurs qui les achètent."

[40] Williams, *The Sociology of Culture,* p. 46.

[41] See Herbert, *Impressionism,* p. 56. The dating of the painting is not agreed upon. Herbert dates it ca. 1873. Lemoisne (no. 335) dated it ca. 1873–75. Reff dates it 1869–71 because of related studies in Degas's notebooks from that period. According to Reff, the picture was posed by Emma Dobigny, a professional model, and Degas's friend Edmond Duranty, the art critic, who had also written an influential essay on physiognomy. He suggests the setting may even have been the bank in the rue de la Victoire owned by Degas's father. He also suggests a relationship to a painting by Degas's friend Evariste de Valernes entitled *Visite au notaire.* See Theodore Reff, *Degas: The Artist's Mind* (New York, 1976), p. 116, note 73; idem, "Degas and de Valernes in 1872," *Arts Magazine,* 56 (September 1981), 126–27. A date closer to the time of the troubles of Degas's father's bank seems feasible, if not likely.

fice. The implied comment on human (and probably sexual) relationships as they are socially affected by money is here pushed a troubling degree farther than in the more neutral yet equally atomized *A Cotton Office*. The increasingly intrusive confrontation with the viewer (through the woman's candid gaze) enhances the disconcerting quality of *Sulking*.

In both paintings framed art comments self-referentially upon its own place within the commercial world. In the Pau version of *A Cotton Office* (see Plate 1), the orthogonal system of the painting diminishes asymmetrically toward (if not exactly to) a framed black wall safe, which appears like a rectangular "halo" (or indeed a fireplace) behind the head of the clerk working at the ledger table on the right edge of the canvas.[42] The shape of this black vault is echoed by that of the picture hung on the wall above it. The spatial and symbolic convergence and juxtaposition of such visual indicators of secure money and framed art may seem to be an apt expression of the central concerns Degas expressed in his entrepreneurial letters from New Orleans about the painting. Yet the displacement of these important signs to the picture's very margin is, albeit typical of the artist, somehow unsettling. In the dramatically cropped Fogg sketch (see Plate 2), the wall safe is eliminated (as is the étagère of cotton samples wrapped in brown paper in the Pau version). Yet the close juxtaposition and similarly painterly treatment of what Degas called the "sea of cotton" and the framed seascape seem to draw a comparable visual analogy between the cotton commodity on the table and the painted *article* on the wall. The Fogg version seems to offer a more adumbrated, condensed, vision of rituals of commercial exchange, in a manner that situates art itself – if only marginally – as a part of that exchange. In *Sulking* (see Plate 5), the positioning of art is more central and its role is more confrontational and unsettling in the represented transaction of unspecified human relations.

A more positive painting on the topic of commerce and, more specifically, art and industry, was Degas's portrait of Henri Rouart of about 1875 (Plate 6), exhibited in the Impressionist show of 1877. Degas seemed genuinely to admire the entrepreneurial success of this friend from school days (who was likewise friends with Lafond and

[42] For identification of this shape as a wall safe, see Brown, *A Cotton Office*, ch. 1, especially a photograph of the only slightly renovated site in 1975.

Cherfils in Pau). Rouart was an artist, collector, and metallurgical engineer whose various industrial inventions included a pioneering ice factory in New Orleans. In a letter to Rouart from New Orleans, Degas had mentioned dining with one Mathieu-Joseph Bujac of Rouart's acquaintance and had expressed the hope of going one day to visit "the ice factory" with him.[43] As Rebecca DeMuth has convincingly documented, Bujac was Rouart's New Orleans manager for the installation and administration of a remarkable ice-making technology invented by Rouart.[44] As a creative scientist in the field of refrigeration mechanics, Rouart had largely been responsible for the design of what was then the largest existing ice factory in the world, built in New Orleans in 1868. Located adjacent to the railroad tracks on Tchoupitoulas Street, between Aline and Delachaise, the Louisiana Ice Manufacturing Company operated an advanced artificial cooling system based on an absorption process involving the compression of liquified ammonia gas in salt water.[45] Rouart's thermodynamic invention, as applied in New Orleans, had far-reaching effects on the refrigeration industry in the United States and Europe. A composite image of the ice plant in New Orleans serves as the adumbrated background of Degas's portrait of Rouart.[46]

As an artist, Rouart exhibited his own paintings in all but the seventh of the eight Impressionist exhibitions and also showed in the friends-of-art salons in Pau. (Given his industrial proclivities, it is ironic, if somehow predictable, that Rouart favored painting largely untroubled landscape scenes.) DeMuth suggests that it was Rouart's position as an industrialist, rather than his reputation as an artist and

[43] *Lettres* (see note 7), no. 3, December 5, 1872, pp. 27, 29; *Letters* (see in note 7), no. 5, p. 26, mistranslates *la fabrique de glace* as "glass factory."

[44] Rebecca R. DeMuth, "Edgar Degas, Henri Rouart: Art and Industry," M.A. thesis, University of Pittsburgh, 1982. See also Arsène Alexandre, *La Collection Henri Rouart* (Paris, 1912), p. 18; Marc S. Gerstein, *Impressionism: Selections from Five American Museums* (New York, 1989), p. 56, no. 17.

[45] See full description of the process in *Graham's Crescent City Directory* (New Orleans, 1870), p. 200. See also M. J. Bujac, *Artificial Refrigeration, Carré's and Mignon and Rouart's Continuous Freezing Apparatus* (Philadelphia, 1870).

[46] Lafond, *Degas,* II, p. 16, was clearly wrong to suggest that Degas painted this portrait *en plein air.* Given the low building in the background and the presence of railroad tracks, it is likewise unlikely that the scene was meant to represent a three-story factory, complete with an apartment for Alexis Rouart, its director, in the Boulevard Voltaire in Paris as suggested by Anne Distel, "Jeanteaud, Linet, Lainé," in Musée d'Orsay, *Degas inédit,* pp. 209–10, note 20.

connoisseur, that Degas acknowledged and represented in his portrait. It seems equally feasible that the painting celebrates a heroic ideal of the modern artist-entrepreneur in an industrial age. The progressive ideal of the marriage of art and industry had been promoted by the socialist Saint-Simon and his followers during the July Monarchy, among the generation of Degas's father.[47] Absorbed and transmuted by the Second Empire's voracious economy, Saint-Simonian principles fueled the expansion of capitalism as much as socialism and were still reverberating during the Third Republic, in the continuing industrial and municipal development campaigns taking place from Paris to Pau.

In a heroizing representation of the successful artist-industrialist, the formal strategies and messages of the Rouart portrait offer a striking and instructive contrast to those of *A Cotton Office in New Orleans*. Situated in an iconic composition reminiscent of Renaissance profile portraiture, Rouart dominates the sketchy factory, which seems to function as an extension of the man. Most notably, the railroad tracks, which transported the coal depicted on the left (necessary for the production of steam), have been manipulated, along with the arrangement of the coal, so as to vortex into a centralized perspective system, something exceedingly rare in Degas's oeuvre as a whole. *A Cotton Office,* by comparison, is as destabilized and careening in its off-centered orthogonal system as the two versions of the *Dance Class* (ca. 1875, Musée d'Orsay, Paris; and ca. 1876, Metropolitan Museum, New York). Rouart himself is not placed in the center, something that gives the portrait a dynamic, asymmetrical sense of potential movement. Yet the vanishing point is located precisely at his eyes – a riveting formal arrangement that Gustave Caillebotte would exploit on a grander scale the following year with his own self-portrait in *Le Pont de l'Europe* (Musée du Petit Palais, Geneva), which was shown in the same Impressionist exhibition as the Rouart portrait. In Degas's painting the centralized authority of Rouart's entrepreneurial-artistic vision becomes the controlling organizational focus and conceptual "raw material" of the industrial

[47] See especially Marguerite Thibert, *Le Rôle social de l'art d'après les Saint-Simoniens* (Paris, 1926). See also Georges Weill, *Un Précurseur du socialisme – Saint-Simon et son oeuvre* (Paris, 1894), pp. 159–60; Sébastien Charléty, *Histoire du Saint-Simonisme (1825–1864)* (Paris, 1931), pp. 352–56.

world he dominates.[48] Whereas Degas's uncle's cotton-factoring business in New Orleans was by its very nature an endangered species and proved unable to survive the vagaries of Reconstruction and the crash of 1873, Rouart's New Orleans ice factory, founded at about the same time, was a growing business in a field of evident and secure future demand. It was perhaps to a notion of the young, creative artist-entrepreneur of the Rouart variety – rather than to a perfunctory role of mere businessman, foregrounded in *A Cotton Office* in the elderly figure of Musson – that Degas aspired as he wrote his ambitious letters about art and business from New Orleans.

A slightly later portrait drawing of another businessman, Hermann de Clermont (ca. 1876–79, Plate 7) is much closer in conception to *A Cotton Office in New Orleans* and, most particularly, to the Fogg sketch (see Plate 2). The subject was the brother of Degas's friend Auguste de Clermont, a painter of horse racing, and the son-in-law of another of Degas's sitters, Mme. Dietz-Monnin, herself married to a rich industrialist and politician. According to members of the Dietz-Monnin family, Degas borrowed quite a bit of money from the Clermont brothers in the wake of the failure of the Degas family bank. In repayment for the loan, Degas is reported to have given works of art to Hermann de Clermont, who also arranged for Degas to paint Mme. Dietz-Monnin when he was in need of more money.[49] Hermann de Clermont owned a tannery and furrier firm, and in this and a companion drawing,[50] Degas portrayed him fingering some pelts in a manner that recalls Michel Musson's perusing of a cotton sample in *A Cotton Office*. But a rather disconcerting quality that seems to arise

[48] A more cynical interpretation might see the pile of coal on the left as embodying a "dark vision" seeming to emanate from Rouart's eyes. But this would be misreading naturalism as expressionism and misinterpreting, in my opinion, the visual analogy implied about the human "raw material" of industrial strength.

[49] Communication from Dietz-Monnin family reported by Richard R. Brettell and Suzanne Folds McCullagh, *Degas in the Art Institute of Chicago* (New York, 1984), pp. 107–8. Degas also did a portrait of M. and Mme. de Clermont which he showed in the fourth Impressionist exhibition of 1879 (no. 79). Pointed out by Götz Adriani, *Degas: Pastels, Oil Sketches, Drawings* (New York, 1985), no. 129. On this project also see Reff, *Notebooks of Edgar Degas*, no. 31, pp. 67, 90. The resemblance of the motif in the drawing to *A Cotton Office* has occasionally caused it to be dated 1872–73; but a date closer to 1878–79 was suggested by Ronald Pickvance, *Degas 1879* (Edinburgh, 1879), no. 50.

[50] The two drawings were framed together in the sale of Degas's studio: Galerie Georges Petit, *Catalogue des tableaux, pastels et dessins par Edgar Degas et provenant de son atelier,* III (Paris, 1919), no. 162.

from the shift from plant fiber to dead animal skins is sustained by the curiously vertiginous spatial organization of the drawing. In substituting the oblique diagonals of *A Cotton Office* for the centralized unity of the Rouart portrait, Degas created a further sense of spatial uncertainty in the Clermont portrait by leaning the figure against what appears to be some kind of parapet, from which one of the draped pelts might slip. Although the basic lines of the composition recall (in reverse) those of the Fogg version of *A Cotton Office*, the effect is more unsettling because the viewer's standpoint is less certainly grounded.

With the final painting in the sequence of pictures on the theme of the masculine world of commerce that began with *A Cotton Office*, the cryptic message is more ostensibly unflattering and antipathetic. In *Portraits, At the Stock Exchange* (1879, Plate 8), the world of the businessmen, who, clad in their Baudelairean black suits, coolly lounge about the open room of *A Cotton Office*, is transformed, reduced, and presented more abruptly, like the segmentalized spaces glimpsed in Degas's other works from the same period behind the scenes at the opera ballet or spied through the keyhole of the demimonde.[51] Exhibiting none of the heroizing clarity of the Rouart portrait, this scene of calculating *flâneurs-financiers* has an illicit, clandestine quality. It represents a world the artist knew all too well: the site of the painting, the steps of the Paris Bourse, was exactly where Achille DeGas had brandished his revolver just four years earlier. The picture could easily take as its caption Degas's previously quoted statement in his *Notebooks* of 1856: "It's as if pictures were being painted by stock exchange players, by friction from people avid for profit."[52]

The central figure is the banker Ernest May, a collector, one of the artist's clients, and a financial backer of the venture to publish the journal *La Jour et la Nuit* (a commercial project undertaken in 1879, but never brought to completion, by Degas, along with artists Mary Cassatt and Camille Pissarro). May is accompanied in the picture by a M. Bolâtre, to whom he bends a professional ear. In Degas's depic-

[51] See the excellent discussion of this picture in Armstrong, *Odd Man Out*, pp. 36–37.

[52] Surely Degas was being ironic or sarcastic when he reportedly said of bankers and *boursiers:* "Les voilà, nos héros d'aujourd'hui." Quoted in Sevin, "Degas à travers ses mots," p. 25.

tion of his patron's Semitic facial features,[53] as well as throughout the composition, including the marginal figures on the left, there is an undeniably caricatural quality. Caricature, as it operates in this picture – and more generally – lends a cynical sense of social attack.[54] There is, in fact, a striking resemblance between Degas's painting and an apparent source, Daumier's lithograph *Robert Macaire Boursier* (Plate 9), which had been published on February 26, 1837, in *Le Charivari.*[55] A great admirer of Daumier, Degas frequently did sketches after the caricaturist's lithographs and learned much from his compositional and physiognomic example.[56] In this case, though, Degas seems to have drawn as much on Daumier's content as on his form. Robert Macaire and his sidekick Bertrand appeared as charlatans and pickpockets throughout the series Daumier had begun in 1836. Adopting various disguises, Macaire was a swindler cast from the same mold as Balzac's Vautrin, a con man who beat the bourgeois at his own game – or, as Champfleury put it, a raven perched on the Bourse. In this instance the conniving Macaire has donned suit and top hat to engage in what appears to be a nineteenth-century form of insider trading.

The conspiratorial flavor is avidly appropriated by Degas, but to rather different ends. Although he makes his central protagonist more detached, he hints nastily, if subtly, at anti-Semitism in the depiction of May's physiognomic traits – this in spite of his being on good terms at the time with other Jewish acquaintances and friends, including Hecht, Halévy, and Pissarro.[57] The prominent visual pun in

[53] In a letter to Félix Bracquemond, Degas referred to May as "a jew" who was "throwing himself into the arts." *Letters* (see note 7), no. 28, pp. 51–52. Linda Nochlin reads the "Jewishness" of this unflattering portrait, along with the "Semitic nose" of one of the marginal figures on the left, as supporting "a whole mythology of Jewish financial conspiracy." She sees the "vulgar familiarity" of the portrait as quite distinct from the "openness of professional engagement" of *A Cotton Office in New Orleans.* See her "Degas and the Dreyfus Affair: A Portrait of the Artist as Anti-Semite," in Norman L. Kleeblatt, ed., *The Dreyfus Affair: Art, Truth and Justice* (Berkeley, Los Angeles, and London, 1987), pp. 96–115, especially pp. 99–101.

[54] See Herbert, *Impressionism,* pp. 55–56.

[55] Cf. the closely related lithograph of Macaire, *Vous êtes banquier, monsieur?,* published in *Le Charivari* July 9, 1838: Loys Delteil, *Le Peintre-Graveur Illustré,* 21, *Honoré Daumier,* II (Paris, 1925), no. 440.

[56] See Reff, *Degas,* ch. II.

[57] Pissarro, himself a Jew and an anarchist, likewise (and astoundingly) adopted distinctively Semitic facial features for a caricatural and allegorical figure of voracious *Capital,* drawn as a part of his *Turpitudes Sociales* series in 1889. On this series, see

which May's effaced right hand can be read in a protocinematic way as double-dealing – as either holding the note being handed to him or as merging with the blurred hands clasped behind the cropped, overlapping figure who strides abruptly in front of him – meanwhile provides a cunning visual elision in which literal artistic legerdemain may be read as other kinds. In this case, though, Degas's critique of business and of his patron seems to have been inflected – several years before the Dreyfus affair, when the artist adopted a vehement anti-Dreyfusard stance – by a perceptible anti-Semitism, which in turn has the effect of complicating and vitiating Daumier's class-directed humor. The fact that Ernest May proceeded to purchase the picture from Degas, without evidently having been offended by it, brings to mind the unfazed acceptance by the Spanish royal family at the beginning of the nineteenth century of Goya's unstintingly uncomplimentary portraits of them.

With this ambivalent painting Degas left behind the explicit subject matter of the male business world. But by this time he was exploring the implicit extension of its protagonists, power, and commercial ideology into the demimonde. That he identified this phenomenon with his close acquaintances is confirmed by a portrait of two friends he showed in 1879, in the same Impressionist exhibition as the *Stock Exchange* – the compositionally similar *Halévy and Cavé Backstage at the Opera* (1878–79, Musée d'Orsay, Paris), which was in turn reminiscent of the Fogg version of *A Cotton Office*. The cropped, disjunctive interchanges between top-hatted, black-suited men (in this specific instance, entrepreneurs of the theater) were transferred more definitively behind the scenes to mingle with cornered, ogled dancers in the *Cardinal Family* monotypes (1876–83; Plate 10) and

Richard Thomson, "Camille Pissarro, *Turpitudes Sociales*, and the Universal Exhibition of 1889," *Arts Magazine*, 56 (April 1982), 82–88. On the Semitic features of *Capital*, see Nochlin, "Degas and the Dreyfus Affair." In a letter explaining the series to his nieces, Alice and Esther Isaacson, Pissarro referred to his drawing of *Capital* as "le portrait d'un Bischoffheim ou d'un Oppenheim, d'un Rothschild, d'un Gould, quelconque." Quoted by Ralph E. Shikes, "Pissarro's Political Philosophy and His Art," in Christopher Lloyd, ed., *Studies on Camille Pissarro* (London and New York, 1986), p. 47. According to Shikes, Pissarro's hostility to Jewish bankers was an attitude motivated by class and politics, "that of the radical, artistic Jew towards the wealthy Jews involved in banks and speculation rather than in what he regarded as creative endeavor." Unlike Degas, Pissarro went on to be staunchly pro-Dreyfus, although he continued to criticize Jewish banks, even in 1898.

related works.[58] In the formally related brothel monotypes, the stealthily observed exchanges often became murky and ugly as sex was reduced to commerce and vice versa (Plate 11, ca. 1879–80). Degas apparently viewed the sex industry, with its efficient and profitable sale of services, as exemplary of modern capitalism. Although the commodity being marketed here was clearly not cotton, the contradictions implicit in Degas's attitudes toward business as a masculine domain were likewise present in his representations of these "businesswomen,"[59] and were further complicated by issues of gender. And whereas his depictions of the public arena of the male business world were intended for exhibition or sale, the brothel images were, for the most part, kept by the artist for private delectation and for the pleasure of a few close friends.

Some of the views of prostitutes exclude men, except as assumed viewers, and concentrate instead on the women's fatigue, their intimate relations with one another (often involving autoeroticism), or on their social relations with their female manager or "madam."[60]

[58] See Eugenia Parry Janis, *Degas Monotypes: Essay, Catalogue & Checklist* (Cambridge, Mass., 1968), nos. 195–231. These prints were done as a project (eventually abandoned) to illustrate a new edition of a volume of stories called *La Famille Cardinal* (1880) by Ludovic Halévy.

[59] Linda Nochlin, "Morisot's *Wet Nurse:* The Construction of Work and Leisure in Impressionist Painting," in her *Women, Art, and Power and Other Essays* (New York, 1988), pp. 43–44, draws a general analogy between the commercial activity in Degas's scenes of businessmen and that of his prostitute scenes. I am aware that the line between prostitute as producer and as marketer becomes blurred here. I am not bothered by that blurring, which seems endemic to the profession. Earlier, prostitutes and courtesans had been apotheosized in both painting (Manet's *Olympia,* 1863) and literature (Goncourt's *La Fille Elisa,* 1877; Huysmans's *Marthe, histoire d'une fille,* 1876; Zola's *Nana,* 1877). See, among others, T. J. Clark, *The Painting of Modern Life: Paris in the Art of Manet and His Followers* (New York, 1985), ch. 2, for an interpretation of prostitutes as potent symbols of the equivocal truth of financial exchange in Haussmann's Paris. See also Charles Bernheimer, *Figures of Ill Repute: Representing Prostitution in Nineteenth-Century France* (Cambridge, Mass., and London, 1989), ch. 4, for a discussion of prostitution in the 1860s and subsequent years "as the most spectacular image of the bourgeoisie's somewhat uneasy will to pleasure" (p. 89). According to Bernheimer (p. 93), prostitutes embodied "the spectacle of commodity fetishism." See Hollis Clayson, *Painted Love: Prostitution in French Art of the Impressionist Era* (New Haven, 1991), pp. 40, 42, on Degas's brothel scenes as representations of a relatively old-fashioned form of commerce in which personhood is canceled by sexual exchange. For the history of prostitution at this time, see Alain Corbin, *Les Filles de Noce: Misère sexuelle et prostitution (19e et 20e siècles)* (Paris, 1978); idem, *Women for Hire: Prostitution and Sexuality in France After 1850,* trans. Alan Sheridan (Cambridge, Mass., and London, 1990); Jill Harsin, *Policing Prostitution in Nineteenth-Century Paris* (Princeton, 1985).

[60] See Janis, *Degas Monotypes,* nos. 58–118; 184–85.

One of the latter scenes, entitled *The Madam's Birthday* (ca. 1879–80, Plate 12), looks unflinchingly at the commercial realities of the *maison close.* The deadpan yet dominant madam is physically and economically linked to the cropped torso on the right, which, stripped of clothes and individuality, becomes an emblem of the sexual commodity being proffered.[61] As several recent studies have argued, Degas's representations of prostitutes are inflected with a curious duality: an oscillation between voyeurism in the choice of subject and point of view and de-eroticism in the formal inversion of conventional physiognomic and bodily vocabularies of desire; a hesitation between a masculine gaze that objectifies the depicted women and a simultaneous revelation of the questionable nature of the commodifying power of that gaze.[62] In this specific case, the tangible presence of the artist's own fingerprints, marking the bodies of the depicted women,[63] offers a rather literal example of what Bernard Berenson would later call "tactile values." A correspondence is established between touch and gaze, so that the depicted prostitutes are fingered visually by the artist and viewer as much as the depicted cotton in *A Cotton Office* is fondled tangibly by the represented buyers, sellers, and brokers. In exposing connections between marketing, consump-

[61] Here I concur with the interpretation given by Richard Thomson, *Degas: The Nudes* (London, 1988), p. 115.

[62] In addition to Thomson, ibid., see Charles Bernheimer, "Degas's Brothels: Voyeurism and Ideology," *Representations,* 20 (Fall 1987), 158–86, reprinted in his *Figures of Ill Repute,* pp. 157–99; Carol Armstrong, "Edgar Degas and the Representation of the Female Body," in Susan Rubin Suleiman, ed., *The Female Body in Western Culture* (Cambridge, Mass., 1985), pp. 223–42; Eunice Lipton, *Looking into Degas: Uneasy Images of Women and Modern Life* (Berkeley and Los Angeles, 1986), chs. 2 and 4; S. Hollis Clayson, "Avant-Garde and Pompier Images of 19th-Century French Prostitution: The Matter of Modernism, Modernity and Social Ideology," in Benjamin H. D. Buchloh et al., eds., *Modernism and Modernity* (Halifax, Nova Scotia, 1983), pp. 43–64; Clayson, *Painted Love,* ch. 2. I am not convinced by a recent attempt to connect Degas's brothel monotypes directly with the anti-prostitution campaign carried on by French feminists in the 1880s, in order to interpret the artist's works as an indictment of the system of state-regulated and sanctioned prostitution. See Norma Broude, "Edgar Degas and French Feminism, ca. 1880: 'The Young Spartans,' the Brothel Monotypes, and the Bathers Revisited," *Art Bulletin,* 70, no. 4 (December 1988), 640–59.

[63] See Bernheimer, *Figures of Ill Repute,* p. 186, note 45. See also Luce Irigaray, *This Sex Which Is Not One* (Ithaca, N.Y. 1985), p. 177 (as quoted by Bernheimer): "Commodities, women, are a mirror of value of and for man. In order to serve as such, they give up their bodies to men as the supporting material of specularization, of speculation. They yield to him their natural and social value as a locus of imprints, marks, and mirage of his activity."

tion, desire, and power, and by reducing human relations to a matter of monetary exchange, the ambivalent imagery of the prostitution monotypes ultimately implicates both the viewer and the artist himself as agents of these visual and economic forces.

Degas's view of another variety of businesswoman, the milliner, was more sympathetic. In one of the largest treatments of the theme in the 1880s (Plate 13),[64] Degas situated the *petite commerçante* so as to make it appear that she "wears" the hat perched adjacent to her on a display stand – a fancy bonnet intended, like the one she currently creates, for an *haute-bourgeoise* consumer – and one that she, in her plain clothes, will probably never wear. Depicting *modistes* in small, self-operated boutiques rather than in large department stores, Degas seemed to admire in these women a quality with which he could identify as an artist, in spite of his higher class status – the shared capacity of being artisans producing and marketing handmade luxury commodities in an increasingly industrialized, consumer society.[65] Yet a backward glance at such temperamentally opposed images as the portraits of Rouart and May, or the scenes of prostitutes and milliners, indicates that the artist's attitudes toward the market, and his place in it, were discontinuous and, at times, contradictory.

By this point in his career, when his visual representations of businesspeople and marketing essentially came to an end, Degas was incrementally making good money, primarily from the growing market for his ballet and racetrack scenes. Although the 2,000 francs he had received for *A Cotton Office* in 1878 was more than the average annual wages of a Parisian shop clerk in the late 1870s,[66] the sum was equivalent to only one-eighth the amount Degas earned with Durand-Ruel in 1880, the first year since 1874 the dealer purchased his

[64] See Grand Palais, *Degas,* no. 235.

[65] Degas, of course, denied that he was producing *objets de luxe* (Vollard, *Degas,* p. 29). In accounting for the tantalizing materiality with which the artist depicted the hats in the milliner scenes, it should be recalled that the artist once proposed to the retailer (and art collector) Georges Charpentier that he publish an edition of Zola's *Au Bonheur des dames* with genuine samples of goods pasted in as illustrations. See *The Correspondence of Berthe Morisot,* ed. Denis Rouart (London, 1957), p. 167, cited in Grand Palais, *Degas,* no. 233. In another respect, Degas's admiration for the milliners has been read as being complicated by issues of gender and the popular reputation these women (like prostitutes) had for sexual availability, although this does not seem to have been Degas's sole emphasis. See Lipton, *Looking into Degas,* ch. 4; Clayson, *Painted Love,* pp. 128–30.

[66] See White and White, *Canvases and Careers,* 130–31.

works.[67] Throughout the 1880s, Degas was successful (if somewhat irregularly so) in selling through dealers to rich businessmen and industrialists, and to the occasional intellectual. His combined annual earnings with Durand-Ruel and, beginning in 1887, with Théo van Gogh at Boussod and Valadon, ranged rather unevenly from 9,000 francs in 1881 to 14,650 in 1882; from only 3,750 in 1889 to a comfortable 21,000 in 1890.[68] As his earnings went up, his productivity went down,[69] indicating the larger prices earned by individual works. During the 1880s, the prices Degas received from dealers for single paintings ranged from 1,000 to 5,200 francs; his drawings and pastels brought in from 75 to 1,000 francs apiece.[70] By 1885, Degas was living well enough to have his own subscription box at the opera, all the while owing unpaid debts to the collectors Faure and Ephrussi.[71] In later years, his cantankerous attitude toward the art market did not improve as he saw his works being resold at tremendous profits – of which he directly received nothing.[72] Indirectly, however, he could

[67] See Raymonde Moulin, *The French Art Market: A Sociological View*, trans. Arthur Goldhammer (New Brunswick and London, 1987), p. 13, for Durand-Ruel's figures from 1880.

[68] See table in Grand Palais, *Degas*, p. 371, note 27. According to Gary Tinterow (ibid., pp. 371–72), Degas's more commercial works during the 1880s can be distinguished by their more finished style. If this is the case, then the two versions of *A Cotton Office* offer a precedent for the practice.

[69] See productivity table in White and White, *Canvases and Careers*, p. 86. Degas produced 38 paintings during the years 1876–80; 26 during 1881–85; 22 during 1886–90; 15 during 1891–95; 15 during 1896–1900. (A major factor was, of course, his shift to pastels.)

[70] For prices of individual works, see stock books in the Archives Durand-Ruel, Paris, as cited by Grand Palais, *Degas*, pp. 375–94. (The painting that went to Durand-Ruel for 5,200 francs on February 14, 1883, was *Course de gentlemen. Avant le départ*, 1862–82, now in the Musée d'Orsay, Paris. On June 18, 1881, he sold *La Leçon de Danse*, ca. 1879, now in the Denver Art Museum, for 5,000 francs to Durand-Ruel, who immediately resold it to Mary Cassatt's brother for 6,000 francs.) For his rising British prices (1872–1918), see Gerald Reitlinger, *The Economics of Taste: The Rise and Fall of Picture Prices 1760–1960* (London, 1961), I, pp. 295–96.

[71] Eugène Manet (brother of artist Edouard Manet and husband of artist Berthe Morisot) commented on this in a letter written during the spring of 1885 to Morisot, quoted in Grand Palais, *Degas*, p. 381. Cf. Degas's letter to Faure, January 2, 1887, about his continuing debt: *Lettres* (as cited in note 7), no. 97, pp. 123–24. According to Guérin, Faure took measures to have Degas deliver the commissioned works the singer was owed. It is not known how the matter was resolved. See "Degas et Faure," in Grand Palais, *Degas*, pp. 221–23.

[72] In 1889, for example, at the sale at Christie's in London of the collection of Captain Henry Hill of Brighton, *L'Absinthe* (now Musée d'Orsay, Paris) brought 180 pounds sterling (see Reitlinger, *Economics of Taste*, p. 295). In 1893, after the painting provoked what McMullen calls a "useful scandal" in London, it was acquired in Paris by Isaac Camondo for 21,000 francs. Another picture (of uncertain title) sold

benefit from the higher prices accordingly commanded by his later works, even though dealers took their share of the profits.

Thus, in the years following 1878, which marked both the official purchase of *A Cotton Office in New Orleans* and the beginning of what has been termed a "crisis" within the ranks of Impressionism,[73] Degas, like other members of the Impressionist group, relied increasingly on dealers as middlemen rather than on artist-initiated direct appeals to the buying public. Durand-Ruel, of course, sought to establish a monopoly on individual artists' works as he accumulated his stock of paintings and projected his sights toward future returns. But he signed no written contracts with artists and settled his accounts in an intermittent and often uneven fashion, depending on prevailing economic and market conditions.[74] Under the circumstances, Degas tried to pursue a relatively free market through competition. Just as he had cultivated Agnew while dealing with Durand-Ruel in the past, he now also sold works through Boussod and Valadon and sought other dealers as well.[75] The more he grappled with the market, the more incorrigible he seemed to become in adopting his mythic, modernist personification of the reclusive yet creative individual, unfettered by materialist concerns and freely producing innovative art. Ironically, Degas's aesthetic progressiveness became his free-market value as dealers and investors now speculated in Degas "futures."

It was through these processes of commodification – what Rémy

for 8,000 francs in 1890 at the auction of the May collection at the Georges Petit Gallery. See McMullen, *Degas,* p. 418. In his memoirs, Paul Durand-Ruel said the following of Degas's mounting prices: "C'étaient des oeuvres de premier ordre. L'une d'elles, une superbe 'Répétition de danse,' que j'avais payée à Degas 3,000 fr. et vendue 200 livres, vaudrait aujourd'hui 500,000 fr. Elle est aussi qu'une autre 'Répétition de danse' que Faure avait payée 4,000 fr. Je la lui ai rachetée plus tard 100,000 fr. et l'ai vendue 125,000 fr. au colonel Payne. Nous la vendrions aisément 500,000 fr. à plusieurs de nos clients en Amérique." Lionello Venturi, *Les Archives de l'Impressionnisme,* II (Paris and New York, 1939), p. 195. (The latter painting is now in the Metropolitan Museum, New York.) The most elevated price a work by Degas brought during his own lifetime was 430,000 francs for the *Danseuse à la barre* (likewise now in the Metropolitan Museum), at the Henri Rouart sale on December 10, 1912, at which time Degas launched his often quoted bon mot comparing himself to "the horse that wins the Grand Prix and is given a bag of oats."

[73] Joel Isaacson, *The Crisis of Impressionism, 1878–1882* (Ann Arbor, 1980).

[74] Moulin, *The French Art Market,* p. 14.

[75] Pissarro wrote to Théodore Duret on December 23, 1880: "Degas a mis le siège devant [Adrien] Beugniet." See Janine Bailly-Herzberg, ed., *Correspondance de Camille Pissarro,* I, *1865–1885* (Paris, 1980), no. 83, pp. 140–41. Degas sold to other dealers during the 1880s, including Alphonse Portier and Clauzet. See Grand Palais, *Degas,* p. 372 and note 34.

Saisselin has called the *bibelotization* of art in the nineteenth century[76] – that Degas (like the Parisian milliners whose small shops were increasingly superseded by the incursion of large department stores including Bon Marché and Printemps) saw the mechanics of the selling of his works increasingly removed from his own hands into the more abstract flux of the market. By a similar economic phenomenon in which speculation was institutionally harnessed, his father's bank had been outdated by anonymous credit banks and his uncle's cotton-factoring firm had been outmoded by collective cotton exchanges. In the late-nineteenth-century shift from small family businesses to monopoly capitalism and from the individual to the oligopoly, financial exchange was increasingly substituted for direct human interaction. This shift, which was one of the messages implied in *A Cotton Office in New Orleans* and made explicit in the brothel monotypes, and which Degas had verbally acknowledged on more than one occasion in the analogies he had drawn between the art and stock markets, now affected his own activities as an artist-entrepreneur.

Thus, Degas's mixed response to the market was ultimately self-reflexive. A self-acknowledged member of the bourgeoisie, he nonetheless suffered chronically from what Eunice Lipton has aptly termed "status anxiety"[77] within the increasingly differentiated ranks of that social class. Degas's haughty disdain for speculation and *arrivisme* should be understood not only in light of the failure of his uncle's cotton company, of René Degas's disastrous speculation in cotton futures, and of the related collapse of the family bank, but also in recalling that Degas's grandfather, René-Hilaire, himself the son of a modest *boulanger,* had begun amassing the family fortune as a professional speculator on the Paris grain market at a time during the Revolution when food shortages were causing riots.[78] Degas, in complaining sardonically about his own role as artist-entrepreneur and in hiding behind his "mask of insensibility," as one friend called it, was in many respects acting out his membership in *la grande bourgeoisie financière,* whose relatively recent claim to social prestige (during the

[76] Saisselin, *The Bourgeois and the Bibelot.*

[77] Lipton, *Looking into Degas,* p. 195. For stratifications within the bourgeoisie, see Adeline Daumard, *Les Bourgeois de Paris au XIXe siècle* (Paris, 1970), especially pp. 95–101, and see pp. 275–76 on the diminution of the enterprising spirit the higher up the monetary scale.

[78] McMullen, *Degas,* p. 2.

July Monarchy) and whose insecure political power were increasingly being challenged and undermined (during the Third Republic) by both monopoly capitalism and social democracy. However biting, Degas's verbal and visual assessments of business and industry were nonetheless no more dissident than those of other artists, writers, and professional bohemians and dandies of diverse, mobile, and assumed class background who, since the days of Romanticism, had adopted notions of an aesthetic aristocracy that supposedly distinguished progressive "high cultural" initiatives from the prosaic enterprises of the money-grubbing bourgeoisie, as well as from the monotonous labor of the working class.[79]

Whether he liked it or not, Degas was both an artist and a businessman; the Romantic (and mythic) dichotomy between the two was not possible in the circumstances of the modern market.[80] Even so, the culture of the market placed the artist in a contradictory position by constructing a sustained belief in aesthetic idealism and artistic disinterestedness – a myth whose function was to elevate art above the material and social conditions of its production and consumption. Any historical account of art in market cultures must closely examine those very conditions.

[79] See Herbert, *Impressionism,* p. 304. Raymond Williams, "The Romantic Artist," in *Culture and Society 1780–1950* (London, 1959), pp. 32–36, pointed out that the artist historically came to think of himself as estranged, unconventional, and alienated at precisely the time when shifts in patronage and the growth of the middle-class market meant that the production of art was beginning to be regarded as just one of a number of kinds of commodity production. Bourdieu, "Flaubert's Point of View," p. 219, on the other hand, sees this new social and commercial situation as potentially liberating for artists. For artistic and literary ambivalence about industrial capitalism and progress, see Elliott Mansfield Grant, *French Poetry and Modern Industry 1830–1870: A Study of the Treatment of Industry and Mechanical Power in French Poetry During the Reigns of Louis Philippe and Napoleon III* (Cambridge, Mass., 1927); Albert Joseph George, *The Development of French Romanticism: The Impact of the Industrial Revolution on Literature* (Syracuse, 1955). On the changing self-concept of the artist, see Maurice Shroder, *Icarus: The Image of the Artist in French Romanticism* (Cambridge, Mass., 1961); Marilyn R. Brown, *Gypsies and Other Bohemians: The Myth of the Artist in Nineteenth-Century France* (Ann Arbor, 1985).

[80] Here I disagree with Colin Campbell's suggestion in the conclusion of *The Romantic Ethic and the Spirit of Modern Consumerism* (Oxford, 1987), pp. 226–27, that "capitalist" and "romantic" values could be somehow separated so that "a career in the arts would seem to allow the middle-class 'Bohemian' child to pass through youth into adulthood without there being much necessity to adopt the commercial, utilitarian attitudes of a 'bourgeois.' " In romantically separating the artist from society, Campbell seems to contradict his own thesis, namely, that "capitalist" and "romantic" strains are integrated in middle-class individuals and in market culture as a whole.

CHAPTER 9

"A Yankee Diogenes": Thoreau and the market

RICHARD F. TEICHGRAEBER III

Thoreau is central to the study of American culture because so many masks seem to fit him comfortably. In *Walden,* he remarked that his own pages "admit of more than one interpretation," and the now voluminous history of commentary and scholarship on his career and work amply justifies that self-description (p. 290).[1] In his own century, Thoreau was recognized as an extreme individualist, an unyielding critic of Christianity, a brilliant self-educated naturalist, a radical abolitionist, and one of America's first conservationists. Portraits by twentieth-century interpreters have included Thoreau the pastoralist, the civic humanist, the democratic individualist, the romantic liberal, and the forerunner of both literary modernism and contemporary "deep ecological" thinking. Small wonder that one recent survey of his various political reputations concluded that Thoreau "seems to be in everyone's camp"; he was almost as heterogeneous as America itself.[2]

Thoreau's reflections on American economic activity and institutions have always loomed large in efforts to understand the variety of his meanings. He wrote in the age of railroads, steamboats, factories, and expanding credit, during the two decades (1840–60) that saw the

An earlier version of this paper was prepared for a conference on "The Culture of the Market," March 9–11, 1990, Murphy Institute of Political Economy, Tulane University. Peter Schwartz commented on the paper at the conference, and I am indebted to him, as well as to Thomas L. Haskell and Bonnie Honig, for several changes.

[1] Henry D. Thoreau, *Walden* in *Walden and Other Writings,* ed. Brooks Atkinson (New York: Modern Library, 1950). Page numbers included in the text refer to this edition.

[2] Michael Meyer, *Several more lives to live: Thoreau's Political Reputation in America* (Westport, Conn.: Greenwood Press, 1977), p. 3.

transformation of the United States into an industrial market society. Many of his contemporaries recognized immediately that his love of nature in some manner represented an alternative to the "pervading worldliness" of their age. An early reviewer of *Walden* for *Putnam's Magazine* called Thoreau "a Yankee Diogenes," and described the aim of his life as "a hermit on the shore of Walden Pond" to be "the very remarkable one of trying to be something, while he lived upon nothing; in opposition to the general rule of striving to live upon something, while doing nothing." But Emerson was arguably too polite in characterizing him simply as a man who "had no talent for wealth."[3] Thoreau seems to have feared and despised America's new economic abundance more deeply than any other major nineteenth-century writer. Among many other things, *Walden* may be the greatest American contribution to a long-lived Western tradition of moral comment on the madness of moneymaking. Thoreau looked upon life in a market society as "life without principle," and his continuing opposition to America's emerging business civilization prompted what may be the single most astonishing piece of social commentary in his work:

> Let us consider the way in which we spend our lives. This world is a place of business. What an infinite bustle! I am awaked almost every night by the panting of the locomotive. It interrupts my dreams. There is no sabbath. It would be glorious to see mankind at leisure for once. It is nothing but work, work, work. I cannot easily buy a blank-book to write thoughts in; they are commonly ruled for dollars and cents . . . I think that there is nothing, not even crime, more opposed to poetry, to philosophy, ay, to life itself, than this incessant business.[4]

Alfred Kazin has called Thoreau "a conscientious objector" to the world of unbridled profit and futile gain.[5] In light of this angry passage, it seems more appropriate to think of him as a figure determined to dispossess America of its material demons.

Yet any careful reader of his work knows that Thoreau's disaffection was by no means consistent or free of paradoxes, was less conscientious than it appears at first glance. While there are radically

[3] *Putnam's Magazine* (October 1854), 443. Ralph Waldo Emerson, "Thoreau," in *Selected Essays*, ed. Larzer Ziff (New York: Penguin Books), p. 395.

[4] "Life Without Principle," in *Walden and Other Writings*, p. 712.

[5] Quoted in Jesse Bier, "Weberism, Franklin, and the Transcendental Style," *New England Quarterly* (June 1970), 185.

antimarket implications in much of his social criticism, he made it clear that he never wanted to be taken as a guide to social reform. He recognized the paradox of poverty in the midst of America's economic progress, but often said this progress had done more to degrade the affluent than the poor. He railed against the commercialization of American life, but conceded that some of the new commercial activity and technology of his time spoke directly to higher spiritual and imaginative sensibilities. In fact, Thoreau frequently chose to convey the joys of a natural and spiritual life in the very language of business and commerce. And finally, to name only one more seeming paradox, he was like other writers of his generation himself a tradesman – one of the "scribbling gentry," as he once put it – whose objects of exchange were his books, essays, poems, and reviews.[6] Thoreau's two years at Walden Pond were not in fact a time when "he lived upon nothing"; most of his waking hours there were probably devoted to writing he later brought for publication and sale in the new and growing literary marketplace of antebellum America.

It may be that Thoreau's students ultimately will provide us with keys that unlock each of these riddles individually. Some paradoxes may have been deliberate and open to easy resolution. It is plausible to see Thoreau's persistent efforts to describe his experience at Walden in economic terms as no more than a parody of the market's means of evaluation, a parody whose ultimate design is to "undermine our commitment to commerce."[7] Yet there will always remain the obstinate fact that there are so many of these riddles, that a number of different paths lead into Thoreau's thinking about the market, that he shifted back and forth from criticism to grudging accommodation, that he had – in short – much greater variety in his response to the market than we have been taught to assume.

In this essay, I want to show that in the end this may well be the most important and interesting thing to accept about Thoreau. Rather than try to decide whether he was finally "for" or "against" the market as he knew it, we should recognize that the variety of his attitudes remains our chief interpretive problem, and seek to make

[6] *The Correspondence of Henry David Thoreau,* ed. Walter Harding and Carl Bode (New York: New York University Press), p. 442.

[7] Judith P. Saunders, "Economic Metaphor Redefined: The Transcendental Capitalist at Walden," in *Modern Critical Interpretations: Henry David Thoreau's 'Walden,'* ed. Harold Bloom (New York: Chelsea House, 1987), p. 67.

better sense of that. Thoreau's name has often been invoked to lend moral authority to protest against the dominance of the market in American life, and with good reason. But we should also acknowledge that a full understanding of his response to the market ultimately requires us to come to terms with his ambivalent attachment as well as with his fierce opposition. To insist on the importance of the question "Given the many-sidedness of Thoreau's talk about the market, how finally should we characterize his attitude toward it?" may be our best guide to what he actually wanted to say.

1

One place to begin to ask that question is with the first three chapters of *Walden,* where Thoreau made his most sustained effort to explain the relationship between his values and those of the marketplace. He introduces himself there as a self-sufficient man dedicated to the pursuit of a simple and independent life free of the "curse of trade" (p. 63). Yet it quickly becomes apparent that the full story of his two years at Walden Pond involved a relationship with the market that became considerably more complex than a complete withdrawal. Recognizing the complexity of that lived relationship – as well as understanding why Thoreau sometimes disguised it – will afford an initial lead into the question of the variety of his views.

The story of Thoreau's settling at Walden Pond moves through two distinct stages. The first recounts the activity involved in building his modest house. Here Thoreau began by stressing that his experiment was not to be seen as any sort of angry retreat from modern society. It represented instead an effort to show that the material wealth of civilization, "though so dearly bought," could be put to much better use than his contemporaries chose to recognize. "It is certainly better to accept the advantages . . . which the invention and industry of mankind offer," Thoreau remarked, than to assume that moral regeneration required us to "live in a cave or a wigwam or wear skins." Although he addressed his experiment to those seeking higher purpose in their lives, then, his message was not that the materials of the market should be shunned altogether but, rather, that "with a little more wit we might use" those materials "to become richer than the richest now are, and to make our civilization a blessing" (p. 36).

This first statement of intentions is important in pointing out that the actual work of building a house at Walden Pond began not with a sudden, defiant act of withdrawal but with the borrowing of tools from others, and that Thoreau's unhurried completion of his work occurred within a fairly elaborate network of social cooperation and economic exchange. First, there was an ax (borrowed from Bronson Alcott) that allowed him to cut and hew timber from the pond's hillside and to shape his studs and rafters; then yet other tools borrowed for the more intricate work of mortising and tenoning his beams. Thoreau started this work near the end of March 1845, and by mid-April – "for I made no haste in my work" – his house was framed and "ready for the raising" (p. 38). Here he also notes in passing, however, that the house was not entirely the creation of his own hands. For while clearing the site for his home, Thoreau had purchased additional boards from James Collins, an impoverished Irishman who lived with his family in a shanty near the pond. By the beginning of May, the entire frame of his house had been set up; and Thoreau comments that while he didn't need assistance from others to raise his modest structure, he nonetheless called on some of his Concord acquaintances for help, so as to "improve so good an occasion for neighborliness" (p. 40). He moved in on July Fourth, delaying completion of his chimney until the fall, while he turned to the more pressing task of tending the two and a half acres of beans he had planted to feed himself and help meet his expenses.

In many of its details, the first stage of Thoreau's experiment tells the story of a figure still ensconced in networks of mutual support and interest-driven reciprocity. Indeed, Thoreau himself is arguably a representative of "civilization," since in using the ax to make a place for himself at the pond, he employs – apparently without being aware of it – one of the chief symbols of civilization in antebellum America. In the second stage, the variety and importance of his relationships become even more apparent. His modest venture in commercial farming – in an effort to earn ten or twelve dollars, Thoreau had planted two and a half acres, chiefly with beans – at the outset required him to "hire a team and a man for the plowing" (p. 49). Thoreau's cash crop ultimately does not bring in enough income to meet all his needs, and so by "surveying, carpentry, and day-labor of various kinds" in Concord he earns additional money to make ends meet (p. 52). He also controls his "pecuniary outgoes" by returning to Concord to have his clothing washed and mended and occasionally to dine out as well (p. 54). In short, although the hut at Walden Pond may have been Thoreau's residence for two years, it turned out to be "less of a home and more of a headquarters" for a figure who sought a measure of self-sufficiency, but not at the cost of complete isolation.[8] A determination to live his own life never prevented Thoreau from dividing and sharing some of the burdens of his existence, or from getting his living by working for wages.

Several details of the story Thoreau tells about the establishment of his household remain open to question. Why the misleading suggestion at the outset of *Walden* that he built his house entirely by himself (p. 3)? Why the misleading description of himself as "merely a squatter" (p. 49)? (Thoreau's friend Emerson was, of course, the owner of the plot of land on which his hut stood.) Moreover, if Thoreau's self-sufficient "life in the woods" embodied a clear-cut alternative to the acquisitiveness of market society, why the sometimes self-mocking humor in Thoreau's detailed description of his personal plan of living? Why the occasional concessions that his experiment had many of the markings of a tall tale? And, finally, why disguise the fact that the chief "private business" he went to Walden to transact had been his writing? It surely seems curious that an author who promises at the beginning of *Walden* to provide "a simple and sincere account" of his life should deliver a self-description so intricate (yet in some respects also incomplete and misleading) that it belies any neat precis (p. 3).

The very intricacy of the story Thoreau provided may point the way to answering some of these questions. For among the things his story asks us to recognize is that Thoreau's search for an escape from the "curse of trade" led him not into a world-transcending economy, but into one that permitted him to slip in and out of the network of economic exchanges. Indeed, it is Thoreau himself who shows us that he never managed to withdraw completely from the market, whatever his original intent may have been. What he came to fashion instead was a way of life perhaps best described as being set up on the margins of the market, entirely free of the material acquisitiveness it

[8] Barbara Novak, *Nature and Culture: American Landscape and Painting, 1825–75* (New York: Oxford University Press, 1980), p. 4; *Correspondence of Henry David Thoreau,* p. 167.

encouraged, yet also dependent on it in important ways for achieving his quest for independence. The temporary embrace of a life of voluntary poverty did not eliminate all motives for exchange in Thoreau's case. Indeed, money transactions not only provided him with the land and some of the materials for his house, they also enabled him to purchase his solitude, since Collins and his family – apparently the only other people living close to the pond in the spring of 1845 – departed once their shanty was bought by Thoreau.

It also turns out that Walden Pond itself was hardly a pristine landscape. To say that Thoreau unwittingly settled in a center of commercial activity would be an obvious exaggeration. But it is remarkable how often such activity intruded upon his existence. Thoreau noted privately in his journal that it was impossible to go walking in the Concord woods during the daylight hours in any season without hearing the sound of the axes, and woodchoppers were a frequent presence during his stay at Walden.[9] Even more conspicuous was the new Fitchburg railroad line, which passed so close to the pond that an arm of it was filled for a high rail embankment that could be seen from almost any point on the pond. Leo Marx has noted that there is scarcely a chapter in *Walden* where Thoreau did not mention seeing or hearing the engine, or walking "over the long causeway made for the railroad through the meadows. . . ." More significantly, it also is clear Thoreau was often elated by the presence of a new invention whose promise in the end seemed to offset its dangers. In *Walden* there was nothing of a "simple-minded Luddite hostility" toward new industrial technology.[10] Thoreau did attack the popular illusion that the improvement of technology was an end in itself. But he held fast to the belief that more extensive commercial activity made possible and encouraged the spread of culture and civility around the world. Indeed, Thoreau twice rehearsed – midway through "Sounds," and again in the last paragraph of "The Pond in Winter" – the already well-established view that commerce was a potentially civilizing process. On the one hand, its material benefits, if properly used, could make men and societies more gentle and refined. For by promoting

[9] Robert D. Richardson, Jr., *Henry Thoreau: A Life of the Mind* (Berkeley: University of California Press, 1986), p. 136.

[10] Leo Marx, *The Machine in the Garden: Technology and the Pastoral Ideal in America* (New York: Oxford University Press, 1964), p. 247.

leisure and travel, it allowed individuals to broaden their tastes and understanding. "I am refreshed and expanded when the freight train rattles past me," Thoreau wrote, "and I smell the stores which go dispensing their odors all the way from Long Wharf to Lake Champlain, reminding me of foreign parts, or coral reefs, and Indian oceans, and tropical climes, and the extent of the globe." On the other hand, commerce also militated against violence by encouraging individuals of different nations to trade rather than to war with one another. Thoreau of course had no desire to engage in international commerce, but he did say that sighting its objects being carried in a train on the shores of Walden Pond made him "feel more like a citizen of the world" (p. 108).[11]

Now all these points might seem obvious enough if we could manage to restrict our attention exclusively to what Thoreau tells us about how and where he pursued his experiment. Yet we are not accustomed to thinking of him as a figure with any needs that were met directly (or indirectly) by market transactions. What, then, deflects our vision away from a fact that Thoreau himself was prepared to acknowledge? Part of an answer is that much of his energy in the opening chapters of *Walden* was spent in didactic and often angry criticism of a society that had come to believe that somehow *all* of its needs could be met by the market. Running parallel to his initial account of his experiment, then, is Thoreau's version of a familiar catalog of follies that countless critics of the market before him had also found reprehensible. The morality the market teaches men is not self-reliance, but success in getting the better of one another, success that comes only by deceiving, supplanting, and betraying one another. Wealth is always created at the expense of some other person, and this means market societies must spawn radical forms of social inequality and dependency. The creation of wealth also depends on an ever-increasing division of labor, a process that produces more

[11] Also see the last paragraph of "The Pond in Winter" (*Walden*, p. 266), where Thoreau concludes his account of the work of ice cutters at Walden Pond by speaking of their customers as "the sweltering inhabitants of Charleston and New Orleans, of Madras and Bombay and Calcutta" who would also "drink at my well." The view that commerce, as an economic process, was central to the process of civilization was particularly widespread in eighteenth-century Western thought. Albert O. Hirschman, *The Passions and the Interests: Political Arguments for Capitalism before its Triumph* (Princeton, 1977) has defined that view as the "*doux-commerce* thesis."

goods but at the cost of making human labor meaningless. The division of labor inevitably results in the division of man. Thoreau also often suggested that everything he understood to represent the promise of American life – that is, the commitments and values at the core of a democratic nation – was being undermined by the wickedness of the market. Indeed, those most in need of moral reform in Concord were those who had apparently succeeded in the market. The poor at least remained mobile, while the rich were weighed down both by possessions and by their dependence on others for the maintenance of their elaborate farms and households.[12]

The force of Thoreau's censure of the materialism of American life should never be underestimated. Yet here again there is no reason why acknowledgment of its power should blind us to the various ways in which Thoreau himself regularly muted or qualified his censure. There are reasons to wonder exactly where he finally stood in the confrontation between spiritual and material values. From the very outset of *Walden,* after all, he stressed that the market's ethic of acquisitiveness was not yet so pervasive that it had resulted in an irreparable loss of values. Nor did he ever locate the main cause of the conformity and spiritual emptiness of American life in the production and exchange of commodities. While obviously dismayed by the "curse of trade," Thoreau was arguably just as concerned to show that it was not too late to give up the worst of the prejudices market economies had created and sustained. One of his chief purposes in writing *Walden* clearly was to provide one example of how men remained free to cultivate those higher faculties of their inner selves, despite living in a society in which "trade curses every thing it handles" (p. 63).

Put another way, what a close reading of the opening chapters of *Walden* tells us is that Thoreau was Janus-faced in his response to the market; he looked in two apparently opposite directions at the same time. Much of the time he seems to be looking backward, usually in anger and despair, to simpler ways of living, free of the artificial needs of life in a market society. In fact, it is the extraordinary force

[12] "I also have in mind," Thoreau wrote at the outset of *Walden,* "that seemingly wealthy, but most terribly impoverished class of all, who have accumulated dross, but know not how to use it, or get rid of it, and thus have forged their own golden or silver fetters" (p. 15).

of Thoreau's censure of the materialism of American life that suggests just how deeply rooted the hold of the market was, and how apparently incorrigible were the new habits of material self-indulgence it nurtured. Yet at the same time his fierce censure also suggests just how determined he was to protect his countrymen from the worst consequences of their own economic success. If America's promise was simply a growing supply of material goods, Thoreau obviously disavowed it. He also went on to insist, however, that there remained much that was new and promising about America, and here there surfaced a side of his thinking – usually unnoticed by students of his social and economic views – that took for granted the affluence of which he was often such a harsh critic. For in the three opening chapters of *Walden,* Thoreau's perspective sometimes shifts entirely from renouncing America's wealth to suggesting alternative better uses for it.

In the first two chapters, the clearest instances of this different attitude can be seen in his perhaps surprising concern for what he sees as the special plight of the so-called degraded rich. In Thoreau's view, his prosperous Concord neighbors were "the most terribly impoverished class of all" not just because they were unable to imagine living full lives without their material goods, but also because they had failed to consider how their wealth might be put to far better use (p. 15). They wasted their money not simply in the purchase of trivial things, the frivolous objects of luxury and fashion, but also because they had failed to seek out "work of *fine* art" instead. In the affluent homes of Concord, Thoreau complained, "There is not a nail to hang a picture on, nor a shelf to receive the bust of a hero or a saint" (p. 33). Later this same complaint is lodged against the town as a whole. Enough of the prosperity of Concord had been spent in conspicuous consumption for the hammered stone of its new public buildings. Far better if its wealth could now find a way to provide for new "halls of free worship or free speech," where its citizens would take more pains "to smooth and polish their manners" and lose that "insane ambition to perpetuate the memory of themselves by the amount of hammered stone they leave" (p. 51).

It is in the chapter entitled "Reading," however, that we see the fullest statement of this largely overlooked side of Thoreau's response to the market. There he provides a more detailed vision of

Concord as a community that would use its wealth to become a cosmopolitan cultural center. Why had his prosperous village not yet seen that it now had in hand resources to "take the place of the nobleman of Europe," by also surrounding itself with whatever conduces to its culture – "genius – learning – wit – books – paintings – statuary – music – philosophical instruments, and the like" (p. 99)? Although still regarded mostly as an inveterate foe of all organized effort, Thoreau clearly did appreciate, as Robert Gross has shown, the possibilities of neighborly cooperation in the realm of culture.[13] It is important to recognize here, however, that he also appreciated that it was precisely America's economic progress that might help to foster a more democratic culture. In Thoreau's view, although the production of wealth had yet to be joined to the production of meaning, the possibility of linking the two still remained open. "New England can hire all the wise men in the world to come and teach her," he insisted, "and board them round the while, and not be provincial at all. That is the *uncommon* school we want" (p. 100). It seems fair to add that the successful establishment and maintenance of such a school also presupposed the continuing uncommon affluence of New England.

2

So far, in considering the three opening chapters of *Walden,* what we have uncovered might be summarized as the grounds for accommodation within Thoreau's criticism of the market – an accommodation that was sometimes surprisingly hopeful, more often reluctant, but usually visible in either form. Thoreau was not wholly of the market, but he was in it, even during his years at Walden Pond. Or putting it in his own language, to keep his "afternoons" free, Thoreau was willing to sell his "forenoons" in the marketplace. His aim was not to find ways of avoiding all work, but simply not to consume the greater part of his days in "getting his living." As with government, Thoreau could abide the workings of the market so long as he did not have to facilitate them or to be largely dependent on them for his continuing

[13] Robert A. Gross, "Much Instruction from Little Reading: Books and Libraries in Thoreau's Concord," *Proceedings of the American Antiquarian Society,* vol. 97, p. 1, (1987), 129–88.

existence. "I can do without," he boasted defiantly in "Resistance to Civil Government" (p. 639). But it would be more accurate to say that he could do without, whenever he chose to do without. Thoreau didn't expect the market somehow to disappear. His goal was to pursue ways of living that left him free to pick and choose the terms on which he would enter into the realm of economic exchange.

One result of adopting this perspective is that we can explain an important part of what Thoreau had in mind when he said that "the success or failure of the present economical and social arrangements" ultimately did not interest him (p. 50). For we can now see more clearly why Thoreau felt his goals could be achieved without fundamental institutional reform. In the end, it was not in fact the market that accounted for the "lives of quiet desperation" led by his prosperous Concord neighbors (p. 7). Their malaise was instead the outcome of the mistaken assumption that the market had created a world in which they were no longer free to choose to reform themselves and thereby to live fuller lives. It may be that the market is a realm of unnecessary and dangerous dependencies, but in Thoreau's view there was as yet no reason to believe that his contemporaries were somehow imprisoned by those dependencies. It "is never too late to give up our prejudices," he insisted, no matter how strong or misconceived they seem to be (p. 8).

This recurring insistence on the possibility of self-reform is important because it also provides a neglected context in which to understand Thoreau's predilection for using the language of the market to express his moral and spiritual values. Now, it may be that this aspect of *Walden* really needs no careful analysis or explanation. If we accept the conventional view of Thoreau as entirely a naysayer in his response to the market, his purpose is finally not so hard to divine. He deliberately appropriated the language of the market, it is frequently said, only to expose it. "What Thoreau is doing," Kenneth Lynn has declared in an early statement of this now familiar approach, "is to destroy the enemy with the enemy's own weapons."[14] But there are difficulties with this line of analysis. It turns, first of all, on a one-sided reading of Thoreau's views of the market that all we have uncovered so far weighs heavily against. One question that arises here is, How

[14] Kenneth S. Lynn, *Visions of America: Eleven Literary Historical Essays* (Westport, Conn.: Greenwood Press, 1973), p. 14.

are we to understand his frequent use of the categories of economic discourse – what Stanley Cavell has described as a "nightmare maze of terms about money and possessions and work" – if the market turns out *not* to be his chief "enemy"?[15] This approach is also problematic because it apparently must ignore a great deal of textual evidence suggesting that Thoreau's predilection for economic categories figured centrally in his effort to show that those who thought their lives were entirely determined by the workings of the market in fact remained free to redeem themselves. Indeed, it is arguable that the pervasiveness of economic language in *Walden* was less the outcome of Thoreau's desire to fault his contemporaries' values than an expression of his determination to show that, even while criticizing their values, he was in important ways still one of them. In this respect, Thoreau can be approached – especially in his recurring use of the language of the marketplace – as a thinker who exemplifies the practices of what Michael Walzer has recently called "the connected critic." He was, in other words, a writer who sometimes sought to earn his authority to criticize by arguing with his fellows in their own language, by adopting their characteristic ways of talking about the world to show them that their ordinary language could be used to express purposes nobler than mere production and exchange.[16]

To offer this as a key to Thoreau's meaning is by no means to suggest that it unlocks all doors into his thinking. The opening chapters of *Walden* remain exceptionally puzzling in many respects, with a depth of irony that is hard to gauge, and a tone that is astonishingly variable. Why did Thoreau so carefully contrast his experiment to the procedures and purposes of businesspeople, if not to shame and embarrass them? Why cast his own spiritual quest as a cost–benefit analysis, replete with meticulously detailed statistics, if not to insist on the fundamental opposition of the spiritual to the material? Sometimes, as Cavell has argued so forcefully, Thoreau's purpose does appear to be little more than a brutal mocking of commercial values,

[15] Stanley Cavell, *The Senses of Walden* (San Francisco: North Point Press, 1981), p. 88.

[16] Michael Walzer, *The Company of Critics: Social Criticism and Political Commitment in the Twentieth Century* (New York: Basic Books, 1988), esp. chs. 1 and 13. Also see Walzer, *Interpretation and Social Criticism* (Cambridge, Mass.: Harvard University Press, 1987), ch. 2. Walzer does not include Thoreau on his list of "connected" social critics, but much of what he says about the practice of such critics informs my treatment of Thoreau here.

"by forcing a finger of the vocabulary of the New Testament" down our throats. For the latter text seems to be the obvious origin of his recurring use of economic imagery "to express, and correct, spiritual confusion: what shall it profit a man; the wages of sin; the parable of talents; laying up treasures; rendering unto Caesar; charity."[17]

Yet sometimes Thoreau, like Emerson, commends – without any trace of sarcasm – the methods of commerce, even as he condemns its ends, and at the same time uses the language of the market to illustrate and embody his own values. "I have always endeavored to acquire strict business habits," he wrote, "they are indispensable to every man" (p. 18). And he makes quite clear that those habits include the confidence to take risks, the habit of keeping careful records, and – more generally – a view of each person's life as consisting of a limited amount of energy and time, which may be saved, spent, conserved, employed, or squandered – much like one's money and property.[18]

The vagaries of tone at the outset of *Walden* undoubtedly will continue to support the familiar view that Thoreau was essentially a naysayer in his thinking about the market. It is arguable, however, that if we examine more carefully some of the various ways in which he employed the language of commerce, what we find is a thinker determined to show that while the market had created spiritual confusion, it had also provided some of its own correctives for that confusion. Thoreau obviously meant to challenge the goals of a market society, but he also wanted to do so in terms he thought would be readily comprehensible to its habitants; or, to state it more directly, he was often measuring the spiritual confusion of his age by internal standards, standards held up in the market itself. What made Thoreau a distinctively "Yankee" Diogenes, according to *Putnam's Magazine,* was that – not unlike his fellow New Englanders – he was finally "too shrewd not to comprehend the advantages of living in what we call the world."[19]

How is the connected critic to assure the subjects of his criticism that he is one of them? One of Thoreau's strategies has been explored recently by Richard and Jean Masteller in a careful demonstration of

[17] Cavell, *The Senses of Walden,* p. 89.

[18] Judith Saunders, "Economic Metaphor Redefined," p. 63. Although I think Saunders assigned too narrow a meaning to Thoreau's use of economic terms, I am much indebted to her provocative analysis.

[19] *Putnam's Magazine* (October 1854), 443.

the ways in which the opening chapters of *Walden* parodied a new genre of house pattern books popular in American culture in the 1840s and 1850s. Works in this genre – the most famous of which were by Andrew Jackson Downing – typically presented a variety of designs for domestic dwellings, including detailed cost estimates, recommendations of particular construction materials, and advice on choosing rural sites for new houses. They also recurrently stressed that building in the countryside would realize a necessary harmony between human beings and the natural world.[20]

There can be no question that *Walden* attacked and parodied many of the key assumptions of this new genre. Where Downing offered thirty-two possible designs for individual dwellings, Thoreau provided a single humble design: a drawing of his one-room dwelling, which would appear on the title page of most editions of *Walden* published in the nineteenth century. Moreover, where the most inexpensive laborer's cottage in Downing's view was estimated to cost $330, Thoreau's itemized list of construction materials – itself a parody of another characteristic feature of the pattern books – amounted to a mere $28 and 12½ cents. It is arguable, however, that *Walden* was not designed to subvert all of the central values of the genre. As the Mastellers themselves argue, the main element of continuity between Thoreau and previous authors of house pattern books lay in a shared assumption that the architectural beauty of a house ought to be the external manifestation of the inward good of its inhabitants. Even while sharply criticizing them on other grounds, Thoreau never quite abandoned this last central assumption. Indeed, he stressed that the issue most dividing him from other authors of house pattern books was a straightforward practical matter:

> The cart before the horse is neither beautiful nor useful. Before we can adorn our houses with beautiful objects the walls must be stripped, and our lives must be stripped, and beautiful housekeeping and beautiful living be laid for a foundation: now, a taste for the beautiful is most cultivated out of doors, where there is no house and no housekeeper. (P. 34)

[20] Richard N. and Jean C. Masteller, "Rural Architecture in Andrew Jackson Downing and Henry David Thoreau: Pattern Book Parody in *Walden*," *New England Quarterly* (December 1984), 483–510. Also see Leonard N. Neufeldt, *The Economist: Henry Thoreau and Enterprise* (New York: Oxford University Press, 1989), who argues that *Walden* was designed to parody the widely popular success-guidebooks published in America from the 1830s through the 1850s.

It would be a mistake, however, to follow the Mastellers in reading this passage as a "dramatic explosion" of the house pattern genre.[21] If nature is the locus of Thoreau's higher values, his encouragement of others to pursue his values has not precluded their eventual return to the project of improving human civilization. The work of adorning houses with beautiful objects clearly remains to be done, and it requires no vision of American culture fundamentally different from that propounded by authors of the house pattern books. If their chief mistake was a matter of putting the cart before the horse, it plainly cannot be the entire cultural program of the genre that Thoreau is rejecting here. What he points to instead is the central confusion in how they hope to realize that program: the facile assumption that good domestic architecture was somehow a sure sign of an already refined, uplifted person. Yet the larger notion that good architecture could in fact be refining and uplifting, as well as the underlying assumption that America's continuing economic affluence might eventually provide for "beautiful objects," are never rejected out of hand. Thoreau did not abandon the hope that the inhabitants of a market society could learn to rule their wealth for what he took to be higher purposes.

Another example of how Thoreau remained a connected critic of his world can be seen in the ways in which he often turns his subtle humor back on himself. Here we also encounter a characteristic feature of his use of market rhetoric that most recent students of this issue have overlooked.[22] Thanks to modern biographers, we today know enough about all the circumstances surrounding Thoreau's experiment at Walden Pond – he remained within easy walking distance of his home; his mother and sisters visited with food every Sunday; he was a "hermit" who returned frequently to Concord – to say that there is something comical about his longstanding reputation as one of the company of rugged American woodsmen and loners.[23] But it

[21] Ibid., p. 507.

[22] Neither Saunders nor Cavell, for example, has anything to say about Thoreau's humor. J Golden Taylor, *Neighbor Thoreau's Critical Humor* (Logan: Utah State University Monograph Series, January 1958), remains a useful introductory study. Also see David S. Reynolds, *Beneath the American Renaissance: The Subversive Imagination in the Age of Emerson and Melville* (New York: Knopf, 1988), pp. 484–85, 497–506.

[23] Leo Marx, *The Pilot and the Passenger: Essays on Literature, Technology, and Culture in the United States* (New York: Oxford University Press, 1988), p. 90.

was Thoreau himself who first drew attention to the sometimes very comic dimensions of his venture. Early in *Walden,* he describes himself punningly as engaged in "trade . . . with the Celestial Empire," and later says that his Concord friends had come to think of him as "a sort of real-estate broker" (p. 73). If we ask about the purpose of such self-descriptions, it makes little sense to say they were designed to serve Thoreau's supposedly larger goal of brutally mocking his contemporaries' commercial values. If there is mockery here, it is being playfully turned back on the critic, and his purpose in punning seems better described as an effort to ingratiate himself with the objects of his criticism by making fun of the sometimes wearyingly solemn story he is telling about himself.

It is arguable that this is also one of the main purposes informing the absurdly detailed "statistics" of the "Economy" chapter. Seen from one familiar angle, the elaborateness of Thoreau's statistics represents a parody of the bookkeeping mentality, an obviously satirical celebration of penny-pinching that outdoes anything to be found in Benjamin Franklin's *Autobiography.* There is a tall tale here that makes persistent fun of a mentality whose principles Thoreau knowingly takes to ludicrous extremes. Yet if he is often twitting both the disciples of Poor Richard and the readers of house pattern books, he is also sometimes using his meticulous statistics to make fun of himself, and in the process again acknowledging the limits of his own success in becoming more self-reliant. The careful "account" of his household expenses, after all, shows plainly that Thoreau never gave up the small luxuries of dining out or of having his clothes washed and mended elsewhere. He even confesses, with self-mocking candor, that since all his wash was done at his mother's home in Concord he had no record of the bills for his laundry.

In short, the often absurdly careful bookkeeping in the first chapter of *Walden* shows Thoreau knew that he had become one of the objects of the tall tale being told in *Walden.* That recognition is important because it serves in the end to diminish some of the distance between Thoreau and his contemporaries. For while Thoreau's chief purpose in *Walden* may have been to show materialistic Americans how to discover and explore a world beyond the market, his satirical use of the statistics can be said to strip that spiritual quest of some of its mysteriousness, since he often defines his own spiritual quest in terms of one of their most characteristic forms of getting and spending, the accountant's ledger. Consider, for example, the paragraph that immediately follows his detailed description of the costs of various materials he used in building his house. He crowed proudly: "I intend to build me a house which will surpass any on the main street in Concord in grandeur and luxury, as soon as it pleases me as much and will cost me no more than my present one" (p. 44). Thoreau, of course, did not intend to build his own mansion, but this tongue-in-cheek bragging is significant because it represents one of several examples in *Walden* of the way in which he was ready to devalue his own pretensions to greatness. If he remained determined not to get into step with his acquisitive Concord neighbors, he was also determined not to stop looking at himself with a skeptical and comic eye. Or put another way, Thoreau was – when he chose to be – a jester in his role as social critic. He was something of a kibitzer as well, since part of what made his criticism of his contemporaries credible was his ability to study himself in light of their own practices of getting and spending. And the sometimes self-mocking humor that emerged from such self-study showed that Thoreau's criticism of his world did not depend simply on detachment and enmity.[24]

Yet Thoreau's use of market language ultimately amounts to more than just parody and satire. It was also designed to serve the more serious and important purpose of showing how self-reform was possible within the confines of a market society. If Thoreau's puns made for self-parody, they also sometimes showed that some of the economic principles in the market could be expanded to serve purposes higher than the production and exchange of things. In the end, all the elaborate financial metaphors and detailed statistics of "Economy" make for what might be called a didactic paradox: Thoreau explains his experiment in terms of what it appears designed to escape, yet he also wants to show that a means of escape is readily at hand, in some of the very methods of commerce itself. Thoreau recognized that the market was in part an economic system that could never have flourished without an adequate supply of self-disciplined individuals attuned to the promptings of economic relationships by inward-turning, self-monitoring habits of thought. Yet he insisted too – and this is

[24] Walzer, *Interpretation and Social Criticism*, p. 61.

precisely why his contemporaries were asked to think of him as a "Yankee Diogenes" – that such habits can be applied to better purposes. We ought to be as attentive to our lives as tradesmen are to their possessions. For if we wish to know better who we are, we too must keep careful records, always observing what comes in and what goes out. We should also get up at sunrise, not to get ahead but because our lives consist of a limited amount of time and energy "which may be conserved, saved, spent, employed, squandered, or hoarded – just like property."[25]

In exploring this side of Thoreau's thinking, Judith Sanders has argued recently that his abundant use in *Walden* of the vocabulary of a Yankee capitalist represented an effort to take his audience's reigning ideological assumptions to their "logical conclusion."[26] But his purpose may be somewhat more complex than this precis manages to suggest. For Thoreau's determination to use the language of the market for his own purposes took at least two distinct forms. The first involved efforts to restore or maintain what might be called a "premarket" understanding of certain key concepts such as "economy" and "profit." Remember what "economy" meant before the coming of the market, Thoreau insisted in the first chapter of *Walden:* the prudent management of a private household, and the practice of a frugality that assured self-subsistence in basic needs. Remember too, he said in *Walden* and elsewhere, that the true "profits" of all one's activities are those benefits that accrue with the full development of one's character. This is not taking market ideology to a "logical conclusion" but is, rather, an effort to *resist* that ideology's sharp restriction on the meaning of its own key ideas.

It would be misleading to suggest, however, that Thoreau's play with market language was primarily conservative in its design. Other passages show that he – like Emerson – also thought that market language might be manipulated to articulate his idealism more directly. One of the least discussed examples of this side of Thoreau's thinking occurs at the outset of the second chapter of *Walden* – "Where I Lived, and What I Lived For." There he briefly recounts an experiment in house building that antedated his venture at Walden Pond.

25 Saunders, "Economic Metaphor Redefined," p. 62.
26 Ibid., p. 63.

His goal then had been the same – a largely "free and uncommitted" life (p. 75) – but the means entirely different, since this earlier quest had taken the form of an imaginative exercise that had required no actual physical labor or relocation.

The experiment unfolded in two related phases. In the first, Thoreau explained that after having surveyed the countryside within a dozen miles of Concord, he decided to buy "in his imagination" all the farms he had visited. "For all were to be bought," he insisted, "and I knew their price" (p. 73). This grand assertion was based in part on an implicit suggestion that there was no actual market price for what Thoreau sought to "own" of the Concord landscape. The highest pleasures he found in the natural world could never come to be the exclusive possessions of individual farm-owners. Nor could those pleasures ever be enhanced by their improving labor. It was precisely Thoreau's proud refusal of the obligations of "actual ownership" – his discovery of "the number of things which he can afford to let alone" (p. 74) – that in his own view made him richer than his friends. For unlike them, he managed to maintain a simple way of life that allowed him to see what was "real" in his man's estate.

For Thoreau, then, it appears that the chief "price" of owning what he thought most valuable was voluntary poverty, never having gotten his fingers "burned by actual possession" (p. 74). Yet it clearly was not that alone, and arguably not necessarily that. In recounting the second phase of his earlier experiment, Thoreau shows that his goal had not been merely leaving things alone. Here, in fact, he admits he had come very close to purchasing a farm – "the Hollowell place" – for himself. The owner changed his mind at the last moment, however, just before the time came to transfer the deed to his property. Thoreau also allowed him to keep his initial ten-dollar tender offer, although he suggests in passing that he had good legal grounds for contesting Hollowell's last-minute refusal.

In looking back on the negotiations, Thoreau again concludes that he had managed to remain "rich" because the failure of his offer ultimately allowed him to maintain his poverty – in fact, given the loss of his tender offer, it clearly served to increase it. But here he also goes on to characterize his wealth in more detail:

I found thus that I had been a rich man without any damage to my poverty. But I retained the landscape, and I have since annually carried off what it yielded without a wheel barrow. With respect to landscapes, –

"I am monarch of all I *survey*,
My right there is none to dispute."

I have frequently seen a poet withdraw, having enjoyed the most valuable part of a farm, while the crusty farmer supposed that he had got a few wild apples only. Why, the owner does not know it for many years when a poet has put his farm in rime, the most admirable kind of invisible fence, has fairly impounded it, milked it, skimmed it, and got all the cream, and left the farmer only the skimmed milk. (P. 74)

The passage illustrates the pleasures of "imaginative ownership" that Thoreau obviously means to distinguish from the drudgery of "actual ownership." It also might be read as a gloss of a brief passage in *Nature* (1836), in which Emerson earlier had called for a "revolution in our notions of property." Like Emerson, Thoreau knew he lived in a society in which property typically meant little more than the right of individuals to the exclusive enjoyment of their lands and goods. Yet, again like Emerson, he insisted that this simple definition had not exhausted all possible understandings of the term. For there was also, as Emerson put it, "a property in the horizon which no man has but he whose eye can integrate all the parts, that is, the poet."[27]

One recent commentator sees Emerson's call for a revolution in our conception of property as evidence for a belief that the human power to make new and imaginative use of language was finally greater than any economic power, and it is plausible to read this belief into the story told at the outset of "Where I Lived, and What I Lived For."[28] (There can be little question that the "real-estate broker" is also an Emersonian poet.) But the message Thoreau finally conveys is too complex to be pinned down so definitively. At first glance, it does appear that market values and transactions stand opposed to all that Thoreau believes in. Yet in the paragraphs that conclude the story of his earlier experiment, his criticism of the world of actual ownership seems to narrow significantly in its scope. He comments, for example, that he had not been unwilling to become a proprietor,

[27] Ralph Waldo Emerson, *Nature*, in *Selected Essays*, p. 38.

[28] Richard Poirier, *The Renewal of Literature: Emersonian Reflections* (New York: Random House, 1987), p. 131.

conceding that he probably would have purchased Hollowell's farm had its owner not refused his offer at the last moment. More strikingly, he also makes it clear that in attempting to buy the farm he had not found himself in the position of being forced to choose between "actual" and "imaginative" ownership of land. Thoreau did not scorn private property per se, so much as what he saw as a needless obsession with improving one's property. "I was in haste to buy" the Hollowell farm, he explained, "before the proprietor finished getting out some rocks, cutting down the hollow apple trees, and grubbing up some young birches which had sprung up in the pasture" (p. 75). If all this is an example of a revolution in our notions of property, it obviously speaks of a change in which the work of relishing and respecting nature takes precedent over the task of improving or mastering it. Yet Thoreau has also imagined here a world in which imaginative and actual ownership are compatible, so long as the first in practice takes precedent over the second. Or put another way, his deep misgivings about the market never allowed for the possibility of taking revolutionary steps against it. What they gave rise to was his determination to define the ideals of new culture independent of the market, yet, also capable of giving it instruction in the higher purposes of human life. And here Thoreau's play with the language of the market might be seen as an instance of his commitment to show how his values might come to fit into market society, not merely stand out in criticism of it.

3

One way of summarizing what we have uncovered in Thoreau's language is to say again that although he was always deeply critical of the materialism of American life, he joined Emerson and other idealistic intellectuals of his time in arguing that Americans could find ways to rule their wealth for higher purposes. Furthermore, where most of his countrymen still assumed there was more wealth to create, Thoreau adamantly insisted that they were already rich enough, and what they most needed now was "magnanimity and refinement" (p. 99). In light of what we've explored in section 2, there also can be little question that one of Thoreau's chief purposes in using commercial language was to drive these points home. True, he used the rhetoric of the market to mock it and to expose its failures, but he also used it to reveal alternative ways of thinking and acting – "buying" the world with imagination rather than with money. The strategy in his play with language was always double-edged: designed to broaden, as well as to expose, the meaning of the vocabulary of trade and wealth.

Yet again it is important not to claim too much for this line of analysis. Thoreau's idealism was never quite so all-inclusive or self-confident as that of Emerson, whose views of the market were otherwise remarkably like his in many respects. Thoreau probably saw more clearly than his friend and mentor how difficult it would be to reconcile the different ambitions of the idealist and the materialist. (He once asked himself in his journal, "But what is the use of trying to live simply . . . when those to whom you are allied insanely want and will have a thousand other things which neither you nor they can raise and nobody else, perchance, will pay for? The fellow-man to whom you are yoked is a steer that is ever bolting right the other way.")[29] Also by comparison to Emerson, the range of moods that informed Thoreau's practice as a connected critic ultimately is astonishing in its variety. He could be patriotic, elegiac, prophetic, scolding, sardonic, angry, and despairing, depending on where one chooses to dip into *Walden*.

It is important to notice, too, that Thoreau was careful to point out that there were certain already established moral accommodations with the market that he found hypocritical and unacceptable. Philanthropy in particular represented a moral balancing act of which he wanted no part. Thoreau saw clearly that, for all the new wealth in antebellum America, a disturbingly large number of his contemporaries lived in poverty and misery. And during his two years at Walden Pond he continued to encounter that paradox, discovering that the area around Walden once had been where the poor Irish and blacks of Concord lived. Yet, despite a genuine sympathy for the poor, Thoreau was no admirer of those who wanted to do more to provide for them. In his view, the profusion and generosity of charitable institutions in New England represented, in large part, what current historians would describe as an exercise in social control. Thoreau thought it naive to see charity as an effort by those with wealth to honor their good fortune by sharing some of it with others. "Philanthropy is

[29] *The Journal of Henry Thoreau,* ed. Bradford Torrey and Francis H. Allen, 14 vols. (Boston: Houghton Mifflin, 1906), vol. 8, p. 8.

almost the only virtue which is sufficiently appreciated by mankind," he conceded, but then added quickly that "it is greatly overrated; and it is our selfishness that overrates it" (p. 68). In Thoreau's view, the new "philosophy of the almshouse" had two main practical results. The first was to justify material acquisitiveness by quieting the souls of the rich. The other was to encourage the dependency of the poor by encouraging them to believe their condition was unavoidable. Neither served to address what Thoreau saw as the chief affliction of poverty: the lack of self-respect among the poor themselves.

Thoreau argued that the aim of true reform was to create a society of individuals largely dependent on themselves and therefore unencumbered by the material things produced for sale in the market. Here philanthropy obviously would be unnecessary. For the ideology of "doing good" for the poor requires the economic inequality that comes with the production and exchange of commodities, and so the practice of charity within a market economy only serves to confirm and uphold the problem it pretends to remedy. If the chief affliction of poverty for the poor themselves was a lack of self-respect, this was entirely the by-product of living in a society where the pursuit of wealth was continually held up as the chief purpose of one's daily existence. When Thoreau discovered the starving and filthy family of John Field, an immigrant Irishman, living near Walden in a miserable hut, he recognized their complete degradation. Yet it clearly was the spiritual, not the material, impoverishment of John Field that troubled him. Thoreau observed that Field himself was an "honest, hard-working, but shiftless" man – shiftless precisely because he had come to America pursuing the illusion "here you could get tea, and coffee, and meat everyday," and despite the failure of all his efforts to realize that dream had yet to give it up (pp. 184–85). Thoreau never wrote about the poor to glorify the dignity of their poverty. What he stressed recurrently was that the question of poverty was inseparable from the larger question, What would America become? So long as the national purpose was seen to be the creation and accumulation of more wealth, Thoreau thought there could never be an effective social remedy for the indignity of poverty. "Superfluous wealth," he wrote, "can buy superfluities only" (p. 293).

The reasons for Thoreau's dismissal of philanthropy as a moral restraint on material acquisitiveness seem straightforward enough: It was, more often than not, counterfeit virtue, rooted in self-righteous concern for the good opinion of others; it unconsciously embraced the materialism of American life, instead of calling it into question. Yet it is precisely here that some modern scholars want to locate what appears to be the most curious paradox in Thoreau's views of the market. He could say repeatedly that money brought more evil than good to America, and warn that riches were of no avail to those who wanted lives with spiritual purpose. Yet it is fair to ask if the apparent extremity of Thoreau's proposed alternative – embodied most famously in his concluding plea that all individuals seek only to "mind your own business" (p. 290) – in the end also served to preclude any systematic effort to prescribe or govern manners for the sake of some higher public good. In fact, Thoreau's consistent refusal to draw a program of reform out of his criticism of the market has recently given rise to the view that he thereby came to demonstrate an "unwitting kinship" with the very behavior he deplored. The final image *Walden* leaves us with, Michael Gilmore has argued, is that of a solitary, self-absorbed individual, a figure utterly indifferent to the common good – and that image ironically enough seems to amount to a distorted "reflection of the laissez-faire individualist pursuing his private economic interest at the expense of the public welfare."[30]

Yet the argument that the Walden Pond experiment created a world as morally restricted in its way as that of the marketplace points to a paradox that dissolves upon close inspection. To begin with, this interpretation turns on a one-sided reading of Thoreau's intentions as a critic of the market, a reading that has been challenged throughout this essay. It is plainly a mistake to say that his views of trade and commerce were marked by absolute opposition or undifferentiated antagonism. Thoreau's experiment, as we have seen, put him a little to the side, not outside, of the market. Moreover, as we shall see, because Thoreau never presented his experiment as the foundation for a complete and self-contained alternative to the market, it makes little sense to approach them as entirely comparable realms of human experience.

The more important interpretive issue this reading raises, however, lies with the question of what practical implications we are entitled to

[30] Michael T. Gilmore, *American Romanticism and the Marketplace* (Chicago: University of Chicago Press, 1985), p. 44.

draw out of Thoreau's venture. Here we ought at least to begin by taking seriously what Thoreau himself said were the *limits* of his accomplishments. He was, as we have noted already, explicit in urging his readers not to take *Walden* as a reformer's manual. He was also explicit in reminding them that his text was a record of an experiment that had long since come to an end. From the outset of *Walden,* Thoreau made it clear that both points taken together cautioned that the importance of the practical details of his way of living at the pond ought not to be overestimated. "I would not have any one adopt *my* mode of living on any account," he wrote, "I desire that there may be as many different persons in the world as possible; but I would have each one be very careful to find out and pursue *his own* way, and not his father's or his mother's or his neighbor's instead" (p. 64). It was, then, a democratic spirit of experiment – a cultural ethos of assertive individualism – that Thoreau championed, not the particular regimen of his days at the pond. Indeed, in his conclusion he explained that he had ended his experiment precisely when it threatened to become another confining routine of the sort he had gone to the pond to escape in the first place:

> I left the woods for as good a reason as I went there. Perhaps it seemed to me that I had several more lives to live, and could not spare any more time for that one. It is remarkable how easily and insensibly we fall into a particular route, and make a beaten track for ourselves. (P. 288)

He then repeated that his life at Walden had never come to represent anything in the way of a utopian alternative to the acquisitiveness of the market. Husbandry surely was one way in which men might build lives characterized by greater self-reliance and minimal involvement in exchange, but it was by no means the only one. In fact, part of what Thoreau discovered at Walden Pond was that his own already chosen occupation as a part-time day laborer was "the most independent life of any," and it was that occupation he resumed when he returned to Concord (p. 63).

What *Walden* affirmed, then, was Thoreau's democratic faith, his confidence that ordinary individuals had the resources to live fuller lives of their own making.[31] "I learned this, at least, by my experi-

[31] George Kateb, "Democratic Individuality and the Claims of Politics," *Political Theory* (August 1984), 331–60, explores this side of Thoreau in much greater detail.

ment," he concluded, "that if one advances confidently in the direction of his dreams, and endeavors to live the life which he has imagined, he will meet with success unexpected in common hours" (p. 288). If every man is potentially his own hero, it surely is a mistake to read Thoreau's concluding plea to "mind your own business" as a prescription for retreat or withdrawal. In fact, if we look at the entirety of the plea he actually made – something most modern commentators seem remarkably unable to do – what we find is a considerably more complex and interesting message.

"Let every one mind his own business," Thoreau wrote, "and endeavor to be what he was made" (p. 290). It is fair to see this as a precis of *Walden* so long as we don't overlook that Thoreau was here repeating a point already made – and perhaps made more clearly – at the outset of the book: The possibilities of self-exploration and self-knowledge remain open to all men, whatever their status or place in society. "Minding your own business" in this setting means attending more carefully to the ordinary activity of one's life, because its benefits potentially are as great as those Thoreau discovered with his deliberate "life in the woods." The life of any individual can mean more, wherever and however one may choose to live it.[32] There is an often fiercely egalitarian sentiment at work throughout *Walden* that rejects any view of life that would restrict access to the higher values in imagination and heroic effort to a select, aristocratic few. Like Emerson before him, Thoreau insisted that, in America at least, the possibilities of a better life were within the grasp of all men. In urging "everyone to be what he was made," however, faithful imitation of his example was hardly what he had in mind. Thoreau never advocated voluntary poverty; he suggested it was merely one possibility.

Yet it is surely too simple to say that the final image *Walden* leaves us with is that of a defiant egalitarian, too easy to replace the hermit with the iconoclast, thereby only trading one cliché for another. Thoreau did urge others to follow him in shaking off habit and convention. He refused to believe that constraints imposed by institutions such as the market might leave individuals powerless to shape their own destinies. "Shall a man go and hang himself," he wrote, simply "because he belongs to the race of pygmies, and not be the biggest

32 Ibid., p. 343.

pygmy that he can?" (p. 290). But it would be misleading to conclude from this that Thoreau's stance ultimately was designed to undermine the values and institutions of the marketplace. Thoreau himself insisted he had no interest in making his world over. Although he despised the materialism and inequality of antebellum America, he clearly had no desire to create a different and more economically just world. The example of his Walden experiment was meant rather to inspire others to pursue more deliberate and thoughtful lives in the world that was given to them. "However mean your life is, meet and live it," he insisted in his conclusion, "do not shun it and call it hard names. It is not so bad as you are. . . . The faultfinder will find faults even in paradise. Love your life, poor as it is" (p. 292).

Thoreau offered no clear way out for others. Despite his own estrangement from his commercial times, that estrangement never dictated either complete withdrawal or unqualified opposition. What Thoreau sought, in the end, might be described as an intellectual position that mirrored an actual place he had once made for himself at Walden Pond: a place both outside and inside the market. Outside because Thoreau obviously wanted to present himself as an arbiter of its value, but inside too because the most he finally expected of his countrymen was acknowledgment of the need for an antipecuniary ethic to restrain their acquisitiveness and recognition that trade and commerce were "but means, and not the end."[33]

4

Gathered together, the various strands of this essay provide what may be a surprisingly straightforward answer to the question raised at the outset: Why were there several sides to Thoreau's thinking about the market? The evidence explored here suggests that the variety of his attitudes finally reflected a readiness to compromise. Given Thoreau's longstanding and well-earned reputation as a slashing critic of the market, that may seem a preposterous claim. But only if we forget that "compromise" has two distinct meanings: compromise in the sense of giving up a single principle, in light of its inapplicability to life, which sounds, and is, wrong as a description of Thoreau's posi-

[33] "Life Without Principle," p. 728.

tion; yet there is also compromise in the sense of recognizing that our principles conflict with one another, and cannot be realized at once, and this is a neglected side of *Walden* to which I've tried to draw more attention here.[34] In fact, it is arguably the best way of making sense of that combination of fierce criticism and ambivalent attachment that marked his thinking about the market. Thoreau, it is true, found his age dull, materialistic, timid, and conformist. Yet while he detested many of the things he saw around him, he also refused to believe he lived in a disenchanted world. The market certainly was not the soil on which the greatness of individuals might blossom, but it was not quite poisoned soil either. Life *with* principle did not require that the market be overthrown, nor did it dictate complete withdrawal. Thoreau never said that he had gone off to Walden simply to show others that if they did not like their world they could move away. Cavell has argued correctly that the main task of *Walden* was "to discover how to earn and spend our most wakeful hours – whatever we are doing," but the last phrase ought to have been italicized.[35] Or put another way, Thoreau finally made it clear that his alternative was neither retreat nor institutional reform, but the fashioning of new individuals who could manage the temptations of a market society – especially its ethic of consumption and its shallow popular culture – without losing their bearings.

This approach may not do full justice to certain other interesting and important aspects of Thoreau's thinking about the market – especially his understanding of the relationship between commerce and slavery. It also may be that no single approach to Thoreau will ever provide a completely satisfactory interpretation of his views. For a growing number of modern readers, the resistance of *Walden* to simplification and straightforward analysis has become its chief claim on our attention.[36] Yet too much can be made of Thoreau's supposed inaccessibility. He did say that his pages admit of more than one interpretation, yet he also said he had no desire to be obscure. Tho-

[34] I am indebted to Thomas S. Schelling, *Choice and Consequence: Perspectives of an Errant Economist* (Cambridge, Mass.: Harvard University Press, 1984), p. 9, for recalling this distinction.

[35] Cavell, *The Senses of Walden*, p. 5.

[36] See, e.g., Walter Benn Michaels, "Walden's False Bottoms," in *Modern Critical Views: Henry David Thoreau*, ed. Harold Bloom (New York: Chelsea House, 1987), pp. 79–95.

reau may at times sound like the inhabitant of a separate world, but that finally was not what he meant to be. Those who insist *Walden* is a supremely difficult text inevitably lose sight of the writer determined to follow Emerson's lead in defining and interpreting the "newness" of America. Like Emerson, Thoreau never thought the ideals he championed were obscure. What he believed was that they were unrealized and yet still immanent in American life. Immanent, it seems, mostly because he divided his nation by generations, not by social or economic classes. For all its flaws, Thoreau's "true America" remained young and therefore still a place of promise. There is nothing in *Walden* of the European Romantics' complaint of having been "born too late," no longing for a past that seemed superior to the present. It was to the "young men" of Concord that Thoreau made a direct appeal at the outset of *Walden.* It was "old men" and their "old deeds" that invited some of his fiercest criticism. "My seniors," he proclaimed, "have told me nothing, and probably cannot tell me anything to the purpose" (p. 8). They had lost sight of, perhaps never even had understood, the real promise of America, choosing dull routines and material comforts over a life dedicated to the free testing and measurement of all their capacities. Yet Thoreau did not see the betrayal of his elders as a closing off of all future opportunities to realize America's promise. At the end of *Walden,* he beckoned his readers to imagine a future America that was to be created in the spirit of his own life: egalitarian, adventurous, critical of established customs and institutions, and engaged with the diversity of nature and human society. The label "alienated" will not stick to Thoreau. For all his complaining, he was, in writing *Walden,* a man who had taken on a cultural mission: to provide – in the carefully recorded example of his own life – the stimulus for a clearer and stronger understanding of that ethos of democratic individualism by which his contemporaries claimed to live.

Finally, to approach Thoreau as a "connected critic" of American institutions also points to some largely unexplored questions concerning Thoreau's place in studying the history of American culture. We are not used to thinking of him as something other than a figure of neglected opposition. But this is a habit we ought to abandon, despite its sometimes distinguished pedigree. The most familiar account of

Thoreau's career, dating back to Emerson's famous obituary essay, concludes that his reputation was a local matter and that his career as a writer was a story of hard times and failure that gave way to modest success late in his life. Assuming Thoreau's obscurity in his own time also fits neatly with the equally familiar view that, because of the extremity of his opinions, few of his contemporaries understood or wanted to hear what he had to say. In a society rushing headlong to embrace the market, it is no surprise to discover that a denigrator of the commercialization of American life failed to gain a popular audience. Recent scholarship, however, suggests that contemporary evaluation of Thoreau was considerably higher than the traditional account allows.[37] This essay has tried to show that we also have something more complex and interesting in Thoreau's criticism of American economic life than the views of an iconoclast. Taken together, these revised portraits suggest that any approach that continues to come to Thoreau by way of Emerson's famous obituary risks at least two fundamental misunderstandings. For Emerson not only misrepresented the cultural standing of Thoreau's work during his lifetime, he also was misleading about Thoreau's general disposition as a social critic. The writer Emerson said "did not feel himself except in opposition" was never in absolute opposition to any of the American institutions of his day, except for slavery.[38] Any adequate understanding of Thoreau, then, must bring more clearly into view two closely related sides of his thinking that Emerson seemed remarkably unable to see: his determination to offer the inhabitants of a market society a good deal more than criticism, and his actual success in overcoming the critic's impulse to be no more than a "faultfinder." Complaining may have been one of Thoreau's specialties, but he took no special pride in it. "The attitude of resistance," he once wrote, "is one of weakness, inasmuch as it only faces an enemy; it has its back to all that is truly attractive."[39] Tossed between his hopes and fears, Thoreau re-

[37] Reynolds, *Beneath the American Renaissance*, pp. 497–506.

[38] Emerson, "Thoreau," in *Selected Essays*, p. 396. It is astonishing how many things about Thoreau Emerson chose to leave out of his eulogy. As R. Jackson Wilson has recently observed, "anyone who read the published version of the eulogy would not have been able to tell that Thoreau had ever published anything." See Wilson, *Figures of Speech: American Writers and the Literary Marketplace, from Benjamin Franklin to Emily Dickinson* (New York: Knopf, 1989), pp. 215–16.

[39] *The Journal of Henry Thoreau*, vol. 9, p. 36.

mained determined to pursue his hopes. In the end, he was unwilling to embrace the frequent pessimism of his own analysis of the condition of American society. It is that refusal – Thoreau's determination to outlast the defeat of his hopes, his insistence that those hopes never embodied "exorbitant demands" – not his more familiar complaints about the materialism of his age, that I have tried to make better sense of in this eassy.

CHAPTER 10

Need and honor in Balzac's *Père Goriot*: reflections on a vision of laissez-faire society

WILLIAM M. REDDY

> You could be *well off* without being *well.* You could be *well,* without being able to lead the life you *wanted.* You could have got the life you *wanted,* without being *happy.* You could be *happy,* without having much *freedom.* You could have a good deal of *freedom,* without *achieving* much. We can go on.
>
> – Amartya Sen[1]

There has always been within economic thought an optimistic current that has treated needs, desires, and tastes as exogenous variables whose character and structure do not require theoretical elaboration.[2] This current has seen monetary exchange as occurring between essentially equal partners, each of which is committed in the same way to increasing her own advantage, or maximizing her individual utility, or satisfying her preferences. By saying this I do not mean to minimize the important differences between the terms "advantage," "utility," or "preferences." I mean only to underline that all these terms have been widely used on the assumption that both parties to a given exchange seek *x* (substitute the appropriate term) in the same way.

But there has also existed, at least since the late eighteenth century, a current within economic thought representing the opposite impulse, the idea that there is what I will call a common hierarchy of needs that

This paper was prepared in connection with a larger research project on early-nineteenth-century French society, which has been supported by a Guggenheim Fellowship, a Fulbright Fellowship, and a grant from the American Philosophical Society.

1 *The Standard of Living: The Tanner Lectures, Clare Hall, Cambridge, 1985* (Cambridge, 1987), 1 (emphasis in original).

2 Marshall Sahlins criticized this aspect of economic thought in his *Culture and Practical Reason* (Chicago, 1976), as has Lester Thurow in *Dangerous Currents: The State of Economics* (New York, 1983).

human beings share and that sets parameters for the functioning and fairness of exchange systems. By this view, parties to exchanges must be differentiated according to which needs, desires, or preferences they seek to satisfy. The great difficulty is that those who bring urgent needs to exchanges are vulnerable to those who bring less pressing desires. Already in 1775 Thomas Spence deplored the concentration of landed property in the hands of a few, because it ensured that the earth would be "cultivated either by slaves, compelled, like beasts, to labor, or by indigent objects [wage laborers] whom they [the landowners] first exclude from a share in the soil, *that want may compel them to sell their labor for daily bread.*"[3] Likewise, Charles Hall, writing in 1805, noted that while "no man is compelled to work at any particular trade," nonetheless, there was "an absolute necessity, under the penalty, the heaviest of all penalties, namely the deprivation of all things that are necessary to him and his family's existence," for the landless laborer to submit to the direction of others.[4] Across the Channel, the recognition that exchange might easily create relations of dominion or authority were central to the sans-culotte ideology of the Year II. Typical of the scandalized tone in which they announced this recognition is the following denunciation by the Hébertiste Chaumette before the Convention on September 5, 1793:

> New lords no less cruel, no less greedy, no less insolent than the old have risen upon the ruins of feudalism. They have bought or leased the property of the old masters, and continue to walk in the paths beaten by crime, to speculate on the public misery [i.e., on the price of grain], to dry up the sources of plenty and to tyrannize over the destroyers of tyranny.[5]

For proponents of this other way of thinking, Ricardo's labor theory of value coupled with his iron law of wages constituted a stark confirmation of their views. Marx in particular recognized that any notion of a subsistence wage as the natural price of labor implied

[3] Emphasis added. From Thomas Spence, *Lecture on Land Reform to the Newcastle Philosophical Society* (1775), quoted in Noel W. Thompson, *The People's Science: The Popular Political Economy of Exploitation and Crisis* (Cambridge, 1984), 40.

[4] Quoted in Thompson, *People's Science,* p. 66, from Charles Hall, *The Effects of Civilization* (London, 1805). Note that the gender implications of the Hall quote, and his reference to family, invoke cultural norms brought into danger by male propertylessness.

[5] Quoted in R. R. Palmer, *Twelve Who Ruled: The Year of the Terror in the French Revolution* (Princeton, N.J., 1941), 46.

what I am calling here a hierarchy of needs, and that such a hierarchy of needs could provide a fertile terrain for the growth of domination.[6]

These two currents have had a long and intricate history, which it is not the intention of this essay to trace. It is worth noting, however, that the debate continues today in, for example, discussions of the work of Amartya Sen, who has criticized the notion of utility and its ancillary vocabulary of "pleasure," "happiness," "desire," and "choice." Sen offers to supplant it with the distinct notions of "functionings" and "capabilities," the former encompassing what is meant by fulfilling "needs" here.[7]

In the age of laissez-faire, economic thinkers were by no means the only ones led to reflect on this matter. Balzac for one, I argue here, made the question of the hierarchy of needs a central theme of his work. In *Père Goriot* in particular Balzac demonstrated the relationship between this common hierarchy of needs and another, opposed (yet dependent) set of motivations that people brought to exchange relationships, motivations clustered around a notion of "honor." Further, he explored the irony that these two motivational clusters dominated the lives of millions in a society whose fundamental principles – recently restructured in a tumultuous revolution – presupposed that exchange relationships involved neither need nor honor but a uniform search for advantage.

Balzac's concerns found their place within a dramatic shift in literary interests that followed upon the French Revolution's laissez-faire reforms. One need only compare Balzac's or George Sand's – or Hugo's or Flaubert's – works with those of, say, Beaumarchais or Rousseau. In *Le mariage de Figaro* or *La nouvelle Héloïse,* penniless protagonists struggle against foes who are endowed with title, privilege, and wealth. The first two, title and privilege, seem in fact to be more important than the last – seem even to be the means by which wealth is monopolized. In postrevolutionary literature, however, the social landscape appears less daunting; the peaks are still very high, but in principle it is now possible for anyone to scale them. Of course, Emma Bovary and Jean Valjean discover that they are not so easily

[6] See, for example, Karl Marx, *Capital: A Critique of Political Economy,* vol. 1, trans. Ben Fowkes (New York, 1977), ch. 27, pp. 880–81.

[7] Sen gives a brief exposition of his theory in *The Standard of Living,* which includes the reactions of a number of other economists.

scalable, each in her or his very different way. In Balzac's world, likewise, money becomes the key that unlocks all doors, but a key that, for very unexpected reasons, turns out to be difficult to obtain and to use. Or, to shift the metaphor, wealth becomes the stairway on which the social hierarchy has arranged itself, but climbing the stairs seems to require much more than just putting one foot in front of the other. Balzac was perfectly aware that this steep hierarchical social order based on wealth – which fascinated and repelled him – was precisely the utopia of freedom that so many late-eighteenth-century men of letters had clamored for. In some of his political writings Balzac forcefully and explicitly condemned the disastrous effects of free competition – that very freedom which the Diderots and d'Alemberts of a previous generation had longed for – on writers and on the book trade.[8]

In his novels Balzac diagnosed the effects of this same free competition on human character more generally.[9] In *Père Goriot* he achieved an unusual clarity in his exploration of these issues; his view of the relationships between money, honor, and need is starkly etched in the structure of the plot itself, and has the kind of originality that can serve as a powerful aid to reflection.

I offer this analysis, which must necessarily be summary in nature, neither as a literary critic nor as an economist but as a social historian who has worked on French society in Balzac's period, the first half of the nineteenth century.

It goes without saying that art cannot be mimetic in any simple sense, that it cannot simply represent or mirror what is around it; instead it engages in what Stephen Greenblatt has called exchanges and negotiations – or what Christopher Prendergast has referred to as contrasts – with the society within which it is born. Frederic Jameson's call for a criticism that attends to the "rifts and discontinuities within the work" and that sees literary products as utterances in an ideological dialogue points toward a similar rejection of any simple account of art as mirror or reflection.[10] But if this is so, then it is

[8] For a discussion of these writings, see Roland Chollet, *Balzac Journaliste: Le tournant de 1830* (Paris, 1983), 17–53.

[9] These effects were only a part of that larger *mal du siècle* that Pierre Barbéris has vividly reviewed, in *Balzac et le mal du siècle,* 2 vols. (Paris, 1970), I, 31–139.

[10] Stephen Greenblatt, *Shakespearean Negotiations: The Circulation of Social Energy in Renaissance England* (Berkeley, Calif., 1988). Christopher Prendergast, *The Or-*

essential for social historians to take "literature" seriously, just as much as it is for critics to reposition literary texts within an appropriate totality of social phenomena. In Balzac's literary productions I see not a "realistic" image of his society, but a seductively packaged critique of his time that yields very different messages depending on the frame of reference within which one reads it. Within the context of economic thought about needs, it represents a very suggestive and original vision.

Goriot's defiance of need

That people have preferences and express them when they buy or sell things might seem to be an unassailable minimum that one could say about monetary exchange. Viewed in one light, the idea that people want what they are getting more strongly than they want what they are giving away, is more tautology than truth. It amounts to saying that people who exchange things want to do what they are indeed doing. However, if it is not a tautology, if it really says something, then this statement must be considered a very optimistic assessment of human nature. It implies that we want things quantitatively and are able to compare readily our different desires and place them accurately in positions along a number line, so that we can finely calculate their relative values. Do you want to have a piano or go on a trip to a distant continent? It is not always easy to compare such weirdly diverse alternatives, despite their similar price tags.

Balzac supposes, on the contrary, that people do not always (may seldom, in fact) know exactly why they are acting as they do, may not give themselves unreservedly to their own decisions, and frequently change their minds – especially about the important things in life. He would have agreed with Amartya Sen that it is "arguable that to think of satisfaction or happiness or pleasure as some kind of a homogeneous magnitude is simply a mistake."[11] Or again that in

der of Mimesis: Balzac, Stendhal, Nerval, Flaubert (Cambridge, 1986), 36–41. Frederic Jameson insists that the "interpretive mission of a properly structural causality will . . . find its privileged content in rifts and discontinuities within the work, and ultimately in a conception of the former 'work of art' as a heterogeneous and (to use the most dramatic recent slogan) a schizophrenic text," and, within the social horizon, calls for the treatment of works of art as "dialogical": *The Political Unconscious: Narrative as a Socially Symbolic Act* (Ithaca, N.Y., 1981), 56, 84.

[11] Sen, *The Standard of Living*, 7.

assessing the well-being and the standard of living of a person, happiness may have direct relevance, and it is plausibly seen as one among various objects of value. . . . But the value of desire has to be assessed, and a person's desire for something he or she does not value correspondingly, and would not do so even on further reflection, may not be a good ground for counting it in the evaluation of that person's well-being or living standard. . . .

The battered slave, the broken unemployed, the hopeless destitute, the tamed housewife, may have the courage to desire little, but the fulfilment of those disciplined desires is not a sign of great success and cannot be treated in the same way as the fulfilment of the confident and demanding desires of the better placed.[12]

Around the central figure of *Père Goriot* swirls a host of nobly perverse characters all chasing their own kind of peculiar bargains with life. Their difficulties arise from trying to translate their complex desires and fears into a simpler numerical calculus, so they can strike deals that move them closer to happiness. Like Goriot they fail – if in varying degrees. An aunt of the young nobleman Eugène de Rastignac sells "her memories" in order to provide him with 1,300 francs. The villain Vautrin arranges a duel for 200,000 francs (which are, however, never paid). Rastignac courts Victorine Taillefer for 3 million francs (which he in the end renounces). An old woman named Michonneau agrees to drug Vautrin and to check his shoulder for the mark of the *bagne* (prison ship) in return for 3,000 francs. The countess Anastasie de Restaud (one of Goriot's pitiless daughters) gives her lover 200,000 francs to keep him near her. (He leaves anyway.)

The baron de Nucingen offers his wife, Delphine (Goriot's other daughter), more spending money if she will make love to him. (She refuses.) The impoverished Rastignac accepts a gold watch from his new love (Delphine again), in spite of the fact that this might be construed as a base payment for services rendered, because, he tells himself, true love allows people to help each other. The same reasoning later allows him to accept the gift of a pretty bachelor apartment from her (price tag: 12,000 francs – picked up by Delphine's father). Besides, Rastignac assures himself, it is only a loan. Later the watch has to be pawned to pay for Goriot's funeral shroud, with 70 francs left over to pay for twenty minutes of praying from the priests.

Of course, to a limited degree, people always know some of the

[12] Ibid., 11.

things that they want. If one is not actively engaged in committing suicide, it follows that one wants to continue breathing, eating, bathing, clothing oneself, and sheltering oneself from the elements. Whatever else one desires, these minimum wants are an inescapable means to the achievement of anything else. Our organic existence thus imposes a degree of order on our desires, less order than some imagine, but far more than zero. The prices of commodities that satisfy our basic organic needs, if they seem high to us, will become the objects of very precise, refined calculations. Such calculations about the prices of "necessities" are the foundation from which all other prices acquire their meaning. (And here, of course, it is important to recognize that not only organic needs may be involved in the determination of what is a necessity. The point is, however, that they predictably do determine a good portion of what is considered necessary. This is all that the notion of a hierarchy of needs is intended to signal.)[13] Imagine what would happen to the prices of paintings, for example, if it were possible to fast for three years in order to save up money to buy one. If the propertyless were able to acquire capital assets merely by painlessly foregoing day-to-day consumption, prices would quickly become incoherent.

This unshakable tie between, on the one hand, needs that must be fulfilled (as the condition and means to fulfilling all other desires) and, on the other hand, prices is one of the threads that knit together the whole plot of *Père Goriot.* Balzac tests its strength by giving us, in Goriot, a limiting case.

The central figure in the novel, Goriot, a retired pasta merchant, gives away the bulk of his considerable fortune to dower his two daughters, marrying them far above his own lowly rank, one to a count, the other to a banking magnate. He reserves enough of his wealth to ensure a comfortable retirement for himself, even if it is

[13] Amartya Sen is critical of the so-called basic needs approach to understanding living standards (see *The Standard of Living*), but the difficulties of operationalizing the notion of need that he points out are not at issue in this essay, so that the term will serve well enough for the time being. It is enough that the reader acknowledge that we all live in a state of medical emergency: about five minutes from death if deprived of oxygen or blood supply, a few hours from death if deprived of shelter in the winter, thirty days from death if deprived of food, vulnerable to lesions, bruises, burns, microbes, cancers, dehydration, concussion, low blood sugar. For present purposes there is no need to sort these out and quantify their relationships, which vary with cultural, personal, and physical circumstance anyway.

only a small portion of what he previously owned. But his daughters continue to turn to him for further financial help. His subsequent gifts to them, much smaller than the initial dowries – and themselves getting smaller and smaller as time goes on – gradually exhaust Goriot's resources. Goriot's devotion to his daughters moves from conventional paternal love through self-sacrifice to ennobling obsession when he starts stripping himself of the bare necessities of life in order to satisfy their caprices. From that moment on, a stark asymmetry emerges between the frivolous or morally questionable uses the daughters have for their father's money on the one hand and the needs Goriot is sacrificing in order to give money to them on the other.[14] Goriot sinks into life-threatening poverty as he helps Anastasie pay off a faithless lover's gambling debts, then helps Delphine furnish an apartment for Rastignac. At the end of the novel he quite literally dies in order to give one of his daughters an evening gown. He sells some plates and buckles – last vestiges of a sumptuous collection of household furnishings – for 600 francs (about a year's salary for a factory worker of the time) and signs away (to the rapacious usurer Gobseck) one year's income on his remaining life annuity for 400 francs more. With this last scrap of his fortune he plans to help Anastasie, his elder daughter, pay off her dressmaker. He is already sick at the time, but rejoices that the thousand-franc bill in his hat will ensure "Nasie" a *soirée pimpante* in her new dress, whereas if he kept the money it would probably only go to the apothecary for medicine. He has nothing by this point, and after a lengthy agony the illness carries him mercifully away.

Goriot has a bit of Christ in him and more than a bit of King Lear. But what distinguishes him most from both of these figures is that he lives in a nineteenth-century capitalist society, under the sway of laissez-faire principles as no society has been before or since, a society in which a flow of money, only recently contained by sturdy legal and customary dikes, seemed to spread across the human landscape unobstructed. Did Balzac choose these models in order to emphasize the strangeness of the new social order?

Goriot's prototypes, King Lear and Jesus, lived in a different world entirely. Lear ceded his feudal sovereignty to his two daughters in one

[14] On the notion of "asymmetry" in use here, see William M. Reddy, *Money and Liberty in Modern Europe: A Critique of Historical Understanding* (New York, 1987).

act and, after that one moment of imprudence, gave them nothing more because he had nothing more to give. Jesus counseled "Give unto Caesar the things that are Caesar's," holding the coin of tribute up like the oddity that it was, a recent import into the land of Judea. But in Goriot's world everything was subject to a refined and minute calculus of cash values. Goriot despoils himself in driblets. He picks away at his fortune, easily transforming his different kinds of property into conveniently sized packets of ready cash to meet his daughters' every whim. And when he is done, when there is no more money to be had and he is worth zero, death follows in a matter of hours. His death itself is insignificant because he is broke. Goriot does not die on the cross by public execution and before public witnesses, he does not die from the effects of exposure after going mad at night on a stormy heath. He dies in his 45-franc-a-month room (rent he can no longer pay) on the top (and therefore cheapest) floor of a *pension bourgeoise* (boardinghouse). His daughters do not come. "Ah, if I were rich," he cries in despair, "if I had kept my fortune, if I had not given it to them, they would be here, they would lick my cheeks with their kisses! I would be staying in a mansion; I would have beautiful rooms, servants, a fire to myself; they would be in tears with their husbands, their children. I would have all that. But nothing. Money gives you everything, even daughters."[15]

"My God, my God, why have you forsaken me?" Jesus cried out from the cross. But Balzac's laissez-faire Jesus cries out in agony on his rented bed that money has forsaken him. Lear in extremis wanders across the land where he once ruled as sovereign, reduced to the company of fools and beggars, full of despairing astonishment at his daughters' disloyalty. But Balzac's bourgeois Lear knew his daughters would disown him the day he gave them their doweries. "No, they won't come!" he says on his deathbed, "I have known that for ten years. Sometimes I told myself they would not, but I dared not believe it."[16]

[15] "Ah! si j'étais riche, si j'avais gardé ma fortune, si je ne la leur avais pas données, elles me lècheraient les joues de leurs baissers! je demeurerais dans un hôtel, j'aurais de belles chambres, des domestiques, du feu à moi; et elles seraient tout en larmes, avec leurs maris, leurs enfants. J'aurais tout cela. Mais rien. L'argent donne tout, même des filles" (237). Page references in parentheses in the notes are to the Garnier Flammarion edition (Paris, 1966).

[16] "Non, elles ne viendront pas! Je sais cela depuis dix ans. Je me le disais quelquefois, mais je n'osais pas y croire" (237).

Because money is such a refined instrument of exchange, Goriot's motives are much more complicated than Lear's in at least one respect. The great advantage of money in the minds of many economic thinkers, its perfect liquidity and transmutability, has for Goriot a frightening disadvantage. He has the option of despoiling himself piecemeal over ten years, but this option also gives him ample opportunity to indulge in second thoughts. Surely this is the lesser of the two evils, one might remark. Just so: To construct a laissez-faire Lear, it was necessary for Balzac to imagine a character who could repeat the error of trust through all the transactions from the formalities of an honorable marriage contract to the miseries of contracting usurious loans, to the forswearing of medicine on his deathbed. What keeps Goriot from being simply a fool is ambivalence: He knows he is mistaken, yet he continues to give. Balzac makes all the major characters of the work both sympathetic and despicable, both pitiful and glorious precisely because of their ambivalent relationships to money, with all the complex choices its refined measurements allow.

The conflict between honor and need

Goriot's sacrifices were Christ-like in their extremism (which extremism is typical of the melodramatic excess that, as Peter Brooks has explained, permeates Balzac).[17] But they were quite normal in another respect. If there is an influence on motives in Balzac's novel strong enough to rival the influence exerted by organic needs, that influence is honor. The implications of this rivalry are spelled out in this section; in the chapter's following two sections they are explored in more depth.

Although the word *honor* appears rarely in the novel, the notion is omnipresent. In this respect Balzac's language faithfully echoed age-old usage. Honor in France had never been explicitly discussed except in cases where it had been injured by an insult.[18] Honor is a

[17] Peter Brooks, *The Melodramatic Imagination: Balzac, James, Melodrama and the Mode of Excess* (New Haven, 1976), 110–52.

[18] Maurice Daumas makes this point concerning the eighteenth century in *L'affaire d'Esclans: Les conflits familiaux au XVIIIe siècle* (Paris, 1988), 81–114; see also François Billaçois, *Le duel dans la société française des XVIe–XVIIe siècles: essai de psychosociologie historique* (Paris, 1986). The same point is also evident from nineteenth-century material I discuss in a forthcoming work on marital separations, "Marriage, Honor, and the Public Sphere in Post-Revolutionary France, 1815–1848."

quality that inhered in appearances, in trappings – even though it was meant to exist on a deeper plane. To aver that specific trappings are inappropriate to a given person was necessarily an insult. Insult challenged appearances, requiring actors to make good on them. To discuss honor at all was often to flirt with insult, unless it was in response to an insult.[19] Before the Revolution, even to advance in honor had been a kind of contradiction in terms, because each person was deemed to possess that honor appropriate to her station – to have too much was as shameful as not to have enough.[20] But the end of the society of orders had destabilized this logic; and this was of great concern to Balzac. Before the Revolution, wealth's relation to honor had been firm, but indirect. Wealth was command over needs, therefore over deference and obedience. For centuries the authority of wealth had subsisted in easy symbiosis with political and military authority, and had shared in – and lent its conspicuous luster to – the honor that clung to such authority. But centralization of the state had deprived the elite of most of its independent political and military authority, until what was left – protocol and precedent, sumptuary regulation, the vestiges of manorialism, the intricacies of privilege, clientage and influence – was transformed into something more like adornments to wealth. Such adornments were the essence of what eighteenth-century lawyers had called, in a usage later picked up by Marx, "feudalism"; and they were what the National Assembly meant when, on the heady night of August 4, 1789, they declared feudalism's demise. Equality before the law granted wealth, by default, a new, unchallenged possession of authority within civil society, and with that authority went all the remaining trappings of honor: aristocratic standards of consumption and social intercourse, family name and personal reputation, polish and self-possession, the deference of employees, servants, tenants, waiters, cabdrivers. But this transition was not an easy one. "Careers open to talent" implied competition for honors that belonged to others, and could therefore easily become "careers open to shame": for no one is more vulnerable to insult than the arriviste, unless, of course, it is the parvenu.

[19] Julian Pitt-Rivers explores this paradoxical facet of honor in his essay "The Anthropology of Honor," in idem, *The Fate of Shechem or the Politics of Sex: Essays in the Anthropology of the Mediterranean* (Cambridge, 1977), 1–17.

[20] Daumas, *L'affaire d'Esclans*.

The attraction of honor was stronger than hunger or cold, it could be stronger even than love. Balzac implies as much when he tells us that young Rastignac's love for Delphine is a love born of ambition, and will easily be eclipsed when Rastignac has exhausted the attachment's capacity to advance his social position. Madame de Beauséant likewise triumphs over the anguish caused by the loss of her lover, the marquis d'Ajuda-Pinto, by protecting her honor. She presides with cool and haughty dignity at a scheduled ball on the very day she hears of her loss, and that same night she retires into obscurity in the countryside. She has lost a lover, but she will submit to no shameful public examination of her pain. On this score, her victory is complete. It was normal in Goriot's world both to be greatly concerned with honor, and to see one's own honor reflected in the honor enjoyed by one's spouse and family relations, as well as in the honor achieved by one's children.

Goriot's sacrifice of everything that remained to him, including his life, for one evening gown is easier to understand once one recognizes the crucial importance of that gown in the protection of Anastasie's, and therefore Goriot's, honor. To wear the gown was an aid in the effort to conceal the scandalous secret that Anastasie had attempted to rob her husband of his family's jewelry. She had rashly stolen the jewels and sold them to get yet more money for her lover. Her husband had been able to recover the jewels, and ordered her to wear them to the ball to squelch rumors of her crime. Hence her desperate need for a suitable dress. If the ballroom floor was a field of battle on which family honor had to be defended at all cost, then Goriot's sacrifice begins to make sense.

Balzac's novels constantly depict such heartrending trade-offs between honor and need. Some characters escape from want by means of dishonorable behavior. (These include criminals like Vautrin, journalists like Lousteau in *Les Illusions perdues,* or young ladies like those at the party in *Peau de Chagrin.*) They sell their affections, their talents, their pens, their bodies for a square meal and a roof that does not leak. Others endure privation in order to purchase scraps of honorable commodities. Young Rastignacs, de Rubemprés, and de Valentins squander meager living allowances on stylish clothing and opera tickets. They give up lunch and dinner for taxi fare, so they can arrive where they are going without mud on their boots.

They gamble away their last coins, since they would rather exist honorably than survive on pennies. Honor is an all-important good for many of Balzac's characters, but one that is confusing in the extreme. Sometimes it is closely associated with other goods – morality, money, hunger, aesthetic pleasure, gift giving – but sometimes it seems diametrically opposed to these same things. Money and honor, in particular, have a strange and exasperating relationship in the works of Balzac: Money brings honor to those who have it, and in some contexts it seems impossible to have honor without it; yet it seems that to get money and the honor it brings, many are forced to dishonor themselves.[21] Moreover, that money alone is sufficient to bring honor is frequently characterized as a shameful feature of contemporary society.

It might seem at first that the wealthy escaped the conflict between honor and need, since they could pursue honor without risk to their appetites. But this freedom from the conflicting pressures of honor and need reflected wealth's special role in the logic of honor. To dress well, to travel in a private carriage, were honorable because excess meant freedom from the need to obey others, from the need to flatter, to ingratiate, to placate, to lie.

The zero point of honor

The interdependence in conflict of honor and need can be most vividly seen in *Père Goriot* by tracing the early stages of Rastignac's painful education in the ways of Parisian society. Rastignac makes his first step along this calvary of innocence when he comes to Paris to

[21] "Mêler l'argent aux sentiments, n'est-ce pas horrible? Vous ne pourrez pas m'aimer," dit-elle.

Ce mélange de bons sentiments, qui rendent les femmes si grandes, et des fautes que la constitution actuelle de la société les force à commettre, bouleversait Eugène, qui disait des paroles douces et consolantes en admirant belle femme, si naïvement imprudente dans son cri de douleur (143).

("It is hideous, is it not," she cried, "to speak in a breath of money and affection? You cannot love me after this," she added.

The incongruity between the ideas of honor which make women so great, and the errors in conduct which are forced upon them by the constitution of society, had thrown Eugène's thoughts into confusion; he uttered soothing and consoling words, and wondered at the beautiful woman before him, and at the artless imprudence of her cry of pain.) This translation from the Everyman's Library edition, trans. Ellen Marriage (London, 1907; 1940), 124.

begin his legal studies, and takes up residence at the boardinghouse of Mme. Vauquer in the Latin Quarter. Balzac depicts this boardinghouse as a bleak place; it serves as a grim point of reference against which to compare the luxurious residences that Rastignac will later visit. It is devoid of grace and charm, its inhabitants are demoralized by their poverty; and this demoralization is directly linked to the refined monetary calculations that have been imposed on them by the difficulty of fulfilling their everyday needs. The necessity of such calculations is in fact shameful. "These seven lodgers," Balzac remarks sarcastically, "were Mme. Vauquer's spoiled children. Among them she distributed, with astronomical precision, the exact proportion of respect and attention due to the varying amounts they paid for their board" (8).[22]

Because *la maison Vauquer* serves as the reference point against which all honor is measured, it is worth looking in some detail at Balzac's characterization of the inhabitants of this boardinghouse.

Balzac first gives a general description of their appearance and their dress, and then considers each of them in turn. We are told no more than what a casual observer could surmise by merely looking at them; but that is enough to sound their souls, because appearance tells of incomes, budgets, and the trying anxieties of a life in straitened circumstances. In the new laissez-faire social order, incomes, budgets, possessions, are what count in placing a person.

First a general description sets the tone:

The dreary surroundings were reflected in the costumes of the inmates of the house; all were alike threadbare. The color of the men's coats was problematical; such shoes, in more fashionable quarters, are only to be seen lying in the gutter; the cuffs and collars were worn and frayed at the edges; every limp article of clothing looked like the ghost of its former self. The women's dresses were faded, old fashioned, dyed and re-dyed; they wore gloves that were glazed with hard wear, much-mended lace, dingy ruffles, crumpled muslin fichus. So much for their clothing; but, for the most part, their frames were solid enough; their constitutions had weathered the storms of life; their

[22] In some cases, as here, the English translations are taken from the Everyman's Library edition, trans. Ellen Marriage; such instances are indicated by page references in parentheses following the quote in the text. (Where no page reference appears, the translation is by the author.) The original of this quote: "Ces sept pensionnaires, étaient les enfants gâtés de madame Vauquer, qui leur mesurait avec une précision d'astronome les soins et les égards, d'après le chiffre de leurs pensions" (32).

cold, hard faces were worn like coins that have been withdrawn from circulation, but there were greedy teeth behind the withered lips. (9)[23]

Here clothes and faces share the attributes of being threadbare, polished by wear (*élimé, glacés, éfacées comme . . . des écus démonétisés*). Subjection to need has brought a moral hardness, a distasteful appetitive vigor (*des corps solidement charpentés, des dents avides*). Following these general remarks each of the individual residents of the pension is described in turn. In these individual descriptions we are told explicitly that, among other things, lack of money destroys personal beauty, or prevents its apprehension. The first is true of old Mlle. Michonneau, the second of young Victorine Taillefer.

Mlle. Michonneau, that elderly young lady, screened her weak eyes from the daylight by a soiled green silk shade with a rim of brass, an object fit to scare away the Angel of Pity himself. Her shawl, with its scanty, draggled fringe, might have covered a skeleton, so meagre and angular was the form beneath it. Yet she must have been pretty and shapely once. What corrosive had destroyed the feminine outlines? Was it trouble, or vice or greed? Had she loved too well? Had she been a second-hand clothes dealer, a frequenter of the backstairs of great houses or had she been merely a courtesan? (9–10)[24]

Here past shameful occupations have, in all probability, transformed a once beautiful woman into a shabbily dressed skeleton of a woman. ("Avait-elle trop aimé?" – even this question points to dishonor, for it implies an extramarital affair that brought disorder to her personal and property relations.)

[23] Aussi le spectacle désolant que présentait l'intérieur de cette maison se répétait-il dans le costume de ses habitués, également délabrés. Les hommes portaient des redingotes dont la couleur était devenue problématique, des chaussures comme il s'en jette au coin des bornes dans les quartiers élégants, du linge élimé, des vêtements qui n'avaient plus que l'âme. Les femmes avaient des robes passées, retintes, déteintes, de vieilles dentelles raccommodées, des gants glacés par l'usage, des collerettes toujours rousses et des fichus éraillés. Si tels étaient les habits, presque tous montraient des corps solidement charpentés, des constitutions qui avaient résistées aux tempêtes de la vie, des faces froides, dures, efacées comme celles des écus démonétisés. Les bouches flétries étaient armées de dents avides (32).

[24] La vieille demoiselle Michonneau gardait sur ses yeux fatigués un crasseux abat-jour en taffetas vert, cerclé par du fils d'archal qui aurait effarouché l'ange de la pitié. Son châle à franges maigres et pleurardes semblait couvrir un squelette, tant les formes qu'il cachait étaient anguleuses. Quel acide avait dépouillé cette créature de ses formes féminines? elle devait avoir été jolie et bien faite: était-ce le vice, le chagrin, la cupidité? avait-elle trop aimé, avait-elle été marchande à la toilette, ou seulement courtisane? (33)

The young Mlle. Victorine Taillefer, as Balzac describes her, is Michonneau at an earlier stage of her existence:

There was the same kind of charm about her too slender form, her faintly colored face and light-brown hair, that modern poets find in medieval statuettes; and a sweet expression, a look of Christian resignation in the dark grey eyes. She was pretty by force of contrast; if she had been happy, she would have been charming. Happiness is the poetry of woman, as the toilette is her tinsel. If the delightful excitement of a ball had made the pale face glow with color; if the delights of a luxurious life had brought the color to the wan cheeks that were slightly hollowed already; if love had put light in to the sad eyes, then Victorine might have ranked among the fairest; but she lacked the two things which create woman a second time – pretty dresses and love-letters. (11)[25]

Not only does poverty destroy beauty and sully female innocence, but even a life of uneventful salaried employment brings inevitable dehumanizing suffering, as in the case of another of Mme. Vauquer's tenants, M. Poiret.

M. Poiret was a sort of automaton. He might be seen any day sailing like a grey shadow along the walks of the Jardin des Plantes, on his head a shabby cap, a cane with an old yellow ivory handle in the tips of his thin fingers; the outspread skirts of his threadbare overcoat failed to conceal his meagre figure; his breeches hung loosely on his shrunken limbs; the thin, blue-stockinged legs trembled like those of a drunken man; there was a notable breach of continuity between the dingy white waistcoat and crumpled shirt frills and the cravat twisted about a throat like a turkey gobbler's; altogether, his appearance set people wondering whether this outlandish ghost belonged to the audacious race of the sons of Japhet who flutter about on the Boulevard Italien. What kind of toil could have so shrivelled him? What devouring passions had darkened that bulbous countenance, which would have seemed outrageous as a caricature? What had he been? Well, perhaps he had been part of the machinery of justice, a clerk in the office to which the executioner sends in his accounts, – so much for providing black veils for parricides, so much for sawdust, so much for pulleys and cord for the knife. Or he might

[25] Sa physionomie roussâtre, ses cheveux d'un blond fauve, sa taille trop mince, exprimaient cette grâce que les poètes modernes trouvaient aux statuettes du Moyen Age. Ses yeux gris mélangés de noir exprimaient une douceur, une résignation chrétiennes. Ses vêtements simples, peu coûteux, trahissaient des formes jeunes. Elle était jolie par juxtaposition. Heureuse, elle eût été ravissante: le bonheur est la poésie des femmes, comme la toilette en est le fard. Si la joie d'un eût reflété ses teintes rosées sur ce visage pâle; si les douceurs d'une vie élégante eussent rempli, eussent vermillonné ces joues déjà légèrement creusées; si l'amour eût ranimé ces yeux tristes, Victorine aurait pu lutter avec les plus belles jeunes filles. Il lui manquait ce qui crée une seconde fois la femme, les chiffons et les billets doux (34).

have been a receiver at the door of a public slaughter-house, or a sub-inspector of nuisances. Indeed, the man appeared to have been one of the beasts of burden in our great social mill; one of those Parisian Ratons whom their Bertrands do not even know by sight; a pivot in the obscure machinery that disposes of misery and things unclean; one of those men, in short, at sight of whom we are prompted to remark that, "After all, we cannot do without them." Stately Paris ignores the existence of these faces bleached by moral or physical suffering; but then Paris is in truth an ocean that no line can plumb. (10)[26]

Note that the employments imagined for Poiret – at the Ministry of Justice, at the slaughterhouse, as health inspector – all involve the dry recording of matters ancillary to death, disease, and violence. To earn a meager living, the Poiret type is exposed year in and year out to the witnessing of horrors in a way that deadens feeling and leaves him "a kind of machine."

Without independence of means, virtue is destroyed, beauty pales, feeling dies; only appetites flourish. Even worse, we soon learn that a shortage of money for basic needs also undermines solidarity, isolating individuals, rendering them indifferent to each other. Since they have nothing to give each other, there is no reason for them to try to persuade each other of anything:

For that matter, there was not a soul in the house who took any trouble to investigate the various chronicles of misfortunes, real or imaginary, related

[26] Monsieur Poiret était une espèce de mécanique. En l'apercevant s'étendre comme une ombre grise le long d'une allée au Jardin des Plantes, la tête couverte d'une vieille casquette flasque, tenant à peine sa canne à pomme d'ivoire jauni dans sa main, laissant flotter les pans flétris de sa redingote qui cachait mal une culotte presque vide, et des jambes en bas bleus qui flageolaient comme celles d'un homme ivre, montrant son gilet blanc sale et son jabot de grosse mousseline recroquevillée qui s'unissait imparfaitement à sa cravate cordée autour de son cou de dindon, bien des gens se demandaient si cette ombre chinoise appartenait à la race audacieuse des fils de japhet qui papillonnent sur le boulevard Italien. Quel travail avait pu le ratatiner ainsi? quelle passion avait bistré sa face bulbeuse, qui, desinée en caricature, aurait paru hors du vrai? Ce qu'il avait été? mais peut-être avait-il été employé au Ministère de la Justice, dans le bureau où les exécuteurs des hautes oeuvres envoient leurs mémoires de frais, le compte des fournitures de voiles noirs pour les parricides, de son pour les paniers, de ficelle pour les couteaux. Peut-être avait-il été receveur à la porte d'un abbatoir, ou sous-inspecteur de salubrité. Enfin, cet homme semblait avoir été l'un des ânes de notre grand moulin social, l'un des ces Ratons parisiens qui ne connaissent même pas leurs Bertrands, quelque pivot sur lequel avaient tourné les infortunes ou les saletés publiques, enfin l'un de ces hommes dont nous disons, en les voyant: *il en faut pourtant comme ça.* Le beau Paris ignore ces figures blêmes de souffrances morales ou physiques. Mais Paris est un véritable océan (33–34).

by the rest. Each one regarded the others with indifference tempered by suspicion; it was a natural result of their relative positions. Practical assistance not one of them could give, this they all knew, and they had long since exhausted their stock of condolence over previous discussions of their grievances. They were in something the same position as an elderly couple who have nothing left to say to each other. The routine of existence kept them in contact, but they were parts of a mechanism which wanted oil. (14)[27]

Not only does poverty isolate the tenants from each other, but it gives Mme. Vauquer a special authority over them by reason of her moderate rents. Where else in Paris could they find edible food and clean rooms for such a price? Therefore: "If she had committed some flagrant act of injustice, the victim would have borne it in silence" (14).[28]

Balzac does not mention honor explicitly in this description; to do so would be to insult his characters openly. He only insinuates, in the usual fashion of informal conversations – as between two gossips entertaining each other with refined caricatures – what his estimation of each person's measure of honor was.[29] Indeed, he heaps disdain on Vauquer's lodgers with every word.

The deformed cursus honorum

At first Rastignac feels no discontent with these surroundings; thrilled by the city, he serves an apprenticeship of Parisian pleasures, "les délices visibles du Paris matériel": theater, museums, courses by famous professors at the Collège de France, "the ins and outs of the

[27] D'ailleurs aucune de ces personnes ne se donnait la peine de vérifier si les malheurs allégués par l'une d'elles étaient faux ou véritables. Toutes avaient les unes pour les autres une indifférence mêlée de défiance qui résultait de leurs situations respectives. Elles se savaient impuissantes à soulager leur peines, et toutes avaient en se les contant épuisé la coupe des condoléances. Semblables à de vieux époux, elles n'avaient plus rien à se dire. Il ne restait donc entre elles que les rapports d'une vie mécanique, le jeu de rouages sans huile (37).

[28] Se fût-elle permis une injustice criante, la victime l'aurait supportée sans se plaindre (37).

[29] The resemblance of description to gossip in this case represents one of those forms of exchange between society and literature discussed by Greenblatt and Jameson (see note 10 above). By imitating gossip, Balzac seeks to solidify the contract between his work and the reader, as well. Indeed, Balzac's form of realism lies much more in his tone of voice than in any descriptive fidelity to a supposed "reality." He draws this tone not only from conversational conventions but also from the new journalism of the Restoration–July Monarchy era.

labyrinth of Paris" (26);[30] he learns the good spots and the bad, the usages and the language of the city.

But on his first vacation back home, he sees his family with new eyes. He sees how they generously hide the distress caused by subtracting 1,300 francs a year to pay for his studies out of their minimal rents of 3,000 francs. He is forced to compare his sisters, who seemed so beautiful to him as a child, with the women of Paris "who had realized the beauty of his dreams" (27).[31] It is here that he first conceives that "soif de distinctions" ("thirst for distinction") that determines him to seek out a distant and very wealthy cousin, Mme. de Beauséant. His family is not in any material need; 3,000 francs was the annual income of a bureau chief in a government ministry or a small-scale plumbing contractor. Theirs is an income, however, that requires great care in its management if everyday needs are to be consistently met. Their impatient son decides on a bold course of action; trading on his wealthy relation, he will seek entry into Parisian high society, and there find a beautiful woman to become his lover and protector.

His cousin Mme. de Beauséant graciously invites him to a ball; there he meets a ravishing beauty, Mme. la comtesse de Restaud, who casually invites him to visit her at any time. Not realizing that this was merely a polite formula, he prepares an expedition to her residence one afternoon shortly thereafter. He dresses in his best clothes and sets out; but the route is a hazardous one. Here Balzac introduces a device that he used more than once in his novels: the confrontation of one of his young heroes with the anguish of traveling on foot in the streets of Paris to visit a wealthy home. Rastignac, while walking along, gave himself over to

> the wild intoxicating dreams which fill a young head so full of delicious excitement. . . . Eugène took unheard of pains to keep himself in a spotless condition, but on his way through the streets he began to think about Mme. de Restaud and what he should say to her. He equipped himself with wit, rehearsed repartees in the course of an imaginary conversation, and prepared certain neat speeches à la Talleyrand, conjuring up a series of small events which should prepare the way for the declaration on which he had based his future; and during these musings the law student was bespattered with mud, and by the time he reached the Palais Royal he was obliged to have his boots

[30] les issues du labyrinthe parisien (48).

[31] qui lui avaient réalisé le type d'une beauté rêvée (49).

blackened and his trousers brushed. "If I were rich," he said, as he changed the five-franc piece he had brought with him in case anything might happen, "I would take a cab, then I could think at my ease." (47)[32]

But instead he is unprepared, and easily disconcerted not only by the imposing character of the Restaud residence, but especially by the casual luxury of Mme. de Restaud's appearance, which is described with all the detail one would expect of a fashion magazine.[33]

Rastignac turned abruptly and saw her standing before him, coquettishly dressed in a loose white cashmere gown with knots of rose-colored ribbon here and there; her hair was carelessly coiled about her head, as is the wont of Parisian women in the morning; there was a soft fragrance about her – doubtless she was fresh from a bath; – her graceful form seemed more flexible, her beauty more luxuriant. Her eyes glistened. A young man can see everything at a glance; he feels the radiant influence of woman as a plant discerns and absorbs its nutriment from the air; he did not need to touch her hands to feel their cool freshness. He saw faint rose tints through the cashmere of the dressing-gown; it had fallen slightly open, giving glimpses of a bare throat, on which the student's eyes rested. The Countess had no need of the adventitious aid of corsets; her girdle defined the outlines of her slender waist; her throat was a challenge to love; her feet, thrust into slippers, were daintily small. (48)[34]

32 à ces espérances étourdiment folles qui rendent la vie des jeunes gens si belle d'émotions. . . . Eugène marchait avec mille précautions pour ne point se crotter, mais il marchait en pensant à ce qu'il dirait à madame de Restaud, il s'approvisionnait d'esprit, il inventait les reparties d'une conversation imaginaire, il préparait ses mots fins, ses phrases à la Talleyrand, en supposant de petites circonstances favorables à la déclaration sur laquelle il fondait son avenir. Il se crotta, l'étudiant, il fut forcé de faire cirer ses bottes et brosser son pantalon au Palais-Royal. "Si j'était riche, se dit-il en changeant une pièce de trente sous qu'il avait prise *en cas de malheur* [sic], je serais allé en voiture, j'aurais pu penser à mon aise" (67–68).

33 See Roland Chollet's discussion of *Le Journal des Dames* and *La Mode* (as well as Balzac's own contributions to the latter), in *Balzac Journaliste: Le tournant de 1830,* 221–77. This description is characteristic of the commodification of persons and things that occurs in Balzac's prose; see Jameson, *The Political Unconscious,* 151–84.

34 Rastignac se retourna brusquement et vit la comtesse coquettement vêtue d'un peignoir en cachemire blanc, à noeuds roses, coiffée négligemment, comme le sont les femmes de Paris au matin; elle embaumait, elle sans doute pris un bain, et sa beauté, pour ainsi dire assouplie, semblait plus voluptueuse; ses yeux étaient humides. L'oeil des jeunes gens sait tout voir: leurs esprits s'unissent aux rayonnements de la femme comme une plante aspire dans l'air des substances qui lui sont propres. Eugène sentit donc la fraîcheur épanouie des mains de cette femme sans avoir besoin d'y toucher. Il voyait, à travers le cachemire, les teintes rosées du corsage que le peignoir, légèrement entrouvert, laissait parfois à nu, et sur lequel son regard s'étalait. Les ressources du busc étaient inutiles à la comtesse, la ceinture marquait seule sa taille flexible, son cou invitait à l'amour, ses pieds étaient jolis dans les pantoufles (69–70).

Even more disconcerting to Rastignac is the presence of a rival for Mme. de Restaud's attention in the form of the dandy Maxime de Trailles, whose appearance Rastignac painfully contrasts with his own:

Rastignac all at once began to hate [the young man] violently. To begin with the sight of the fair, carefully arranged curls on the other's comely head had convinced him that his own crop was hideous; Maxime's boots, moreover, were elegant and spotless, while his own, in spite of all his care, bore some traces of his recent walk; and, finally, Maxime's overcoat fitted the outline of his figure gracefully, he looked like a pretty woman, while Eugène was wearing a black coat at half-past two. The quick-witted child of the Charente felt the disadvantage at which he was placed beside this tall, slender dandy, with the clear gaze and pale face, one of those men who would ruin orphan children without scruple. (49)[35]

Here again the supreme importance of money impresses itself on Rastignac, money to assure proper self-adornment and self-presentation, money, the lack of which may be apparent in the most elusive details of one's self-presentation (most tellingly here, in the "légère teinte de boue" that remains on Rastignac's boots).

Within minutes of his arrival Rastignac renders himself hateful to his hostess by an innocent misstatement that deeply wounds her honor. He simply asks why he has seen "Père Goriot" (which might be translated as "Pop Goriot" or "old man Goriot") leaving the Restauds' hôtel. He does not realize that the aging pauper is the countess's father. He is mystified by her distress. "Monsieur," interjects her husband, "you might at least have said Monsieur Goriot!"[36]

Confused by his inadvertent insult, he determines to go at once and ask his cousin Mme. de Beauséant to explain his error. Damning the expense, he takes a carriage so he can at least arrive at her hôtel in a respectable manner. But to his surprise, her lackeys smirk at his "vulgar bride's conveyance."[37] Introduced into her private apart-

[35] Rastignac se sentit une haine violente pour ce jeune homme. D'abord les beaux cheveux blonds et bien frisés de Maxime lui apprirent combien les siens étaient horribles. Puis Maxime avait des bottes fines et propres, tandis que les siennes, malgré le soin qu'il avait pris en marchant, s'étaient empreintes d'une légère teinte de boue. Enfin Maxime portait une redingote qui lui serrait élégamment la taille et le faisaint ressembler à une jolie femme, tandis qu'Eugène avait à deux heures et demie un habit noir. Le spirituel enfant de la Charente sentit la supériorité que la mise donnait à ce dandy, mince et grand, à l'oeil clair, au teint pâle, un de ces hommes capables de ruiner des orphelins (70).

[36] "Monsieur, vous auriez pu dire monsieur Goriot!" s'écria-t-il (74).

[37] équipage de mariée vulgaire (76).

ment, he sees "for the first time a great lady among the wonderful and elegant surroundings that reveal her character and reflect her daily life" (56).[38] In her beautiful salon, description fails; we are given few details. Rastignac simply realizes that the conspicuous display of Mme. de Restaud is coarse by comparison. Daughter of a self-made man, Mme. de Restaud was, he now sees, "[in love with] the gilding, the ostentatious splendor, the unintelligent luxury of the parvenu, the riotous extravagance of a courtesan" (69).[39] Whereas in Mme. de Beauséant's apartment, Rastignac, "taken aback by the glistening of marvelous wealth, believed in the reality of the *Arabian Nights*."[40] This "richesse merveilleuse" is not enumerated, in stark contrast to Balzac's careful cataloging of furniture and dress for both the pension Vauquer and the residence of Mme. de Restaud. It is as if Mme. de Beauséant is so wealthy and so habituated to wealth that display is of no concern for her. Her indifference silences, humbles the novelist's voice.

In the end Balzac concludes as follows on Rastignac's educational experiences:

> Between Mme. de Restaud's blue boudoir and Mme. de Beauséant's rose-colored drawing-room he had made a three years' advance in a kind of law which is not a recognized study in Paris, although it is a sort of higher jurisprudence, and when well understood, is a kind of high road to success of every kind. (60)[41]

As a result, "The demon of luxury gnawed at his heart, greed burned in his veins, his throat was parched with the thirst of gold" (58).[42]

Again Maurice Daumas's sensitive discussion on honor in the eighteenth-century context helps us to understand the situation Rastignac was in. Honor, Daumas observes, could be increased, but "no one ever spoke of this."

[38] pour la première fois les merveilles de cette élégance personnelle qui trahit l'âme et les moeurs d'une femme de distinction (77).

[39] amoureuse, des dorures, des objets de prix en évidence, le luxe inintelligent du parvenu, le gaspillage de la femme entretenue (89).

[40] étourdis par les scintillements d'une richesse merveilleuse, croyait à la réalité des contes arabes . . . (79).

[41] Entre le boudoir bleu de madame de Restaud et le salon rose de madame de Beauséant, il avait fait trois années de ce *Droit parisien* dont on ne parle pas, quoiqu'il constitue une haute jurisprudence sociale qui, bien apprise et bien pratiquée, mène à tout (81).

[42] Le démon du luxe le mordit au coeur, la fièvre du gain le prit, la soif de l'or lui sèche la gorge (79).

Full honor is inconceivable except in a position of full belonging to a group. Acquiring honor is even more paradoxical than acquiring belonging: How can one find oneself, by definition, with a "shortage of honor"? To wish to advance in honor is therefore incompatible with *dike* [moderation in speech], and damages the symbolic possessions of others, because the system of honor functions as a zero-sum game.[43]

Thus Rastignac wished to possess luxuries or gold not for their own sake, but because he could not gain honor except by appearing already to possess the increased honor he sought. This is why it was so important to appear already rich, to act as if one was already familiar with the peculiar customs and expectations of the *beau monde parisien.* Only in this way could one surreptitiously advance in honor. Only this requirement of the prevailing honor code finally instilled in our young hero a pure and febrile thirst for gain, that peculiar motive whose universality was political economy's first principle.

Having appreciated the scope of his problem, Rastignac's first step is to send for extra spending money from his family and to find a tailor willing to extend him credit. Indeed Rastignac discovers that his tailor fully understands the nature of the struggle he is undertaking; the tailor, as it turns out, considers himself to be "a stepping-stone between a young man's present and future" (81).[44] Later, Balzac remarks, Rastignac would make a fortune for this tailor, by passing along in certain company the following remark: "I have twice known a pair of trousers turned out by him make a match [marriage] of twenty thousand livres a year!" (81)[45]

An essential feature of Rastignac's education is his acceptance of the deformation of gender identity that conflict between need and honor works on the individual. Women are depicted as suffering from an array of painful constraints on their behavior that men do not experience. Here honor takes on a grim, repressive visage; in its

43 "Le plein-honneur ne se conçoit qu'en position d'autochtonie. Et acquérir (de) l'honneur est encore plus paradoxical qu'acquérir (de) l'autochtonie: comment se trouverait-on, par nature, en 'manque d'honneur'? Vouloir augementer son honneur serait d'ailleurs incompatible avec la diké [paroles, modérées, raisonables], porterait atteinte au bien symbolique d'autrui, puisque le système de l'honneur fonctionne selon le principe des vases communicants, c'est-à-dire du bien limité." Daumas, *L'affaire d'Esclans,* 105.

44 un trait d'union entre le présent et l'avenir des jeunes gens (102).

45 "Je lui connais, disait-il, deux pantalons qui ont fait faire des mariages de vingt mille livres de rente" (102).

name Delphine and Anastasie suffer near imprisonment at the hands of their husbands; in its name Mme. de Beauséant embraces permanent exile from the capital; and in its name the loving young Mlle. Taillefer languishes in loneliness and poverty. Rastignac must worry about keeping his boots clean in public; these women must wonder whether they shall even be allowed to see a public space. Poverty for women is a subordinate issue: the implication is that they always have (dishonorable) means at hand to fulfill their needs; whether they shall preserve their honor is their only concern. Everywhere one looks, Balzac shows women's possibilities of love and fulfillment dashed by the needs of family honor and the happenstances of those property arrangements honor dictates. Men are at least allowed to have ambition. Balzac was no feminist, but his opposition to the Civil Code's treatment of women was systematic.[46]

Nonetheless, in Balzac's rendition, both male and female suffer from the deforming effects of the lifelong effort to avoid both deprivation and shame. The two sexes offer to each other satisfaction of an appetite that is not exactly a need, as well as publicly visible relationships that can contribute greatly to an individual's honor or shame. There are immediate benefits but also a most formidable danger, therefore, in trafficking in sex either to satisfy more pressing needs (as we are invited to surmise was the case with Mlle. Michonneau) or to advance in honor (as does Rastignac). To turn love into money as he intends to do, Rastignac finally recognizes,

> he must swallow down all sense of decency, and renounce all the generous ideas which redeem the sins of youth. He had chosen this life of apparent splendor, but secretly gnawed by the canker-worm of remorse, a life of fleeting pleasure dearly paid for by persistent pain. (131)[47]

Secret remorse at best, public shame at worst, may plague the actor who makes this choice. At the same time, it is impossible to give oneself wholly and sincerely to someone of the other sex unless both

[46] Jean Forest, *Des femmes de Balzac* (Montreal, 1984); Marie-Henriette Faillie, *La femme et le Code civil dans la Comédie humaine d'Honoré de Balzac* (Paris, 1968); Maité Albistur and Daniel Armogathe, *Histoire du féminisme français,* 2 vols. (Paris, 1977), II, 386–89.

[47] il fallait avoir bu toute honte, et renoncer aux nobles idées qui sont l'absolution des fautes de la jeunesse. Cette vie extérieurement splendide, mais rongée par tous les *taenias* du remords, et dont les fugitifs plaisirs étaient chèrement expiés par de persistentes angoisses, il l'avait épousée (149).

parties are free of that calculus of gain imposed by the (even faint) proximity of need. This double bind applies to all.

Need and *démoralisation*

Throughout this account, Balzac's description of the social world of Paris fully supports the lessons that Rastignac learns. That is, the novelist's voice implies Rastignac is on the right path, even if it is not a particularly happy path. Only money can lift one out of shame and into the light of honor and self-respect; and only great quantities of money can really banish shameful calculation from one's consciousness.[48] At least in *Père Goriot* and certain other novels, Balzac presents as truly desirable only objects that bring honor within society as it was then constituted, and treats as dishonorable (and not desirable) the mere satisfaction of day-to-day needs. Balzac's constant appeal for the reader's complicity, for the reader's acceptance of the protagonist's perceptions and goals, is another facet of the vital exchange going on between novel and social praxis.

But there is a great problem with the complicity of the novelist's voice in the lessons the young law student learns. Who would doubt, on reflection, that many forms of solidarity flourished, then as now, among the poor, that people of all strata of society, then as now, had their own notions of honor and were not demoralized by their inability to live up to the standards that prevailed among the rich and the super-rich? This question in fact became a controversial one, for the first time in history, in Balzac's own day. The controversy was spurred by the discovery (or one should say the invention) of poverty.[49] In old

[48] "In Balzac . . . it has for whatever historical reason become necessary to secure the reader's consent, and to validate or accredit the object as desirable, before the narrative process can function properly. . . . [T]his narrative apparatus depends on the 'desirability' of an object whose narrative function would have been a relatively automatic and unproblematical secondary effect of a more traditional narrative structure." Jameson, *The Political Unconscious*, 156.

[49] The notion that poverty was in a sense "invented" in this period has been argued for England by Gertrude Himmelfarb in *The Idea of Poverty: England in the Early Industrial Age* (New York, 1984). Himmelfarb is right to insist that "poverty" has an intricate intellectual history, a point missed entirely by earlier influential students of this problem, such as Louis Chevalier, whose *Laboring Classes and Dangerous Classes in Paris in the First Half of the Nineteenth Century* (Princeton, N.J., 1973) has been rightly criticized for its native reading of sources. I have argued forcefully elsewhere that observers of the poor in early-nineteenth-century France misapplied middle-class standards (and a notion of human morality inspired by the market model) in their

regime social thought it was understood that each *corps* and *communauté* had its own form of honor, even down to the thieves and beggars, who were believed to have their own fraternities, their own secret languages, and their own "kings." But the Revolution put an end to this method of configuring the poor and the marginal.[50] In the late 1820s a new kind of investigative literature on the poor began coming out in a steady stream; in these investigative studies, the problem of *démoralisation* became central. Could one live in very straitened circumstances without losing all sense of shame? Could a family, for example, sleep in one bed without falling into incest, or send their children to work in factories without failing to care for them? To answer this question in the negative was to invent "poverty" in the nineteenth-century sense of that term: an amalgam of inescapable deprivation and shame. The argument cut across political boundaries, as can be seen in the way it was taken up by novelists; Eugène Sue's *Mystères de Paris* (1843), an enormously successful novel that probed the amoral criminal underworld of the poor and preached the benefits of socialism, was countered by, for example, George Sand's romantic evocations of goodness and endurance among poor rural women in *La mare au diable* (1845) or *La petite fadette* (1848).

The overwhelming consensus among social historians working today would be that fear of inevitable demoralization among the poor was a middle-class obsession that represented a profound misunderstanding of how the laboring poor lived and worked.[51] This is not to argue that persons without property and dependent on limited-wage incomes were able to pursue their preferred forms of interpersonal relationships free of difficulties, nor even that they escaped the hard-

attempt to gauge the relation between impoverishment and immorality. See William M. Reddy, *The Rise of Market Culture: The Textile Trade and French Society, 1750–1900* (Cambridge, 1984), 138–84.

[50] See, for example, Dominique Julia and Roger Chartier, "Le monde à l'envers," *L'Arc* 65 (1976), 43–53; or Jacques-Louis Ménétra, *Journal de ma vie: Jacques-Louis Ménétra, Compagnon vitrier au XVIIIe siècle,* ed. Daniel Roche (Paris, 1982). On the consequences of the Revolution for perceptions of the poor, see Louis Chevalier, *Laboring Classes* – who, however, wrongly supposes that the new literary images of the poor accurately reflected a changing reality.

[51] See, for example, William H. Sewell, *Work and Revolution in France: The Language of Labor from the Old Regime to 1848* (Cambridge, 1980); Maurice Agulhon, *La république au village* (Paris, 1970); Katherine A. Lynch, *Family, Class, and Ideology in Early Industrial France: Social Policy and the Working-Class Family 1825–1848* (Madison, Wis., 1988).

ships of deprivation and the requirements of deference and obedience without damage to their self-concepts or their capacities for closeness. In the midcentury dialect literature of the factory town of Lille, for example, lack of money is indeed commonly depicted as a moral test, in apparent conformity to the views of middle-class social investigators of the day. But in the popular dialect poetry, workers are frequently depicted as victorious over the constraints of poverty, whereas the social investigators depict a whole community sunk in vice.[52] Consideration of Balzac's novel offers a possible explanation of the origins and plausibility of this misguided obsession, even though Balzac himself, to people his social world, seldom looks beyond what he would call the middle class, and says next to nothing of the truly poor.

That *démoralisation,* as it was then called – which we might translate as a proclivity to shamelessness – was readily supposed to go with poverty is rendered comprehensible by Balzac's account of Mme. Vauquer's boardinghouse. Its inhabitants are in a position analogous to that of the families of wage laborers, as depicted in the pessimistic investigative accounts of the period. (That they retain the pretensions and the faded symbols of middle-class status only makes their poverty seem that much more somber.) They lack solidarity because they have nothing to give each other, no surplus of goods upon which to found steady exchange relationships; they are subject to the authority of property owners (employer, landlord) because they bring far more urgent needs to their exchange relationships with property owners than do the property owners themselves. A factory owner could permit himself most egregious acts of injustice toward his needy employees, just as could Mme. Vauquer toward her needy tenants.[53]

By the same token, the needy poor – required, as if inadvertently, to submit to the authority of those with property (inadvertently because after the Revolution all parties to contracts were deemed in law to be equals) – establish by their obeisance a strong link between property and authority. The link is quantitative; the more property one has, the more authority one exercises. But just as it brings authority over the poor, a surplus of property in turn brings deference and

[52] For an extensive analysis of this literature, see Reddy, *Rise of Market Culture,* 253–88.
[53] For further discussion, see Reddy, *Money and Liberty.*

consideration from all, because it endows one with the capacity to give. Besides receiving the obedience and respect of one's employees or tenants, those with great surpluses enjoyed the respect of their fellow property owners, who hope to strike favorable deals with them, to sell them land or breeches at high prices, to marry their daughters advantageously. This is why inherited notions of honor, closely associated with military and political authority, could survive into the nineteenth century in association with purely "private" proprietary or contractual authority.

Rastignac's family, for example, has a small amount of property, enough to finance his legal studies, and is therefore beholden to no one. He may choose his associates freely and he stands on a footing of equality with other property owners. But to advance beyond this bare minimum in income (and therefore in authority and honor) he must become a suppliant, a courtier, and strive to make his homage acceptable to wealthy patrons or patronesses.[54] In a social order devoid of legally sanctioned distinctions between persons (such as sumptuary codes or rules of precedence, protocol, or *dérogeance*), wealth alone suffices to bring the trappings of honor that become difficult to distinguish from honor itself, which become, in effect, by a scandalous magic, honor itself.[55] These were Rastignac's very thoughts as he left the "grandiose hôtel de Beauséant" on that fateful day:

> As his fancy wandered among these lofty regions in the great world of Paris, innumerable dark thoughts gathered in his heart; his ideas widened, and his conscience grew more elastic. He saw the world as it is; saw how the rich lived beyond the jurisdiction of law and public opinion, and found in success the *ultima ratio mundi.* "Vautrin is right, success is virtue!" he said to himself. (69)[56]

No figure in the novel more clearly establishes these linkages between surpluses, gift giving, authority, and honor than Goriot him-

[54] Even the normative cursus honorum for a person in Rastignac's position – that is, a provincial law practice, a minor post in the judiciary, a marriage alliance with a prefect's daughter – required self abasement, as Vautrin's cynical exposition establishes (106–18).

[55] See Pitt-Rivers, "The Anthropology of Honor," for an in-depth analysis of honor's duality as, at once, a code of conduct and a purely external, ceremonial, and institutional quality.

[56] Son imagination, transportée dans les hautes régions de la société parisienne, lui inspira mille pensées mauvaises au coeur, en lui élargissant la tête et la conscience. Il vit le monde comme il est: les lois et la morale impuissantes chez les riches, et vit dans la fortune l'*ultima ratio mundi.* "Vautrin a raison, la fortune est la vertu!" se dit-il. (89).

self, whose gradual decline within Mme. Vauquer's boardinghouse – from being an object of attention, respect, flattery, marital designs, to become finally a target for general derision, the constant butt of humiliating jests – coincides perfectly with the gradual depletion of his remaining wealth. He enters the boardinghouse a feared and respected figure; as he begins changing rooms to economize on rent, contempt creeps into the voice and demeanor of Mme. Vauquer and her other tenants. Goriot confronts the dilemma of all who seek honor by giving: that they thereby fritter away the very source of their honor. By the end he is reduced to the role of witless buffoon.

However implausible, therefore, is the affirming voice of the novelist as it approves all Rastignac's hard-learned lessons, this voice nonetheless speaks the language of a dominant logic that would likely apply in one form or another to any social order in which needs are satisfied by relatively unregulated monetary exchanges. In this respect, Balzac's voice upholds and advances, even as it deplores, universal subjection to the rule of wealth. It would certainly be a mistake to imagine that the disdain for close calculation and parsimony expressed in this novel (a disdain that necessarily tainted everyone except for the super-rich) represented merely a holdover of feudal or precapitalist values. Such disdain is implicit in that very excess of consumption whose skillful manipulation and display are the raison d'être of saving and economizing. There would be no reason to calculate closely and to save in the first place, after all, if there was no possibility of winning honor through largesse at the end. This is why aristocratic excess could survive so easily into the nineteenth century; it retained a living relationship to the regime of private property.

"Conspicuous consumption," to recall Veblen's famous formulation, appears in Balzac's *Père Goriot* as the outcome of a meticulous calculus of asymmetries. Goriot forgoes medical care for an evening gown; Rastignac exhausts a week's expense budget in an effort to arrive with his boots clean at the hôtels of de Restaud and de Beauséant (yet he is still plagued by that "legère teinte de boue"). These odd trade-offs of need for honor (just two salient examples from hundreds in Balzac's oeuvre) are founded on the inescapable authority that accrued to those with surpluses of property. That authority sought outward display in refined consumption and in a complex protocol of routine ceremony – both of which easily became ends in themselves, as well as possible means to acquire that which they sought to display, as Rastignac's tailor understood. That authority was exercised within and outside of families, and passed with property through family ties. It called for a certain subordination of women. Rastignac mimicked the display and obeyed the protocol despite his relative poverty, because by acquiring or retaining honor he controlled the means to establish relationships that might bring money and property his way. Money and property are then in turn a means to a more solid achievement of honor. Distinctions between means and ends on such a plane could not be maintained. Indeed, it was the general infection of all possible ends (such as, for example, genuine sexual fulfillment) with the taint of ulterior motives (whether desire for honor or for gain) that prevented Balzac's characters from ever acting without ambivalence or remorse.

Granted *homo economicus* is dead. *Requiescat in pace.* But what figure shall we replace him with? *Père Goriot* offers the vision of personalities struggling to master an inescapable conflict between honor and need. Need is born of our physical nature, which sets universal limits on our pursuit of goals (we must all eat, breathe, etc.). Because the propertyless must urgently seek money to satisfy their daily needs, authority inevitably attaches itself to those with significant surpluses of property. As a result, honor contributes its aura to all the commodity forms that signify the availability of surpluses – even down to the absence of slight traces of mud on a pair of boots. Honor is thus born of need, in opposition to it, in a context in which need must be satisfied by the daily acquiring and spending of money. And from the conflict between these two is born, in turn, that peculiar state of ambivalence characteristic of the Balzacian hero, that state which Goriot and Rastignac share and which establishes a bond of friendship between them, a state only exacerbated by money's greatest virtue: its perfect liquidity. This is the state in which the choice between medicine and an evening gown or between dinner and a shoeshine can become a decisive, identity-defining moment in one's life.

PART IV

Agency and structure

CHAPTER 11

The reformist dimension of Talcott Parsons's early social theory

HOWARD BRICK

Historians have rightly assumed that the development of the social sciences in the United States can be illuminated by examining their relationships to contemporary movements and ideologies of social reform. Commentators debate whether the main current of modern social theory in Europe is better understood as originating within the "party of change" or the "party of order," but little question remains about the historical associations of social theory in the United States. The roots of the nineteenth-century American Social Science Association in antebellum reform movements or the links between social-scientific "realism" and Progressivism are only two examples suggesting that the bulk of writers in the developing fields of social studies had some intention of remaking society as they strove to understand it.[1]

The work of Talcott Parsons (1902–79), the preeminent theoretical

[1] I borrow the phrases "party of change" and "party of order" from Arno Mayer's way of describing modern European politics in, for example, *Political Origins of the New Diplomacy 1917–1918* (New Haven, Conn.: Yale University Press, 1959). For the most part, Göran Therborn's account, *Science, Class and Society: On the Formation of Sociology and Historical Materialism* (London: NLB, 1976), situates the early development of social theory in the reform party, at least in supposing that social theory was intended to understand and help consolidate the new order that emerged from the social and political revolutions of the seventeenth and eighteenth centuries. Robert A. Nisbet's *The Sociological Tradition* (New York: Basic Books, 1966), on the other hand, sees sociology as expressing the conservative reaction against the modern revolutions, in defense of community, tradition, and hierarchy. For the United States, see Thomas Haskell, *The Emergence of Professional Social Science: The American Social Science Association and the Nineteenth-Century Crisis of Authority* (Urbana and Chicago: University of Illinois Press, 1977); Morton White, *Social Thought in America: The Revolt Against Formalism* (New York: Viking Press, 1949); and James T. Kloppenberg, *Uncertain Victory: Social Democracy and Progressivism in European and American Thought 1870–1920* (New York: Oxford University Press, 1986).

sociologist in the United States after World War II, ought to be situated in such a field of reform-oriented purposes and perceptions. In this vein, Fred Matthews has explained the ascendancy of Parsons's "structural-functional" theory of society, starting in the late 1930s, as a manifestation of new perspectives on managed social change. Parsons's depiction of society as a system in homeostatic equilibrium, according to Matthews, reflected the clinical temperament of New Deal reformers who considered society an objective entity, something that could be "operated on."[2] Indeed, Matthews's judgment has a measure of biographical accuracy regarding Parsons's personal political inclinations that is superior to those interpretations associating Parsons's work with the hard conservatism of Harvard physiologist L. J. Henderson and his legendary "Pareto circle" of the 1930s.[3] Notwith-

[2] Fred Matthews, *Quest for an American Sociology: Robert E. Park and the Chicago School* (Montreal: McGill–Queen's University Press, 1977), pp. 181–82.

[3] On the Pareto circle, see Barbara Heyl, "The Harvard 'Pareto Circle,' " *Journal of the History of the Behavioral Sciences* 4 (1968): 316–34. There is no question of the deep conservatism of L. J. Henderson, organizer of the Pareto study group, manifested in his frank elitism and contempt for the social reforms and democratic rhetoric of the Roosevelt administration. George Homans, a prominent young figure in the group and an acolyte of Henderson's, shared this conservatism, as indicated in his memoirs, *Coming to My Senses: The Autobiography of a Sociologist* (New Brunswick, N.J.: Transaction Books, 1984). The Pareto circle as a whole ought not be identified with such quasi-aristocratic conservatism, however, for as Seymour Martin Lipset and Everett Carll Ladd, Jr., have shown, the members included several with liberal or left-wing orientations. See Lipset and Ladd, "The Politics of American Sociologists," in *Varieties of Political Expression in Sociology* (Chicago: University of Chicago Press, 1972), pp. 79–80.

Although Parsons is often associated with Henderson, there is little evidence of deep intellectual sympathy between them. Parsons had encountered Vilfredo Pareto's work independently of Henderson, at first under the influence of Joseph Schumpeter, whose seminar on general economics (1927–28) Parsons took. At that time Pareto interested Parsons for his views on the nature of scientific theory and the distinction between economic and sociological concerns, properly speaking. Parsons completed his first long essay on Pareto, "Pareto and the Problems of Positivistic Sociology," in the spring of 1932, *before* Henderson began his renowned Pareto seminar in fall 1932. Furthermore, although they shared an interest in Pareto, and Parsons thanked Henderson for a close reading and critique of his book manuscript, Henderson openly disdained Parsons's interests in Durkheim and Weber, and Parsons, according to his son, "never felt completely comfortable" with Henderson.

One work that attributes crucial significance to Henderson's "Pareto circle" in Parsons's development is Geoffrey Hawthorn, *Enlightenment and Despair: A History of Sociology* (Cambridge: Cambridge University Press, 1976), pp. 213–14. See Talcott Parsons [hereafter "TP"], "A Short Account of My Intellectual Development," *Alpha Kappa Deltan* 29 (1959): 6–7; TP, "On Building Social System Theory: A Personal History," *Daedalus* (1970): 828; "Dialogues with Parsons," in G. C. Hallen, Michael V. Belok, Martin U. Martel, R. Prasad, eds., *Essays on the Sociology of Parsons: A Felicitation Volume* (New Delhi, 1977), p. 6; letters, L. J. Henderson to TP, October

standing those critical sociologists of the 1960s and 1970s who saw a deep conservative bias in Parsons's emphasis on studying mechanisms of social stability, Parsons in the 1930s was far from being a conservative in any sense corresponding to contemporary American political labels.[4] Rather, he hoped to subject the automatism of economic life to social controls and reshape social institutions in ways imagined by the most ambitious New Dealers.

Insofar as the New Deal "saved capitalism," however, Matthews's association of Parsons's social theory and contemporary reform seems perhaps only to reassert the conservative character of his work in a somewhat different sense. Parsons's work then would fit neatly with the thesis of historians like Warren Susman and Richard Pells, who have stressed how essentially conservative midcentury liberal reform, marked by an overriding desire for order, really was.[5] Such a view, savoring of "corporate liberal" interpretations that depict New Deal reform as a conservative program of social change managed from above to restore and maintain a corporate system, proves inadequate, however, as a more nuanced portrait of the period's politics and ideology emerges.[6] Recent historiography, best represented in Steven

26, 1936, Parsons Papers, Harvard University Archives [hereafter "PP"], section 42.41, box 2; and Walton Hamilton to TP, June 10, 1932, PP. Author's interview with Charles D. Parsons, Columbia University, New York, November 23, 1987.

4 Early critics of Parsons's conservatism included Lewis Coser, *The Functions of Social Conflict* (Glencoe, Ill.: Free Press, 1956); Ralf Dahrendorf, *Class and Class Conflict in Industrial Society* (Stanford, Calif.: Stanford University Press, 1959); Donald N. Levine, "Simmel and Parsons: Two Approaches to the Study of Society" (Ph.D. diss., University of Chicago, 1957); C. Wright Mills, *The Sociological Imagination* (New York: Oxford University Press, 1959). The mounting criticism of Parsons in the 1960s was capped by Alvin Gouldner, *The Coming Crisis in Western Sociology* (New York: Basic Books, 1970).

5 Warren I. Susman, "The Culture of the Thirties," pp. 150–83, in *Culture as History: The Transformation of American Society in the Twentieth Century* (New York: Pantheon, 1984); Richard Pells, *Radical Visions and American Dreams: Culture and Social Thought in the Depression Years* (New York: Harper, 1973). Terry A. Cooney offered an insightful critique of the Susman–Pells thesis in his paper "Cultural Stability in the 1930s," annual meeting of the Organization of American Historians, St. Louis, Missouri, April 7, 1989.

6 Key works on "corporate liberalism" include Gabriel Kolko, *The Triumph of Conservatism: A Reinterpretation of American History 1900–1916* (New York: Free Press, 1963); James Weinstein, *The Corporate Ideal in the Liberal State 1900–1918* (Boston: Beacon Press, 1968); Barton Bernstein, "The New Deal: The Conservative Achievements of Liberal Reform," in Bernstein, ed., *Towards a New Past: Dissenting Essays in American History* (New York: Vintage Books, 1968); and Ellis Hawley, "The Discovery and Study of a 'Corporate Liberalism,' " *Business History Review* 52 (Autumn 1978): 309–20.

Fraser and Gary Gerstle's edited volume *The Rise and Fall of the New Deal Order,* has begun to draw a portrait of the New Deal not as the mere realization of corporate liberal aims but, rather, as a long process of protest, reform, resistance, and reaction taking place over almost two decades.[7] In this view, the long-term result of that process – a limited welfare state at midcentury more or less suited to the maintenance and growth of American capitalism – failed to fulfill the liberal aspirations of many New Dealers who had greater ambitions for institutional innovations in the political economy of the United States. To recover those ambitions and reconstruct the intellectual milieu that fostered them might provide a better sense of political meanings in 1930s social theory than the "corporate liberal" view of the period has offered.

While the New Deal established certain forms of nationalized social insurance for the first time in American history, reformers ranging from left-wing New Dealers like Rexford Tugwell and his associates in the Resettlement Administration to those radical intellectuals outside the administration whom Alan Lawson has called "independent liberals" had expected and promoted more ambitious programs of social planning. Their aspirations found expression, for instance, in campaigns for many regional development authorities like the Tennessee Valley Authority (TVA) or for integral communities in the "greenbelt towns," and the latter program was one of the initiatives in social planning that only barely got started before being stalled or rolled back on the eve, and in the midst, of World War II.[8] As the concept of "social planning" subsequently disappeared from the agenda of reform, U.S. liberalism passed a watershed, variously described by writers like Alan Brinkley or Alan Wolfe as a shift from "planning" to "growth" strategies or from "regulatory" to "fiscal liberalism."[9] Both terminologies imply that liberalism dropped its most daring chal-

[7] Steven Fraser and Gary Gerstle, eds., *The Rise and Fall of the New Deal Order* (Princeton, N.J.: Princeton University Press, 1989).

[8] Bernard Sternsher, *Rexford Tugwell and the New Deal* (New Brunswick, N.J.: Rutgers University Press, 1964); Joseph L. Arnold, *The New Deal in the Suburbs: A History of the Greenbelt Town Program 1935–1954* (Columbus: Ohio State University Press, 1971); R. Alan Lawson, *The Failure of Independent Liberalism 1930–1941* (New York: Capricorn Books, 1971).

[9] Alan Wolfe, *America's Impasse: The Rise and Fall of the Politics of Growth* (New York: Pantheon Books, 1981); Alan Brinkley, "The New Deal and the Idea of the State," in Fraser and Gerstle, eds., *Rise and Fall of the New Deal Order,* pp. 85–121.

lenges to existing economic institutions and corporate prerogatives while embracing a program of sustained economic growth, which was expected to fund social relief programs ancillary to the marketplace. In other words, social reform gave way to welfare liberalism.[10]

Such an appreciation for the discontinuous development of twentieth-century liberalism suggests that the outcome of reform efforts (and their functional fit with capitalist prosperity) need not be identified with the motives and intentions of social reform – thus opening to view a bygone world of liberal thought. It is that world which provided the context for, and enables us to assess the meaning of, Talcott Parsons's early work. His first major work in social theory, *The Structure of Social Action* (1937), should be read neither as a wholly abstract treatise on the premises of sociological reasoning nor as a reflection of the conservatizing force of New Deal styles of administration but, rather, as a concerted argument defending the possibility of collectivizing economic practices at a time when the very status of private property in modern society was in some respects open to question. There was, in other words, a reformist dimension of Parsons's early work with aspirations surpassing the boundaries of achieved New Deal reforms. *The Structure of Social Action* may thus be recognized as a specific theoretical manifestation of the practical aims summed up in the style of liberalism here named "social reform."

The political current I have named "social reform" may be considered a manifestation of a larger intellectual phenomenon, the rise of a social-democratic liberalism that James Kloppenberg, in his book *Uncertain Victory,* has found in the early twentieth century.[11] According

[10] Postwar liberalism in the United States assumed a more modest stance than earlier advocates of social-reform liberalism had, but that modesty may have been self-defeating in the long run. So argued Allen Matusow, who showed how "transfer" programs in the 1960s, organized to fund social services for the poor without altering the maldistribution of wealth in the United States, often failed to achieve their goals. Paul Starr's description of Medicare/Medicaid innovations in the 1960s (under the heading "Redistribution Without Reorganization") pointed out how federally administered relief programs characteristically refrained from challenging preexisting economic (and professional) institutions. See Matusow, *The Unraveling of America: A History of Liberalism in the 1960s* (New York: Harper & Row, 1984), pp. 97–127, 217–42; Starr, *The Social Transformation of American Medicine* (New York: Basic Books, 1982); Ira Katznelson, "Was the Great Society a Lost Opportunity?" in Fraser and Gerstle, eds., *Rise and Fall of the New Deal Order,* pp. 185–211.

[11] Kloppenberg, *Uncertain Victory.*

to Kloppenberg, some of the most prominent U.S. intellectuals of the time, along with like-minded Europeans, promoted a convergence or mediation of liberal and socialist political principles and a corresponding resolution of old dilemmas in ethics and epistemology. In fact, such a synthetic style of thought, associated with aspirations to radical reform, continued to have influence in intellectual life beyond the chronological limit of Kloppenberg's study (1920), lasting virtually until World War II. Particularly in those intellectual circles that developed new social-scientific disciplines, there appeared key tenets of this experimental and ambitious reformism: vigorous arguments for a socialized conception of the individual and of the springs and consequences of action, a general suspicion of classic liberal tenets tied to the market ideal, a strong interest in economic institutions as fundamental components of social organization, a desire to justify epistemological and political activism, and the general expectation that modern social evolution yielded more organized, or collectivized, forms of economic and political practice.[12] Much of Talcott Parsons's early work shared the general values and assumptions of American social reform in the 1920s and 1930s, including assumptions regarding the given trend toward collectivism and the centrality of economic institutions. This essay is intended to locate the reformist dimension of Parsons's early intellectual development and show how *The Structure of Social Action* can be interpreted in its light.

"A College for Training Parsons"[13]

Talcott Parsons was born December 13, 1902, to a middle-class professional family in Colorado Springs. The last of six children, he was given the maiden name of his maternal grandmother. His parents had solid bourgeois credentials and liberal inclinations. Edward S. Parsons, the son of a modestly successful Brooklyn, N.Y., box manufacturer, had turned away from a business career to join the Congre-

[12] While not necessarily *socialist,* such notions implied a deep skepticism of *capitalism* and a tropism toward collective social organization in some form. On the early socialist proclivities of a major prewar theorist with broad influence thereafter, see Dmitri N. Shalin, "G. H. Mead, Socialism, and the Progressive Agenda," *American Journal of Sociology* 93 (January 1988): 913–51.

[13] Title of chapter 1 in Thomas LeDuc, *Piety and Intellect at Amherst College* (New York: Columbia University Press, 1946).

gational clergy and espouse the Social Gospel. Talcott's mother, Mary Augusta (Ingersoll) Parsons, daughter of a prominent Cleveland business family, supported woman suffrage and other reform causes.

Edward Parsons had attended Amherst College, as most Parsons men did.[14] Founded in 1821 as a center of opposition to Harvard's Unitarianism, Amherst combined Congregational orthodoxy, evangelical spirit, and devoted scholarship – a dual allegiance, a historian of the college writes, to "piety and intellect." Through the nineteenth century, the campus was swept by waves of student revivals, the last one touching Edward Parsons. Drawn to the social meliorism of liberal theology, he studied briefly with one of the early leaders of social Christianity, Lyman Abbott, and contributed to the movement redefining Christianity in more moral than doctrinal terms with his short book *The Social Message of Jesus.*[15] From the East Coast, Edward had followed the call to a pulpit in Greeley, Colorado, in 1888, but he held it for only four years before taking a professorship in English at Colorado College, in Colorado Springs, serving also as the college's vice-president from 1898 to 1916. In the Congregational tradition, his literary interests ran to Milton.[16] After working briefly in New York City, helping to organize war-related services of the YMCA, Edward Parsons assumed the presidency of Marietta College, a small Congregational school in Ohio, in June 1919.

[14] His brother Frank had also attended Amherst College, but Frank followed a more conventional career path, becoming a wealthy corporate attorney in New York City and later a benefactor of his academically inclined nephew, Talcott. An older and a younger brother of Talcott's also attended Amherst. Obituary for Frank H. Parsons, *New York Times,* October 14, 1937, p. 25; author's interview with Charles Parsons; author's interview with Helen W. Parsons, Somerville, Mass., October 15, 1987.

[15] LeDuc, *Piety and Intellect at Amherst College,* pp. 2, 13–21, 27–28, 34, 94–98, 109, 141–45. On the tendency to a moral definition of religion in Anglo-American liberal Christianity, see James Turner, *Without God, Without Creed* (Baltimore, Md.: Johns Hopkins University Press, 1985), pp. 82–96, and Stanley Pierson, *Marxism and the Origin of British Socialism* (Ithaca, N.Y.: Cornell University Press), pp. 7–8. Edward S. Parsons, *The Social Message of Jesus: A Course of Twelve Lessons* (National Board of the YWCA, 1912).

[16] Martin U. Martel, "Talcott Parsons," *International Encyclopedia of the Social Sciences,* vol. 18, ed.. David Sills (New York: Free Press, 1979), pp. 609–30. *Amherst College Biographical Record: Centennial Edition 1821–1921* (Amherst, Mass.: Amherst College, 1927); *The Decennial Record of the Class of Eighty-Three: Amherst College 1883–1893* (New York: New York Printing Co., 1893); *National Cyclopaedia of American Biography,* vol. 33 (New York, 1947). Author's interview with Charles D. Parsons; author's interview with Helen W. Parsons.

By the time Talcott reached Amherst College in 1920, the era of student revivals had long passed. What survived into the early twentieth century was a strong ethic of service combined with sophisticated study in the natural sciences, although there were times when the service ideal was almost overshadowed by the rising social status of the alumni and students, the domination of student life by fraternities, and the growing enthusiasm for college sports.[17] Talcott apparently took after his father – congenial, but grave and even ponderous. Gently mocked as "Little Talcott, the gilded cherub" (he was not much taller than five feet), Parsons was pictured in the 1924 Amherst yearbook with a caption that asked, "Why do you talk Latin and German in your sleep?"[18] His older brother Charles appeared quite different. Graduating from Amherst ten years before Talcott, Charles was described by his college classmates as a jovial "rah-rah boy" whose rambunctiousness, they thought, must conceal deeper reserves of integrity and purpose.[19] Indeed, he went on to show there was "something more solid underneath"; returning from a summer stint as a volunteer with the medical missions of the philanthropist Wilfred Grenfell in Labrador, Charles decided to become a physician. After his training, he spent ten years managing one of Grenfell's hospitals in the distant outpost of Twillingate, Newfoundland, and became one of Grenfell's closest aides. Charles's career stood as an exemplar of Talcott's notion of "service" as a professional ideal.[20]

Amherst College in the early 1920s was a place vibrant with intellectual and political activity, belying the image of complacent retrench-

[17] LeDuc, *Piety and Intellect.* On the social status of Amherst students by the first third of the twentieth century, see David O. Levine, *The American College and the Culture of Aspiration 1915–1940* (Ithaca, N.Y.: Cornell University Press, 1986), pp. 54, 128.

[18] *The Olio* (Amherst College, 1924).

[19] *Senior Class Book 1913* (Rutland, Vt.: Tuttle, 1913), p. 69.

[20] On the career of Charles Edwards Parsons (1892–1940), see letter, TP to Dr. Abraham Myerson, March 8, 1941, PP, section 15.2, box 15; obituary, "Dr. Charles Parsons, Ex-Aide of Grenfell," *New York Times,* January 1, 1941, p. 23; *Amherst College Biographical Record, Centennial Edition 1821–1921* (1927).

One of Talcott's sisters, Elizabeth Ingersoll Parsons, also worked in medicine, taking a doctorate in 1925 at Johns Hopkins in immunology and devoting a thirty-year career to work in several public health agencies. The oldest of the Parsons children, Esther, stayed home and cared for her parents. *Notable American Women 1935–1940* (Detroit: Gale Research, 1981), p. 688; obituary for Elizabeth Ingersoll Parsons, *New York Times,* September 12, 1957.

ment attributed to the postwar years. Although checked and excluded from the old parties, the reform spirit nurtured before the war survived nationwide in the first few years of the new decade and even radicalized a shade as third-party farmer–labor activism brought reformers and "progressive" unionists together in promotion of "industrial democracy."[21] Amherst College under the leadership of Alexander Meiklejohn was a center for the "progressive bloc" of American intellectuals, and it was cited at the time by Upton Sinclair in his scathing account *The Goose-Step* as an exception to the upper-class conservative bias of American colleges.[22] Young laborite intellectuals like Paul Douglas and Carter Goodrich were welcomed on the faculty in the years of Talcott Parsons's stay there.

During his tenure as president, Meiklejohn hired young faculty with backgrounds in the settlement house movement, brought the British Fabian R. H. Tawney to campus, and fostered the local growth of the Intercollegiate Socialist Society and its successor (after 1921), the Student League for Industrial Democracy (SLID).[23] In the early twenties, Meiklejohn backed a Labor College cosponsored by Amherst and the trade unions of nearby Holyoke and Springfield. Active in the program were Talcott's favored teachers, Otto Glaser and Henry Plough, the biologists he studied with while he still intended to follow his brother and pursue premedical training, and the iconoclastic institutional economists Walton Hamilton and Clarence Ayres, who introduced him to the social sciences.[24]

Meiklejohn antagonized several different constituencies in the college community by leading a campaign against intercollegiate sports,

[21] On the Left after World War I, see James Weinstein, "Radicalism in the Midst of Normalcy," *Journal of American History* 52 (1966): 773–90; Paul W. Glad, "Progressives and the Business Culture of the 1920s," *Journal of American History* 53 (1966): 75–89; and David Montgomery, *The Fall of the House of Labor* (Cambridge: Cambridge University Press, 1987), pp. 399–401.

[22] Upton Sinclair, *The Goose-Step: A Study of American Education* (Pasadena, Calif.: The author, 1923), p. 432.

[23] Cynthia Stokes Brown, ed., *Alexander Meiklejohn: Teacher of Freedom* (Berkeley, Calif.: Meiklejohn Institute, 1981), pp. 1–56; Ross Terrill, *R. H. Tawney and His Times: Socialism as Fellowship* (Cambridge, Mass.: Harvard University Press, 1973), pp. 56–57; Max Horn, *The Intercollegiate Socialist Society 1905–1921: Origins of the Modern American Student Movement* (Boulder, Colo.: Westview Press, 1979), p. 67. On Amherst faculty, see *The Olio,* 1924, and *Amherst Student,* January 17, 1921, September 21, 1922.

[24] *Amherst Student,* October 4, 1920, p. 1; *The Olio,* 1924.

struggling with the older, established faculty over administrative prerogatives, and showing a marked distaste for vigorous fund-raising. He was forced to resign by the college trustees in June 1923.[25] The young Parsons belonged "to the group who were most agitated by the events and who were among [Meiklejohn's] strongest partisans." Along with a comrade named Addison Cutler, Parsons wrote a report on the Meiklejohn affair for *The New Student,* the publication of the National Student Forum, a left-liberal network of college clubs that discussed the influence of big business on higher education, encouraged students to take industrial jobs, argued over whether students should assume a partisan alignment with working-class interests, and reported on the worker education movement.[26] After making a false threat to quit the college in protest, Parsons's group vowed to carry on the spirit of Meiklejohn's program in progressive education. As Hamilton, Ayres, and others left Amherst in the wake of the controversy, Meiklejohn's student supporters took their place at the helm of the Labor College classes and organized for themselves an independent "group major," an interdisciplinary set of courses in economics, political science, history, and philosophy devoted to current social problems, under the rubric "Control in the Economic Order." Reminiscing in the late 1970s, Parsons described himself then as an engaged student, one of the "enthusiasts for the Russian Revolution and for the rise of the British Labor Party . . . firmly in the opposition to the current United States regime during the presidencies of

[25] On the controversy over Meiklejohn's tenure as Amherst College president, and Parsons's role in it, see Richard M. Jones and Barbara Leigh Smith, eds., *Against the Current: Reform and Experimentation in Higher Education* (Cambridge, Mass.: Schenkman, 1984), pp. 326, 337–39; Claude M. Fuess, *Stanley King of Amherst* (Columbia University Press, 1955), pp. 127–28, 136, 139, 141–42, 144–46; Addison T. Cutler and Talcott Parsons, "A Word from Amherst Students," *The New Student,* October 20, 1923, pp. 6–7; "Controversy over President Meiklejohn Over-Aired," *Amherst Student,* June 16, 1923.

[26] George P. Rawick, "Introduction," Greenwood reprint of *The New Student* (Westport, Conn.: Greenwood Press, 1970). See founding statement of the National Student Federation, *The New Student,* April 19, 1922, p. 2; reports on workers' education, *The New Student,* March 3, 1922, p. 1; June 7, 1922, pp. 1, 5; October 20, 1923, p. 7. On industrial jobs, see *The New Student,* May 5, 1923, p. 6; June 2, 1923, p. 7. On students and labor, see *The New Student,* October 6, 1923, p. 5; November 17, 1923, pp. 6–7; January 5, 1924, p. 5; and especially Paul Blanshard of the SLID, "Facing Toward Labor," January 19, 1924, p. 2, versus J. E. Ozanne, "Labor's Tyranny over Thinkers," January 19, 1924, pp. 2–3; on the role of big business in higher education, see *The Student Conference at Hartsdale, N.Y., December 26–29, 1922,* supplement to *The New Student,* January 13, 1923.

Harding and Coolidge." At Amherst, Parsons chaired his college chapter of the Student League for Industrial Democracy.[27]

Parsons was a child of Progressivism in both a familial and educational sense. From all corners he was inculcated with belief in the unity of "knowledge, responsibility, and reform" as James Kloppenberg defined the essence of Progressive doctrine. Paramount in his Amherst education, Parsons and his friend Cutler declared in 1923, was the lesson "that the economic and social order was a matter of human arrangements, not one of inevitable natural law, and hence that it was subject to human control."[28] He was also heir to the contradictions implicit in the Progressive mentality. Combining piety and intellect, Amherst was perfectly constituted to reflect the affiliation and tension of two principles that historian Daniel Rodgers has distinguished as hallmarks of Progressive-era thought: the moral idealism inherent in the new notion of "social bonds," and the instrumental rationality promoted under the rubric of "social efficiency."[29]

All three of the major Amherst influences on young Parsons – Alexander Meiklejohn and his allies Walton Hamilton and Clarence Ayres – were critics of capitalism, Meiklejohn from a communitarian standpoint rooted in Scottish moral philosophy and the institutionalists from a standpoint derived from Thorstein Veblen's critique of economic dogma. All three recognized the reality of "social bonds," at least insofar as they shared the theoretical premise that all aspects of social life were knit together, "interdependent" or "organically" combined.[30] The institutionalists embraced a kind of organicism when they criticized the orthodox economists' artificial and one-sided emphasis on the profit-maximizing behavior of individuals, proposing instead to study "the whole economic life process" in which cultural practices and social organizations shaped the conduct of pro-

[27] Letter, TP to Harry Laidler, September 8, 1958, Harry Laidler Papers, Tamiment Library, New York University; "Student Economists – An Adventure in 'Workers Education,' " *The New Student,* March 15, 1924, p. 3; TP, "Clarence Ayres's Economics and Sociology," in William Breit and William Patton Culbertson, Jr., eds. *Science and Ceremony: The Institutional Economics of C. E. Ayres* (Austin: University of Texas Press, 1976), p. 176.

[28] Cutler and Parsons, "A Word from Amherst Students," p. 6.

[29] Daniel T. Rodgers, "In Search of Progressivism," *Reviews in American History* 10 (1982): 123–27.

[30] On concepts of interdependence and organicism, see Thomas L. Haskell, *The Emergence of Professional Social Science;* Morton White, *Social Thought in America;* James T. Kloppenberg, *Uncertain Victory.*

ductive (and unproductive) activity. As a communitarian philosopher who strove to foster union among his students as a single body, Meiklejohn promoted a notion of social bonds with a more distinctly moralist flavor. A philosophical idealist, he defined community as a body founded on the centrality of shared moral ideas, and he promoted general education courses in the hope of providing students with a common experience of ethical discourse countering capitalism's tendency to erode the collective, public experience of politics.[31] His communitarian moralism fit at best uncomfortably with the cold instrumental rationalism of the institutionalists, who had difficulty admitting a place in modern society for motivations other than the pursuit of productive efficiency.

Young Parsons was drawn to both parties. Though not noticeably devout, he had learned enough from his father to embrace moral idealism and consider religious belief and motive a signal element of human experience. On the other hand, he also freely adopted the institutionalist style of argument, distinguishing as Ayres did between "technological" and "ceremonial" aspects of social behavior and treating the latter dismissively for the most part, as the province of "leisure class motives . . . with no rational justification."[32] Parsons did not, however, appear content to leave matters there, for even in his college papers of 1923 there were hints of an attempt to adjudicate the rationalist and moralist positions. Writing for Ayres, Parsons added to the "technological"–"ceremonial" dichotomy a third sphere of social behavior he called "institutional," where compromises among individuals' interests were arranged in order to smooth social interaction. In the rough, something of Parsons's mature perspective was already apparent, for in the strain between moral idealism and instrumental rationality – between religion and science, piety and intellect at Amherst – there appeared the conflict of idealism and posi-

[31] Jones and Smith, eds., *Against the Current,* pp. 299–300; Gerald Grant and David Riesman, *The Perpetual Dream: Reform and Experiment in the American College* (Chicago: University of Chicago Press, 1978), pp. 43–50, 291n; Levine, *The American College and the Culture of Aspiration,* pp. 96, 106, 160.

[32] Clarence E. Ayres, *The Theory of Economic Progress* (Chapel Hill: University of North Carolina Press, 1944), pp. 89–102; TP, "A Behavioristic Conception of the Nature of Morals," PP, section 42.8.2, box 2. Parsons's remark on "leisure class motives" appears in a discussion of esthetics, where he adopted the point of view Ayres had maintained in a series of highly publicized campus debates with the classicist Walter R. Agard. See *Amherst Student,* January 18, 1923, and January 25, 1923.

tivism that his great treatise *The Structure of Social Action* was dedicated to resolve.[33]

When Parsons set off in 1924 for a year of study at the London School of Economics (LSE), his Amherst teachers provided him with introductions to the preeminent social-democratic intellectuals there, Harold Laski and R. H. Tawney.[34] According to a friend he met in Vienna during the summer of 1925, Parsons was then a socialist. During the next year (1925–26), he studied at the most liberal of German universities, Heidelberg, where he knew Karl Mannheim and studied Marxism with Emil Lederer, one of the few Social Democratic Party intellectuals in the German academy and a pioneer in the sociological analysis of the modern "white collar" class. Under the direction of Edgar Salin, a popular lecturer who edited the papers of Friedrich List, founder of German historical economics, Parsons wrote a doctoral dissertation on Werner Sombart's and Max Weber's theories of capitalism.[35] When he completed the dissertation in the summer of 1927, the agenda for his first major study project was all but determined, bound to issue ten years later in his *Structure of Social Action.*

The agenda of 1927

Parsons commenced his professional academic career in the fall of 1927 by moving to Harvard and taking a post as instructor in the Economics Department renowned nationwide as the citadel of economic orthodoxy in the United States. He had spent the preceding academic year teaching economics and sociology at Amherst, sandwiched between his studies at Heidelberg and his return to Germany in the summer of 1927 to defend his dissertation. Amherst had

[33] The central problems of *The Structure of Social Action* were those of rationality and order. Parsons asked what role in social behavior should be accorded to instrumental reason and to nonrational motivations and how one might account for the existence of societies as ongoing processes of human action. The two issues melded into one. While treating rational action as an ideal norm and the starting point for a complex schema of types of action, Parsons argued in *The Structure of Social Action* that social order was inconceivable if one ascribed only instrumentally rational motivations to human actors.

[34] Letter, John M Gaus to TP, June 21, 1924, PP, section 42.8.2, box 2.

[35] F. M. Godfrey, "The Salin Festschrift," *Contemporary Review* (November 1962): 250–51. See also Herman Lebovics, *Social Conservatism and the Middle Classes in Germany 1914–1933* (Princeton, N.J.: Princeton University Press, 1969), pp. 79–108.

changed since his college days there, having brought Richard Meriam, a young Harvard-trained economist, to campus to replace the departed institutionalists. It was Meriam who suggested to Parsons that he needed to learn formal economics and that Harvard would be a good place to do it. Having just encountered the work of Weber, whose neo-Kantian methodology sustained a critique of German historical economics and a justification of formal economic theory, Parsons was inclined to take the advice. This impetus to move away from the institutionalist school came at a time when Veblen's reputation was declining, since his theses on business restrictionism seemed outmoded by unprecedented prosperity and the beginnings of mass distribution of durable consumer goods.[36] Once at Harvard, furthermore, Parsons found two resident authorities, Alfred North Whitehead and the physiologist L. J. Henderson, whose critical philosophy of science seemed to challenge the institutionalists' arguments against orthodox economic theory. The empiricism of the institutionalists – their critique of economic theory as unrealistic and their intention to build by observation and description a truer vision of "the economic life-process as a whole" – now appeared naive. Whitehead's strictures against "misplaced concreteness" in interpreting scientific theory, and Henderson's insistence that the definition of "fact" depended on the theory that framed it, seconded Weber's ideas about the necessary role of abstraction in scientific reasoning, the selectivity of observation, and the inevitable artificiality of scientific models that ought not be simply identified with empirical reality.[37] Consequently, Parsons turned to defend the scientific validity of orthodox economics, at least if it were treated as an abstract conceptual scheme that was frankly artificial in extracting only one element (rational economizing action) from the complexity of social process. For the sake of analysis, then, aspects of behavior other than rational economizing action could be abstracted from the concrete social whole and studied by other, complementary social sciences.[38]

[36] Joseph Dorfman, *Thorstein Veblen and His America* (New York: Viking Press, 1934), p. 499. Needless to say, those theses were to regain enormous influence in the Depression decade.

[37] Whitehead, a recent arrival on the Harvard faculty, had published *Science and the Modern World* (1925), then enjoying great popularity in liberal student circles for its attempt to heal the rift between spiritual and scientific ideas.

[38] The argument was laid out in a series of articles on the relations between economics and sociology: TP, "Wants and Activities in Marshall," *Quarterly Journal of Econom-*

Parsons's institutionalist heritage remained strong enough, however, to color his first professional publications. In two articles of 1928 and 1929, drawn from his German dissertation on the concept of capitalism in the work of Sombart and Weber, Parsons criticized "Anglo-American economic thought" for failing to recognize the historical specificity of capitalism as an integral social whole, something Parsons said German theorists from Marx onward had grasped. Furthermore, in probing Sombart's and Weber's notions of organicism or systemic order in capitalism, Parsons was able to reflect on problems of social reform that had arisen in his early education. Both Sombart and Weber, Parsons wrote, concurred with Marx in seeing capitalism as a compulsive system that exerted force over individuals regardless of their intentions and wishes, and it was precisely the systemic character of its institutional structure which demanded that any imaginable social reform be radical – or as Parsons put it, not mere "tinkering with some parts independently of others."[39]

Still, Parsons judged, any theory that took the organic principle to extremes would lead to conservative pessimism, unable to propose a way of breaking the bounds of a fully integrated capitalist order; always more an optimist than his German mentors, Parsons chose to preserve the possibility of reform by emphasizing lines of continuous development from one social order to another:

> There seems to be little reason to believe that it is not possible on the basis which we now have to build by a continuous process something more nearly approaching an ideal society. . . . *In the transition from capitalism to a different social system surely many elements of the present would be built into the new order.*[40]

Though this passage was aimed against Sombart in particular, Parsons's optimistic and progressive dissent applied to Weber as well. The "analytical" logic that allowed Weber to accept the validity of

ics 46 (1931): 101–40; "Economics and Sociology: Marshall in Relation to the Thought of His Time," *Quarterly Journal of Economics* 46 (1932): 316–47; "Some Reflections on 'The Nature and Significance of Economics,' " *Quarterly Journal of Economics* 48 (1934): 511–45; "Sociological Elements in Economic Thought, I. Historical," *Quarterly Journal of Economics* 49 (May 1935): 414–53; "Sociological Elements in Economic Thought, II. The Analytical Factor View," *Quarterly Journal of Economics* 49 (August 1935): 646–67.

39 TP, " 'Capitalism' in Recent German Literature: Sombart and Weber," *Journal of Political Economy* 36 (December 1928): 652–53, 658–59.

40 Ibid., p. 653, emphasis added.

formal economics served to help Parsons in turn draw modernity out of Weber's iron cage. According to Parsons, Weber's cultural despair was rooted in an "empiricist" error of identifying the *element* of bureaucratic rationality in contemporary society with the whole of social order, thus painting a false picture of modern ossification.[41]

In the coming years, Parsons would find ways of both reading Weber in a progressive light and framing progressive reform in a Weberian light. The Weberian premises most important to Parsons were the insistence on studying society "from the subjective point of view" (or in terms of the motives guiding action) and the neo-Kantian emphasis on the role of theory in structuring scientific observation. The first premise led Parsons to conclude that although individual behavior was subject to "systemic" constraints, those trans-individual constraints had to be understood in terms of internal, subjective regulation of motives rather than objective, outer compulsion: understanding *motivation* was thus the heart of sociological inquiry. The second encouraged Parsons to focus his attention on abstract, conceptual issues in social science. Thus, he recalled years later, completion of his dissertation in 1927 led him to turn "from the idea of 'capitalism' as a socio-economic system, to that of the relations between economic theory and the theory of the social system."[42] Despite Parsons's neo-Kantian claim to be absorbed in pure theory, however, a sensitive reading of all his writings from 1927 to 1937 can elucidate the connections in Parsons's mind between the concept of capitalism, the status of economic theory, and the problem of motivation – and show, consequently, how practical political and moral imperatives continued to guide his work through the 1930s.

After publishing parts of his dissertation and his translation of Weber's *Protestant Ethic and the Spirit of Capitalism* (1930), Parsons began a detailed study of the English economist Alfred Marshall, pioneer of marginalist theory and founder of contemporary economic orthodoxy. Parsons's essays in 1930 and 1931 gave a sympathetic

[41] TP, " 'Capitalism' in Recent German Literature: Sombart and Weber – Concluded," *Journal of Political Economy* 37 (1929): 33–36, 48–50. Leon Mayhew stresses Parsons's lifelong inclination to defend modern society as such and the process of continuous development within its structural framework, in the Introduction to *Talcott Parsons on Institutions and Social Evolution* (Chicago: University of Chicago Press, 1982), pp. 61–62.

[42] "The Circumstances of My Encounter with Max Weber," paper presented to Eastern Sociological Association, Philadelphia, April 1, 1978, in PP, section 15.75.

portrait of Marshall, leading his former Amherst mentor Walton Hamilton to charge him with "apostasy" and "quietism."[43] Though his solicitude for formal economics might have appeared to be a *volte-face,* Parsons's new start at Harvard should be seen rather as a turning point, where interests and concerns surviving from his earliest intellectual and political dispositions were translated into new terms that set an agenda for a long effort. As he strove to uncover those lines of continuous development that promised to bring modern society beyond capitalism to a "new order," he embarked on a ten-year theoretical project aimed at legitimating new, socially constituted motivations suited to a collectivized, postcapitalist order in which economic theory might serve as an instrumental means to meaningful ends. *The Structure of Social Action* ought to be understood as the by-product and culmination of that reformist project.

Reading *The Structure of Social Action*

Certainly the tone of *The Structure of Social Action* betrayed little of the empirical interests in contemporary capitalism and dynamics of social change that characterized Parsons's college years and his Sombart–Weber articles. Posed as a study of the "immanent" development of social-scientific theory over the preceding half century, *The Structure of Social Action* tried to demonstrate how the works of otherwise disparate figures – Alfred Marshall, Vilfredo Pareto, Emile Durkheim, and Max Weber – showed incipient features of a common "voluntaristic theory of action," which would – when fully fleshed out – successfully mediate the tension between positivism and idealism in sociological theory while resolving as well other profound empirical, epistemological, and methodological problems.

The Structure of Social Action identified scientific development with the emergence of a paradigm, where agreement among a community of practitioners on a single framework of basic questions or concepts serves to "found" a science, in this case, sociology.[44] Although Parsons described a gradual, evolutionary drift toward a new formula

[43] Letters, Walton Hamilton to Parsons, December 11, 1931, and June 10, 1932, PP, section 42.8.2, box 2.

[44] This paragraph examines Parsons's book roughly in terms of the model of theoretical development in science offered in Thomas Kuhn, *The Structure of Scientific Revolutions* (Chicago: University of Chicago Press, 1962).

or "frame of reference" for social thought, thus dulling the sharpness of the paradigmatic break Thomas Kuhn says marks a scientific revolution, Parsons clearly thought he was recording a theoretical development that had revolutionary import in his field. For Parsons, the obsolete paradigm of prior social thought, the "utilitarian theory of action," foundered on a particular empirical problem – the explanation of social order – which the emergent theory of voluntarism promised to overcome.

From Hobbes through Locke, the tradition that Parsons named utilitarian explained the order (or stability and continuity) of society by reference to a superior sovereign authority or a foundational natural reason. Both factors lay outside society as such and both contradicted other important presuppositions of utilitarian theory, namely that individuals are motivated to pursue ends that are in principle independent of (i.e., have no necessary relation to) the ends of others. Pushed further to account for social action in its entirety – including the question of how actors' goals are determined – utilitarian thought proved its "positivist" bent, Parsons explained: it assumed that humans acted either "rationally," in adapting to their environment, or lawfully, according to instinctual patterns of behavior. In either case – rational adaptation or instinctual drives – the ends that humans pursued were collapsed into the *conditions* of action, appearing as something given rather than something chosen by an actor. Defining "action" schematically in terms of four elements – given conditions, the ends actors pursued, the means they used, and the norms that determined how they chose the means of action – Parsons sought a theory of social action that preserved all these essential elements in their integrity, granting each a degree of independence and resisting any kind of reductionism that would define social elements in naturalistic terms. Here Parsons broached a distinctly *theoretical* problem, in addition to the empirical problem of explaining social order.[45]

In addition to these empirical and theoretical problems, *The Structure of Social Action* insistently probed related issues of a methodological and epistemological character. The methodological problem focused on how to define the object, society, considering the conflict of nominalism and sociologism that had long troubled attempts to

[45] TP, *The Structure of Social Action: A Study in Social Theory with Special Reference to a Group of Recent European Writers* (New York: Free Press, 1968), pp. 43–125.

found sociology as a science: Was "society" only a conventional abstraction referring to the interaction of concrete individuals who are the sole real components of social existence, or was society a substantive reality unto itself – sui generis – apart from constituent individuals?[46] Parsons's *epistemological* problem – the need to escape the quandary posed by the alternative of empiricism and skepticism – emerged in a lengthy discussion of Durkheim's frustrated attempts to define the "social element" in terms suited to scientific norms of objective observation. Assuming that the "facts" available to scientific observation were, as objects, exterior to human minds, Durkheim first assumed that the "social element" could be observed in the regulations imposed (by law or other means of control) on individuals from the outside. Dissatisfied with that Hobbesian approach, but still insistent on a standard of exteriority, Durkheim sought the "social element" in collective ideas, though by imagining them to lie outside individual minds he was committed to an idealist position that invested ideas themselves with a metaphysical reality. Finally, the empiricist standard of objective observation itself had to be challenged. In his late work, Durkheim argued that sciences could not account for their knowledge without reference to prior mental categories that organize observational data – and that those categories were given not in the nature of mind but by the form of social experience. Consequently, however, Durkheim adopted a "sociological epistemology" – basic categories of perception varied from society to society – that implied complete relativism and denied objective validity to all knowledge. Parsons asked, then, how could one escape empiricism without collapsing into thorough skepticism?[47]

Parsons described the "voluntaristic theory of action" he championed as one that resolved these fundamental problems, giving a compelling account of social order while mediating and surpassing both positivism and idealism. The voluntaristic theory depicted society in the form of "systems of action," or a complex interweaving of "action chains" (sequences of means and ends, elements of which might be considered alternatively products of past actions or ingredients of future actions). Many actors, each initiating a plurality of acts, were drawn together in mutual relations by their participation in these

[46] Ibid., pp. 74, 248.
[47] Ibid., pp. 364–443.

woven chains, where one person's end was another one's means. This web of action, as it were, was rooted on one end in nature (those ultimate conditions and means that were not in turn ends of prior human action) and tied together at the other end in culture (those ultimate ends and norms that were not merely means to other projects). Social order in this scheme was thus understood in terms of the stitching that kept the web from unraveling: For Parsons, it lay in a system of "ultimate ends" legitimated by values held commonly by all actors in a society. This phenomenon at the top of the web, which Parsons called "common-value integration," in some sense, then, enabled social action at all lower levels.

Parsons claimed that positivistic theories focused one-sidedly on conditions and means (nature) whereas idealistic theories focused one-sidedly on ends and norms (culture). While Parsons's voluntaristic sociology provided an immanent explanation of social order, relying on no extrasocial source of integration (in sovereign power or natural harmony), it avoided, he claimed, both positivistic and idealistic extremes by analyzing social action insofar as it was structured by shared values. In Parsons's mind, this approach was distinct from a study of values in and of themselves, for such a study would focus on culture alone.[48]

There is a striking dialectical form to Parsons's argument throughout *The Structure of Social Action.* Not only did the voluntaristic theory mediate and surpass positivism and idealism; it also went beyond both the methodological dichotomy of nominalism and sociologism and the epistemological dichotomy of empiricism and skepticism. Understood as an analytical abstraction from, rather than empirical reflection of, an infinitely complex concrete reality, "society" was neither nominal nor reified; rather, as the *aspect* of action systems that grants them coherence via common values, it was a "real" part of human experience without appearing as a discrete entity in itself. As for epistemology, Parsons responded to the danger of corrosive skepticism arising from antiempiricism by providing a neo-Kantian justification for the validity of the voluntaristic theory itself. Ultimately, the voluntaristic theory was proven valid not by empirical means but by reference to prior intersubjective principles of under-

[48] Ibid., p. 768.

standing. As Parsons scholar Harold Bershady has pointed out, Parsons rested the case for voluntarism on the grounds that *it alone* elaborated the "action schema" (the combination of conditions, means, ends, and norms) in a *logically complete* way, while the "action schema" itself constituted the necessary, conditional framework for any knowledge of society at all, serving a purpose, Parsons wrote, "analogous to [that of] the space–time framework of physics."[49]

This reading of *The Structure of Social Action* remains on an abstract and formal plane, but there is another way of looking at Parsons's argument that reveals its practical content. Examined rhetorically, Parsons's argument resembled contemporary forms of (predominantly left-wing) political argument. As already indicated, Parsons opened his book with a critique of the "utilitarian theory of action," his name for the dominant preexisting current of Anglo-American social thought. Sociologist Charles Camic has pointed out how inadequate Parsons's portrait was as a descriptive history of utilitarian philosophy per se, but this criticism almost misses the point of Parsons's discussion: Essentially, the "utilitarian theory" served Parsons as a rarefied version of liberal market theory and his criticism of it stood as a more sophisticated recapitulation of the institutionalist attack on economic orthodoxy.[50] For Parsons, "utilitarianism" was the theory of *homo economicus:* It treated actors as atomic individuals, treated their ends as exogenous factors (varying "randomly"), and assumed that the only norm they used for selecting means of action was that of rational efficiency. Besides being inadequate to explain social affairs, Parsons suggested, this theory was also decadent, tending to devolve into debased forms (various kinds of "radical positivism" explaining action in terms of instinctual drives or rational adaptation to given conditions) that violated its founding principles of human freedom. In this respect Parsons's rhetoric uncannily evoked that of left-wing polemics on the crisis of capitalism in the mid-1930s. Parsons's terms in the early pages of *The Structure of Social Action* look almost like code when set alongside the left-wing trope that described the collapse of capitalism, the looming threat of fascist

[49] Ibid., p. 733. Harold Bershady, *Ideology and Social Knowledge* (New York: Wiley, 1973).

[50] Parsons states that the utilitarian system has been "clearly worked out" in "the modern economic doctrine of utility." *Structure of Social Action,* p. 60.

regimentation based on reactionary appeals to "blood and soil," and the need to avert that fate by commencing socialist reforms. Parsons described "the inherent instability of the utilitarian system" and showed how it "breaks down," devolving into a "mechanistic determinism" that explains human action solely in terms of "heredity and environment." To avoid that theoretical fate, Parsons urged a move in the "opposite direction" – away from biological reductionism to reaffirm the role of reason and the possibility of freedom – by "radically revising" the utilitarian system's "whole framework."[51] Exchange the word "utilitarianism" for "capitalism" and the discussion resembles a common left-wing tract for socialist reform as the key to preserving the liberal tradition.[52]

Talcott Parsons was far from being a revolutionary socialist, although he might very well have qualified as a reformist social democrat. In any case, it is clear Parsons believed he was living in revolutionary times. An unpublished paper of 1932 asked impatiently, "Is the stability and permanence of the present politico-economic regime to go entirely unquestioned?" Similar sentiments marked the opening pages of *The Structure of Social Action,* where Parsons wrote, "Is it not possible that the future holds in store something other than 'bigger and better' industrialism . . . that instead of this, contemporary society is at or near a turning point . . .[?]"[53] It is striking, however, how little the body of the book, at least on the surface, related to such immediate practical concerns of politics and social change. One might ask why Parsons so quickly fled the question of contemporary dynamic change raised in the book's first pages. Furthermore, what connection might be drawn at a deeper level between the abstract theoretical argumentation and those concrete, practical questions that played some role in sparking Parsons's reflections? In asking such questions I have supposed that Parsons had motives larger in

[51] *Structure of Social Action,* pp. 99–100, 102, 114, 120–22, 165–67.

[52] The typical form of left-wing warning was manifested, for instance, in the 1932 manifesto of the League of Professional Groups for Foster and Ford, but this structure of argument characterized a broader stream of left-wing intellectuals than those who flocked to the Communist Party as either members or fellow travelers. To some extent, John Dewey's political books of the 1930s, *Liberalism and Social Action* and *Freedom and Culture,* made similar arguments about the need for economic collectivism to avert the worst consequences of capitalist instability.

[53] TP, "Pareto and the Problems of Positivistic Sociology," PP, p. II-III-35; *Structure of Social Action,* p. 4.

scope than a purely professional concern with elaborating the most general theoretical foundations of his discipline.[54] Parsons seems to have taken for granted a basic trend of modern social evolution – that capitalist society was yielding to something much more collectivist in form – and to have assumed, consequently, that the most significant remaining social problem was a moral one. In effect, *The Structure of Social Action* posed this question: In a society ideologically so dependent on the liberal (utilitarian) tradition, what resources are available to morally justify individuals' acceptance of and commitment to new collective forms of political economy? To see how the book may be understood as a reflection on this question, however, it is necessary to go outside the book itself to a series of articles and unpublished documents Parsons composed over the years during which his book took shape.

Morality and economics

The problem Parsons saw in relating morality and economics can be highlighted by contrasting two significant articles he published in the early and middle 1930s. His 1933 essay "Service," in the *Encyclopedia of the Social Sciences,* joined the Weberian notion of secularization with a kind of social-Christian critique of capitalism, arguing that "the individualistic economic developments of early modern times" had eroded "ethical sanctions of service" and left no doctrines extant with "the power of justifying to the individual a real submergence of his self-interest."[55] Two years later, though, another essay suggested an entirely different use of Weber. Reviewing the work of British economic historian H. M. Robertson, Parsons claimed Weber had shown that capitalism could not be understood as "economic individualism" at all, or as the "pursuit of self-interest" unfettered by moral restraint. Rather, capitalism had arisen because "stringent ethical control" was applied in new ways to economic behavior. And Parsons added, "the element of positive ethical value" Weber discovered at

[54] For an interpretation of *The Structure of Social Action* as solely motivated by professional disciplinary concerns, see Charles Camic, "*Structure* After 50 Years: The Anatomy of a Charter," *American Journal of Sociology* 95 (July 1989): 38–107.

[55] TP, "Service," *Encyclopedia of the Social Sciences,* vol. 13 (1933), pp. 672–74.

the *origin* of capitalism "remained and still remains as a basic element in the modern economic order."[56]

In between these two articles – in the years 1933 and 1934 – Parsons had studied the work of Emile Durkheim intensively, and this encounter might explain the new way he dealt with Weber's work in response to Robertson.[57] For Parsons, Durkheim had illustrated the so-called noncontractual bases of contract (the shared norms necessary for people to enter into contract to begin with) and thus refuted the utilitarian individualism of classic liberal theory by demonstrating the existence of a common ethical element in social interaction. Furthermore, Durkheim suggested that even individualism was a moral postulate held collectively, to be distinguished from *anomie* or loss of moral regulation per se. From these premises, Parsons concluded that the social-Christian or ethical-socialist view of contemporary market society – an amoral cutthroat world corrosive of social bonds – accepted as fact (while condemning on principle) the mistaken liberal assumption that modern societies consisted of atomized individuals. On the contrary, Parsons insisted, contemporary society had a moral element, a communal dimension, and that element was nothing other than Weber's calling (*Beruf*) – or, depending on your translation, *profession*. With Durkheim's help, then, Parsons turned Weber on his head: instead of *der Beruf* stimulating economic action that ultimately undermined its own initial ethical imperatives, the professional commitment implied in the Calvinist calling in fact survived, perhaps providing a means of controlling (or even superseding) the economic individualism of the marketplace.

Parsons's reversal of opinion on the validity of one of the most common ethical critiques of capitalism was not intended to rehabilitate the moral repute of contemporary capitalism as such. His reversal on the validity of the institutionalist assault on economic orthodoxy should be understood similarly. Accepting the scientific status of orthodox economics did not commit Parsons to justifying capitalist social relations. These he still insisted were historically relative. In a

[56] TP, "H. M. Robertson on Max Weber and His School," *Journal of Political Economy* 43 (October 1935): 688–96.

[57] See Parsons, "Revisiting the Classics Throughout a Long Career," in Buford Rhea, ed., *The Future of the Sociological Classics* (Boston: Allen & Unwin, 1981), pp. 183–94, and "A Short Account of My Intellectual Development," pp. 1–12.

1930 draft essay on Alfred Marshall, the prevailing theorist of orthodoxy in Anglo-American economics, Parsons set out to prove that Marshall's advocacy of "laissez-faire" (a phrase Parsons used by then as a kind of code word for capitalism) was not logically entailed in Marshall's economic theory per se; Parsons repeated the point in a 1936 essay that attacked certain unnamed "dogmatists" for wedding economic theory to "defense of a particular empirical social order." (Almost certainly Parsons had in mind the antisocialist arguments of F. A. Hayek and Ludwig von Mises, whose *Collectivist Economic Planning* had appeared the year before.)[58] Parsons considered most economists to be as naively empiricist as the institutionalists, and he consistently challenged the reification that would construe orthodox abstractions of economic man, rational motivation, and optimal efficiency as real descriptions of actual social life.[59] In fact, taken by themselves, the descriptive judgments that institutional economists made of the American economy – namely, the steady growth of business concentration that rendered the old liberal idea of thrifty, competitive individualists hopelessly obsolete – were unobjectionable, Parsons found.[60]

Thus, in a 1934 article on conservative British economist Lionel Robbins, Parsons asserted that economic laws were to be understood not as faithful descriptions of necessary connections among existing social facts but, rather, as logical propositions bearing a conditional character: *If* one strove toward efficiency, the laws formulated the means toward it. In this sense, he indicated, economics like all social

[58] See TP, "Outline of a Study on the Sociological Background of Alfred Marshall's Economic Theory" and "Marshall and Laissez-Faire: A Sociological Study" (typescript), PP, section 42.45.4, box 11, pp. 1–6. In the draft, "Marshall and Laissez Faire: A Sociological Study," Parsons refers on p. 4 to "laissez faire, or free enterprise as he [Marshall] calls it," and on p. 79 to "the system of capitalism or free enterprise." From the published version of this piece, Parsons dropped the term "capitalism" altogether except to contrast Marx's concept of it to Marshall's definition of "free enterprise." See TP, "Wants and Activities," p. 127n. TP, "On Certain Sociological Elements in Professor Taussig's Thought," in *Explorations in Economics: Notes and Essays Contributed in Honor of F. W. Taussig*, ed. Jacob Viner (New York: McGraw-Hill, 1936), pp. 363–64. *Collectivist Economic Planning: Critical Studies on the Possibilities of Socialism*, ed. F. A. Hayek (London: Routledge & Kegan Paul), had appeared in 1935.

[59] See, for instance, Parsons's review of *Economics and Sociology*, by Adolf Lowe, *American Journal of Sociology* 42 (1937): 477.

[60] See, for instance, Parsons's essay, "Thrift," in *Encyclopedia of the Social Sciences*, vol. 14 (1934), pp. 623–26, and "Outline of a Study on the Sociological Background of Alfred Marshall's Economic Theory."

science assumed a purposive standpoint.[61] Formally, his argument resembled that of the market socialists, professional economists like Oskar Lange, Abba Lerner, and H. D. Dickinson, who sought in the mid-1930s to drive a wedge between what they considered the scientific price theory of neoclassical economics and capitalist society: The latter, because of its vast wastefulness, did not operate in an "economic" fashion at all, and the former, they asserted, could serve as a tool of planning in a collectivist regime.[62] This formal similarity does not indicate, in itself, that Parsons advocated a full-scale socialist economic plan, but it does suggest that he occupied a discursive universe, one of neoclassical economics on the eve of the Keynesian revolution, in which free-market principles had given way to various theories of macroeconomic management, ranging from A. C. Pigou's welfare economics to Lange's market socialism. Parsons's personal files included a bibliography of all the major works of the 1930s on market socialism, suggesting that he was at least familiar with this body of thought.[63]

Parsons's reformist interests emerged in an unusually clear form in the 1936 article in which he attacked the so-called economic dogmatists. In that essay, a critical appreciation of Harvard economist and dean of American orthodoxy Frank Taussig, Parsons rejected the view that monetary incentive was the sole motive of social action or even the prime mover of economic growth. Weber had shown, Parsons argued, that the early bourgeois were driven not by egoism but by "disinterested" ethical concerns (that is, Puritan concerns over election and proof) – a fact suggesting that new moral motivations

[61] "Some Reflections on 'The Nature and Significance of Economics,' " p. 540.

[62] The key statement of "market socialist" principles, Oskar Lange's "On the Economic Theory of Socialism," a direct response to *Collectivist Economic Planning,* appeared in *Review of Economic Studies* 4 (1936–37). Lange's essay was reprinted in Oskar Lange and Fred M. Taylor, *On the Economic Theory of Socialism,* ed. Benjamin E. Lippincott (Minneapolis: University of Minnesota Press, 1938). See also H. D. Dickinson, "Price Formation in a Socialist Community," *Economic Journal* 43 (June 1933); A. P. Lerner, "Economic Theory and Socialist Economy," *Review of Economic Studies* 2 (October 1934); "A Note on Socialist Economics," *Review of Economic Studies* 4 (October 1936); and "Statics and Dynamics in Socialist Economics," *Economic Journal* 47 (June 1937).

[63] In the festschrift for Frank Taussig, *Explorations in Economics* (New York: McGraw-Hill, 1936), Parsons was responsible for editing the section called "The Social Setting of Economic Activity," which featured an essay by Alan R. Sweezy, "The Economist in a Socialist Economy," citing the work of Dickinson, Lange, and Lerner.

might emerge in lieu of pure monetary incentive to drive economic activity just as effectively. Thus Parsons found no reason to conclude that equalizing income would necessarily degrade work motivations or innovation. He added:

> In so far as money income has become, as is largely the fact in our society, the dominant symbol of achievement and social status, the explanation is not to be looked for in any intrinsic nature of economic motivation, which if interfered with will bring disaster [as the dogmatists had suggested], but in what may roughly be called 'institutional' causes *which are historically variable.*[64]

Thus framed by a debate with free-market dogmatists, the question of economic motivation was tied closely to issues of social reform, particularly the feasibility of collectivism. To be sure, Parsons strove for a tone of objectivity and impersonality, which required him to soft-pedal or obscure expressions of practical motivation in his writing, always maintaining the aim of building a value-free science. In the Taussig article, Parsons presumed only to raise the question of economic motivation and the feasibility of collectivism – to be resolved, he said, by further scientific work. He added, however, that a key to answering the question was "an explicit analytical theory of human motivation."[65] Insofar as such a theory was a goal of *The Structure of Social Action,* his own work in progress, it is plausible to infer that Parsons saw the construction of his work in relation to pressing problems of social reform, namely, the possibility of new kinds of motivations for economic activity in a nonindividualistic system where profit drives no longer held unchallenged primacy. It is possible, also, to see how his focus on economic motivation provided Parsons with a peculiarly Weberian "action" perspective on the problem of social-democratic change – that is, a focus on the social construction of motivations vis-à-vis economic activity in a dawning collectivist order.

Although Parsons did not explicitly present this problem as the unifying theme of *The Structure of Social Action,* hints of it appeared in a research study of the medical profession Parsons began in 1934 and

[64] TP, "On Certain Sociological Elements in Professor Taussig's Thought," pp. 377–78, emphasis added. The fact that the burden of Parsons's piece in the Taussig festschrift was merely to affirm the *possibility* of collectivist reform suggests he was responding to Hayek and von Mises, who sought to deny it.

[65] Ibid., p. 378.

carried on as he completed the book. Parsons never completed the program of field work he initially intended to serve as the empirical basis of this research study, but some of his reflections on medical practice informed articles of the time, particularly "Education and the Professions" (1937), "The Professions and Social Structure" (1939), and "The Motivation of Economic Activities" (1940).[66] Throughout, the professions provided a model of motivations, not exclusively self-interested or based on expectations of monetary reward, that sustained a high level of productive activity and social service. The fact that Parsons later recalled the original medical study as a "crucial experiment" for the sociological theory elaborated in *The Structure of Social Action* is further evidence for the argument that the problem of economic motivation, along with the reformist issues it raised, can be considered to be implicitly at the core of that book.[67]

Capitalism, the professions, and social reform

The place of the professions in Parsons's theoretical and practical agenda must be understood in terms of the meaning he gave to the concept of "institutions," the proper subject, he believed, of sociological inquiry. His theory of institutions was cast in a distinctly Durkheimian mold, not only because he based his definition of institutions on Durkheim's sharp dichotomy between collective, moral factors and individual, instrumental factors but also because he, like Durkheim, considered professions (or "occupational groups") as one of the central "institutional" forms of social solidarity in modern life and hence the fulcrum of a social reform strategy.[68] In his unpublished 1935 paper, "Prolegomena to a Theory of Institutions," Parsons defined "institutions" as those social arrangements regulating human action *primarily* by the force of moral commitment rather than by

66 "Remarks on Education and the Professions," *International Journal of Ethics* 47 (1937): 365–69; "The Professions and Social Structure," *Social Forces* 17 (1939): 457–67; "The Motivation of Economic Activities," *Canadian Journal of Economics and Political Science* 6 (1940): 187–203.

67 Parsons referred to his unfinished study of the medical profession as a "crucial experiment," in "A Short Account of My Intellectual Development," p. 9.

68 Steven Lukes, *Emile Durkheim, His Life and Work* (Stanford, Calif.: Stanford University Press, 1985), pp. 16–24, and Jeffrey C. Alexander, *Theoretical Logic in Sociology, vol. 2: The Antinomies of Classical Thought: Marx and Durkheim* (Berkeley: University of California Press, 1982), pp. 75–160, 211–96.

positive or negative sanctions appealing to self-interest. He did not doubt that utilitarian considerations naturally arose as "secondary" supports for institutionalized behavior, and among these secondary supports he counted specifically "political" measures, defined as such by their reliance on coercive power. But all these secondary supports would prove bankrupt, he wrote, should "moral attachment . . . dissolve away."[69] This argument was telling, for at a time when dramatic social reform was usually identified with expanding the capacity of the state to intervene in and manage economic affairs, Parsons cast doubt on the efficacy of purely "political" measures of control. Since "political" measures depended for their efficacy on a preexisting moral bond secured in social institutions, the real locus of reform lay not in the state but in civil society. Although such arguments could be considered hostile to the contemporary direction of social change, it is more plausible to see in them this claim: Only in civil society could new institutions, a source of moral renovation, provide the necessary *foundation* for mounting tendencies toward establishment of some kind of planning regime.

Parsons's 1934 prospectus for his research study of the medical profession reveals the relationship between his theoretical reflections on institutional regulation and the problem of capitalism. In the prospectus, Parsons proposed to study the relation between the American medical profession's "formal structure" of "competitive individualism," that is, the fee-for-service system of private practice, and its governing professional ethics, based on traditional nonmarket commitments to provide care.[70] Parsons claimed that the medical profession provided "a peculiarly favorable test case" for the Durkheimian thesis that institutional norms underlay individualistic behavior, and thus Parsons suggested that the nonmarket motivations were at least as deeply rooted as market individualism. His discussion at this point suggests that the professions embodied for him what Karl Polanyi somewhat later called a "counter-movement" to the market, a merger

[69] TP, "Prolegomena to a Theory of Social Institutions," PP. Published in *American Sociological Review* 55 (June 1990): 319–33.

[70] See draft, "Sketch of a proposed study of the informal functioning of social institutions as an agency of control over the individual interests and activities of members of the medical profession," n.d., PP, section 15.75, box 3. Parsons began the study in the fall of 1934, according to a letter, TP to Sorokin, October 4, 1935, PP, section 42.8.2, box 2.

of moral and economic elements that limited the market's sway in modern society.[71]

In this context, it is possible to reinterpret Parsons's well-known 1939 essay "The Professions and Social Structure," which ostensibly offered an ideological defense of modern capitalism. Parsons's claim there that "the problem of self-interest itself has been exaggerated" cut two ways. While it challenged the tendency to distinguish business occupations from professions on an axis of "egoism and altruism" – and thus seemed to undermine the anticapitalist ethical critique of writers like R. H. Tawney – it also implied a stiff challenge to capitalist ideologues who identified egoism and efficiency. Professional and business occupations, Parsons wrote, shared functionally similar commitments to rationality, specialization, and so forth, and as individuals, professionals and businessmen were probably equally motivated by a mix of self- and other-regarding concerns. Parsons did not deny, however, that between the two lay "a clear-cut and definite difference on the *institutional* level" – that is, the primacy of monetary incentive in business. Given his view of institutions as historically relative and changeable forms, such remarks recall the complex of concerns voiced in his 1936 essay on Taussig and incentives: the nature of economic motivation and the possibility of changing its governing institutional norms. Indeed, "Professions and Social Structure" ended with the suggestion that a sociology of professions could "throw much light . . . on certain . . . possibilities of dynamic change." He did not neglect to point out how highly valued professional organization already was in modern society, particularly in the pursuit of knowledge and the provision of medical care.[72]

What kinds of "dynamic change" did Parsons have in mind? Could the functional similarities between business and the professions be considered a smooth path conducive to a program of reshaping the

[71] Karl Polanyi, *The Great Transformation* (Boston: Beacon Press, 1944). See also Fred Block and Margaret R. Somers, "Beyond the Economistic Fallacy: The Holistic Social Science of Karl Polanyi," in Theda Skocpol, ed., *Vision and Method in Historical Sociology* (Cambridge: Cambridge University Press, 1984), pp. 47–84. Cf. Magali Sarfatti Larson, *The Rise of Professionalism: A Sociological Analysis* (Berkeley: University of California Press, 1977), pp. 53–63, which relies on Polanyi's notion of the "counter-movement" to define "anti-market and anti-capitalist components" of professional organization.

[72] TP, "The Professions and Social Structure," pp. 457–67.

first to resemble the second, reconstructing business enterprise in professional organizational forms? In 1928, Parsons had raised the hope, contra Sombart, of discovering some line of continuity between existing social structure and a proposed future state. Was he now implying that the professions – representing (as forms of consensual, collegial self-regulation) the survival of community within modern society – provided a model for achieving control of economic life, establishing a kind of collectivism based on norms already present in the existing social order? Indeed, in view of Parsons's early motives, we can interpret his basic theoretical assertions of the 1930s – on the nature of price theory, the historical mutability of institutions, the significance of common moral motivations, and the effectiveness of sanctions – as part of a coherent, though unvoiced and implicit, political argument: that a future economic order based more on planning than market incentives *was* possible *if* state control were undergirded by generalized professional values gearing personal behavior in the economic sphere to commonly accepted definitions of the public good and the public trust.[73]

In the 1930s (and early 1940s), professionalism had not entirely lost the anticapitalist ideological overtones it had carried for some writers of the Progressive period.[74] Left-wing writers in the Depression decade continued to see middle-class professionals as a swing group that

[73] This formulation is an interpretative reconstruction extrapolating from Parsons's various writings of this time.

[74] In his essay "Professionalism *versus* Capitalism: R. H. Tawney, Emile Durkheim, and C. S. Peirce on the Disinterestedness of Professional Communities," in Haskell, ed., *The Authority of Experts: Studies in History and Theory* (Bloomington: Indiana University Press, 1984), pp. 180–225, Thomas Haskell recalls this Progressive-era heritage, although he minimizes Parsons's debt to it and exaggerates his departure from it.

In our time, the liberal sociology of the professions, emphasizing service norms, has come under vigorous attack for expressing, at best, the pious self-satisfaction of academic intellectuals and, at worst, an ideology of middle-class careerism and elite domination. The narrow and self-serving meanings of professionalism highlighted in this critique may be most evident at those periods, like our own, when reform movements are at low ebb and middle-class life in general is most committed to the status quo. The formation of radical caucuses in the professions and the construction of "alternative" community services in the 1960s and 1970s, for example, provide a quite different example, suggesting ways in which motives toward social reform and political activism survived in the professional ideal.

Professional motives conducive to social activism were recalled in an essay written by Parsons's son Charles to introduce *Philosophy and Political Action*, eds. Virginia Held, Kai Nielsen, and Charles Parsons (New York: Oxford University Press, 1972), pp. 3–12. Charles Parsons recalls that his father approved of his arguments in this essay. Author's interview with Charles Parsons.

might be recruited to the left or lost to the right.[75] In some of the scenarios of social change drawn in those years, furthermore, managers were expected to play a *professional* role in a social-democratic order. Lewis Corey's 1942 book *The Unfinished Task,* for instance, argued in Veblenian fashion that the local management of business, if disengaged from (absentee) private ownership and unalloyed profit maximization, could serve as a skilled, professional staff in public enterprises.[76] The market socialists' view of the role of managers, acting independently under the price-setting authority of a central planning board, was not much different. Even those with less radical notions, like left-liberals in the cooperative movement or in the trade union leadership, foresaw an expanded role for public enterprise – as "yardstick industries" established to set standards for private corporations – which would have required managers to perform a "disinterested" public function.[77]

The robustness of this discursive community suggests the mild left-wing tinge that Parsons's reflections on the professions had in their historical context. Indeed, Parsons's letters of the time make it clear that he viewed the professional model as something that could be extended to new spheres of social life, effectively removing them from the sway of market forces. To a student, he wrote that the newspaper, for instance, might "evolve in a direction that brings it closer to the fiduciary professional organizations like universities, hospitals, and so on," resting on endowments rather than profit seeking and freeing the journalist to act as a true professional.[78] Even in his favored case of medicine, Parsons clearly did not consider the established mix of market and nonmarket motivations unchangeable: In an unpublished 1939 book review, he mocked the "romantic" individualist propaganda of the American Medical Association while

[75] In his book *The Crisis of the Middle Class* (New York: Covici, Friede, 1935), Lewis Corey appealed to the new middle classes on the grounds that their professional motives would best be realized under a socialist order.

[76] Lewis Corey, *The Unfinished Task: Economic Reconstruction for Democracy* (New York: Viking Press, 1942). On Corey's resort to Veblen, see "Veblen and Marxism," review of *What Veblen Taught,* ed. Wesley C. Mitchell, in *Marxist Quarterly* 1 (January–March 1937): 162–68.

[77] See, for instance, the program of the Michigan Commonwealth Federation adopted in early 1944, discussed by Lewis Corey, "Program for a New Party?" *Antioch Review* 4 (Fall 1944): 465–69.

[78] Letter, TP to William Pinkerton, June 30, 1941, PP, section 15.2, box 15.

showing some sympathy for "the most important experiments in organization which have departed from the 'orthodox' private practice."[79] Parsons's presentation of "the doctor as the analogy to social planning," in a discussion over the summer of 1937 with University of Chicago social scientists Louis Wirth and Charles Merriam, also suggests that he viewed a program of generalizing the form of professional organization as the foundation for wide-ranging reform.[80]

Parsons's personal associations from the beginning of his Harvard career also suggest it is correct to situate him in a left-liberal intellectual milieu.[81] Parsons's friends among Harvard's young economics instructors in the late 1920s and early 1930s included Edward Mason, whose early interest in the history of European socialism led to publication of a book on the Paris Commune, and Redvers Opie, who decried the influence Hayek and von Mises came to wield at the London School of Economics.[82] Parsons was close as well to colleagues of his LSE days who would become lifelong friends, Arthur R. Burns and Eveline Burns, Columbia economists and left-wing New Dealers who spent their summers during the 1930s near the Parsonses in New Hampshire.[83] Eveline Burns worked for Roosevelt's Committee on Economic Security and later on the National Resources Planning Board, where she acted as a conduit bringing the

[79] Typescript reviews, n.d., of *What It Means to Be a Doctor,* by Dwight Anderson (1939), and *American Medicine Mobilizes,* by James Rorty (1939), in PP, section 42.41, box 2.

[80] See notes on discussions held in Chicago, August 22, 1937, and signed by Louis Wirth, Charles E. Merriam, and Parsons, "Shaping the Future," PP, section 42.8.2, box 2. The notes cite discussions on the issues of "what is planning" and "social planning vs. the planned society."

[81] One of Parsons's leading interpreters, Jeffrey C. Alexander, also notes Parsons's proximity to social-democratic values, adding that Parsons moved from "a dynamic and activistic liberalism [in the 1930s] to a more static and quiescent position" in the 1950s. Jeffrey C. Alexander, *Theoretical Logic in Sociology, vol. 4: The Modern Reconstruction of Classical Thought: Talcott Parsons* (Berkeley: University of California Press, 1983), pp. 133, 195, 389. Charles Parsons defined his father politically as a kind of New Dealer with social-democratic leanings, who continued after World War II to express his admiration for the British Labour Party government of 1945–51 and for Swedish social democracy. Author's interview with Charles Parsons.

[82] Letters, "Edward" to TP, November 16, 1931, and Opie's letter to TP from LSE after Parsons's publication of his 1934 essay on Robbins, PP, section 42.8.2. Mason, *The Paris Commune: An Episode in the History of the Socialist Movement* (Macmillan, 1930).

[83] Author's interview with Helen W. Parsons; author's interview with Charles D. Parsons.

British welfare-planning ideas of the Beveridge Report to American government. Earlier, in the late 1920s, Arthur Burns regarded his times as marked by "a struggle over the place which private property is to take in the world of the future" and recorded in his diary a discussion with Parsons that was friendly to the apparent successes of economic planning in the Soviet Union.[84]

By the 1930s, then, Parsons's examinations of the status of economic theory, the problem of motivation, and the concept of capitalism came together in a focus on the professions as the potential source of an alternative model of economic motivation appropriate to a society where a degree of social planning and a purposive use of economic theory prevailed. It is clear, however, that Parsons regarded the primary and crucial question of social reform as a moral one – that of disseminating, as he put it in his short essay on "Education and the Professions," "disinterested" motives in place of the rampant "love of money."[85] There is a sense in which Parsons's thinking on the professions – regarded as collectivities mobilizing the moral commitments of their members – recalled Emile Durkheim's notion of 1902 that "occupational groups" could serve as agencies of solidarity helping to reform an individualistic society; in another sense, this argument recalled that feature of the American Progressive mind highlighted by Richard Hofstadter's analysis of the "age of reform" – its typical moralist cast.[86] By mounting a moral project of extending already existing norms of professional practice, Parsons believed that contemporary society (to invert the Marxian formulation) held the seeds of its own salvation. The problem was merely that existing values and moral orientations were insufficiently concretized in institutions.

The meanings of voluntarism

Talcott Parsons shared the Depression decade's preoccupation with economic institutions and institutional reform – notwithstanding the

[84] A. R. Burns, *American Diary* (Columbia University Archives), July 25, and August 4, 1928.

[85] TP, "Remarks on Education and the Professions," pp. 365–69.

[86] Durkheim, "Some Notes on Occupational Groups," in *The Division of Labor in Society,* trans. George Simpson (New York: Macmillan, 1933), pp. 1–31. Hofstadter, *The Age of Reform* (New York: Vintage, 1955).

charge of critics then and since that his penchant for abstract, formal theory was distant from political affairs and by nature quietist.[87] Parsons's personal commitment to social reform was evident in a rarely cited passage of his 1937 treatise, *The Structure of Social Action,* where he aimed at Emile Durkheim a charge he would later suffer himself. Durkheim, he wrote, showed an excessive preoccupation with order and stability, and so firmly identified moral norms and social cohesion as to endorse mere conformism and "eliminate the creative element of action altogether." By contrast, Parsons brought attention to the gap between ideal norms and the social conditions that block their realization. Here, he wrote, there arose the specifically voluntaristic category of "will and effort," and in this striving to effect ethical ends – to realize a society's own ethical affirmations – were to be found, he said, "the dynamic processes of social change."[88] This passage helps tie *The Structure of Social Action* as a whole to the body of reform-minded ideas more evident in Parsons's contemporaneous articles. It also helps determine the meanings implied in the name Parsons gave to his social theory – "voluntaristic." One of its meanings, it appears in this context, was a reformist imperative: the will to make social change by compelling a society to live up to its founding ethical ideals.

Another key meaning of Parsons's "voluntarism" – one that was tied to his theory of institutions – also helps reconnect the lengthy and abstract theoretical discourse of *The Structure of Social Action* to the contemporary political interests only alluded to in the book's introductory pages. In his unpublished 1935 essay, "Prolegomena to a Theory of Institutions," Parsons applied the term "voluntaristic" to a *type* of social action. Although his general "voluntaristic theory" mediated the bygone opposites of positivistic and idealistic social theory, this essay described "voluntaristic *action*" as that (analytically separable) sphere of behavior governed by normative regulation in institutions. This type of action mediated the worldly focus of what he called "intrinsic" (instrumentally rational) action and the otherworldly focus of so-called symbolic (ceremonial) action. The typology Parsons of-

[87] Walton Hamilton accused him in 1931–32 of letting an interest in abstract, formal theory divert him from pressing issues of social and economic life (see note 43); C. Wright Mills, himself having had an institutionalist training as a student of Clarence Ayres in the 1930s at the University of Texas, repeated the charge in *The Sociological Imagination.*

[88] TP, *The Structure of Social Action,* pp. 445–50.

fered here strikingly evoked his undergraduate paper of 1923, which added "institutions" as a third, harmonizing sphere to Clarence Ayres's dichotomy of "technological" and "ceremonial" behavior.[89] Indeed, it appears that Parsons's "voluntaristic theory of action" was above all a theory of institutions, and institutions as Parsons understood them were significant for the peculiar kind of control or constraint they imposed on individual self-interest: a kind of constraint that was, by the internalization of rules, chosen as part of one's orientation to action, a matter of free (volitional) concession to social regulation.

This reflection on the meaning of institutions carried enormous weight in a discussion of basic trends in contemporary social affairs, particularly the question raised early in *The Structure of Social Action* about whether "contemporary society is at or near a turning point." Parsons shared the view that modern society created increasingly complex forms of large-scale social organization that effectively limited the sway of individualistic action as understood in classic liberal theory. That tradition, Parsons stressed repeatedly in his writings of the 1930s, was deeply marred by outmoded assumptions. In particular, he attacked its dogged insistence on a metaphysical individualism, its belief in linear progress based on continuous economic growth, its facile assumption that a "natural identity of interests" held all members of a market society together, and its neglect of the element of coercion in economic affairs (which, he recognized, Marx had analyzed so acutely).[90] Its resources for conceiving social order, especially at a time of sharp conflicts, were profoundly weak. In this context, Parsons's book set off in search of a postliberal theory that could explicate the kinds of motivations required to effectively sus-

[89] TP, "A Behavioristic Conception of Morals" and "Prolegomena to a Theory of Social Institutions"; for an illuminating discussion of the three-part schema, see David Sciulli, "The Practical Groundwork of Critical Theory: Bringing Parsons to Habermas (and vice versa)," in Jeffrey C. Alexander, ed., *Neofunctionalism* (Beverly Hills, Calif.: Sage, 1985), pp. 27–30.

[90] In "Some Reflections on 'The Nature and Significance of Economics,' " p. 528, for instance, Parsons challenged the " 'liberal' bias" of economic theory that fails to broach "the question of the role of coercive power." He considered problems of inequality and coercion again in "On Certain Sociological Elements in Professor Taussig's Thought," pp. 366–68, and at times applauded Marx for relating politics and economics and thus integrating the coercive element. See "Sociological Elements in Economic Thought, I," p. 430; "Some Reflections," p. 543; and *Structure of Social Action,* p. 109.

tain the moral legitimacy of a collectivized order that was already emerging – for such a volitional, moral bond as was promised in "institutions" (epitomized by the professions) was necessary if *coercive* forms of collectivization, all too evident in his times, were to be avoided. Thus Parsons's view of the contribution a voluntaristic sociology made to understanding and resolving the crisis of modernity justifies the analogy offered earlier between the rhetorical form of Parsons's argument over utilitarianism and contemporary left-wing analyses of capitalist collapse. The voluntaristic theory of action made the nature of organization, which as Max Weber had pointed out became all-embracing in the modern world, consistent with the preservation of free will. Not at all unlike the left-wing rhetoric of combating or averting the threat of fascism, Parsons's voluntaristic theory sought to chart a way out of the danger of accelerating coercion in modern social life, a way of preserving liberal values by surpassing the classic liberal system of theory and action.

Such a reconstruction of Parsons's theory may help explain why Parsons's reform motivations expressed themselves in such rarefied theoretical terms as those of *The Structure of Social Action* and why, as some of his recent critics have averred, his focus there lay so one-sidedly (and in so "idealistic" a fashion) on "common-value integration" as the key to explaining social order.[91] Parsons viewed the contemporary social crisis essentially as a moral or ideological crisis, occasioned by the obsolescence of classic liberalism; in that context, merely to demonstrate the force of "common-value integration" in maintaining social interaction was sufficient to combat the baleful ideological inheritance of liberal individualism. To do this and take market models of social order off the pedestal was Parsons's achievement.

In some sense, this aspect of Parsons's argument did not go far beyond what his predecessors of the Progressive era, like George Herbert Mead, had already argued in promoting a socialized conception of the individual. Nonetheless, the historical affiliation of Parsons in this period with the Progressive generation of social theory in the United States goes far toward illuminating the nature of Parsons's early work. In *Uncertain Victory,* James Kloppenberg has portrayed the Progressive generation as the promoter of a powerful, new manner of thought

[91] Cf. Camic, "*Structure* After 50 Years."

that overcame a series of disabling dilemmas in epistemology, ethics, and politics – between empiricism and idealism, moral absolutism and utilitarianism, and finally between liberalism and socialism. As already indicated, the structure of Parsons's thought, as evident in the formal arguments of *The Structure of Social Action,* had the same dynamic impulse to mediate inherited dichotomies. The synthetic method, furthermore, was at work in Parsons's treatment of the professions. Parsons's notes of the 1930s were filled with geometric and categorical jottings that repeatedly treated the professions as a tertiary mediation of two initial terms. Typically, Parsons laid out a distinction between the individualistic and contractual term *Gesellschaft* and the collectivist or familistic term *Gemeinschaft.* Breaking each of these down into component elements, he sought to show that professions combined elements of both *Gesellschaft* and *Gemeinschaft,* borrowing in particular the universalistic and specialized aspects of behavior from the former and the "disinterested" (as opposed to self-interested) aspects of behavior from the latter. Parsons's formulation of the professions manifests the same kind of "convergence" of individual and collective elements Kloppenberg identified as a trait of the prewar reform thinkers. As in Kloppenberg's cases, Parsons's manner of thinking suggested in political and economic terms a mediation of liberal and socialist premises, or what Parsons himself later came to call a "social liberal" ideology.[92]

Talcott Parsons has long been viewed as a conservative in social theory, a sociologist whose preoccupation with the mechanisms of social order and stability helped turn the tide against the change-oriented social thought of the early twentieth century – that is, the pragmatism of John Dewey, the critical realism of Thorstein Veblen, and the conflict-based notions of social ecology promoted by Robert Park's "Chicago school" of sociology. I have argued, however, that Parsons's early work, culminating in his first great treatise, *The Structure of Social Action* (1937), is only properly understood as a late manifestation of the reformist inclinations of the social-scientific intelligentsia in the United States. Indeed, *The Structure of Social Action* was a study of social theory catalyzed by Parsons's preoccupation with the problem of economic motivation, and that problem, framed ab-

[92] TP, "The Distribution of Power in American Society" (1960), in *Politics and Social Structure* (New York: Free Press, 1969).

stractly and impartially in most of his writings of the 1930s, was actually rooted in a social-democratic disposition to discover routes of reform capable of surpassing capitalist social relations on the basis of communal resources still potent in modern society.

By considering Parsons's early theory in conjunction with the course of social-reform ideology, we are compelled to take account of the historical discontinuity in liberal ideas uncovered in recent historical studies of the New Deal legacy and the implications of that breach for social theory. The most ambitious New Dealers of the middle and late 1930s held to a program of social reform that called for various kinds of social and economic planning to intrude on and limit the sway of market forces. Although never a major force in American politics, nor the most influential element in the Roosevelt administration, this current at least represented a respectable body of opinion makers, academic experts, government administrators, and leaders of farm and labor organizations, sharing a fairly coherent set of proposals for substantial reforms. Identified with liberalism as a crusading ideology of social change, this current voiced itself in the demand for "many TVAs," in the initial aspirations and rationale of the greenbelt town program (putting integral planning of local social services in place of unregulated market-driven "development"), and in the hope of "realigning" the Democratic Party as a wholehearted reform party. By 1942 or 1943, however, such talk of "social planning" had waned, and by the early postwar years the prevailing agenda of reform proposed by American social-democratic liberalism had been substantially remade.[93] In the view of postwar liberalism, improved delivery of health, education, and welfare services was to be grafted onto existing but unchallenged economic institutions by means of fiscal management of federal revenues.[94] No matter how ambitious its vi-

[93] The "social reform" ideology appeared not only in the more ambitious programs of the New Deal but in a broader political current with such varied manifestations as the farmer–labor party ventures of the middle 1930s; the reformist vigor of such mid-1930s "New Dealers" as Mordecai Ezekiel, Isador Lubin, Lauchlin Currie, and others; the American Labor and Liberal Party organizations in New York; and the Union for Democratic Action (UDA) in the early years of World War II. The election of the right-wing Congress in 1942 and the dumping of Vice-President Henry Wallace from the Roosevelt ticket in 1944 were recognized as marked setbacks for this liberal current.

[94] See Alan Brinkley, "The New Deal and the Idea of the State," in Gerstle and Fraser, eds. *Rise and Fall of the New Deal Order,* pp. 105–12, on the new fiscal liberalism.

sions of a social-service state, this agenda no longer included a program of rebuilding the terrain of fundamental economic institutions in American life.

This shift seems to have had a theoretical echo in Parsons's work after *The Structure of Social Action,* for in the years around World War II, his theory took a turn away from the preoccupations with the nature of modern capitalism and the centrality of economic institutions that had governed his early period. Instead of orienting his theoretical enterprise in sociology toward its disciplinary boundary with political economy, he shifted toward sociology's proximate relations with social psychology and anthropology. Although an investigation of that shift is beyond the scope of this essay, the change – acknowledged in Parsons's autobiographical statements – suggests that a significant paradigm shift in American social theory occurred not with the inception of Parsons's project but at a later point, cutting across his own path of theoretical development.[95] In this sense, later works like *The Social System* (1951) – which has a more complacent flavor than *The Structure of Social Action* – should not be considered simply the maturation of a germ present in his earliest treatise. Speaking from within the bygone world of a lost reformist liberalism – which at least had the virtue of making the place of the market in modern society an acute theoretical and practical problem – Parsons's early work had a distinct character. To recognize its time-bound character is not to limit its range of reference or discard it but to disclose in it a depth and a critical edge that decontextualized accounts of theoretical development in the social sciences have not recognized.

[95] Historian of science Henrika Kuklick has argued that a "scientific revolution" occurred in sociology with a shift toward preoccupation with mechanisms of "socialization" (i.e., the means of relating the individual to social structure as a whole). Parsons himself had recognized his growing interest during the early 1940s in "socialization" – a phenomenon he said eluded categories of political and economic organization – as the issue that catapulted him beyond a preoccupation with "the capitalism/socialism dichotomy." See Henrika Kuklick, "A 'Scientific Revolution': Sociological Theory in the U.S., 1930–1945," *Sociological Inquiry* 43 (1973): 3–22, and TP, "On Building Social System Theory: A Personal History," p. 838.

Plate 14. Portrait of David Riesman, cover of *Time* magazine (September 27, 1954). Copyright 1954 Time Inc. Reprinted by permission.

CHAPTER 12

The strange career of *The Lonely Crowd:* or, the antinomies of autonomy

WILFRED M. MCCLAY

In the realm of ends everything has either a *price* or a *dignity.* Whatever has a price can be replaced by something else as its equivalent; on the other hand, whatever is above all price, and therefore admits of no equivalent, has a dignity.

– Immanuel Kant

When the distinctively modern self was invented, its invention required not only a largely new social setting, but one defined by a variety of not always coherent beliefs and concepts.

– Alasdair MacIntyre

1

When Henry R. Luce and Britton Hadden, ambitious young journalists freshly graduated from Yale (class of 1920), first began to think of establishing a new weekly newspaper called *Facts,* they actually had in mind a publication that would do more, and less, than relate the facts. By the time their idea had crystallized into a prospectus, and the publication's name had been changed to *Time,* its character, and market, had become clear. Its mission would be to condense conventional news accounts down to four-hundred-word distillations, dealing "*briefly* with EVERYTHING OF IMPORTANCE" in the world, not only relating therein the bare "facts" but providing interpretation, telling

I am grateful to the Murphy Institute for its support for the preparation of this essay, and to both of this volume's editors for their helpful comments and criticisms of an earlier draft. I would also like to acknowledge my indebtedness to Patrick Allitt, Joyce Appleby, Thomas Bender, Richard Latner, Kenneth Lynn, Matthew Mancini, Samuel Ramer, John Shelton Reed, Douglas Rose, David Steiner, Peter Schwartz, Teresa Toulouse, and Robert Wuthnow, each of whom offered valuable comments. A special thanks to David Riesman for his characteristically generous, candid, and thoughtful reactions to what I have written about him and his work.

the impatient reader "what the news *means.*" Its readership would be the busy middle-class man (and, as Luce later averred, also the mythical "lady from Dubuque" whom Harold Ross's *New Yorker* had disdained), who was interested in following national and international affairs, but who did not have the time or energy to make sense of the reams of newsprint generated by the established newspapers. That would be *Time*'s job. When Volume 1, Number 1, appeared on March 2, 1923, it consisted entirely of material Luce and Hadden had sifted and lifted from the voluminous pages of the staid *New York Times,* and reworked into a snappy, vivid, signature *Time* style. The two men were not reporting the news; they were doing something more important – deciding what the news really was, and artfully packaging it for a mass, national market.[1]

In an era of American ascendancy, Luce publications would supply many of the pictures in Americans' heads, becoming a veritable fountain of shared national imagery. Men and women who appeared on the cover of *Time* took a place, for a time, in the iconography of American public life (and the journalistic marketplace), certified by the editors as being "of importance." Hence the importance of *Time*'s cover for the issue of September 27, 1954, given over to the countenance of a decidedly un-Lucean figure: a sober, unillusioned, graying, tweedy, lawyerly, bespectacled liberal sociologist from the University of Chicago named David Riesman – a certifiable Fifties "egghead" and principal author of a best-selling study of American society, *The Lonely Crowd* (Plate 14).

"Social Scientist David Riesman," inquired the caption, "What is the American Character?"; and the cover art ominously limned some of the answers it was thought Riesman had provided. Behind and beneath Riesman stretched an enormous sea of anonymous human heads, perhaps the herdlike audience for some unspecified mass-cultural spectacle. Rising out of the crowd, in the middle ground, are

[1] James Baughman, *Henry R. Luce and the Rise of the American News Media* (Boston, 1987); Robert T. Elson, *Time, Inc.: The Intimate History of a Publishing Enterprise, 1923–1941* (New York, 1968); John Kobler, *Luce: His Time, Life, and Fortune* (New York: 1968); W. A. Swanberg, *Luce and His Empire* (New York, 1972); Allan C. Carlson, "Luce, *Life,* and 'The American Way,' " *This World,* 13 (Winter 1986), 56–74. See also Michael Schudson's important study *Discovering the News* (New York, 1978). Kobler (53) notes that when Luce and Hadden began publication, their reference library consisted of unindexed files of the past twenty years of the *New York Times,* a copy of *Who's Who,* and a copy of *Roget's Thesaurus.*

two crisscrossing striated beams of light, upon each of which stands a man. The first man, dressed in a dark Victorian suit and wearing long, bushy nineteenth-century sideburns, seems to stride briskly and purposefully away from the reader, oblivious to all but his quest, a giant gyroscope strapped to his back. The second man, dressed in a light-colored suit, is a more "modern" twentieth-century man, perhaps a salesman; he is facing in the opposite direction. Following the conventions of graphic design, the second man faces forward, into the book, into the future, by facing to the reader's right; by facing left, the other man faces backward, into the spine, into the past. The second man extends his left arm in an extravagant posture of beckoning friendliness, while to his back is strapped a small radar dish, a device mysteriously integral to his designs. Meanwhile, in the near foreground, we see social scientist Riesman gazing forward coolly and unflappably, his back turned to both men, and to the mob.[2]

This striking image marked the first time in the magazine's thirty-one years that a sociologist had ever graced the cover of *Time,* in itself a notable enough fact, bespeaking the rising status of intellectuals in postwar American life. As Steven Weiland has pointed out, *Time* intended to present Riesman as "the model American intellectual," a heroic example of the prototypical "autonomous man" celebrated by *The Lonely Crowd.*[3] The accompanying article and photographs thus served not only to summarize the findings of *The Lonely Crowd,* which they did rather well, but to afford glimpses into the life of such an exemplary man. In a biographical sidebar entitled "An Autonomous Man," we learn all about him. "Author David Riesman tries to be an autonomous man," we are told, "and many of his friends think that he achieves a high degree of success." We watch while Riesman and his wife and children rehearse Mozart chamber music together. We are told that he has a large Chicago house with two servants, and owns a Vermont dairy farm; that he plays "vigorous, competent, year-round tennis," that he is "interested in his clothes and his food," that he "keeps a good wine cellar," that he drinks "orange juice mixed with soda," and that (to show a trace of the common touch) he "likes movies," so long as they are not "mes-

[2] *Time,* September 27, 1954, cover and 22–25.

[3] Steven Weiland, "Social Science Toward Social Criticism: Some Vocations of David Riesman," *Antioch Review,* 44, no. 4 (Fall 1986), 446–47.

sage movies." This ode to Riesman's well-rounded, well-tempered, vibrant existence was so lavish a public valentine as to be embarrassing.[4] It was as if Riesman had been made a victim of his own intellectual success.

That was not the only irony inherent in *Time*'s extraordinary attention to Riesman. For one thing, *The Lonely Crowd*'s examination of "the changing American character" had often been highly critical of the very mass media that were now transforming Riesman into a national celebrity and putting his ideas at the tip of everyone's tongue. Would the power of Riesman's observations be counteracted by eager absorption – "co-opted," to use the parlance of a later decade, by the very forces he undertook to describe and criticize? Could the *Time*sters transform anything, even a critic of their own modus operandi, into grist for their mills?

There was yet another, more serious, irony. Riesman was already beginning to feel deep reservations about the arguments put forward in *The Lonely Crowd,* doubts that rose even as the book's popularity rose, doubts that would begin to surface clearly in the preface to the book's 1961 edition and that have been surfacing regularly ever since.[5] A playful, protean thinker who always regarded his writings as exploratory and provisional in nature, and whose mind was as a consequence perpetually open to revision, Riesman had already expanded his thinking beyond the confines of *The Lonely Crowd*'s formulations.[6] But the book was propelled forward by its own momentum, for its portrait of modern American society was so compelling that

[4] As, indeed, it was for Riesman, who has throughout his career consistently shunned notoriety, even to the extent of adamantly refusing ever to appear on television, despite myriad requests. When he learned that *Time* was preparing a cover story on *The Lonely Crowd,* he was horrified, and attempted to persuade the magazine's managing editor (like Riesman, a *Crimson* alumnus, graduating from Harvard in 1932, the year after Riesman) to refrain from running it. The editor replied no, and furthermore requested Riesman's cooperation in allowing photographs to be taken, to which the latter reluctantly consented – much to his later regret. David Riesman to the author, April 1, 1992, and interview in Winchester, Massachusetts, July 16, 1992.

[5] David Riesman et al., *The Lonely Crowd: A Study of the Changing American Character* (New Haven, 1969), xxiii–lx. (This preface has been retained in the 1969 Yale abridged edition, along with a new 1969 preface; I use the pagination from that more readily available edition.) This material was drawn from a more detailed attempt to answer critics in Riesman's "*The Lonely Crowd:* A Reconsideration in 1960," which appeared in Seymour Martin Lipset and Leo Lowenthal, eds., *Culture and Social Character: The Work of David Riesman Reviewed* (Glencoe, Ill., 1961), 419–58.

[6] See, for example, his essays in *Individualism Reconsidered* (Glencoe, Ill., 1954).

four years after its initial 1950 publication, it was still being read by many and discussed by many more. Four years after its publication, Riesman would still be "current" enough to make the cover of the nation's leading current affairs weekly – whether he wanted to be there or not.[7]

If *Time* had to choose "the" American intellectual of the mid-1950s – and it is in the iconographic nature of such magazines to do such things – it could hardly have done better. Although *The Lonely Crowd* was coauthored with Nathan Glazer and Reuel Denney, in the end it bore Riesman's unmistakable intellectual stamp: in the suppleness, clarity, and unsolemnity of its style; in the amazingly catholic reading in the social sciences and humanities it drew upon; in the intuitive leaps and worldly savvy of its social and cultural observations; and in the remarkable agility with which it deployed an eclectic armory of concepts. As an intellectual who seemed to be equally comfortable working inside the university, like a thoroughbred academic man, or outside it, like the legendary *Partisan Review* writers of New York, Riesman seemed to span the variegated possibilities of American intellectual life. These qualities were not only a function of Riesman's unusually capacious and versatile mind, and the special advantages inherent in his patrician Philadelphia upbringing; they were also a product of a protracted vocational search, which brought him to the discipline of sociology very late in his life.[8] As he recently wrote, he and his collaborators were, for better or worse, "undersocialized as sociologists." By this he meant not only that they were not professional sociologists, but that in his own case, he had neither a Ph.D. in *any* field nor any substantial formal sociological training.[9] He had, however, built up an unusually rich fund of experience,

[7] By the time the *Time* article appeared, the amazingly productive Riesman had also published a sequel, *Faces in the Crowd* (1952), a biographical study of *Thorstein Veblen* (1953), and a superb collection of essays entitled *Individualism Reconsidered* (1953).

[8] On his upbringing, see Weiland, "Social Science Toward Social Criticism," 444–57; and several articles by Riesman: "A Personal Memoir: My Political Journey," in Walter W. Powell and Richard Robbins, eds., *Conflict and Consensus: A Festschrift in Honor of Lewis A. Coser* (New York, 1984), 327–64; "Two Generations," *Daedalus* 93 (1964), 72–97; and "Becoming an Academic Man," in Bennett M. Berger, ed., *Authors of Their Own Lives: Intellectual Autobiographies by Twenty American Sociologists* (Berkeley, 1990), 22–74. I am also indebted to a letter from Riesman to the author, April 24, 1985.

[9] David Riesman, "Innocence of *The Lonely Crowd*," *Society*, 27, no. 2 (January–February 1990), 78.

particularly (although not exclusively) of the white-collar social world he would analyze so compellingly in *The Lonely Crowd.*

His vocational search led him on a winding route, although he generally excelled at whatever he did. After majoring in biochemistry at Harvard, he graduated from Harvard Law, clerked for Supreme Court Justice Louis Brandeis, worked as a trial lawyer in Boston, taught law at the University of Buffalo, worked in the New York District Attorney's office, and, during World War II, was employed as a contract termination manager for the Sperry Gyroscope Company. In 1946, at thirty-seven, after undergoing several years of psychoanalysis under German émigré Erich Fromm,[10] and after amassing an impressive fund of practical experience in American legal, academic, and corporate cultures, he accepted a position as an assistant professor on the social science faculty of the University of Chicago, at a time when Chicago's faculty was abundantly endowed with both established and rising stars of the sociological firmament – Edward Shils, Milton Singer, Everett Hughes, Lloyd Warner, Robert Redfield, Daniel Bell, Morris Janowitz, and Philip Rieff, among others. Riesman had turned down two offers of college presidencies to become an untenured assistant professor, mainly because he wanted the kind of "colleagueship" that would help him to "educate myself more fully in the social sciences."[11] A mere four years later, he would be one of the most famous sociologists in the world.

The Lonely Crowd was a certifiable event in American intellectual and cultural history, a book of both importance and significance, if these rough synonyms may be distinguished from each other, as it is sometimes useful to do, by reference to their etymological roots. *The Lonely Crowd* was intrinsically important in its contributions to American intellectual life; it imported or carried into American social thought a brilliant and endlessly suggestive perspective on the social psychology of the burgeoning new professional-managerial middle

[10] Weiland points out how little is known about this phase of Riesman's life; see "Social Science Toward Social Criticism," 454. Riesman also downplays its significance, asserting that he underwent analysis "not because I thought I needed it," but "to please my mother, who wanted to be able to talk with me during the time she was an analysand of Karen Horney, who had recommended Fromm to her for me" ("Becoming an Academic Man," 45–46). Certainly, however, the protracted vocational search that Weiland argues for would also place Riesman's psychoanalysis in a key, if forever inscrutable, position in the process of Riesman's formation.

[11] Riesman, "Becoming an Academic Man," 34.

class, and the ways in which that social psychology might represent a dramatic departure from previous American precedents. Unlike the narrow empirical studies so characteristic of Riesman's contemporaries, it stands squarely in the rich sociological tradition of such early masters as Max Weber, Georg Simmel, Emile Durkheim, and Alexis de Tocqueville, who saw their work as part and parcel of the Western philosophical and literary tradition. Moreover, it is a book that still seems strikingly fresh and relevant even after forty years, for it anticipates many of the most salient themes in subsequent American social and political analysis.[12]

But its significance, the cultural meaning that its appearance and reception in the postwar era signify, lies elsewhere. The resonances it set off in the minds of the American reading public suggest that, aside from the innovative content of its arguments, it was also a sign of the times. As H. Stuart Hughes rightly asserted, *The Lonely Crowd* "both reflected and stimulated a mood of national soul-searching" in the Fifties; hence the often disturbing image of themselves that contemporary Americans discovered in its pages did not deter them from taking Riesman's critique seriously, and from appropriating the book's irresistible taxonomy of "inner-directed" and "other-directed" modal personalities to account for their dissatisfaction with the changing character of their neighbors, their colleagues, and perhaps even themselves.[13]

The book's great public success, then, and the resultant recognition embodied in the *Time* cover, clearly indicated that beneath the triumphant surface of postwar American culture ran a subterranean stream of doubt. *The Lonely Crowd* was far from being the only book to express the darker half of this dualism; indeed, one could argue that the flush, ebullient postwar years also produced the most trenchant and enduring works of social and cultural criticism in American history. The very existence of such works as Lionel Trilling's *The Liberal*

[12] As a recent tribute, see the contribution by Jackson Lears to Lary May, ed., *Recasting America: Culture and Politics in the Age of the Cold War* (Chicago, 1989). See also Peter Rose, "David Riesman Reconsidered," *Society,* 19, no. 3 (March–April 1982), 52–61; Leon Botstein, "Children of *The Lonely Crowd,*" *Change,* 10, no. 5 (May 1978), 16–20, 54; Anne Lowrey Bailey, "Riesman on Riesman," *Change,* 17, no. 3 (May–June 1985), 51–57. For comic relief, see also Michael Parenti, "How to Write a Best Seller in the Social Sciences," *Social Policy,* 2, no. 6 (March–April 1972), 22–24.

[13] H. Stuart Hughes, *The Sea Change, 1930–1965* (New York, 1975), 134.

Imagination (1950), C. Wright Mills's *White Collar* (1951), Reinhold Niebuhr's *The Irony of American History* (1952), David Potter's *People of Plenty* (1954), Louis Hartz's *The Liberal Tradition in America* (1955), William Whyte's *The Organization Man* (1956), John Kenneth Galbraith's *The Affluent Society* (1958), Daniel Bell's "Work and Its Discontents" (1960), Paul Goodman's *Growing Up Absurd* (1960), Daniel Boorstin's *The Image* (1961), and Dwight Macdonald's *Against the American Grain* (1962), among many others, ought at least to complicate the conventional wisdom about the postwar era's insufferable complacency and cultural uniformity.[14] Indeed, as the radical critic Russell Jacoby has recently lamented, such a collection of writers may well represent the last generation of American "public intellectuals," writers whose critical perspectives were meant to be both intellectually rigorous and available to a broad, nonspecialist public audience.[15]

Nevertheless, many of these works addressed themselves, in one way or another, to issues that fit under the imprecise rubric of "conformity." Many, as a consequence, evinced a deep concern that the integrity and independence of the individual, benchmark values of a liberal order, were endangered by the encroachments inherent in the transformation of the United States into an increasingly organized, corporate, bureaucratized, mass-consumption society. Such concerns would likely have arisen in any event, as an economy oriented toward industrial production began to give way to a postindustrial order built around the provision of services and consumer goods; such questions were just beginning to be raised in the 1920s, before the cataclysms of Depression and war distracted Americans' attention from them.[16]

[14] Richard Pells, *The Liberal Mind in a Conservative Age: American Intellectuals in the 1940s and 1950s* (New York: 1985), x.

[15] Russell Jacoby, *The Last Intellectuals: American Culture in the Age of Academe* (New York, 1987). It is well worth noting that several of the intellectuals whose work Jacoby praises highly, such as James Agee, Daniel Bell, John K. Galbraith, Dwight Macdonald, and William Whyte, wrote regularly for Henry Luce. As Jacoby mentions in an aside, "Even Henry Luce of the *Time* magazine empire, often denounced as a master propagandist, employed and even liked mavericks and dissenters" (232).

[16] Lippmann's *Public Opinion* began to raise such questions, as did Robert S. and Helen M. Lynd, *Middletown: A Study in Contemporary American Culture* (New York, 1929). On the latter, see Richard Wightman Fox, "Epitaph for Middletown: Robert S. Lynd and the Analysis of Consumer Culture," in Richard Wightman Fox and T. J. Jackson Lears, eds., *The Culture of Consumption: Critical Essays in American History, 1880–1980,* 101–41.

But the multifaceted complex of issues raised by the Cold War caused them to be posed in an especially intensified form, particularly for intellectuals who, like most of the authors just mentioned, found themselves actively involved in defending the autonomy of intellectual life, and resisting the totalistic demands of both McCarthyism and Stalinism. Certain specific fears still smolder and flicker in the background of these works: fears of internal subversion by organized Communists, countered by fears of internal tyranny at the hands of authoritarian anti-Communists; fears of a militant totalitarianism abroad, pitted against fears of a totalitarian potential from within.

That last potential, too, might manifest itself in less sinister but no less worrisome form, as part of modern Western intellectuals' persistent but growing concern over the fate of individuality in an age of mass society.[17] John Stuart Mill's *On Liberty* held a prominent place in that literature; so, too, did Emerson's hymns to self-reliance.[18] Perhaps more powerfully felt in the postwar years was the specter of the great, mild, quasi-paternal supervisory power of which Mill's friend Alexis de Tocqueville wrote in the second volume of *Democracy in America.* After having fallen into near obscurity, Tocqueville enjoyed a spectacular revival in the postwar era, becoming a virtual substitute for Marx – the Marx of Mass Society, so to speak.[19] When Dwight Macdonald railed against the "spreading ooze" of Mass Culture, or when Lionel Trilling embraced Freudianism as a biologically based *terra firma* protecting the individual from the pliability of "culture," or when William Whyte warned against the potential tyranny of a "social ethic," all had the threat of this Tocquevillean "soft" totalitarianism, and the special challenge it represented to independent intellectual life, very much in mind.[20] So, too, did *The Lonely*

17 See the illuminating essays of Edward Shils contained in *The Intellectuals and the Powers, and Other Essays* (Chicago, 1972), particularly "Mass Society and Its Culture" (229–47) and "Daydreams and Nightmares: Reflections on the Criticism of Mass Culture" (248–64). See also Rupert Wilkinson, *The Pursuit of American Character* (New York, 1988), 71–86, on Americans' "fear of being owned."

18 John Stuart Mill, *On Liberty* (London, 1859); Ralph Waldo Emerson, "Self-Reliance," from *Essays, First Series* (Boston, 1841).

19 Robert Nisbet, "Many Tocquevilles," *American Scholar* 46 (Summer 1976), 59–76. For a helpful explication of the way in which Tocqueville replaced Marx, for a time, see John P. Diggins, *The American Left in the Twentieth Century* (New York, 1973), 136–38.

20 Dwight Macdonald's "A Theory of Mass Culture" is contained in Bernard Rosenberg and David Manning White, eds., *Mass Culture: The Popular Arts in America*

Crowd, which by virtue of its poetic title alone pointed toward a desolate combination of emptiness and passivity, anomic isolation combined with the mentality of the herd, settling over the nation. Riesman owed that theme, and much else besides, to the haunting imagery of the *Democracy*'s more abstract, sociological, and brooding second volume.[21]

In fact, *The Lonely Crowd* contained some intellectual connections between the conceptions of "hard" and "soft" totalitarianism, many of them arising out of Riesman's intimate contact with German refugees from Hitler. This interest in German refugees derived less from his own German-Jewish roots, which actually appear to have mattered very little to him, than from his generous, cosmopolitan outlook and his close relationship with the German-born Harvard political scientist Carl Joachim Friedrich. The author of one of the principal studies of totalitarianism, among many other books, Friedrich became Riesman's mentor at Harvard and later his close friend; it was Friedrich who introduced Riesman to many of the refugee intellectuals who flocked to Cambridge in the 1930s.[22] The rise of Hitler loomed understandably large in the minds of these German émigrés, and some part of their powerful conceptions was also imparted to Riesman. Many of the book's fundamental ideas closely parallel the work of Riesman's friend and analyst Erich Fromm, whose *Escape from Freedom,* published in early 1941, had argued that the attraction of totalitarian movements arose from the inability of modern men

(Glencoe, Ill., 1957); Lionel Trilling, *Beyond Culture: On Literature and Learning* (New York, 1965); William Whyte, *The Organization Man* (New York, 1956).

21 When the *Democracy* was originally published in French, it appeared in two two-volume installments, published in 1835 and 1840 respectively; it is, however, customary to refer to the 1835 volumes as Volume 1 and the 1840 volumes as Volume 2. Many readers have been struck by the differences between the two volumes, the first being highly reportorial or descriptive of the specific American scene, and the second being more analytical, more "sociological," more reflective, and perhaps more pessimistic. André Jardin provides an account of this change in his magisterial *Tocqueville: A Biography* (New York: 1988), 199–281; see also George Pierson, *Tocqueville and Beaumont in America* (New York, 1938); and James T. Schliefer, *The Making of Tocqueville's Democracy in America* (Chapel Hill, 1980).

22 Riesman, "A Personal Memoir," 336; and "Becoming an Academic Man," especially 30–54. Friedrich himself was of an earlier, pre-Hitler generation of German immigrants; but his contacts with the arriving émigrés were considerable. It was because of those contacts that Riesman was moved to serve as executive director of a project for relocating refugee lawyers. It is indicative of the warmth and durability of their friendship that Riesman and Friedrich bought a farmhouse together in Brattleboro, Vermont, in 1933.

and women to cope with the radical freedom that modernity had bestowed upon them.[23] And, in the late 1940s, Riesman approached Hannah Arendt, whose influential *Origins of Totalitarianism* he would later read with enormous enthusiasm in manuscript, to see if she would be willing to contribute a historical chapter for *The Lonely Crowd,* dealing with the development of Western social character. "I have the feeling," he wrote her, "that nobody understands our times so well as you, that nobody has such an extraordinarily acute sense of what has *changed.*"[24]

It is perhaps not so surprising that Arendt declined the offer; it is a little difficult to imagine such an independent thinker, especially given her animus toward the social sciences, being comfortable taking part in a collaborative study in sociology. But when she returned the favor and read Riesman's manuscript, she also returned his enthusiasm, confessing that she was "wondering all the time" about the similarities and differences between the phenomena he described and those of her own work. The other-directed man's "craving for being loved and accepted is new after all," she asserted, indicating a "being lost in the world which is similar" to the situation of "mass-man in Europe" – although in America "these phenomena arise as it were out of society, without . . . anyone doing anything about it," a fact that "frightened" her.[25] Riesman was grateful for her praise, and confided to her, in June 1949, "I have a new title tentatively, which really gets at what we are both discussing now, 'Passionless Existence in America.' "[26] The "mass man" and Riesman's "other-directed" man appeared to have a good deal in common; both were pathetically adrift in a structureless, normless world.[27]

[23] Erich Fromm, *Escape from Freedom* (New York, 1941). The London edition of the book, published by Kegan Paul, Trench, Trubner, and Co., was called *The Fear of Freedom.*

[24] David Riesman to Hannah Arendt, June 7, 1949, and May 25, 1948. Arendt Papers, Library of Congress. See also Elisabeth Young-Bruehl, *Hannah Arendt: For Love of the World* (New Haven, 1982), 252.

[25] Hannah Arendt to David Riesman, June 13, 1949. Arendt Papers, Library of Congress.

[26] Riesman to Arendt, June 14, 1949. Arendt Papers.

[27] Stephen Whitfield, *Into the Dark: Hannah Arendt and Totalitarianism* (Philadelphia, 1980), 98. Whitfield makes clear the degree to which Arendt's view of totalitarianism derives from and is built upon earlier theories of the origins and pathologies of mass society. It seems very likely that the concluding section on loneliness that Arendt added to her revised 1966 edition of the *Origins* reflected Riesman's influence.

From the perspective offered by a longer view of American intellectual history since the Civil War, there was considerable irony in this circling of the intellectual wagons around the imperiled individual. For in many respects it represented a repudiation of what had been one of the most consistently iterated and vigorously pursued goals of the most energetic American social thinkers in the post–Civil War decades – the overcoming of Americans' stubborn tendency toward atomistic individualism, to be achieved by integrating them into more rational, more efficient, more unified, more socially conscious, more equitable, and more humane modes of social and economic relatedness. The shift that John Higham perceived in the imaginative horizons of Americans during the middle years of the nineteenth century, a movement from "boundlessness" to "consolidation," may serve us equally well as a broad characterization of that entire century's gradually shifting social ideal. As the country became economically and politically knit together, the need for a knitting together of its awareness of itself arose as well.[28]

The consolidating tendency began, of course, with the great convulsive effects of the Civil War, which in its waging as well as its results represented a decisive step in forging a national consciousness, and in casting intellectual doubt on the freewheeling individualism endorsed by the most prominent Northern thinkers of the antebellum years.[29] But a distinctive new intellectual perspective began to emerge in the 1880s, when Lester Frank Ward published his reform-Darwinist tract *Dynamic Sociology* (1883), a brief for "sociocracy"; and when Edward Bellamy's wildly popular utopian novel *Looking Backward* (1888) drew thousands of Americans to join clubs devoted to the study of the collectivist social vision that he had, significantly, named Nationalism. The "consolidationist" perspective grew and developed well into the next century, finding expression in Edward A. Ross's influential 1901 textbook *Social Control,* in Herbert Croly's Progressive manifesto *The Promise of American Life* (1909), and, perhaps most impressively and subtly of all, in the multitudinous works of John Dewey. Indeed, the question of the individual's proper relation

[28] John Higham, *From Boundlessness to Consolidation* (Ann Arbor, 1969); Robert Wiebe, *The Search for Order, 1877–1920* (New York: 1967).

[29] George Fredrickson, *The Inner Civil War: Northern Intellectuals and the Crisis of the Union* (New York, 1965).

to society always lay near the heart of Dewey's many efforts in the fields of social, educational, and moral philosophy, and his manner of approaching the question was consistent:

> The idea that the outward scene is chaotic because of the machine . . . and that it will remain so until individuals reinstate wholeness within themselves, simply reverses the true state of things. The outward scene, if not fully organized, is relatively so in the corporateness which the machine and its technology have produced; the inner man is the jungle which can be subdued to order only as the forces of organization at work in externals are reflected in corresponding patterns of thought, imagination, and emotion. The sick cannot heal themselves by means of their disease, and disintegrated individuals can achieve unity only as the dominant energies of community life are incorporated to form their minds.[30]

Dewey was, of course, a far more subtle thinker than such a quote might seem to imply; his aversion to dualism led him to insist time and again upon the interactive mutuality of self and society. There was, moreover, no more ardent foe of totalitarianism, no firmer believer in participatory democracy.[31] But when read in the wake of Hitler and Stalin, and of other modern despots who sought to "subdue to order" the "inner man," such words could carry overtones rather different from those conveyed in the 1920s. Was it not, after all, precisely the stubborn "jungle" of the self that a cultural critic like Lionel Trilling – who (like many of his milieu) was deeply affected by his brushes with Stalinism in the 1930s – was so anxious to preserve?[32] It was also in the context of such concerns that a book like *The Lonely Crowd* was written and read.

Dewey, by then in his eighties, had already begun to sense a neo-individualism afoot in America after World War II – and he most emphatically did not approve. Five years before *The Lonely Crowd* was published, Dewey wrote an indicative article for *Commentary*'s

[30] John Dewey, *Individualism, Old and New* (New York, 1930), 65.

[31] See Robert Westbrook's masterful interpretation of Dewey in his *John Dewey and American Democracy* (Ithaca, 1991).

[32] See Trilling's "Freud: Within and Beyond Culture," in *Beyond Culture,* 89–118. Trilling has attracted a good deal of scholarly attention, in addition to the many accounts of him in memoirs and histories of the New York intellectuals; I have especially profited from William Chace, *Lionel Trilling: Criticism and Politics* (Stanford, 1980); Stephen Tanner, *Lionel Trilling* (Boston, 1988); Mark Krupnick, *Lionel Trilling and the Fate of Cultural Criticism* (Evanston, Ill., 1986); and especially an account of Trilling's ideas by a sympathetic clinical psychologist, Edward Joseph Shoban, Jr., *Lionel Trilling* (New York, 1981).

Crisis of the Individual series. The very title of the series was significant – but Dewey's article, entitled "The Crisis in Human History: The Danger of the Retreat to Individualism," was filled less with worries about the individual than with misgivings about the current "swing back to magnification of something called *the individual*," and to an outlook that ascribes "independent reality and ultimate value to the individual person alone."[33] Such a characterization – a swing *back* – suggests that Riesman was doing more than adapting the social thought of refugees from Hitler, who might have been thought especially prone to read Dewey's words as a brief for benign *Gleichschaltung*. Riesman was also tapping into the energies of venerable American intellectual traditions, traditions that Dewey had so often attacked.[34] He was, in part, reaching back to precisely the individualistic outlooks that the "consolidationist" thinkers had been struggling to overcome. The concerns that stood at the heart of Tocqueville, Mill, and Emerson, the concerns animating nineteenth-century liberalism, were brought back to center stage by *The Lonely Crowd*. There was something of the same gesture in the "New Frontier" label affixed a decade later to the presidential campaign of John F. Kennedy – a name that not only tapped the mythic vein of the Old West but, more directly, recalled the classical-liberal conceptions of the individual implicit in Frederick Jackson Turner's "frontier thesis."

2

It is not at all clear that Riesman and his collaborators meant to do anything of the sort. In fact, they explicitly denied that they were, in the preface to the 1961 edition of the book: "The authors of *The Lonely Crowd* are not conservatives harking back to a rugged individualism that was once a radical Emersonian ideal."[35] That they felt compelled to make such a denial, however, is as significant as the denial itself. So, too, is the fact that by 1969 the book had accumulated fifty pages of prefatory material, most of it devoted to correctives, amplifications, and explications designed to correct and answer

33 John Dewey, "The Crisis in Human History," in *Commentary* 1 (March 1946), 1–9, esp. 8.

34 See Dewey's essay "The American Intellectual Frontier," in *Character and Events,* 1:448; originally appearing in *New Republic,* May 10, 1922.

35 Riesman, *The Lonely Crowd* (1969 revised edition), xxxii.

readers' errors and misunderstandings. It may have been a losing battle. As C. Vann Woodward has ruefully observed, remembering the discomfort he experienced as his *Strange Career of Jim Crow* came to be used in ways he had never anticipated, authorship of a celebrated work can be a decidedly mixed blessing for a scholar.[36] The anxiety of influence can be equaled by the anxiety of being influential: the anxiety of losing control over your book's meaning and watching it become a possession of the culture, which can mean becoming associated with thoughts you do not share and movements you do not endorse. By the 1969 edition, Riesman seemed to feel this regret acutely, as he indicated in a "cautionary preface." *The Lonely Crowd* had "entered the picture many Americans . . . have of ourselves," he averred; as such, it has "contributed to the climate of criticism of our society and helped create or reaffirm a nihilistic outlook among a great many people who lay claim to moral or intellectual nonconformity."[37] More recently, he rued the fact that "individuals seeking to show that they were not 'other-directed,' that they were unconstrained by parents and peers found extravagant ways to flaunt their supposed authenticity."[38] Although Riesman has more than once asserted that he and his collaborators "had no expectation" that the book would appeal to a wide audience, that assertion is belied not only by the book's fluid and witty expository style, but by his own admission to Arendt in 1949 that he was "trying to organize [the book] in such shape that I can appeal to a wider audience than academic people."[39] Unfortunately, he got his wish.

One has to admire Riesman's openness and willingness to engage in such searching self-criticism; few authors ever do the same. But one also observes that his regrets are not without a tinge of bitterness at times; an understandable feeling, particularly understandable to any author who feels his work has been widely and consistently misused. But was it really? Or, more precisely, is it possible that the alleged "misuse" of *The Lonely Crowd* is in fact the key to its signifi-

[36] C. Vann Woodward, *Thinking Back: The Perils of Writing History* (Baton Rouge, 1986), 81–99; see also his *The Future of the Past* (New York, 1989), 295–311.
[37] Riesman, *The Lonely Crowd* (1969 edition), xii.
[38] Riesman, "Innocence of *The Lonely Crowd*," 77. See also the remarks on *The Lonely Crowd* in Robert Bellah et al., *Habits of the Heart: Individualism and Commitment in American Life* (Berkeley, 1985), 49.
[39] Riesman to Arendt, June 14, 1949. Arendt Papers.

cance, and a window onto the antinomies it attempted to contain? To find out, it is necessary to go back and take a closer look at the book's argument, keeping alert along the way for hints of ambiguity and ambivalence.

The Lonely Crowd is above all else a study of what Riesman, following Erich Fromm, called "social character" – the modes of psychological conformity which a society inculcates in its members, and by which it holds together. As such, it was far from alone in its time, since similar "culture and personality" studies, which attempted to connect individual psychology with the distinctive practices of a given culture, had proliferated during and after World War II, produced by such writers as Ruth Benedict, Fromm, Geoffrey Gorer, Karen Horney, Abram Kardiner, and Margaret Mead.[40] What was distinctive about *The Lonely Crowd,* however, and what made for its wide readership, were the personality typologies it introduced and the dynamic element in its argument – its assertion that the social character of Americans had changed dramatically since the nineteenth century, from "inner-directed" personality types, self-reliant souls who navigated their way through life by relying doggedly on principles inculcated early in life, especially by parents; to "other-directed" types who were brought up to look to external cues from others – not only their parents but their peers, their co-workers, their co-professionals, the mass media, and the like – as a guide to proper behavior and beliefs.[41] Riesman best expressed the difference between the two by navigational analogy, comparing the mechanism of inner-direction to

[40] See Lowenthal and Lipset, *Culture and Social Character,* 15–26; Riesman, *The Lonely Crowd,* 4.

[41] I have left out of my account here a very important part of the original argument, which any reader of the work will immediately notice, but from which Riesman quickly distanced himself when it came under attack. That was his attempt to relate his character types to population patterns, which he believed, following the biometrician Raymond Pearl and the demographer Frank W. Notestein, to have traced an S-curve over the long term. Tradition-direction corresponded to societies of "high growth potential" (high birth and death rates); inner-direction to "transitional growth" (declining death rate); and other-direction to "incipient population decline" (moving toward a net decrease in population). (Riesman, *The Lonely Crowd,* 7–31). Aside from the obvious peculiarity that Riesman put this theory forward in the midst of an American "baby boom," both the demographics and the correlations were immediately questioned, and Riesman was concerned that this might distract readers from the typologies and make his argument seem too mechanistic; so he quickly backed away from the demographic part of his argument. See Lipset and Lowenthal, *Culture and Social Character,* 156–58, 241–42.

the self-contained gyroscope – shades of Sperry Gyroscope! – and that of other-direction to radar, which takes its measure of the world by sending out electromagnetic pulses and attending carefully to what comes back.[42] Thus *Time*'s cover artist chose to depict these modal personalities, not only in period dress with characteristic gestures but with their indispensable tool of social navigation readily at hand.

Both types differed significantly from the "tradition-directed" person who had preceded them: a type whose characteristics were generated by older, tradition-bound, static, highly ascriptive social orders, wherein the individual stood in a well-defined functional and status relationship to the rest of the group. (Significantly, the tradition-directed man was not depicted on the *Time* cover.) The tradition-directed stood on the "before" side of all the classic sociological dualisms: status versus contract (Maine); *Gemeinschaft* versus *Gesellschaft* (Tönnies); mechanical solidarity versus organic solidarity (Durkheim); feudalism versus capitalism (Marx); communal relationships versus associative ones (Weber); primary versus secondary groups (Cooley). Individuality was kept to a minimum in the tradition-directed order; correctness of behavior rather than inward disposition was emphasized; and the characteristic weapon of social sanction was shame or expulsion.[43]

With inner-direction, however, we are in the emerging capitalist world, where flux is the only constant, where strictly behavioral norms are undermined, and where, therefore, parents must psychologically equip their children to find their own way, like intrepid explorers venturing into unstable and unpredictable environments. Hence the appropriateness of the metaphorical gyroscope as the navigational tool.[44] Ideally, the inner-directed family instilled within the souls of its children a "rigid though highly individualized character," which could be a kind of internal substitute for the comprehensive traditional social systems modern life had left behind, using guilt rather than shame as its sanctioning mechanism. In Riesman's description, the inner-directed personality resembled the type of Freudian psychoanalytic theory, largely by virtue of Freud's emphasis on the introjections of parental

[42] Riesman, *The Lonely Crowd*, 25–26.
[43] Ibid.
[44] Riesman, *The Lonely Crowd*, 65–66, 94, for his example of Lord Chesterfield's letters to his son.

(and especially paternal) ideals and authority to form the powerful, and highly compulsive, superego.[45] Inner-direction was suggestive, too, of Max Weber's quintessential pioneering capitalist, a characterological type whose accumulating and rationalizing discipline flowed from, or was in any event crucially supported by, the internal restraints of the Protestant ethic.[46]

Inner-direction was appropriate to the era of capitalist expansion. In a production-oriented age ruled by a psychology of scarcity, the force of productive labor was concentrated on conquering "the hardness of the material," work and play were severely differentiated, and pleasure was a "sideshow," a fleeting escape from care that principally served to refresh oneself for a return to life's battle. Like self-propelled economic monads, inner-directeds relied on "the invisible hand" to provide social coordination for their actions, which meant that in day-to-day social existence they asked for, and gave, little quarter. The tendency of a society in which inner-direction was dominant was "to protect the individual against the others at the price of leaving him vulnerable to himself." This tendency had its positive aspects, for it relieved the individual of the oppressive requirement to meet the standards of others; but it also left that individual vulnerable to the searing wounds of his own self-criticism. Life was a continual struggle for self-approval, in which even the achievement of one's goals did not relieve the burden of striving, for "mere behavioral conformity cannot meet the characterological ideal."[47] Salvation, so to speak, was achieved not by works, but by faith alone.

With the national economic transformation, commencing just after the turn of the century, from a production- and extraction-oriented economy into a consumption-oriented one, the need for a different kind of person, and a different mode of conformity, soon became manifest. Inner-direction was rapidly becoming outmoded. Instead of the "hardness" of material, the crucial tasks of work now increasingly revolved around the "softness" of men; therein lay the great opportunity and challenge for the ambitious and upwardly mobile. This change

[45] Sigmund Freud, *New Introductory Lectures on Psychoanalysis,* trans. James Strachey (New York, 1965), 60–62.

[46] Max Weber, *The Protestant Ethic and the Spirit of Capitalism,* trans. Talcott Parsons (London, 1930).

[47] See Riesman, *The Lonely Crowd,* 13–17, 113–29.

flowed not only from the manipulative demands of a consumption-driven national economy, as exemplified in the bevy of skilled and alluring advertisers and other such siren songsters that came to national prominence in the 1920s.[48] It also flowed from the often intense demands created by the increasingly interpersonal and bureaucratic patterns of office work, the professions, and even industrial labor, characteristic of a less freewheeling, increasingly corporate and monopolistic phase of capitalism.[49] The new kinds of industry arising in the United States would rely on higher levels of formal education in the work force; it would be built around "techniques of communication and control" relating to both the morale and the efficiency of employees, as well as to the demands of the marketplace; and hence would find unprecedented uses for "men whose tool is symbolism and whose aim is some observable response from people" – a group, in short, rather like that sometimes designated by the imprecise term "the new class."[50]

Riesman vivified this transformation from inner-direction to other-direction through a set of his own dualisms, often quite as witty as they were revealing: "From Morality to Morale"; "From Craft Skill to Manipulative Skill"; "From Free Trade to Fair Trade"; "From the Bank Account to the Expense Account"; "From the Wheat Bowl to the Salad Bowl"; "From the Invisible Hand to the Glad Hand."[51] And all these changes can be correlated, as was true for the previous two types, with changes in family and child-rearing practices. In the "other-directed round of life," the severe internal discipline of the inner-directed family unit is largely abandoned, since the rigidity of the inner-directed "character" had become irrelevant, even a liability, in a brave and fluid new world of consumer-oriented abundance and people-oriented work. (Accordingly, the more appropriate psychological model for socialization is not that of the patriarchal Freud, but the more fluid and interpersonal emphases of the American psychiatrist

48 T. J. Jackson Lears, "From Salvation to Self-Realization: Advertising and the Therapeutic Roots of the Consumer Culture, 1880–1930," in Fox and Lears, *The Culture of Consumption*, 1–38.

49 Cf. Riesman, *The Lonely Crowd*, 131–32.

50 Ibid. On the matter of the "new class," a useful critical examination is Daniel Bell, "The New Class: A Muddled Concept," in *The Winding Passage: Essays and Sociological Journeys, 1960–1980* (New York: 1980), 144–64.

51 Riesman, *The Lonely Crowd*, 130–48.

Harry Stack Sullivan.) The parents must learn to accept a supporting, or at best costarring, role in the drama of their children's formation; for the child's peer group has became "much more important to the child." Well-informed, progressive-minded parents readily accepted this demotion; indeed, the principal reason they would be likely to intervene authoritatively in their child's affairs is "not so much about his violation of inner standards as about his failure to be popular or otherwise to manage his relations with these other children."[52]

For Riesman, these priorities both acknowledged and furthered the gestation of a new kind of person, the product of a dense new network of socialization forces whose immense aggregate force often left parents feeling like nervous bystanders. Unlike their inner-directed predecessors, such children look to their contemporaries as "the source of direction for the individual – either those known to him or those with whom he is indirectly acquainted, through friends and through the mass media."[53] Their individual worth, the appropriateness of their behavior, the acceptability of their tastes, and so on – all are judged, in the end, by "a jury of their peers"; hence there is good reason to have one's radar in good operating order. In that peer group, contemporaries compete against one another to achieve "marginal differentiation," even as they appeal to one another for approbation – a paradoxical combination of the sociable and the unsociable that Riesman labeled "antagonistic cooperation."[54] And, as Riesman repeatedly emphasized, the mass media play a critical role in this characterological transformation. "Increasingly," Riesman observed, "relations with the outer world and with oneself are mediated by the flow of mass communications"; a statement, it should be remembered, made when television broadcasting was still in its infancy.[55]

[52] Ibid., 22. In the 1961 edition Riesman himself added a note mentioning the Sullivan–Freud contrast (30). See also Harry Stack Sullivan, *The Interpersonal Theory of Psychiatry,* ed. Helen Swick Perry (New York, 1953); and Perry's superb biography of Sullivan, *Psychiatrist of America: The Life of Harry Stack Sullivan* (Cambridge, 1982).

[53] Riesman, *The Lonely Crowd,* 22.

[54] Ibid., 82–83. This insight is also applicable to the professions; for what is peer review but judgment by a jury of one's peers? For an examination of the inability of professions to achieve internal disinterestedness, see Thomas L. Haskell, "Professionalism *versus* Capitalism: R. H. Tawney, Emile Durkheim, and C. S. Peirce on the Disinterestedness of Professional Communities," in Thomas L. Haskell, ed., *The Authority of Experts: Studies in History and Theory* (Bloomington, Ind., 1984), 180–225.

[55] Riesman, *The Lonely Crowd,* 21–22.

The consequences of that mediation were especially striking in the business of child rearing. Children were now "bombarded by radio and comics from the moment [they] can listen and just barely read"; and such exposure not only began the child's absorption into a distinctive peer culture, but initiated the socially important task of training him as a consumer. Consumer taste became a crucial part of the other-directed child's social equipment, virtually a substitute for etiquette in easing one's way into the group and allowing one to grasp the "socialization of consumer preferences" so indispensable to membership in good standing. (Are Chevys to be preferred to Fords? McDonald's to Burger King? Coca-Cola to Pepsi? As anyone with school-age children knows, the answers to these inconsequential questions might turn out to be very consequential indeed.) Riesman also looked closely at the attributes of children's stories, always an important agency of character formation and socialization, and there too he saw change. Instead of the quintessentially inner-directed story "The Little Engine That Could," other-directed parents were reading to their children stories like "Tootle the Engine," a "cautionary tale" in which the adventurous young engine Tootle lands in trouble because of his unwillingness to "stay on the tracks" with the other engines, as his instructors have repeatedly warned him to do. Riesman also supplied the following example, which is not quite so tongue-in-cheek as it may first seem:

> We may mark the change by citing an old nursery rhyme:
>
> "This little pig went to market;
> This little pig stayed at home.
> This little pig had roast beef;
> This little pig had none.
> This little pig went wee-wee-wee
> All the way home."
>
> The rhyme may be taken as a paradigm of individuation and unsocialized behavior among children of an earlier era. Today, however, all little pigs go to market; none stay home; all have roast beef, if any do; and all say "we-we."[56]

The new other-directed sensibility, then, is most clearly visible in children growing up under the new dispensation; it is not quite so evident in their parents, who must dwell in the twilight zone of transition. Even adults who in effect accepted the other-directed regime, at

[56] Ibid., 98–99.

the same time still held conscious convictions acquired under the auspices of inner-direction; and contemporary social institutions also still reflected an admixture of these convictions. But the characterological shift was no less real for these ambiguities:

> The parents, harking back as they do in their character structures to an earlier era, are themselves competitive – more overtly so than the children. Much of our ideology – free enterprise, individualism, and all the rest – remains competitive and is handed down by parents, teachers, and the mass media. At the same time there has been an enormous ideological shift favoring submission to the group, a shift whose decisiveness is concealed by the persistence of the older ideological patterns. The peer-group becomes the measure of all things; the individual has few defenses the group cannot batter down.[57]

A far cry, indeed, from the language of chaotic inner jungles needing to be tamed.

3

Other-direction, then, did not seem an acceptable resting place for the development of the American character; and it was for this reason that Riesman elected, in the book's concluding pages, to put forward an alternative, to both inner- and other-direction, that he called "autonomy." In so doing, he rather abruptly modulated the discussion into a different key – a more fluid, more optimistic, less deterministic key whose tonic was one of the resounding concepts of classical liberalism, and moreover a crucial underpinning for a morality compatible with "the culture of the market." There is some reason to wonder, however, whether such a reappropriation was really possible for Riesman. A brief excursus into the history of the concept of autonomy may help illuminate the grounds of this problem.

Although "autonomy" is an ancient Greek word, it designates a largely modern idea, the idea of the individual's moral self-governance.[58] This understanding of autonomy can be understood as a

[57] Ibid., 82.

[58] Of course, I am speaking here strictly of its meaning in the context of moral philosophy, not in the context of political institutions or biological organisms. It is interesting that the *Oxford English Dictionary* gives priority to those meanings, and presents the Kantian sense of autonomy as metaphorical. The liberal conception of autonomy has antecedents in Stoic writers like Epictetus and Marcus Aurelius. See John Gray, *Liberalism* (Minneapolis, 1986), 59–61.

product of the Reformation's freeing of the individual conscience, although even the Lutheran notion of "the priesthood of the believer" presumed ultimate obedience to God, not an individual's empowerment to do-as-thou-wilt. In Kant's view, too, autonomy was really a fairly rigorously circumscribed concept. It stood for the capacity of a rational being to subject himself or herself to self-generated – but *rational,* and therefore universal – laws. Kant was just as dissatisfied as Riesman was with the compulsive quality of much of what passed for morality; autonomy was for him truly "the basis of the dignity of both human nature and every rational nature."[59] He even contrasted "autonomy" with "heteronomy," a word that could be almost exactly translated as "other-direction."

But autonomy actually entailed an enormous responsibility, that of imaginatively legislating for the rest of humanity, by the terms of the famous categorical imperative – "Act only according to that maxim by which you can at the same time will that it should become a universal law."[60] In that sense, the autonomous person was no more "free" to create his or her own values than was Luther, or Sophocles's Antigone. But such a standard arguably made the concept of freedom more meaningful, especially in a world still glowing in the contented early Enlightenment belief in a lawful universe. Yes, the will was subject to the law, "but subject in such a way that it must be regarded also as self-legislative and *only for this reason* as being subject to the law (of which it can regard itself as the author)."[61] Autonomy is thus also distinguished from mere self-indulgence or appetitive license; instead of being governed – "directed" – by religious precepts, by the traditional *nomoi,* or by whims, appetites, and other compulsive forces within and without, one could declare one's independence, and become the constitutional monarch of one's own soul. That constitution, though, was not easily amended.

In retrospect we are likely to see Kant's formulations as one of the most impressive efforts in a brave *arrière-garde* effort to save rules of morality from the terrors of an entirely individual, "emotivist" standard – no standard at all, really, since it cannot refer persuasively

59 Immanuel Kant, *Foundations of the Metaphysics of Morals,* trans. Lewis White Beck (Indianapolis, 1954), 54.
60 Ibid., 39.
61 Ibid., 49. My emphasis.

to anything outside of itself. Utilitarianism, too, was involved in the same fight, putting forward the principle of "utility" as a practical teleological substitute for divinely sanctioned moral principles. But neither was able to hold back the antinomian tide that would be so powerfully embodied in Nietzsche.[62] A wild and vital experience of radical freedom swept in, demolishing rational authority in the process; "the price paid for liberation from what appeared to be the external authority of traditional morality," writes Alasdair MacIntyre, "was the loss of any authoritative content from the would-be moral utterances of the autonomous agent." The moral agent in his radical freedom "spoke unconstrained by the externalities of divine law, natural teleology, or hierarchical authority; but why should anyone else now listen to him?"[63] The marketplace of moral ideas had become a consumer's paradise; but many of the goods were of questionable value.

One can see this development as both the culmination and failure of what MacIntyre calls "the Enlightenment project of providing [the autonomous moral agent] with a secular, rational justification for his moral allegiances."[64] It was "Nietzsche's historic achievement to understand more clearly than any other philosopher . . . that what purported to be appeals to objectivity were in fact expressions of subjective will."[65] The "death of God" – the death of an ultimate external authority – is both a cause and a consequence of this unmasking. Yet it is important to remember that at roughly the same moment in Western intellectual history, the Enlightenment project was in the process of erecting another, entirely different, self-negating criticism, arising out of the new discipline of sociology. As Robert Nisbet has pointed out, the nineteenth century witnessed a reorientation of social thought that was, in many respects, as momentous as that which the Enlightenment originated:

> In widening areas of thought in the nineteenth century we see rationalist individualism (kept alive, of course, most impressively by the utilitarians, whose doctrines provide negative relief for so many sociological concepts) assailed by theories resting upon a reassertion of tradition, theories that would have been as repugnant to a Descartes or a Bacon as to a Locke or a

[62] Alasdair MacIntyre, *After Virtue: A Study in Moral Theory* (Notre Dame, 1981), 60.
[63] Ibid., 65–6.
[64] Ibid., 65.
[65] Ibid., 107.

Rousseau. We see the historic premise of the innate stability of the individual challenged by a new social psychology that derived personality from the close contexts of society and that made alienation the price of man's release from these contexts. Instead of the Age of Reason's cherished natural order, it is now the institutional order – community, kinship, social class – that forms the point of departure for social philosophers as widely separated in their views as Coleridge, Marx, and Tocqueville. From the eighteenth century's generally optimistic vision of popular sovereignty we pass to nineteenth century premonitions of the tyranny that may lie in popular democracy when its institutional and traditional limits are broken through. And finally, even the idea of progress is given a new statement: one resting not upon release from community and tradition but upon a kind of craving for new forms of moral and social community.[66]

In other words, at the very same time that Nietzsche disdainfully pushed aside the dream of rational autonomy, the new discipline of sociology was pulling the rug out from under it, asserting that the binding irrational force of its master concepts or root metaphors – such as community, status, authority, alienation, the sacred – inevitably transformed the autonomous actor back into an inescapably social and "heteronomous" creature. Ironically, as the willingness to believe in God or divine law receded from intellectual life, the willingness to believe in the inexorable human need for "authority" and "the sacred" gained ground. At the same time that individuals more and more freely declared their independence from norms, the assertion that norms were ultimately indispensable to any kind of social order seemed more and more persuasive.[67]

Which brings us back again to the questions raised earlier about *The Lonely Crowd*. By taking up the cudgel for autonomy, was Riesman not only battling the recent past of American intellectual history, and the current social and cultural tendencies of postwar America – but also disregarding the very structural presuppositions of his discipline, and skipping by the mounting evidence that "autonomy" was, at best, a problematic ideal?[68] Was he, in a sense, writing an antisociological work of sociology, by creating powerful typologies of

[66] Robert Nisbet, *The Sociological Tradition* (New York, 1966), 9.

[67] One should also take note of the odd combination of tribute and demystification that concepts like "norms," "authority," and "the sacred" capture. The vocabulary of social science stands in a strange, characteristically modern stance in that respect, for it renders less accessible the very things whose necessity it proclaims.

[68] I have not even mentioned the problems presented Riesman by the multiplicity of the self in modern depth psychology.

social character, and then exhorting the reader to cast them aside? If the norms embodied in "social character" are to be a genuine prerequisite for social cohesion, then how can one pick and choose which ones to obey? By what standard?[69]

So far as the text of *The Lonely Crowd* is concerned, the answers to these questions are elusive, since the discussion of autonomy is not nearly so concrete and well developed as what precedes it. This deficiency became a factor influencing the book's critical reception. Although many reviewers lauded the book, some rather pointedly exempted the ending from their praise, which was precisely the part of the book in which Riesman put forward the ideal of autonomy. *Commonweal*'s reviewer, for example, called the book "one of the most penetrating and comprehensive views of the twentieth century urban American you're likely to find," but with a "disappointing happy ending."[70] The *New Yorker*'s critic believed the book was admirably "spirited," beautifully written, and "full of sharp and disturbing conclusions," but that its "chief weakness is its ending, which leaves us entirely up in the air, uncertain of where we go next."[71]

Riesman himself later acknowledged this fault in the book. It would have been hard for him not to, since, as he remarked in the 1961 preface to *The Lonely Crowd,* "most articulate readers of *The Lonely Crowd* . . . tended to regard inner-direction and autonomy as much the same thing." He believed that "the confusion between autonomy and inner-direction that many readers fell into reflects our own inability to make the idea of autonomy a more vivid and less formal one – to give it content, as inner-direction gained content because the concept called to mind many historical exemplars available to everyone's experience."[72] In an article published early in 1990, he went further, acknowledging that "the notion of autonomy was rather thinly sketched," and that "[a]s it was interpreted by many readers, it proved to be at best an ambiguous and at worst a harmful ideal"; it "strengthened the cult of candor," and gave rise to "a new hypocrisy" in which "we disguised even from ourselves our virtuous selves, our impulses of caring and concern toward others."[73] It be-

[69] Wiebe, *The Search for Order,* 144, has a useful formulation of this same problem.
[70] *Commonweal,* October 5, 1951, 621.
[71] *New Yorker,* November 4, 1950, 166.
[72] Riesman, *The Lonely Crowd* (1969 edition), lvi.
[73] Riesman, "Innocence of *The Lonely Crowd,*" 77.

came, in short, a sanction for a kind of low-grade Nietzschean individualism. It negated the categories of compulsion, but without supplying a sufficient philosophical basis for moral freedom.

This is far from being the only serious criticism of *The Lonely Crowd.*[74] Not only was the book unclear about the distinction between inner-direction and autonomy, but it was confusing in its judgment about the relative merits of inner- and other-direction. When looking at the matter from a strictly developmental standpoint, though, Riesman was likely to suggest that other-direction was more advanced than inner-direction, and therefore would more easily evolve into a state of autonomy. For example,

> other-direction gives men a sensitivity and rapidity of movement which under prevailing American institutions provide a large opportunity to explore the resources of character . . . and these suggest to me at least the possibility of an organic development of autonomy out of other-direction.[75]

This optimism, so characteristic of the book's "Autonomy" section, had much to do with some of the specific features of autonomy that the book identified. To deal with the problem of other-directed "false personalization" in the workplace ("the spurious and effortful glad hand"), he recommended a general "de-personalizing" of work, so that other-directed workers would be able to save their precious

[74] Some of the most penetrating critiques of the book were offered by historians, who quarreled with Riesman's claim of a characterological shift. Carl Degler argued that Americans had *always* been other-directed, and that there was essential continuity between the nineteenth and twentieth centuries; see his "The Sociologist as Historian: Riesman's *The Lonely Crowd,*" *American Quarterly,* 15, no. 4 (1963), 483–97. See also the spirited response to Degler by Cushing Strout, "A Note on Degler, Riesman, and Tocqueville," *American Quarterly,* 16, no. 1 (1964), 100–102. David Potter disputed the validity of Riesman's cultural generalizations, arguing that, like those of Frederick Jackson Turner and others before him, these extrapolated exclusively from male experience; see his "American Women and the American Character," in John A. Hague, ed., *American Character and Culture in a Changing World: Some Twentieth-Century Perspectives* (Westport, Conn., 1979), 209–25. For our purposes, however, the interest lies less in the historical validity of Riesman's argument, although that issue ultimately cannot be ignored, than in a consideration of the significance of the Riesman argument as a reflection of its own times.

[75] Riesman, *The Lonely Crowd* (1969 edition), 260. In the original unrevised 1950 edition, this passage is far more rambling and obscure: "his very other-direction gives [the adjusted other-directed man] a sensitivity and rapidity of movement that may be historically new. That part of his social character which fits him for his roles at work is a smaller part of his total character than among most tradition-directed and inner-directed types. To be sure, he has been strenuously socialized and has lost much of himself in the process" (306). Surely the revision represented a clarification.

"emotional reserves" for use in play – play having become "the sphere for the development of skill and competence in the art of living."[76] Therefore, "competence in play" was precisely what is wanted for the transition to autonomy. This training in competence was heavily oriented toward consumership, the development of taste, the discovery of fun and fulfilling leisure pursuits (through the assistance of "avocational counselors"), and the liberation of fantasy. (One is reminded of *Time*'s sidebar portrait of Riesman as, above all, a discerning consumer.) For example, he suggested "the creation of model consumer economies among children," offering a description of a "world's fair for children" that is eerily reminiscent of the economic system depicted in Bellamy's *Looking Backward:*

> A group of advertisers . . . might issue scrip money to groups of children, allowing them to patronize some central store – a kind of everyday world's fair – where a variety of "luxury" goods ranging from rare foods to musical instruments would be available for their purchase. At this "point of sale" there would stand market researchers, able and willing to help children make their selection but having no particularly frightening charisma or overbearing charm or any interest on the employers' side in pushing one thing rather than another. These "experiment stations" might become the source of revealing information about what happens to childhood taste when it is given a free track away from the taste gradients and "reasons," as well as freedom from the financial hobbles of a given peer-group. In precisely such situations children might find the opportunity to criticize and reshape in their own minds the values of objects. In the "free store" they would find private alcoves where they might enjoy books and music, candy and comics, in some privacy.[77]

This remarkable passage, which is perhaps the most specific exemplification of autonomy in the book, suggests several things about Riesman's conception. First, that autonomy is well modeled in a market situation, but a market in which consumer choices are artificially purged of all adulterations, such as needs, advertising, sales pressure, peers – and "reasons." The buyer is not a Kantian will, or even a Freudian ego, but a kind of unmoved mover-connoisseur whose freedom lies precisely in his or her imperviousness to external influences. Yet Riesman also believed there was political value in such experiments. "Market research," he remarked, "has for many years seemed to me one of the most promising channels for demo-

[76] Riesman, *The Lonely Crowd,* 326.
[77] Ibid., 339–40.

cratic control of our economy," since market researchers "can be employed to find out not so much what people want but what with liberated fantasy they might want."[78] On the seventh day of creation, it seems, God rested in peace, while the autonomous went shopping.

In short, Riesman's conception of autonomy is empty or, at best, a negative concept, since it negates whatever is compulsory in his other characterological types without supplying anything tangible to take its place. He makes no effort to struggle with the paradoxes of autonomy that Kant so painstakingly addressed. His vision of a radically unconditioned self is remarkably benign; there is no Nietzschean abyss or heroic amoralism anywhere to be seen. And, to repeat a point that must be frequently stressed about *The Lonely Crowd,* it assumed that economic abundance was here to stay, that the problems of economic production had been solved; therefore, the conflicts that typified a scarcity economy would no longer be a significant factor in Americans' lives.[79]

This is not to heap even more criticism onto Riesman's own self-criticism, but to point out that the "misreadings" he lamented were thoroughly legitimate. Indeed, it is no wonder that readers who followed the book's argument to the point where "autonomy" is introduced became badly confused. For in the first three-fourths of the book's pages, *The Lonely Crowd* presented a chilling (if humorously related) story of the embattled individual whose very socialization was yoked to the consumption preferences of his peers, and of a society that has corrupted the meaning of its governmental institutions into "politics as an object of consumption."[80] Just as important, if much more difficult to pin down, was the tone of that portion of his account, which often suggested (albeit without ever stating) an ironic, even Veblenian disdain for his subject. In the case of Veblen, his peculiar literary style is crucial to his meaning, since its severe, defamiliarizing detachment conveys a mocking and supercilious undercurrent that is all the more effective for being unstated.[81] Riesman

[78] Ibid., 341.

[79] A similar presumption lies at the base of David Potter, *People of Plenty: Economic Abundance and the American Character* (Chicago, 1954).

[80] Riesman, *The Lonely Crowd,* 210–17.

[81] It is important to recognize, though, that Riesman was not a Veblenian, as Colin Campbell seems to assert in *The Romantic Ethic and the Spirit of Modern Consumerism* (New York, 1987), 8. See, for example, David Riesman, *Thorstein Veblen: A Critical Interpretation* (Boston, 1953).

and his collaborators are far less consistent in, and exert less control over, the messages conveyed by their stylistic choices; but the following passage may be taken as one of many possible instances when a Veblenian undercurrent appears:

> Business is supposed to be fun. . . . The demand to have fun is one that the inner-directed businessman never faced. He could afford to be properly gloomy and grim. The shortening of hours . . . has extended the requirements for office sociability largely in the top management of business, government, and academic life. Here people spend long hours in the company of their office peer-group. Their lunches are long; their golf games longer still. Much time in the office itself is also spent in sociability: exchanging office gossip ("conferences"), making good-will tours ("inspection"), talking to salesmen and joshing secretaries ("morale"). In fact, depleting the expense account can serve as an almost limitless occupational therapy for men who, out of a tradition of hard work, a dislike of their wives, a lingering asceticism, and an anxiety about their antagonistic cooperators, still feel that they must put in a good day's work at the office. But, of course . . . this kind of sociability, carrying so much workaday freight, was [not] free or sociable.[82]

It is hard to disentangle the satirical from the descriptive in such a passage; that is part of its charm. The satire is carried by the very way the scene is observed and narrated, by the observer's implicit distancing of himself from all that he is observing. It recalls the comic stance of social-observation stylists that Kenneth Lynn called "the style of a gentleman," a pose that conveys to the reader, in detailed but mildly amused prose, one's superiority to one's subject – a subject, moreover, for whom the author wants to make certain he cannot be mistaken. It is a style, therefore, especially useful in a fluid social world, like that of Addisonian London or colonial America – or Riesman's own upwardly mobile Fifties.[83]

But the comparison of Veblen's view with the modus operandi of *The Lonely Crowd* would surely elicit a howl of protest from Riesman, and not without reason. He has often taken great pains to stress explicitly his abhorrence of elitism, his distaste for those critics who snobbishly stigmatize popular culture and popular tastes, his serious intellectual and conceptual differences with Veblen.[84] All of that is

[82] Riesman, *The Lonely Crowd,* 142.
[83] Kenneth S. Lynn, *Mark Twain and Southwestern Humor* (Boston, 1959), 3–22.
[84] See Riesman, *Thorstein Veblen;* and J. L. Simich and Rich Tilman, "On the Use and Abuse of Thorstein Veblen in Modern American Sociology, I: David Riesman's

readily granted, but the problem remains: Does the style, intentionally or not, communicate a distaste for other-directed men that clashes with the explicit disclaimers? Is *The Lonely Crowd* a book moving, like surf waters, in two different directions at once? If so, is the force of its incoming waves enfeebled by the great power of its undertow, so that the reader is not propelled joyfully forward into the direction of autonomous consumption but is instead pulled backward – to echo Dewey's phrase one more time – into a yearning for inner-direction?

The answer cannot be a simple one. To be sure, the book sometimes genuinely attempts a tone of ethnography, an air of scientific neutrality; but then that may unexpectedly give way to a strong suggestion of moral critique. Too many pages pass an unfavorable judgment upon the other-directed, whether explicitly or implicitly, and the cumulative effect is too unrelievedly negative to be entirely disposed of by Riesman's claim that he was trying to "develop a view of society which accepts rather than rejects new potentialities for leisure, human sympathy, and abundance."[85] Even the book's most ardent admirers admitted the problem. No one cheered *The Lonely Crowd* more loudly than Lionel Trilling, who called it "one of the most important books about America to have been published," as well as "one of the most interesting books that I have ever read"; who mused after reading it whether sociology was not "taking over from literature one of literature's most characteristic functions, the investigation and criticism of morals and manners," for Riesman had shown he could write "with a sense of social actuality which Scott Fitzgerald might have envied." This was almost unimaginably high praise, coming from such a high priest of the literary imagination. But Trilling nonetheless tempered his praise in one important respect, observing that

> Mr. Riesman remarks that he had found it almost impossible to make a comparison of the two forms of character-direction without making inner-direction seem the more attractive. I don't agree with Mr. Riesman that the

Reductionist Interpretation and Talcott Parsons' Pluralist Critique," *American Journal of Economics and Sociology,* 42, no. 4, 417–29, especially 419–22. The latter is a somewhat unfair attack on Riesman, which nevertheless illuminates his differences with Veblen, and the extent of his Freudianism and tendency to psychologize Veblen's work as an "internalized colloquy between his parents."

85 Riesman, *The Lonely Crowd* (1969 edition), 160.

preference is a mere prejudice which we must guard against. . . . it is still inner-direction that must seem the more fully human, even in its excess.[86]

Hence, it is hardly surprising that many readers were inclined to agree with Trilling, and to find the central part of the book – the invidious contrast between inner- and other-direction – was the only part that really spoke to them, or the only part they heard.[87] Thus, they read *The Lonely Crowd* selectively, conflating inner-direction and autonomy, and ignoring Riesman's utopian-consumerist flights of fancy. For that central opposition between inner- and other-direction spoke powerfully to a long-standing repertoire of Americans' most enduring fears. The British scholar Rupert Wilkinson recently argued that what he calls "the four fears" have been especially characteristic of Americans: the fear of "being owned"; the fear of "falling apart"; the fear of "falling away"; and the fear of "winding down."[88] These distinctions deserve more attention than is possible here, but they can be roughly described. The first relates precisely to the loss of independence and autonomy; the second, to the dissolution of the community into egoism and chaos; the third, to the specter of moral and spiritual decline; and the fourth, to the loss of personal economic dynamism, and the competitive spirit. These fears are also related to one another, as polarities: the first against the second, and the third against the fourth. All but the second are powerfully present in *The Lonely Crowd.*

4

That, then, returns us to the rumbling anxieties stirring beneath the placid surface of America's postwar preeminence; and it appears that *The Lonely Crowd* may have mirrored its times rather exactly, turning out to be significant even in its ambivalences. This may be more frequently the case than we know. "The whole history of ideas,"

[86] Lionel Trilling, "A Change of Direction," in *The Griffin,* 1, no. 3 (1952), 5. This essay, combined with a later, even more admiring essay on *Individualism Reconsidered,* is reprinted in Trilling's "Two Notes on David Riesman," in *A Gathering of Fugitives* (Boston, 1956), 85–100.

[87] See the shrewd account in James Gilbert, *Another Chance: Postwar America, 1945–85* (Chicago, 1986), 117, although it is worth noting that Gilbert makes no mention of the difference between inner-direction and autonomy.

[88] Wilkinson, *The Pursuit of American Character,* 71–117.

declared the anthropologist Mary Douglas, "should be reviewed in the light of the power of social structures to generate symbols of their own."[89] Perhaps a "symbolic" way of reading *The Lonely Crowd* would dwell less on its internal inconsistencies than on its cultural consistencies, they way in which its internal tensions are just as meaningful – perhaps more meaningful – than its explicit argument. What I mean by this may be illuminated by another criticism that can be leveled at the book.

This criticism revolves around the very central concept of "social character," part of Riesman's Frommian patrimony. It is, so to speak, the opposite number to "autonomy," and as such, suffers in the end from the same ambiguities and antinomies that beset autonomy. On the one hand, the inculcation of "social character" is absolutely necessary for the smooth and integrated functioning of a society; on the other, it can and should be set aside at will, by hardy men and women who have the psychological wherewithal for true individuation. With this paradox, we have arrived, by a different route, at familiar ground, the conjunction of the "sociological" and "Nietzschean" critiques of rational autonomy. But if we look carefully at the account Riesman gives of certain phenomena he observes – if, as D. H. Lawrence put it, we trust the tale and not the teller – we may detect a somewhat different, and possibly more fruitful, perspective on this impasse.[90]

If it is really imperative that something called "social character" be inculcated by a society, we should see it most clearly when we look at child rearing and schooling. But much of Riesman's evidence, if followed disinterestedly, appears to point to the conclusion that those institutions are doing a very bad job of it. (And if they are doing a bad job, how imperative can his conception of "social character" be?) Consider, for example, the passage quoted near the end of section 2 of this essay, which concludes with the Protagorian proclamation that "the peer-group becomes the measure of all things." It is an impressive sentence; but one's reaction becomes complicated by what follows:

> The competitive drives for achievement sponsored in children by the remnants of inner-direction in their parents come into conflict with the cooperative

[89] Cited in Warren Susman, *Culture As History: The Transformation of American Society in the Twentieth Century,* 271.

[90] D. H. Lawrence, *Studies in Classic American Literature* (New York, 1923), 8.

demands sponsored by the peer-group. The child therefore is required to channel the competitive drive for achievement, *as demanded by the parent,* into his drive for approval. . . . Neither parent, child, nor the peer-group is particularly conscious of this process. As a result all three participants in the process may remain unaware of *the degree to which the force of an older individualistic ideology provides the energies for filling out the forms of a newer, group-oriented characterology.*[91]

The more one looks at these words, the more one feels the phenomenon is being forced into Procrustean categories that do not quite explain what is going on. Suppose, for example, we were to look at the same phenomena from a more or less functionalist position. Would we not ask different questions? For example, what social purpose does this somewhat confusing mixture of messages, of individualism and group-consciousness, serve? Why do our institutions of character formation work in the way that they do? Is it possible that they *have* to work in that way, to produce the kind of person the society needs? Is it possible, moreover, that the closest we can come to a *social* description of moral autonomy is to envision a shifting balance between inner- and other-direction?

The Lonely Crowd's famous chapter entitled "Americans and Kwakiutls" provides an even better example of its tendency to interpret ideological inconsistency as misperception. Riesman asked students who had read Ruth Benedict's classic work *Patterns of Culture* to tell him which of three "primitive societies" depicted in its pages the United States most closely resembled: the mild and cooperative Pueblo, the aggressive Dobu, or the competitive Kwakiutl. No students, according to Riesman, chose the Pueblo, despite its arguable similarities to the emerging culture of other-direction; apparently these students were still too thoroughly imbued with individualist "legends about America that are preserved in our literature" to recognize that the world they will live in does not correspond to those hoary narratives. At the same time, though, these students do not hesitate to say they "would prefer to live in the Pueblo culture," remarked Riesman, adding with amazement, that "while this choice is in itself not to be quarreled with, the important fact is that they do not know that they already are living in such a culture."[92]

[91] Riesman, *The Lonely Crowd,* 83. My emphasis.
[92] Ibid., 271–82.

Again, the same questions arise, and they might be summarized by asking: Are the students not, at the very least, living in a culture that could, in a way that is essential rather than incidental, accommodate features of both Pueblo and Kwakiutl cultures? Is their own perception of America to be so airily dismissed? Isn't there something wrong with a conception of social character that is so diametrically at odds with the experience of the world that its supposed possessors have? Is that not yet another change rung on the charge of false consciousness – a charge that, strangely, takes the students to task for convincing themselves that their world is *worse* than it actually is?

The problems raised by these questions might be lessened, if not solved, were Riesman to have envisioned inner- and other-direction as coexisting polar opposites, resembling in some respects the Jungian psychological distinction between introversion and extraversion, inevitably in tension with one another; and that their *simultaneous* inculcation is the social goal of schools and parents.[93] Whatever consequences that might bring for his broader historical argument, it would better highlight what the book's contemporary readers found to be so powerful in it – the palpable tensions that it depicted, tensions that individuals could easily discover in themselves and those they knew, between inner and outer, freedom and compulsion, in an increasingly organized world. Americans' social character, in this view, would have a polar or bifurcated aspect built into it, not an imperfectly unitary one. A critic looking for monolithic consistency in social character would be put off by Wilkinson's "four fears" because they are contradictory, mutually exclusive. How can a people fear such wildly different things? But as Erik Erikson observed in *Childhood and Society,* a book published in the same year as *The Lonely Crowd,* "whatever one may come to consider a truly American trait can be shown to have its equally characteristic opposite."[94] A culture that values, indeed thrives on, the antagonism of opposites must find a way to feed the fires of both.

As for the matter of the book's historical dimension, its claim on

[93] C. G. Jung, *Two Essays in Analytical Psychology,* trans. R. F. C. Hull (Princeton, 1953), 41–63; and *Psychological Types,* trans. H. G. Baynes and R. F. C. Hull (Princeton, 1971), 330–407.

[94] Erik Erikson, *Childhood and Society* (New York, 1950), 285.

the reader's attention as a view of "the changing American character," that too may benefit from some reconsideration. Just as the early modern market elicited and legitimated traits of character that were already present in many individuals but had hitherto lacked an institution in which they might express themselves – so, too, do organized modern societies with large bureaucracies and powerful mass media call forth and reinforce certain traits of character. But it may be more accurate to see this change not as a shift from one typology to another, but as a shift towards a coexistence of (and friction between) the two. Not only would this formulation better capture the experience of Riesman's contemporary readers – *The Lonely Crowd* as cultural symbol, uniting the pulls of inner-direction and other-direction, along with a glance toward autonomy – but it might also suggest a different kind of social explanation, and even a different approach to the great sociological dualisms.

This last possibility has been explored by Thomas Bender in an intriguing book tracing conceptions of community and social change in America. Looking at the most influential of all sociological dualisms – *Gemeinschaft* and *Gesellschaft* – Bender proposes that it be understood, not as designating strictly discrete and sequential phases in the evolution of human social relations, but as signifying two different kinds of relations that, particularly in a modern society, coexist and contend with one another. "The task of the cultural historian," Bender argues, "is not to date the moment when one of the worlds of social relations is replaced by the other," but to "probe their interaction and to assess their relative salience to people's lives in specific situations" – to discover a perspective that takes in "the simultaneous polarity and reciprocity of these two patterns of human interaction."[95] One benefit of this approach is that it helps us account for the ways that premodern, traditional, and *Gemeinschaftlich* ways and values coexist with, and even interpenetrate, the characteristic ways of the modern world, contrary to a more monolithic understanding of modernization. Perhaps the typologies of *The Lonely Crowd* may best be understood in a similar way – as contending polarities, neither of which entirely vanquishes the other – indeed, each of which stands in a compensatory relationship to the other.

[95] Thomas Bender, *Community and Social Change in America* (New Brunswick, 1978), 1–43.

5

But there is an important difference between these sets of dualisms. *Gemeinschaft* was the world of the traditional community, and *Gesellschaft* was, among other things, the world of the market, and of rational, calculating, commerce-minded individuals engaging in instrumental, functional transactions; indeed, "the historical development of the market," Bender reminds us, "constitutes a crucial element in the emergence of a bifurcated society described in Tönnies's *Gemeinschaft und Gesellschaft*."[96] The combination of the two elements in the bifurcation – community and society, traditional and modern – play off one another, compensating for one another's weakness. In particular, the persistence of the traditional "community" form of relationship continued to be a rich resource for the kind of nonpecuniary values that a strictly calculating "society" did not cherish.

The worlds that correspond to inner- and other-direction, however, are *both* market worlds – expressions, perhaps, of two somewhat different "cultures of the market," corresponding roughly to entrepreneurial and corporate capitalism. But given the weakness of tradition-direction in Riesman's vision, he can offer no countervailing polarity to mitigate the social shaping force of the market. This is perhaps merely a way of arguing that America was born modern and liberal, as so many observers from Tocqueville to Louis Hartz have asserted.[97] As a comprehensive historical understanding of American political and social thought, that view may have its limitations, as Richard B. Latner argues elsewhere in this collection.[98] But one easily may judge, particularly by observing the strenuousness of scholarly efforts in the past three decades to resuscitate lost or abandoned strains of American political and social thought, how thoroughly these languages were submerged by the time Riesman was writing.

"Republican" ideas have recently been thriving in the protected and climate-controlled environment of academe; Marxism has been thriving there even longer; there has even been a renaissance (or *naissance*)

[96] Ibid., 111.
[97] Louis Hartz, *The Liberal Tradition in America* (New York, 1955).
[98] Richard B. Latner, "Preserving 'The Natural Equality of Rank and Influence': Liberalism, Republicanism, and Equality of Condition in Jacksonian Politics," Chapter 6 of this volume.

of traditionalist-conservative thought in the postwar decades; but once the Petri dishes are opened to public scrutiny, the delicate microorganisms contained therein are often snuffed out by the inhospitable atmosphere.[99] A similar fate nearly always befalls efforts to bring religious ideas into American public life openly as principles of moral organization. Again, this has certainly not always been the case in American history; but it certainly *was* the case for Riesman, whose near complete silence on the subject of religion in *The Lonely Crowd* is in itself an emphatic position.[100] For all the historical inaccuracies with which Louis Hartz's *Liberal Tradition in America* has been tasked, its fundamental *cri de coeur* – where is there to be found a vital and survivable alternative? – retains its force.

In that respect, with Riesman and Hartz we find ourselves very comfortably ensconced in the limitations of our own time; *The Lonely Crowd* speaks not only of and for its time, but of and for our own. Perhaps that is one reason why Riesman's portrait of autonomy seems especially disappointing and unsatisfactory, since its mere intensification of selected features of inner- and other-direction really did not alter the terms of discussion in any decisive or illuminating way. The problems remain, of where the means can be found to articulate what Americans should render unto the market, what they should reserve for higher things, and what might be the grounds for such a reservation; and it is not at all clear that question can be effectively answered under the capacious bigtop of liberalism, which prides itself chiefly on its claim to fit everything in.[101] There are writers both on the left and the right who concur in a principled unwillingness to embrace what William Reddy calls "the liberal illusion," an unwillingness to accept the process of exchange as a moral arbiter. This confluence is not to be airily dismissed by the adage *les extrêmes se touchent.*

[99] On the renaissance of conservative ideas, see George Nash, *The Conservative Intellectual Movement in America Since 1945* (New York, 1976); and Paul Edward Gottfried, *The Search for Historical Meaning: Hegel and the Postwar American Right* (DeKalb, Ill., 1986), as well as the forthcoming study by Professor Patrick Allitt of Emory University, of the influence of Roman Catholicism on the postwar conservative movement.

[100] Russell Kirk, *Prospects for Conservatives* (Washington, D.C., 1989), 77–88.

[101] See William Reddy, *Money and Liberty in Modern Europe: A Critique of Historical Understanding* (New York, 1987), ix–32, for a critique of "the liberal illusion." The lack of any going alternative to the liberal tradition is also illustrated, in several ways, by Bellah et al., *Habits of the Heart.*

For Burke and Marx, archetypal *extrêmes,* actually shared certain important elements of common ground; both believed that much that was precious and life-sustaining had been destroyed, in ways both blatant and subtle, by the pitiless demystifications through which the modern order was made. The market, like the Edenic serpent, is perhaps the subtlest of demystifiers, simply by virtue of its avowedly voluntary modus operandi. For its function is to translate a wider and wider range of human interactions into voluntary exchanges of quantifiable and commensurable things. The positive features of this are evident enough; they are the great virtues of full-blown market societies, wherein the individual is liberated from the hereditary and ascriptive limitations that held him or her back in a traditional social order, and is made to feel free to act in a clearly defined economic sphere as an autonomous agent.

Yet, particularly when it is most successful, the market's very operation also tends to subject more and more of the world to the denatured and disenchanted standard of commensurability, and therefore to the peril of becoming just another commodity in a world in which everything has its price. Thus cuts the double edge of demystification. The liberated individual is free to buy the queen's chalice; but only at her estate auction, where it retains little more mystique than what the canny auctioneer chooses to put there. In this view, then, the doctrine of consumer sovereignty, operating as it were through a kind of economic Heisenberg principle, alters the world over which it holds sway. At the same time that it empowers the individual to make his or her own choices, it diminishes the value of the things to be chosen. The deification of individual choice, through the institutionalization of the market, forecloses a host of real, and extremely venerable, human possibilities.

To be sure, there is sometimes an unattractive whiff of snobbishness and paternalism in this criticism, as there is in so many of the critiques of "mass society" and "consumer culture," whether they emanate from the left or the right; but it is a criticism that deserves a better answer than the surly *ad hominem.*[102] One way of answering it might be to remember that the market ethos's penetration into all

[102] Rosenberg and White, *Mass Culture,* contains many of the most important documents in this debate.

dimensions of life was neither envisioned nor advocated by the market's earliest advocates.[103] Indeed, "the market" as such originally designated an independent economic institution that stood outside the network of social, kinship, religious, and cultural ties in which most economic activity had formerly been embedded. Its purpose was the establishment of a space in which such activity was legitimate in its own right, not the elimination of those older ties.[104] It depended, as do all liberal institutions, on the possibility of a theoretical and practical separation of spheres of activity – religious, social, political, economic.

It also presumed a moral counterweight, something akin to the Kantian sense of the *dignity* of things, a notion of unexchangeable and incommensurable worth that a too exclusively market-oriented society violates. Such a one-sided society violates the liberal separate-sphere principle undergirding the original understanding of "the market" just as surely as did a traditional order, where all economic exchange was deeply embedded in, and beholden to, social and cultural institutions. Yes, answers the critic of liberalism, but the fact remains that the one grew out of the other – if, indeed, it was not present from the beginning. Whether one attributes that fact to the overriding importance of economic institutions, or to the ongoing overthrow of all traditional cultural authority that the growth of market relations required, or some combination of the two, the result suggests the great historical fragility of the separate-spheres principle.

The possibility remains, however, that these warnings of the market's conquest of consciousness are overheated and overdrawn; that, as Bender has suggested, traditional ways are not wholly obliterated by modernization; that the notion of tradition itself is far more fluid and more durable (and more profoundly indispensable) than Riesman's account allowed;[105] that metaphors of polarity and polyva-

[103] Richard F. Teichgraeber, *'Free Trade' and Moral Philosophy: Rethinking the Sources of Adam Smith's Wealth of Nations* (Durham, 1986), esp. 121–78; Albert O. Hirschman, *The Passions and the Interests: Political Arguments for Capitalism Before Its Triumph* (Princeton, 1977); and Irving Kristol, *Two Cheers for Capitalism* (New York, 1978).

[104] Bender, *Community and Social Change,* 113. See also Jerry Z. Muller, "Capitalism: The Wave of the Future," *Commentary,* 86, no. 6 (December 1988), 21–26, which also points to the persistence of "community-like institutions" (or what Bender might call *Gemeinschaftlich* institutions) under capitalism.

[105] See Jaroslav Pelikan's insightful *Vindication of Tradition* (New Haven, 1984), based on his 1983 Jefferson Lecture in the Humanities; Edward Shils, *Tradition* (Chicago,

lence, rather than that of separate spheres, may be the better way of coming to terms with the crosscurrents in which we live; that, contra Marx, cultural contradiction is not only inescapable but essential to our condition as historical beings. As José Ortega y Gasset put it, the European man "has been 'democratic,' 'liberal,' 'absolutist,' 'feudal,' " and does "in some way continue being all these things; he does so in the 'form of having been them.' " Or, as the Hungarian-born American historian John Lukacs more succinctly put it, "Nothing in history passes away completely."[106]

6

We return, then, after a second excursus, to look one final time at the ambivalences and polyvalences revealed in our examination of *The Lonely Crowd,* and to a fact about the book that connects it, in the most direct way imaginable, to a consideration of the culture of the market. It is a simple, brute fact, but one that should not be overlooked: the fact that the book *sold,* and kept on selling – by the early 1970s, more than a million copies had sold in the abridged Anchor Books paperback edition – as it continues to sell even today, and to be widely cited and used in the classroom.[107] Why has this been so? If Mary Douglas is right, the answer must be that the culture of the market, too, like any social structure, generates symbolic formulations and figurations of itself – self-portraits, so to speak, of its condition. Those may include complex, self-critical, polyvalent ones such as *The Lonely Crowd,* and such freighted icons as the heroic rendering of the "autonomous" David Riesman and his "directed men" that appeared on the cover of *Time* – or, for that matter, the many other works of social criticism that were published, and sold briskly, in the 1950s. Such self-mirrorings bespeak, and speak to, the dividedness of a highly self-conscious people. Interestingly, the only critic of *The Lonely Crowd* who has taken the full measure of this fact was a

1981); and S. N. Eisenstadt, "Post-Traditional Societies and the Continuity and Reconstruction of Tradition," *Daedalus* 102 (1973), 1–27.

106 John Lukacs, *Outgrowing Democracy: A History of the United States in the Twentieth Century* (New York, 1984), 7.

107 Nathan Glazer, "From Socialism to Sociology," in Berger, ed., *Authors of Their Own Lives,* 202.

German, the sociologist Ralf Dahrendorf, whose words on this subject have about them the wise perspective of cultural distance:

> It is often forgotten that critics like the authors of *The Hidden Persuaders, The Organization Man,* and *The Lonely Crowd* are after all Americans. Their books, although not primarily addressed to a large audience, have become almost best sellers. Nobody is more prepared to deplore the trends they describe than their readers themselves – those, in other words, to whom their criticisms are intended to apply. It is a problem for the sociologist of literature to decide whether the reception is a proof or a refutation of the theses of the studies in question. In any case, it seems clear that so long as this reception is possible there is little reason to claim that American society is as yet a democracy without liberty at the mercy of the hidden persuaders of advertising, run by organization men for whom the Protestant ethic is but a distant myth, and made up of other-directed characters without any internal gyroscope of life.[108]

Whether the reception is a proof or a refutation: this shrewd observation points us back once again to a recognition of the divided consciousness characterizing the very people that Riesman has studied. They recognized Riesman's typologies operating in their own lives; indeed, one can speculate that only those with some degree of other-direction would feel the compulsion to run out and read this book about other-direction, the book about which tout le monde was talking. But the same people would not respond so favorably to the book's unflattering view of other-direction, unless they felt themselves to be (like the author) distinct from that type. Such a conundrum suggests the complexity of the social phenomena *The Lonely Crowd* was registering. It also suggests the tensive space between descriptive typology and jeremiad, social science and social criticism, in which *The Lonely Crowd* itself stands; for it is a work that struggles to reconcile, or at least to contain, the different demands of proof and refutation, description and prescription, detachment and engagement, neutrality and admonition. These contradictions and ambivalences are finally a source of the book's appeal, for they reflect, even more effectively than the authors meant them to, the complicated world with which the book was struggling.

An even more basic element in *The Lonely Crowd,* though, is the related problem of autonomy, one of the fundaments of liberalism,

[108] Ralf Dahrendorf, "Democracy Without Liberty: An Essay on the Politics of Other-Directed Man," in Lipset and Lowenthal, *Culture and Social Character,* 206.

and the foundation for any claim of moral legitimacy to be made on behalf of market culture. A yearning for autonomy was limned in the *Time* portrait of Riesman; yet autonomy, as we have seen, is besieged by antinomies on either side: on its "left" by an extreme Nietzschean (or Emersonian) subjectivism; on its "right" by a social-scientific (or Marxist, or traditionalist) vision of embeddedness.[109] It is sandwiched between the most extreme forms of boundlessness and consolidation. But autonomy is not thereby crushed, or rendered entirely a chimera; it is, for us, like the Kantian conception of moral freedom, a kind of phenomenological irreducible and an inevitable premise of our speech and our action – much as could be said of the concept of objectivity itself, which is subject to the pull of precisely the same antinomies.[110] We cannot live without either. Antinomies are contradictions that cannot be evaded, cannot be reconciled, cannot be denied, cannot be rendered unproblematic, must be lived with, and within.

It is easy to castigate the market on any number of grounds. But it has proved exceedingly difficult to find a palatable and workable substitute. For better or worse, a principled commitment to cultural dissensus has become increasingly axiomatic to the way we live. Riesman saw this development with unusual clarity, and understood it to be an identifying mark of market culture. The market, he wrote in 1952, was one of the social inventions that constituted the "glory of modern large-scale democratically-tending society," precisely because it allows us "to put forward in a given situation only part of ourselves . . . while retaining the privilege of private conscience and of veto."[111] In an environment of cultural dissensus, economic exchange at least provides a common denominator – Riesman called it "a procedural consensus" – a coherence built upon the low but solid ground of commensurability. The market creates, however imperfectly, a space in which people who are radically different from one another can interact freely, respectfully, without having to sacrifice

[109] See Thomas L. Haskell, "Persons as Uncaused Causes: John Stuart Mill, *The Spirit of Capitalism,* and the 'Invention' of Formalism," Chapter 13 of this volume.

[110] Thomas L. Haskell, "Objectivity Is Not Neutrality: Rhetoric vs. Practice in Peter Novick's *That Noble Dream,*" in *History and Theory,* 29, no. 2, 129–57; Thomas Nagel, *The View from Nowhere* (New York, 1986).

[111] Riesman, "Values in Context," in *Individualism Reconsidered,* 18; the essay originally appeared in *American Scholar,* 22, no. 1 (1952).

precious elements of their identity to one another.[112] Voltaire made graphic the virtues of this distinctive social space in a famous passage from his *Lettres philosophiques:*

> Take a view of the Royal Exchange in London, a place more venerable than many courts of justice, where the representatives of all nations meet for the benefit of mankind. There the Jew, the Mahometan, and the Christian transact together as though they all professed the same religion, and give the name of Infidel to none but bankrupts.[113]

Voltaire's dry wit should not conceal the degree to which he was describing a new kind of fidelity, a new ground for consensus. To be sure, one easily can disparage the banality of the common faith displayed here. One could, for example, wistfully contrast it with the higher dignity of precisely those rich traditions and particularistic identities the assembled representatives did *not* share. But not without first granting full recognition to the achievement being here described. If the market is not itself a sufficient source of enduring values, it is at least tolerant of nearly all others, so long as its own are allowed to flourish. Perhaps that last clause represents a high price to pay. But it may be the best that a polyvalent, pluralistic, tradition/inner/other-directed soul, yearning somehow to be both autonomous and connected, but often feeling merely lonely and crowded, can aspire to.

[112] Muller, "Capitalism," 26: "The market may erode noneconomic values, *yet it also permits their expression,* by allowing those with diverse goals to cooperate without agreement on some ultimate common purpose." (My emphasis.)

[113] Voltaire, "On the Presbyterians," from *Letters Concerning the English Nation,* in Peter Gay, ed., *The Enlightenment: A Comprehensive Anthology* (New York, 1973), 150–51.

CHAPTER 13

Persons as uncaused causes: John Stuart Mill, the spirit of capitalism, and the "invention" of formalism

THOMAS L. HASKELL

During the later returns of my dejection, the doctrine of what is called Philosophical Necessity weighed on my existence like an incubus. I felt as if I was scientifically proved to be the helpless slave of antecedent circumstances; as if my character and that of all others had been formed for us by agencies beyond our control, and was wholly out of our own power. I often said to myself, what a relief it would be if I could disbelieve the doctrine of the formation of character by circumstances.

– John Stuart Mill, *Autobiography,* 175, 177

For, behold, this is what it is to be human . . . a creature with a will, at once bound and free.

– Pope Gregory I[1]

We humans obviously were not cut out to understand the problem of free will and determinism. That does not prevent us from trying. Year after year, generation after generation, the books and essays issue forth, not only those addressing the problem directly (shelved under "theology" and "philosophy") but also those bearing labels such as

The original version of this essay was prepared for a conference on "The Culture of the Market," sponsored by the Murphy Institute of Political Economy, Tulane University, in March 1990. Jonathan Riley commented on the paper at the conference and I am indebted to him for several changes, none of which are likely to persuade him. Richard Teichgraeber, the Director of the Murphy Institute, provided useful advice, as did Marilyn Brown, Allen Kahan, Wilfred McClay, and Martin Wiener. Later versions of the essay benefited from the comments of John Daly, Thomas Grey, Charles Lockhart, Bruce Mazlish, and Carole Pateman.

[1] Gregory I, quoted in Peter Brown, *The Body and Society: Men, Women, and Sexual Renunciation in Early Christianity* (New York: Columbia University Press, 1988), 434.

"history," "social science," "hermeneutics," "structuralism," or "deconstruction" that stumble into its coils more or less inadvertently. Many a proud discovery amounts to nothing more than an unwitting echo of Pelagius or Augustine; few authors find anything more profound to say than Gregory I, who candidly admitted defeat. To be in the grip of convictions about freedom and fate that are at once compelling and irreconcilable is evidently part of what it means to be human.

The famous "dejection" or "mental crisis" that John Stuart Mill experienced as a young man can serve as a reminder that the conundrums of freedom and fate are not exclusively philosophical, but also psychological. Whatever else it may be, freedom is in the first instance a matter of perception. To be "free" instead of determined is to perceive oneself, or one's choices and actions, as causes instead of effects, as origins that reach creatively into the future, rather than terminations foreordained by antecedent events. It is, at least provisionally, to perceive oneself as an uncaused cause. Yet after Darwin it is no longer clear how there can be any such thing as an uncaused cause. Thus we stumble over the problem of freedom every time we attribute causal status to ourselves, other persons, things, conditions, or events – which is to say we are always stumbling over the problem, for attributing causation is a game we humans play incessantly.[2]

Like all games, the game of causal attribution has rules, but they do not cover all situations, they remain open to dispute, and they often are observed in the breach. Even when played by the rules, the game is afflicted by all the infirmities that predictably characterize human thinking about freedom and fate. Still, like other norms, the rules of causal attribution prevail on the whole and in the main, loosely governing the way the game is played, even when the players are not conscious of them and quite incapable of putting them into words.

It is by means of this rule-bound game that we construct and sustain, moment by moment, the cultural universe in which we live. To know how people play the game of causal attribution is to know

[2] Needless to say, in speaking of causal attribution as a game I mean to stress its conventional and rule-bound character, not any lack of seriousness. My interest in causal attribution was first sparked by Fritz Heider, "Social Perception and Phenomenal Causality," *Psychological Review* (November 1944), 358–74, and much influenced by H. L. A. Hart and A. M. Honoré, *Causation in the Law* (London: 1959), and Joel Feinberg, "Causing Voluntary Actions," in *Doing and Deserving: Essays in the Theory of Responsibility* (Princeton: Princeton University Press, 1970), 152–86.

nearly all there is to know about their form of life, for the web of cultural meanings in which we human beings suspend ourselves is largely made up of cause and effect relations. But for our perception of causal connection, experience would collapse into a heap of unrelated bits and pieces. Causation, as one British philosopher put it, is the "cement," or glue, that holds our world together.[3] We play the game, organizing our experience into meaningful configurations, every time we connect one element to another causally – every time we feel proud for the good we have done, or guilty for the bad; every time we praise others for what they have accomplished, or blame them for their failings; every time we welcome the punishment of a criminal, or rejoice at the vindication of an innocent person; every time we curse our fate or thank our lucky stars; every time we explain events by saying, "This happened because of that," or "This produced that," or "She made it," or "He did it," or "I've got the flu."

We cannot fry an egg, drive to work, please a lover, or explain why we are late without drawing on our knowledge of causal relations. Tacit imputations of causation enable us to make the distinctions we depend on every day between innocence and complicity, originality and imitation, spontaneity and deliberateness, exploitation and just compensation, accident and design. Perceptions of causal relations permeate everything we think, say, or do, and it could not be otherwise for the rules of causal attribution are, after all, the rules of change itself; of being and nonbeing, of how things come into, and go out of, existence. All our judgments, moral and factual alike, depend on deciding what is cause, what is effect. Nothing could be more fundamental, or more paradoxical.

Much of our confusion about freedom and fate stems from the fact that the rules governing the game of causal attribution are themselves in play. They change; they too (within limits) come into and go out of existence, and thus different eras, different cultures, or even different factions within a single culture may play the game differently. This essay will touch upon such a change, one of such immense scale that we might better describe it as an upheaval, and one that is intimately associated (as cause? as effect?) with the rise of market culture.

Our focal point is the experience of one man, the philosopher John

[3] J. L. Mackie, *The Cement of the Universe: A Study of Causation* (Oxford: Oxford University Press, 1974).

Stuart Mill, who, in 1826, as a young man of twenty, was temporarily paralyzed by the fear that, despite all appearances to the contrary, he was a passive "stock or stone," destitute of emotional vitality, incapable of originating action, merely a "helpless slave of antecedent circumstances" – a being whose freedom to choose and think and act was, in his own eyes, empty and merely formal.[4] The mental crisis occupies a large place in Mill's *Autobiography* and has attracted the attention of many scholars, but none, I think, have taken Mill literally enough. He himself described his crisis as a matter of causal attribution. So persuaded was he of the force of circumstances in shaping character that he found it impossible, for a time, to cast himself in a causal role. He came to regard himself as literally inconsequential, as devoid of agency, incapable of having effect. What dejected him, he said, was the fear that in spite of all subjective appearances to the contrary everything he did and thought originated not with him, but in the antecedent circumstances that had made him the person he was.

On his own account, in other words, the crisis arose out of the *transitivity* of cause-and-effect relationships, the fact that anything we call a "cause" (including even the voluntary choices and actions of apparently free human agents) can upon logical reflection be regarded as the *effect* of prior causes, thereby compromising its causal status. How we distinguish one link in a chain or network of cause-and-effect connections, and construe it as "the cause" of subsequent events (a construal that always requires us to exclude from consciousness another set of reflections that would instead construe it as an effect of antecedent events) is one of the abiding problems in the philosophy of causal attribution, and one that holds immense practical significance for the interpretation of human affairs. Indeed, in this regard the rules of the attributive game, by allocating causation between the self and the circumstances that impinge upon it, quite literally constitute personhood. Whatever else the self may be, it is at least that shadowy region where the influence of environing circumstances seems to leave off and awareness of conscious choice and action seems to begin. Insofar as the rules of the game prompt us to see the relation between environing circumstance and human action

[4] John Stuart Mill, *Autobiography and Literary Essays,* ed. John M. Robson and Jack Stillinger, vol. 1 of *The Collected Works of John Stuart Mill,* ed. John M. Robson (Toronto and Buffalo: University of Toronto Press, 1981), 175.

in an intransitive light, we experience the self as an uncaused cause, a pure point of origin, a kind of cornucopia in which purposeful activity arises out of nothing and surges into the world. When, on the contrary, we construe that relation in a more transitive light, as Mill did in the depths of his dejection, fate expands at the expense of freedom and the very existence of the self can be placed in jeopardy.

Since a person can be regarded as free only to the extent that he or she is construed as causally efficacious, the problem of transitivity is the classic problem of freedom and fate, recast in psychological and attributive rather than philosophical terms.[5] As Gregory I observed so long ago, depending on the angle of view taken, the human will can always be seen as either "bound" (a product of external and antecedent circumstances), or "free" (not merely one link among others in a causal chain originating elsewhere, but an *origin* of such chains). Compelling evidence can be cited for either view and the choice between them can be momentous, but to embrace fully the truth of one, as Mill found, is to negate the equally compelling truth of the other.

Although other writers have not been unaware that Mill talked about the crisis in terms of causal attribution, they have seen little significance in the terms he chose. Several have treated his causal language as an intellectualization of something more visceral: the young man's Oedipal rebellion against his father, James Mill, whose Draconian project for educating his children could hardly help but leave them feeling that they had been "formed . . . by agencies beyond our control." Without denying in the least the father's dominance, the son's rebellion, or even the overtones of sexual rivalry that a Freudian interpretation would give to their relationship, I contend that the younger Mill got it right the first time: His problem was first

[5] To construe the question as one of causal attribution is, of course, to construe it in terms other than those actually employed by most of the principal contributors to the great controversy over freedom and fate. There is some risk in this strategy, some danger of forcing diverse perceptions into a Procrustean mold, but there are also certain advantages, especially when the contributor's own language approximates that of causal attribution as closely as Mill's obviously does. In a recent study notable for its compendious coverage and strict reporting of the actual language of the debate, John R. Reed observed, "After all, during the nineteenth century, though men had many models of the self from which to choose, in the end they were forced to make only a few central decisions. Either the self was coherent and directed from within, or it lacked integrity and depended upon external energy." *Victorian Will* (Athens: Ohio University Press, 1989), 24.

and foremost the transitivity of causation. His progenitor's domineering ways presented that problem in such an acute manner that it could not be evaded, but the problem was not confined to James Mill, or to domineering fathers generally. Compelled by his father's intrusiveness to grapple with the problem of transitivity, the young man was among the first to discover that the resources supplied by market culture are not well suited to that task.

It was not accidental, I shall argue, that the young man who underwent this crisis was raised in a family whose spiritual history so closely corresponds to the momentous trajectory that Max Weber traced from a pious "Protestant ethic" in the seventeenth century, to a utilitarian and secular ethic, highly conducive to capitalism, by the end of the eighteenth. Nor was it accidental, I believe, that this especially acute episode of anxiety about freedom and consequentiality should have occurred in the world's most advanced market economy just as it was setting forth on the rocky road to full-scale industrial capitalism.

Least of all is it incidental that this youth, who feared in 1826 that his self might be swallowed up in a sea of circumstantiality, only a few years earlier had been euphorically confident of his power to outwit fate and construct a future of his own choosing. John Stuart Mill's youthful oscillation back and forth between the extremes of voluntaristic euphoria and fatalistic dejection was, I believe, precisely the experience that enabled him to become, as a mature adult, one of the principal intellectual architects of a new market-oriented form of life, one that subtly and profoundly altered ancient boundaries between freedom and fate in Western culture. In later years Mill wrote influentially on the logic of science, rescued Utilitarianism from the eccentricities of Jeremy Bentham, pioneered in the fledgling discipline of political economy, and authored such cornerstones of the Liberal tradition as "On Liberty" and "The Subjection of Women." Although we customarily associate Max Weber's famous thesis with those who truck and trade in the marketplace, there is a broader sense, recognized by Weber, in which the utility-maximizing "Spirit of Capitalism" found in John Stuart Mill its most sophisticated exemplar.

That such an astute observer, and one so well placed to discern the innermost tendencies of a market-oriented form of life, should have chosen to make the story of his youthful "mental crisis" the central event of his *Autobiography* reveals something important about the precariousness of selfhood and the evanescence of the experience of freedom in the culture of capitalism. And that, in turn, can tell us something important about an upheaval in the conventions of causal attribution that began over two centuries ago and that continues to shake the foundations of Western culture today.

Mill's mental crisis embodies in psychological miniature an attributive predicament that by the end of the nineteenth century had assumed the proportions of a culturewide malaise. Today's culture is perpetually riven by seemingly unresolvable disputes between "formalists" and "antiformalists," between those who construe persons as autonomous agents, only intransitively related to the circumstances of their lives, and those who construe persons transitively, as products of a circumstantial setting that profoundly influences everything they think or do, quite literally making them the persons they are. For convenience I speak of two fixed and opposed poles, but in truth "formalism" and "antiformalism" are inherently relative, constantly in motion, and very much matters of degree. One generation's bold new antiformalism has often become the next generation's stale formalism; both can reside uncomfortably in a single troubled mind; each calls the other into being by labelling and condemning it.

Ancient though the dilemmas of freedom and fate undoubtedly are, it is only in the form of life spawned by the market that the rules of the attributive game become so elastic and unstable that every event is open to multiple interpretations, ranging from "formalistic" ones, which construe thinkers and actors as uncaused causes, to "deep," "structural," or "radical" ones, which treat conscious choice and perception as reflexes of underlying realities. Market culture on this interpretation creates a world of depths and surfaces, in which politics involves not only a clash of interests but also a struggle between incommensurable modes of interpretation, each professing allegiance to its own distinctive pattern of causal attribution and incredulous of all alternatives. To intellectuals, those members of the culture who specialize in interpretive virtuosity, no cause is uncaused, no choice spontaneous, no act uninterested, no person unselfish, no interpretation immune to the charge of formality. As an uncommonly articulate eyewitness to the early stages of the upheaval that produced this disturbing situation, and an early victim of the fears it aroused, John Stuart Mill deserves our close attention.

Before examining Mill's own account of his mental crisis it is important to note a quirk of perspective that threatens to mislead us about his role in history. When Oliver Wendell Holmes, John Dewey, Thorstein Veblen, Charles Beard, and other American intellectuals embarked upon their highly successful "revolt against formalism" at the beginning of this century, they pointed to John Stuart Mill as a prime exemplar of the brittle formalities they hoped to sweep away.[6] Like the Foucauldians and Derrideans of the 1980s, the antiformalists of Dewey's generation armed themselves with a broadly historicist critique of reason, but (again like their "postmodern" counterparts) their historicism was no guarantee of sensitivity to the historicity of the debate in which they were engaged. In choosing Mill as their target they displayed ironically short historical memories, for in his own day Mill and his utilitarian friends were for good reason regarded as "philosophic radicals," who delighted in unmasking formalities and demonstrating that behind all fine words and high ideals the real motor of human affairs was interest. Interest itself they understood to be the conscious trace of an inborn urge to maximize pleasure and minimize pain, not much less mechanical in its operation than the tendency of plants to turn away from shadow and toward light. "Interest" has been a rallying cry of antiformalists ever since, for when we discount the reasons people give for their choices and insist instead upon the driving force of interest, we depict them as creatures of circumstance, actors whose conduct becomes all too predictable once their needs and wants, their most urgent contingencies and dependencies, have been identified.[7]

[6] Morton White, *Social Thought in America: The Revolt Against Formalism* (Boston: Beacon Press, 1957), 14, 21–27.

[7] Macaulay's skepticism about the explanatory power of "interest" is worth recalling. In his criticism of James Mill's *Essay on Government,* Macaulay called it but a "truism" that men act always from self-interest. "This truism the Utilitarians proclaim with as much pride as if it were new, and as much zeal as if it were important. But in fact, when explained, it means only that men, if they can, will do as they choose. When we see the actions of a man, we know with certainty what he thinks his interest to be. But it is impossible to reason with certainty from what *we* take to be his interest to his actions. [It is idle] to attribute any importance to a proposition, which, when interpreted, means only that a man had rather do what he had rather do.

"If the doctrine that men always act from self-interest, be laid down in any other

That Mill could be construed by his own generation as a militant antiformalist and by the next generation as virtually the inventor of formalism says something, of course, about his ambivalence, and the ambivalence that must be felt by anyone who thinks deeply on these issues. It says still more about the succession of ever more militant versions of antiformalism that cascaded down through the nineteenth century, each triumphantly relabeling its predecessors "formalistic." This was, after all, the century that began with Kant and ended with Nietzsche. It began, that is, with a philosophy that profoundly subverted common sense by conceding that reason, forever imprisoned within the circumstances of its own structure, could never achieve certainty about things-in-themselves, and it ended with Nietzsche, who dismissed all talk of a world beyond the phenomenal and construed reason itself in a radically transitive light, as nothing more than sheep's clothing for the dark cunning of the will.

But more important for my immediate purposes, Mill's reputation for antiformalism in his own generation and formalism in the next says worlds about the singularity of his moment in history. He was one of the first post-Christian theorists of human agency, and among all such theorists he was perhaps the very first to strive for a complete and balanced view of the matter.[8] Unlike Helvétius and La Mettrie and other materialists of the eighteenth century, who, in the face of stiff resistance, were content to score polemical points against the monolithic voluntarism of the Church, Mill did not feel embattled and did not bother to attack (or defend) any religious conception of the relation between persons and circumstances. "I was brought up from the first," he said, "without any religious belief, in the ordinary acceptation of the term. . . . I am thus one of the very few examples, in this country, of one who has, not thrown off religious belief, but

sense than this – if the meaning of the word self-interest be narrowed so as to exclude any one of the motives which may by possibility act on any human being, – the proposition ceases to be identical; but at the same time it ceases to be true." T. B. Macaulay, "Mill's Essay on Government: Utilitarian Logic and Politics" (1829), in *Utilitarian Logic and Politics: James Mill's Essay on Government, Macaulay's Critique and the Ensuing Debate,* ed. Jack Lively and John Rees (Oxford: Oxford University press, 1978), 124–25. Italics in original.

8 David Hume has perhaps the best claim to being first, and was no doubt a deeper thinker than Mill, yet he never displayed Mill's concern to develop a complete and balanced view of the subject. See Hume, *Inquiries Concerning Human Understanding and Concerning the Principles of Morals,* ed. L. A. Selby-Bigge, 3rd ed., revised by P. H. Neddich (Oxford: Clarendon Press, 1975 [1777]), 92.

never had it: I grew up in a negative state with regard to it."[9] Growing up in no faith at all was sufficiently eccentric in Mill's youth that his father, James Mill, an agnostic and an outspoken champion of candor and free speech, advised his son to hide his unbelief from the world, a pretense that the boy found vexatious but prudent. By the time the younger Mill wrote his *Autobiography* in the 1850s, candid avowals of unbelief had become acceptable in intellectual circles, but this was a dramatic change: he called it a "great advance in liberty of discussion . . . one of the most important differences between the present time and that of my childhood."[10]

As a distinctively secular thinker, one of the principal lessons that Mill drew from his youthful mental crisis and then developed in his mature philosophy was that in matters bearing on freedom and fate the only safe ground lay in the middle. The extreme positions lying to either side were untenable – "free will" because it imputed to mankind an implausible capacity for transcendence, and "determinism" because it led to the fatalism and paralysis that Mill knew all too well from firsthand experience. To define the problem this way, as a matter of seeking a *via media* between rejected extremes, is the distinctive feature of the secular worldview that Western intellectuals adopted as religion lost its grip on their world. As we shall see, the Christian framework that had once reigned supreme and that during Mill's lifetime still retained the loyalty of most of his contemporaries, defined the problem in a quite different way, which did not attach any particular premium to a middle path. Although for believers it safeguarded the integrity of the self more effectively than any secular scheme is ever likely to do, it also paradoxically allowed for a much fuller acknowledgment of the role played by circumstantiality.

Mill may well strike us today as he struck John Dewey's generation, as excessively formal. He certainly could never have said with Hans Georg Gadamer that "the self-awareness of the individual is only a flickering in the closed circuits of historical life."[11] Yet Mill's thought is far more akin to our own than that of Samuel Taylor Coleridge or others among his contemporaries whose allegiance to Christian conceptions of the soul and providential modes of interpretation re-

[9] John Stuart Mill, *Autobiography,* 41, 45.

[10] Ibid., 47.

[11] Gadamer, *Truth and Method* (New York, 1975), 245.

mained intact. However we may differ from him, he shares our secular assumptions, and in the broad sweep of history that makes him one of us. To see how differently the problem of transitivity was dealt with in the Christian era and how pioneering Mill's treatment of it was, consider the contrast between his attitude toward circumstantiality and that of Martin Luther, writing three centuries earlier in an era of uncompromised faith.

Luther published *Bondage of the Will* in 1525 as a refutation of Erasmus. In it the world is depicted as a cosmic contest between adversaries of such stupendous power that no thought of human freedom could plausibly arise. "All Christians know," wrote Luther, "that there are in the world two kingdoms at war with each other. In the one, Satan reigns. . . . In the other kingdom Christ reigns. His kingdom continually resists and wars against that of Satan; and we are translated into His kingdom, not by our own power, but by the grace of God, which delivers us from this present evil world and tears us away from the power of darkness." Human autonomy being out of the question in such a world, the only issue was which master to serve, which army to join. "The knowledge and confession of these two kingdoms, ever warring against each other with all their might and power, would suffice by itself to confute the doctrine of 'free will,' seeing that we are compelled to serve in Satan's kingdom if we are not plucked from it by Divine power. The common man, I repeat, knows this, and confesses it plainly enough by his proverbs, prayers, efforts and entire life."[12]

Given the necessity of submitting either to Satan or to God, a variety of radical situatedness became not only acceptable to Luther, but the proper goal of life. The abandonment of any pretense to autonomy or intransitivity was all to the good, just so long as one could be sure it was the hand of God in which one was situated. Autonomy thus held no appeal for Luther and, still more surprising in modern eyes, circumstantiality held no terror.

> I frankly confess that, for myself, even if it could be, I should not want "free will" to be given to me, nor anything to be left in my own hands to enable me to endeavor after salvation; not merely because in face of so many dangers, and adversities, and assaults of devils, I could not stand my ground and hold fast my "free will" (for one devil is stronger than all men, and on these terms

[12] Martin Luther, *The Bondage of the Will,* ed. J. I. Packer and O. R. Johnston (n.p.: Fleming H. Revell, 1957), 312.

no man could be saved); but because, even were there no dangers, adversities, or devils I should still be forced to labour with no guarantee of success, and to beat my fists at the air. If I lived and worked to all eternity, my conscience would never reach comfortable certainty as to how much it must do to satisfy God. Whatever work I had done, there would still be a nagging doubt as to whether it pleased God, or whether he required something more. The experience of all who seek righteousness by works proves that; and I learned it well enough myself over a period of many years, to my own great hurt. But now that God has taken my salvation out of the control of my own will, and put it under the control of His, and promised to save me, not according to my working or running, but according to His own grace and mercy, I have the comfortable certainty that He is faithful and will not lie to me, and that he is also great and powerful, so that no devils or opposition can break him or pluck me from Him.[13]

The contrast between Mill and Luther could not be more striking. Mill was terrorized by the thought that he was the "helpless slave of antecedent circumstances," but Luther welcomed the bondage of his will and drew strength from the thought that his every choice and act originated not in him, but in antecedent circumstances that had been willed by (or were identical with) his ever active, omnipotent Creator. Mill and Luther played the game of causal attribution by very different rules, and the heart of the difference was Mill's inability to believe in a Divine Being whose essence was precisely that He was the cause of everything, including the circumstances in which the self was situated.

To put the matter in terms that are highly anachronistic (and theologically indelicate), but nonetheless instructive from a secular, twentieth-century point of view, we might say that the whole point of theology – of speculations about a Being who is understood to be the Creator and First Cause of all that exists – is to confront the problem of causal transitivity in the most thoroughgoing way, and take the sting out of it once and for all. To conceive of oneself as snugly nestled in the palm of a beneficent God, and to feel that the active will of the omnipotent Creator manifests itself in all one's acts and choices, is, after all, an experience of radical situatedness – but not a displeasing or debilitating one. In effect, religion resolves the problem of transitivity and banishes the terrors that circumstantial determination arouses by first conceding that the self is not an uncaused cause, but then simultaneously insisting that what the self is the effect of, what it owes its

[13] Ibid., 313–14.

existence to, is neither the endless and aimless interweavings of natural causal processes, nor the banalities of happenstance, but the First Cause Himself. "If we cannot be uncaused causes," religionists as much as say, "let us be the unmediated effects of the First Cause." If our lives must be seen in part as the unwitting products of a particular circumstantial setting, let us divinize the circumstances that hold us in thrall by construing ourselves as the creatures of a loving Creator, and the setting itself as the instrument by which His will be done.[14]

The quintessentially causal language in which God was customarily addressed – "Maker," "Father," "First Cause," "Prime Mover," "Creator" – says much about the game of causal attribution that prevailed in the Christian era. Insofar as people felt in their lives the active presence and power of such a supremely causal entity, the question of transitivity simply could not arise in its modern form. As long as persons and their choices were understood to be the products of God's will, evidence of transitivity could only flatter their self-esteem, for it was a token of their Godliness, their intimate proximity to the First Cause. As Mill's friend Coleridge put it,

In the Bible each agent appears and acts as a self-subsisting individual: each has a life of its own, and yet all are one life. The elements of necessity and

[14] Calvin went even farther than Luther in divinizing the circumstantial setting of life. "The providence of God, as it is taught in scripture, is opposed to fortune and fortuitous accidents," wrote Calvin. "If any one falls into the hands of robbers, or meets with wild beasts; if by a sudden storm he is shipwrecked on the ocean; if he is killed by the fall of a house or a tree; if another, wandering through deserts, finds relief for his penury, or, after having been tossed about by the waves, reaches the port, and escapes, as it were, but a hair's breadth from death, – carnal reason will ascribe all these occurrences, both prosperous and adverse, to fortune. But whoever has been taught from the mouth of Christ, that the hairs of his head are all numbered (Matt. x:30), will seek further for a cause, and conclude that all events are governed by the secret counsel of God." *Institutes of the Christian Religion,* excerpted in *European Origins of American Thought,* ed. David D. Van Tassel and Robert W. McAhren (Chicago: Rand McNally, 1969), 4–5. As Michael Walzer observes, "In Calvinist thought nature ceased altogether to be a realm of secondary causation, a world whose laws were anciently established and subject to God's will only in the extraordinary case of a miracle. Providence no longer consisted in law or in foresight: 'providence consists in action.' The eternal order of nature became an order of circumstantial and particular events, the cause of each being the immediate, active (but inscrutable) will of God. . . . 'no wind ever rises or blows, but by the special command of God.' " Walzer notes that although Calvin's God "required an obedience so precise and total as to be without precedent in the history of tyranny, he also freed men from all sorts of alternative jurisdictions and authorities." Michael Walzer, *Revolution of the Saints: A Study in the Origins of Radical Politics* (New York: Atheneum, 1969), 35 (quoting Calvin), 152.

free-will are reconciled in the higher power of an omnipresent Providence, that predestinates the whole in the moral freedom of the integral parts. Of this the Bible never suffers us to lose sight. The root is never detached from the ground. It is God everywhere: and all creatures conform to his decrees, the righteous by performance of the law, the disobedient by the sufferance of the penalty.[15]

Insofar as God's omnipotence was understood to extend "everywhere," crowding out the influence of mere mundane circumstances, or divinizing them, harnessing them to His ends, even the most insistent contingencies could not pose any threat to the integrity of the self or undermine the self's suitability for praise and blame. Mill's dejection arose precisely from the fear that his motives were not truly his, having been created by circumstances beyond his control. On the Christian interpretation that fear was misplaced. That a person's motives did not arise *de novo* from his or her understanding, but were the products of antecedent circumstances, did not bother Coleridge in the least, because he was confident that what stood behind the understanding of the faithful was a beneficent God. "The understanding may suggest motives, may avail itself of motives, and make judicious conjectures respecting the probable consequences of actions," said Coleridge. "But the Knowledge taught in the Scriptures *produces* the motives. . . . Strange as this will appear to such as forget that motives can be causes only in a secondary and improper sense . . . motives themselves are effects, the principle of which, good or evil, lies far deeper."[16]

Danger lay not in admitting the situatedness of the self, but only in getting the situation wrong – mistaking the hand of Satan for that of God. The anxious balancing act between autonomy and dependence that makes Mill look familiar to us today could not begin until the First Cause had faded from sight, for only then could circumstantiality take on its present appearance as a debilitating miasma that, if not kept at arm's length, threatens to engulf the self. Virtually everyone today takes it for granted, as Mill did in his mature writing, that the extreme positions on either side of the debate are to be avoided. What we want today, and what each optimistically imagines himself

[15] Samuel Taylor Coleridge, *Lay Sermons*, ed. R. J. White, vol. 6 of *Collected Works*, (n.p.: Routledge & Kegan Paul, and Princeton University Press, 1972), 31–32.

[16] Ibid., 21. Italics in original.

or herself to have achieved, is an understanding of the relation between persons and circumstances that "does justice" to both autonomy and dependence, that "balances" the opposing claims of agency and structure, of free will and determinism – that, in the astute words of Michael Sandel, avoids both the "radically disembodied subject" toward which formalism tends, and the "radically situated subject" toward which antiformalism tends.[17] We agree, in other words, that persons are neither independent of their circumstances, nor seamlessly interwoven with them and that the relation between self and circumstance is neither wholly intransitive nor wholly transitive. Able to agree about little else, we carve out a "middle path" and wonder why everyone else's "middle path" fails to correspond with our own.[18] No one, let it be noticed, no matter how sensational their structuralist rhetoric (e.g., "the author is dead") admits personally to being a mere "creature of circumstance," undeserving of either credit or blame for anything that happens in the world. Today even the most reckless secular antiformalist will admit, at least when pressed, that the very idea of personhood seems to require some degree of autonomy, for if the self were nothing more than an empty conduit through which environmental forces surged, unhindered and unchanged, it would be literally inconsequential, incapable of having effect in the world, and thus no proper self at all.[19] It was precisely the loss of this autonomy, and fear that he was, indeed, a "radically situated subject," incapable of truly originating anything, unsuitable for either praise or blame, that plunged the young John Stuart Mill into such deep despair.

[17] Michael J. Sandel, *Liberalism and the Limits of Justice* (Cambridge: Cambridge University Press, 1982), 21.

[18] James T. Kloppenberg, *Uncertain Victory: Social Democracy and Progressivism in European and American Thought, 1870–1920* (New York and Oxford: Oxford University Press, 1986), 26–28.

[19] As Joel Feinberg argues, the key question in the debate between free will and determinism is not *whether* we are "plugged into" nature, but *how*: "If the determining influences are filtered through our own network of predispositions, expectations, purposes, and values, if our own threshold requirements are carefully observed, if there is no jarring and abrupt change in the course of our natural bent, then it seems to me to do no violence to common sense for us to claim the act as our own, even though its causal initiation be located in the external world. In short, the more like an easy triggering of a natural predisposition and external cause is, the less difficulty there is in treating its effects as a voluntary action." Feinberg, "Causing Voluntary Actions," 172.

Indispensable though some saving residue of autonomy is to our sense of balance, we seem unable to justify our intuitions about it. We wonder if autonomy is but a pale substitute for "soul." Jon Elster speaks for us all when he confesses that "I can offer no satisfactory definition of autonomy."

> Just as there are persons known for their judgement, there are persons that apparently are in control over the processes whereby their desires are formed, or at least are not in the grip of processes with which they do not identify themselves. Yet the identity and even the existence of such persons is much more controversial than in the case of judgement. . . . One might fear that when the list of non-autonomous processes of desire formation is extended, as it has been in the past, and surely will be in the future, it will come to gobble up all our desires, leaving nothing to autonomy.[20]

Most of us muddle along, steering clear of all obvious exaggerations of either freedom or fate, only vaguely aware of our residual reliance on a notion of autonomy that we are not at all sure how to defend. It is some comfort to know that in this respect we share a good deal with our pre-Christian ancestors in fifth-century Athens. A central preoccupation of ancient Greek thought, Martha Nussbaum eloquently observes, was a hope at once "splendid and equivocal:"

> However much human beings resemble lower forms of life, we are unlike, we want to insist, in one crucial respect. We have reason. We are able to deliberate and choose, to make a plan in which ends are ranked, to decide actively what is to have value and how much. All this must count for something. If it is true that a lot about us is messy, needy, uncontrolled, rooted [like a growing plant] in the dirt and standing helplessly in the rain, it is also true that there is something about us that is pure and purely active, something that we could think of [as Plato did] as being "divine, immortal, intelligible, unitary, indissoluble, ever self-consistent and invariable."[21]

Much as secular Western intellectuals strive today for a *via media* between rejected extremes, so the Greeks, on Nussbaum's interpretation, tried to balance "the pursuit of self-sufficiency" and the "effort to banish contingency from human life" against their own "vivid sense of the special beauty of the contingent and the mutable." Their "love

[20] Jon Elster, *Sour Grapes: Studies in the Subversion of Rationality* (Cambridge: Cambridge University Press, 1983), 21.

[21] Martha Nussbaum, *The Fragility of Goodness: Luck and Ethics in Greek Tragedy and Philosophy* (Cambridge: Cambridge University press, 1986), 2, quoting Plato, *Phaedrus.*

for the riskiness and openness of empirical humanity," Nussbaum explains, found poignant expression in "recurrent stories about gods who fall in love with mortals."[22]

Christianity told a less equivocal story, about a God who monopolized causal potency throughout the universe and assumed human form only in order to redeem the faithful and rescue them from mortality itself. Not content to leave the "splendid hope" a plaything of fate or capricious gods, Christians conceived of a God whose irresistible influence extended everywhere and pervaded mundane affairs, domesticating and divinizing them for the benefit of His followers. Protestants went even farther than traditional Christians by accentuating the Augustinian theme of predestination and stressing providential modes of interpretation. Theirs was a world in which fortune and fate were regarded as words of the heathen. Everything that happened happened because God willed it to happen, if not directly then indirectly through the gift of moral freedom bestowed on those whom He predestined for salvation.

The gradual decay in the West of the ancient practice of construing the events of this world as the effects of divine will is the most dramatic change in the game of causal attribution that history records. "Secularization," the opaque and uninformative label customarily given to this change, heralded the emergence of a new attributive game in which the self, no longer sheltered from the random play of undivinized circumstance, would be obliged to abandon time-honored assumptions about its place in the world and devise new strategies suitable for a temporally and causally boundless universe. Unable to construe the events of this world as effects set in motion by the First Cause, Mill found himself unable also to share Luther's calm acceptance of "radical situatedness," for when inquiry into the sources of the self cannot find any sure stopping place in the Creator, the chains of causal linkage run off to infinity and the "splendid hope" of freedom is in perpetual danger of being swallowed up by fate. If Mill's struggles to reconceive the relation between self and world do not win the approval of twentieth-century readers because they seem halfhearted and residually "formal," it is not because we have found any satisfactory solution to the dilemmas he confronted.

22 Ibid., 3.

Max Weber was on to something important when he identified the rise of capitalism with changes in religious sensibility. Indeed, I suspect that the relation between religion and economic change is even more intimate than he imagined. The change in religious sensibility that figures most prominently in Weber's thesis is the development within Christianity of an ethic of worldly asceticism, culminating in the Protestant Reformation. The inculcation of this ethic by Protestant divines, said Weber, unintentionally recruited large numbers of people into the self-monitoring, calculating, deliberate mode of life – a preparation for the life of "economic man" – without which the market's capacity for allocative efficiency could never have been fully realized. The discipline of supply and demand had little impact on people incapable of self-restraint or inattentive to economic self-interest. No reader of *The Protestant Ethic and the Spirit of Capitalism* could fail to recognize the importance of the Protestant ethic, but it is easy to overlook another change of religious sensibility that is logically just as important to Weber's argument. That change is secularization. Weber did not explore secularization or try to explain it, but simply asserted it as a ready-made explanation for the otherwise puzzling conjunction that made up his title: How did the "Protestant Ethic" evolve into the "Spirit of Capitalism"? Weber's none too illuminating answer was secularization, which drained the Protestant ethic of its original purpose of glorifying God, and thus left behind a dry husk of habit, devoid of religious meaning, which obliged its adherents to labor diligently in their callings; to strive always to maximize their assets, whether personal or material; and to do so as an end in itself, neither having nor seeming to require any higher justification. As we turn now to the first part of the story leading up to Mill's mental crisis, it is important to recall that he embodied both of the changes in religious sensibility that Weber referred to: Mill was both an heir to the Protestant ethic and the architect of a form of life that was distinctively both economic and secular.

James Mill, who was raised in the church and trained as a Scotch Presbyterian preacher, took care to instruct his children in ecclesiastical history. His son remembered being encouraged "to take the strongest interest in the Reformation, as the great and decisive contest against priestly tyranny for liberty of thought." But the elder Mill ultimately repudiated the religion he was licensed to preach and threw aside even Deism on the moral grounds that any all-powerful being would have to be regarded as the author of unspeakable evils. The most important religious lesson that John Stuart Mill remembered learning from his father was agnostic. That lesson took just the form one would predict of a person who had once expected to see the hand of God in all the events of this world, but who found that mode of causal attribution impossible to sustain and therefore had to adapt to another, in which certain questions, once answerable in terms of divine will, no longer could even be asked. The lesson, explicitly causal, was this: "The manner in which the world came into existence was a subject on which nothing was known [and] the question 'Who made me?' cannot be answered."[23]

In the absence of a benign First Cause, the question "Who [or what] made me?" tugs at the lid of a Pandora's box full of transitive possibilities. That question would haunt Mill during his "mental crisis," but during the years of his youth leading up to that event he seems to have been preoccupied with another question, equally causal, but pointing, as it were, in exactly the opposite direction: *What can I make, or do?* The latter question, which casts the self in the role of maker instead of thing made, cause instead of effect, disembodied subject instead of situated object, had about it in Mill's lifetime an aura of novelty and excitement and open-ended hopefulness that we jaded denizens of the twentieth century can scarcely imagine. It was the question on which utilitarianism was built, and it was a question that in the very asking tended to draw a veil over its increasingly alarming counterpart in the game of causal attribution, "Who [or what] made me?"

Under the tutelage first of his father ("The last of the eighteenth century," as the son later called him[24]) and then Jeremy Bentham, the younger Mill was led to believe that the horizons of what was called "human improvement" were in his lifetime expanding by leaps and bounds in every direction, opening up a bright new world of possibilities for human mastery after millennia of abject acquiescence in fate. Futile though reason might be when inquiring into first causes and the origins of selfhood (Who made me?), an agnostic of the Millian variety saw no reason for dismay, for what mattered was one's ability

[23] John Stuart Mill, *Autobiography,* 45. See also 41, 43.
[24] Ibid., 213.

cogently to assess the circumstances of the present and chart a course toward a desirable future (What can I make?). The paramount question was about not the past, but the future, about not what made the self, but what sort of world the self could make. And as to the world's plasticity, and the power and creativity of the self to use reason instrumentally to bring about future states of the world by actions taken in the present – as to all these matters pertaining to human agency, the younger Mill was taught to have no doubts at all. About his ability to help make a new and better world, he was initially as confident as a proper Scots Presbyterian would have been about tracing the origins of *his* highest self back to the amazing and undeserved grace of the Creator, thus answering unequivocally the question "Who made me?"

But just as a shadow of doubt always accompanied the scrupulous Presbyterian's confidence that his true self had been molded by the hand of God, so the younger Mill's confidence in his own capacity to make a better world was subtly undercut from the beginning. As is well known, his father enthusiastically embraced the environmentalism of John Locke, David Hartley, and the French philosophes, and took it to justify, or rather require, an unprecedented extension of parental responsibility for the education of the young. Of all the enlightened doctrines that James Mill stood for, none was more fundamental to his thinking, according to his son, than that which taught "the formation of all human character by circumstances, through the universal Principle of Association, and the consequent unlimited possibility of improving the moral and intellectual condition of mankind by education."[25] The wonder, from our retrospective vantage point, is that the generations of reformers who embraced this doctrine so enthusiastically construed it entirely as a measure of their own "unlimited" power and responsibility to shape the future – not as an unsettling reminder that their own character was susceptible to similar shaping forces and their own autonomy no more than a fragile hope. The result of the doctrine in James Mill's case was an educational regime for his son so aggressive that although its explicit lesson may have been free agency, it also conveyed a tacit message of a very different kind.

The younger Mill's instruction began with Greek at age three and

[25] Ibid., 111.

proceeded at breakneck pace from *Aesop's Fables,* the first Greek text he read, to Plato's dialogues, including the *Theætetus,* which he read (finding it "totally impossible" to understand) by the age of seven.[26] The boy's schoolday began before breakfast, as he accompanied his father on walks through the countryside, telling him of the books he had read and taken notes on the day before: Xenophon on Socrates; the histories of Robertson, Hume, and Gibbon; McCrie's *Life of John Knox,* Sewall's and Rutty's histories of the Quakers; accounts of Drake and Cook and the great voyages, among many others. "He was fond of putting into my hands books which exhibited men of energy and resource in unusual circumstances, struggling against difficulties and overcoming them."[27] The day continued at James Mill's writing table, where he cleared a space for his son and, although hard at work on his own *History of India* – and "one of the most impatient of men" – allowed himself to be interrupted every time the boy came to a Greek word he did not know.[28] Latin training commenced at age eight; Aristotle's *Organon* was tackled at twelve; a "complete course" of political economy, including the recently published work of David Ricardo, a friend of the family, at age thirteen.[29]

John Stuart Mill looked back upon this "unusual and remarkable" education with gratitude for the "advantage of a quarter of a century" that it gave him over his contemporaries, but his gratitude was mixed, as we can well imagine, with a good deal of ambivalence about the intensity of his father's influence over him.[30] Convinced of the power of circumstances and the plasticity of character, the elder Mill set out to fashion for his son a character that would be autonomous and creative in the highest degree. The son's subsequent career suggests that the father's project substantially succeeded. But the means to that end required that he lay siege to the child, annihilating today's autonomy for the sake of tomorrow's. "Whether I was more a gainer or a loser by his severity," John Stuart Mill later "hesitate[d]" to say, but he was sure that "the element which was chiefly deficient in his moral relation to his children, was that of tenderness."[31] "I was con-

[26] Ibid., 9.
[27] Ibid., 11.
[28] Ibid., 9.
[29] Ibid., 13, 21, 31.
[30] Ibid., 5, 33.
[31] Ibid., 53.

stantly meriting reproof by inattention, inobservance, and general slackness of mind in matters of daily life."[32] Standards seem to have been deliberately set impossibly high: "He was often, and much beyond reason, provoked by my failures in cases where success could not have been expected."[33] Other children were kept away, lest their influence intrude upon the father's. "Extreme vigilance" was exercised to prevent the boy from hearing himself praised. "From his own intercourse with me, I could derive none but a very humble opinion of myself; and the standard of comparison he always held up to me, was not what other people did, but what a man could and ought to do."[34]

John Stuart Mill never forgot the place in Hyde Park where he and his father were walking when, at age fourteen, as the boy was about to leave the household for the first time, his father explained to him "that whatever I knew more than others, could not be ascribed to any merit in me, but to the very unusual advantage which had fallen to my lot, of having a father who was able to teach me, and willing to give the necessary trouble and time."[35] When some years later a friend, impressed by his sensitivity to poetry, admitted that at first Mill had seemed to him "a 'made,' or manufactured man," there can be little doubt about who Mill thought, or feared, his maker might be.[36]

Still, the overt message of his early education was not to fret about ultimate origins or the grounding of selfhood, but instead to take his place confidently in the ranks of those fighting for the improvement of mankind. In that mission Jeremy Bentham rapidly assumed a tutorial status higher even than that of his father. Although Mill's education under his father had already been one long "course of Benthamism," when he read for himself the first pages of Bentham's *Traité de Législation* at age fifteen, the principle of utility "burst upon me with all the force of novelty."

> The reading of this book was an epoch in my life; one of the turning points in my mental history. . . . The feeling rushed upon me, that all previous moralists were superceded, and that here indeed was the commencement of a new era in thought. . . . Under the guidance of the ethical principle of Pleasurable and Painful Consequences, followed out in the method of detail introduced

[32] Ibid., 39.
[33] Ibid., 31.
[34] Ibid., 35.
[35] Ibid., 37.
[36] Ibid., 163.

into these subjects by Bentham, I felt taken up to an eminence from which I could survey a vast intellectual domain, and see stretching out into the distance intellectual results beyond all computation. As I proceeded farther, there seemed to be added to this intellectual clearness, the most inspiring prospects of practical improvement in human affairs.

The elevated language of Mill's recollections, looking back on that moment from middle age, soars still higher:

When I laid down the last volume of the *Traité*, I had become a different being. The "principle of utility," understood as Bentham understood it, and applied in the manner in which he applied it through these three volumes, fell exactly into its place as the keystone which held together the detached and fragmentary component parts of my knowledge and beliefs. I now had opinions; a creed, a doctrine, a philosophy: in one among the best senses of the word, a religion; the inculcation and diffusion of which could be made the principal outward purpose of a life.[37]

There is no more striking textual specimen than this of the limitless confidence so characteristic of late-eighteenth- and early-nineteenth-century reformers, as their causal horizon billowed outward and brought within what seemed easy reach of instrumental reason an immense range of opportunities for doing good – "opportunities" that had hitherto seemed impossibly remote and intractable, and therefore not really opportunities at all. In this heady experience lies the origin of the humanitarian sensibility, for with every new opportunity came new responsibilities, new sources of guilt, new occasions for the commission of evil through omitting to do good.[38] The heightened sense of agency struck the young Mill with all the force of a religious conversion, supplying him at one stroke with an identity and a mission in life – a "religion," he did not hesitate to call it. That sense of power had been centuries in preparation, but what crystallized it for him was Bentham's daring delineation of cause-and-effect linkages suitable for the use of reform-minded legislators aiming at the reengineering of man and society. No wonder the shock of recognition left the boy feeling whole for the first time, a "different being," viewing the world from on high, intellectually in command of a vast domain. He knew how powerfully circumstances could shape

[37] Ibid., 69.

[38] For a more extensive discussion of these points, see my "Capitalism and the Origins of the Humanitarian Sensibility" (Part I), *American Historical Review*, 90 (April 1985), 339–361; and ibid., (Part II) (June, 1985), 547–66.

character. After all, Bentham's recipes for altering individual and social character by manipulating the circumstances of people's lives differed only in scale and scope of ambition from the ones Mill's father had employed so successfully in making him the singularly well-educated person he was.

The word "utilitarianism" was given its modern signification in the winter of 1822–23, when Mill, still a boy of sixteen, formed the idea of a fortnightly gathering of young disciples in the home of Bentham, who lived nearby. Mill christened it the "Utilitarian Society," borrowing the unfamiliar term from a novel about a Scots clergyman who warned his parishioners not to "leave the Gospel and become utilitarians."[39] The society continued to meet until 1826, when Mill turned twenty and the "mental crisis" struck.

During the three and a half years between John Stuart Mill's discovery of Bentham and his breakdown, there was little to suggest that his father's project had been anything but successful. In 1823 the precocious lad was given a sinecure in the East India Company, working as a clerk under the direct supervision of his father in the office of the Examiner of East India Correspondence. Although he was still in his teens, his letters and articles on parliamentary affairs, defects of the law, and religious freedom began appearing in such Liberal and quasi-radical organs as *The Traveller* and *The Morning Chronicle.* Bentham took him on for a year as editor (and in some passages coauthor) of the five-volume *Rationale of Judicial Evidence,* in Mill's mature opinion "one of the richest" of all Bentham's productions.[40] The creation of the *Westminster Review* as the quasi-official organ of the "philosophical radicals" gave Mill a receptive vehicle for his views and he became its most prolific contributor. It was, he observed, "a time of rapidly rising Liberalism," and the *Review* "made a considerable noise in the world [giving] a recognized *status* . . . to the Benthamic type of radicalism, out of all proportion to the number of its adherents."[41]

At an age when most people are still struggling to escape adolescence, Mill was associating with an increasingly illustrious set of friends and engaging in public debates with experienced orators

[39] John Stuart Mill, *Autobiography,* 81.
[40] Ibid., 119.
[41] Ibid., 101. Italics in original.

twice or thrice his age. He was already a full-fledged political intellectual with a growing reputation and a brilliant future. Yet the chapter of his *Autobiography* in which he recounts his early publishing exploits in the *Westminster Review* is titled "Youthful Propagandism," and in retrospect he credited himself with little originality and only the appearance of self-possession. He took pains to note that although Bentham was the chief intellectual inspiration of the radicals, his father "exercised a far greater personal ascendancy": It was his father's opinions "which gave the distinguishing character to the Benthamic or utilitarian propagandism of the time." He gave his father credit for having "perfect command over his great mental resources" and never met anyone who "could do such ample justice to his best thoughts in colloquial discussion." The elder Mill's opinions "flowed from him in a continuing stream," and in the face of such a torrent the younger Mill could conceive of himself as no more than a "channel" through which his father's energy poured into the world – a metaphor that in its perfect passivity says much about the young man's inability to cast himself successfully in the role of a genuinely creative causal agent.[42] The same message is conveyed by his abject confession that during these years the common complaint against Benthamite radicals, that they were "mere reasoning machine[s], [was] not altogether untrue of me."[43]

The utilitarian philosophy that so intoxicated the young John Stuart Mill was, from the neo-Kantian perspective of Max Weber, simply the "spirit of capitalism" in its most systematic, intellectualized aspect. Utilitarianism and the "spirit of capitalism" are nearly synonyms in Weber's vocabulary; they refer to the same dry husk of habit left behind when the Protestant ethic lost its anchorage in Christian piety. He spoke, for example, of the religious roots of the Protestant ethic dying out and "giving way to utilitarian worldliness," and of the "great religious ethic of the seventeenth century" bequeathing a pharisaically good conscience to its "utilitarian successor." Near the end of *The Protestant Ethic and the Spirit of Capitalism,* acknowledging the study's limitations, Weber said that in order to complete it one would have to trace the emergence of secular

[42] Ibid., 105.
[43] Ibid., 111.

rationalism through all the areas of ascetic religion, from the "medieval beginnings of worldly asceticism to its dissolution into pure utilitarianism."[44]

In Mill's day utilitarianism was less a philosophy than a celebration and technical elaboration of human consequentiality. Its roots lay in the heightened sense of worldly agency that the Protestant ethic cultivated. Consider the words of Benjamin Franklin, another heir of the Protestant ethic whose utilitarian cast of mind is well known, and who served as Weber's prime exemplar of the "Spirit of Capitalism":

> Remember, that *time* is money. He that can earn ten shillings a day by his labour, and goes abroad, or sits idle, one half of that day, though he spends but sixpence during his diversion or idleness, ought not to reckon *that* the only expense; he has really spent, or rather thrown away, five shillings besides. . . .
>
> Remember, that *credit* is money. If a man lets his money lie in my hands after it is due, he gives me the interest. . . .
>
> He that kills a breeding-sow, destroys all her offspring to the thousandth generation. He that murders a crown, destroys all that it might have produced, even scores of pounds. . . .
>
> He that loses five shillings, not only loses that sum, but all the advantage that might be made by turning it in dealing, which by the time that a young man becomes old, will amount to a considerable sum of money.[45]

"That this is the spirit of capitalism which here speaks in characteristic fashion," wrote Weber in *The Protestant Ethic and the Spirit of Capitalism,* "no one will doubt, however little we may wish to claim that everything which could be understood as pertaining to that spirit is contained in it."[46] There is indeed little reason to doubt that Franklin's words embody the spirit of capitalism. What may be more surprising, in spite of Weber's routine association of utilitarianism with the "spirit of capitalism," is the thought that these same words also express vital elements of the worldview that the younger Mill embraced when he embarked on a career of idealistic utilitarian and humanitarian reform. The suggestion seems at first glance counterintuitive. Capitalists, after all, pursue self-interest. Humanitarian reformers aim at altruistic ends, and over the course of the past two centuries it has often been private property and its bourgeois possessors that have

[44] Weber, *Protestant Ethic,* 176, 183.
[45] Ibid., 48–50.
[46] Ibid., 51.

blocked reform. What concern is it of the idealistic reformer that "time is money," or that lost shillings and dead breeding-sows entail what economists call "opportunity costs"?

Although Benjamin Franklin addressed his advice to young tradesmen who wanted to get rich, and Jeremy Bentham addressed his to legislators who presumably aspired to the greatest good for the greatest number, the two men's advice is crucially similar in what it presupposes about human agency. The two men played by the same rules of causal attribution. Both took for granted an audience whose members were alert to opportunity and confident of their ability to intervene in the course of human affairs and thereby to shape events to their own will. Both writers aimed to inculcate in their readers still greater alertness and self confidence. The advice of both men embodied a novel attitude toward time, one that radically annexed the future to the present and made it malleable in the hands of the deliberate, farsighted actor. For Franklin and Bentham, as for James and John Stuart Mill, the future is not something distant and inexorable that happens to us, regardless of our choices, but something that in large measure we are already creating, moment by moment, by both our actions and our omissions to act in the present. So immediate is the future's relation to the present, so certain is the actor's capacity to shape it by embarking *now* on the preferred course of action, that the design and production of the future becomes a duty. To allow an unintended future to come about is to be careless, to betray a norm of responsibility.

Although Weber never spoke in terms of causal attribution, his highest ambition in *The Protestant Ethic and the Spirit of Capitalism* was to trace the historical emergence of this sense of duty, for he was convinced this was the principal contribution that religion made to the rise of capitalism. Granting that capitalists "make tallow out of cattle and money out of men," Weber nonetheless sharply distinguished the spirit of capitalism from acquisitiveness per se, and focused instead on a "peculiarity of this philosophy of avarice . . . above all the idea of a duty of the individual toward the increase of his capital, which is assumed as an end in itself."

Truly what is here preached is not simply a means of making one's way in the world, but a peculiar ethic. The infraction of its rules is treated not as foolishness but as forgetfulness of duty. That is the essence of the matter. . . .

> And in truth this peculiar idea, so familiar to us to-day, but in reality so little a matter of course, of one's duty in a calling, is what is most characteristic of capitalistic culture, and is in a sense the fundamental basis of it. It is an obligation which the individual is supposed to feel and does feel toward the content of his professional activity, no matter in what it consists, in particular no matter whether it appears on the surface as a utilization of his personal powers, or only of his material possessions (as capital).[47]

The altruistic Benthamite reformer and the calculating, leather-aproned shopkeeper cherished different goals, but both lived with one foot in the future and both displayed a heightened sense of causal agency that carried with it new obligations. Some of these new obligations were moral, some merely prudential. A person who felt obliged to honor the precept that "time is money" might, of course, fulfill that obligation entirely in prudential, self-serving ways. But once habituated to the idea that future and present are so closely and predictably related that it would be a breach of obligation to pass up any opportunity to make capital grow, some people were bound to transpose that future-oriented dutifulness into the moral sphere, and to conclude that it was a still greater breach of obligation to pass up opportunities to "do good" in a larger, more public sense. The sense of duty is the same in both cases, and so is the logic of causal attribution: the person who passes up opportunities, however slight, to make money must bear responsibility for the earnings forgone; similarly, the person who passes up opportunities to do good – even indirect ones, like signing petitions and taking all the other complex steps necessary to uproot an institution as deeply entrenched as slavery – must bear responsibility for the continued existence of evil.

Morally, of course, there is a vital contrast between people whose felt obligation toward the future extends only to matters of self-interest and those whose concerns embrace the public interest as well. But what was historically novel in the period 1750–1850 was the perception of the future as plastic and the self as able, even duty-bound, to shape it. Thus for our purposes the businessman who mined the future for profit and the reformer who sculpted it in hopes of improving mankind had more in common with each other than either had with the people Weber called "traditionalists," who, because they ordinarily felt incapable of controlling the future – and

[47] Ibid., 51, 54.

certainly acknowledged no duty to do so – perceived themselves to be living in a different sort of world.[48]

Weber, keenly aware of the artificiality of ideal types, but also cognizant of their heuristic indispensability, characterized the world of traditionalism as the reversed mirror image, as it were, of the "spirit of capitalism." The traditionalist saw in tradition an adequate guide to conduct, failed to see present acts and choices as having any very close or reliable instrumental relationship to the future, and displayed an attitude of resignation toward whatever life might bring. From this perspective, not intrinsically any less respectable in Weber's eyes than the one that prevails today, the present appeared to be an extension of the past, moving inexorably toward an unknowable destination under the influence of forces that dwarfed human volition. Since traditionalists did not view their present as a staging ground for the production of the future, they seldom encountered the most distinctive features of modern life, "opportunities," those curious temporal interfaces that permit us almost magically to reach through time, as it were, and secure particular futures by actions we take in the present. The very idea of an "opportunity" presupposes the possession of "recipe knowledge," predictable instrumental relations between present actions and future events that played little part in the traditional imagination. Thus the traditionalist laborer, when offered higher piece rates for getting the harvest in on time, instead quit working as soon as his or her customary wage was earned, leaving the crop to rot on the vine. "A man does not 'by nature' wish to earn more and more money," observed Weber, "but simply to live as he is accustomed to live and to earn as much as is necessary for that purpose. Wherever modern capitalism has begun its work of increasing the productivity of human labour by increasing its intensity, it has encountered the immensely stubborn resistance of this leading trait of pre-capitalistic labour."[49]

Before Adam Smith's "invisible hand" could allocate goods and resources in its relentless but singularly efficient manner, there had to exist in the population substantial numbers of "economic men," peo-

[48] For Weber's characterization of traditionalism see ibid., 59–69, and passim.

[49] Ibid., 60. For the significance of "recipe knowledge," on which the perception of "opportunity" depends, see my "Capitalism and the Origins of the Humanitarian Sensibility" (Part I), 356–61.

ple of a calculating and manipulative frame of mind, who did not take tradition as their guide and were not content with things as they have always been. They had to be alert to opportunity, attentive to the subtle disciplinary pressures created by changes in prices and wages, and willing to alter their modes of conduct so as to maximize every advantage. Weber recognized full well that capitalism had existed in isolated enclaves long before the Protestant Reformation. He also recognized that the market itself, by rewarding some character types and penalizing others, encouraged the development of the utility-maximizing sort of person that its efficient operation demanded. But he did not believe that the market by itself could ever have created – out of a population militantly averse to change and ideologically well armed against the *auri sacra fames* – sufficiently large numbers of "economic men" to account for the massive transformation of the western European economy that did, in fact, occur in the centuries following the Reformation.

> Thus the capitalism of to-day, which has come to dominate economic life, educates and selects the economic subjects which it needs through a process of economic survival of the fittest. But here one can easily see the limits of the concept of selection as a means of historical explanation. In order that a manner of life so well adapted to the peculiarities of capitalism could be selected at all, i.e. should come to dominate others, it had to originate somewhere, and not in isolated individuals alone, but as a way of life common to whole groups of men. This origin is what really needs explanation.[50]

What made the traditionalist's transformation into "economic man" so difficult to explain was that the traditionalist's most distinctive trait, his comparative blindness to opportunity, ruled out an entire range of explanations. Ordinarily we explain what people do by showing that they had something to gain from it, that they were acting on interest, responding to incentives. But to speak of "gain," "interests," and "incentives" is to presuppose that the actor perceives opportunity as we do. Having defined traditionalists as people insensitive to the existence of opportunity, it obviously would not do for Weber to say that they adopted a radically new, opportunity-perceiving style of life because of the opportunities such a life offered. The emergence of "economic man" would be no puzzle at all if one could assume that opportunities for personal enrichment (or public improvement) were fixed facts with

[50] Weber, *Protestant Ethic,* 55.

uniform and transparent meanings, sure to be grasped as such in any and all cultural settings. But Weber knew that this was not the case. Traditional society condemned the pursuit of mammon, viewed change of all kinds with deep suspicion, and was populated by people whose understanding of the relationship between present and future discouraged perceptions of opportunity. Why had all this changed? Why would such people have ever abandoned their tradition-oriented way of life and adopted one of perpetual busy-ness and self-aggrandizement? What had induced the cognitive shift necessary to the emergence of "opportunity"? From our retrospective vantage point it is all too easy to say that the prospect of a higher standard of living should have been more than enough to lure people out of traditional ways of life, which usually entailed penury, if not grinding poverty. But the prospect of affluence, even supposing it could have been brought into focus, could not have had any leverage on people who were traditionalists in the specific sense Weber so carefully defined – that is, who were *unresponsive* to incentives and *genuinely content* to do as they had always done. How, then, can we account for the change?

As is well known, Weber found a solution to the puzzle in religion. Although traditional culture prized stability and discouraged people from even recognizing the existence of material incentives for changing their lives, that culture did a great deal to sensitize them to religious incentives. In the intensely religious atmosphere of the sixteenth and seventeenth centuries, the one opportunity to shape the future that was deeply etched in the minds of all who were exposed to the teachings of the Church was that of salvation. For the sake of eternal life, Weber suggested, perhaps even traditionalists would abandon tradition, give up a life of satisfaction with things as they had always been, and embark upon a life of restless striving and ceaseless self-advancement.

For the purposes of the present argument, what is most important about Weber's thesis is his suggestion that the heightened sense of personal agency and obligation to grasp opportunity and construct the future that characterized the capitalist entrepreneur (and, by extension, altruistic reformers such as John Stuart Mill) was originally inculcated, paradoxically, by a religious doctrine that was stunningly deterministic. One of Weber's principal achievements in *The Protestant Ethic* was his demonstration that the logical implications of predestination, which undoubtedly pointed in the direction of fatalism and resignation to the will of God, were massively overshadowed by the psychological implications, which pointed in just the opposite direction.[51] The language of causal attribution developed in the preceding pages helps reinforce Weber's point. By reviving the Augustinian theme of predestination and hammering home the Protestant message of God's omnipotence and the utter impotence of the natural man to accomplish anything at all toward his own salvation, Calvin, like Luther before him, was carrying out a thoroughgoing divinization of the circumstances underpinning human existence. Calvin's human subject was, with a vengeance, "radically situated," for without an infusion of divine grace the natural man was wholly incapable of merit, and even the saint was understood to be dependent at every instant upon his Maker's gratuitous and undeserved mercy. In the words of a latter-day Calvinist, Jonathan Edwards, "The constant exercise of the infinite power of God is necessary to keep bodies in being."[52] To adopt the Protestant conviction that man was saved by "faith alone" was to insist on the transitivity of all cause-and-effect relations not originating directly in God, and to come very close to depicting God, not merely as the First Cause, but as the sole authentic cause in the universe. Nonetheless, for Calvin as for Luther, the resulting bondage to circumstance was sweet and liberating because the circumstances that shaped the conduct and personhood of the elect were understood to be the very substance of God's grace.[53]

[51] "Fatalism is, of course, the only logical consequence of predestination. But on account of the idea of proof the psychological result was precisely the opposite." Ibid., 232n.

[52] Quoted in Perry Miller, *Jonathan Edwards* (New York: Dell, 1967), 91.

[53] One could argue that Weber's insight into the psychological dynamics of predestination was incomplete. The doctrine had not one, but two faces: threatening and consoling. It threatened irrevocable damnation, but also offered assurance that the circumstantial setting of life was, in spite of all appearances to the contrary, an instrument of divine purpose. Weber assumed that the doctrine struck fear into the hearts of adherents and drove them in sheer terror to cling to the idea of the calling as one's only spiritual life raft. But predestination could have been a comforting doctrine for people already disturbed by the eruption of contingency in their lives and eager to believe that even the most disruptive events reflected the will of God. An interpretation of predestination stressing its tendency to divinize the circumstances of human existence and thereby assure people that they were not mere "creatures of circumstance" would reinforce Michael Walzer's suggestion, contra Weber, that the effect of predestination was less to induce anxiety than to "confirm and explain in theological terms perceptions men already had of the dangers of the world and the self." Walzer, *Revolution of the Saints*, 308.

Who was elect? Everything hinged on this. No scrupulous Calvinist could ever be sure of the answer. But as Weber showed in his discussion of the "doctrine of proof," believers were encouraged to look for signs of election in their everyday affairs, their "calling," and it was in this search that the "economic man" was forged. God in his inscrutable wisdom had predestined some to eternal life and others to an eternity of suffering. Convinced that the ways of God were inaccessible to human reason, but convinced also that the smallest and homeliest detail of everyday existence might signal the will of an omnipotent and ever active Being, believers anxiously examined the trajectory of their daily experience in hopes of catching glimpses of divine favor. Since God's grace was all that kept even the saints from sinking into the bottomless corruption of the natural world, any success in holding oneself upright had to be attributed only proximately to oneself and ultimately to God.

The logical impossibility of ascertaining one's own state of grace with certainty made self-surveillance all the more important and supplied believers with an unparalleled psychological incentive to become self-conscious, self-monitoring agents, who conceived of their lives as careers extending from past to present to future and who constantly adjusted their conduct so as to bring about the closest possible fit between present intentions and future consequences – all the while crediting whatever success they might achieve to an infusion of divine Grace. "Only a life guided by constant thought could achieve conquest over the state of nature," Weber observed.[54] What Calvin demanded of his followers was "constant self-control" and a "systematic rational ordering of the moral life as a whole."[55] Under the leadership of the Protestant reformers, Christian asceticism "slammed the door of the monastery behind it" and "strode into the market-place of life," seeking to discipline the spontaneity of the impulses and to penetrate the routine of everyday life with its methodical rigor. And the vital step in fashioning a new form of life that would allow people to live in the world, but be neither of nor for this world, was to persuade them to "act upon [their] constant motives"[56] – or, as we might say, to *intentionalize* their lives, acting al-

[54] Weber, *Protestant Ethic,* 118.
[55] Ibid., 126.
[56] Ibid., 119.

ways in such a way as to render their experience, insofar as possible, a product (proximately, of course) of their own God-fearing intentions rather than of tradition, chance, accident, or the will of other human beings. Only persons bent upon the intentionalization of their lives and equipped with the "recipe knowledge" that the intentional life presupposes can construe the production of the future as a duty. And only insofar as people took that duty to heart, argued Weber, could capitalism burst the bonds of tradition and transform the culture of Europe. In their campaign to humble all rivals to God's causal omnipotence Protestants declared "fortune" and "fate" to be words of the heathen and construed their own agency in a radically transitive light, as the inexorable unfolding of a divine plan formed outside time. But in so doing they unintentionally created a niche in traditional culture within which, without incurring the sanctions either of conscience or community, they could act for all the world as if they were duty-bound to pursue opportunities, respond to material incentives, make their own lives, and even become, for all practical purposes, "self-made men."

That a doctrine logically so deterministic, and so candidly designed to rid the universe of all agents but One, could in psychological practice sharpen the boundaries of personhood and powerfully heighten people's sense of responsibility for the conduct of their own lives, will always remain paradoxical, notwithstanding all Weber's elucidations. The paradox is testimony to the immensely different configuration that the problem of relating persons to their circumstances had under religious auspices as compared with its configuration today, when with some brave exceptions it is only the uneducated who continue to construe the world as a stage cunningly designed by God for the enactment of a drama of redemption. Among intellectuals living in the wake of Darwin – and in the wake of all the social and economic changes of the nineteenth and twentieth centuries that conspired palpably to reinforce Darwin's message of endless flux and contingency – design has disappeared from the universe and the circumstantial setting of human existence seems beyond any possibility of divinization.

We have seen the fruitfulness of Weber's insight that the psychological implications of a belief system need not correspond with its logical implications; that a doctrine pointing logically toward fatalism and resignation, can, in practice, foster the most intense sort of activism. What Mill's mental crisis suggests is that the reverse is also true: A doctrine whose logical implications highlight the power of humans to make the world what they will, can, in practice, induce feelings of inconsequentiality and a beleaguered sense of self. Just as predestination can lead in practice to a keen awareness of all the respects in which the world depends upon the self, so the doctrine of utility, in spite of its overt celebration the boundlessness of human agency, can lead to an oppressive sensitivity to all the respects in which the self depends upon the world. The truth of the proposition is plainly evident in the relation between James Mill and his son. It was an expansive sense of agency and a corresponding alertness to opportunity and feeling of obligation to superintend his son's education that led the father to intrude upon the boy's life, depriving him of every semblance of autonomy and leaving him convinced that he was "a 'made,' or manufactured man." The relation between father and son illustrates in miniature the peculiar dynamics of freedom and fate in the wider culture, for insofar as actors occupy the same world, and are exposed to the consequences of one another's actions, the agency of one cannot fail to intrude upon and undermine the autonomy of others. In the world of proliferating technique and technological innovation that the market fosters, every new capacity to act breeds feelings of incapacity in those who are acted upon, and every expansion of causal horizons for some renders more fragile the perceptions of intransitivity upon which the autonomy of others depends. Far from being a polar opposition, the relation between freedom and fate begins to take on the ominous appearance of an identity.

The fifth chapter of the *Autobiography* is devoted to the "mental crisis" and the "important transformations in my opinions and character" that Mill attributed to it. He began his account of the crisis by recalling its "origin," the euphoria that swept over him upon reading Bentham. That he should thus identify his dejection and paralysis with the voluntaristic enthusiasm that immediately preceded it is a matter of considerable significance within the present interpretive framework, and a point to which we shall want to return. "From the winter of 1821, when I first read Bentham," he wrote, "I had what might truly be called an object in life; to be a reformer of the world. My conception of my own happiness was entirely identified with this object. . . . my whole reliance was placed on this."

This did very well for several years, during which the general improvement going on in the world and the idea of myself as engaged with others in struggling to promote it, seemed enough to fill up an interesting and animated existence. But the time came when I awakened from this as from a dream. It was in the summer of 1826. I was in a dull state of nerves, such as everybody is occasionally liable to; unsusceptible to enjoyment or pleasurable excitement; one of those moods when what is pleasure at other times, becomes insipid or indifferent; the state, I should think, in which converts to Methodism usually are, when smitten by their first "conviction of sin."

Mill was keenly aware that his experience, although on his view wholly secular, conformed rather closely to a pattern etched by centuries of Christian teachings about conversion and spiritual rebirth. The pursuit of happiness on which his "whole reliance" had hitherto been placed lost its dreamlike charm; pride and self-confidence gave way to the anguish and self-revulsion of the the sinner; and life quite literally lost the only point it could have on utilitarian premises. The question *What can I make, or do?* no longer entranced him:

In this frame of mind it occurred to me to put the question directly to myself, "Suppose that all your objects in life were realized; that all the changes in institutions and opinions which you are looking forward to, could be completely effected at this very instant: would this be a great joy and happiness to you?" And an irrepressible self-consciousness distinctly answered "No!" At this my heart sank within me: the whole foundation on which my life was constructed fell down. All my happiness was to have been found in the continual pursuit of this end. The end had ceased to charm, and how could there ever again be any interest in the means? I seemed to have nothing left to live for.[57]

No longer inspired by visions of the better world that he and other friends of human improvement could make through their own expansive agency, his "whole foundation" collapsed and the question his father and Jeremy Bentham had taught him not to ask, "Who made me?" pressed in upon him as never before. A cloud settled over his life that neither sleep nor his favorite books were able to dispel. "I carried it with me into all companies, into all occupations." Feeling that his distress was neither interesting nor respectable, and that he

[57] John Stuart Mill, *Autobiography,* 137, 139.

deserved no sympathy, he spoke to no one about it. Although it would have been natural, he said, to turn to his father for advice, he was "the last person" to approach in a "case such as this." "Everything convinced me that he had no knowledge of any such mental state as I was suffering from, and that even if he could be made to understand it, he was not the physician who could heal it. My education, which was wholly his work, had been conducted without any regard to the possibility of its ending in this result; and I saw no use in giving him the pain of thinking that his plans had failed, when the failure was probably irremediable, and at all events, beyond the power of *his* remedies."[58]

The Oedipal overtones of the episode are unmistakable. Mill himself attributed his cure in part to the poetic inspiration of Wordsworth, in part to his formulation of the balanced, nonfatalistic view of liberty and necessity that he eventually set forth in his *System of Logic,* but also in part to a flood of tears mysteriously triggered by a passage he happened to read in Jean François Marmontel's *Memoirs.* The passage described the death of a father, the plight of his wife and children, and the daring resolution of his son, a "mere boy," to "supply the place of all that they had lost."

> A vivid conception of the scene and its feelings came over me, and I was moved to tears. From this moment my burthen grew lighter. The oppression of the thought that all feeling was dead within me, was gone. I was no longer hopeless: I was not a stock or a stone. I had still, it seemed, some of the material out of which all worth of character, and all capacity for happiness are made. Relieved from my ever present sense of irremediable wretchedness, I gradually found that the ordinary incidents of life could again give me some pleasure. . . . Thus the cloud gradually drew off, and I again enjoyed life: and though I had several relapses, some of which lasted many months, I never again was as miserable as I had been.[59]

There is no reason to challenge Bruce Mazlish's conclusion that "the 'dejection' of Mill's experience, the 'depressing and paralyzing' nature of that experience, was intimately connected to his feeling that he had been 'made,' *completely determined,* by his father." How his own character had been formed became for this dutiful son "*the* most pressing and constant question of his life," and one that could not fail to implicate the man who had fathered him and so minutely superintended his

[58] Ibid., 139. Italics in the original.
[59] Ibid., 145.

education.[60] Freud's understanding of "overdetermination" leaves ample room for us to construe Mill's later writings on liberty and necessity both as worthy philosophical efforts in their own right and as manifestations of a deeply rooted personal need to come to terms with the suffocating influence of his father. The only mistake would be to think that the dread "incubus" of "Philosophical Necessity" was for Mill merely a surrogate for his domineering progenitor. The possibilities that choice is a subjective illusion, that human action is fully determined by the conditions in which it occurs, that the self originates nothing and is, in truth, inconsequential – these possibilities define a dread-inspiring state of mind, quite apart from whatever amplification they may receive from Oedipal associations. Being conceived is, after all, the most elemental form of being caused, or "made," and thus biological descent raises in microcosm all the problems of transitivity.

Mill's own efforts to trace the sources and explain the consequences of his crisis veered somewhat erratically between emotional and intellectual planes of interpretation. At the emotional level he treated his dejection as a result of impoverished feelings. His emotional reaction to Marmontel's *Memoirs* seemed relevant to him, of course, not because he recognized any sexual rivalry with his father, but simply because his tears reassured him that all feeing was not dead within him, that he "was not a stock or a stone."[61] The Romantic reaction against the Enlightenment that Mill reported was "streaming in upon me" at the time supplied him with a ready-made interpretation of melancholia as the result of impoverished feelings, and lay the blame for impoverished feelings squarely on the analytical habits of mind that his father and Bentham had so assiduously cultivated in him.[62] The identification of good psychic health with the exercise of, or "being in touch with," the emotions was not then the cliché it has since become, but it was already sufficiently commonplace that Mill took pains to note that he had "always before received with incredulity" what he now came to accept: "that the habit of analysis has a tendency to wear away the feelings."[63]

[60] Bruce Mazlish, *James and John Stuart Mill: Father and Son in the Nineteenth Century* (New York: Basic Books, 1975), 227, 404. Italics in the original.

[61] The absence of any mention of his mother in the *Autobiography* only fuels twentieth-century suspicions of denial. See ibid., 16.

[62] John Stuart Mill, *Autobiography,* 169.

[63] Ibid., 141.

Mill never entirely abandoned the associationist framework of Locke and Hartley, according to which analysis was the indispensable means of detecting false associations, separating ideas that had come to be associated only through accident or prejudice. By analytically sifting out false associations we attain "our clearest knowledge of the permanent sequences in nature; the real connexions between Things . . . natural laws." These laws, in turn, "cause our ideas of things that are joined together in Nature, to cohere more and more closely in our thoughts."[64] Mill's crisis persuaded him that the analytical habit, however "favourable to prudence and clearsightedness," was a "perpetual worm at the root both of the passions and of the virtues." His father, using the familiar instruments of praise and blame, reward and punishment, had striven to make the good of mankind the object of the boy's existence by contriving to associate feelings of happiness with everything promoting the general good. But to no avail.

> My education, I thought, had failed to create these feelings in sufficient strength to resist the dissolving influence of analysis, while the whole course of my intellectual cultivation had made precocious and premature analysis the inveterate habit of my mind. I was thus, as I said to myself, left stranded at the commencement of my voyage, with a well equipped ship and a rudder, but no sail. . . . The fountains of vanity and ambition seemed to have dried up in me, as completely as those of benevolence. . . . There seemed no power in nature sufficient to begin the formation of my character anew, and create in a mind now irretrievably analytic, fresh associations of pleasure with any of the objects of human desire.[65]

Thomas Carlyle's first great essay, "Signs of the Times," appeared in the *Edinburgh Review* in 1829, during the "later stages" of Mill's dejection. It was a tirade against the very philosophy in which Mill had been trained and a trenchant commentary on the implications of that philosophy for the psychology of human agency. When Carlyle condemned the "Age of Machinery" and lamented a generation "grown mechanical in head and heart," one of his principal targets was the British associationist tradition from Locke to Bentham, and the danger he identified with that tradition was precisely that of drowning human agency in a sea of circumstantiality. "The Philoso-

[64] Ibid., 141, 143.
[65] Ibid., 143.

pher of this age," he argued, "is not a Socrates, a Plato, a Hooker, or Taylor, who inculcates on men the necessity and infinite worth of moral goodness, the great truth that our happiness depends on the mind which is within us; but a Smith, a De Lolme, a Bentham, who chiefly inculcates the reverse of this, – that our happiness depends entirely on external circumstances; nay, that the strength and dignity of the mind within us is itself the creature and consequence of these."[66]

Although Carlyle's early writings at first struck Mill as a "haze of poetry and German metaphysics," their "wonderful power" eventually made a "deep impression."[67] The first meeting of the two men took place in 1831, shortly after Mill's recovery. In composing the account of his crisis that appears in the *Autobiography,* Mill seems to have relied extensively on Carlylean language. After all, Carlyle, by attacking "Mechanism" and identifying it closely with the "doctrine of circumstances," held out to Mill a very appealing interpretation of his mental crisis, one that lifted it out of the realm of accident and personal idiosyncrasy and gave it a cultural, or even cosmic, dimension. In words that must have seemed full of resonance to the young man in his misery, Carlyle declared that "our favourite Philosophers have no love and no hatred; they stand among us not to do, nor to create anything, but as a sort of Logic-mills, to grind out the true causes and effects of all that is done and created." In the eyes of such philosophers, complained Carlyle, not only precocious youngsters with domineering fathers, but even history's greatest and most heroic figures, were "simply so many mechanical phenomena, caused or causing."[68] Identifying utilitarianism with a leaden stress on circumstantiality, and linking it closely to Adam Smith and the pursuit of

[66] Thomas Carlyle, *A Carlyle Reader: Selections from the Writings of Thomas Carlyle,* ed. G. B. Tennyson (New York: Modern Library, 1969), 34, 37, 40–41.

[67] John Stuart Mill, *Autobiography,* 181, 183. Speaking of Carlyle's early articles, Mill also observed that "for a long time I saw nothing in these (as my father saw nothing in them to the last) but insane rhapsody" (169). Mill did not deem himself a competent judge of Carlyle, whom he regarded as a "poet" and a "man of intuition," and he credited Harriet Taylor with "interpreting" Carlyle for him (183).

[68] Carlyle, *A Carlyle Reader,* 46–47. "Speak to any small man of a high, majestic Reformation, of a high majestic Luther; and forthwith he sets about 'accounting' for it; how the 'circumstances of the time' called for such a character, and found him, we suppose, standing girt and road-ready, to do its errand; how the 'circumstances of the time' created, fashioned, floated him quietly along into the result; how, in short, this small man, had he been there, could have performed the like himself!" (47).

profit, Carlyle depicted the antiformalist world of the Benthamites as a seamless web of causal contingency, inimical to passion, corrosive of all high values, and unfit for human habitation. In doing so, he described the very symptoms Mill was then experiencing, and traced those symptoms straight to the market-bred dilemma of transitivity:

> The infinite, absolute character of Virtue has passed into a finite, conditional one; it is no longer a worship of the Beautiful and Good; but a calculation of the Profitable. Worship, indeed, in any sense, is not recognized among us, or is mechanically explained into Fear of pain, or Hope of pleasure. . . .
>
> By arguing on the "force of circumstances," we have argued away all force from ourselves; and stand leashed together, uniform in dress and movement, like the rowers of some boundless galley. . . . Practically considered, our creed is Fatalism; and, free in hand and foot, we are shackled in heart and soul with far straiter than feudal chains. Truly may we say, with the Philosopher, "the deep meaning of the Laws of Mechanism lies heavy on us"; and in the closet, in the marketplace, in the temple, by the social hearth, encumbers the whole movements of our mind, and over our noblest faculties is spreading a nightmare sleep.[69]

Perceptive though Carlyle's diagnosis was, his prescription for cure amounted to little more than an obstinate refusal to accept the disturbing message of circumstantiality to which consciousness exposed him. Here again, Mill seems to have followed Carlyle's lead. Of the two great lessons that Mill drew from his crisis, the first was a theory of life that he himself acknowledged had "much in common with . . . the anti-self-consciousness theory of Carlyle."[70] As if in repudiation of the Calvinist imperative to monitor experience constantly and adjust conduct so as to make life, insofar as possible, a product of one's own deliberate intentions, Mill now sang the praises of serendipity, spontaneity, and unconsciousness. "Ask yourself whether you are happy and you cease to be so," he observed. "The only chance is to treat, not happiness, but some end external to it, as the purpose of life. Let your self-consciousness, your scrutiny, your self-interrogation, exhaust themselves on that; and if otherwise fortunately circumstanced, you will inhale happiness with the air you breathe, without dwelling on it or thinking about it . . . or putting it to flight by fatal questioning. This theory now became the basis of my philosophy of life."[71]

[69] Carlyle, *A Carlyle Reader*, 46, 51.
[70] John Stuart Mill, *Autobiography*, 145.
[71] Ibid., 147.

Although elements of the "anti-self-consciousness theory" were already apparent in "Signs of the Times," Carlyle developed the theme more fully in "Characteristics," published in 1831, which continued his attack on "Utilitarianism, or Radicalism, or the Mechanical Philosophy, or by whatever name it is called," and identified it with a larger "fever of Skepticism [that] must needs burn itself out."[72] Noting that in all departments of life the "Voluntary and the Conscious" bear only a small proportion to the "Involuntary and Unconscious," Carlyle opted wholeheartedly for the latter, contending that unconsciousness was a sign of "wholeness" and "right performance."[73] "Boundless as is the domain of man, it is but a small fractional proportion of it that he rules with Consciousness and by Forethought," he argued. Rhetorically he asked, "Is it the skillful anatomist that cuts the best figure at the Sadler Wells? or does the boxer hit better for knowing that he has a *flexor longus* and a *flexor brevis*?"[74]

What Carlyle wanted from life was what he found missing from the literature of the age, "spontaneous devotedness to the object, being wholly possessed by the object, what we can call Inspiration."[75] For him, as for Mill, the "choking incubus"[76] that drained away all possibility of spontaneity was an all too acute awareness of the causal force of circumstance in a setting that resisted every effort at divinization. "Freewill no longer reigns unquestioned and by divine right," he observed, "but like a mere earthly sovereign, by expediency, by Rewards and Punishments: or rather, let us say, the Freewill, so far as may be, has abdicated and withdrawn into the dark, and a spectral nightmare of a Necessity usurps its throne."[77] Unlike Karl Marx, who warned of the formalist fantasies of autonomy and self-sufficiency the market might foster, Carlyle warned of a market-bred attentiveness to circumstance and preoccupation with contingency that threatened to eviscerate the very idea of freedom and induce a kind of self-inflicted paralysis.

> Never since the beginning of Time was there, that we hear or read of, so intensely self-conscious a Society. . . .

[72] Carlyle, *A Carlyle Reader,* 102, 100.
[73] Ibid., 75, 73, 77.
[74] Ibid., 71.
[75] Ibid., 86.
[76] Ibid., 103.
[77] Ibid., 74.

> Truly it may be said, the Divinity has withdrawn from the earth; or veils himself in that wide-wasting Whirlwind of a departing Era, wherein the fewest can discern his goings. Not Godhead, but an iron, ignoble circle of Necessity embraces all things; binds the youth of these times into a sluggish thrall, or else exasperates him into a rebel. Heroic Action is paralysed; for what worth now remains unquestionable with him?[78]

The second lesson that Mill drew from his crisis followed from the first. In order to silence the nagging voice of consciousness and restore unity to a self that seemed intolerably divided and becalmed on a glassy sea of disenchantment, he concluded that one must cultivate the feelings, the region of elemental and spontaneous energies, the source of the "winds" without which even the best-equipped ship could not sail. He vowed to give "its proper place, among the prime necessities of human well-being, to the internal culture of the individual. . . . The maintenance of a due balance among the faculties, now seemed to me of primary importance. The cultivation of the feelings became one of the cardinal points in my ethical and philosophical creed."[79]

Coleridge and Harriet Taylor would become Mill's chief guides in matters of feeling, but here, too, the influence of Carlyle seems unmistakable. In "Signs of the Times" Carlyle had distinguished between the "inward" or "Dynamical" province and the "Mechanical" or "outward" one. The former he identified with "the primary, unmodified forces and energies of man, the mysterious springs of Enthusiasm, Poetry, Religion."[80] He conceded that excessive cultivation of the "Dynamical province" could lead to "idle, visionary, impracticable courses" and even to "Superstition and Fanaticism," but he insisted that undue cultivation of the Mechanical – although "productive of many palpable benefits" – would prove to be equally pernicious because of its tendency to destroy "Moral Force . . . the parent of all other Force." The good life, then, required a balanced cultivation of both the inward and the outward dimensions of life, and since the present age exceeded all others in its development of the Mechanical, the time had come to cultivate the Dynamical, even if it meant a diminished role for the intellect – even, indeed, if it meant loss of consciousness.[81]

[78] Ibid., 83, 92.
[79] John Stuart Mill, *Autobiography*, 147.
[80] Carlyle, *A Carlyle Reader*, 42.
[81] Ibid., 46.

> If in any sphere of man's life, then in the Moral sphere, as the inmost and most vital of all, it is good that there be wholeness; that there be unconsciousness, which is the evidence of this. Let the free, reasonable Will, which dwells in us, as in our Holy of Holies, be indeed free, and obeyed like a Divinity, as is its right and effort: the perfect obedience will be the silent one.[82]

In the autumn of 1828, before he read Carlyle and while he was still dejected and desperate for a renewed sense of spontaneity, Mill had come upon the poetry of William Wordsworth. He recorded the occasion as an "important event" in his life.[83] What made Wordsworth's poems "a medicine for my state of mind," he said, "was that they expressed, not mere outward beauty, but states of feeling, and of thought coloured by feeling, under the excitement of beauty. They seemed to be the very culture of the feelings, which I was in quest of."[84] The delights of reading Wordsworth reassured him that human beings had access to a "source of inward joy, of sympathetic and imaginative pleasure" that could never be exhausted. Here was a "perennial source of happiness" that would continue to give life a purpose, even when all the goals of utilitarian reform had been achieved, even "when all the greater evils in life shall have been removed."[85]

Here, indeed, was a solution of sorts to the crisis itself, for the strength of his response to Wordsworth convinced Mill that by reading poetry, listening to music, and otherwise cultivating the inward, "Dynamical" world of the feelings, he might safely continue the very practice on which he blamed his dejection – his analytical mode of inquiry. "The delight which these poems gave me, proved that with culture of this sort, there was nothing to dread from the most confirmed habit of analysis."[86] By counterbalancing inward and outward culture, he felt that he could fill his slack sails and yet also keep his bearings. The irony of "cultivating" the emotions as a deliberate, instrumental means of achieving spontaneity seems to have escaped him.

Thus, in the end the great lessons Mill learned from his crisis did not require him to repudiate his original self, or to disavow the father who had played such a large role in fashioning it, but only to supple-

[82] Ibid., 73.
[83] John Stuart Mill, *Autobiography,* 149.
[84] Ibid., 151.
[85] Ibid.
[86] Ibid., 153.

ment that original self with a greater openness and sensitivity to the emotive dimension of life. For the remainder of his life Mill prided himself on his balanced appreciation of the emotional and the intellectual. Indeed, straddling fences, embracing both sides of issues that lesser thinkers regarded as irreconcilable, became one of his trademarks as a thinker. Although raised as a utilitarian and always ready to bring the principle of utility to bear on new questions, he would never again give his sole allegiance to utility or any other principle or system; although moved by romanticism, and deeply indebted to it for the interpretive framework in which he cast his mental crisis, no one would ever mistake him for a romantic. In the great debate between the eighteenth and the nineteenth centuries he adopted Goethe's motto of "manysidedness," acknowledging truths on both sides and marveling at the "blind rage with which the combatants rushed against one another."[87] Far from giving up his "early opinions" – "in no essential part of which I at any time wavered" – he claimed in the end that all the new thinking he did under the pressure of his dejection "only laid the foundation of these [early opinions] more deeply and strongly" while clarifying their effect.[88] In resolving the crisis he had moved a "great distance" from his father's "tone of thought and feeling."[89] But for better or worse John Stuart Mill was still his father's son, and he knew it.

Mill was proud of his resolution of the crisis and believed that others might benefit from knowledge of it. Accordingly it forms the pivotal event of the *Autobiography*, overshadowing even the story of his unconventional and transformative relationship with Harriet Taylor. What seems to have pleased him most is the tense philosophical reconciliation between liberty and necessity that he briefly summarized in the *Autobiography* and developed further in his *System of Logic*. It was in connection with this – a recapitulation, as it were, of the ultimate meaning for posterity of John Stuart Mill's mental crisis – that he wrote the passage that stands at the head of this essay, which can now be reproduced in full:

During the later returns of my dejection, the doctrine of what is called Philosophical Necessity weighed on my existence like an incubus. I felt as if I

[87] Ibid., 171.
[88] Ibid., 175.
[89] Ibid., 189.

was scientifically proved to be the helpless slave of antecedent circumstances; as if my character and that of all others had been formed for us by agencies beyond our control, and was wholly out of our own power. I often said to myself, what a relief it would be if I could disbelieve the doctrine of the formation of character by circumstances; and remembering the wish of Fox respecting the doctrine of resistance to governments, that it might never be forgotten by kings, nor remembered by subjects, I said that it would be a blessing if the doctrine of necessity could be believed by all *quoad* the characters of others, and disbelieved in regard to their own. I pondered painfully on the subject, till gradually I saw light through it. I perceived, that the word Necessity, as a name for the doctrine of Cause and Effect applied to human action, carried with it a misleading association; and that this association was the operative force in the depressing and paralyzing influence which I had experienced. I saw that though our character is formed by circumstances, our own desires can do much to shape those circumstances; and that what is really inspiriting and ennobling in the doctrine of freewill, is the conviction that we have real power over the formation of our own character; that our will, by influencing some of our circumstances, can modify our future habits or capabilities of willing.

Assuring his readers that this formulation was not an abandonment of the doctrine of circumstances but, rather, "that doctrine itself, properly understood," he drew a sharp distinction between the doctrine of circumstances and "Fatalism," and discarded altogether the misleading word "Necessity." Thus stripped of its thorns, the heritage impressed upon him by Bentham and his father – "the last of the eighteenth century" – could be embraced once again, both for its truth and its goodness.

The theory [of circumstances] which I now for the first time rightly apprehended, ceased altogether to be discouraging, and besides the release to my spirits, I no longer suffered under the burthen, so heavy to one who aims at being a reformer in opinions, of thinking one doctrine true, and the contrary doctrine morally beneficial. The train of thought which had extricated me from this dilemma, seemed to me, in after years, fitted to render a similar service to others; and it now forms the chapter on Liberty and Necessity in the concluding Book of my *System of Logic.*[90]

Mill's confidence that other people had experienced something like his crisis, and would want to know how he had extricated himself from it, was surely correct. Yet any reader who turns from the *Autobiography* to the *System of Logic,* hoping for further illumination, is

[90] Ibid., 175, 177.

likely to be disappointed, for even when spelled out fully Mill's resolution of the problem of transitivity seems less than decisive.

Although uncomfortable with the connotations of the word "necessity," Mill made clear in this, his most complete formulation, that his own position in the long controversy dating back to Pelagius was much closer to "Necessity" than to "Free Will." In the *System of Logic* he rejected out of hand the Christian doctrine handed down from Aquinas which held that the will, unlike other phenomena, is not determined by its antecedents, but solely by itself.[91] The question he set himself was how to reconcile necessity – the view that the will is determined by character, and character by circumstance – with our subjective sense of freedom. Some people, he argued, imagine that the predictability of our conduct is, in itself, enough to destroy our feeling of freedom. But predictability need not conflict at all with our sense of freedom, he contended, once we see the significance of Hume's discovery that "there is nothing in causation but invariable, certain, and unconditional sequence."[92] Since in both material and mental matters there is no "intimate connexion," no "peculiar tie," or "mysterious constraint" linking cause and effect, we can acknowledge the predictability of our conduct in the eyes of those who know us well, and admit even the corollary of strict causal regularity in human affairs, without undermining our feeling of freedom. These concessions to necessity did not bother Mill, because they successfully skirted the principal danger he wished to avoid, namely, the implication that we are ever "compelled, as by a magical spell, to obey any particular motive."[93]

What Mill was most eager to conserve was the primordial insight of

[91] "Now it is a law of providence that everything is moved by its proximate cause. . . . But the proximate moving cause of the will is the apprehended good, which is its object, and the will is moved by it as sight is by color. Therefore no created substance can move the will except by means of the apprehended good – in so far, namely, as it shows that a particular thing is good to do; and this is *to persuade*. Therefore no created substance can act on the will, or cause our choice, except by way of persuasion." *Basic Writings of St. Thomas Aquinas,* ed Anton C. Pegis, 2 vols. (New York, 1945), 2: 168–69 [Summa Contra Gentiles, Book III, ch. 88]. Italics in original.

[92] John Stuart Mill, *A System of Logic, Ratiocinative and Inductive: Being a Connected View of the Principles of Evidence and the Methods of Scientific Investigation,* vol. 8 of *The Collected Works,* ed. J. M. Robson (Toronto and Buffalo: University of Toronto Press and Routledge & Kegan Paul, 1974), 837.

[93] Ibid., 838.

asceticism: the possibility of authentically opposing one's own motives, of the self standing in genuine opposition to itself and thus participating in its own making. In stark opposition to the ascetic possibility stood fatalism. "A fatalist believes, or half believes (for nobody is a consistent fatalist), not only that whatever is about to happen, will be the infallible result of the causes which produce it, (which is the true necessitarian doctrine,) but moreover that there is no use in struggling against it; that it will happen however we may strive to prevent it." And in the *System of Logic,* unlike the *Autobiography,* he specifically identified fatalism with the followers of Robert Owen.

In the words of the sect which in our own day has most perseveringly inculcated and most perversely misunderstood this great doctrine, [man's] character is formed *for* him, and not *by* him; therefore his wishing that it had been formed differently is of no use; he has no power to alter it. But this is a grand error. He has, to a certain extent, a power to alter his character. Its being, in the ultimate resort, formed for him, is not inconsistent with its being, in part, formed *by* him as one of the intermediate agents. His character is formed by his circumstances (including among these his particular organization); but his own desire to mould it in a particular way is one of those circumstances, and by no means one of the least influential.[94]

Although this argument earned the voluntarist conclusion it aimed at – that "we are exactly as capable of making our own character, *if we will,* as others are of making it for us" – Mill knew that it could not carry the day. He continued: "Yes (answers the Owenite), but these words, 'if we will,' surrender the whole point: since the will to alter our own character is given us, not by any efforts of ours, but by circumstances which we cannot help; it comes to us either from external causes, or not at all."[95] Faced with an infinite regression, Mill slipped out of the mode of demonstrative argument and appealed to considerations that in the hands of William James and John Dewey would come to be known as "pragmatic." In a spirit closely akin to that which James would later adopt in his famous essay "The Will to Believe," Mill observed that "to think that we have no power of altering our character, and to think that we shall not use our power unless we desire to use it, are very different things, and have a very

[94] Ibid., 840. Italics in original. The masthead of the Owenite periodical (more or less weekly) *The New Moral World* carried the motto "The Character of Man is Formed for Him and not by Him."

[95] Ibid. Italics in original.

different effect on the mind."[96] Having no doubt that the conditions of human existence could only grow worse if people lost confidence in the possibility of improving their character, Mill opted for the conclusion that would do the most good. However far beyond proof the authenticity of freedom might remain, all risk of error was overwhelmed by the desirability of believing in it. Without ever overcoming the danger of infinite regression or proving that our efforts at self-reform really originate with the self, Mill was content in the end merely to observe how inconvenient it would be to accept the contrary conclusion. In so doing, he tacitly conceded that on secular premises the problem of transitivity was insoluble, even as he insisted that life could (and should) go on as if it were.

Mill did not associate his mental crisis with Robert Owen or with socialism. He mentioned the Owenites only once in the *Autobiography* and that single mention occurs in the chapter preceding the one devoted to his mental crisis. Obviously the "doctrine of the formation of character by circumstances" was not anything he learned from Owen, for it had been his father's guiding principle. Still, the timing of his encounter with the Owenites is intriguing, for it occurred in 1825, the year before the onset of the mental crisis. A group of Owenites calling themselves the Cooperative Society were holding weekly public debates in Chancery Lane when Mill and his circle of brilliant young intellectuals in the Utilitarian Society heard about them and began attending. "Some one of us started the notion of going there in a body and having a general battle," he wrote, and the result was a "*lutte corps-à-corps*" between Owenites and political economists that continued for three months and drew large audiences, including many from the Inns of Court. Distinguished orators spoke on each side. Mill regarded one of his own opponents, the distinguished barrister Connop Thirlwall, as the best speaker he had ever heard. Mill called it a "perfectly friendly dispute" and stressed that the two sides had "the same objects in view," but acknowledged that the Owenites regarded the political economists as their most "inveterate opponents."[97]

It is, of course, appropriate that Mill, exemplar of the spirit of

[96] Ibid., 841.
[97] John Stuart Mill, *Autobiography*, 127, 129.

capitalism, should battle Owen, the first socialist – and even more appropriate, given the present interpretive framework, that the battle should have revolved around the suitability of the self for causal attribution. Because the debate between capitalism and socialism has been under way now for the better part of two centuries and the affairs of the entire globe have hinged upon it, the issues that initially sparked the debate have long since been lost to view beneath layers of impassioned rhetoric and the accumulated debris of discarded theoretical epicycles. The supercession of Owenite socialism by the Marxian variety, with its celebration of proletarian revolution and ponderous, quasi-mystical Teutonic vocabulary, has obscured the simple question about causal attribution and transitivity with which the great debate began: "Who [or what] made me?"[98]

That, after all, was the question Owen was tacitly asking and answering in 1813, when he published *A New View of Society; or, Essays on the Principle of the formation of the Human Character,* the text that launched the socialist movement in England. He took direct aim at the widespread but erroneous notion that "each individual man forms his own character, and that therefore he is accountable for all his sentiments and habits, and consequently merits reward for some, and punishment for others." This exaggerated view of human responsibility was, Owen asserted, the "true and sole origin of evil." Although he regarded the presumption of individual autonomy as "the Evil Genius of the world" and an "error that carries misery in all its consequences," he was optimistic that its days were numbered.

> This error cannot much longer exist; for every day will make it more and more evident THAT THE CHARACTER OF MAN IS, WITHOUT A SINGLE EXCEPTION, ALWAYS FORMED FOR HIM; THAT IT MAY BE, AND IS CHIEFLY, CREATED BY HIS PREDECESSORS; THAT THEY GIVE HIM, OR MAY GIVE HIM HIS IDEAS AND HABITS, WHICH ARE THE POWERS THAT GOVERN AND DIRECT HIS CONDUCT. MAN, THEREFORE, NEVER DID, NOR IS IT POSSIBLE HE EVER CAN, FORM HIS OWN CHARACTER.[99]

Transitivity was not a problem for Owen or his followers, for they cheerfully and naively accepted the "radical situatedness" of the self,

[98] On the supercession of Owenism by Marxism, see Gregory Claeys, *Machinery, Money and the Millennium: From Moral Economy to Socialism* (Cambridge: Polity Press, 1987), 156–83.

[99] Robert Owen, *A New View of Society* (Glencoe, Ill.: Free Press, n.d. [3rd. ed., 1817]), 90–92. The passage was repeated over and over in Owenite literature, and usually printed in boldface.

seeing no more danger in it than Luther had (on wholly different premises) three centuries earlier. Putting "society" in the place that God once occupied as the first cause and creator of man, they waved farewell to individual autonomy and moral responsibility without so much as a backward look. Protestant divines had always taken great pains to show that God's overruling Providence in no way lessened human moral responsibility, but Owen failed even to acknowledge the problem.[100] He was sure that "all goodness, wisdom, and happiness" would accrue to mankind with recognition of the great truth that "all the faculties of humanity are created for the individual, without his consent or knowledge; that these faculties are well or ill cultivated from birth *for* the individual, by society; and that society alone should be responsible for the inferior or superior, good or bad, cultivation of every one."[101] The question why, given the complete transitivity of all human choices, anyone *ought* to seek justice, or *ought* to oppose evil, troubled Owen not at all. His followers did not hesitate to draw the "very obvious deduction," namely, "that virtue and vice were equally necessitated, and [that] the ascription of merit or demerit to the agent who manifested the operation of this unchangeable and uncontrollable law, was a *non sequitur,* and an injustice."[102] Unable to divinize the circumstances in which the self was sunk (a project that Auguste Comte actually undertook with his "religion of Humanity,") the Owenites offered as a substitute the socialization of those circumstances in a distant rational future, a strategy on which the revolutionary varieties of socialism did not significantly improve.[103] It should not surprise us that Owen attacked "all the existing false religions of the world" more bitterly than he did either the property-owning classes or the social system that worked to their advantage. Nor should it surprise us that the initial resistance to Owenite socialism came not from the owners of property so much as from outraged religionists, to whom it seemed sacrile-

[100] Luther, for example, held that "necessity does not destroy moral responsibility." *Bondage of the Will,* 185.

[101] Robert Owen, *The Revolution in the Mind and Practice of the Human Race: or the Coming Change from Irrationality to Rationality* (Clifton, N.J.: A. M. Kelley, 1973 [1849]), 144.

[102] *The New Moral World: or Gazette of the Universal Community of Rational Religionists,* vol. 6, no. 48 new series (September 21, 1839), 753.

[103] Gertrude Lenzer, ed. and intro., *Auguste Comte and Positivism: The Essential Writings* (New York: Harper & Row, 1975).

gious for human society to be assigned the causal status hitherto belonging to God.[104]

If the importance of Mill's struggle to make sense of transitivity was lost on the Owenites, his efforts were also unsatisfactory to traditional Christians. The latter were more likely than the Owenites to appreciate what was at stake, but in their eyes Mill's attempt to rescue the self failed because it conceded far too much to a world of circumstantiality, unredeemed by any hint of divine purpose. Of all the Protestant denominations the Unitarians were most eager to assimilate new learning, most willing to water down the supernatural element in Christianity, and most likely to welcome sophisticated defenses of voluntarism. Yet the leading Unitarian in England, James Martineau, found little to admire in the "middle" path Mill had struck between freedom and fate. From the vantage point of even the most avant-garde religionists, Mill was, like Owen or Bentham, an antiformalist radical, whose conception of the self practically snuffed out autonomy and left human beings mere creatures of circumstance.

> Our author's whole picture of man exhibits him as a natural product, shaped by the scene on which he is cast; and he rejects every theory without exception which has been set up in psychology, in logic, in morals, to vindicate the autonomy of human reason and conscience. . . .
>
> If, in his aim to supplement Bentham, our author yielded to an idealistic impulse, he remained true, in what he retained in the great utilitarian, to the materialistic tendencies of the school. The inward side of ethics is made, in every aspect, dependent on the outward. Do we ask what determines the moral quality of actions? we are referred, not to their spring, but to their consequences. Do we inquire how we came by our moral sentiments? by contagion, we are told, of other people's approbation and disapprobation, not by any self-reflective judgment of our own. Do we seek for the adequate sources of a man's guilt or goodness? we are presented with an enumeration of the external conditions which made his character, like his health, just what it is.[105]

John Stuart Mill, it should now be clear, did not invent formalism. What he "invented" (or reinvented, in view of its antiquity) was a precarious balancing act that enabled him to maintain a modicum of poise in the midst of an unprecedented upheaval in the conventions governing causal attribution. The balance he struck appeared exces-

[104] Robert Owen, *The Life of Robert Owen*, vol. 1 (London: Frank Cass, 1967 [1857]), 159–64, quotation 160.

[105] James Martineau, *Essays, Reviews, and Addresses*, vol. 3 (London: Longman's Green, 1891), 520, 527.

sively formal to a few of his most radical contemporaries, such as the Owenites, but insufficiently so to many more, who, like James Martineau, complained that Mill treated mankind merely as "a natural product, moulded by surrounding pressures." Eager though Mill was to reaffirm the ascetic possibility of the self standing in genuine opposition to itself, Martineau's complaint was precisely that Mill had left too little room for "self-formation, the evolution from within towards an unrealized type of perfection."[106]

In the eyes of believers, Mill's final formulation of the problem of freedom and fate could not satisfy, for in truth it left the self open and exposed to the same process of disenchantment that Scottish philosopher Thomas Reid had observed at work on natural objects in the eighteenth century. "As philosophy advances," wrote Reid, "life and activity in natural objects retires, and leaves them dead and inactive. Instead of moving voluntarily, we find them to be moved necessarily; instead of acting, we find them to be acted upon; and nature appears as one great machine, where one wheel is turned by another, and that by a third; and how far this necessary succession may reach, the philosopher does not know."[107] The perceptions of transitivity that lay at the heart of this process of disenchantment would, by the end of the nineteenth century, no longer be confined to natural objects, and Max Weber saw as perceptively as anyone of his generation what it would mean for disenchantment to overtake and pervade the entire world of self and society.

Weber showed in the Protestant ethic thesis that a doctrine pointing logically toward fatalism can, in psychological practice, foster voluntarism. Mill's mental crisis, as we have seen, suggests that the reverse is also true: A doctrine that is logically enabling can, in practice, carry psychological implications that are paralyzing. On the face of things it seems extremely paradoxical that a radically heightened sense of agency should, in and of itself, lead to a radically constricted one, yet Mill thought this was true in his own case. His Benthamite euphoria did not merely precede his dejection but was its "origin," he said. On

[106] Ibid., 527.

[107] Reid, quoted in John Stuart Mill, *A System of Logic,* vol. 7 of *The Collected Works,* ed. J. M. Robson, intro. R. F. McRae (Toronto and Buffalo: Toronto University Press and Routledge & Kegan Paul, 1973), 358.

his own associationist premises, reinforced, as we have seen, by Carlyle's vitalistic derogation of self-consciousness, Mill had no way of accounting for this sudden transmutation of voluntaristic euphoria into fatalistic depression except by invoking what he himself had always regarded as a cliché, the idea that analytical thinking eroded the feelings. An account more plausible to twentieth-century minds comes into view as soon as we step outside Mill's own associationist framework and think in terms of causal attribution.

Environmentalist arguments of the sort that Mill and the Utilitarians subscribed to have always carried paradoxical implications about human agency. If the character of human beings is a product of their environment, then human beings have the power to change their character by changing their environment. But this accession of power is ironically drained of content because consistency requires us to acknowledge that we who act to shape a new future are no less malleable than those we act upon. Our present power over the future implies an equivalent power of the past over the present, thus raising Mill's question of transitivity: How can we know that our apparent power over the future is anything more than the power of the accumulated past, acting through us, its unwitting and deluded agents? As long as we think only of our power over the future, environmentalism is an enabling doctrine that flatters the self and promises ever higher levels of mastery. But if, as environmentalism assumes, all events of this world are sewn together by relations of contingency, then, being consistent, we cannot well deny that we ourselves, and all our present acts and choices, are the effects of equally compelling environmental contingencies for which we deserve neither blame nor credit. Environmentalism leaves no secure space for uncaused causes. If we allow our gaze to drift away from the happy panorama that unfolds when we think about our power over the future, and think instead about the past influences of which we, even in the act of willing, are passive effects, the implications of environmentalism are hideously reversed and become deeply unflattering to the self and its sense of autonomy.

Since environmentalism is a style of causal attribution, the same paradox can be put in another way that highlights the role of knowledge. The optimism of the environmentalist, who gazes into the future and is gratified to think of the new world he or she can make, presupposes knowledge of a host of necessary causal connections between present acts and future states of the world. Without "recipe knowledge" charting causal linkages between present acts and future events, no opportunities for reform or control could be perceived. The more ample the fund of recipe knowledge, the farther into the future it reaches, and the more certain the connections it discloses between cause and effect, the more expansive the actor's sense of agency, the broader the actor's causal horizon, and the more gratifying the prospect.

But human beings are not only causes, they are also effects. They not only gaze into the future and ponder what effects their acts and omissions might one day have, they also (sometimes) look over their shoulders at the past, and ask themselves, "Of what am I the effect?" or, in Mill's vocabulary, "Who made me?" In this second sphere of causal attribution the motive is explanatory rather than pragmatic. And when it comes to explaining how we got to be who we are, the ample fund of far-reaching causal recipes that seemed so enabling, as long as it was confined to the pragmatic sphere, blows up in our face. The psychological significance of our knowledge of causal relations reverses as we pass from one sphere to the other. In the pragmatic, future-facing sphere of causal attribution (What can I make?), the more certain the connection between cause and effect, the more powerful we feel, for in that sphere we cast ourselves in the role of cause and welcome necessity, since it assures us that our recipes will work. But in the retrospectively oriented explanatory sphere where we cast ourselves in the role of effect (What made me?), the more necessary the connection, the less basis we have for feeling that our acts truly originate with us. The very element that in the pragmatic sphere assured us our choices would be effectual, in the explanatory sphere undermines the authenticity of choice itself. In the pragmatic sphere, the richer and more complex our knowledge of causal relations becomes, the finer our control over the future appears to be; but in the explanatory sphere, the richer and more complex our knowledge, the greater the perceived force of circumstance in our lives, the more contingent our existence seems, and the less original and consequential we feel. Freedom and fate, then, are not the north and south poles of human possibility, defining by their remoteness from each other the most extreme of oppositions. Instead, if Mill's experience is any guide, in our culture they are two faces of a single coin, separated by only the coin's thickness and about equally likely, once put in motion, to land facing up.

Capitalism puts the coin in motion. It does so by fostering a form of life in which technique proliferates explosively because, as Weber showed, people feel duty-bound to "intentionalize" their experience, perpetually struggling to minimize unintended outcomes and achieve technical mastery over the future. Although the intentionalizing motive has its roots in religious doctrine, what sustains it in a mature economy is not religion but the competitive discipline of supply and demand. Weber is easy to misunderstand on this point. The power of the market to produce the kinds of people and practices it needs is easily underestimated because Weber was eager to show that religion was no mere reflex of economic change and that the market could not flourish until Calvinism had provided it with an ample supply of self-monitoring "economic men." But Weber knew full well that capitalism needed the personality-transforming power and sweeping recruitment capacity of religion only in order to breach the walls of traditionalism and gain a dominant position. Once it prevails, he recognized, the market no longer needs the support of religion because it independently "educates and selects the economic subjects it needs through a process of economic survival of the fittest."[108] In the circular manner that often holds between institutions and character, the practices and traits of personality that the market presupposes as a condition of its existence, it also induces and perpetually reinforces. And insofar as those traits and practices aim at the production of an intended future, the market cannot fail to encourage habits of remote causal attribution.

The "economic man" initially fostered by religion and then continually re-created and reinforced by the market itself cannot do the work cut out for him unless he has wide causal horizons and an ample fund of techniques, or "recipe knowledge," linking present acts to future outcomes. For such a person, as we have seen, the present must be construed as a staging ground for the production of the future, and the instrumental relation between present acts and future outcomes must appear so certain, so necessary, that failure to attend to the production of a desirable future will be interpreted as a breach of

[108] Weber, *Protestant Ethic,* 55.

obligation. He must think causally: and since thinking causally consists in linking present choices to consequences more or less remote in time by techniques or recipes that map a route from one to the other, the market man (or woman) must be both a voluntarist and a virtuoso of technique, attentive to the remote consequences of behavior and acutely conscious of ways in which the world can be bent to one's will. The market by its very nature encouraged the production, proliferation, circulation, and preservation of recipe knowledge. As Joyce Appleby observed in her study of economic theory and ideology in seventeenth-century England, the extension of the market worked to "activate the participants' imaginative powers" and stimulate "long-range planning through rational calculations."[109] The most distinctive feature of the character induced by the market, then, is its habit of remote causal attribution, its readiness to perceive its own choices as the cause of distant events – "distant" not only in time and space, but also in terms of the counterintuitive qualitative transformations involved in their production. To say all this is merely to unfold the implications of Franklin's quintessential formulation of the Spirit of Capitalism, "Time is money" – three deceptively simple words that neatly collapse "then" into "now," "there" into "here," and one qualitative order of things, "time," into another, "money."

Yet, as we have just seen, human beings do not spend all their lives in the future-oriented, pragmatic sphere of causal attribution. And when they shift their attention to the retrospective, explanatory sphere, the one in which we ask "Who [or what] made me?" the psychological implications of their market-induced habit of remote causal attribution can take on a very different meaning. Both the entrepreneur and the humanitarian reformer feel lifted up to a commanding eminence, as Mill did, by their possession of far-reaching recipe knowledge; but the rich fund of recipe knowledge that sustains far-flung causal horizons and a vaulting sense of agency in the pragmatic mode, merely highlights and magnifies the inescapable dependence of self on world whenever considerations of consistency allow it to seep into the explanatory sphere. Having learned in the everyday, pragmatic world of the marketplace to think in terms of extended chains of causal linkage, and having learned in particular to distrust

[109] Joyce Oldham Appleby, *Economic Thought and Ideology in Seventeenth Century England* (Princeton: Princeton University Press, 1978), 246, 84.

proximate causal attribution because of its superficiality, its failure to take into account the full range of future events that are within the power of the will to shape and anticipate, the modern self plays by rules of causal attribution that can, when transposed into the explanatory sphere, promote feelings of powerlessness and inconsequentiality more extreme, one suspects, than anything felt by our ancestors in traditional society, who never dared imagine that they could command the future or escape the past. Although it is only human to be in the grip of contradictory convictions about freedom and fate, there is reason to believe that the form of life spawned by the market exacerbates the contradiction.

Perhaps that should not surprise us, for we have always known that capitalism allows the individual unprecedented liberty to do as he or she pleases, but only on the unspoken condition that each individual be exposed to the relentless, if "invisible," discipline of supply and demand, which ensures – at least in theory – that what truly pleases will also conform in the long run to the harsh dictates of allocative efficiency. C. B. Macpherson expressed the paradox succinctly. "The market makes men free; it requires for its effective operation that all men be free and rational; yet the independent rational decisions of each man produce at every moment a configuration of forces which confronts each man compulsively. All men's choices determine, and each man's choice is determined by, the market."[110]

Consistency being among the most ephemeral of human motives, most of us do not find it difficult to compartmentalize our lives, reserving our far-flung causal horizons for pragmatic matters, where they make us feel good, and excluding such perceptions from explanatory inquiries, where they can be so troublesome. John Stuart Mill, among the most consistent of men, was at greater risk than most of us. But in a world shaped by market discipline, remote causal attribution is always a live option even when it does not prevail, and the "radical" or "deep" forms of explanation and perception to which it gives rise can never be ruled out of court. Nor should we want them to be. Indeed, we might observe that the market, by creating a culture in which every human act or event is susceptible to multiple interpretations depending on whether its causes are construed to lie on the

[110] C. B. Macpherson, *The Political Theory of Possessive Individualism: Hobbes to Locke* (London: Oxford University Press, 1962), 106.

"surface," or to be more "deeply" situated, creates also the possibility of a class of people specializing in "deep" explanation. Would it be too much to suggest that for the past century or two there has existed such a class, known ever since the Dreyfus affair of the 1890s as the "intellectuals"? And to suggest also that the politics of market societies have for the past century been largely a contest between those who see the plight of the poor and the downtrodden to be a product of deep-lying structural conditions over which the victims have no control, and those who, on the contrary, see them more nearly as free agents, deeply complicit in their own difficulties? Different modes of causal attribution, and thus of explanation, create the principal political chasms that divide us.

Certainly from Mill's day down to our own, the smugness of the "self-made man" – the person who imagines that his or her comfortable situation in life owes much to personal merit and little to luck, circumstance, or communal nurturance – has helped knit together political and cultural radicals in a common campaign to "make paste" of the bourgeoisie: to expose the formalist pretensions not only of bourgeois politics and economics, but also of law, science, art, and religion, and thereby to roll back ideological mystification and pave the way for a more authentic life, one that acknowledges the precariousness of personhood and takes into account the inescapable "situatedness" of us all. The defining characteristic of the "self-made man" is his evident imperviousness to Mill's troubling insight that causation may be transitive; that even one's freest choices and most creative acts may be the effects of causal factors lying outside the self. And, in turn, the most distinctive and emblematic characteristic of the modern literary or humanist intellectual has been disdain for, and knowing superiority to, those who imagine themselves to be "self-made" – or, to speak generically, superiority to the formalist, the person who exaggerates autonomy and underestimates the role that circumstances play in shaping the way people think and act and become who they are.

Among intellectuals today it is widely assumed that formalism thrives in market societies for all the same reasons that ideologies of individualism do. Liberalism, individualism, and formalism seem to go together and to be mutually reinforcing. The reason seems obvious: class interest. The bourgeoisie has good reason to relax the bonds of community, to celebrate the entrepreneurial autonomy of its own members, and to pretend, at least, that everyone in liberal society, whether rich or poor, enjoys the same extensive liberty to think and do whatever they please. The ideological functions of formalism seem plainly evident in the classic case of the "free" laborer who, unlike the slave, the serf, or the apprentice, is physically unconstrained and legally free to sell his or her labor to the highest bidder, but who discovers how empty formal freedom is when trying to negotiate a favorable wage contract with a supposed "equal," the wealthy factory owner. Inequalities of bargaining power make all the difference, and those inequalities remain invisible as long as they are seen through the distorting lenses of formalism.[111] Still other layers of antecedent circumstance come into view as we extend our vision back into the past, noticing that the worker belongs to a class deprived of access to the means of production by an enclosure movement or by other, still earlier, forms of primitive accumulation. Formalism, by magnifying autonomy and shrinking circumstance, is thus said to veil the dominance of the ruling class, to legitimate the exploitation of wage labor, and to render invisible the structural conditions that confine choice within safe channels and define the status quo. As Mill's contemporary Karl Marx put it in *The German Ideology,* "in imagination, individuals seem freer under the dominance of the bourgeoisie than before, because their conditions of life seem accidental; in reality, of course, they are less free, because they are more subjected to the violence of things."[112]

There are important elements of truth in this classic scenario, just as there are in the ancient suspicion that, in the end, all of us are indeed "creatures of circumstance," notwithstanding all our "splendid hopes" to the contrary. Yet if the interests of the ruling class under capitalism are so well served by formalism, it is not at all easy to understand why, over a period during which capitalism has marched from victory to victory, formalism has been forced to beat one retreat after another. Nor is it easy to understand, if the circumstance of class interest has exerted such a powerful influence over the thought and

[111] For a brilliant reassertion of this insight, and an attempt to disentangle it from the categories of traditional Marxist analysis, see William Reddy, *Money and Liberty in Modern Europe: A Critique of Historical Understanding* (Cambridge: Cambridge University Press, 1987), especially ch. 3, "Growth of the Liberal Illusion."

[112] Karl Marx, *The German Ideology,* excerpted in *The Marx–Engels Reader,* ed. Robert C. Tucker (New York: Norton, 1972), 163.

experience of the formalists, how antiformalist intellectuals (most of whose origins have been bourgeois) have managed to exempt themselves from its power. In the present context the question of consistency must arise. Have antiformalists themselves been entirely free of illusions of self-creation and autonomy, as they have embarked, generation after generation, on the exhilarating and manifestly self-affirming project *pour épater la bourgeoisie*? In attacking formalism, have radicals been struggling against the tide and striking at the soft underbelly of the enemy, as they have believed? Or could it be that in adopting the posture of antiformalism they have unwittingly been riding in the swift central current of cultural transformation, echoing and even amplifying the very market forces they set out to master, occupying as it were an attributive niche that the market itself carved out for them? These questions about the relation between capitalism and formalism take on special significance today, when the emancipatory aspirations that once accompanied the critique of bourgeois culture seem in some quarters to have evaporated, leaving behind a residue of antiformalist *ressentiment* (often masked as *jouissance*) that aims merely at the "deconstruction" of any and all construals of reality – as if hunting down settled convictions were a self-justifying activity, even after all hope of arriving at superior convictions (truer, more realistic, more just) has been given up.

The question becomes, What sort of culture does the market foster? The one sketched by Marx, in which interest prompts people (nonradicals, at least) habitually to mistake formal freedom for the real thing and impute to themselves and others a degree of autonomy that the world cannot actually supply? Or the one that Mill sensed in the depths of his despair and that was most memorably characterized by Carlyle – a culture organized around the habit of remote causal attribution, in which even the greatest freedoms to which humans can plausibly aspire are apt to seem, at least to sensitive souls, unreal and unsatisfying (merely "formal"), thereby stimulating an appetite for sensations of spontaneity, self-sufficiency, and authenticity more intense than any society can satisfy?

These are ambitious questions and I do not claim to answer them decisively. The principal argumentative burden of the preceding pages has been simply that the relation between capitalism and formalism is more complex than the conventional story would have it, and that the conventional story errs most grievously in supposing that "interest" is the only way economic developments can influence consciousness. The market teaches not one but many lessons. Some, of course, serve the interests of those who benefit most from the market's existence; but others cut against the grain of interest, creating, for instance, the very possibility of perceiving the beneficiaries of the market as a "ruling class," whose authority stems neither from nature nor God, but merely from mutable circumstances of the sort that human beings can hope to understand and influence.

It will not do to say either that the market fosters formalism, or that it fosters antiformalism: What it fosters is precisely the debate between the two. The market makes possible the emergence of a game of causal attribution whose rules are sufficiently indeterminate that every event has both "formal" and "deep" interpretations, and which therefore allows for the emergence of rival elites, each committed to its own mode of explanation. Knowing this does not discredit either elite. Having once sampled the explanatory fruits of remote causal attribution, there is no turning back; those of us who take what used to be called the "life of the mind" seriously cannot rest content with a mode of explanation that we regard as superficial, or set in advance any fixed limits on how deep explanation should run. But neither are we obliged to succumb to the illusion that depth always equals truth. The commonsense explanations yielded by "proximate" causal attribution are inescapable and can never be rendered wholly obsolete by their deeper rivals. "Deep" explanations deliver nothing more than another perspective, shaped like all other perspectives by the perceiver's time, place, and situation. Thus, when we set about the destructive work of stripping away the masks that shelter someone else's self from the world, we should do so in the full knowledge that we, too, rely on a conception of self that, when stripped of all claims to autonomy, ceases to exist. Perhaps the most obvious lesson to draw from John Stuart Mill's mental crisis is simply that although our claims of autonomy vary in degree and in kind, in the end (in practice, even if not in rhetoric) we are all "formalists," all claimants to an autonomy we cannot conclusively justify. To play the game of causal attribution is to construe at least one self, one's own, intransitively. What life would be like in the absence of that game, I find it impossible to imagine.

Index

Lightning Source UK Ltd.
Milton Keynes UK
UKOW050718201011

180593UK00001B/84/P